Consumer Society in
American History

Consumer Society in American History

A READER

*Edited with an Introduction
and Bibliographic Essay by*

Lawrence B. Glickman

Cornell University Press

Ithaca and London

First published 1999 by Cornell University Press
First printing, Cornell Paperbacks, 1999

Printed in the United States of America

Library of Congress Cataloging-in-Publication Data

Consumer society in American history : a reader / edited by Lawrence B. Glickman
p.   cm.
Includes bibliographical references and index.
ISBN-13: 978-0-8014-8486-5 (pbk. : alk. paper)
ISBN-10: 0-8014-8486-3 (pbk. : alk. paper)
1. Consumption (Economics)—United States—History. I. Glickman, Lawrence B., 1963–
HC110.C6C574   1999
339.4'7—dc21   99-34304

Cornell University Press strives to use environmentally responsible suppliers and materials to the
fullest extent possible in the publishing of its books. Such materials include vegetable-based,
low-VOC inks, and acid-free papers that are recycled, totally chlorine-free, or partly composed
of nonwood fibers. For further information, visit our website at www.cornellpress.cornell.edu.

Paperback printing   10   9   8   7   6   5

Contents

Preface   vii

Introduction: Born to Shop? Consumer History and
American History   1
LAWRENCE B. GLICKMAN

Part I. Frameworks and Definitions

1. Consumer   17
   RAYMOND WILLIAMS

2. Consuming Goods and the Good of Consuming   19
   COLIN CAMPBELL

3. Consumer Society   33
   JEAN BAUDRILLARD

4. What Is an Economy For?   57
   JAMES FALLOWS

5. An Environmentalist's Perspective on Consumer Society   78
   ALAN DURNING

Part II. Roots of American Consumer Society

6. The First Consumer Revolution   85
   JAMES AXTELL

7. Narrative of Commercial Life: Consumption, Ideology, and
   Community on the Eve of the American Revolution   100
   T. H. BREEN

8. Consumption in Early Modern Social Thought   130
   JOYCE APPLEBY

Part III. Class, Gender, and Modernity, 1880–1940

9. Encountering Mass Culture at the Grassroots: The Experience of
   Chicago Workers in the 1920s   147
   LIZABETH COHEN

10. Familiar Sounds of Change: Music and the Growth of
    Mass Culture   170
    GEORGE SANCHEZ

11. From Scarcity to Abundance: The Immigrant as Consumer   190
    ANDREW HEINZE

12. Consuming Brotherhood: Men's Culture, Style and
    Recreation as Consumer Culture, 1880–1930   207
    MARK A. SWIENCICKI

13. "Don't Buy Where You Can't Work"   241
    CHERYL GREENBERG

Part IV. Consumerism Since World War II

14. The 'Work' Ethic and 'Leisure' Activity: The Hot Rod
    in Post-War America   277
    H. F. MOORHOUSE

15. The Commodity Gap: Consumerism and the Modern Home   298
    ELAINE TYLER MAY

16. The Revolution Will be Marketed: American Corporations
    and Black Consumers During the 1960s   316
    ROBERT E. WEEMS, JR.

17. All Work and No Play. It Doesn't Pay   326
    JULIET B. SCHOR

18. When High Wage Jobs Are Gone, Who Will Buy What We Make? 328
    KIM MOODY

19. The Green Consumer   333
    JOHN ELKINGTON, JULIA HAILES, AND JOEL MAKOWER

Part V. Critiques and Celebrations

20. Delectable Materialism: Second Thoughts on Consumer Culture 341
    MICHAEL SCHUDSON

21. The Tyranny of Choice   359
    STEVEN WALDMAN

22. The Pleasures of Eating   367
    WENDELL BERRY

23. Coming Up for Air: Consumer Culture in Historical Perspective 373
    JEAN-CHRISTOPHE AGNEW

    Bibliographic Essay   399
    LAWRENCE B. GLICKMAN

    Contributors   415

    Index   419

Preface

In the last decade there has been a revolution in the study of American consumer history. This revolution has been both thematic and chronological. It has also entailed a historical shift from narrow and peripheral to broad and central significance. Where once consumption was studied, if at all, as an element in the history of popular and commercial culture, it is now seen as being intertwined with the major themes of national identity and American history—including economic, political, foreign policy, intellectual, cultural, environmental, labor, racial, ethnic, and gender history. Similarly, where once consumer history was a topic limited to the twentieth century and even to particular decades—typically the 1920s or the 1950s—it is now seen as playing an important role in all phases of American history, including the colonial period. The study of consumption has become a framing device for many approaches to, and all eras of, American history.

This thematic and chronological expansion, however, has not resulted in a new and widely accepted synthesis of U.S. consumer history. The meaning of consumption has been complicated, not simplified, by the new scholarship. Whereas scholars (that is those few who did not reject it out of hand as a trivial topic) in the past thought they knew what consumption was and when it was important, today's students of American consumer society lack such assurance. In place of these mistaken certainties lies a recognition that the study of consumption is not a marginal subfield, but a central element of American history.

Consumer Society in American History: A Reader is designed to provide students and scholars alike with a convenient selection of some of the best of recent consumer scholarship. Juxtaposing rarely linked types of contemporary consumer studies, it includes many perspectives and vocabularies. Rather than leaving the reader with a unified history and meaning of American consumption, this book shows that the history and meaning of American consumption can be profitably approached in a variety of ways.

Readers may notice that two of the topics most commonly associated with the phrase "consumer society"—advertising and popular culture—are not heavily presented in this volume. Similarly, the subject of consumption by women receives less attention than might be expected. The underemphasis of these topics is due, in part, to the fact that excellent studies of these issues are readily available and are, for the most part, well-known to aspiring consumer historians. In addition, these topics do not account for the full range of roles that consumption has played in American history. The "consumer society" described in this volume challenges stereotypes that readers might bring to the topic: it looks at people not usually thought of as consumers (such as Native Americans, working people, and Revolutionary Era Americans); it examines the ways in which consumption has intersected with class relations, race, and ethnicity; it emphasizes the connection between consumption and politics; and it focuses to a greater extent on the reception and response to goods and consumption than on the businesses, media outlets, and advertisers who produce and promote the goods.

By shifting the traditional focus, it is hoped that this volume will provide an impetus for historians and other scholars to begin thinking more systematically about the history and meaning of American consumer society. There are many fine examples of consumer history and the topic is clearly becoming of interest to a growing number of scholars. But as of yet, there is no field known as American consumer history; no journal or professional organizations exclusively devoted to the topic; no academic prizes awarded for outstanding scholarship; nor is it yet a standard topic for graduate student qualifying examinations. While individual works of scholarship are recognized, it is not yet seen by the historical profession as a field of study that stands on its own. The status of American consumer history is analogous to women's history or African American history prior to the "new social history" that brought those fields from the margin to the center of historical scholarship in the 1960s and 1970s.

This volume, however, does not provide conclusive evidence that consumer scholarship should become a separate field. The attraction of the readings in this book stems from their diversity (ranging from theory, to history, to journalism), the number of different vocabularies and methodologies they employ, the way they come to divergent conclusions, that they locate radically different subjects as exemplifying consumer society, and the fact that they resist any attempt to make them part of a "consumer synthesis." Indeed, the essays reveal such a level of interconnection with the main themes of American history that it might be ill advised to isolate consumer history as a unique field of study. It is precisely this degree of interconnection between consumption in all its forms and American history in general that this book showcases.

The essays in *Consumer Society in American History: A Reader*—selected from a growing pool of superb scholarship and commentary—capture the scope and variety of the rapidly evolving and expanding field of consumer history, one that was barely recognized a generation ago. Indeed, the biggest problem in compiling the selections was one of omission—space limitations forced many excellent works to be passed over. Partially to rectify the problem of these omissions and more generally to recognize this excellent scholarship, the "Bibliographic Essay" section provides a compilation of the key books and articles in the field.

I have incurred many debts in producing this book. I would especially like to thank the sudents in my consumer history classes and seminars over the last decade at the University of South Carolina and the University of California, Berkeley. My students became collaborators; they asked hard questions, took the subject seriously, and encouraged me to think that this anthology would find an appreciative audience.

I would also like to thank the contributors to this volume (as well as their publishers), the dozens of generous colleagues who responded to Cornell University Press's query and commented on the selections and framework of this volume, as well as the scholars whose works are cited in the bibliographical essay. Kathryn Kish Sklar, who first suggested this volume several years ago, deserves special thanks as do the other members of the Consumer History Study Group who supported this project. My editor Peter Agree has consistently supported this project over the many years of its germination. Thanks also to the staff at Cornell University Press and Textbook Writers Associates, Inc. for superb assistance. Finally, I owe a great debt to Jill Frank, Marilyn Halter, Daniel Horowitz, and an anonymous reader for helpfully critiquing early drafts of the "Introduction" and "Bibliographic Essay."

Consumer Society in
American History

Born to Shop? Consumer History and American History

Lawrence B. Glickman

"The American Dream is a vision of men as consumers, and the American story is the story of an inveterate struggle to embody this dream in the institutions of American life."

—Horace Kallen, 1936

"The basic myth of our culture is that consumption is the goal of life."

—Dallas Smythe, 1972

Consumption has long been central to American identity, culture, economic development, and politics. More than one commentator has called consumption the "national pastime" of the United States.[1] But America's long engagement with consumption has not been unchanging. The term itself has undergone a significant transformation. Once "consumption" was synonymous with wastefulness—a meaning that has not completely disappeared among critics, as several essays in this volume reveal. Over the course of the industrial revolution, however, consumption came to take on the more neutral, or even positive, connotation of productive social activity in a market economy. Even within any given era, "consumerism" has had a plurality of distinct and not always consistent significations: sometimes defined as excessive materialism, sometimes as a political movement of organized consumers.[2] It has been treated as moral danger, popular culture, economic policy, political activity, and as a symbol of modernity itself. The tension among these meanings throughout American history is emblematic of the ambivalence that Americans have felt—and continue to feel—about the part consumption plays in their lives. As James Gilbert has observed, "While American society is the most consumer-oriented in the world (in terms of the sheer number of material objects), it is also a society that quizzes itself endlessly about the effects of materialism, of inauthenticity, of defining oneself in terms of consumer objects."[3]

Despite transformations in both its significance and its sites of practice (consumption has shifted from the trading post to the internet, from the corner store to the department store, from the farm to the factory), consumption has been central to American national identity from the period of European

1

exploration to the present. Equally important have been the longstanding, and unresolved, debates about the moral, economic, and political consequences of consumption, and the near constant stream of consumer philosophizing. For every advocate of the idea that simple living is the embodiment of the American spirit, there have been as many proponents of the contention that a deep and abiding materialism is the root of the nation's unique greatness. This is why both epigraphs at the beginning of this introduction are apt: consumption is central to both the material and ideological components of American identity; it is simultaneously a concrete institution and a guiding myth.[4]

A synopsis of consumption in American history suggests the important, if continually changing, place it holds.

- Commercial exchange was central to the earliest colonial encounters between Europeans and native Americans and transformed both cultures in what James Axtell calls "The First Consumer Revolution." Well before the industrial revolution made mass consumption possible, a commercial and nascent global economy placed consumption at the center of the cross-cultural exchange in the "Age of Exploration."
- During the colonial period, as the American population doubled every twenty-five years, the growing "middling classes" in the colonies began to purchase manufactured goods which they proudly displayed in their homes. Growing demand, a result of a marked increase in per capita wealth among colonists, spurred the industrial revolution, first in England and eventually in the United States.
- American religious leaders expressed concern about the potential for commercial avarice in the New World. New England Puritan ministers strove to ensure that merchants charged only "just prices," not market prices, for their ever-expanding array of imported goods. Yet at the same time the language of the market began to creep into religious discourse—a tension that has continued into the twentieth century as churches have aimed for limits on consumption while embracing parishioners as consumers.
- The American Revolution was in part a consumer revolution. The identity of the colonies as a nation, an "imagined community" to borrow Benedict R. O'G Anderson's phrase, grew out of the practices of wearing homespun clothing and boycotting British goods, most notoriously during the Boston Tea Party. The revolutionaries became the first in a long line of Americans to link consumption—or its withdrawal—and politics.
- The market revolution of the early nineteenth century brought mass-produced goods first to the urban, middle-classes and eventually to small-town America. As America shifted economically (in an uneven process) from a rural, subsistence society to an urbanizing, market-based one, the meaning of what constituted "necessities" changed. Rather than consuming only what was needed, Americans began to raise their standards of consumption.
- In the shorter hours movement, begun in antebellum America and intensifying with the eight-hour movement of the 1870s and 1880s, workers de-

manded more leisure. They argued that, to the extent that they produced the nation's goods, they deserved to enjoy their fair share of the fruits of their labor. For most American workers the work week steadily declined: from sixty-four hours in 1850, to sixty by 1890, to fifty-five by 1914, to forty by the 1930s.

- Along with the shorter hours movement, workers' demand for "living wages" (defined as reward for consumption needs rather than simply a productive equivalence) became central to organized labor's "consumerist turn" in the late nineteenth century. Thus the store and the cash register joined the shop floor as a place of labor struggle and activism.
- With the rise of the union label, first popularized in the immediate post-Civil War years, workers and labor reformers developed a model of solidarity based on consumption. The idea that consumption was not merely an individualist activity had already been argued by the American revolutionaries who ascribed social meaning to market activities; but in the late nineteenth century, consumerist solidarity began to take on its characteristically modern form. The twentieth century has seen it become one of America's dominant modes of political activism.
- Following the Revolution, but particularly after the Civil War, minority peoples frequently used boycotts and consumer activism as a political tactic to make claims for justice in the public sphere. Emboldened by a demand for what the historian Robin D. G. Kelley calls "consumer entitlement" through activism, African Americans, for example, boycotted Jim Crow streetcars in southern towns and cities in the 1890s when segregation was applied to the public transportation systems.[5]
- Through criticism by those identifying themselves as "white," of the standard of consumption of others (often in derogatory-gendered or racial language), consumption has also been a tool for injustice and discrimination, a way of marking outsiders. Even as the purchase of goods was being acclaimed as a key to American identity and citizenship, the business practices of "red lining" (keeping stores away from minority neighborhoods) and of making products and services unavailable to blacks served to exclude racial minorities from consumption. A 1906 pamphlet by Samuel Gompers and Herman Gustadt, *Meat vs. Rice: American Manhood against Asiatic Coolieism. Which Shall Survive?* made a consumerist argument for resuming the practice of legally preventing Chinese immigration.
- N. W. Ayer & Son, the first advertising agency, was created in 1877. By the end of the century, advertising had become a big business, a linchpin of the new corporate economy and a crucial purveyor of the American Dream. By 1900, corporations spent $95 million a year on advertising; by the end of World War I, American advertising had become a half a billion dollar a year industry.[6]
- In the nineteenth century, mail order catalogs led to the creation of what Daniel Boorstin calls "consumption communities," groups of Americans

united by their purchases into the web of consumer culture. This form of purchase, which allowed anyone to buy national brands at standard prices through the anonymity of the postal system, appealed to African Americans and others who often faced maltreatment at the local store. Rural Americans, who lived far from stores able to offer them a big selection, also became enthusiastic catalog shoppers, especially after the late nineteenth-century advent of Rural Free Delivery.

- In the nineteenth century, consumption became what it continues to be today: a central part of American commercial and popular culture. "Cheap amusements"—commercial entertainments such as amusement parks, theaters, and dance halls—transformed the urban landscape, providing the arena for a new heterosocial public life and the abandonment of Victorian culture. Department stores, "palaces of consumption," created a new consumer landscape for the largely female middle-class shoppers and working-class clerks: John Wanamaker's, A. T. Stewart's, R. H. Macy's, Gimbel's, Jordon Marsh, and Filene's included amenities such as restaurants, electric displays, and wide varieties of merchandise. The new disease of "kleptomania" arose during this period as Victorian middle-class women faced the social pressures of the new consumer culture.

- Immigrants and urban newcomers, while continuing to assert their ethnic identity, also assimilated through what Andrew Heinze calls the "bridge" of consumer culture. It enabled the immigrants of the late nineteenth and early twentieth century (whether Mexican Americans in Los Angeles, Jews in the metropolises of the Northeast, or Central Europeans in Chicago) to Americanize on their own terms, carving out identities as hyphenated Americans neither inhabiting the cultural world of the old country nor leaving behind their culture for an American one.

- Consumption became a gendered phenomenon, particularly in the late nineteenth century. For many families, shopping was a form of women's work; at the same time, the new commercial world afforded women new opportunities in the worlds of work and leisure.

- Two works of turn-of-the-century fiction politicized the meaning of "consumer society." Edward Bellamy's *Looking Backward* (1887) depicted an American utopia in which widespread consumerism obviated the need for class conflict. Upton Sinclair's *The Jungle* (1906) popularized the consumer movement and, with its stomach-turning depictions of the meatpacking industry, gave impetus to the Pure Food and Drug Act of 1906.

- In the most influential critique of the decadent consumer culture of the Gilded Age upper class, Thorstein Veblen's *Theory of the Leisure Class* (1899) brought the phrase "conspicuous consumption" into the national vocabulary.

- At the turn of the twentieth century a new kind of politicized consumption emerged. Known as the "consumer movement," it was a characteristically Progressive Era form of middle-class political engagement, with a special appeal for women. The founding of the New York Consumers League (1890) and the National Consumers League (1899) were key to the politicization of middle-class consumers. As Kathryn Kish Sklar notes in discussing women's political activism in the nineteenth century, it has often been the case that "consumer consciousness built political consciousness." In 1914, at the peak of the Progressive Era, Walter Lippmann wrote, "We hear a great deal about the class-consciousness of labor; my own observation is that, in America, today's consumer's consciousness is growing much faster."[7]

- During the Progressive Era, another facet of modern consumer society emerged: the assembly line. Henry Ford mass-produced the reasonably priced Model T and paid his workers $5 per day so they could afford his cars and other fruits of mass production. The automobile became, in Daniel Boorstin's words, "the omnipresent symbol of American consumption communities" and the leading edge of the "Fordist" mass production/mass consumption model that dominated American business practices until the late twentieth century.[8]

- In 1927, the consumer movement, dormant in the immediate postwar years, was revived with the publication of Stuart Chase's and F. J. Schlink's *Your Money's Worth*. It became known as the "*Uncle Tom's Cabin*" of the consumer movement, a best seller, and a selection of the Book-of-the-Month Club.

- The 1930s saw the proliferation of a wide range of consumer organizations ranging from the Consumers Union to the League of Women Shoppers (slogan: "Use your buying power for justice") to consumer cooperatives. In addition to formal organizations, a number of grassroots movements emerged—including the "Don't Buy Where You Can't Work" campaign of African American city dwellers. During this decade, the politicians and economists came to agree that underconsumption played a significant role in setting off the Great Depression. The New Deal responded with a host of measures aimed at bolstering the purchasing power of ordinary Americans.

- President Franklin D. Roosevelt's 1941 State of the Union Address laid out "Four Freedoms," one of which was "freedom from want." In the speech, FDR called for "the enjoyment of the fruits of scientific progress in a wider and constantly rising standard of living."[9]

- The 1950s witnessed a new kind of American affluence dominated by suburbs and automobiles. Shopping malls proliferated from eight in 1945 to 3,840 by 1960. In two articles in the late 1950s, "Rocketing Births: Business Bonanza" and "A New, $10-Billion Power: The U.S. Teen-Age Consumer," *Life* magazine argued that the baby boom generation—both infants and teens—was leading America to new levels of consumption, some of it family oriented (diaper services, clothing, food) and much of it individual (automobiles, record purchases, beauty care products).[10]

- In the mid-1950s, a new phase of consumerist protest, starting with the Montgomery Bus Boycott, launched the modern Civil Rights Movement.

Several years later, sit-ins in Greensboro, Nashville, and elsewhere expanded the connection between consumption and civil rights. "Close your charge account with segregation, open up your account with freedom" was one of the slogans of the drive to integrate the lunch counter at Rich's department store in Atlanta.[11]

- With the 1959 "kitchen debate," consumption entered foreign policy as Vice President Richard Nixon used the presence of modern appliances in American homes to make the case for the superiority of free market capitalism and Western democracy.
- President John F. Kennedy's 1962 message to Congress called for a "Consumer's Bill of Rights" which included the right to safety, the right to be informed, the right to choose, and the right to be heard in governmental decision making.
- David Caplowitz's *The Poor Pay More* (1963) brought national attention to the high cost of consumption for impoverished Americans.
- Rachel Carson's *Silent Spring* (1964) revived national concern about the environmental consequences of mass consumption.
- In 1964, President Lyndon Johnson created the White House post of Special Assistant for Consumer Affairs and selected longtime consumer activist Esther Peterson to serve in the position.
- Ralph Nader's *Unsafe at Any Speed* (1965) launched the contemporary consumer movement with his claim that consumers were "manipulated, defrauded, and injured not just by 'fly-by-night' hucksters but by blue-chip business firms." Nader suggested that, "Giving consumers the know-how to help themselves is one of the most creative functions of government." The next year, Senator Philip Hart's (D–MI) "Truth in Packaging" bill was passed and signed into law. [12]
- Beginning in the late 1960s, the United Farm Workers brought consumption into the labor struggle once again. Agricultural workers urged middle-class consumers to refrain from purchasing grapes, so long as growers resisted union organizing campaigns and industry conditions remained dangerous.
- Throughout the 1960s and 1970s, apostles of the "simple life" revived this old American ideal even as the counterculture became a source of profits for big business.
- President Jimmy Carter's 1979 "Crisis of Confidence" speech warned Americans that "too many of us now worship self-indulgence and consumption. Human identity is no longer defined by what one does, but by what one owns. But we've discovered that owning things and consuming things do not satisfy our longing for meaning. We've learned that piling up material goods cannot fill the emptiness of lives which have no confidence and purpose."[13]
- In the 1980s, critiques of Yuppie consumerism were outweighed by celebrations of American affluence. Don Delillo's novel *White Noise* (1985) parodied the emptiness—and danger—of American affluence by depicting trips

to the supermarket in competition with an "airborne toxic event" for the attention of the townspeople.

• Even as the 1990s witness new levels of consumer spending, marketing, and advertising, the decade also brings a revival of older notions of consumerism. Scorning companies that produce goods with cheap labor abroad and sweat shop labor at home, many critics have been led to call for a revival of consumer responsibility. Calling for a "Civic Consumers Coalition," the political theorist Benjamin Barber argues that consumers "can do plenty of things . . . to nurture greater corporate virtue."[14] Concern about long work hours and declining real wages are also leading Americans to ponder once again the relationship between work and leisure.

The History of American Consumer History

The preceding capsule summary demonstrates that throughout American history, consumption has been widely practiced and encouraged. Consumerism (the various ideologies and movements built around consumption) has been central to economics and politics—hence the description of the United States as a "consumer society." Yet what exactly do these phrases mean? Despite the endless labeling of America as being a consumer society—sometimes with praise, other times with blame—until recently there were few serious analyses of the meaning and history of America's consumer society. Although central to the American experience, consumption has not been central to our frameworks for interpreting that experience.

The result has been a rather stale view of the history of America's consumer society: it appeared briefly in most textbooks as a phenomenon emerging alongside mass production in the 1920s; it then reappeared in these same texts as a part of the discussion of post-World War II affluence. These mentions in textbooks notwithstanding, few scholars treated the origins and development of a consumer society as a topic worthy of historical inquiry. (The "Classics" section of the "Bibliographic Essay" at the end of this collection lists a number of important works on the subject, many of them best sellers, written in early- and mid-twentieth century America; but rarely were these treatments historical in approach.)

For much of the twentieth century, intellectuals either celebrated or derided America's consumer society. What they rarely did was to treat it as a serious object of study. There were a few exceptions to this rule, such as David Potter's *People of Plenty* (1954). Yet even Potter held a curiously static view of consumption. Consumption to Potter was what the frontier was to Frederick Jackson Turner: the defining component of national character.[15] (The difference was that whereas Turner worried about the declining frontier, Potter was made uneasy by the increasing flood of affluence.) In arguing that Americans were fundamentally a people of plenty and that the only variable that changed over time was how much "plenty" the people had, Potter understated the transformations in the meaning and practice of consumption over the course of American history.

Dominated by the pious celebrations of cold war politicians—who conflated consumption and capitalism as the hallmark of the free world—and the moralistic and sometimes elitist dismissals by most scholars and public intellectuals—who denigrated consumer society for producing robotic suburban conformity—public discourse about consumption was equally impoverished. During the 1950s, Americans learned from Vice President Nixon, in the famous "kitchen debate," that modern, affordable appliances were proof of the superiority of the West. (Nixon had not been the first to invoke consumption in the battle against communism. Two decades earlier, Franklin D. Roosevelt had claimed that if he could give one book to the Soviets to teach them about the West, it would be the Sears Catalog.) From intellectuals they heard complaints that the consumer society was making them corporate drones inordinately susceptible to peer pressure. They learned about the degrading character of the books they read, the movies they watched, and the music to which they listened. Interestingly, radicals and conservatives, who could agree on little else, found common ground on this issue: the left worried about the anaesthetizing impact of the consumer society on the masses and the right worried about the tendency of mass culture to level society to the lowest common denominator. Those with unconventional views advocating neither of these extremes—for example, the popular writer Vance Packard—were drowned out by convergence of the mass culture critique and the jingoistic celebration.[16]

The 1960s changed the nature of public discussion but had little discernable impact on scholarly treatments of consumerism. During this period, serious criticism of the meaning of consumer society emerged from a variety of quarters, alongside transformations in practices of consumption. Many counterculturists challenged the consensus view that affluence was altogether a good thing. Hippies "dropped out," leaving behind the superficial pleasures of the world of material goods for what they claimed was a deeper, purer, and simpler existence. Environmentalists warned against the dangers of overconsumption. During the Vietnam War era, the imperial relation between the developed world and the so-called Third World was scrutinized, particularly as it related to the West's use of the raw materials of the non-Western World. The fact that the United States held six percent of the world's population but used approximately forty percent of its resources ceased to be proof of American greatness and came to be seen as a serious problem. Ralph Nader's consumer movement called on ordinary citizens to check the power of large corporations; ecologists challenged Americans to take into account the longterm effects of their consumption; Civil Rights activists made some of their most powerful claims for justice in the realm of consumption. "Every human has a vote every time he makes a purchase," is how the ex-athlete and Civil Rights activist Jackie Robinson linked consumer and citizen.[17]

Yet the 1960s also produced countervailing forces that reinforced and greatly extended consumer society. Baby boomers became a huge niche audience for corporations producing magazines, records, films, foods, and restaurants that appealed to their countercultural sensibilities. Notwithstanding these crosscurrents, scholars examining these movements did not place consumption at the center of their analyses, nor did they produce a vocabulary or mode of analysis for understanding consumption.

It was only in the late 1970s and 1980s that historians began to treat consumption as an important part of the fabric of American life, one worthy of serious study. Attempting to move beyond the clichés of the survey textbook and the Manichean public discourse, many young scholars began to look anew at the meaning of consumption and to explore how consumption was interwoven with the American experience. Alongside this phenomenon came a recognition that an adequate understanding of consumer society required more than studying those who vocally opposed it. The area most fruitfully reconsidered in this pioneering consumer scholarship was popular culture, especially commercialized leisure. The scholarship examined consumption's more visible cultural manifestations—the amusement park, the department store, advertising—attending to the inequalities of power based on class, race, and gender. At the same time, it pointed out the sometimes surprising topsy-turviness of the new commercial world in which, for example, working-class female clerks in department stores gained power from their interactions with middle-class female customers due to their insiders' taste.[18] This scholarship produced more complicated frameworks and nuanced views. Showing the limits of the binarism that had long dominated the discourse of consumerism, it demonstrated that unlike the intellectuals and politicians who tended to declare themselves for or against consumer society, most Americans lived, however ambivalently, firmly within consumer society. Their experiences could not be reduced to a simple thumbs up or down: they negotiated with consumer society; were occasionally seduced by it; and sometimes found ways to use it to increase their power.

Many of the authors in this collection treat consumerism as a problem even as they posit, however uneasily, its centrality to the American economy and identity. Building on the recognition that the actual behavior of Americans has conformed neither to moralistic mass culture criticism nor to cold war celebration, the current wave of consumer history scholarship—as represented in this collection—broadens the domain of inquiry beyond mass culture and commercial leisure. In the process, it discovers ranges of activity and thought that make consumption central not only to the history of mass consumption, but to American history more generally—including labor, environmental, gender, African American, political, business, immigration, religious, and intellectual history. Many of the scholars included here uncover the roots of current consumer practices in the eighteenth and nineteenth centuries not by invoking mythic—and largely untested—ideas about American abundance, but by studying nitty-gritty social and cultural history. The study of consumer society now extends to the examination of working-class families and budgets, labor ideology and practice, immigrant life, gender relations, the discourse of religious leaders, political activism, and many other aspects of life that for a long time had seemed far removed from consumer culture.

These scholars do not take the meaning of consumer society for granted. Showing that it is an essentially contested concept, they explore the question of whether consumer society should be understood as a level of material wealth; an infrastructure (i.e., corporations, advertisers, public relations agents, department stores, mail order catalogs, and gourmet coffee bars); a mindset that includes both self-description and self-consciousness as consumers; an economy in which mass production and mass consumption predominate; a political tactic; or a national identity. Collectively, the answer proposed in this volume is: all of the above. Rather than treating consumer society as an object of moral judgment (although, as Part V shows, it will, and should, remain subject to normative scrutiny), the new consumer historians use it as a window into understanding a broad range of issues in American history.

Consumer Society in American History is organized into six sections: Part I "Frameworks and Definitions"; Part II "Roots of American Consumer Society"; Part III "Class, Gender and Modernity, 1880–1940"; Part IV "Consumerism Since World War II"; Part V "Critiques and Celebrations"; and "Bibliographic Essay." The book begins with definitions and theories, and concludes with assessments of the meaning of American consumer society. The middle three historical sections move chronologically from colonial America to the present, with an emphasis on the period from the end of the Civil War through the present. Addressing, from a historical point of view, the ways Americans in a wide range of contexts and time periods have talked about consumption and practiced it, this reader presents a number of scholarly frameworks (not all of them American) available for studying it. In an etymological analysis, Raymond Williams charts the history of the word "consumer" in Chapter 1, linking the change in the connotation of the word to the economic transformations of the industrial revolution. Colin Campbell suggests in Chapter 2 that consumption, which we tend to think of as one of our basest material activities, has an ethical, indeed idealistic, dimension. Individual pleasure has little to do with the real meaning of consumer society, Jean Baudrillard claims in Chapter 3. Rather, consumers society makes "pleasure a duty," and consumption a "system of needs" in which we are surrounded by, but cannot appreciate, objects. In Chapter 4 James Fallows shows, in a comparison of Japan and the United States, that cultural explanations cannot fully explain how consumer societies emerge—that social policy affects consumer practices. In the final chapter of Part I, environmentalist Alan Durning harkens back to the older meaning of consumption as he warns of the ecological dangers of overconsumption.

In Part II, Chapter 6, James Axtell shows that consumption played a significant role in New World encounters between Native Americans and Europeans. T. H. Breen then argues in Chapter 7 that consumption played a role in forging American identity during the revolutionary era. Chapter 8 is devoted to Joyce Appleby's exploration of the reason consumption has been the "linchpin of our modern social system," though it has "never been the linchpin of our theories to explain modernity." As Lizabeth Cohen, George Sanchez, and Andrew Heinze demonstrate in Chapters 9, 10, and 11 of Part III, immigrants have used consumer society to help them Americanize while maintaining their ethnic identities. Then Mark Swienciki explains, in Chapter 12, that nineteenth-century men, despite their attempt to pin the label of "consumer" on women, spent a good deal of money on consumer activities. In Chapter 13 Cheryl Greenberg shows that the less powerful can use consumption to make claims, in her analysis of the "Don't Buy Where You Can't Work" campaigns organized by Harlem's African American community during the 1930s.

Part IV opens with H. F. Moorhouse arguing, in Chapter 14, that although it was a form of leisure, the culture of hot rodders was one that stressed hard work and despised convenient commercial short cuts. In Chapter 15 Elaine Tyler May links consumption and domestic ideology to the Cold War. Then, in Chapter 16, Robert E. Weems, Jr., examines the phenomenon of corporations taking advantage of racial identities to sell products. Chapter 17 by Juliet B. Schor and Chapter 18 by Kim Moody note that time and money, key aspects of consumer society, are intimately connected to the quality of workers' lives. John Elkington, Julia Hailes, and Joel Makower advocate market-based environmentalism in Chapter 19.

The contention of Michael Schudson in Part V, Chapter 20 is that analysts of consumer society have repeatedly echoed three persistent lines of criticism: Puritan, Quaker, and Republican. In Chapter 21 and 22, Steven Waldman and Wendell Berry extend the tradition of the jeremiad in forceful critiques of the political and moral consequences of modern consumer culture. Jean-Christophe Agnew postulates in Chapter 23 that perhaps the most salient characteristic of American consumer society is the continually debated significance of that society.

As the essays in this collection reveal, to say that America is a "consumer society" is to say many things. Key issues that emerge from this collection include:

America's long engagement with consumption. Obviously, the practices of consumption and the ideologies of consumerism have changed dramatically over time; but they are not recent phenomena. They are deeply-rooted, if constantly changing, components of American society.

The transition question. Is there a "critical point," as David Potter posited, when "society shifts from production to consumption"? When did the United States become a consumer society? Has it always been one? Were Americans born to shop? Did they learn to do so? Or were they coerced?

These are questions for history as well as politics, questions about when the transition occurred and about national identity. For every Horace Kallen who argued in 1936 that consumption was an American "birthright," meaning a fundamental and original characteristic of national identity, there is a William Leach who argued that Americans were forcibly "enticed into consumer pleasure and indulgence" by the new corporate culture of the twentieth century. No longer is consumer society automatically equated with a particular era or set of economic or technological features. Rather than a single transition, there has been a continuous tension in American history between consumer and producer values.[19]

Work. While labor and consumption are opposites in common parlance, consumption is frequently described as a form of work or an unworthy replacement for work. Indeed, American consumer scholarship began with Thorstein Veblen's *Theory of the Leisure Class* (1899) which expressed the view that consumer society undermined the "instinct of workmanship." It valorized *homo consumens* rather than *homo faber* when, Veblen believed, it is the latter that gives humanity true happiness and satisfaction. In consumer society, many critics argue, echoing Jean Baudrillard, play becomes work as it turns pleasure into a product that we are rather joylessly compelled to seek and buy. "In the modern world," John Lukacs writes, "the production of consumption has become more important than the consumption of production."[20] The movement of goods, in the view of these writers, becomes more important than the making or the enjoyment of them; the "good life" has become confused with the "goods life." So while work and consumption seem to be worlds apart, in consumer society the two become linked in a variety of ways.

Gender. Consumption has always been a gendered phenomenon. That is to say, men and women have experienced consumption differently. Women's consumption (i.e., grocery shopping) has often been a form of unpaid labor. In addition, as the Victorian era waned, one of the ways in which women entered the public sphere was through the commercialized world of consumption—the department store, the amusement park, the movie theater, all became acceptable sites for middle-class women to appear.

Discourse. The practices of consumption have contributed to the making of the United States as a consumer society, but equally important—perhaps more so—has been the constant stream of talk about consumption. This discourse has taken many forms, from acute anxiety (owing to concern about the moral damage done by consumption) to boisterous celebration (because widespread consumption has been seen as proof of freedom). Indeed, from the beginning, America's relation to consumption has been profoundly ambivalent. While it has been consistently linked to personal and political freedom in addition to the health of the economy, it has also been deemed central to economic inequality, the eclipse of traditional values, and the valorization of artifice.

Incorporation and Difference. Consumption is often described as a homogenizing force (the gist of the "mass culture critique" that reigned as the primary mode of analysis of consumer society for much of the twentieth century), or as a trivializing force which reduces politics to shallow materialism. As one historian has recently written, "At its root, twentieth-century consumer capitalism stood for a new kind of equality . . . the right of every American to push a shopping cart and to decide what brought happiness."[21] Yet consumption is also a site at which matters of power and difference are played out. Gender, class, ethnicity, and nationhood have all been heavily shaped by consumption.

Freedom. Consumption and freedom have long been linked; to some the linkage is illusory and to others it is very real. Marketplace choice, personal fulfillment, and political justice have all been connected to consumption, as has the corresponding critique that these values can never be gained through the commercial nexus of consumption. Consumption has been closely linked to the crusade for social justice in the following variations: 1) all Americans have a right to the bounty that the American people create—to a so-called American standard of living; 2) justice demands that one person's money is as good as another's; 3) the right to consumption, in a capitalist democracy, should not be restricted to particular groups.

Organized non-consumption. As many of these essays note, in American history the withdrawal of consumption has occasionally been as important as the act of consumption. In a consumer society, choosing not to consume—and encouraging or forcing others not to do so—has been claimed as a political act by Americans from the Revolution to the present day.

Consumption is woven into the fabric of American life—it is bound up with national unity as well as fragmentation; democracy as well as inequality; conformity but also protest; work and play. Through their explorations of these tensions in consumer society, the essays in this volume help explain American history itself.

Notes

1. Alan Thein Durning *How Much is Enough: The Consumer Society and the Future of the Earth*, (New York: Norton, 1992): 8; Barry Schwartz, *The Costs of Living: How Market Freedom Erodes the Best Things in Life* (New York: Norton, 1994): 162. Durning notes: "In the perception of most of the world's people, the consumer life-style is made in America."(8)

2. Roger Swagler, "Evolution and Application of the Term Consumerism: Themes and Variations," *Journal of Consumer Policy* 18 (1995): 347–60. For other helpful attempts to define these terms see, Juliet B. Schor, *The Overspent American: Upscaling, Downshifting and the New Consumer*, (New York: Basic Books, 1998): 224; Zygmunt Bauman, *Work, Consumerism and the New Poor* (Buckingham, U.K.: Open University Press, 1998): 23–6; and, in this book, Mark A. Swiencicki, "Consuming Brotherhood."

3. James B. Gilbert, "Introduction: From Power to Culture," *The Maryland Historian* 19 (Spring-Summer 1988): 2–3.

4. The epigraphs are drawn from the following sources: Horace Kallen, *The Decline and Rise of the Consumer: A Philosophy of Consumer Cooperation* (New York: Appleton, 1936): 198; Dallas Smythe, "Buy Something," in *In the Marketplace: Consumerism in America*, ed. Frank Browning et al. (San Francisco: Canfield Press, 1972): 167.

5. August Meier and Elliot Rudwick, "Negro Boycotts of Jim Crow Streetcars in Tennessee," *American Quarterly* 21 (Winter 1969), 755–63; Robin D. G. Kelley, " 'We Are Not What We Seem': Rethinking Black Working-Class Opposition in the Jim Crow South," *Journal of American History* 80 (June 1993): 75–112. Quotation 104.

6. Figures cited in Thomas J. Schlereth, *Victorian America: Transformations of Everyday Life, 1876–1915*, (New York: HarperPerennial, 1991): 157.

7. Kathryn Kish Sklar, *Florence Kelley and the Nation's Work*, (New Haven: Yale University Press, 1995): 23; Lippmann quoted in *Encyclopedia of the Consumer Movement*, ed. Stephen Brobeck et al. (Santa Barbara: ABC-CLIO, 1998): 586.

8. Daniel J. Boorstin quoted in James D. Norris, *Advertising and the Transformation of American Society*, (Westport, Conn.: Greenview Press, 1990): 168.

9. Franklin Delano Roosevelt, State of the Union Address, January 6, 1941.

10. "Rocketing Births: Business Bonanza," *Life* (June 15, 1958): 83–9; "A New, $10-Billion Power: The U.S. Teen-Age Consumer," *Life* (August 31, 1959): 78–85.

11. See the recollections of Julian Bond and Lonnie King in Howell Raines, *My Soul is Rested: Movement Days in the Deep South Remembered* (New York: Penguin, 1977): 88.

12. Ralph Nader, *Unsafe at Any Speed* (1972; New York: Grossman, 1965): xxvi.

13. Jimmy Carter, "The Crisis of Confidence," July 15, 1979.

14. Benjamin R. Barber, *A Place for Us: How to Make Society Civil and Democracy Strong* (New York: Hill and Wang, 1998): 101–4.

15. For a recent version of Turner's famous 1893 address, see *Rereading Frederick Jackson Turner: "The Significance of the Frontier in American History" and Other Essays*, with commentary by John Mack Faragher (New York: Henry Holt, 1994).

16. Jackson Lears writes in a review of Daniel Horowitz's *Vance Packard and American Social Criticism*, "the major critics of consumption failed to see how consumption and display can play crucial roles in any society's development of art, ritual, and shared social meaning." See "The Hidden Persuader," *New Republic* (October 3, 1994): 32–6.

17. Jackie Robinson, "Must Project a More Realistic Image of Negro," *Advertising Age* (July 1964): 84.

18. Susan Porter Benson, *Counter Cultures: Saleswomen, Managers, and Customers in American Department Stores, 1890–1940* (Urbana: University of Illinois Press, 1986).

19. Kallen, *Decline and Rise of the Consumer*: 94; William Leach, *Land of Desire: Merchants, Power, and the Rise of a New American Culture* (New York: Pantheon, 1993): 3–4. See also Jackson Lears, "Beyond Veblen: Rethinking Consumer Culture in America," in *Consuming Visions: Accumulation and Display of Goods in America, 1880–1920*, ed. Simon J. Bronner (New York: Norton, 1989): 73–97. Lears writes on p. 77, "it may be a mistake to argue a shift from the plodding nineteenth century to the carnivalesque twentieth: the carnival may have been in town all the time."

20. Quoted in Colin Campbell, *The Romantic Ethic and the Spirit of Modern Consumerism* (Oxford: Basil Blackwell, 1989): 36.

21. David Farber, *The Age of Great Dreams: America in the 1960s*, (Hill and Wang: New York, 1994): 64. But Farber points out on the very next page that African Americans were justifiably angry about their exclusion from the bounty that came to seen as a birthright of those born in the "American Century."

P A R T   I

Frameworks and Definitions

CHAPTER 1

Consumer

Raymond Williams

In modern English **consumer** and **consumption** are the predominant descriptive nouns of all kinds of use of goods and services. The predominance is significant in that it relates to a particular version of economic activity, derived from the character of a particular economic system, as the history of the word shows.

Consume has been in English since C14, from fw *consumer*, F, and the variant *consommer*, F (these variants have a complicated but eventually distinct history in French), rw *consumere*, L—to take up completely, devour, waste, spend. In almost all its early English uses, **consume** had an unfavourable sense; it meant to destroy, to use up, to waste, to exhaust. This sense is still present in 'consumed by the fire' and in the popular description of pulmonary phthisis as **consumption**. Early uses of **consumer**, from C16, had the same general sense of destruction or waste.

It was from mC18 that **consumer** began to emerge in a neutral sense in descriptions of bourgeois political economy. In the new predominance of an organized market, the acts of making and of using goods and services were newly defined in the increasingly abstract pairings of *producer* and **consumer**, *production* and **consumption**.

Yet the unfavourable connotations of **consume** persisted, at least until lC19, and it was really only in mC20 that the word passed from specialized use in political economy to general and popular use. The relative decline of *customer*, used from C15 to describe a buyer or purchaser, is significant here, in that *customer* had always implied some degree of regular and continuing relationship to a supplier, whereas **consumer** indicates the more abstract figure in a more abstract market.

The modern development has been primarily American but has spread very quickly. The dominance of the term has been so great that even groups of informed and discriminating purchasers and users have formed *Consumer's Associations*. The development relates primarily to the planning and attempted control of markets which is inherent in large-scale industrial capitalist (and state-capitalist) production, where, especially after the depression of lC19, manufacture was related not only to the supply of known needs (which *customer* or *user* would adequately describe) but to the planning of given kinds and quantities of production which required large investment at an early and often predictive stage. The development of modern commercial *advertising* (persuasion, or *penetration* of a market) is related to the same stage of capitalism: the creation of needs and wants and of particular ways of satisfying them, as distinct from and in addition to the notification of available supply which had been the main earlier function of *advertising* (where that kind of persuasion could be seen as *puff* and *puffery*). **Consumer** as a predominant term was the creation of such manufacturers and their agents. It implies, ironically as in the earliest senses, the using-up of what is going to be produced, though once the term was established it was given some appearance of autonomy (as in the curious phrase **consumer choice**). It is appropriate in terms of the history of the word that criticism of a wasteful and 'throw-away' society was expressed, somewhat later, by the description **consumer society**. Yet the predominance of the capitalist model ensured its widespread and often overwhelming extension to such fields as politics, education and health. In any of these fields, but also in the ordinary field of goods and services, to say *user* rather than **consumer** is still to express a relevant distinction.

CHAPTER 2

Consuming Goods and the Good of Consuming

Colin Campbell

There has long been a tendency in both academic and intellectual circles to devalue, and often to denigrate, that field of human conduct which falls under the heading of "consumption." This is due to the existence of a powerful tradition of thought that generally regards consumption with some suspicion, inclining us to believe that, even if it is not exactly "bad," it can have nothing whatever to do with that which is good, true, noble, or beautiful.

Two factors can be identified as largely responsible for this attitude of suspicion. One is the discipline with which the term "consumption" is most commonly associated: economics. For it is inherent in the basic paradigm adopted by economists that *production* is singled out as the activity that matters. Although in theory consumption is the sole end and justification for all production, it is quite clear that production, not consumption, is the more valued and morally justifiable activity. A second reason for the bias in favor of production is to be found in that Puritan inheritance which itself gave rise to modern economics (if indirectly, via utilitarianism), and that, more pertinently, also encouraged successive generations to place work above leisure, thrift above spending, and deferred above immediate gratification. It is this generalized asceticism that is largely responsible for the contemporary denigration of consumption.[1]

However, even the Puritans did not condemn all consumption; what they accepted as legitimate was consumption directed at satisfying needs, while fiercely condemning any expenditure in excess of what was deemed necessary to meet these needs. In other words, it was luxury consumption which was roundly condemned, not consumption in general. One of the main reasons modern consumption has such a bad press is that it is generally seen to be mainly "luxury" or "want-based" in character. Consequently, even the little moral legitimacy consumption once possessed has today largely been swept away.[2]

In contemporary society, then, there are essentially two attitudes toward consumption. First, it may be viewed as a matter of satisfying "genuine" needs (what we may call "basic provisioning"), in which case, even if this is considered a mundane matter of routine, day-to-day decision-making and habit, it is at least seen as a legitimate activity by most intellectuals. Alternatively, consumption is viewed as largely a matter of gratifying wants and desires by means of goods and services that are viewed as nonessential (that is, luxuries), in which case it is typically regarded as an arena of superficial activity prompted by ethically dubious motives and directed toward trivial, ephemeral, and essentially worthless goals.

Now there are two distinct yet closely associated points to note about this latter attitude. The first concerns the idea that want-driven consumption concerns the "unnecessary" and hence the unimportant things in life; this leads to condemnations of consumption on the grounds that it involves people in superficial or frivolous activities. Consumption is thus contrasted with "real," significant activities such as work, religion, or politics. The second and related point is that involvement in trivial activities, and especially the tendency to take them seriously, is assumed to stem from questionable motives: no one guided by high-minded or noble concerns, it is assumed, would ever become involved in such dubious pursuits. Consequently, consumption is viewed as the realm in which the worst of human motives prevail—motives such as pride, greed, and envy. Any social scientist who wishes to understand consumption is forced to confront both of these moral judgments, since they are central to most theories of consumption.[3]

The question, therefore, is whether our understanding of the activities of consumption does indeed justify the condemnation with which it generally meets. In short, is consumption bad for us? In addressing this question, one is not concerned with whether consuming is harmful in the literal sense that our health or well-being is threatened by the nature of the items we consume. Rather, the focus is on the claim that consuming is deleterious because it is an activity (or a set of activities) that "brings out the worst in us"; that is to say, because it encourages us to behave in morally reprehensible ways. Does consumption lead us to be greedy, materialistic, avaricious, or envious? The predominant concern is with the motives (and to a lesser extent the goals) that are presumed to underlie modern consumption behavior.[4]

The thesis advanced here will be that the usual antipathy toward the motives of consumption is, if not entirely without justification, extremely one-sided, if only because the social science theories that buttress it are hardly plausible. Close attention to why people actually do consume goods suggests the presence of an idealistic, if not exactly ethical, dimension. Therefore, we must first outline a somewhat different view of the nature of consuming in contemporary industrial (or postindustrial) society from those which currently prevail.

Modern Consumption

Why people consume goods is understandably a central question for social science. Essentially, there have been two general answers to this question—one economic, the other sociological. The inadequacies of the economic paradigm (in which the origin of wants is simply not explored) have been well documented elsewhere and will not be pursued here. On the other hand, the sociological model, which in practice means Thorstein Veblen's model, is still widely employed and its inadequacies are rarely noted.

In essence, Veblen's model assumes that consumption is a form of communication in which "signals" concerning the wealth (and thus, it is argued, the social status) of the consumer are telegraphed to others. In addition, it is assumed that individuals seek to use such "conspicuous consumption" as a way of improving their social standing, aiming ultimately to "emulate" that "leisure class" which, it is claimed, stands at the pinnacle of the class system. This view of consumption links it directly with an ethically dubious activity, social climbing. In assuming that consumers' main interest in goods is as symbols of status, Veblen asserts that consumers are motivated by a mixture of anxiety (over how others may view them) and envy (of those in a superior position). It is hardly surprising that, with the widespread acceptance of such a theory, consuming is commonly viewed as ethically suspect.

There are, however, many problems with Veblen's model, which generally can be said to be theoretically incoherent where it is not empirically false.[5] The key deficiency is that it does not account for the dynamism that is so typical of modern consumption. Status competition through conspicuous display does not require novel products; it coexists happily with an unchanging, traditional way of life.[6] In this respect, both the economic and the sociological models have the same central failing: they attempt to provide an ahistorical general theory that fails to recognize crucial differences between traditional and modern consumption. The question is not. Why do people consume? Rather it is, Why do we consume as we do? That is to say, why do *modern* individuals consume as they do?

The Problem of Consumerism

It is a fundamental mistake to imagine that modern consumption, or consumerism, is simply traditional consumption writ large, as if all that separates the two phenomena was a question of scale. Therefore, it is misleading to assume that modern consumption equals mass consumption. Consumption in modern societies may well be consumption "for the masses," something that could not occur until modern techniques made large-scale production possible; but what really distinguishes it is its dynamic character. The very high levels of consumption typical of modern societies do not stem primarily from the fact that large numbers of people consume; rather, they stem from the very high levels of individual consumption, which in turn stem from the apparent insatiability of consumers and the fact that their wants appear never to be exhausted. While technological innovation and planned obsolescence both have a part to play in keeping consumption levels high, the greatest contribution is consumers' almost magical ability to produce new wants immediately after old ones are satisfied. No sooner is one want satisfied than another appears, and subsequently another, in an apparently endless series. No modern consumer, no matter how privileged or wealthy, can honestly say that there is nothing that he or she wants. It is this capacity to continuously "discover" new wants that requires explaining.

What makes consumerism even more puzzling is that we typically discover that we desire novel products, ones with which we are unfamiliar. We cannot possibly know what "satisfaction" (if any) such products might yield when we desire them. Indeed, it would seem that it is principally this preference for novel goods and services that lies behind the apparent inexhaustibility of wants itself, as manifest, for example, in the central modern phenomenon of fashion.

These, then, are the features that distinguish the modern from the traditional consumer. The latter generally tends to have fixed needs rather than endless wants, and hence consumes the same products repeatedly, as and when these needs arise. This pattern of consumption does not, as economists often seem to imply, simply result from the lack of resources to consume more. Rather, the pattern represents all the consumption that the "needs" dictated by traditional ways of life require.[7] The problem to be addressed when attempting to account for modern consumption, therefore, is how it is possible for inexhaustible wants—often wants for novel products and services—to appear with such regularity.

A Hedonistic Approach

It is possible to provide at least a partial solution to this problem by regarding modern consumption activity as the consequence of a form of hedonism. In saying this, it is important to recognize that what is meant by hedonism or pleasure-seeking has nothing in common with that theory of satisfaction-seeking, deriving from utilitarianism, which traditionally underlies most economic theories of consumption.

The latter model is built around the idea that human behavior is concerned with the elimination of deprivation or need. Consequently, it assumes that individuals interact with objects so as to make use of their "utility" to "satisfy" these "needs." Such conduct may bring pleasure to the individual, but not only is this not guaranteed, it is not the reason the object was desired. Thus, economic theory is not centrally concerned with pleasure-seeking behavior. The principal reason for this is that whilst utility is a real property of objects, pleasure is a judgment that individuals make about stimuli they experience. As such, pleasure is not necessarily connected with extracting utility from objects. Trying to satisfy needs usually requires engaging with real objects in order to discover the degree and kind of their utility in meeting pre-existing desires. Searching for pleasure means exposing oneself to certain stimuli in the hope that they will trigger an enjoyable response. Hence, whilst one typically needs to make use of objects in order to discover their potential for need satisfaction, one need only employ one's senses to experience pleasure. What is more, whereas an object's utility is dependent upon what it is, an object's pleasurable significance is a function of what it can be taken to be. Only reality can provide satisfaction, but both illusions and delusions can supply pleasure.

However, since the elimination of basic human needs is generally experienced as pleasurable (as in the experience of eating when one is attempting to eliminate the deprivation caused by hunger), pleasure-seeking has traditionally been perceived as bound up with efforts to meet needs. This perception becomes less valid as the advance of civilization causes fewer people to experience the frequent deprivation of their basic needs, so that the pleasure associated with need-fulfilment tends to become more and more elusive.[8] the traditional hedonist's response is to try to recreate the gratificatory cycle of need-satisfaction as often as possible.

Traditional hedonism hence involves a concern with "pleasures" rather than with "pleasure," there being a world of difference between valuing an experience because (among other things) it yields pleasure, and valuing the pleasure an experience can bring—that is, focusing upon a distinct aspect or quality of the experience. The former is the ancient pattern. Human beings in all cultures seem to agree on a basic list of activities that are "pleasures" in this sense, such as eating, drinking, sexual intercourse, socializing, singing, dancing, and playing games. But since pleasure is a quality of experience, it can, at least in principle, be judged to be present in all sensations. Hence the pursuit of pleasure in the abstract is potentially an ever-present possibility, provided that the individual's attention is directed to the skillful manipulation of sensation rather than to the conventionally identified sources of enjoyment.[9]

Modern Hedonism

All too often, then, it has been assumed that hedonistic theories of human conduct emphasize sensory pleasures. This, however, is not necessarily the case, for although all pleasure-seeking can be said to have a sensory base, there is no reason that hedonism should concentrate exclusively, or even primarily, on the "baser" appetites. Indeed, while an emphasis on the sensory may have characterized traditional hedonism, it is not characteristic of its contemporary counterpart; modern hedonism focuses less on sensations than on emotions.

Emotions have the potential to serve as immensely powerful sources of pleasure, since they constitute states of high arousal. Any emotion—even the so-called negative ones, such as fear, anger, grief, and jealousy—can provide pleasurable stimulation. However, for the stimulation associated with such emotions to be experienced as pleasant, the extent of the arousal must be adjustable: it must be possible for the individual to "control" the emotion. An ability to self-regulate emotion is much more than a mere capacity to suppress (though this is its starting point), but extends to the "creation" of a given emotion at will.

Such emotional cultivation is achieved largely through the manipulation of what an individual believes to be the nature of his or her condition or environment, particularly through adjustments in the degree to which certain things are held to be the case. For example, to the extent that people can convince themselves that they have been harshly treated by life and don't deserve their bad luck, they will be able to enjoy the "pleasure" of self-pity. To a large extent, however, the deliberate cultivation of an emotion for the pleasure derived from experiencing it does not center around efforts to reconstruct what is believed about the real environment in this way. Rather, it tends to focus on the somewhat easier task of conjuring up imaginary environments that are sufficiently realistic to prompt an associated emotion. This modern, autonomous, self-illusory hedonism is called, in everyday language, daydreaming.

Daydreaming

Daydreaming is an integral part of the psychic lives of modern men and women, yet there is a tendency either to ignore its presence and/or to deny its importance. Nearly everyone in modern society both daydreams and fantasizes; this is a regular, daily activity for both sexes and all ages.[10]

Yet there has been little recognition of the importance of this phenomenon or of the fact that it is characteristically a modern practice, largely dependent on the development of individualism, literacy (that is to say, silent reading), and the novel. There is little doubt that the impulse lying behind daydreaming is a hedonistic one, as individuals turn away from what they perceive as an unstimulating real world in order to dwell on the greater pleasures imaginative scenarios can offer. In this context, the individual can be seen as an artist of the imagination, someone who takes images from memory or the immediate environment and re-arranges or otherwise improves them so as to render them more pleasing. Such daydreams are experienced as convincing; that is to say, individuals react subjectively to them as if they were real (thereby gaining an emotional response), even while realizing that they are not. This is the distinctly modern faculty the ability to create an illusion that is known to be false but felt to be true.

Generally speaking, the way reality is typically adjusted by the daydreamer so as to give pleasure is by simply omitting life's little inconveniences, as well as by adding what, in reality, would be happy (if not extraordinarily unlikely) coincidences. In this way, imagined experience characteristically comes to represent a perfected vision of life, and from what are often quite small beginnings, individuals may develop daydreams that become "alternative worlds"—that is, elaborate works of art—deviating more and more from what might reasonably be expected of reality.

Although daydreaming is commonly dismissed as an inconsequential phenomenon, there are grounds for believing that it has significant effects. For example, although daydreaming is typically prompted by boredom, the pleasures it supplies mean that daydreamers are likely to experience "real life" as more boring than they did before, increasing the probability that further daydreaming will occur. Thus, like all forms of pleasure, day-dreaming can easily become addictive and result in a certain tendency to withdraw from ordinary life.

However, daydreaming differs from straightforward fantasizing in that it concerns events and scenarios that might actually occur at some point in the future. Indeed, daydreams often begin with simple, anticipatory imaginings surrounding real, upcoming events, such as holidays. This makes it more or less inevitable that actuality is going to be compared—in terms of pleasure gained—against the standard set by the anticipatory daydream, and hence generally experienced as (quite literally) disillusioning. For no matter how pleasant the real-life experience turns out to be, it is impossible for it to resemble the perfection attained in imagination. Consequently, disillusionment is very likely to prompt still more daydreaming, and thus, inevitably, further disillusionment. This suggests that daydreaming creates certain permanent dispositions: a sense of dissatisfaction with real life and a generalized longing for "something better."

The Spirit of Modern Consumerism

Such an understanding of the dynamics of how dreams and experiences of real life interact may make it possible to explain those mysterious features of modern consumerism identified above. These include not simply the question of where wants come from (and indeed go to), but also how it is that consumers have an inexhaustible supply of them, and why it is that they have such a strong preference for novel, as opposed to familiar, goods. We can now suggest that modern consumers will desire a novel rather than a familiar product, largely because they believe its acquisition and use can supply them with pleasurable experiences that they have not so far encountered in reality. One may project onto the novel product some of the idealized pleasure that has already been experienced in daydreams, but that cannot be associated with products currently being consumed (as the limits to the pleasure they provide are already familiar). For new wants to be created, all that is required is the presence in the consumer's environment of products that are perceived to be new.[11] Hence, we can say that the basic motivation underlying consumerism is the desire to experience in reality that pleasurable experience the consumer has already enjoyed imaginatively.

Only new products are seen as offering any possibility of realizing this ambition. But since reality can never provide the perfected pleasures encountered in daydreams (or, if at all, only very occasionally and in part), each purchase naturally leads to disillusionment; this helps explain how wanting is extinguished so quickly, and why people disacquire goods almost as rapidly as they acquire them. What is not extinguished, however, is the fundamental longing that daydreaming itself generates. For the practice of daydreaming continues (and indeed may be strengthened), and hence there is as much determination as ever to find new products to serve as replacement objects of desire.

This dynamic interplay between illusion and reality is the key to an understanding of modern consumerism (and modern hedonism generally), for the tension between the two creates longing as a permanent mode, with the concomitant sense of dissatisfaction with what is and the yearning for something better. Daydreaming turns the future into a perfectly illusioned present. Hence, individuals do not so much repeat cycles of sensory pleasure-seeking (as in traditional hedonism) so much as they continually strive to close the gap between imagined and experienced pleasures. Yet this gap can never be closed, for whatever one experiences in reality can be adjusted in imagination so as to be even more pleasurable. Thus the illusion is always better than the reality, the promise more interesting than actuality.[12]

This theory of consumerism is inner-directed. It does not presume that consumption behavior is either guided by, or oriented to, the actions of others. In that sense, it breaks with the long-standing sociological tradition that presents consumption as an essentially social practice.[13] On the other hand, this theory does not present consumption as driven by material considerations. The idea that contemporary consumers have a magpie-like desire to acquire as many material objects as possible (the acquisitive society thesis) represents a serious misunderstanding of the basic motivational structure that leads consumers to want goods. The acquisitive society thesis is particularly at odds with the facts, for modern consumer society is characterized as much by the extent to which individuals dispose of goods as the extent to which they acquire them. Consumerism involves a high *turnover* of goods, not merely a high level of their acquisition. This fact is consistent with the claim that the true focus of desire is less the object itself than the experience the consumer anticipates possessing it will bring.

Consumerism and the Counterculture

By extricating modern consumption from its presumed connection with other-directed status striving and envy on the one side, and crude materialism and acquisitiveness on the other, an understanding of this sphere of activity may be reached that does not automatically carry with it overtones of moral disapproval or condemnation. Unfortunately, this aim does not appear to have been achieved, since, by closely associating consumption with hedonism, it seems inevitable that consumerism will remain an object of moral disapproval. Indeed, one could claim that the present theory only makes matters worse, as, in some quarters at least, pleasure-seeking is even more objectionable than the consumption of "luxury" goods. Certainly we can say that, on the whole, pleasure has been the one constant target of moralists over many generations, largely because of the hostile attitude originally taken by the early Christian fathers and typically still held in our own day by fundamentalists and other representatives of the religious right.[14]

There is, however, an alternative moral tradition that not only defends the pursuit of pleasure, but associates it directly with the highest moral and spiritual ideals. This tradition of thought was represented historically by Antinomianism and then, in more recent times, by Romanticism. It is still very much alive, with its last significant efflorescence occurring in the 1960s in the form of the movement we know as the "counterculture."[15]

Central to the Romantic creed is the belief that the true and the good are both subsumed under the beautiful, and consequently that they, too, are to be discerned by means of the imagination. It also follows that these ideals, like beauty itself, can be recognized by their capacity to give pleasure, with the natural consequence that the path to virtue and enlightenment is identical with the pursuit of pleasure. This is recognizable as the faith that inspired many of the young counterculturalists of the 1960s; yet it is only fair to observe that they were hardly renowned for their defense of the consumer society. On the contrary, they launched the very critique of commercial and material values that has, to a large extent, laid the basis for much of our current unease about the state of modern life. While the counterculturalists defended pleasure-seeking, they also attacked what they saw as the evil of consumerism. How is this paradox to be explained?

To some extent it can be accounted for by the fact that the counterculturalists, like the spokespersons for the conventional morality they claimed to reject, held to that erroneous view of the nature of consumption mentioned above. Hence, they accepted the assumption that consumerism involved status envy, acquisitiveness, and materialism, whilst being perhaps understandably reluctant to recognize that their own high valuation of pleasure might be connected in some way with their experience as the first generation to be reared in a climate of widespread affluence.

In contrast to this explanation of the paradox, what one might call the "official" explanation is that the Romantic identification of pleasure with the ideal realm of virtue and beauty means that there is an understandable hostility to any trivialization or "prostitution" of this central dimension of human experience—hostility, in other words, to any tendency to treat the pursuit of pleasure as a simple end in itself, a mere "recreation" in which push-pin could be re-garded as on a par with poetry. Thus, the Romantics' principal objection to consumption (it is said) was not that it was prompted by a search for pleasure (even less that it gave pleasure), but that pleasure seeking was not being taken seriously enough. In other words, Romanticism gives the highest possible legit-imation to the pursuit of pleasure, especially the pursuit of imaginatively med-icated pleasure, whilst condemning not merely simpleminded and crass plea-sures, but hedonism itself, when it is not associated with a high moral purpose.

The Goods of Consumerism

However, to suggest that one can approve of pleasure-seeking when it is part and parcel of the pursuit of high ideals, yet disapprove of it when, separated from such ideals, it is engaged in simply for personal gratification, presumes that it is possible to tell which is which. Unfortunately, this is not so easy. For example, the practice of taking drugs, especially LSD, was defended by many in the 1960s on the grounds that it was an important means of attaining en-hanced self-awareness and spiritual enlightenment. But for many hippies and quasihippies, drugs were probably used with no such end in view, but simply because of the "high" they yielded. It is difficult to distinguish between these two positions because, in practice, they often merge into one another; or per-haps, more accurately, the one can easily become the other over time. Individ-uals may set out to take drugs merely to gain a high, only to find that their awareness is transformed; or, alternatively, those who take drugs because they hope to attain enlightenment might, on the contrary, merely develop an addic-tion to a particular form of intense physical stimulation.

It might be objected that this is to make heavy weather of what is really a fairly simple matter, since as far as most consumption activity is concerned, purely selfish, or at least self-interested, motives are obviously at work. Unfor-tunately for this argument, the presence of selfish interests is not incompatible with more high-minded concerns. Whilst some consumption is merely a matter of mundane provisioning, much of it is of considerably less prosaic interest to those involved. Obviously, buying a house, a car, a boat, or a set of furniture is, for most people, an act of some moment, linked to what might be consid-ered their "life projects." Understandably, then, major purchases of this kind often figure prominently in people's thoughts, where they play a crucial role as both incentives and rewards. In other words, such acts of consumption are critically interwoven into the motivational structures of individuals, providing the energy they need to carry through difficult tasks as well as the gratification necessary if they are to believe subsequently that their efforts were worthwhile. In this direct and obvious sense, not merely actual consuming, but also imagi-nary, "anticipatory consuming" can indeed be said to be good for us, since without it, we might lack good reasons for doing anything at all.

It does not necessarily follow, however, that because purchasing goods plays such an important part in the reward system of individuals, there is no idealistic or ethical dimension present in those projects around which individuals organize their lives. After all, although people's daydreams differ, a common factor, apart from the quality of pleasure, is the representation of the dreamer in an idealized manner. Thus, the pleasure people derive from daydreaming is not separate from their moral life; it is intimately associated with it: doing good—or more accurately, perhaps, imagining oneself doing good and being good—often constitute an important part of the pleasures of daydreaming.

In this respect, the pleasures associated with imagining perfect scenarios relate directly to imagining oneself as a perfect person, one who exemplifies certain ideals. This point can be illustrated by considering two important aspects of modern consumption: fashion and tourism.

The theory outlined above helps explain why modern consumers should be so eager to "follow fashion," without, however, having to resort either to the implausible suggestion that they are forced to do so, or that they are merely striving to "keep up with the Joneses." Since fashion is an institution that guarantees the controlled introduction of a degree of novelty into goods with high aesthetic significance, the taste for novelty generated by the widespread practice of self-illusory hedonism helps explain the importance and persistence of this institution.

Unfortunately, there has been a consistent tendency for intellectuals to decry fashion, to treat it as a trivial, insignificant, even worthless phenomenon. Yet if we use the term properly, to refer to a consistent process of changes in style (rather than simply a synonym for custom or practice), opprobrium is entirely inappropriate. For fashion necessarily involves an aesthetic ideal, and those who dedicate themselves to keeping up with fashion—or even more interestingly, perhaps, to "taking the lead in fashion"—can be said, quite justifiably, to be striving to bring their lives into line with the ideal of beauty. That there may be an element of narcissism involved, or that the conduct in question may be strengthened by the presence of such motives as pride or vanity, does nothing to negate the ideal dimension of such behavior, since all forms of moral conduct probably require the helping hand of self-interest. "Following fashion" may indeed, in some instances, be little more than a mindless and morally worthless endeavor, but it can also be the high-minded pursuit of a serious ideal.

Much the same can be said of tourism which is increasingly becoming a central component, not merely of modern consumerism, but of modern life. Tourism does not involve the purchase of products, but of experiences; yet, as with fashion, novelty is the most critical quality in defining the parameters of desire. Here, too, there has been a tendency in some circles to caricature and despise the "tourist" whilst celebrating, by contrast, the genuine "traveller." But this bias is hard to justify, since the acquisition of valued experiences is crucial to the goals that find favor in modern society (and especially, perhaps, in the contemporary United States). The human potential and encounter-group movements of the 1960s and 1970s, as well as their successors, the quasireligious and psychotherapeutic movements of the 1990s, stressed the importance of critical "experiences" in helping individuals to discover their "true selves" and hence maximize their potential. Such phrases are also often to be found in statements defining the goals of education, therapy, and art. If the acquisition of "experiences," especially those of a highly novel kind, is accorded such critical importance in contexts such as these, how is it that it should be denied this status when occurring under the heading of "tourism"?

Is Consumption Good for Us?

I do not know. Such a question suggests both that we can agree on what constitutes the good life and that we know exactly what effects our current consuming practices are having on ourselves and our society. In addition, it is difficult to speak of "consumption" as if it were a single, undifferentiated activity. However, as I have tried to show, there is something distinctive about modern consumption. By elucidating this I have endeavored to shed some light on whether the motives and goals embedded in such activity can be considered good. Obviously there is no simple answer, for consumerism is a complex phenomenon.

However, it is clear that both self-interested and idealistic concerns are involved in consumerism. Indeed, consumerism is prompted by concerns and guided by values that underpin many other modern institutions, yet which, in those other contexts, are usually regarded favorably. It is not as if the theory I have outlined applies only to consumption. It applies with equal force to all forms of behavior in which imaginative pleasure-seeking or desire plays a significant role. Romantic love is one such phenomenon, so one could ask, with equal justification, whether love is good for us.[16]

Hence, it is delusory to imagine that one can cordon off consumption from the larger moral and idealistic framework of our lives and dub it "bad" without, in the process, significantly affecting the total moral landscape of our world. Consumerism probably reflects the moral nature of contemporary human existence as much as any other widespread modern practice; significant change here would therefore require no minor adjustment to our way of life, but the transformation of our civilization.

Notes

1. Another moral dimension to this discussion is associated with gender. Much consumption activity (especially shopping) has long been seen as primarily "women's work," whilst production has been judged "men's work." This can also be seen as a major influence on the ethical judgments passed on consumption.

2. It has often been suggested that a new "ethic" has arisen that serves to legitimate consumerism: see William H. Whyte, *The Organization Man* (New York: Doubleday-Anchor Books, 1957); David Reisman et al., *The Lonely Crowd: A Study in the Changing American Character* (New York: Doubleday-Anchor, 1966); and Daniel Bell, *The Cultural Contradictions of Capitalism* (London: Heineman, 1976). Tellingly, such claims are made by writers who do not themselves endorse the new ethic, but, on the contrary, seek to condemn it, often from a perspective of apparent support for the old ascetic Protestant values. Consequently an attitude of suspicion, if not hostility, toward consumerism still typifies academic and intellectual discussions in this field.

3. This view sometimes places the blame on individuals for engaging in such practices, while at other times it exonerates them by arguing that consumers are typically coerced or manipulated into this form of behavior by others (usually manufacturers or advertisers). In either case, however, consumerism itself is judged to be bad, whether the source of the evil lies in individuals or in the organization of the society.

4. This extremely negative view of modern consumption is not typically shared by consumers themselves; indeed, one suspects that it is not actually shared by academics and intellectuals, either, when actually acting as consumers. In fact, there has recently been a movement among intellectuals and some academics to view consumerism as far more significant; see Steven Connor, *Postmodernist Culture: An Introduction to Theories of the Contemporary* (Oxford: Blackwell, 1989); David Harvey, *The Condition of Postmodernity* (Oxford: Blackwell, 1989); Mike Featherstone, *Consumer Culture and Postmodernism* (London: Sage, 1991); and Frederic Jameson, *Postmodernism, Or the Cultural Logic of Late Capitalism* (London: Verso, 1991). Here, there is a tendency to regard consumption as the central focus of the efforts of individuals to create and maintain their personal identity. However, despite this development, there is little evidence of any change in moral tone. For such conduct is still likely to be despised, if not actually condemned.

5. In the first place, the picture of a single leisured elite whom all other classes seek to emulate (either directly or indirectly) inaccurately portrays the complex stratification system of modern societies. Second, what determines the consumption habits of this elite remains a mystery, as *they* have no one to emulate. Third, new fashions in the consumption of goods do not always or even commonly originate with a social elite and then "trickle down" the status ladder as a result of imitation and emulation by those in inferior positions. In fact, fashions "trickle up" or even "across" just as often as they trickle down (see Paul Blumberg, "The Decline and Fall of the Status Symbol: Some Thoughts on Status in a Post-Industrial Society," *Social Problems* 21 [1974]: 480–98). Fourth, social standing is not determined simply by wealth (let alone only by conspicuously displayed wealth); other qualities, most obviously birth, can still be important. Finally, treating wealth and leisure as equivalents, both signifying "waste," is seriously misleading given the important Protestant tendency to applaud the first whilst deploring the second, as well as the Bohemian inversion of this view. For a full account of the emulation model of consumption see Thorstein Veblen, *The Theory of the Leisure Class* (London: George Allen & Unwin, 1925); for a critique, see Colin Campbell, "The Desire for the New: Its Nature and Social Location as Presented in Theories of Fashion and Modern Consumerism," in *Consuming Technologies: Media and Information in Domestic Spaces*, ed. Roger Silverman and Eric Hirsch (London: Routledge, 1992), and idem, "Conspicuous Confusion? A Critique of Veblen's Theory of Conspicuous Consumption," *Sociological Theory* 12, no. 2 (1994).

6. See, for example, Melville J. Herskovits, *Economic Anthropology: A Study in Comparative Economics* (New York: Alfred A. Knopf, 1960).

7. See Elizabeth E. Hoyt, "The Impact of a Money Economy upon Consumption Patterns," *Annals of the American Academy of Political and Social Science* no. 305 (1956); 12–22; and Kusum Nair, *Blossoms in the Dust: The Human Factor in Indian Development* (New York: Frederick A. Praeger, 1962).

8. See the argument in Tibor Scitovsky, *The Joyless Economy: An Inquiry into Human Satisfaction and Consumer Dissatisfaction* (New York: Oxford University Press, 1976).

9 These two orientations involve contrasting strategies. In the first, the basic concern is with increasing the number of times one is able to enjoy life's "pleasures"; thus the traditional hedonist tries to spend more and more time eating, drinking, having sex, and dancing. The hedonistic index here is the incidence of pleasure per unit of life. In the second, the primary object is to squeeze as much of the quality of pleasure as one can out of all the sensations one actually experiences during one's life. All acts are, from this perspective, potential pleasures, if only they can be approached or undertaken in the right manner; the hedonistic index here is the extent to which one is actually able to extract the fundamental pleasure that "exists" in life itself.

10. See J. L. Singer, *Daydreaming* (New York: Random House, 1966).

11. Products need not actually be new; they merely have to be presented or packaged in such a way that it is possible for consumers to believe they are new.

12. That there is a close relationship between people's daydreams and their selection, purchase, use, and disposal of goods and services is revealed, for example, by the nature of advertisements. But one should not assume from this that advertising *creates* daydreaming, as the latter appears to be an intrinsic feature of the mental life of modern humans and does not depend on external agencies to prompt or support it.

13. See Veblen and Riesman.

14. To suggest that consumerism is driven by pleasure-seeking is to raise the possibility that ecological and anticonsumerist movements might have something in common with earlier Puritanical movements. Perhaps an important underlying (if not openly admitted) impulse behind such movements might indeed be a hostility to pleasure. Could such movements represent a new Puritanism in their calls for us to sacrifice our energy-expensive and "wasteful" way of life?

15. See, for the Romantic nature of this movement, Colin Campbell, *The Romantic Ethic and the Spirit of Modern Consumerism* (Oxford: Blackwell, 1987); Frank Musgrove, *Ecstasy and Holiness: Counter-Culture and the Open Society* (London: Methuen, 1974); and Bernice Martin, *A Sociology of Contemporary Cultural Change* (London: Blackwell, 1981).

16. The question has of course been posed before, and the answer much debated. See Jacqueline Sarsby, *Romantic Love and Society* (Harmondsworth: Penguin, 1983); Ethel Spector Person, *Love and Fateful Encounters: The Power of Romantic Passion* (London: Bloomsbury, 1989); and Stanton Peele, *Love and Addiction* (New York: Taplinger, 1975).

CHAPTER 3

Consumer Society

Jean Baudrillard

Today, we are everywhere surrounded by the remarkable conspicuousness of consumption and affluence, established by the multiplication of objects, services, and material goods. This now constitutes a fundamental mutation in the ecology of the human species. Strictly speaking, men of wealth are no longer surrounded by other human beings, as they have been in the past, but by *objects*. Their daily exchange is no longer with their fellows, but rather, statistically as a function of some ascending curve, with the acquisition and manipulation of goods and messages: from the rather complex domestic organization with its dozens of technical slaves to the "urban estate" with all the material machinery of communication and professional activity, and the permanent festive celebration of objects in advertising with the hundreds of daily mass media messages; from the proliferation of somewhat obsessional objects to the symbolic psychodrama which fuels the nocturnal objects that come to haunt us even in our dreams. The concepts of "environment" and "ambiance" have undoubtedly become fashionable only since we have come to live in less proximity to other human beings, in their presence and discourse, and more under the silent gaze of deceptive and obedient objects which continuously repeat the same discourse, that of our stupefied (*medusée*) power, of our potential affluence and of our absence from one another.

As the wolf-child becomes wolf by living among them, so are we becoming functional. We are living the period of the objects: that is, we live by their rhythm, according to their incessant cycles. Today, it is we who are observing their birth, fulfillment, and death; whereas in all previous civilizations, it was the object, instrument, and perennial monument that survived the generations of men.

While objects are neither flora nor fauna, they give the impression of being a proliferating vegetation; a jungle where the new savage of modern times has trouble finding the reflexes of civilization. These fauna and flora, which people have produced, have come to encircle and invest them, like a bad science fiction novel. We must quickly describe them as we see and experience them, while not forgetting, even in periods of scarcity or profusion, that they are in actuality the *products of human activity*, and are controlled, not by natural ecological laws, but by the law of exchange value.

> The busiest streets of London are crowded with shops whose show cases display all the riches of the world: Indian shawls, American revolvers, Chinese porcelain, Parisian corsets, furs from Russia and spices from the tropics; but all of these worldly things bear odious white paper labels with Arabic numerals and then laconic symbols £SD. This is how commodities are presented in circulation.[1]

Profusion and Displays

Accumulation, or *profusion*, is evidently the most striking descriptive feature. Large department stores, with their luxuriant abundance of canned goods, foods, and clothing, are like the primary landscape and the geometrical locus of affluence. Streets with overcrowded and glittering store windows (lighting being the least rare commodity, without which merchandise would merely be what it is), the displays of delicacies, and all the scenes of alimentary and vestimentary festivity, stimulate a magical salivation. Accumulation is more than the sum of its products: the conspicuousness of surplus, the final and magical negation of scarcity, and the maternal and luxurious presumptions of the land of milk and honey. Our markets, our shopping avenues and malls mimic a new-found nature of prodigious fecundity. Those are our Valleys of Canaan where flows, instead of milk and honey, streams of neon on ketchup and plastic—but no matter! There exists an anxious anticipation, not that there may not be enough, but that there is too much, and too much for everyone: by purchasing a portion one in effect appropriates a whole crumbling pyramid of oysters, meats, pears or canned asparagus. One purchases the part for the whole. And this repetitive and metonymic discourse of the consumable, and of commodities is represented, through collective metaphor and as a product of its own surplus, in the image of the *gift*, and of the inexhaustible and spectacular prodigality of the *feast*.

In addition to the stack, which is the most rudimentary yet effective form of accumulation, objects are organized in *displays*, or in *collections*. Almost every clothing store or appliance store presents a gamut of differentiated objects, which call upon, respond to, and refute each other. The display window of the antique store is the aristocratic, luxurious version of this model. The display no longer exhibits an overabundance of wealth but a *range* of select and complementary objects which are offered for the choosing. But this arrangement also invokes a psychological chain reaction in the consumer who peruses it, inventories it, and grasps it as a total category. Few objects today are offered *alone*, without a context of objects to speak for them. And the relation of the consumer to the object has consequently changed: the object is no longer referred to in relation to a specific utility, but as a collection of objects in their total meaning. Washing machine, refrigerator, dishwasher, have different meanings when grouped together than each one has alone, as a piece of equipment (*ustensile*). The display window, the advertisement, the manufacturer, and the *brand name* here play an essential role in imposing a coherent and collective vision, like an almost inseparable totality. Like a chain that connects not ordinary objects but *signifieds*, each object can signify the other in a more complex super-object, and lead the consumer to a series of more complex choices. We can observe that objects are never offered for consumption in an absolute disarray. In certain cases they can *mimic* disorder to better seduce, but they are always arranged to trace out directive paths. The arrangement directs the purchasing impulse towards *networks* of objects in order to seduce it and elicit, in accordance with its own logic, a maximal investment, reaching the limits of economic potential. Clothing, appliances, and toiletries thus constitute object *paths*, which establish inertial constraints on the consumer who will proceed *logically* from one object to the next. The consumer will be caught up in a *calculus* of objects, which is quite different from the frenzy of purchasing and possession which arises from the simple profusion of commodities.

The Drugstore

The drugstore is the synthesis of profusion and calculation. The drugstore (or the new shopping malls) makes possible the synthesis of all consumer activities, not least of which are shopping, flirting with objects, idle wandering, and all the permutations of these. In this way, the drugstore is more appropriately representative of modern consumption than the large department store where quantitative centralization leaves little margin for idle exploration. The arrangement of departments and products here imposes a more utilitarian approach to consumption. It retains something of the period of the emergence of department stores, when large numbers of people were beginning to get access to *everyday* consumables. The drugstore has an altogether different function. It does not juxtapose categories of commodities, but practices an *amalgamation of signs* where all categories of goods are considered a partial field in a general consumerism of signs. The cultural center becomes, then, an integral part of the shopping mall. This is not to say that culture is here "prostituted"; that is too simple. It is *culturalized*. Consequently, the commodity (clothing, food, restaurant, etc.) is also culturalized, since it is transformed into a distinctive and idle substance, a luxury, and an item, among others, in the general display of consumables.

A new art of living, a new way of living, claims advertising, (and fashionable magazines): a pleasant shopping experience, in a single air-conditioned location; one is able to purchase food, products for the apartment or summer home, clothing, flowers, the latest novel, or the latest gadget in a single trip, while husband and children watch a film; and then later you can all dine together on the spot.

Cafe, cinema, book store, auditorium, trinkets, clothing, and many other things can be found in these shopping centers. The drugstore recaptures it all in a kaleidoscopic mode. Whereas the large department store provides a marketplace pageantry for merchandise, the drugstore offers the subtle recital of consumption, where, in fact, the "art" consists in playing on the ambiguity of the object's sign, and sublimating their status and utility as commodity in a play of "ambiance."

The drugstore is neo-culture universalized, where there is no longer any difference between a fine gourmet shop and a gallery of paintings, between *Playboy* and a *Treatise on Paleontology*. The drugstore will be modernized to the point of offering a bit of "gray matter":

> Just selling products does not interest us, we would like to supply a little gray matter . . . Three stories, a bar, a dance floor, and shops; trinkets, records, paperbacks, intellectual books, a bit of everything. But we are not looking to flatter the customer. We are actually offering them "something": a language lab on the second floor; records and books where you find the great trends that move our society; music for research; works that explain an epoch. Products accompanied by "gray matter," this is the drugstore, but in a new style, with something more, perhaps a bit of intelligence and human warmth.[2]

A drugstore can become a whole city: such as Parly 2,[3] with its giant shopping center, where "art and leisure mingle with everyday life"; where each residential group encircles a pool club (the center of attraction), a circular church, tennis courts ("the least of things"), elegant boutiques, and a library. Even the smallest ski resort is organized on the "universalist" model of the drugstore, one where all activities are summarized, systematically combined and centered around the fundamental concept of "ambiance." Thus Idleness-on-the-Wasteful[4] simultaneously offers you a complete, polymorphic and combinatorial existence:

> Our Mt Blanc, our Norway spruce forest; our Olympic runs, our "park" for children; our architecture, carved, trimmed, and polished like a work of art; the purity of the air we breathe; the refined ambiance of our Forum, modeled after Mediterranean cities where, upon return from the ski slopes, life flourishes. Cafes, restaurants, boutiques, skating rinks, night clubs, cinemas, and centers of culture and amusement are all located in the Forum to offer you a life off the slopes that is particularly rich and varied. There is our closed-circuit TV; and our future on a human scale (soon, we will be classified as a work of art by the department of cultural affairs).

We have reached the point where "consumption" has grasped the whole of life; where all activities are sequenced in the same combinatorial mode; where the schedule of gratification is outlined in advance, one hour at a time; and where the "environment" is complete, completely climatized, furnished, and culturalized. In the phenomenology of consumption, the general climatization of life, of goods, objects, services, behaviors, and social relations represents the perfected, "consummated,"[5] stage of evolution which, through articulated networks of objects, ascends from pure and simple abundance to a complete conditioning of action and time, and finally to the systematic organization of ambiance, which is characteristic of the drugstores, the shopping malls, or the modern airports in our futuristic cities.

Parly 2

"The largest shopping center in Europe."

"Printemps, B.H.V., Dior, Prisunic, Lanvin, Frank et Fils, Hediard, two cinemas, a drugstore, a supermarket, Suma, a hundred other shops, all gathered in a single location!"[6]

In the choice of shops, from groceries to high fashion, there are two requirements: progressive marketing and a sense of aesthetics. The famous slogan "ugliness doesn't sell" is outmoded, and could be replaced by "the beauty of the surroundings is the precondition for a happy life": a two-story structure . . . organized around a central mall, with a main street and promenades on two levels; the reconciliation of the small and large shop and of the modern pace with the idleness of antiquity.

The mall offers the previously unexperienced luxury of strolling between stores which freely (*plain-pièd*) offer their temptations without so much interference as glare from a display window. The central mall, a combination of rue de la Paix and the Champs-Elysées, is adorned by fountains and artificial trees. Kiosks and benches are completely indifferent to seasonal changes and bad weather. An exceptional system of climate control, requiring eight miles of air conditioning ducts, creates a perpetual springtime.

Not only can anything be purchased, from shoestrings to an airline ticket, or located, such as insurance company, cinema, bank or medical service, bridge club and art exhibition, but one need not be the slave of time. The mall, like every city street, is accessible seven days a week, day or night.

Naturally, the shopping mall has instituted, for those who desire, the most modern form of payment: the "credit card." The card frees us from checks, cash, and even from financial difficulties at the end of the month. Henceforth, to pay you present your card and sign the bill. That's all there is to it. Each month you receive a bill which you can pay in full or in monthly installments.

In the marriage between comfort, beauty, and efficiency, Parlysians discover the material conditions of happiness which the anarchy of older cities refuses them.

Here we are at the heart of consumption as the total organization of everyday life, as a complete homogenization. Everything is appropriated and simplified into the translucence of abstract "happiness," simply defined by the resolution of tensions. Expanded to the dimensions of the shopping mall and the futuristic city, the drugstore is the *sublimation* of real life, of objective social life, where not only work and money are abolished, but the seasons disappear as well—the distant vestige of a cycle finally domesticated! Work, leisure, nature, and culture, all previously dispersed, separate, and more or less irreducible activities that produced anxiety and complexity in our real life, and in our "anarchic and archaic" cities, have finally become mixed, massaged, climate controlled, and domesticated into the simple activity of perpetual shopping. All these activities have finally become desexed into a single hermaphroditic ambiance of style! Everything is finally *digested* and reduced to the same homogeneous fecal matter (this occurs, of course, precisely under the sign of the disappearance of *"liquid" currency*, the still too visible symbol of the *real* excretion (*fecalité*) of real life, and of the economic and social contradictions that previously haunted it). All that is past (passed): a *controlled*, lubricated, and *consumed* excretion (*fecalité*) is henceforth transferred into things, everywhere diffused in the indistinguishability of things and of social relations. Just like the Roman Pantheon, where the gods of all countries coexisted in a syncretism, in an immense "digest," the super shopping center,[7] our new pantheon, our pandemonium, brings together all the gods, or demons, of consumption. That is to say, every activity, labor, conflict and all the seasons are abolished in the same abstraction. The substance of life, unified in this universal digest, can no longer have any *meaning*: that which produced the dream work, the poetic work, the work of meaning, that is to say the grand schemas of displacement and condensation, the great figures of metaphor and contradiction, which are founded on the lived articulation of distinct elements, is no longer possible. The eternal substitution of homogeneous elements alone remains. There is no longer a symbolic function, but an eternal combinatory of "ambiance" in a perpetual Springtime.

Towards a Theory of Consumption

The Autopsy of Homo Economicus

There is a fable: "There once was a man who lived in Scarcity. After many adventures and a long voyage in the Science of Economics, he encountered the Society of Affluence. They were married and had many needs." "The beauty of *homo economicus*," said A. N. Whitehead, "was that we knew exactly what he was searching for." This human fossil of the Golden Age, born in the modern era out of the fortuitous conjunction of Human Nature and Human

Rights, is gifted with a heightened principle of formal rationality which leads him to:
1. Pursue his own happiness without the slightest hesitation;
2. Prefer objects which provide him with the maximum satisfaction.

The whole discourse on consumption, whether learned or lay, is articulated on the mythological sequence of the fable: a man, "endowed" with needs which "direct" him towards objects that "give" him satisfaction. Since man is really never satisfied (for which, by the way, he is reproached), the same history is repeated indefinitely, since the time of the ancient fables.

Some appear to be perplexed: "Among all the unknowns of economic science, needs are the most persistently obscure" (Knight).[8] But this uncertainty does not prevent the advocates of the human sciences, from Marx to Galbraith, and from Robinson Crusoe to Chombart de Lauwe,[9] from faithfully reciting the litany of needs. For the economists, there is the notion of "utility." Utility is the desire to consume a specific commodity, that is to say, to nullify its utility. Need is therefore already embedded in commodities on the market. And preferences are manipulated by the arrangement of products already offered on the market: this is in fact an elastic demand.

For the psychologist there is the theory of "motivation" which is a bit more complex, less "object oriented"[10] and more "instinct oriented,"[11] derived from a sort of ill-defined, preexisting necessity. For the sociologist and psychosociologist, who arrived last on the scene, there is the "sociocultural." The anthropological postulate, of the *individual* endowed with needs and moved by nature to satisfy them, or of a consumer who is free, conscious and aware of his needs, is not put into question by sociologists (although sociologists are suspicious of "deep motivations"). But rather, on the basis of this idealistic postulate, sociologists allow for a "social-dynamics" of needs. They activate models of conformity and competition ("Keeping up with the Joneses")[12] derived from the pressure of peer group, or they elaborate grand "cultural models" which are related to society in general or to history.

Three general positions can be identified: for Marshall, needs are interdependent and rational; for Galbraith, choices are imposed by motivation (we will come back to this); for Gervasi (and others), needs are interdependent, and are the result of learning rather than of rational calculation.

Gervasi: "Choices are not made randomly. They are socially controlled, and reflect the cultural model from which they are produced. We neither produce nor consume just any product: the product must have some meaning in relation to a system of values."[13] This leads to a perspective on consumption in terms of integration: "The goal of the economy is not the maximization of production *for the purposes of the individual*, but the maximization of production in relation to society's value system" (Parsons).[14] Similarly, Duesenbury will claim that the only choice is, in fact, varying one's possessions according to one's position in the social hierarchy. In effect, the differences in choice from one society to another, and the similarity of choices within a society, compel us to view consumer behavior as a social phenomenon. The economist's notion of "rational" choice has been changed into the model of choice as conformity, which is significantly different. Needs are not so much directed at objects, but at values. And the satisfaction of needs primarily expresses an *adherence to these values*. The fundamental, unconscious, and automatic choice of the consumer is to accept the life-style of a particular society (no longer therefore a real choice: the theory of the autonomy and sovereignty of the consumer is thus refuted).

This kind of sociology culminates in the notion of the "standard package,"[15] defined by Riesman as the collection of products and services which constitutes the basic heritage of the middle-class American. Constantly on the rise and indexed on the national standard of living, the standard package is a minimum ideal of a statistical kind, and a middle-class model of conformity. Surpassed by some, only dreamed of by others, it is an *idea* which encapsulates the American way of life.[16] Here again, the "standard package" does not so much refer to the materiality of goods (TV, bathroom, car, etc.) as to *the ideal of conformity*.

All of this sociology gets us nowhere. Besides the fact that the notion of conformity is nothing more than an immense tautology (in this case the middle-class American defined by the "standard package," itself defined by the statistical mean of consumed goods—or sociologically: a particular group which consumes a particular product, and the individual consumes such a product because he or she belongs to such a group), the postulate of formal rationality, which in economics determined the individual's relation to objects, is simply transferred to the relation of the individual to the group. Conformity and satisfaction are interrelated: the resulting similarity in the subject's relation to objects, or to a group *posited as a distinct entity*, is established according to the logical principle of equivalence. The concepts of "need" and "norm" respectively are the expressions of this miraculous equivalence.

The difference between the economic notion of "utility" and the sociological notion of conformity is identical to the distinction Galbraith establishes between the pursuit of profit and economic motivation, which is characteristic of the "traditional" capitalist system, on the one hand, and the behavior of identification and adaptation, which is specific to the era of organization and of the technostructure, on the other. The *conditioning of needs* becomes the central issue for both the psycho-sociologists of conformity, and for Galbraith. This is never an issue for economists (and for good reasons), for whom consumers, with their ultimate rational calculation, remain ideally free.

Since Packard's *The Hidden Persuaders* and Dichter's *The Strategy of Desire* (and some others as well),[17] the conditioning of needs (particularly through advertising) has become the favorite theme in the discourse on consumer society. The celebration of affluence and the great lament over "artificial" or "alienated needs," together have fueled the same mass culture, and even the intellectual discourse on the issue. Generally this discourse is grounded in the antiquated moral and social philosophy of a humanist tradition. With Galbraith, however, it develops into a more rigorous economic and political theory. We will therefore remain with him, starting from his two books, *The Affluent Society* and *The New Industrial State*.

Briefly summarizing his position, we could say that the fundamental problem of contemporary capitalism is no longer the contradiction between the "maximization of profit" and the "rationalization of production" (from the point of view of the producer), but rather a contradiction between a virtually unlimited productivity (at the level of the technostructure) and the need to dispose of the product. It becomes vital for the system at this stage to control not only the mechanism of production, but also consumer demand; not only prices, but what will be asked for the price. Either prior to production (polls, market studies) or subsequent to it (advertising, marketing, conditioning), the general idea "is to shift the locus of decision in the purchase of goods from the consumer where it is beyond control to the firm where it is subject to control.[18] Even more generally:

> The accommodation of the market behavior of the individual, as well as of social attitudes in general, to the needs of producers and the goals of the technostructure is an inherent feature of the system [it would be more appropriate to say: a *logical* characteristic]. It becomes increasingly important with the growth of the industrial system.[19]

This is what Galbraith calls the "revised sequence," in opposition to the "accepted sequence" whereby the consumer is presumed to have the initiative which will reflect back, through the market, to the manufacturers. Here, on the contrary, the manufacturers control behavior, as well as direct and model social attitudes and needs. In its tendencies at least, this is a total dictatorship by the sector of production.

The "revised sequence," at least, has the critical value of undermining the fundamental myth of the classical relation, which assumes that it is the individual who exercises power in the economic system. This emphasis on the power of the individual largely contributed to the legitimation of the organization; all dysfunctions, all nuisances, the inherent contradictions in the order of production are justified, since they enlarge the consumer's domain of sovereignty. On the contrary, it is clear that the whole economic and psychosociological apparatus of market and motivation research, which pretends to uncover the underlying needs of the consumer and the real demand prevailing in the market, exists only to generate a demand for further market opportunities. And it continuously masks this objective by staging its opposite. "Man has become the object of science for man only since automobiles have become harder to sell than to manufacture."[20]

Thus everywhere Galbraith denounces the boosting of demand by "artificial accelerators," which the technostructure carries out in its imperialist expansion, rendering the stabilization of demand impossible.[21] Income, luxury goods, and surplus labor form a vicious and frantic circle. The infernal round of consumption is based on the celebration of needs that are purported to be "psychological." These are distinguished from "physiological" needs since they are supposedly established through "discretionary income" and the freedom of choice, and consequently manipulable at will. Advertising here of course plays a capital role (another idea which has become conventional) for it appears to be in harmony with commodities and with the needs of the individual. In fact, says Galbraith, advertising is adjusted to the industrial system: "It appears to place a significance on products only in so far as it is important for the system, and it upholds the importance and prestige of the technostructure from the social point of view." Through advertising, the system appropriates social goals for its own gain, and imposes its own objectives as social goals: "What's good for General Motors . . . "

Again we must agree with Galbraith (and others) in acknowledging that the liberty and sovereignty of the consumer are nothing more than a mystification. The well-preserved mystique of satisfaction and individual choice (primarily supported by economists), whereby a "free" civilization reaches its pinnacle, is the very ideology of the industrial system. It justifies its arbitrariness and all sorts of social problems: filth, pollution, and deculturation—in fact the consumer is sovereign in a jungle of ugliness, where *the freedom of choice is imposed on him*. The revised sequence (that is to say, the *system* of consumption) thus ideologically supplements and connects with the *electoral system*. The drugstore and the polling booth, the geometric spaces of individual freedom, are also the system's two mammary glands.

We have discussed at length the analysis of the "technostructural" conditioning of needs and consumption because it is currently quite prominent. This kind of analysis, thematized in multiple ways in the pseudo-philosophy of "alienation," constitutes a representation of society which is itself part of consumerism. But it is open to fundamental objections that are all related to its idealist anthropological postulates. For Galbraith individual needs can be stabilized. There exists in human *nature* something like an *economic principle* that would lead man, were it not for "artificial accelerators," to impose limits on his own objectives, on his needs and at the same time on his efforts. In short, there is a tendency towards satisfaction, which is not viewed as optimizing, but rather as "harmonious" and balanced at the level of the individual, a tendency that would allow the individual to express himself in a society that is itself a harmony of collective needs, instead of becoming caught up in the vicious circle of infinite gratifications described above. All this sounds perfectly utopian.

1. Galbraith denounces the "specious" reasoning of economists on the issue of "authentic" or "artificial" gratification: "There is no proof that an expensive woman obtains the same satisfaction from yet another gown as does a hungry man from a hamburger. But there is no proof that she does

not. Since it cannot be proven that she does not, her desire, it is held, must be accorded equal standing with that of a poor man for meat."²² "Absurd," says Galbraith. Yet, not at all (and here classical economists are almost correct in their opposition to him: quite simply, they position themselves to establish the equivalency of satiable demands and thereby avoid all the problems). It is nevertheless the case that, from the perspective of the satisfaction of the consumer, there is no basis on which to define what is "artificial" and what is not. The pleasure obtained from a television or a second home is experienced as "real" freedom. No one experiences this as alienation. Only the intellectual can describe it in this way, on the basis of a moralizing idealism, one which at best reveals him as an alienated moralist.

2. On the "economic principle," Galbraith claims: "What is called economic development consists in no small part in devising strategies to overcome the tendency of men to place limits on their objectives as regards income and thus on their efforts."²³ And he cites the example of Filipino workers in California: "The pressure of debt, and the pressure on each to emulate the most extravagant, quickly converted these happy and easygoing people in a modern and reliable work force."²⁴ In addition, in underdeveloped countries the introduction of Western gadgets is the best form of economic stimulation. This theory, which we could call economic "pressure," or disciplined consumption, and which is connected to forced economic growth, is seductive. It makes it appear that the forced acculturation to the processes of consumption is a *logical development* in the evolution of the industrial system. An evolution which progresses from the discipline of timetables and everyday behavior (to which workers have been subjected since the nineteenth century) to the processes of industrial production. Once having asserted this, we need to explain *why* consumers "take the bait," why they are vulnerable to this strategy. It is much too easy to appeal to "a happy and carefree" disposition, and mechanically to assign responsibility to the system. There is no "natural" inclination to a carefree disposition any more than there is to the work ethic. Galbraith does not take into consideration the logic of social differentiation. Hence he is forced to represent the individual as a completely passive victim of the system. These processes of class and caste distinctions are basic to the social structure, and are fully operational in "democratic" society. In short, what is lacking is a socio-logic of difference, of status, etc., upon which needs are reorganized in accordance to the *objective* social demand of signs and differences. Thus consumption becomes, not a function of "harmonious" individual satisfaction (hence limited according to the ideal rules of "nature"), but rather an infinite social *activity*. We will eventually come back to this issue.

3. "Needs are in reality the fruits of production," says Galbraith, pleased with himself for having put it so well. Expressed in a clear and demystified tone, this thesis, as he understood it, is nothing more than a subtle version of the natural "authenticity" of certain needs and of the bewitching character of

the "artificial." What Galbraith means is that without the system of production a large proportion of needs would not exist. He contends that, in the production of specific goods and services, manufacturers simultaneously produce all the powers of suggestion necessary for the products to be accepted. In fact, they "produce" the need which corresponds to the product. There is here a serious psychological lacuna. Needs are strictly specified in advance in relation to *finite objects*. There is only need for *this or that object*. In effect, the psyche of the consumer is merely a display window or a catalog. Certainly once we have adopted this simplistic view of man we cannot avoid the psychological reduction: empirical needs are the specular reflections of empirical objects. At this level, however, the thesis of conditioning is false. We are well aware of how consumers resist such a precise injunction, and of how they play with "needs" on a keyboard of objects. We know that advertising is not omnipotent and at times produces opposite reactions; and we know that in reference to a single "need," objects can be substituted for one another. Hence, at the empirical level, a rather complicated strategy having a psychological and sociological nature intersects with the strategy of production.

The truth is not that "needs are the fruits of production," but that *the system of needs* is *the product of the system of production*, which is a quite different matter. By a system of needs we mean to imply that needs are not produced one at a time, in relation to their respective objects. Needs are produced as a *force of consumption*, and as a general potential reserve (*disponibilité globale*) within the larger framework of productive forces. It is in this sense that we can say that the technostructure is extending its empire. The system of production does not "shackle" the system of pleasure (*jouissance*) to its own ends (strictly speaking, this is meaningless). This hypothesis *denies* autonomy to the system of pleasure and substitutes itself in its place by reorganizing everything into a system of productive forces. We can trace this *genealogy of consumption* in the course of the history of the industrial system:

1. The order of production produces the productive machine/force, a technical system that is radically different from traditional tools.
2. It produces the rationalized productive capital/force, a rational system of investment and circulation that is radically different from previous forms of "wealth" and modes of exchange.
3. It produces the wage-labor force, an abstract and systematized productive force that is radically different from concrete labor and traditional "workmanship."
4. In this way it produces needs, the *system* of needs, the productive demand/force as a rationalized, controlled and integrated whole, complementary to the three others in a process of the total control of productive forces and production processes. As a system, needs are also radically different from pleasure and satisfaction. They are produced *as elements of a system*

and not *as a relation between an individual and an object*. In the same sense that labor power is no longer connected to, and even denies, the relation of the worker to the product of his labor, so exchange value is no longer related to concrete and personal exchange, nor the commodity form to actual goods, etc.

This is what Galbraith does not see and along with him all of the "alienists" of consumption, who persist in their attempts to demonstrate that *people's relation to objects, and their relation to themselves is falsified*, mystified, and manipulated, consuming this myth at the same time as the object. Once having stated the universal postulate of the free and conscious subject (in order to make it reemerge at the end of history as a happy end[ing],[25] they are forced to attribute all the "dysfunctions" they have uncovered to a diabolic power—in this case to the technostructure, armed with advertising, public relations, and motivation research. This is magical thinking if there is such a thing. They do not see that, taken one at a time, needs are *nothing*; that there is only the system of needs; or rather, that needs are nothing but *the most advanced form of the rational systematization of productive forces at the individual level*, one in which "consumption" takes up the *logical* and necessary relay from production.

This can clear up a certain number of unexplained mysteries for our pious "alienists." They deplore, for example, the fact that puritan ethics are not abandoned in periods of affluence, and that an outdated moral and self-denying Malthusianism has not been replaced by a modern ethos of pleasure. Dichter's *Strategy of Desire* is determined to twist and subvert these old mental structures "from below." And it is true: there has not been a revolution in morals; puritan ideology is still in place. In the analysis of leisure, we will see how it permeates what appear to be hedonistic practices. We can affirm that puritan ethics, and what it implies about sublimation, transcendence, and repression (in a word, morality), *haunts* consumption and needs. It is what motivates it from within and that which gives needs and consumption its compulsive and boundless character. And puritan ideology is itself reactivated by the process of consumption; this is what makes consumption the powerful factor of integration and social control we know it to be. Whereas from the perspective of consumption/pleasure, this remains paradoxical and inexplicable. It can all be explained only if we acknowledge that needs and consumption are in fact an *organized extension of productive forces*. This is not surprising since they both emerged from the productivist and puritan ethics which was the dominant morality of the industrial era. The generalized integration of the "private" individual ("needs," feelings, aspirations, drives) as a productive force can only be accompanied by a generalized extension, at this level, of the schemas of repression, of sublimation, of concentration, of systematization, of rationalization (and of "alienation" of course!), which, for centuries, but especially since the nineteenth century, have governed the structuration (*edification*) of the industrial system.

The Fluidity of Objects and Needs

Until now, the analysis of consumption has been founded on the naive anthropology of *homo economicus*, or at best *homo psychoeconomicus*. It is a theory of needs, of objects (in the fullest sense), and of satisfactions within the ideological extension of classical political economy. This is really not a theory. It is an immense tautology: "I buy this because I need it" is equivalent to the claim that fire burns because of its phlogistic essence. I have shown elsewhere[26] how this empiricist/teleologist position (the individual taken as an end in itself and his or her conscious representations as the logic of events) is identical to the magical speculation of primitive peoples (and of ethnologists) concerning the notion of mana. No theory of consumption is possible at this level: the immediately self-evident, such as an analysis in terms of needs, will never produce anything more than a consumed reflection on consumption.

The rationalist mythology of needs and satisfactions is as naive and "disabled" as is traditional medicine when confronted with psychosomatic or hysterical symptoms. Let us explain: within the field of their objective function objects are not interchangeable, but outside the field of its denotation, an object becomes substitutable in a more or less unlimited fashion. In this field of connotations the object takes on the value of a sign. In this way a washing machine *serves* as equipment and *plays* as an element of comfort, or of prestige, etc. It is the field of play that is specifically the field of consumption. Here all sorts of objects can be substituted for the washing machine as a signifying element. In the logic of signs, as in the logic of symbols, objects are no longer tied to a function or to a *defined* need. This is precisely because objects respond to something different, either to a social logic, or to a logic of desire, where they serve as a fluid and unconscious field of signification.

Relatively speaking, objects and needs are here interchangeable just like the symptoms of hysterical or psychosomatic conversion. They obey the same logic of shifts, transferals, and of apparently arbitrary and infinite convertibility. When an illness is *organic*, there is a necessary relation between the symptom and the organ (in the same way that in its role as equipment there is a necessary relation between the object and its function). In the hysterical or psychosomatic conversion the symptom, like the sign, is (relatively) arbitrary. Migraine, colitis, lumbago, angina, or general fatigue form a chain of somatic signifiers along which the symptom "parades." This is just like the interconnection of object/signs, or of object/symbols, along which parades, not needs (which remain tied to the object's rational goal), but desire, and some other determination, derived from an unconscious social logic.

If we trace a need to a particular locus, that is, if we satisfy it by taking it literally, as it presents itself, as a need for a *specific object*, we would make the same error as if we performed traditional therapy on an organ where the symptom is localized. Once healed it would reappear elsewhere.

The world of objects and of needs would thus be a world of *general hyste-*

ria. Just as the organs and the functions of the body in hysterical conversion become a gigantic paradigm which the symptom replaces and refers to, in consumption objects become a vast paradigm designating another language through which something else speaks. We could add that this evanescence and continual mobility reaches a point where it becomes impossible to determine the specific objectivity of needs, just as it is impossible in hysteria to define the specific objectivity of an illness, for the simple reason that it does not exist. The flight from one signifier to another is no more than the surface reality of a *desire*, which is insatiable because it is founded on a lack. And this desire, which can never be satisfied, signifies itself locally in a succession of objects and needs.

In view of the repeated and naive confusion one finds when faced with the continual forward flight and unlimited renewal of needs—which in fact is irreconcilable with a rationalist theory claiming that a satisfied need produces a state of equilibrium and a resolution of tensions—we can advance the following sociological hypothesis (although it would be interesting and essential to articulate both desire and the social): if we acknowledge that a need is not a need for a particular object as much as it is a "need" for difference (the *desire for social meaning*), only then will we understand that satisfaction can never be *fulfilled*, and consequently that there can never be a *definition* of needs.

The fluidity of desire is supplemented by the fluidity of differential meanings (is there a metaphoric relation between the two?). Between them specific and finite needs only become meaningful as the focus of successive conversions. In their substitutions they signify, yet simultaneously veil, the true domain of signification—that of lack of difference—which overwhelms them from all sides.

The Denial of Pleasure

The acquisition of objects is *without an object* ("objectless craving,"[27] for David Riesman). Consumer behavior, which appears to be focused and directed at the object and at pleasure, in fact responds to quite different objectives: the metaphoric or displaced expression of desire, and the production of a code of social values through the use of differentiating signs. That which is determinant is not the function of individual interest within a corpus of objects, but rather the specifically social function of exchange, communication and distribution of values within a corpus of signs.

The truth about consumption is that it is *a function of production* and not a function of pleasure, and therefore, like material production, is not an individual function but one that is *directly and totally* collective. No theoretical analysis is possible without the reversal of the traditional givens: otherwise, no matter how we approach it, we revert to a phenomenology of pleasure.

Consumption is a system which assures the regulation of signs and the integration of the group: it is simultaneously a morality (a system of ideological values) and a system of communication, a structure of exchange. On this basis, and on the fact that this social function and this structural organization by far transcend individuals and are imposed on them according to an unconscious social constraint, we can formulate a theoretical hypothesis which is neither a recital of statistics nor a descriptive metaphysics.

According to this hypothesis, paradoxical though it may appear, consumption is defined as *exclusive of pleasure*. As a social logic, the system of consumption is established on the basis of the denial of pleasure. Pleasure no longer appears as an objective, as a rational end, but as the individual rationalization of a process whose objectives lie elsewhere. Pleasure would define consumption *for itself*, as autonomous and final. But consumption is never thus. Although we experience pleasure for ourselves, when we consume we never do it on our own (the isolated consumer is the carefully maintained illusion of the *ideological* discourse on consumption). Consumers are mutually implicated, despite themselves, in a general system of exchange and in the production of coded values.

In this sense, consumption is a system of meaning, like language, or like the kinship system in primitive societies.

A Structural Analysis?

In the language of Lévi-Strauss we can say that the social aspect of consumption is not derived from what appears to be of the realm of nature (satisfaction or pleasure), but rather from the essential processes by which it separates itself from nature (what defines it as a code, an institution, or a system of organization). Consumption can be compared with the kinship system, which is not determined in the final analysis by consanguinity and filiation, by a natural given, but rather by the arbitrary regulation of classification. In the final analysis, the system of consumption is based on a code of signs (object/signs) and differences, and not on need and pleasure.

Rules of marriage represent the multiple ways of assuring the circulation of women within the social group. It is the replacement of a consanguineous system of relations of biological origin by a sociological system of alliance. Thus, rules of marriage and kinship systems can be seen as a kind of language, that is, a set of operations intended to assure, between individuals and groups, a certain kind of communication. The same is true for consumption: a sociological system of signs (the level characteristic of consumption) is substituted for a bio-functional and bio-economic system of commodities and products (the biological level of needs and subsistence). And the essential function of the regulated circulation of objects and commodities is the same as that of women and words. It is designed to assure a certain type of communication.

We will come back to the differences between these various types of "languages": they are essentially related to the mode of production of the values exchanged and to the type of division of labor associated with it. Commodities obviously are produced, whereas women are not, and they are produced differently from words. Nevertheless, at the level of distribution, commodities and objects, like words and once like women, constitute a global, arbitrary, and coherent system of signs, a *cultural* system which substitutes a social order of values and classifications for a contingent world of needs and pleasures, the natural and biological order.

This is not to claim that there are no needs, or natural utilities, etc. The point is to see that consumption, as a concept specific to contemporary society, is not organized along these lines. For this is true of all societies. What is sociologically significant for us, and what marks our era under the sign of consumption, is precisely the generalized reorganization of this primary level in a system of signs which appears to be a particular mode of transition from nature to culture, perhaps *the* specific mode of our era.

Marketing, purchasing, sales, the acquisition of differentiated commodities and object/signs—all of these presently constitute our language, a code with which our entire society *communicates* and speaks of and to itself. Such is the present day structure of communication: a language (*langue*) in opposition to which individual needs and pleasures are but the *effects of speech (Parole)*.

The Fun-System, or the Constraint of Pleasure[28]

The best evidence that pleasure is not the basis or the objective of consumption is that nowadays pleasure is constrained and institutionalized, not as a right or enjoyment, but as the citizen's *duty*.

The puritans considered themselves, considered their actual being, to be an enterprise to make profit for the greater glory of God. Their "personal" qualities, and their "character," which they spent their lives producing, were capital to be invested wisely, and managed without speculation or waste. Conversely, yet in the same way, man-as-consumer considers the *experience of pleasure an obligation*, like an *enterprise of pleasure and satisfaction*; one is obliged to be happy, to be in love, to be adulating/adulated, seducing/seduced, participating, euphoric, and dynamic. This is the principle of the maximization of existence by the multiplication of contacts and relations, by the intensive use of signs and objects, and by the systematic exploitation of all the possibilities of pleasure.

The consumer, the modern citizen, cannot evade the constraint of happiness and pleasure, which in the new ethics is equivalent to the traditional constraint of labor and production. Modern man spends less and less of life in production, and more and more in the continuous production and creation of personal needs and of personal well-being. He must constantly be ready to actualize all of his potential, all his capacity for consumption. If he forgets, he will be gently and instantly reminded that he has no right not to be happy. He is therefore not passive: he is engaged, and must be engaged, in continuous activity. Otherwise he runs the risk of being satisfied with what he has and of becoming asocial.

A *universal curiosity* (a concept to be exploited) has as a consequence been reawakened in the areas of cuisine, culture, science, religion, sexuality, etc. "Try Jesus!" says an American slogan. *Everything* must be tried: since man as consumer is haunted by the fear of "missing" something, any kind of pleasure. One never knows if such and such a contact, or experience (Christmas in the Canaries, eel in whisky, the Prado, LSD, love Japanese style) will not elicit a "sensation." It is no longer desire, nor even "taste" nor a specific preference which are at issue, but a generalized curiosity driven by a diffuse obsession, a *fun morality*,[29] whose imperative is enjoyment and the complete exploitation of all the possibilities of being thrilled, experiencing pleasure, and being gratified.

Consumption as the Rise and Control of New Productive Forces

Consumption is a sector that only *appears* anomic, since, following the Durkheimian definition, it is not governed by formal rules. It appears to surrender to the individualistic immoderation and contingency of needs. Consumption is not, as one might generally imagine (which is why economic "science" is fundamentally averse to discussing it), an indeterminate marginal sector where an individual, elsewhere constrained by social rules, would finally recover, in the "private" sphere, a margin of freedom and personal play when left on his own. Consumption is a collective and active behavior, a constraint, a morality, and an institution. It is a complete system of values, with all that the term implies concerning group integration and social control.

Consumer society is also the society for the apprenticeship of consumption, for the social indoctrination of consumption. In other words, this is a new and specific mode of *socialization* related to the rise of new productive forces and the monopolistic restructuration of a high output economic system.

Credit here plays a determining role, even though it only has a marginal impact on the spending budget. The idea is exemplary. Presented under the guise of gratification, of a facilitated access to affluence, of a hedonistic mentality, and of "freedom from the old taboos of thrift, etc.," credit is in fact the systematic socioeconomic indoctrination of forced economizing and an economic calculus for generations of consumers who, in a life of subsistence, would have otherwise escaped the manipulation of demands and would have been unexploitable as a force of consumption. Credit is a disciplinary process which extorts savings and regulates demand—just as wage labor was a rational process in the extortion of labor power and in the increase of productivity. The case cited by Galbraith, of the Puerto Ricans who, having been passive and carefree, were transformed into a modern labor force by being motivated to consume, is striking evidence of the tactical value of a regulated, forced, instructed, and stimulated consumption within the modern socioeconomic order. As Marc Alexandre demonstrates, this is achieved through credit (and the discipline and budget constraints it imposes), by the mental indoctrination of the masses to a planned calculus and to "basic" capitalist investment and behavior.[30] The rational and disciplinary ethics, which according to Weber was at the origin of modern capitalist productivism, in a way, has come to inhabit a whole domain which previously escaped it.

We don't realize how much the current indoctrination into systematic and organized consumption is *the equivalent and the extension, in the twentieth century, of the great indoctrination of rural populations into industrial labor, which occurred throughout the nineteenth century*. The same process of rationalization of productive forces, which took place in the nineteenth century in the sector of *production* is accomplished, in the twentieth century, in the sector of *consumption*. Having socialized the masses into a labor force, the industrial system had to go further in order to fulfill itself and to socialize the masses (that is, to control them) into a force of consumption. The small investors or the sporadic consumers of the pre-war era, who were free to consume or not, no longer had a place in the system.

The ideology of consumption would have us believe that we have entered a new era, and that a decisive "human revolution" separates the grievous and heroic Age of Production from the euphoric Age of Consumption, where justice has finally been restored to Man and to his desires. But there is no truth in this. Production and Consumption are *one and the same grand logical process in the expanded reproduction of the productive forces and of their control*. This imperative, which belongs to the system, enters in an inverted form into mentality, ethics, and everyday ideology, and that is its ultimate cunning: in the form of the liberation of needs, of individual fulfillment, of pleasure, and of affluence, etc. The themes of expenditure, pleasure, and non-calculation ("Buy now, pay later") have replaced the "puritan" themes of thrift, work, and patrimony. But this is only the appearance of a human revolution. In fact, this is the substitution of a new system of values for one that has become (relatively) ineffective: an internal substitution in a system essentially unchanged; a substitution within the guidelines of a more general process. What could have been a new finality, has become, stripped of any real content, an imposed mediation of the system's reproduction.

Consumer needs and satisfactions are productive forces which are now constrained and rationalized like all the others (labor power, etc.) From whichever perspective we chose (briefly) to examine it, consumption appeared quite opposite to the way we experience it as ideology, that is, as a dimension of constraint:

1. Governed by the *constraint of signification*, at the level of the structural analysis.
2. Governed by the *constraint of production* and the cycle of production in the analysis of strategies (socio-economico-political).

Thus, affluence and consumption are not the realization of Utopia, but a new objective state, governed by the same fundamental processes, yet overdetermined by a new morality. This corresponds to a *new* sphere of productive forces in the process of directed reintegration within the *same* expanded system. In this sense there is no objective "progress" (nor *a fortiori* "revolution"): it is simply the same thing and something else. What in fact results from the total *ambiguity* of affluence and consumption, which can be observed at the level of daily events, is that these are always lived as *myth* (the assumption of happiness, beyond history and morality), while they are simultaneously *endured as an objective process of adaptation* to a new type of collective behavior.

On the issue of consumption as a civic restraint, Eisenhower stated in 1958: "In a free society, government best encourages economic growth when it encourages the *efforts* of individuals and private groups. The government will never spend money as profitably as an individual tax-payer would have were he freed from the burden of taxation." He implies that consumption, not being directly imposed, could effectively replace taxation as a social levy. "With nine billion dollars of fiscal deductions," adds *Time* magazine, "the consumer went to two million retail stores in search of prosperity ... They realized that they could increase economic growth by replacing their fans with air conditioners. They *ensured the boom* of 1954 by purchasing five million miniaturized television sets, a million and a half electric knives, etc." In short, they performed their civic duty. "Thrift is un-American," said William H. Whyte.[31]

Regarding needs as productive forces, the equivalent in the heroic epoch to "manual labor as natural resource," an advertisement for movie advertising claims:

> The cinema allows you, thanks to its large screen, to present your product on site: colors, forms, conditioning. Each week 3,500,000 spectators frequent the 2,500 cinemas in our advertising network; 67 per cent of them are between the ages of fifteen and thirty-five. These are consumers *in the fullness of their needs*, who want and are able to purchase ...

Exactly, they are individuals in full (labor) force.

The Logistic Function of the Individual

> The individual serves the industrial system not by supplying it with savings and the resulting capital; he serves it by consuming its products. On no other matter, religious, political, or moral, is he so elaborately and skillfully and expensively instructed.[32]

The system needs people as workers (wage labor), and as economizers (taxes, loans, etc.), but increasingly they are needed *as consumers*. Labor productivity is increasingly replaced by the productivity obtained through technological and organizational improvements and increasingly investments are being redirected to the level of the corporation.[33] *But as consumer, the individ-*

ual has become necessary and practically irreplaceable. In the process of the extension of the techno-bureaucratic structures we can predict a bright future and the eventual realization of the individualist system of values, whose center of gravity will be displaced from the entrepreneur and the individual investor, figurehead of competitive capitalism, to the individual consumer, subsequently encompassing all individuals.

At the competitive stage, capitalism still sustained itself, for better or for worse, with an individualist system of values bastardized with altruism. The fiction of a social, altruistic morality (inherited from traditional spiritualism) "softened" the antagonisms of social relations. The "moral law" resulted from individual antagonisms, just as "the law of the market" resulted from competitive processes; they preserved the fiction of stability. For a long time we have believed in individual salvation for the community of all Christians, and in individual rights limited only by the rights of others. But this is impossible today. In the same way that "free enterprise" has virtually disappeared giving way to monopolistic, state and bureaucratic control, so the altruistic ideology is no longer sufficient to reestablish a minimum of social integration. No other collective ideology has come to replace these values. Only the collective constraint of the state has thwarted the exacerbations of multiple individualisms. From this arises the profound contradiction of civil and political society as "consumer society": the system is forced to produce more and more consumer individualism, which at the same time it is forced to repress more and more severely. This can only be resolved by an increase in altruistic ideology (which is itself bureaucratized, a "social lubrication" through concern, social reform, the gift, the handout, welfare propaganda and humane relations). But this incorporation of altruism in the system of consumption will not be sufficient to stabilize it.

Consumption is therefore a powerful element in social control (by atomizing individual consumers); yet at the same time it requires the intensification of *bureaucratic control* over the processes of consumption, which is subsequently heralded, with increased intensity, as the *reign of freedom*. We will never escape it.

Traffic and the automobile provide the classic example of this contradiction, where there is the unlimited promotion of individual consumption; the desperate call to collective responsibility and social morality; and increasingly severe restraints. The paradox is the following: one can not simultaneously remind the individual that "the level of consumption is the just measure of social merit" and expect of him or her a different type of social responsibility, since in the act of personal consumption the individual already fully assumes a social responsibility. Once again, consumption is *social labor*. The consumer is conscripted and mobilized as a laborer at this level *as well* (today perhaps just as much as at the level of "production"). All the same, one should not ask the "laborer of consumption" to sacrifice his income (his individual satisfactions) for the collective good. Somewhere in their social subconsciousness, these millions of consumers have a sort of practical intuition of their new status as alienated laborer. The call for public solidarity is immediately perceived as a mystification. Their tenacious resistance here is simply a reflex of *political* defense. The consumer's "fixated egoism" is also the gross subconscious recognition of being the new exploited subject of modern times, despite all the nonsense about affluence and well-being. The fact that resistance and "egoism" drives the system to insoluble contradictions, to which it responds by reinforcing constraints, only confirms that consumption is a gigantic *political* field, whose analysis, as well as that of production, is still to be achieved.

The entire discourse on consumption aims to transform the consumer into the Universal Being, the general, ideal, and final incarnation of the human species. It attempts also to make of consumption the premise for "human liberation," to be attained in lieu of, and despite the failures of, social and political liberation. The consumer is in no way a universal being, but rather a social and political being, and a productive force. As such, the consumer revives fundamental *historical* problems: those concerning the ownership of the means of consumption (and no longer the means of production), those regarding economic responsibility (responsibility towards the *content* of production), etc. There is here the potential for a deep crisis and for new contradictions.

Ego Consumans

Nowhere, up to the present day, have these contradictions been consciously manifested, except perhaps in a few strikes among American housewives and in the sporadic destruction of commodities (May 1968, the *No Bra Day*[34] when American women publicly burned their bras). "What does the consumer represent in the modern world? Nothing. What could he be? Everything, or almost everything. Because he stands alone next to millions of solitary individuals, he is at the mercy of all other interests."[35] One must add that the individualist ideology is an important element here (even though, as we saw, its contradictions are latent): since it affects the collective domain of social labor, exploitation by *dispossession* (of labor power), it produces (at a certain point) an effective solidarity. And this leads to a (relative) class consciousness. Whereas the directed *acquisition* of objects and commodities is individualizing, atomizing, and dehistoricizing. As a producer, and as a consequence of the division of labor, each laborer presupposes all others: exploitation is for everyone. As a consumer, humans become again solitary, cellular, and at best *gregarious* (for example in a family viewing TV, the crowd at a stadium or in a movie house, etc.) The structures of consumption are simultaneously fluid and enclosed. Can we imagine a coalition of drivers against car registration? Or a collective opposition to television? Even if every one of the million viewers is opposed to television advertising, advertisements will nevertheless be shown. That is because consumption is primarily organized as a discourse to oneself, and has a tendency to play itself out, with its gratifications and deceptions, in this minimal exchange. The object of consumption isolates. The private sphere lacks concrete negativity because it is collapsed on objects which themselves lack negativity. It is structured from outside by the system of production, whose strategy is no longer ideological at this level, but still political; whose strategy of desire invests the materiality of our existence with its monotony and distractions. Or, as we saw, the object of consumption creates distinctions as a stratification of statuses: if it no longer isolates, it differentiates; it *collectively assigns* the consumers a place in relation to a code, without so much as giving rise to any *collective solidarity* (but quite the opposite).

In general then consumers, as such, are unconscious and unorganized, just as workers may have been at the beginning of the nineteenth century. As such consumers have been glorified, flattered, and eulogized as "public opinion," that mystical, providential, and *sovereign* reality. Just as The People is glorified by democracy provided they remain as such (that is provided they do not interfere on the political or social scene), the sovereignty of consumers is also recognized ("powerful consumers," according to Katona),[36] provided they do not try to act in this way on the social scene. The People—these are the laborers, provided they are unorganized; the Public, or public opinion—these are the consumers, provided they are content to consume.

Notes

1. Karl Marx, *Contribution to a Critique of Political Economy* (NY: International Publishers, 1970) p. 87. [Trans.]
2. Baudrillard appears to be quoting from an advertising brochure here, and elsewhere in the text. But at times they sound contrived, and can easily be read as fictional. [Trans.]
3. Parly 2: a planned community (etymologically and geographically) between Paris and Orly (the airport in the southern suburb of Paris). Baudrillard offers his own description in the next section. [Trans.]
4. "Idleness-on-the-Wasteful" would be one anglo-saxon version of "Flaine-la-Prodigue," Baudrillard's parody of suburban communities around Paris. "Flaine": perhaps the conjunction of "flemme" (laziness) and "flâneur" (idle/loafer); "Prodigue" (extravagant/wasteful).[Trans.]
5. See Chapter 2, note 24. [Trans.]
6. Printemps, B. H. V., Dior, Prisunic, Lanvin, Frank et Fils are department stores. [Trans.]
7. Originally in English.[Trans.]
8. Knight: unable to identify the source of this quotation. [Trans.]
9. A French sociologist, author of *Pour une sociologie des aspirations* (Paris: Denoël, 1969). [Trans.]
10. Originally in English. [Trans.]
11. Ibid.
12. Ibid.
13. The translator is unable to identify the source of this quotation.
14. The translator is unable to identify the source of this quotation from Talcott Parsons.
15. Originally in English. [Trans.]
16. A study in *Sélection du Reader's Digest* (A. Piatier: *Structure et perspectives de la con-*

sommation européenne), found that consumption in Europe is the activity of a minority, in contrast to the large middle class in the USA, a consuming elite (the As) which serves as a model for a majority that does not yet have access to this display of luxury (sports car, stereo system, summer home), without which there are no Europeans worthy of the name.

17. For these references see chapter 2, nn. 9 and 11. [Trans.]

18. John Kenneth Galbraith, *The New Industrial State* (New York: Signet, 1967) p. 215. [Trans.]

19. Ibid., p. 222.

20. The translator and editor are unable to locate this wonderful reference from Galbraith.

21. This is the "anticoagulant" effect of advertising (Elgozy).

22. Galbraith, *The New Industrial State*, p. 281. [Trans.]

23. Ibid., p. 279. [Trans.]

24. Ibid., p. 280. [Trans.]

25. 'Happy end' was originally in English. [Trans.]

26. "The ideological genesis of needs," in *For a Critique of the Political Economy of the Sign*, trans. Charles Levin (St. Louis: Telos Press, 1981).

27. Originally in English. [Trans.]

28. 'Fun-system' was originally in English. [Trans.]

29. Originally in English. [Trans.]

30. Marc Alexandre, "Sur la société de consommation," *La Nef*, 37.

31. Originally in English. The translator is unable to identify the source of this quotation.

32. *The New Industrial State*, p. 49. [Trans.]

33. Cf. Paul Fabra's article in *Le Monde*, June 26, 1969, "Les superbenefices et la monopolization de l'epargne par les grandes enterprises."

34. Originally in English. [Trans.]

35. *Le Cooperateur*, 1965.

36. Originally in English from George Katona, *The Mass Consumption Society* (New York: McGraw-Hill, 1964). The translator is unable to identify the page of this citation.

CHAPTER 4

What Is an Economy For?

James Fallows

Every country and culture is unique, and the "Asian" economic system naturally is something different in Singapore from what it is in Thailand or Japan. There are comparable variations among European and North American styles of capitalism. In their emphasis on industrial guidance and national policy, France and Germany are more Asian than they are American. In their approach to leisure and the good life, the Europeans are less like the new Asian model than like Americans. Still, four main patterns distinguish the Asian system from the prevailing Western model. Some of them are descended from old clashes between German and Anglo-American philosophies of economic competition. . . . They involve:

- The *purpose* of economic life. In the American-style model the basic reason for having an economy is to raise the consumer's standard of living. In the Asian model it is to increase the collective national strength. Ideally, the goal is to make the nation independent and self-sufficient, so that it does not rely on outsiders for its survival. The American-style goal is materialistic; the Asian-style goal is political, and comes from long experience of being oppressed by people with stronger economies and technologies.

- The view of *power* in setting economic policies. Anglo-American ideology views concentrated power as an evil ("Power corrupts, and absolute power . . ."). Therefore it has developed elaborate schemes for dividing and breaking up power when it becomes concentrated. The Asian-style model views concentrated power as a fact of life. It has developed elaborate systems for ensuring that the power is used for the long-term national good.

- The view of *surprise* and unpredictability. The Anglo-American model views surprise as the key to economic life. We believe that it is precisely because markets are fluid and unpredictable that they work. The Asian-style system deeply mistrusts markets. It sees competition as a useful tool

"What is an Economy For?" by James Fallows reprinted from *The Atlantic Monthly* (January 1994). Used by permission of *The Atlantic Monthly* and James Fallows.

for keeping companies on their toes, but not as a way to resolve any of the big questions of life—how a society should be run, in what direction its economy should unfold. This is, in Western terms, a military view of economics. Within the American military the Army competes with the Navy for funds, and competition within each branch keeps both the Army and the Navy sharp. But the services don't cast votes or place bids to decide where the nation should fight. Decisions like that are not left to a market.

- The view of *national borders* and an us-versus-them concept of the world. People everywhere are xenophobic and exclusive, but in the Anglo-American model this is thought to be a lamentable, surmountable failing. The Asian-style model assumes that it is a natural and permanent condition. The world consists of us and them, and no one else will look out for us.

Consumers or Employees?

By the tenets of post-Second World War Anglo-American economics, "What is an economy for?" isn't a very difficult question. In fact, it answers itself. Economic development means "more." If people have more choice, more leisure, more wealth, more opportunity to pursue happiness, society as a whole will be a success. In theory, any deal that the market permits will in the long run be good for society as a whole.

The Anglo-American system is long on theories. It is easy to pick up any English-language textbook and find theories proving that whatever gives more to the consumer is best for everyone. The Asian system is not so explicitly theoretical. Yet the fundamental purpose of the Asian model is evident from its performance. Its goal is to develop the productive base of the country—the industries either within the country or under the control of the country's citizens around the world. When it comes to a choice between the consumer's welfare and the producer's, it's really no choice at all.

In countless ways the most successful of today's Asian societies reveal their bias in favor of the producer. A few illustrations:

- Japan and Korea are famous for protecting their rice markets. Even though the small plots, high land prices, and aged rural work force together make the cost of rice several times as high as it is elsewhere in the world, neither country gives its consumers the option of buying from overseas. In the Western world this is usually taken to be a quaint affectation. After all, Japanese and Korean spokesmen usually defend their policy in emotional terms ("our precious heritage"), and even if the markets were thrown wide open, there is a limit to how much foreign rice the Japanese or the Koreans could eat. (Because of crop failures following last year's wet summer, the Japanese government will allow emergency rice imports this year, but says it will close the market when the emergency has passed.)

In fact rice policy reveals a major, consequential pro-producer bias. Especially in Japan, but also in Korea and Taiwan, farm protectionism is the crux of a sweeping anti-consumer social bargain. If there is a single factor limiting consumption in these countries, it is the extremely high price of land; and if there is a single force that keeps the price up, it is the system that sets aside so much land (one quarter of the nonmountainous land in Japan) for the production of very expensive crops. "High land prices have caused the Japanese to act in ways they would not have otherwise," Susan Hanley, of the University of Washington, wrote in 1992. "It is not Japan's Asian cultural heritage that sets it apart . . . so much as the result of its artificially high land prices."

• The more successful the economy in Asia, the more likely it is to have a rigged, anti-consumer, high-priced retail system. Japan's is the most successful, and its retail economy is the most cartelized and expensive. It's not simply that imported goods are expensive; Japanese-made goods are too. According to a survey at the end of 1991, clothes cost twice as much in Tokyo as in New York, food about three times as much, gasoline about two and a half times as much, and so on.

Anglo-American economic theory can explain why Japanese prices are so high: the retail system is full of cartels and monopolies. A network of laws, contracts, and commercial agreements in Japan discourages discounting and price competition. Until it was relaxed in the early 1990s, Japan's famous *dai ten ho*, or "big store law," effectively outlawed supermarkets, since it required that small local merchants give their approval (or be bribed into doing so) before a big store could be built. It is hard for familiar economic theory to accept that such an inefficient and anti-consumer system might last for many decades, with the apparent approval even of the victimized population of consumers.

The immediate reason the system lasts is the political power of small merchants, who—along with farmers and the construction industries—are big donors to the powerful Liberal Democratic Party in Japan. The more basic reason it lasts is that it helps producers, and in ways that offset the penalty to consumers. When competition in Europe or America pushes down the price of VCRs, cars, and semi-conductor chips, Japanese producers can maintain high prices within Japan. In effect, producers wring monopoly profits out of their own people in order to build a war chest for competition overseas. When the yen doubled in value against the dollar from 1985 to 1988, retail prices in Japan should have fallen significantly—but they barely budged. Japanese corporations were taxing their own people with artificially high prices so that they could maintain artificially low prices in export markets in Europe and North America. In return for this tax the Japanese got strong organizations and full employment. This may not be an attractive bargain from the Western viewpoint, and no individual Japanese or Korean likes paying higher prices. But as a social bargain it is seen as keeping the nation's producers strong and thereby keeping the social fabric intact.

The closest counterpart in American experience is AT&T before its breakup. Ma Bell penalized consumers in many ways. Rates were higher than they might have been. All equipment had to be "authorized" by AT&T. At the same time, Bell used the money to fund its research labs and all its other operations. This is a version of everyday practice in Japanese business: consumers have fewer choices than they might ideally have, and corporations absorb and redeploy the money they save.

- In their own role as consumers even corporations in Japan and Korea reveal the anti-consumer bias of the Asian system. Their workers have for several decades traded artificially low wages for the promise of full employment. The wages are artificially low because through much of the postwar era earnings have lagged behind the increase in corporate productivity. By Western economic logic wages should have been rising much more rapidly. Similarly, Japanese and Korean corporations have traded artificially low profits for their equivalent of full employment, which is an ever-growing market share. In 1991 a business survey listed the thirty most profitable large companies in the world. Twenty-three of them were American, four were British, and none were Japanese.

- The parts of Japanese, Korean, and Taiwanese life that encourage consumption are made difficult. The parts that encourage savings, investment, and deferred gratification are made easy and attractive—the way it was in America during the Second World War. The automobile market in Japan, for instance, is dominated by the *shaken* racket. The word *shaken* (pronounced "shah-ken" rather than like the English word "shaken") literally means "car ticket." In effect a *shaken* is a reinspection certificate that each car in Japan must have in order to remain legally on the road. The *shaken* policy originated during the infancy of the Japanese auto industry, when domestic cars were such unreliable rattletraps that bureaucrats thought it would be dangerous to let them on the road without constant safety checks. The public-safety rationale for reinspections obviously no longer applies. Nonetheless, after three years and then every two years thereafter Japanese drivers must take their cars in for a new *shaken*, and every two years they are saddled with hugely expensive "necessary" repairs. By the time a car is three or five years old, it can cost so many thousands of dollars to meet *shaken* standards that it makes sense to buy a new car, even though new cars themselves cost much more than the same models outside Japan. It is a way to turn the population into a captive market for producers.

- The experience of the past generation has taught most Asian countries one dramatically clear lesson. They can't really go wrong by giving consumers too little, but they can easily go wrong by giving consumers too much. During the collapse of Japan's bubble economy, in 1991 and 1992, government officials said privately that an atmosphere of hardship was useful. Consumerism had been getting out of hand, and the bubble's collapse would have a tonic effect—without imposing real hardship on Japan or endangering Japan's long-term prospects. (Business-failure rates among Japanese manufacturing and construction firms were actually lower during the "crash" years of the early 1990s than they had been on average during the booming 1980s.)

In Korea the late 1980s were heady, pro-consumer years. The 1988 Seoul Olympics did for the country what the 1964 Tokyo Olympics had done for Japan. Anything seemed possible. In the fashionable parts of Seoul young women wore miniskirts and young men hung out all night. By 1990 the trade surplus was heading for the cellar, and the government had to fight back with a huge "anti-luxury" campaign. With economic growth slipping, the national tax office announced that "extravagance beyond one's reported means" would invite tax scrutiny. In effect this meant that anyone who bought a Mercury Sable, Lincoln Continental, Mercedes, or BMW could expect to be put through the tax wringer—a more serious threat in Korea than in some other countries, because so much business is off the books. Tariffs and other barriers had already raised the price of these cars to more than twice what they would cost in the United States. That hadn't choked off sales, but the tax threat did; sales of the Sable virtually stopped after the tax men stepped in.

Beyond all these economic calculations is a question of human nature. Anglo-American economic theory boils people down to their roles as consumers. Life experience, even in America, tells us that people have more in mind than getting the cheapest possible price and the highest possible wage. In certain circumstances people *like* to work hard, and save, and sacrifice themselves. Even though lottery winners typically don't have society's most desirable jobs, many of them decide to keep working even after they have cashed in. For years and years studies have shown that people who own small businesses behave in a self-exploitative, economically irrational way. They typically work longer hours than normal employees and earn less money than they could if they sold off their assets and invested the proceeds. Decisions like these are oddities in the Anglo-American economic world, where they are explained away with little theories about the "utility" of work. They are central to the Asian model of individual and collective life.

The Emperor's Legacy

In the United States the effort to break up political power and the attempt to prevent the concentration of economic power have been seen as parallel steps toward liberty. The United States has a three-branch government because of fear that any one branch will become too dominant. The great reformers in the American tradition have generally risen to strike down excessive concentrations of power, from Jefferson (in his battle with Hamilton) to Andrew Jackson to Teddy Roosevelt to Ralph Nader to Ronald Reagan, in their varying ways. The people who have argued for centralizing and exercising power have generally had the excuse of wartime: Abraham Lincoln, Woodrow Wilson, Franklin D. Roosevelt, John F. Kennedy, and Lyndon Johnson.

The deepest criticism of Japanese politics, made by the Dutch writer Karel van Wolferen, is that it lacks a definable center of political accountability. In the French or American system a President must finally make big choices, whereas in the Japanese system (as Van Wolferen explains it) the buck never stops anywhere.

The classic illustration of this problem is Japan's apparent paralysis during the first month after Iraq invaded Kuwait. The standard critique outside Japan was that the country was not doing its fair share. This entirely missed the point. Eventually Japan came up with quite a large sum of money, when it could have made the case for not contributing money at all. (The case would have been that it was foolish to go to war over this issue, and that if other countries had emulated Japan, by conserving their use of oil, they could have afforded to take a longer-term view.) Rather, the problem was that Japan seemed incapable of deciding what its position was. The Foreign Ministry announced one policy, the Finance Ministry disavowed it. The Prime Minister at the time, Toshiki Kaifu, was scheduled to go on a trip to the Middle East. Officials in the Foreign Ministry called the trip off. Feuding occurs in any government, but in this government not even the Prime Minister had the authority to resolve it.

Most other Asian societies do have a center of power. Indeed, this center has often been one dominant figure—a military strongman, as in Thailand, Indonesia, and often Korea; a statesman-leader, epitomized by Lee Kuan Yew, of Singapore; a sheer tyrant, as in North Korea and Burma; or a political boss, as in Malaysia and often Taiwan.

But whether the center of politics has been weak, as in Japan, or strong, as everywhere else, the political system as a whole has generally been authoritarian in Asia. Compared with any Western societies, and especially the Anglo-American system, Asian states have been less embarrassed and more explicit about the government's role in shaping society. The contrast is obviously sharper with America than with, say, France, which operates a Japanese-style *dirigiste* system without the social control. The Japanese system also resembles the most successful parts of government-business interaction in the United States, such as nuclear-weapons design and medical research. And it has analogues in many parts of Asia.

Some scholars contend that the heavy hand of government is the living legacy of Confucius. Anglo-American ideology warns against the abuse of power, and therefore tries to restrict Kings, Prime Ministers, and Presidents. The traditional Confucian "mandate of heaven" approach assumes that there will be an Emperor, asking only whether he exercises power well or poorly. Other scholars argue that such theories are merely cultural window-dressing, used by ruling groups to rationalize their hold on power.

Either way, the history of powerful governments in East Asia has made most governments both more competent and more legitimate when they work with businesses. They are more competent because the great prestige of the civil service continues to attract the best-educated people in the country. For a variety of historical and social-status reasons, jobs in the government bureaucracy are still among the most desirable ones in Korea, Japan, Taiwan, and other Confucian-influenced East Asian societies. Ambitious young graduates compete for positions in the Japanese Ministry of Finance or with the Korean Economic Planning Board the way ambitious young Americans compete for jobs at what we drolly call "investment" banks. (In 1990 Wasserstein Perella & Company, the mergers-and-acquisition house that was spun off from First Boston, received more than 30,000 applications for eight positions for college graduates.)

Today's Asian bureaucrats always complain that the thrill is gone, that they're not paid enough, that the long hours are driving out the real talent, and so on. For instance, early in 1992 the *Yomiuri Shimbun*, Japan's largest paper, said that the bureaucrats were groaning because they were about to be switched to a mandatory work week of five (rather than six) days, as part of Japan's efforts not to work so hard. Their grievance was that it would just mean more overtime during the regular week. Still, by international standards the Asian governments attract very skillful people into their ministries, and the ministers have both personal and institutional legitimacy.

A Fundamental Mistrust of the Market

The dynamic view of economics is connected to the main spirit of American culture. People's lives should change! The future should be full of surprise!

This is not the spirit of most Asian societies, least of all Japan. The more familiar you become with Japanese customs, the more you are impressed with the virtue of doing the expected thing. (Letters to friends in Japanese, for instance, are always supposed to begin with comments about the weather.) The ideal Japanese life is one from which uncertainty has been removed as early as possible—by getting into the right school, by joining the right corporation. In 1989 pollsters asked citizens in seven countries to react to the statement "It is boring to live like other people." In America 69 percent of respondents agreed with the statement. In Japan only 25 percent did.

In a much broader sense, the Asian systems mistrust the uncertainty the market brings. The Asian and Anglo-American models both trust the market to decide which products will succeed or fail, which companies will beat which others. The Anglo-American model trusts political and economic markets with larger decisions as well: what is a good society, what is the right course for economic growth. The Asian model shrinks in horror from this possibility—as American parents would shrink from the idea that "the market," in the form of music videos, TV shows, and shopping malls, should teach their children what is right and wrong.

"The peoples of China, North Korea, South Korea, Japan, and other Confucian cultures deeply believe that the state ought to provide not only material wherewithal for its peoples but moral guidance," the Korean scholar Jung-en Woo wrote in 1991. "By and large, Westerners have no way to understand this point except to assert that the Asian countries suffer from a series of absences: no individual rights, no civil society, no Englightenment, and thus a weak or absent liberalism." The individual may sometimes feel these lacks, but what is more important is that the system roll on.

According to most Western political theory—displayed in America at its extreme—the state has no legitimate power to say what makes a good life or a healthy economy. Everyone makes such choices for every day; the choice for the society emerges naturally from these decisions. If everyone wants to avoid taxes, taxes stay low. If people want to buy computers—or guns, or X-rated videos—that industry flourishes. The genius of this system is that it can use people's hungers and jealousies as a tool. It perfectly melds political and economic theories: political liberalism and economic laissez-faire, each of which says to leave the individual alone. The flaw is that the system suffers from "market failures," as economists and political scientists call them. Most people would be better off if the society invested more in schools or roads, but no one wants to vote for higher taxes. Everyone feels worse off when there are very wide social divisions, but no individual can make choices that narrow them.

In reality, the largest questions of right and wrong have been settled outside the market system—through religion, or family prejudice, or patriotism, or ethnic loyalty. But it is hard for the American-style system to argue that anything profitable is wrong if a willing seller and a willing buyer can agree on a price.

No government in Asia believes such things. Many individuals do, people being the same everywhere. But governments, with the possible exception of Hong Kong's, think that they, not individuals, should make the big decisions of right and wrong.

Time and again the visitor to Japan hears the phrases "confusion in the market" and "excessive competition." These are shorthand for the dangers of letting market forces get out of control. Each time these phrases come up, they raise intriguing translation problems. You can almost hear the interpreters saying the phrase as if it had quotation marks around it in English—"confusion in the market." There are no comparable terms in English, because the very concepts do not exist. What the Japanese and Koreans call "excessive" competition is what Western economics texts call "perfect" competition.

A deeper idea is the fundamental distinction between the market as a means and the market as an end in itself. Every healthy society knows that market incentives are necessary—real price competition, failure for products that don't make the grade, reward for innovation and enterprise. But only in the Western model is nothing besides the market necessary.

In the early stages of their economic development, especially after the Second World War, Asian governments found it easy to set targets and plans. Above all else they had to catch up to the Western lead. Even now Asian systems reveal their faith that the goals should be chosen, rather than left to the market to decide. For example:

• The Korean government has for decades divided up the work of national development among Korea's major companies. One group of companies must run the shipyards; another must collaborate with the Americans on semiconductor projects. In Taiwan the government requires companies to set aside a certain share of their sales revenue for research-and-development expenses. "Such measures would probably strike those South Koreans [and Taiwanese] who have absorbed the *political* ideals of the Anglo-Saxon model as flagrant violations of liberty," the economist Alice Amsden wrote in 1991.

Yet this is a very Anglo-Saxon view of democracy, not a universal one. It could just as well be argued that to leave in private hands investment decisions that have the potential to make a major impact on the welfare of society is itself inherently undemocratic.

• The Anglo-American system tries to permit as many deals to be made as possible. In general, anything that's profitable should be legal, unless there's a compelling argument against it. The only loyalties that are not supposed to be for sale are within a family and to the country. More generally, friendship is supposed to operate outside the market system. But in Asia, and especially in Japan, *business* relationships are also supposed to operate outside the market, with loyalty to one's employer being more important than whether the relationship is immediately profitable or not. A Japanese scholar named Michio Morishima pointed out, in *Why Has Japan "Succeeded"?*, that

the "loyalty" market is opened only once in a lifetime to each individual, when he graduates from school or college. It is in this market that those who are able to provide loyalty meet those who are looking for it, their "lords."

• During the Japanese stock market's long slide from 1989 to 1992, Japanese analysts contended that computer-program trading, introduced into the Tokyo stock market by American firms, was driving the market to daily lows. This strengthened the general feeling that the way to save the market was to restrict its flexibility—to make it more regulated again rather than to perfect its market forces. A Japanese report at the time said, "Deregulation of brokers' commissions in the US caused securities industry profits to fall and forced many firms into high-risk areas, such as aggressive mergers

and acquisitions, a report by the Securities Industry Council charged."
That is, letting too many decisions be made by the market created instability for all.

- In the summer of 1991, when scandals were being revealed practically every day in the Japanese securities industry, a strange scandal was also unfolding in the earth-moving industry. Many of the competitors of the large Komatsu Corporation had been paying spies to provide secrets about Komatsu's master plan. The *Nihon Keizai Shimbun* reported, with a worried tone, that after the revelations "many [initially] thought confusion would reign in the construction industry." But, the paper said with relief, "it has been as calm as a lake in the morning—nary a ripple."

One of the reasons for this camaraderie is the fact that the Japan Construction Equipment Manufacturers Association, the "club" of the construction machinery industry, has just been organized. Until the "club" was organized, the industry was one huge price war. And, if the war went on, no one would make a profit and all would lose. Sensing that they were cutting each other's throats, the industry finally got together. So Komatsu didn't want to ruin all that effort.

Once the industry had formed its cartel, everyone felt secure again.

In 1955 the American novelist Richard Wright, the author of *Black Boy* and *Native Son*, went to Bandung, in newly independent Indonesia, for the historic conference of the nonaligned countries. This was the first real postcolonial muscle-flexing by Asian and African countries, led by the likes of Jawaharlal Nehru, Gamal Abdel Nasser, and Sukarno. As a black American, Wright had gone expecting to feel fellowship with those who had been controlled by white colonialists. His book about the conference, *The Color Curtain*, reflected his increasing puzzlement over, and estrangement from, the nonaligned policies. Although he did not put it this way, mistrust of the market was one of the traits that struck him most.

Still another and, to the Western mind, somewhat baffling trait emerged from these Asian responses. There seemed to be in their consciousness a kind of instinct (I can't find a better word!) toward hierarchy, toward social collectivities of an organic nature. In contrast to the Western feeling that education was an instrument to enable the individual to become free, to stand alone, the Asian felt that education was to bind men together.

The point for the moment is that one economic system assumes that it does not have to make the largest decisions about national purpose except when the system is being attacked from outside, in time of war. The other assumes that the state *always* has a role in guiding the nation. It is the clash between these visions, rather than the rightness or wrongness of either of them, that creates current problems.

Borders and Borderlessness

In Western economics it's hard to come up with a theoretical reason for concentrating on national economic well-being. In the Asian model this is not a problem at all; it's taken for granted.

In daily life there is no shortage of nationalistic spirit in Western countries in general or the United States in particular. The flag waves constantly in American TV commercials. Crowds chant "USA" at international sporting events. But the principles that guide economic policy in the Anglo-American approach avoid the concept of national interest except in strictly military terms.

Most Anglo-American concepts in fact treat national economic interests as if they didn't really exist. Companies move their plants overseas, because that is what business logic says they should do. When it comes to politics, we're able to explain—but just barely—why one person should be inconvenienced for the good of all. I pay taxes because I'm part of a political community, even though in any given year I may pay more into the government than I directly get out. In the Anglo-American model there really isn't an economic community that justifies anyone's paying higher prices than he absolutely has to, or preferring to deal with someone from the same country rather than buying from overseas.

This outlook seems advanced and tolerant from the Western, liberal perspective. The world should be "borderless." In the summer of 1990 Roger Porter, who was then President Bush's chief domestic-policy adviser, gave a speech about America's outlook on world trade. Some people, he said, clung to the "old notion of nations, companies, and markets rigidly defined by national borders." But in this modern age, he concluded, such a notion was "outdated and dangerous." Porter was making a partisan argument in behalf of the Bush economic program, but his assumption that consciousness of nationality was "outdated and dangerous" reflected an educated Western view that has nothing to do with party.

In the United States discussions of corporate nationality have stuck mainly to the realm of theory. According to American assumptions, it is only natural for businesses to operate in rootless, global fashion. Therefore most Americans assume that denationalization has already occurred. American discussion on this point has been heavily influenced by the writings of Robert Reich, who was a lecturer at Harvard's John F. Kennedy School of Government before he became Secretary of Labor in the Clinton Administration. Since the mid-1970s Reich has been proposing solutions to America's long-term economic problems, and his ideas about industrial policy have attracted a broad following. During the Bush years Reich wrote several influential articles in the *Harvard Business Review* and a subsequent book called *The Work of Nations*, which argued that corporations had grown past the point where they could sensibly be considered American or German or Japanese. With headquarters in one country, research centers in another, factories in yet other countries, and customers all around the world, Reich said, big diversified corporations could be loyal only to their own economic interests. Though Chrysler had its headquarters in Detroit and Matsushita was based in Osaka, neither would necessarily care about the government or labor force of its home country. Each would go wherever the money, the market, and the skilled work force drew it. In an age of global corporations, Reich concluded, a nation's well-being rises or falls with the skills of its workers. Therefore he vigorously advocated plans for improving American education and retraining American workers.

In practical terms, Reich said in a 1990 article titled "Who Is Us?," published in the *Harvard Business Review*, this blurring of corporate nationality meant that the U.S. government should not try to help American-owned companies solely because they were American-owned. The government owed its loyalty to citizens and workers within its borders, and companies from Europe, Japan, Mexico, or anywhere else might have more to offer the American work force. When the U.S. government gave contracts to Boeing, provided bailouts to Chrysler, or negotiated on behalf of Motorola or Zenith, by Reich's analysis it might not have been helping American workers in any direct way. There was no telling where the companies would build the products that federal money was subsidizing. If Toyota was building plants in America and Chrysler was moving plants to Mexico, then Toyota should be considered at least as "American" as Chrysler.

As a theoretical matter, this proposition is sensible and appealing. Daily life abounds with cases that seem to confirm the point. American plants move to Mexico; Japanese and German plants open up in the United States. A large number of American commentators have embraced the "Who Is Us?" assumption, usually crediting Reich for having precisely defined the shift to a world in which corporations no longer have citizenship. Yet many of the specific illustrations on which this changed perspective is based turn out to be misleading. For instance:

- In the summer of 1989 Reich published an article in *The New Republic* that provided a perfect illustration of the way a preference for home-based companies could backfire. U.S. trade negotiators, he said, had been hammering at the Japanese government to open the country's market to cellular phones made by Motorola. The irony, he said, was that in helping Motorola the government was doing little or nothing for American workers, because the phones Motorola wanted to sell were actually designed and made in Kuala Lumpur.

As a recent resident of Kuala Lumpur, I was surprised when I read this assertion, since I had known Motorola officials there and had never heard them say that they made cellular phones. As it turns out, they didn't. Motorola officials wrote immediately to *The New Republic* pointing out that the phones were made in the United States. James P. Caile, the director of marketing for

Motorola's Cellular Subscriber Group, said in his letter that the telephones in question were designed and made in Arlington Heights, Illinois.

Half a year later Reich published his seminal article, "Who Is Us?" Once again he used Motorola as a main illustration of the difference between the welfare of American companies and the welfare of American workers. Motorola, he said this time, "designs and makes many of its cellular telephones in Kuala Lumpur, while most of the Americans who make cellular telephone equipment in the United States for export to Japan happen to work for Japanese-owned companies."

After this article appeared, Richard W. Heimlich, Motorola's director of international strategy, wrote to the *Harvard Business Review*, pointing out once more that the phones were made in America, not Malaysia. Heimlich's letter also questioned Reich's claim that some "Japanese-owned companies" were building cellular phones in America and exporting them to Japan. Heimlich's letter was published in the *Harvard Business Review*; Reich replied in the magazine about cellular telephones thus: "One of those [Motorola's] Southeast Asian plants, by the way, does make parts for cellular telephones, according to industry sources."

Heimlich also wrote directly to Reich, offering to discuss the issue further. Reich sent back an angry personal letter (which Motorola officials gave me when I asked for their side of the story), saying that he resented having his intellectual and academic integrity challenged. This letter referred Heimlich to a book by Edward Graham and Paul Krugman, which Reich said would substantiate his claims.

The book is called *Foreign Direct Investment in the United States*. I found when I looked at it that it says nothing at all about Motorola in Kuala Lumpur, and in a broader sense its argument is the opposite of Reich's. Its perspective is clearly internationalist, and one of its intentions is to rebut irrational American fears about the effects of foreign investment. Nevertheless the data Krugman and Graham examined show that corporate nationality does matter, and that it matters most for Japanese-owned firms.

At least in the United States, foreign-owned companies behave differently from American-owned firms in many ways. The biggest difference is that foreign-owned firms are far more likely to import their components from suppliers in the home country than to buy them locally. This difference is most pronounced for Japanese-owned firms. In December of 1991 Edward Graham published a comparison of Japanese-owned and American-owned manufacturing firms operating in the United States. He found that the Japanese-owned firms were less likely to produce goods for export from the United States, less likely to produce goods for export from the United States, less likely to invest R&D funds in America—and four times as likely to import components, instead of manufacturing or buying them in the United States.

In the Winter, 1991, issue of *The American Prospect*, Reich once again used Motorola to illustrate the borderless nature of the new, integrated world, and Heimlich once again protested in a letter to the editor. Later that year Reich published *The Work of Nations*. It included a full-scale presentation of the borderless argument, including "one example" that summed up the folly of the U.S. government's working in behalf of U.S.-based corporations—the same example.

The power of the Motorola-in-Malaysia story depends on the assumption that it is one of many possible illustrations of a widespread trend. If there really were a large number of examples to choose from, it's hard to explain why an author would have stuck with such a troublesome case. After I made numerous calls to the Labor Department to ask Reich why he seemed so attached to this one story, he replied through a press representative at the department that he had "seen no evidence to change his mind" about the Motorola case.

- Last year, after he became Labor Secretary, Reich presented another perfect example of the "coming irrelevance of corporate nationality." The example came in a memorandum he sent to President Bill Clinton on March 23, concerning trade and "competitiveness" strategies. "Our efforts should focus on opening foreign markets to American *exports*, rather than merely to U.S. products," he said, sensibly. American exports would employ workers in America; mere "U.S. products," for instance Coca-Cola sold overseas, might do little for America's work force. Then came the example:

Japan's agreement to purchase 20 per cent of its semiconductors from non-Japanese firms, for example, does not necessarily promote high-wage production in the United States. Close to 75 per cent of the chips which Japan purchased last year from U.S. firms were fabricated in Japan.

If true, this illustration would be even more powerful than the Motorola story in showing that corporations had transcended nationality. It would also mean that the semiconductor agreement had completely backfired, "forcing" Japanese purchasers, Brer Rabbit–like, into buying more output from factories based in Japan. But this account of the agreement's effects also turns out to be inaccurate. According to figures collected by the U.S. Trade Representative's office, the percentage of such American-brand chips that were made in Japan was 30, not "close to 75." The semiconductor agreement had in fact achieved its stated purpose: most of the American chips sold in Japan were indeed designed and made in the United States.

- In the same memorandum Reich gave another illustration of the borderless paradox. The U.S. government at that time was evaluating how to get involved in the emerging technologies of high-definition television. The main decisions lay with the Federal Communications Commission, which was to decide which transmission system, among several competing proposals, should be the standard for HDTV broadcasts within the United States. At the time Reich wrote his memo, three business consortia were vying to have their standards selected. One was led by the electronics makers Thomson, based in France, and Phillips, based in Holland. The other two were all-American, in that the main partners in them were all U.S.-based institutions: an alliance between Zenith and AT&T, and a group led by the Massachusetts Institute of Technology and the Chicago firm General Instruments. (A fourth group, led by Japanese firms, dropped out of the competition when it became clear that its analog transmission system would lose in competition against the digital systems proposed by each of the other teams.)

In his memorandum to the President, Reich said that the government should look beyond strictly technical issues to see "which standard is likely to generate the greatest amount of high-wage production in the United States." He added,

(Interestingly, the only consortium which has pledged to develop and manufacture its high-definition televisions in the United States is the Dutch-French group [Phillips-Thompson-Sarnoff] [*sic*]; the AT&T-Zenith group will not do so, because Zenith is moving all its television production to Mexico.)

Like the Motorola and semiconductor examples, this one seemed to show the folly of helping American corporations. But as with the other examples, the real facts of this case undercut the "Who Is Us?" argument.

The French-Dutch consortium did indeed plan to do the final assembly of its TV sets in America. Zenith planned to do its final assembly in Mexico. But this stage of the process boils down to "screwdriver jobs": final assembly is the bolting together of sophisticated, high-value components made somewhere else. Most of the value of an HDTV, which in turn means most of the sophisticated, high-wage jobs, would come from designing and producing those components. The most important and valuable components would be the many diverse semiconductors that would control the conversion and display of incoming digital signals. The high-resolution, large-scale picture tubes would be the next most valuable components. Where these specialized products were made, rather than where the sets were put together, would determine where the highest-value jobs from HDTV would end up.

If Thomson-Philips eventually leads the HDTV industry, the advanced semiconductors for its sets will almost certainly come from Thomson's factories in France. If the AT&T-Zenith group does, the semiconductors will come from AT&T in the United States. In a letter to Reich, Zenith's chairman, Jerry K. Pearlman, had emphasized that since the "American" consortium would make its advanced components in the United States, it would produce more highly skilled jobs for Americans than the European consortium would.

Pearlman is hardly an impartial observer, but his account of HDTV supply patterns conforms to most other accounts in the industry. It is "interesting," as Reich had said in his memorandum to the President, to speculate that the foreign-based consortium would create more high-value jobs within the United States, but this is probably not the reality. Most other evidence, both anecdotal and analytic, confirms the antique-seeming idea that corporations do their most valuable work in the country where they are based.

Them Against Us

Anglo-American theory instructs Westerners that economics is a "positive-sum game," from which all can emerge as winners. Asian history instructs many Koreans, Chinese, Japanese, and others that economic competition is a form of war. To be strong is much better than to be weak; to give orders is better than to take them. By this logic the way to be strong, to give orders, to have independence and control—to win—is to keep in mind the difference between us and them. This perspective comes naturally to Koreans when thinking about Japan, or to Canadians when thinking about the United States, or to Chinese or Japanese when thinking about what the Europeans did to their nations. It does not come naturally to Americans.

But, again, it comes naturally in the Asian system. There are more examples from Japan than from the other countries, because Japan got there first; Korea, for instance, would love to be just as nationalistic, but under the current balance of power in Asian economies it doesn't have a chance.

Here are a few ways in which Asian economies are more nationalistic than ours.

• *Intra-industry trade.* Theory seems to call for international trade to become more specialized by region as time goes on. Wine and cheese will come from France, magazine editors from England, cars from Japan, wool from New Zealand, and vodka from the Russian potato lands. Each country will develop its own national skill.

In fact just the opposite occurs. Since the end of the Second World War the fastest-growing type of international trade had been "intra-industry" trade. German car companies like Mercedes, Audi, and BMW make cars that are attractive to customers in France, Japan, and America—but some people in Germany want non-German cars like Ferraris, Toyotas, Volvos, and Fords. Germany also has a very active auto-parts industry. It sells to other auto makers around the world, and its own makers buy parts from non-German makers, notably in the United States.

The result is that Germany actively sells automobiles and auto parts to the rest of the world—and actively buys the same things. This pattern, of sales *and* purchases within an industry, is intra-industry trade. It is measured on a scale that runs from zero to 100. An intra-industry trade rate of zero means that trade in a certain industry all runs one way: a country only sells or only buys a certain product. (For instance, Saudi Arabia's trade rate for oil sales would be zero.) A rate of 100 means that a country sells exactly as much of a certain product as it buys.

Countries that have very low intra-industry trade rates are typically Third World countries or others with unbalanced economies. The classic banana republic would sell only raw materials and would import nearly all the machinery it used. The intra-industry trade rate in most developed countries is high and steadily rising. Depending on the industry, countries in Western Europe have recently had intra-industry trade rates in the low 60s through the low 80s. The U.S. rates are slightly lower than the European ones, which is not surprising, since the U.S. economy is bigger and less influenced by foreign trade.

Japan does not fit this pattern. First, its overall rate has been unusually low. Edward Lincoln, of the Brookings Institution, in his 1990 book *Japan's Unequal Trade*, calculated that Japan's overall rate was 25, which was one third the overall rate for France and far below that of any other industrial power. This means in practice that the Japanese economy buys only the goods it simply cannot make: fuel, food, raw materials, and certain advanced products (notably airplanes) in which its industries cannot yet compete.

Second, Japan's rate has rarely risen. For the rest of the developed world intra-industry trade has been the main engine of trade growth during the postwar years. Countries started with different rates, but all the rates went up. Japan's stayed low through most of the postwar era and, according to Edward Lincoln, rose only modestly in the late 1980s, when Japanese manufacturers moved some of their plants overseas. It is not necessary to say that Japan's low rate is wise, unwise, or some mixture: its effect is to divide the world into "us" and "them" production zones, and to keep as many industries as possible in the hands of "us."

• *Management.* The board members of U.S. companies are still mainly American white men, but there are exceptions. For instance, in May of 1992 *The Wall Street Journal* provided a long list of executives of major American corporations who were born outside the United States. The computer industry is full of people who started in other countries. The magazine world is full of the English.

Most Asian countries have a far more nationality-conscious policy. It would be inconceivable for a non-Korean to run one of the major Korean enterprises. Although it is difficult to find reliable figures for the number of non-Japanese who serve on the boards of directors of major Japanese companies (Japan's big-business federation, the Keidanren, says it has "no information" on this subject), the number, as best I can determine, is in the single digits. Japanese firms doing business around the world had a much higher proportion of Japanese managers than American firms had of Americans, or European firms had of their own nationalities. At the end of 1991 the *Nihon Keizai Shimbun* surveyed Japanese-owned companies in America. It concluded, "Only about 5 percent of executives are American and delegation of authority to local companies just isn't happening."

- *Incoming investment.* During the late 1980s Americans debated about the higher levels of foreign investment coming into their country, and whether it was racist to be concerned about investment from Japan rather than, say, from Holland. One answer to this question is that there was more of it from Japan. During the late 1980s Japanese investors overtook the Dutch to hold the second largest amount of U.S. assets. (The leading holders were the British.) In terms of new investments the Japanese were far ahead of everyone else in the late 1980s.

The real reason for the complaint about Japanese investment was that European investment did not seem profoundly foreign. European-owned companies in America were mainly run by Americans. Japanese-owned companies were to a much larger extent run by Japanese. During the 1988 campaign Michael Dukakis made a famous gaffe by denouncing foreign ownership at an auto-parts factory that turned out to be owned by Italian interests. The fact that on his visit he didn't notice that it was foreign-owned pointed up the underlying message: he would never have made that error with Mitsubishi.

Moreover, the British and Dutch economies were wide open for American investment. Japan's economy was not. Indeed, the share of Japan's economy that is owned by foreigners is the nation's most distinctive economic trait—because it is so tiny. Systems for measuring foreign ownership vary, but approximately 10 percent of the U.S. economy is now foreign-owned. For most European nations the foreign-owned share is higher, since the countries are smaller and their economies are more integrated. Yet for Japan the foreign-owned share is about one percent, and is virtually zero in certain crucial industries. The foreign-owned share of North American and European economies has been steadily rising. The foreign-owned share of Japan's economy has fallen for several years—despite the collapse of prices on the Japanese stock market in the early 1990s, which should theoretically have attracted bargain hunters from overseas.

For the first few decades after the Second World War, Japanese laws flatly prohibited foreigners from buying Japanese companies. The handful of foreign companies that are well established in Japan—Coca-Cola, IBM—are the exceptions that prove the rule. For various reasons they were able to grandfather themselves into the system. Their success is usually cited as proof that anyone who tries hard enough can find a way into the Japanese system. But most other companies were forbidden to do the same thing thirty or forty years ago, when it would have been cheap—and they can't afford to do it now.

Dennis Encarnation, of the Harvard Business School, has pointed out that when Japanese enterprises invest in plants in Europe or North America, they almost always buy a controlling interest—100 percent if possible, 51 percent at least. When foreigners have bought shares of Japanese firms, they have almost always ended up as minority owners, and often receive no seats on the board of directors.

- *Technology*. There is a final point to emphasize about a nationality-conscious business policy: it goes with an aversion to relying on foreigners. This desire for autarky is completely understandable in historical and psychological terms, although it is considered irrational in the realm of economics.

When Japan suddenly became industrialized, in the opening decades of this century, it lost the ability to feed its own people from its own soil. When its leaders and general considered making war on America, in the 1930s, what drove them was the fear that they would run out of oil. One nightmare they faced was that their shipping would be cut off and they would be starved out. Today is a very different time—supplier cartels can be broken, as with OPEC; people who have money, as Japan does, can find food to buy. Yet much the same mentality runs through many Japanese—and other Asian—approaches to technology. In ways that no economic theory can fully explain, the goal of national policy is to bring control of the technology into Japanese (or Korean, or Chinese) hands—even if this is irrational, even if it violates the spirit of the borderless world.

Japanese corporations do practice a form of conventional economic competition, but all within their own borders. This is known as the "one-set" philosophy: each big company makes a set of products that includes one of each kind. Each beer maker produces a draft beer, a "dry" beer, a lager, and so on; each electronics company tries to produce a full range of radios, TVs, and fax machines. Successful Japanese students are expected to get top marks in every subject. Economists say that specializing in everything is in principle not possible. But in practice the urge to be on top in *every* field, rather than concentrating on some and leaving the rest to competitors, is a stronger impulse in Japanese society than in most others.

Americans may complain about the decline of their steel and semiconductor industries—that is, areas where the United States once enjoyed a lead and has had to watch factories shut their doors. But few Americans really think it is a problem if we have to buy our entire supply of CD players from overseas. The United States has no government project under way to create a domestic fax-machine industry, and when government guidance is proposed—for semiconductors, HDTVs, and superconductors—it is always controversial. The Japanese assumption is very different. In 1988, after an agricultural-trade conference in Montreal, a Japanese negotiator spoke to a Canadian colleague. "You know what really makes Japan unusual?" he said. "We are the only major industrial power that is not also a food exporter. If we could improve the productivity of our rice farming by fifteen percent a year, in eight years we would be competitive with California." Not even Japan's least competitive industry, agriculture, should be conceded to foreign competition.

The Japanese emphasis on the country's "unique" capacity for high-quality manufacturing provides an argument for national self-sufficiency. In 1985 the most disastrous crash in Japanese air history occurred outside Tokyo. A Boeing 747 owned by Japan Air Lines took off from Tokyo's Haneda Airport, bound for Osaka. Shortly afterward it crashed into a mountainside, killing 520 passengers. Officials from Japan Air Lines visited the bereaved families to express the company's contrition. On investigation it proved that the principal cause of the crash was a faulty repair job carried out by Boeing engineers, which had left one of the plane's pressure bulkheads in a weakened state.

Many lessons might be drawn from the catastrophe. The high death toll was in part an indictment of bureaucratic infighting within Japan's Self-Defense Force, which squabbled for hours over which branch would do what in going to aid the victims. Autopsies showed that many people had survived the crash but died later of exposure or injuries; they could have been saved with a faster response. Nonetheless the crash was taken in Japan as a symbol of the across-the-board shoddiness of American equipment; over the next few years I heard it mentioned in that context dozens of times.

I moved to Japan half a year after the JAL crash, and less than a month after the space shuttle *Challenger* blew up shortly after being launched. Several times during the next year I heard quite similar responses from Japanese: if we had done it, it wouldn't have happened. A Canadian friend was at the Japanese space center that day and recalls the air of schadenfreude. The unspoken mood was, what can you expect? This gloating was unwarranted on the part of Japanese quality-control experts, since their country's own H-2 rocket, usually described in the press as the first "pure" Japanese aerospace project, kept blowing up on the launch pad in the late 1980s and early 1990s.

But the general perception of shoddy American production perfectly reinforces the Japanese view of the JAL crash and the *Challenger* explosion. Early in 1992, when the speaker of the Japanese House complained about American work habits, a *Wall Street Journal* story quoted a Japanese pollster, Takayoshi Miyagawa, as saying that the comment "represents a general perception of Japanese people on the quality of American labor." The result of the JAL crash and similar U.S.-made catastrophes, he said, is that "the Japanese people think we should make by ourselves whatever concerns human life."

Sometimes the strategy of saving lives by restricting imports backfires. In 1988 Japan's Ministry of Health and Welfare coordinated a drive by the country's three largest vaccine-making companies to produce an alternative to an American vaccine that had not been approved for sale in Japan. The American vaccine, produced by the Merck Corporation, had the trademarked name of MMR and was used to protect children against measles, mumps, and rubella (German measles) with one inoculation. Merck's vaccine was extremely safe; after it had been used on more than 100 million children, no cases of serious side effects had been confirmed. Japanese doctors at the time administered three separate shots for the three diseases. To promote the growth of Japan's pharmaceutical industry, and to avoid using Merck's product, the Japanese government asked each of the three companies to produce its best vaccine for one of the diseases covered by MMR. These the government combined into a new vaccine, which it also called MMR. When the vaccine was ready, in early 1989, the Ministry of Health and Welfare began a mandatory nationwide inoculation program for children. "Rather than use foreign products, we wanted Japanese products because they are of better quality," an official of Japan's Association of Biologicals Manufacturers told Leslie Helm, who reported the story in the *Los Angeles Times*.

In fact Japan's MMR was of much worse quality than the foreign alternatives. Based on the safety record of Merck's MMR and similar foreign vaccines, the Ministry of Health and Welfare had expected that its vaccine would produce side effects in no more than one case per 100,000 inoculations—but the incidence of side effects was at least 100 times as great as predicted. The most serious side effects were meningitis and encephalitis, which killed some children and left others paralyzed or brain-damaged. By the end of 1989 the government had made the Japanese MMR vaccine optional rather than mandatory, but it left the vaccine on the market while the remaining stocks were used up and did not approve the safer Merck product for sale in Japan. (Japanese doctors have now returned to giving separate immunizations for the three diseases.)

The preferences of such a system cannot be explained by a desire to save lives—or to protect consumers. By modern Western standards such preferences seem illogical and self-defeating at best, brutally misguided at worst. Yet they are in keeping with the belief, widespread outside the English-speaking world, that inconvenience to consumers is less damaging in the long run than weakness of a nation's productive base. The fastest-growing modern economies, in East Asia, reflect this view. Like it or not, we live in the world that Asian success stories have shaped. We need to figure out how to compete in it.

CHAPTER 5

An Environmentalist's Perspective on Consumer Society

Alan Durning

Q: What is consumption, and why is it an environmental issue in the U.S.?

Durning: I use the word consumption to mean the utilization of economic goods. But the Oxford Dictionary defines it in a way that's more appropriate. It defines consumption as making away with or destroying, wasting or squandering, using up. America is the most materially successful civilization in the history of the planet. That is at once a wonderful thing and at the same time an environmental problem. We consume our body weight each day in basic raw materials extracted from forests and farmlands, range lands and mineral ores. And that consumption accounts for a larger share of the world's environmental problems than almost anything besides—possibly—global population growth.

Q: What is the difference between being materialistic and being consumptive, and which poses the greater environmental threat?

A: People often speak of Americans as being materialistic. To me, real materialism means caring about things and taking care of them. Environmentally speaking, materialism isn't necessarily a bad thing. Consumerism, on the other hand, is the philosophy that ever more stuff is the route to ultimate satisfaction. I think this is incompatible with an environmentally sound economy. Unfortunately, I think it better characterizes the way [Americans] have been behaving for the last 50 years.

Q: Doesn't our current economic system demand that we make consumption our way of life?

A: Our current economic system is driven by consumption—by indices like consumer confidence and intentions to buy. If we make a transition to a post-consumer way of life—where we have enough material comforts but we make them last longer—and we have other non-material sources of fulfillment—things like time spent with friends, and time to enjoy the out-of-

Reprinted from "Personal Perspective: An Interview with Alan Durning" (1997) at the following website: www.iwla.org/iwla/sep/efl/issue3/intervw.html. Used by permission of the Izaac Walton League of America and Alan Durning.

doors—then some industries are going to suffer because our industrial structure has developed to feed these [unsustainable] consumption patterns. Jobs in those sectors of the economy would be lost.

Q: Must the transition to a post-consumer lifestyle be disruptive and endanger the economic security of individuals and communities?

A: If we do the transition right, we could secure sources of livelihood. One example: If we switch from an exclusive dependence on automobile transportation and move toward a wider mix of options including walking, bicycling, buses and rail, as well as automobiles, then we could actually see employment in the transportation sector increase. For every mile you travel on a train you employ more people than you do driving a car for a mile. I think the transition of employment patterns will help employment in the long run, not hurt it.

Q: How do we measure consumption?

A: We do not measure consumption in dollars. It's measured in physical units—kilowatts, tons of steel, cubic meters of wood. Nature doesn't care about how many dollars get spent. It cares about how many tons of carbon dioxide get emitted into the atmosphere, and how much habitat is left undisturbed to support its original compliment of species.

Q: What would life be like in a post-consumer society?

A: As we move [toward a post-consumer society], we'll figure out better and better ways to do things with the resources that we do consume. We'll move to a vision far better than anything I can imagine right now, because Americans are enormously resourceful people.

Here are some thoughts. Basic technologies that have been around for a long time along with some new, advanced technologies will provide many services to consumers without using a lot of resources. For example, we might see a future where people ride more bicycles and use more lap-top computers, where we have more satellite dishes for telecommunications and also more clothes-lines. A future where you could walk to more of the places that you were going because dwelling and commercial areas would be more compactly designed. Where people would eat fewer high-fat foods and live longer as a consequence. Where high-speed trains and ocean liners would be primary modes of long-distance travel. Where we would participate in [home and community] activities that take time. Where America will win from moving beyond the consumer society to a sustainable society.

Q: Do you think that consumer moderation can be restored as the American norm without the threat of dramatic resource shortages?

A: I think that moderation can be restored as the norm. It will take many changes. The first will be educating people so that they understand the implications of their current lifestyles. This is not a matter of pointing fingers or blaming people for the way they were brought up to live. Our society has sanctioned this lifestyle and can take pride in having created the material affluence that we enjoy. The challenge now is to consolidate our gains, maintain the real comforts we have, but dramatically reduce the impact on natural systems that is caused by this comfort [level].

Q: What steps should be taken nationally to aid in the transition to a post-consumer society?

A: I think the single most important thing is to eliminate the long list of perverse subsidies that make destruction of natural resources cheaper than conservation of them. We subsidize extraction of timber from old growth forests. We subsidize the removal of water from rivers. We subsidize overgrazing. We subsidize urban sprawl through the most generous mortgage interest deduction program in the world. We subsidize extraction of raw materials and we subsidize highway transportation. There are many ways in which the government subsidizes overconsumption, but we provide none of these kinds of subsidies for recycling or conserving. Imagine the day when everybody recycles and conserves because it's what their pocketbook, rather than their conscience, tells them to do.

Q: How do American patterns of consumption influence the desired levels of resource consumption for other parts of the world?

A: We in the United States have been setting the standard for what is success worldwide. The American dream has become the operative definition of international development. We judge other countries by how close they are to American consumption standards and that makes those standards the premier environmental challenge. If we deal successfully with the consumption challenge, I think that our country's place in the history of the world will be cemented as that of the greatest nations that has ever been.

Q: What encouraging signs do you see that indicate that Americans are ready or willing to reduce their consumption of natural resources?

A: I think that there are a lot of signs that Americans are fed up with crass consumerism. There is opinion data that shows this and there are new movements toward frugality and voluntary simplicity. There are more than 50 newsletters in the U.S. in which folks share tips about how to save money and enjoy life more. Even in the corporate world more people are asking what it is that makes their lives worth living. Not everyone is coming to the conclusion that the thing to do is reduce consumption, but the fact that they are searching for new values is a hopeful sign.

The search for new values requires a new and different consumption ethic. This ethic must recognize that even our best attempts to use resources at responsible, sustainable rates are based on our very limited knowledge of the complex functioning of natural systems—systems we will never fully understand.

The new ethic must also address the disparity between the consumption patterns of the haves and have-nots. "Most of the world's looming environmental threats, from groundwater contamination to climate change, are byproducts of affluence," Durning writes in an earlier work, Poverty and the Environment. *"But poverty can drive ecological deterioration when desperate people exploit their resource base, sacrificing the future to salvage the present."*

Growing populations multiply the environmentally destructive effects of consumption, and restrict everyone's consumption level worldwide. In this light, *"how much is enough?"* is becoming an increasingly urgent question—not just for conservationists, but for everyone with a stake in the future of this planet.

Roots of American Consumer Society

CHAPTER 6

The First Consumer Revolution

James Axtell

We Have Celebrated Two Important Revolutions in recent years, the American and the French, and we are in the midst of observing another event of revolutionary proportions, the Columbus Quincentenary. Each of these revolutions has a publicly accepted inaugural date—July 4, 1776, July 14, 1789, October 12, 1492—which enables us to fill our calendars with commemorative events. But the latest addition to the revolutionary pantheon comes without a birth certificate or scholarly consensus about its credentials and pedigree. I refer to the English "consumer revolution," which claims no kinship to the more famous English revolutions of Tudor government, civil war, or 1688.

It's small wonder that scholars cannot agree about the causes, timing, effects, and long-range importance of this latest revolution because they discovered it only within the last ten years or so. Another reason for the lack of consensus owes to its nature: this is one of the first "revolutions" to be discovered by the Early Modern practitioners of the "new" social history, rather than by political historians of a conventional stripe. Given the scope of their questions and the quicksilver quality of their evidence, social historians seldom agree about anything, and the consumer revolution is no exception. Yet the outlines of the phenomenon are becoming clearer with each passing article.

It seems that sometime between 1690 and 1740, first in England and Scotland and soon in England's mainland American colonies, consumers of the gentle and particularly "middling" classes began to purchase an unprecedented number and variety of manufactured goods and to use many of them in conspicuous displays of leisure, social ritual, and status affirmation (or arrogation). Thanks to a pronounced increase in per capita wealth and disposable income, consumers not only upgraded their necessities, such as bedding, eating utensils, and clothing, but chose from a veritable Sears catalogue of competitively priced luxury goods and amenities, which reached the remotest corners of the land in peddlers' packs and the inventories of myriad country stores. Often patterned after the latest of the ever-changing fashions of Paris and London and vigorously promoted by window displays, newspaper advertisements, and word-of-mouth, these goods quickly spread from responsive English manufactories across regions and classes in a wide but standardized repertoire. This had the effect of forging strong material bonds between mother country and colonies, even as political fissures were beginning to appear in their union, some the result of mounting debts incurred by colonial shoppers anxious to keep up with the Carters and the Schuylers.[1]

One might legitimately ask, Why is the purchase—even the widespread, cross-class purchase—of satin waistcoats, looking glasses, japaned dressing tables, Wedgwood china, forks, and matching tea services considered "revolutionary"? The experts offer a number of answers. The first is that, unlike the later Industrial Revolution, the consumer revolution was made, less by increased, more efficient, and more competitive productivity on the supply side, than by unprecedented and particular consumer demand, which called forth the supply and inspired many of the technological and organizational advances of the Industrial Revolution. This demand, in turn, was moulded by new techniques of mass marketing and the conscious creation of "imaginary necessities." "As wealth and population increased," explained an English visitor to colonial Baltimore, "wants were created, and many considerable demands, in consequence, took place for the various elegancies as well as the necessaries of life."[2]

Enjoying for the first time so many economic choices, consumers, especially women, were empowered by a heady sense of personal independence and the ability to fashion themselves with the material trappings of "gentility." In the American colonies, however, this heavy dependence on the credit extended by English merchants and manufacturers led to fears of economic enslavement. These fears, in turn, exacerbated fears of political tyranny from the Stamp Act on and gave rise to such consumer boycotts as the Association to halt importation of the "effeminating" and enervating "Baubles of Britain." In other words, when the British government injected coercion into its relations with the colonies, the ties of loyalty that bound the colonists to an empire of free-flowing goods quickly came undone. "A constitutional crisis transformed private consumer acts into public political statements" and many Americans "discovered political ideology through a discussion of the meaning of goods."[3]

In sketching the outlines of this eighteenth-century British revolution, I have a strong sense of *déjà vu*. Where have I seen this before? The answer, as might be expected from an ethnohistorian of colonial North America, is in the Indian communities of seventeenth-century North America. Such an answer will undoubtedly be greeted with a certain amount of reasonable skepticism. After all, don't we all know that the American Indians were poor and spiritual people who lived from hand-to-mouth in a precarious environment and put their faith in strange gods and spirits rather than earthly things? Don't we know that their "nomadic" lifestyle and their communal ethic of sharing militated against the senseless acquisition of material comforts? Perhaps unlikelier candidates for a *consumer* revolution could not be found, certainly not fifty or seventy-five years before their "civilized" and admittedly materialistic English counterparts experienced one.

Such skepticism is unwarranted. The Indians of the Eastern Woodlands experienced a consumer revolution every bit as revolutionary as that experienced by their European suppliers, though not identical in every respect, and they did so many years earlier, usually as soon as the commercial colonists founded trading posts, *comptoirs*, and nascent settlements. How, if the natives lived in penury, was this possible? Without gold or silver mines like those in Mexico and Peru, how did native North Americans across the social spectrum (which was not wide in any case) find the purchase price of any European goods, much less goods in sufficient quantity and variety to warrant a "revolutionary" denomination?

The per capita wealth of Indian America, though it cannot be measured in native currencies, increased dramatically from the earliest stages of contact because European traders were willing and eager to pay top pound, franc, and florin for American animal pelts and skins, which the Indians were adept in curing and procuring for their own domestic uses. Three kinds of pelts were the most lucrative for the Indians. Beaver, for which the natives had little use before the trade, became the best seller because its soft, microscopically barbed underfur was in great demand for the manufacture of broad-brimmed felt hats for Europe's gentlemen. A ready market also existed for rare and luxurious "small furs," such as marten, otter, and black fox, which were used to trim the rich gowns of the high-born. And beginning in the last quarter of the seventeenth century, the Indians of the Southeast could sell any number of humbler but larger deerskins, which provided scarce leather for Continental breeches, saddlebags, bookbindings, and workingmen's aprons. The European demand for skins the natives regarded as commonplace was seemingly insatiable and enabled all male hunters of a tribe to participate in the search for income-producing pelts if they wished.

To judge by the traders' export figures, a substantial majority of native hunters did quite well in the new European market. The Mahicans and eastern Iroquois brought about 8,000 beaver and otter skins to the Dutch posts at Fort Orange and New Amsterdam in 1626. Nine years later they had doubled their take. By the late 1650s, 46,000 pelts were pouring into Fort Orange alone.[4] The French in Canada were even better supplied by their native partners.

In 1614, only six years after the founding of Quebec, 25,000 skins, mostly beaver, were shipped to France's hatters. By the 1620s the Montagnais on the north shore of the St. Lawrence were trading 12–15,000 pelts at Tadoussac every year. In flotillas of 60–70 canoes, some 200 Huron traders from southern Ontario brought 10,000 skins a year to Quebec. Twenty years later, even as their population was cut in half by disease and intertribal warfare, the Hurons produced 30,000 beaver pelts annually.⁵ In New England, the Plymouth colony was able to pay off its English creditors only because Abenaki hunters on the Kennebec River in Maine kept them supplied with animal skins: about 8,000 beavers and 1,156 otters between 1631 and 1636 alone. Even then the lion's share of Abenaki pelts went to French traders from Acadia.⁶

To the south, the natives of the interior supplied outgoing ships with 54,000 deerskins a year between 1700 and 1715. Between 1740 and 1762 the take was up to 152,000 skins a year. The best hunters were the Muskogees or Creeks of Alabama and Georgia. In 1720 they traded more than 80,000 skins to South Carolina and French Mobile. Forty years later, with a new market in Savannah, they were killing 140,000 deer every season.⁷ In the 1750s and Cherokees took 25,000 skins annually from the mountains of North Carolina, Georgia, and Tennessee, an average of 12 deer for each of 2,000 warriors. In the twenty years between 1739 and 1759, Cherokee hunters alone reduced the southeastern deer population by 1.25 million.⁸

Clearly, the natives of eastern America controlled resources that were in great demand in Europe. But did they realize their profit potential? Or did they kill all those animals for a few cheap trinkets and a swot or two of rotgut rum, leaving themselves no better off than they were before the advent of the white man? British traders in particular knew that the natives, whose simple lives required few necessities, had to be given a sense of personal "Property" if their American business was ever to thrive. For a notion of material accumulation, "though it would not increase their real Necessities, yet it would furnish them with imaginary Wants."⁹ By 1679, Indians from Hudson Bay to the Carolinas had discovered that "many Things which they wanted not before because they never had them are by . . . means [of the trade] become necessary both for their use & ornament."¹⁰ They had been, in a stay-at-home European's words, "cosoned by a desire of new-fangled novelties."¹¹

But had they? To hear both native hunters and knowledgeable Europeans tell it, the Indian was nobody's fool and certainly felt that he made out like a bandit in his dealings with the rubes from the Old World. For ordinary skins "which cost them almost nothing," the Indians received novel trade goods superior to their own artifacts of skin, bone, stone, and wood.¹² A Montagnais hunter once exclaimed that " 'The Beaver does everything perfectly well, it makes kettles, hatchets, swords, knives, bread, in short it makes everything.' He was making sport of us Europeans," explained his Jesuit guest, "who have such a fondness for the skin of this animal and who fight to see who will give the most to these Barbarians, to get it." Some while later, the same Indian said to the Frenchman, holding out a very beautiful knife, " 'The English have no sense; they give us twenty knives like this for one Beaver skin.' "¹³

While the natives didn't easily understand price fluctuations obedient to Western laws of supply and demand, they were shrewd enough to advance their own bargaining position by playing European competitors against each other, by avoiding superfluities that had no place in their own culture, and by being extremely finicky about the quality and style of goods they would accept. In 1642 Roger Williams noted how the Narragansetts of Rhode Island "will beate all markets and try all places, and runne twenty, thirty, yea, forty mile[s] and more, and lodge in the Woods, to save six pence."[14] Likewise, testified a Recollect priest who knew them well, the Iroquois and natives of the Great Lakes "are rather shrewd and let no one outwit them easily. They examine everything carefully and train themselves to know goods."[15] A Virginia trader in Chesapeake Bay in 1630 complained, to no avail, that his Indian customers were "very long and teadeous" in viewing his array of trade goods and did "tumble it and tosse it and mingle it a hundred times over."[16] Four years later, a trade on the coast of Maine groused to his English boss that "The Indians are[e] now so well seen Into our trading Commodities, that heare is litle to be got by yt." Not only did the competing French and English traders undersell one another in a frenzy to acquire furs, but the Indians refused to buy short English coats, coverlets that were not "soft & warme," or unlined hats without bands.[17] A half-century later, in the mountains of Virginia and North Carolina, William Byrd's Indian customers would have no truck with large white beads (instead of small ones), porous kettles, light (instead of dark) blue blankets, guns with weak locks, or small (instead of large) hoes.[18] "They are not delighted in baubles," Thomas Morton had observed as early as 1632, "but in usefull things."[19] As European trader after trader quickly learned, in native America the customer was always right.

The customer was not only right, he held the upper hand in the struggle over payment. Because his necessities and even his acquired tastes were so few and relatively inelastic, in the establishment of trade the Indians needed the European trader less than he needed them. The sharp competition between company traders, *coureurs de bois*, and government factors for most Indian customers, even those in the *pays d'en haut*, only increased the natives' leverage. So they quickly demanded and received credit from the traders.

In late summer or early fall, the trader advanced the Indians on account the goods, arms, ammunition, and food they needed for the winter hunt. When the hunters returned in the late spring or early summer with their catch, the trader cancelled their debts and, if they had a surplus, furnished them with supplies and luxuries. If the hunters had a poor season, they often escaped the consequences of their growing debts by simply moving to new hunting grounds and striking up business with a new trader, who was only too happy to purchase their pelts and to extend them a line of credit. As a Swedish governor complained of his native trading partners in 1655, "If they buy anything here, they wish to get half on credit, and then pay with difficulty."[20] Traders in Hudson Bay, New France, New England, New Amsterdam, and the Carolinas felt the same crunch early in their relations with the fur-toting natives.

If we are going to declare these new Indian purchases a "consumer revolution," similar to the later English one, we should also analyze in some detail the kind and quantity of trade goods the Indians preferred. We have two major ways to learn about native preferences. One is from the work of archaeologists, whose excavations of Indian villages and burials turn up the broken and discarded material of native life as well as the most treasured possessions buried with the dead. The second way is from the hand of traders' clerks and government officials, who made detailed lists of trade items and diplomatic gifts to be shipped to Indian villages by canoe or packtrain. These two sources can be supplemented to some extent by the findings of underwater archaeologists at the feet of cold northern river rapids, where French canoes overturned with all their bright new cargoes headed for Indian country.[21] These beautifully preserved objects can tell us what in the peddlers' packs may have attracted the Indians, but they do not necessarily tell us whether the natives purchased them or used them in ways that Europeans would expect.

According to all our sources, the *nouveaux-riches* natives bought five kinds of European goods: tools, clothing, decorations, novelties, and occasionally food. Even before they had direct and regular access to European traders, the Indians acquired a variety of utilitarian and decorative items from sea-going traders, abandoned colonial facilities, shipwrecks, or natives who had access to these sources. Many native communities met their first European objects in the sixteenth century, long before the English or the French established lasting colonies in North America. When Gaspar Corte-Real sailed to Newfoundland or a nearby coast in 1501, for example, he met one Indian man clutching a piece of an Italian gilt sword and another sporting a pair of Venetian silver earrings.[22]

The earliest items favored by both native men and women were metal tools to make their work go easier and faster. Since the natives were already fully equipped with the requisite tools to manage their environment, they purchased the same kinds of European implements made of superior materials. Processed metal was brighter, more durable, and held and edge longer than annealed native copper, bone, fired clay, stone, or wood. So the natives sensibly spent their first fur paychecks on iron axes (to save the time involved in burning large trees down), hatchets (to gather firewood and crack enemy skulls), awls (to punch leather and drill shell beads), ice chisels (to break-open beaver lodges), butcher knives (to replace more breakable and costly flint knives), swords (to point spears and arrows with pieces of broken blade), fish-hooks (to replace unbarbed bone hooks), wide hoes (to replace deer scapula or short digging sticks), and brass or copper kettles (to replace heavier, thicker, and more fragile clay pots).

We know a good deal about the metal goods the Indians purchased because they survive well in the ground and frequently end up in caring museums. But their numbers are somewhat deceiving, for the best-selling item in native (as in English and colonial) markets from the seventeenth century on was cloth of all kinds.[23] Unfortunately, cloth does not fare well in the ground over centuries unless it happens to be parked next to some copper or brass, whose salts during oxidation preserve vegetable matter. We do have a few archaeological cloth remnants, but most of our knowledge of the Indian appetite and stylistic preferences for cloth comes from lead seals used to certify cloth at its source (which turn up in archaeological contexts) and from the letterbooks and inventories of traders. They make it clear why most of the early Indian names for Europeans meant "Cloth makers" or "Coat-men" when they were not called "Iron-Workers" or "Swordmen."[24]

Why would the natives spend their fur proceeds on European cloth when they already had perfectly adaptable fur and skin clothing? Woolen blanketing or duffels was the single biggest seller for several reasons: it was lighter than and as warm as a fur mantle or *matchcoat*, it dried faster and remained softer and suppler than wet skins and was even warm when wet, it came in bright colors which natural berry and root dyes could not duplicate (though most Indians preferred "sad" hues of red and blue), and, with metal knives and scissors, it could quickly be fashioned into leggings, breechclouts, tie-on sleeves, or mantles by women who no longer had to laboriously cure and dress several skins. Another potential advantage was seldom realized because the Indians almost never washed their clothes and literally wore them off their backs.[25] Soap was not in the trader's kit until the more fastidious nineteenth century, and since the dead were always buried in their best clothes, cloth heirlooms and hand-me-downs were rare. With the "bargains" offered by the European traders, the natives found it easier to buy new threads than to slave over a soapy stream.

While cloth was in great demand in Indian country, a few items were unpopular. There was almost no market for tight or fitted clothing, for example. Until the genteel eighteenth century, no native man would have been caught dead in a pair of European breeches: they impeded running and other natural functions (southern men, at least, squatted to urinate).[26] Elaborate military-style coats with braid, buttons, and capacious cuffs were worn only by a handful of favored chiefs and head warriors on ceremonial occasions. The only fitted pieces of clothing that sold relatively well were brightly patterned calico shirts, which the men wore open at the neck and flapping in the breeze.

We can be very brief about the food trade because it was rare. In the seventeenth century the native hunters of eastern Canada occasionally bartered a beaver for some durable ship's biscuit or bread when they couldn't find Indian corn among their agricultural neighbors. But prunes and raisins never caught on except as gifts, and sugar, flour, and tea made their way very slowly into native larders, and then only if colonial settlements were close by.[27]

From the earliest indirect contact with Europeans, the Indians sought to enhance their beauty and status with decorations of foreign material or manufacture. Chinese vermilion, sold in tea-bag-sized paper packets, gradually supplanted native red ochre, and verdigris added a brand new color to harlequin faces. As the Portuguese explorer Corte-Real discovered, silver earrings found a male as well as female market. Copper and brass bracelets, tin finger rings (particularly engraved Jesuit rings with religious motifs, initials, and hearts), bangles or jingling cones made from sheet brass, necklaces of Venetian glass beads in both solid colors and stripes, mostly red, white, and blue, corkscrew wire ear dangles, and, in the eighteenth century, German silver brooches, pins, and gorgets custom-made for the Indian trade were among the most popular European jewelry. While several of these items were new in form and function, the natives made more familiar jewelry from thimbles (by attaching a leather thong through a hole cut in the bottom to make jinglers), scraps of kettle or sheet copper (cut into pendants, gorgets, and even sweat scrapers in the Deep South), and gold and silver coins (perforated and worn around the neck as pendants).[28] With jewelry as with most things, the Indians used, adapted, and interpreted Europe's introductions in traditional ways.

This is less but still true of the final category of Indian trade goods, what we must call novelties because they had no native counterparts. Part of the revolutionary character of native consumerism is attributable to the effects some of these material innovations had on native life. Mouth harps, bells, and clothing fasteners (buttons, buckles, and lace points) played only bit parts in transforming Indian culture in the seventeenth and early eighteenth centuries. But guns, alcohol, and even mirrors were center stage.

An arquebus or flintlock was, in one sense, only a noisy bow and arrow. It was also heavier, harder to make and repair, more expensive, less reliable in wet weather, much slower, and incapable of surprise after the first round. Despite the many deficiencies of firearms, however, the Indians rushed to acquire them as soon as they had seen them in action. For guns drove fear into enemy breasts as often as balls, smashed bones and did more internal damage than razor-sharp arrowheads, and heralded the status of their owners in ways that traditional weapons never could. Against traditional wooden slat armor and old-time massed armies, the gun won hands down.[29] One major effect of the advent of firearms, therefore, was the natives' sole reliance on dispersed guerilla tactics executed behind trees or from ambush. Sir William Johnson, the Superintendent of Indian Affairs for the British northern department, was of the opinion that the authority of chiefs had also declined since the introduction of firearms because, he said, "They no longer fight in close bodies but every Man is his own General."[30]

The effects of alcohol upon Indian society were nearly as destructive. Cadwallader Colden, an expert on the Iroquois, thought that drunkenness among the American tribes "has destroyed greater Numbers, than all their Wars and Diseases put together."[31] He was wrong about the magnitude but right about the seriousness of the problem which the advent of brandy kegs, rundlets of rum, and case bottles of wine posed for native communities. Although—or perhaps because—the Woodland Indians had no previous experience with intoxicating beverages or hallucinogens, they took to liquid spirits with frightening abandon. And they drank only to become fully inebriated, in which state they felt invincible, capable of making anti-social mayhem with a perfect excuse, and perhaps (though the evidence is weak) more susceptible to

the dreams in which "guardian spirits" conveyed their sacred secrets for success.[32] When the "water-that-burns" arrived in sufficient quantity in a village,
the place was soon turned into the very "image of hell." Drunken "frolics"
lasting several days often produced several victims of shootings, stabbings,
brawls, burning, biting, and bawdry. Neither resident missionaries nor native
leaders were very successful in persuading the traders to halt the profitable
flow, although they used two compelling arguments: the Indians were dying in
excessive numbers from drink-related murders (and, we know also, from exposure and increased susceptibility to colds, pneumonia, and other diseases),
and the temperance issue "produce[d] all Evil and Contention between man
and wife, between the Young Indians and the Sachims."[33] Alcohol was clearly
one trade good the natives could well have done without.

By contrast, mirrors seem terribly tame as novelties go. But the first "look-
ing-glasses" and mirror boxes, which reached the remote Senecas of western
New York by the 1620s, may have promoted a preoccupation with personal
fashion as much as full-length hanging mirrors did among the genteel colonists.
Among the Indians, however, "the men, upon the whole, [were] more fond of
dressing than the women" and carried their mirrors with them on all their journeys, which the women did not.[34] As a vehicle of vainglory, the mirror was a
necessity, especially for young warriors who now had more income to spend on
imported face paints, jewelry, and other finery. Before the advent of mirrors, a
native coxcomb had to have his face painted "by some woman or girl," which
curtailed his independence and let some of the air out of his vanity.[35] With his
own mirror, which he wore constantly around his wrist or over his shoulder, he
could arrange his hair, refurbish his scalp-lock, and paint his face to his heart's
content in the privacy of his own toilette. One unfoppish Frenchman who
knew the Great Lakes tribes well believed that "if they had a mirror before
their eyes they would change their appearance every quarter of an hour."[36] But
the tell-tale object, like all spiritual power, was capable of bringing bad news as
well. During the great smallpox epidemic of 1738, which killed half of the
Cherokee population, "a great many" Indians "killed themselves" by shooting,
cutting their throats, stabbing, and throwing themselves into fires because they
had seen themselves disfigured by the pox in their ubiquitous mirrors and,
"being naturally proud," could not stand the literal loss of face.[37]

We can now appreciate the amazing variety of European goods that reached
Indian customers in the seventeenth and eighteenth centuries. To constitute a
revolution comparable to the later English one, however, these material products had to arrive in native villages in such quantities that tribesmen and
women up and down the social scale had their lives altered by the pursuit,
purchase, and use of them. There are basically two ways to establish these
quantities. The indirect way is to look at the substantial leap in exports from
England to the American colonies in the seventeenth century. It is surely no
coincidence that exports of woolens and metalwares doubled between the
1660s and 1700, and miscellaneous manufactures, including tableware and

sewing accoutrements, increased threefold.[38] Most of those items were the mainstays of the Indian trade, which we know was burgeoning, even as the native population was declining from disease, wars, and dislocation.

The more direct way is to register the changes in Indian villages, either above or below ground, at the time or later. Obviously, we don't have comparable evidence for every tribe in every region. But what we do have is strongly suggestive. For example, on both Seneca and Onondaga Iroquois sites from 1600 to 1620, only 10–15 percent of the artifacts found by archaeologists are European in origin. From sites dated 1650–55, fully 75 percent of the assemblages are European (and this, remember, grossly underestimates the amount of cloth used).[39] Small wonder, then, that in 1768 Eleazar Wheelock, the master of an Indian school in Connecticut, conducted a frustrated search among the eastern Iroquois nations for a native artifact that was "perfectly Simple, and without the least Mixture of any foreign Merchandise" to send as a gift to the Earl of Dartmouth, the benefactor of his future college. A "small specimen" was all he could find because, he apologized, "our Traders have penetrated so far into their Country." Only "some articles which were defaced by Use" were crafted from the traditional materials he sought. Perhaps he shouldn't have been so surprised, for two years earlier one of his English missionary-teachers had written that the Iroquois were "in some measure like those in New England much degenerated, both as to their Customs, their Dress and their Impliments."[40]

"Degeneration" is the wrong term to describe any cultural change, unless, of course, we believe that the only bona fide Indian looks and acts like his pre-Columbian ancestors. But New England's native population, largely converted to Christianity and settled in "praying towns," had indeed felt the forces of acculturation in the century since the Reverend John Eliot began to proselytize them. Many lived in English frame houses complete with standard colonial furniture, plowed their fields with horses or oxen, kept cattle, dressed in English garb, cooked in iron kettles and skillets, and ate off glazed earthenware with spoons and forks. Even those who still lived in wigwams, such as Phebe and Elizabeth Moheege of Niantic, Connecticut, cooked in an iron pot suspended from a trammel, drank at a tea table, ate at another table in a chair (presumably not at the same time), stored their cups and plates in a wall cupboard and their prized possessions in two wooden chests.[41]

Another symbol of the revolutionary changes in the lives of virtually all eastern American natives lived just down the road from the Moheeges, across the Rhode Island line. There in a house or "palace" lived "King George Ninigret," the chief of the once-mighty Narragansetts. When Dr. Alexander Hamilton of Annapolis rode by in 1744, King George owned 20–30,000 acres of "very fine level land" upon which he had "many tennants" and "a good stock of horses and other cattle." "This King," Hamilton noted with evident approval, "lives after the English mode. His subjects have lost their own government [sic] policy and laws and are servants or vassals to the English here.

His queen goes in a high modish dress in her silks, hoops, stays, and dresses like an English woman. He educates his children to the belles lettres and is himself a very complaisant mannerly man. We pay'd him a visit, and he treated us with a glass of good wine."[42]

King George, of course, was atypical of his American brethren in the degree of his apparent success. He was, after all, a chief. But he was a new kind of chief, one who sold his tribal lands to white men and pocketed most of the proceeds, rather than consulting the will of his people and distributing the revenues among them. Nor did he share his personal property as a traditional chief would have a century earlier. This Indian looked out for Number One in good capitalist fashion: he gave many thoughts to his own family's future but far fewer to that of his "subjects" who labored menially for his English models and neighbors.[43]

But most Indians in colonial America were unable to ride the crest of change like King George and were caught instead in the undertow and dragged into dependence and debt. In their initial rush to acquire the material marvels of Europe, they gave no thought to the future and hunted out the game that gave them access to foreign markets. When the beaver and whitetail deer disappeared, the natives were left with nothing to sell but their land, their labor, or their military services, which the proliferating colonists were only too glad to buy at bargain rates. Those prices, paid always in desirable trade goods, were low because, with the game diminished, the Indians had little leverage left and had become dangerously dependent on their European suppliers for an ever-growing list of "necessities." In 1705 Robert Beverley noticed that "The *English* have taken away great part of their Country, and consequently made everything less plenty amongst them. They have introduc'd Drunkenness and Luxury amongst them, which have multiply'd their Wants and put them upon desiring a thousand things they never dreamt of before."[44] These "artificial Wants," as Ben Franklin called them, were so numerous that even the Indians admitted, particularly in the early eighteenth century, that "they could not live without the English" and that they would "always be ruled by them."[45]

Yet, like their colonial neighbors who later formed the Association to rid themselves of foreign debt and debilitating "luxury," many tribesmen in the eighteenth century sought to recapture their autonomous aboriginal past by participating in what anthropologists call "revitalization movements."[46] In 1715 the Yamasees and several Muskogee groups resorted to all-out, purifying war with the South Carolinians because they had accumulated tribal debts of 100,000 deerskins, which, in the face of greatly diminished herds in the increasingly settled coastal region, they had little hope of ever paying off.[47]

But the most famous revitalization took place among the Delawares of western Pennsylvania and the Ohio Valley, where in the early 1760s they were called to action by several messianic prophets. Their message was much the same: if the Indians wished to get to their own heaven and to make life on earth bearable in the meantime, they had to revive their "old" ceremonies and to make several sacrifices. The most onerous but the most purifying was to "learn to live without any trade or connections with the white people, clothing and supporting themselves as their forefathers did."[48]

Such a message was particularly welcome in the camps of the Great Lakes Indians who followed Pontiac into major "rebellion" against the British in 1763. The major cause of their discontent was material: once the French competitors of the British were driven from North America, the British felt free to raise the prices of their trade goods, drastically cut the number of goods (including ammunition) distributed as gifts in the long-standing protocol of diplomacy, and prohibited the sale of liquor, all in a spirit of unmasked contempt for native life and values. No longer able to live without the "Baubles of Britain," Pontiac's warriors decided on a course of action every bit as revolutionary as that followed by the colonists themselves thirteen years later.[49]

Notes

1. For the British phase of the revolution, see Neil McKendrick, John Brewer, and J. H. Plumb, eds., *The Birth of a Consumer Society: The Commercialization of Eighteenth-Century England* (Bloomington, Ind., 1982); Lorna Weatherill, *Consumer Behavior and Material Culture in Britain, 1660–1760* (London, 1988); Joan Thirsk, *Economic Policy and Projects: The Development of a Consumer Society in Early Modern England* (Oxford, 1978); Eric Jones, "The Fashion Manipulators: Consumer Tastes and British Industries, 1660–1800," in Louis P. Cain and Paul J. Uselding, eds., *Business Enterprise and Economic Change: Essays in Honor of Harold F. Williamson* (Kent, Ohio, 1973), 198–226; Carole Shammas, *The Pre-industrial Consumer in England and America* (Oxford, 1990).

On the American side, see Shammas, *ibid.*; T. H. Breen, "An Empire of Goods: The Anglicization of Colonial America, 1690–1776," *Journal of British Studies*, 25 (Oct. 1086), 467–99; Breen, " 'Baubles of Britain': The American and Consumer Revolutions of the Eighteenth Century," *Past and Present*, no. 119 (1988), 73–104; Breen, "The Meaning of Things: Interpreting the Consumer Economy in the Eighteenth Century" (William Andrews Clark Memorial Library Lectures: The Birth of Consumer Societies, 1988–89); Gloria L. Main and Jackson T. Main, "Economic Growth and the Standard of Living in Southern New England, 1640–1774," *Journal of Economic History*, 48:1 (March 1988), 27–46; Lois Green Carr and Lorena S. Walsh, "The Standard of Living in the Colonial Chesapeake," *William and Mary Quarterly*, 3d ser. 45:1 (Jan. 1988), 135–59; Carr and Walsh, "Consumer Behavior in the Colonial Chesapeake," in Cary Carson, Ronald Hoffman, and Peter J. Albert, eds., *Of Consuming Interests: The Style of Life in the Eighteenth Century* (Charlottesville, 1992); Cary Carson, "The Consumer Revolution in Colonial British America: Why Demand?," *ibid.*

2. William Eddis, *Letters from America*, ed. Aubrey C. Land (Cambridge, Mass., 1969), 51–52.

3. Breen, " 'Baubles of Britian,' " 88, 90.

4. George T. Hunt, *The Wars of the Iroquois: A Study in Intertribal Trade Relations* (Madison, Wis., 1940), 33; Allen W. Trelease, *Indian Affairs in Colonial New York: The Seventeenth Century* (Ithaca, N.Y., 1960), 43, 131.

5. Marcel Trudel, *Histoire de la Nouvelle-France. II: Le comptoir, 1604–1627* (Montreal, 1966), 207; Bruce G. Trigger, *The Children of Aataentsic: A History of the Huron*

People to 1660, 2 vols. (Montreal, 1976), 286, 336–37, 603–5 (continuous pagination); Conrad Heidenreich, *Huronia: A History and Geography of the Huron Indians, 1600–1650* (Toronto, 1971), 280.

6. William Bradford, *Of Plymouth Plantation, 1620–1647*, ed. Samuel Eliot Morison (New York, 1952), 286–89; Ruth A. McIntyre, *Debts Hopeful and Desperate: Financing the Plymouth Colony* (Plymouth, Mass.: Plimoth Plantation, 1963).

7. Verner W. Crane, *The Southern Frontier, 1670–1732* (Ann Arbor, 1956, 1929), 111, 330 (table 4); Joel W. Martin, "The Creek Indian Deerskin Trade, 1670–1805" (manuscript), table 1.

8. Gary C. Goodwin, *Cherokees in Transition: A Study of Changing Culture and Environment Prior to 1775*, U. of Chicago, Dept. of Geography, Research Paper No. 181 (Chicago, 1977), 98.

9. John Hardman, Liverpool merchant, 1749, quoted in E. E. Rich, "The Indian Traders," *The Beaver*, outfit 301 (Winter 1970), 5–20 at 18.

10. Joseph and Nesta Ewan, eds., *John Banister and His Natural History of Virginia, 1678–92* (Urbana, Ill., 1970), 42.

11. *The Essays of Michael Lord of Montaigne*, trans. John Florio, 3 vols., Everyman ed. (London and Toronto, 1910), 1:170 ("Of cannibals").

12. Nicolas Denys, *The Description and Natural History of the Coasts of North America (Acadia)*, ed. and trans. William F. Ganong (Toronto: The Champlain Society, 1908), 441.

13. Reuben Gold Thwaites, ed., *The Jesuit Relations and Allied Documents*, 73 vols. (Cleveland, 1896–1901), 6:297, 299.

14. Roger Williams, *A Key into the Language of America* (London, 1643), 163.

15. *Father Louis Hennepin's Description of Louisiana*, ed. and trans. Marion E. Cross (Minneapolis, 1938), 167.

16. Quoted in Albright G. Zimmerman, "European Trade Relations in the 17th and 18th Centuries," in Herbert C. Kraft, ed., *A Delaware Indian Symposium*, Pennsylvania Historical and Museum Commission, Anthropological Series No. 4 (Harrisburg, 1974), 57–70 at 66.

17. James Phinney Baxter, ed., *Documentary History of the State of Maine. III: The Trelawny Papers* (Portland, Me., 1884), 25–26, 29.

18. Marion Tinling, ed., *The Correspondence of the Three William Byrds of Westover, Virginia, 1684–1776*, Virginia Historical Society Documents 12–13 (Charlottesville, 1977), 29, 30, 57, 60, 64, 66.

19. Thomas Morton, *New English Canaan* (London, 1632), in Peter Force, comp., *Tracts and Other Papers, Relating Principally to the Origin, Settlement, and Progress of the Colonies in North America*, 4 vols. (Washington, D.C., 1836–47), vol. 2, no. 5, p. 40.

20. Governor Johan Rising, June 14, 1655, in Albert Cook Myers, ed., *Narratives of Early Pennsylvania, West New Jersey, and Delaware, 1630–1707*, Original Narratives of Early American History (New York, 1912), 157. See also Toby Morantz, " 'So Evil a Practice': A Look at the Debt System in the James Bay Fur Trade," in Rosemary E. Ommer, ed., *Merchant Credit and Labour Strategies in Historical Perspective* (Fredericton, N.B., 1990), 203–22.

21. Robert C. Wheeler *et al.*, eds. *Voices from the Rapids: An Underwater Search for Fur Trade Artifacts, 1960–73*, Minnesota Historical Archaeological Series No. 3 (Minneapolis: Minnesota Historical Society, 1975).

22. James Axtell, *After Columbus: Essays in the Ethnohistory of Colonial North America* (New York, 1988), ch. 9, esp. p. 154.

23. Kenneth E. Kidd, "The Cloth Trade and the Indians of the Northeast during the Seventeenth and Eighteenth Centuries," Royal Ontario Museum, Division of Art and Archaeology, *Annual* (Toronto, 1961), 48–56; Louise Dechêne, *Habitants et marchands de Montréal au XVII siècle* (Paris, 1974), 507 (graphique 11); Peter A. Thomas, "Cultural Change

on the Southern New England Frontier, 1630–1665," in William W. Fitzhugh, ed., *Cultures in Contact: The Impact of European Contacts on Native American Cultural Institutions, A.D. 1000–1800* (Washington, D.C., 1985), 146; Joel W. Martin, *Sacred Revolt: The Muskogees' Struggle for a New World* (Boston, 1991), 57–58; Dean L. Anderson, "Perishable Trade Goods: Documentary Material Data and Historical Period Indian Research" (paper presented at the annual meeting of the Society for Historical Archaeology, Savannah, Jan. 7–11, 1987).

24. Axtell, *After Columbus*, 135.

25. *Peter Kalm's Travels in North America: The English Version of 1770*, ed. Adolph B. Benson, 2 vols. (New York, 1966), 520 (continuous pagination); William Wood, *New England's Prospect* [London, 1634], ed. Alden T. Vaughan (Amherst, Mass., 1977), 84; Stanley Pargellis, ed., "The Indians in Virginia . . . 1689," *William and Mary Quarterly*, 3d ser. 16 (1959), 230.

26. James Axtell, *The European and the Indian: Essays in the Ethnohistory of Colonial North America* (New York, 1981), 58.

27. Trigger, *Children of Aataentsic*, 358–59; Bruce G. Trigger, *Natives and Newcomers: Canada's "Heroic Age" Reconsidered* (Kingston and Montreal, 1985), 138, 204, 238; Paul A. Robinson, Marc A. Kelley, and Patricia E. Rubertone, "Preliminary Biocultural Interpretations from a Seventeenth-Century Narragansett Indian Cemetery in Rhode Island," in Fitzhugh, *Cultures in Contact*, 119.

28. Axtell, *After Columbus*, ch. 9.

29. Brian J. Given, "The Iroquois Wars and Native Arms," in Bruce Alden Cox, ed., *Native People, Native Lands: Canadian Indians, Inuit and Métis*, Carleton Library Series No. 142 (Ottawa, 1988), 3–13; Axtell, *The European and the Indian*, 259–63; Thomas Abler, "European Technology and the Art of War in Iroquoia," in Diana Claire Tkaczak and Brian C. Vivian, eds., *Cultures in Conflict: Current Archaeological Perspectives*, Proceedings of the Twentieth Annual Conference of the Archaeological Association of the U. of Calgary (Calgary, 1989), 273–82.

30. James Sullivan et al.., eds., *The Papers of Sir William Johnson*, 14 vols. (Albany, N.Y., 1921–62), 12:952 (Johnson to Arthur Lee, March 28, 1772).

31. Cadwallader Colden, *The History of the Five Indian Nations of Canada* (London, 1747), 13–14.

32. Axtell, *The European and the Indian*, 257–59. There are only two sources for the much-cited connection between inebriation and the dream or vision quest, and neither provides direct evidence that the natives themselves took to alcohol as a short cut to visions: Edmund S. Carpenter, "Alcohol in the Iroquois Dream Quest," *American Journal of Psychiatry*, 116:8 (Aug. 1959), 148–51, and André Vachon, "L'eau-de-vie dans la société indienne," Canadian Historical Association, *Report* (1960), 23. R. C. Dailey, "The Role of Alcohol Among North American Indian Tribes as Reported in The Jesuit Relations," *Anthropologica*, 10 (1968), 48–50, and Maia Conrad, "From Visions to Violence: Iroquoian Alcohol Use in the Seventeenth Century" (paper presented at the annual meeting of the American Society for Ethnohistory, Chicago, Nov. 5, 1989) are more circumspect about the lack of direct evidence.

33. [François Vachon de] Belmont's History of Brandy," ed. and trans. Joseph P. Donnelly, *Mid-America*, 34 (1952), 60.

34. Kalm, *Travels in North America*, 520–21.

35. Thwaites, *Jesuit Relations*, 44: 283.

36. Nicholas Perrot, "Memoir on the Manners, Customs, and Religion of the Savages of North America," in Emma Helen Blair, ed. and trans., *The Indian Tribes of the Upper Mississippi Valley and Region of the Great Lakes*, 2 vols. (Cleveland, 1911), 1: 142.

37. [James] *Adair's History of the American Indians* [London, 1775], ed. Samuel Cole Williams (New York, 1966), 245.

38. Ralph Davis, "English Foreign Trade, 1660–1700," *Economic History Review*, 2d ser. 7:2 (Dec. 1954), 150–66.

39. James W. Bradley, *Evolution of the Onondaga Iroquois: Accommodating Change, 1500–1655* (Syracuse, N.Y., 1987), 130; Charles F. Wray, "The Volume of Dutch Trade Goods Received by the Seneca Iroquois, 1600–1687 A.D.," *New Netherland Studies*, Bulletin KNOB, 84:2/3 (June 1985), 100–112.

40. Papers of Eleazar Wheelock, Dartmouth College Library, Hanover, N.H., catalogued in *A Guide to the Microfilm Edition of the Papers of Eleazar Wheelock* (Hanover, N.H.: Dartmouth College Library, 1971), 766554 (Theophilus Chamberlain to Wheelock, Oct. 4, 1766), 768672 (Wheelock to Dartmouth, Dec. 22, 1768). See also *Travels of William Bartram* [Philadelphia, 1791], ed. Mark Van Doren (New York, 1955), 401: "As to the mechanic arts or manufacturers, at present [the Indians of the Southeast] have scarcely any thing worth observation, since they are supplied with necessaries, conveniences, and even superfluities by the white traders."

41. William C. Sturtevant, "Two 1761 Wigwams at Niantic, Connecticut," *American Antiquity*, 40:4 (Oct. 1975), 437–44; Kathleen J. Bragdon, "The Material Culture of the Christian Indians of New England, 1650–1775," in Mary C. Beaudry, ed., *Documentary Archaeology and the New World* (Cambridge, 1988), 126–31; Daniel Mandell, " 'To Live More Like My Christian English Neighbors': Indian Natick in the Eighteenth Century," *William and Mary Quarterly*, 3d ser. 48 (Oct. 1991), 552–79.

42. Carl Bridenbaugh, ed., *Gentleman's Progress: The Itinerarium of Dr. Alexander Hamilton, 1744* (Chapel Hill, 1948), 98.

43. John A. Sainsbury, "Indian Labor in Early Rhode Island," *New England Quarterly*, 48 (1975), 378–93.

44. Robert Beverley, *The History and Present State of Virginia* [London, 1705], ed. Louis B. Wright (Charlottesville, 1968), 233.

45. Albert Henry Smyth, ed., *The Writings of Benjamin Franklin* (New York, 1907), 10:97; John Phillip Reid, *A Better Kind of Hatchet: Law, Trade, and Diplomacy in the Cherokee Nation During the Early Years of European Contact* (University Park, Pa., 1976), 194–95.

46. Anthony F. C. Wallace, "Revitalization Movements: Some Theoretical Considerations for Their Comparative Study," *American Anthropologist*, 58 (1956), 264–81.

47. Richard L. Haan, "The Trade Do's Not Flourish as Formerly': The Ecological Origins of the Yamassee War of 1715," *Ethnohistory*, 28:4 (Fall 1981), 341–58.

48. Howard H. Peckham, *Pontiac and the Indian Uprising* (New York, 1970, 1947); Charles E. Hunter, "The Delaware Nativist Revival of the Mid-Eighteenth Century," *Ethnohistory*, 18:1 (Winter 1971), 39–49; Anthony F. C. Wallace, *The Death and Rebirth of the Seneca* (New York, 1969), 114–22. Gregory Evans Dowd, "The French King Wakes Up in Detroit: 'Pontiac's War' in Rumor and History," *Ethnohistory*, 37:3 (Summer 1990), 254–78 at 259–61, reminds us that Neolin, the major Delaware prophet, made a partial exception for the gift-giving French.

49. Peckham, *Pontiac and the Indian Uprising*, 101–2; Michael McConnell, *A Country Between: The Upper Ohio Valley and Its Peoples, 1724–1774* (Lincoln, Neb., 1992).

CHAPTER 7

Narrative of Commercial Life: Consumption, Ideology, and Community on the Eve of the American Revolution

T. H. Breen

On the eve of Independence, Americans interpreted imperial politics in highly unusual ways. Indeed, historians of the Revolution report that colonists—even educated leaders of church and state—enthusiastically endorsed conspiratorial forms of thought.[1] The popular appeal of such forms of explanation is not surprising. After all, mid-eighteenth-century Americans had to make sense of rapidly changing economic and political conditions for which there was no precedent in their experience. Parliament aggressively asserted its sovereignty by taxing the colonists at about the same time that a flood of British manufactured items transformed the American marketplace. When Stephen Hopkins, Rhode Island's governor, surveyed the relation of the colonies to an expanding empire in 1765, he concluded, as did many contemporaries, that "the scene seems to be unhappily changing."[2]

Uneasy perceptions of this sort provoked a creative cultural response. Americans such as Hopkins interpreted for themselves and for their neighbors as best they could the mysterious engines of political and economic transformation. Drawing on the language and beliefs of ordinary people, they told stories that helped situate Americans within an unstable world that had rendered problematic much that they took for granted about provincial society. Some of the tales invented during this period serve as apposite illustrations of a dependent culture struggling to control change by giving it plausible local meaning. These hermeneutic efforts generated what can be termed new narratives of everyday life.

By reconstructing the mental framework that informed one of the central narratives of the mid-eighteenth century—in this case, an elaborate story of misunderstood American consumers—we shall better understand how the

"Narrative of Commercial Life: Consumption, Ideology, and Community on the Eve of the American Revolution" by T. H. Breen reprinted from *William and Mary Quarterly* 3rd Series, Vol. L. (July 1993). Used by permission of the *William and Mary Quarterly*.

colonists came to imagine themselves within an expanding empire of trade, how at a moment of extreme political crisis a bundle of popular ideas and assumptions about commerce suggested specific styles of resistance, and finally, how a boycott movement organized to counter British policy allowed scattered colonists to reach out to each other and to reimagine themselves within an independent commercial empire.

In 1763, no one could have foreseen that the translation of a "Genius of Commerce" into political protest would produce radical new forms of liberal community in America.[3] It was the unintended consequences of commercial ideas that made the Revolution genuinely revolutionary.[4] We shall look initially at the evolution of a popular narrative of commercial life and then explore the broad experiential and ideological context in which this bizarre account briefly but powerfully flourished.

Although the origins of folk explanations are difficult to isolate, we can with reasonable confidence begin the investigation of the new commercial narrative in the early 1760s. It was during this period that Americans first focused their attention on why British authorities had redefined the rules that had governed the empire for as long as anyone could remember. In this context, the Sugar Act of 1764 seemed so precipitate, so destructive to the normal flow of trade, so ill conceived that it defied easy explanation. But Americans accepted the interpretive challenge, probing connections between parliamentary oppression and the consumption of British goods.

The first troubled response appeared in Boston. Although the author of an anonymous pamphlet of 1764 entitled *Considerations Upon the Act of Parliament* did not proclaim a full-blown conspiracy, he suggested that Americans themselves bore responsibility for deteriorating relations with England. During the Seven Years' War, the colonists not only had lived too well but had done so too publicly. Their opulent consumption of British manufacturers strongly impressed "the gentlemen of the army and others at present and lately residing in the maritime towns." These outsiders learned that the Americans "spend full as much [on] the luxurious British imports as prudence will countenance, and often much more."[5]

The next year, the commercial interpretation of parliamentary taxation acquired fuller definition. John Dickinson, a respected Pennsylvania lawyer, traced the imperial crisis in part to a stunning misinterpretation in Great Britain of American consumer habits. "We are informed," Dickinson noted in *The Late Regulations*, "that an opinion has been industriously propagated in *Great-Britain* that the colonies are wallowing in wealth and luxury." That conclusion, he insisted, represented a pernicious misreading of colonial culture. The streets of America were not paved with gold, and in any case, impoverished colonists could not possibly pay new taxes. During the Seven Years' War, European visitors had witnessed an abnormal economy, artificially fueled by large military expenditures. Americans, Dickinson claimed, were ordinarily and mostly quite poor. British observers had been misled because the colonists, "having a number of strangers among us," were too generous and hospitable for their own good. The Americans had "indulged themselves in many uncommon expenses." This "imprudent excess of kindness" was simply an ill-conceived attempt to impress British visitors.[6]

Other writers took up the narrative of commercial life, adding innovative elements of their own. In 1768, for example, an anonymous New York pamphleteer situated Anglo-American consumption within a larger historical framework. Readers of *The Power and Grandeur of Great-Britain*—one of the more impressive political discussions of this period—learned that the original New World settlers had overcome "a thousand discouragements" and only recently had managed to establish themselves as "a numerous people." Whatever hardships they endured, the struggling colonists had contributed generously to English prosperity. As loyal consumers on a distant shore, they purchased "merchandize of an almost infinite variety, numberless useful and useless articles [that] are now yearly furnished to three millions of people." The profits of this trade flooded back to England. Even during the mid-century wars against France, commercial revenues increased. For the privilege of obtaining these goods uncomplaining colonists ransacked "the seas and the wilds of America . . . to make payment for them, and the improved lands are cultivated chiefly for the same purpose." Like other colonial authors, the New Yorker described the Seven Years' War as the crucial moment in the development of an empire of goods. In its aftermath, Britain turned the ingenuity of American consumers into a justification for parliamentary taxation, based on the reports of visitors "who saw a great display of luxury, arising from the wealth, which many had suddenly acquired during the wars."[7]

At this point, the author added a sociological dimension to an evolving commercial explanation of political crisis. It was not so much that the reports of extravagant American market behavior had been erroneous. Rather, the colonists were parvenu consumers who had failed to master the etiquette of a polite society. "It is an old observation," the pamphleteer confessed, "that those who suddenly plunge into unexpected riches, in ostentation greatly exceed those who either derive them from their ancestors, or have gradually acquired them by the ordinary course of business." Contemporary imperial policy, therefore, was the product of shoddy anthropology. The British refused to appreciate that, despite their superficial glamour, eighteenth-century Americans remained provincial bumpkins, too poor to pay parliamentary taxes and too untutored to display their wealth tastefully.[8]

In 1768, William Hicks of Philadelphia heightened the conspiratorial element in this broad folk discourse. It was no accident, he announced, that ordinary English people accepted inflated estimates of colonial prosperity as truth, for unnamed sources had systematically distorted reports of economic conditions in America. Hicks protested that "the estimates of our wealth which have been received from ignorant or prejudiced persons, are, in every calculation, grossly erroneous. These misrepresentations, which have been so industriously propagated, are very possibly the offspring of political invention, as they form the best apology for imposing upon us burthens to which we are altogether unequal." This interpretive framework—what was becoming for Hicks a conspiracy of commerce—carried extremely sinister implications for the colonists' happiness within a commercial empire. Boldly linking consumption and politics, Hicks asked Americans to remember exactly how Parliament had first reacted to the false reports of wealth. Had that body not immediately imposed new taxes? Were not these revenue acts an ominous hint of future assaults? Without money, what would the colonists be able to afford? The plot was obvious. The British wanted to keep the Americans poor, marginal consumers just able to pay the rising taxes but never "suffered to riot in a superfluity of wealth." Industrious colonists could surrender their dreams of luxury, their expectations of sharing the material culture of Britain. "Whatever advantages may hereafter present themselves, from an increased population, or a more extended trade," lamented Hicks, "we shall never be able to cultivate them to any valuable purpose; for, how much soever we may possess the ability of acquiring wealth and independence, the partial views of our selfish brethren, supported by the sovereignty of Parliament, will most effectually prevent our enjoying such invaluable acquisitions."[9]

Narratives of commercial life—a fluid assemblage of popular notions about consumption and politics—echoed through the colonial newspapers, indicating that the tale of hospitable American consumers and bemused British visitors, of luxury and poverty in a changing economy, had become a staple of popular culture on the eve of Independence. Writing in the *New-London Gazette*, "Incultus Americanus" reminded readers that the Seven Years' War had been responsible for "an insatiable itch for merchandizing; and the folly and extravagance of the people in imitating the customs and dress of foreigners." Self-indulgence had been the colonists' undoing. "Our extravagant dress and luxury had this fatal effect . . . , that Europeans concluded we were a people abounding with wealth, and well able to furnish largely for defraying the national debt."[10] The *Boston Evening-Post* noted that the British belief in "our being in affluent and flourishing circumstances, was grounded upon a mistake or the misrepresentation of travellers or others."[11] By 1771, the argument for disjuncture between appearance and reality had become standard fare. "A Friend of the Colony of Connecticut" explained in the *New-Haven Post-Boy* that "a large consumption of unnecessary foreign articles . . . has given us the false and deceitful appearance of riches, in buildings, at our tables, and on our bodies. Which has attracted the attention if not raised the envy of our neighbors, and perhaps had its influence in making the late grievous unconstitutional revenue acts."[12]

Even as the contest with Great Britain intensified and the possibility of armed conflict loomed, Americans maintained that the political crisis was somehow related to their own participation in a new Anglo-American marketplace. One example appeared in 1774. The Reverend Ebenezer Baldwin of

Danbury, Connecticut, published a short sermon explicitly directed to ordinary farmers living in isolated communities who were "not under the best advantages for information from the news papers and other pieces wrote upon the controversy." How had it come to pass, Baldwin asked these rural people, that Americans were contemplating armed resistance against the British empire? For answers one needed to look no further back in time than the Seven Years' War. "As America was much the seat of the last war," Baldwin recounted, "the troops sent here from the mother country, opened a much freer communication between Great Britain and the Colonies, [and] the state of the colonies was much more attended to in England, than it had been in times past."

Such familiarity generated only superficial understanding. British visitors failed to appreciate just how much the social dynamics of America differed from those of England. "In a country like this," Baldwin reminded the farmers, "where property is so equally divided, every one will be disposed to rival his neighbor in goodness of dress, sumptuousness of furniture, &c. All our little earnings therefore went to Britain to purchase mainly the superfluities of life." Economic leveling in the colonies stimulated status competition; consumer goods were the primary means by which men and women sorted themselves out in society. "Hence the common people here make a show, much above what they do in England," Baldwin asserted. Here was the source of a profound cultural misunderstanding. "The luxury and superfluities in which even the lower ranks of people here indulge themselves," the Connecticut minister observed, "being reported in England by the officers and soldiers upon their return, excited in the people there a very exalted idea of the riches of this country, and the abilities of the inhabitants to bear taxes."[13] Whatever their former excesses as consumers may have been, Baldwin thought that Americans could still save the political situation. All they had to do was reform their buying habits, putting aside the imported goods that had made them seem richer than they actually were. The moment had arrived for the "lower ranks" of society to appreciate that their private decisions in the marketplace had helped to precipitate and could influence the greatest political event of their lives.

Versions of the commercial narrative had strong popular appeal. In 1774, for example, "A Citizen of Philadelphia" submitted a story of naïve American consumers to several urban newspapers. This form of the evolving story was more elaborate and less sophisticated. To be sure, the Seven Years' War brought British troops to America. These had not been average soldiers, however, for as A Citizen explained, the officers were upper-class figures, "many of them sons of the best families." Other eminent Englishmen accompanied the military to the New World. "Gentlemen on their travels extended their route to America," the writer explained, "and even Peers of the realm landed on our shores." Sudden attention from such distinguished personages flattered the colonists, who worked hard to make a favorable impression on their elite guests. A Citizen recaptured their effusive hospitality: "we lavished the fruits of our industry, in social banquets,—We displayed a parade of *wealth*, beyond the bounds of moderation and prudence; and suffered our guests to depart, with *high ideas of our riches*." As the prodigal Americans soon learned, these socially prominent officers and gentlemen lost no time informing well-connected friends in England about the affluent consumers they had encountered in the New World. Perhaps these reporters meant no harm; perhaps they did not consciously engage in conspiracy. There was no disputing, however, that as England "was oppressed with a heavy load of debt, . . . how natural then, was it for Parliament, to hunt out fresh resources?"[14]

The narrative of commercial life gained what may have been a final reformulation in David Ramsay's *History of the American Revolution*. Published in 1789, this sedulously researched account of the War for Independence strove to avoid the shrill partisan tone that marred many early patriot histories. Like others who reviewed the conflict, the South Carolina physician and army veteran found it difficult to understand why Parliament decided to tax the Americans in the first place. He located the answer in Britain's willingness to accept "exaggerated accounts" of Americans' wealth. "It was said," Ramsay explained, " 'that the American planters lived in affluence, and with inconsiderable taxes, while the inhabitants of Great-Britain were borne down.' " The culprits again seem to have been British soldiers serving in America. "Their observations were founded on what they had seen in cities, and at a time, when large sums were spent by government, in support of fleets and armies, and when American commodities were in great demand." Kind Americans spared no expense in feting their British allies in the great struggle against France. "To treat with attention those, who came to fight for them," Ramsay asserted, "and also to gratify their own pride, the colonists had made a parade of their riches, by frequently and sumptuously entertaining the gentlemen of the British army." The visitors mistakenly concluded that the colonists lived very well. It was a natural error. These officers "judging from what they saw, without considering the general state of the country, concurred in representing the colonists, as very able to contribute, largely, towards defraying the common expenses of empire."[15]

These various versions of the commercial narrative joined other discourses that Americans invented to explain to themselves why relations with England had soured so suddenly. Although other tales circulated widely throughout the colonies during this period—for example, stories of massive political corruption in Great Britain—this largely overlooked account of eager, misunderstood colonial consumers possesses unusual interest. It represents an imaginative, often entirely plausible response to two distinct crises in the Anglo-American world of the mid-eighteenth century. The colonists had to accommodate not only the demands of a new consumer marketplace that inundated the homes of free men and women with alluring goods but also the aggressive Parliament that threatened to destroy a delicate commercial system that made it possible to pay for these goods.

The commercial narrative that enjoyed popularity for over two decades effectively linked these separate challenges. For one thing, it established a shared chronology. Change accelerated during the Seven Years' War, setting the stage for a cultural misinterpretation so profound that the Americans could never again persuade Parliament that they were in fact poor. The interpretation turned on the consumption of English manufactures by Americans who were overly hospitable, remarkably self-indulgent, and socially insecure. Versions of the story came from all regions of the continent, from different classes and backgrounds, from people who seemed in retrospect to have felt a little guilty that their own excesses had given off such confusing signals. The narrative of commercial life explained that it was not the goods that had hurt the Americans but, rather, their misuse; not the purchase, but the vulgarity.

Historians have failed to give the commercial perspective proper interpretive standing. Another body of thought has long dominated the search for the ideological origins of the American Revolution. According to Bernard Bailyn, who more than any other has set the terms of this debate, eighteenth-century colonists subscribed to a controlling set of "assumptions, beliefs, and ideas—the articulated world view—that lay behind the manifest events of the time."[16] This complex mental framework, often labeled "republican," marginalized the language and experience of commercial capitalism.[17] In this interpretive perspective, colonial Americans were not trying to accommodate to a rapidly changing world economic system; instead, they resisted it. They condemned the modern commercial mentality. They were backward looking, suspicious of trade and banking, fearful of spreading political corruption produced by financial revolution in Great Britain. Americans of republican persuasion spent their days exposing plots consciously designed to pervert Britain's ancient constitution, schemes to establish a standing army, efforts to silence the press—in short, conspiracies to crush liberty. These shrill anxieties helped Americans to see the evil hand behind British policy, and by 1776 colonial readers of John Trenchard and Thomas Gordon had transformed themselves into armed rebels against the empire. So runs the "republican synthesis."[18]

Historians critical of this dominant interpretation have argued that the colonists' political ideology before the Revolution was more liberal and Lockean than we had been led to believe. Others have tried to restore elements of traditional Protestant theology to the ideological mix, but with the notable exceptions of Joyce Appleby and Isaac Kramnick, few seem comfortable with a political discourse that owed much to the experiences of ordinary men and women in a new consumer marketplace.[19] To construct a persuasive explanation of the dialectic between experience and ideology on the eve of Independence, one would need to address two separate interpretive problems about which current historiography has little to say.

First, we should focus on the elusive relation between the events of everyday life and the stories that contemporaries invented to make sense of those events.

This is not an exercise that necessarily gives interpretive privilege to the writings of highly educated colonial leaders—for example, to the pamphlets produced by great planters, successful lawyers, and prominent ministers. These familiar sources have obvious utility, but we should cast the net more broadly to include elements of popular thought—inchoate, sometimes contradictory ideas and assumptions that persons of very different economic and regional backgrounds came to share by mid-century.[20]

Second, we should consider how artisans and farmers—the sort of folk who may have heard the Reverend Baldwin—confronted a mid-eighteenth-century world that impinged ever more insistently on their sense of self. The great value of the local studies produced by American historians over recent decades is that they powerfully draw attention to ordinary men and women making decisions about the conduct of their lives. The drama of the past reveals itself most poignantly within small units, within communities trying to explain environmental change, within families experiencing the joys and disappointments connected to cycles of life and death, within the minds of individual men and women attempting to work out their sexual, racial, and ethnic identities.

Local analysis, however, cannot be its own reward. Throughout recorded history, ordinary people have found that they must express agency within larger frameworks, such as capitalism and nationalism—forces that puzzled and frightened, that demanded personal response, and that presented an unprecedented range of choice.[21] In mid-eighteenth-century America, the outside world often spoke most seductively through imported consumer goods, and because they imagined themselves within an empire of commerce, colonists who had previously not had much to do with each other came to see it a matter of common sense to respond to the disruption of their economic and political lives through specific commercial strategies such as an ever-wider boycott movement. Political actions grew out of a popular ideology. What no one anticipated was that mass political mobilization within a consumer marketplace would radically transform how Americans construed community so that by the 1770s their experience provoked them to imagine a powerful commercial empire of their own.

Americans brought to the final political crisis a complex bundle of ideas about the British empire that were products of long commercial experience. This set of popular assumptions provided an interpretive lens through which the colonists viewed parliamentary claims to absolute sovereignty. Jonathan Mayhew, a leading Boston clergyman, understood these patterns of thought as well as any colonist, and he was therefore an appropriate person to celebrate in 1766 the repeal of the Stamp Act with a sermon entitled *The Snare Broken*. Mayhew used the occasion to reexamine what membership in the British empire meant to colonial Americans. He concentrated on shared assumptions—what he termed "commonly-received opinions" and notions generally "taken for granted"—that he believed had shaped popular political identity.[22] At that happy moment, Mayhew must have sensed that scholarly arguments would not spark the desired emotional response. To be sure, Americans cared deeply about the empire to which they swore allegiance. It was just that their thoughts about this subject were a bit fuzzy—a loose amalgam of beliefs about the balanced constitution, the common law tradition, and the sanctity of the Protestant succession. These disparate elements had somehow contributed to their own freedom and prosperity.[23] Certainly, there was no denying success. According to one American writing in 1768, "Britain seems now to have attained to a degree of wealth, power, and eminence, which half a century ago, the most sanguine of her patriots could hardly have made the object of their warmest wishes."[24]

On one point Americans expressed near universal agreement. They believed that the empire owed its ascendance almost entirely to international commerce, that trade was the indispensable source of national wealth and military power, and that trade even sustained political liberty.[25] World history, they claimed, demonstrated that commercial societies were freer and happier than those that had not experienced its marvelously transforming effects. Thus writer "X" in the *Connecticut Journal* insisted that "the experience of every age, and nation from the remotest knowledge, down to the present-day, join in asserting this fact; that no nation, ever became rich or poor, but in proportion to the increase, or decrease of their trade." For "X," the British empire brought Americans more than economic prosperity: commerce went "hand in hand with liberty; rose, flourish'd and declin'd together."[26]

Colonial newspapers regularly reaffirmed the lesson. Commerce distinguished the British empire from other empires, from despotic systems that could never deliver the peace, security, and coherence that eighteenth-century Americans now took for granted. "Commerce is the most solid foundation of civil society," the *Boston Evening-Post* announced in 1764. "By this our necessities, conveniences, and pleasures are supplied from distant shores; every region is amazed to find itself abounding in foreign productions, and enriched with a thousand commodities unknown to itself, and promoting its welfare and serving to make life more agreeable."[27] Mid-century Americans imagined themselves within a great circulation of money and goods, a practically Newtonian marketing system connecting them in mutually beneficial ways to strangers throughout the empire.

For Americans, trade implied reciprocity. All groups within the empire stood to gain something by exchanging goods. Commercial relations between peoples and societies were analogous to private contracts, all parties negotiating and each party compromising a little in an effort to reach agreement. To take advantage of a partner's weakness, to take more from a relationship than one returned, was condemned as shortsighted as well as avaricious. A young man chosen in 1766 to deliver a prize-winning dissertation on "The Reciprocal Advantages of a Perpetual Union Between Great-Britain and Her American Colonies" voiced the common wisdom: "I hope . . . to make it appear," he de-

clared, "that a reciprocal emolument will arise from a perpetual union between *Britain* and her *American* Colonies; as she may by their means greatly
enlarge her trade and commerce . . . , as they will reap the advantage of her
riches and power, by being protected from their enemies, and supplied with the
conveniences of life at a cheaper rate, and of a better quality than if manufactured by themselves." [28] From this perspective the empire was a bargain.
Members of an Annapolis trade inspection committee expressed the point less
effusively in 1770, but they too assumed reciprocity. "The Province of Maryland," they explained, "and the whole Continent of *British America*, had for
more than an Hundred Years, carried on a very extensive Commerce with
Great-Britain, which gave a quick Progress to the Population of America, and
advanced greatly the Strength, Wealth and Grandeur of *Great-Britain*." [29]

While the commercial model assumed balance and fairness within the empire, the colonists—even before the crisis over parliamentary taxation—routinely betrayed a sense of their own vulnerability. American rhetoric often
sounded more anxious than descriptive. Writers seemed overly eager to persuade the British—perhaps their fellow colonists also—that trade did in fact
benefit the metropolitan core as well as the distant peripheries. The key to any
positive assessment of imperial trade was the Americans' rising consumption of
manufactured goods. In 1764, for example, Governor Thomas Fitch lectured
the people of Connecticut that "the Colonies and Plantations in *America* are,
indeed, of great Importance to their Mother Country and an Interest worthy of
her most tender Regard." The provinces were partners, not competitors. "The
more they prosper and increase in Number, Riches and Commerce," Fitch
noted defensively, "the greater will be the Advantage not only to them but also
to the Nation at Home." The colonies provided an ever-expanding market for
"almost all Sorts of *British* Manufactures, and of many and various Kinds of
Goods of the Produce of other Countries, first imported into *Britain*." [30] In Massachusetts, Oxenbridge Thacher asserted that it was common knowledge "that
the greatest part of the trade of Great-Britain, is with her colonies." As the
Americans prospered, so too would the British. Thacher observed that "doubtless even the luxury of the colonists is the gain of G. Britain." [31]

Colonial observers understood something fundamental about the imperial
connection that modern historians have generally ignored: mid-century Americans confronted a situation that was genuinely new. Before the 1740s, few
would have described their relation with Great Britain within the framework
of a rapidly expanding consumer marketplace. After that date, the commercial
connection became much more invasive, more manifest—a development demanding adjustment and accommodation and one that touched the lives of
people living in all parts of America.

Contemporaries were fully aware of the changes that had dramatically
transformed the face of a provincial material culture. A quotidian world had
taken on a different appearance. People dressed more opulently and more col-
orfully. They purchased more manufactured items that made them feel hap-

pier, warmer, or better looking.[32] As William Smith observed in his *History of the Late Province of New-York*, "In the city of New-York, through our intercourse with the Europeans, we follow the London fashions. . . . Our affluence, during the late war [Seven Years' War], introduced a degree of luxury in tables, dress, and furniture, with which we were before unacquainted."[33] Other Americans testified to the suddenness of the change. "I am now forty-four years old," a "Countryman" told the readers of the *Boston Gazette* in 1769, "and to see the difference in the times really astonishes me. I never had, Mr. Printers, believe me, nothing better to go to meeting in, than a pair of sheepskin breeches, a felt hatt, and homespun-made coat with horn buttons." According to the Countryman, his neighbors now demanded "English-made cloth that cost . . . a guinea a yard."[34]

Statistical evidence abundantly supports contemporary impressions. Trade figures compiled for the eighteenth century reveal that England's exports to the mainland colonies increased over 50 percent between 1720 and 1770. The sharpest rise occurred between 1750 and 1770, and the per capita expenditures on British manufactures equaled, perhaps even exceeded, the phenomenal rate of growth of the American population. Cloth of various types was the major item for sale, but judging from analyses of colonial probate records, men and women also rushed to purchase household amenities such as clocks and china that were just then becoming available at prices that most middle-class families could afford.[35]

Increasing opportunities to consume triggered intense print controversies about the character and limits of luxury, the moral implications of credit, the role of personal choice in a liberal society, and the relevance of traditional status hierarchies in a commercial world that encouraged people to fashion protean public identities.[36] Heated debates on these issues represented an initial effort by large numbers of Americans throughout the colonies to gain intellectual control over the marketplace, to make sense of their new experiences, and to bring ideology into line with a commercial system that they found inviting as well as intimidating. These controversies were facets of a more general struggle to reach accommodation with a particular form of preindustrial capitalism. Similar debates occurred in eighteenth-century Scotland, Ireland, and France, for in those nations a flood of manufactured goods also forced ordinary people to rethink the meaning of traditional cultures. The market compelled a response, and even without political revolution, Americans would inevitably have had to adjust to its demands.[37]

This developing commercial mentality was neither premodern nor anticapitalist. Americans welcomed improved living standards, and they would have regarded calls to restore an earlier, largely subsistence economy as sheer lunacy.[38] By the mid-eighteenth century the simple life had come to be associated with a dull, savage existence. James Otis, the Massachusetts lawyer, who may have been the most radical democrat in America before Thomas Paine, dismissed market asceticism out of hand. Writing in the *Boston Gazette* in 1761,

Otis observed that "luxury is a very vague & loose term, [and] if by it is meant the importation of many foreign commodities, the more we have the better. . . . I know it is the maxim of some, that the common people in this town and country live too well; however I am of a quite different opinion, I do not think they live half well enough."[39]

During the 1760s, Parliament revised the rules of empire in an effort to reduce a huge national debt. For Americans, the revenue acts came as a shock. They could see no compelling reason to tinker with a commercial system that seemed to be working well enough. To be sure, both sides grumbled from time to time about specific trade problems—smuggling, breaches of the Navigation Acts, inadequate supplies of currency, and the like—but new parliamentary taxes were certainly not the proper solution. As "A Friend to this Country" explained in the *Boston Evening-Post*, "it is an argument in the mouth of almost everyone, 'that the whole profit of our lives center in Britain, & that 'tis folly for them to tax us to gain in themselves what they already secured by a trade, the balance of which is wholly in their favor.' "[40]

The escalating dispute raised fundamental constitutional issues, and while Americans passionately defended their positions on rights and representation, they also worried about their continued participation in the consumer marketplace. In their attempts to comprehend the sudden shift in British policy, they drew as much on their own recent commercial experience as they did on abstract theories of republican governance. The stories they told themselves about prodigal American consumers entertaining British soldiers were a part of this general response. So, too, were decisions about specific forms of political mobilization. The colonists evolved instruments of protest within a mental framework that was largely a product of living in a commercial empire.[41]

The most striking aspect of the Revolutionary boycotts is their utter novelty. No previous popular rebellion had organized itself so centrally around the consumer. That the Americans did so is an additional indication of their modernity. Yet historians have not viewed the boycott movement as problematic: it just happened; it was a reflexive response to taxation without representation.[42] And so it must have seemed to most colonial Americans. While they defended their constitutional goals, fiercely affirming their rights, they seldom bothered to consider the rationale of nonimportation. Shared consumer assumptions and experiences flowed smoothly into the taken-for-granted of resistance. As a Philadelphia broadside declared, "the Stopping the Importation of Goods is the only probable Means of preserving to us and our Posterity . . . Liberty and Security."[43]

The first boycotts of 1765–1766, contested the Stamp Act. Similar protests occurred in 1768–1770 and 1774–1776. Over time, the nonimportation movement grew larger, more successful, and more democratic. Groups of local merchants usually planned and executed the initial efforts, but the driving force behind the various committees and associations gradually passed to the people. Throughout the colonies, extralegal bodies seized control of the boycott movement; as they did so, their members increasingly spoke in the name of a newly constituted American public.

While the boycott was rapidly becoming the distinctive signature of American political protest, colonists began to resituate themselves in an evolving commercial discourse. Their focus shifted away from reciprocity, away from a mutually beneficial exchange with Great Britain, to outright claims of American preeminence. "I think it may justly be said," boldly declared a Philadelphia writer, "that THE FOUNDATION OF THE POWER AND GLORY OF GREAT BRITAIN ARE LAID IN AMERICA."[44]

Although this booster may not have believed that the American tail really wagged the British dog, he and others made a strong case for Britain's economic dependence on American consumers. Thacher, for example, likened commerce within the British empire to "a grand chain" and concluded that Parliament could not remove the American links "without greatly endangering the whole."[45] In 1769, the *South-Carolina Gazette* suggested that consumption of imported goods was really a source of political empowerment. Americans, the editor argued, "know themselves to be the best customers Great-Britain has, for her wares." They did not have to pay the oppressive taxes. Britain's rulers should learn that "every American has an indisputable right to lay his money out [on goods] as sparingly as he pleases." If Americans supported the boycott, then no one could predict what might happen. British merchants might suffer large losses; British workers might find themselves out of work. "Must not such a number of idle hands, in the heart of the country, be extremely alarming?" inquired the South Carolinian.[46]

If riots in the Midlands of England failed to win parliamentary concessions, Americans had another card to play: they could go into manufacturing themselves. This had not been a topic of broad colonial interest before the passage of the Stamp Act, but once it became part of a general commercial conversation, it opened up new creative possibilities. Insistence that Americans were capable of satisfying their own consumer demand—something that they would not achieve for many decades—made it easier for people to imagine genuine economic independence. In any case, there is not much evidence that Revolutionary Americans wanted to roll back the commercial progress of the eighteenth century. If a recalcitrant Parliament forced their hand, explained a letter in the *Boston Chronicle*, "the people of America, must from necessity, if not from motives of interest, set up manufacturers of their own: which must gradually diminish, and in consequence put an end to that mutual beneficial commerce, that has hitherto subsisted between us."[47]

Such plausible, though exaggerated, economic claims fed the boycott movement, continuously strengthening the political resolve of individual consumers. Local associations organized to promote nonimportation and manufacturing represented initial, often tentative steps toward a radical reconstitution of civil society.[48] For in point of fact, Americans of the time were experimenting with new forms of community, founded not on traditional religious affiliations but on shared commercial interests. Only those who insist that preindustrial capitalism inevitably sparked destructive individualism will be surprised by popular attempts to construct interpretive communities around a temporary withdrawal from an Atlantic marketplace.

The truth of the matter is that a liberal market ideology proved capable of sustaining interpretive communities—indeed, of mobilizing ordinary men and women into associations unequivocally dedicated to the common good. As a "Tradesman" writing for the *Pennsylvania Chronicle* in 1770 well understood, civil society in America could develop from sources other than republicanism. He explained that "as we form a considerable, independent, and respectable Body of the People, we certainly have an *equal Right* to enter into Agreements and Resolutions *with others* for the public Good, in a sober, orderly Manner, becoming Freemen and loyal Subjects. . . . [L]et us determine, *for the Good of the Whole*, to strengthen the Hands of the Patriotic Majority, by agreeing not to purchase *British Goods*."[49]

The link between commerce and community energized a pamphlet published in Boston in 1762. The anonymous author of *Debtor and Creditor* launched his argument with an observation to which few American readers would have objected. God's blessing, he observed, is the "Foundation of Happiness to any Community." He moved quickly to less familiar intellectual ground; other factors merited consideration. "The Number, Riches, and Unanimity of the People are the secondary Constituents of this Happiness," and these elements were in turn a function of "Commerce and Government." "Extensive Commerce and an happy Government will soon introduce a flourishing Nation," he noted in the expansive language of the Scottish Enlightenment. The "Commerce" that the writer had in mind strengthened community, stimulated cooperation, and in these respects, "is like our spiritual Race. In the Spiritual Race we labour for Happiness hereafter, and should not only press towards Heaven ourselves, but, likewise, give all possible Assistance to others in their Labours therein." The analogy with commerce was obvious. In this sphere, too, the individual would work for the common good. "In the Race of Commerce," the writer explained, "not only our own private Advantage, but also that of the Body of which we are Members, should be in View." He imagined a powerful self-regulating community in which "it is our Duty to look on every Addition to our Fortune as an additional Obligation on us to assist and forward the Designs of those who, perhaps, are more indigent, tho' equally industrious."[50]

The nonimportation movement—in effect, a communal experiment in applied ideology—exposed a radical egalitarian strand within the commercial discourse. To appreciate this development one must remember that the consumer market of the mid-eighteenth century was open to almost any white person able to pay the price. Generous credit, paper currency, and newspaper advertisements encouraged broad participation.[51] Usually, free producers were also consumers. And on the eve of Revolution, the success of the colonial boycotts depended on all these consumers temporarily deciding to become non-consumers. The argument for the liberating possibilities of agency in the new Anglo-American marketplace is not intended to mitigate the exploitative and oppressive effects of eighteenth-century capitalism. The development of an Atlantic economy meant that African-American slaves and indentured servants—indeed, unfree people of all sorts—worked very hard, often under extremely harsh conditions. New forms of self-fashioning were built on the suffering of laborers in England and America who made mass consumption possible.

Since in the politicization of private economic choice every free voice counted, it is not surprising that the promoters of the boycott movement tried to legitimate their activities through appeals to the popular will. They presumed to speak for the majority, however defined. Exclusiveness ran counter to the spirit of this powerful mobilizing discourse, and it was a happy moment when a town could report—as did Norwich, Connecticut, in September 1770—that "there was as full a Town Meeting as [was] ever known when the Town voted, almost unanimously, to adhere to their . . . Non-Importation Agreement."[52]

The so-called subscription lists also testify to the egalitarian thrust of eighteenth-century commercial thought. These instruments extended the boycott movement to large numbers of people who normally would not have had a voice in public affairs. The lists presented individual consumers with a formal declaration of purpose, followed by an oath or pledge. The goal of subscription was in part indoctrination. The forms reviewed a growing catalogue of grievances and announced that in the short term only nonimportation could preserve liberty and property. More significant, the ritual of signing gave birth to new collectivities. The ordinary consumer who accepted the logic of the argument and signed the paper thereby volunteered to support a community protest.

Surviving subscriptions resonate with religious as well as contractual language. A Boston agreement drafted in 1767 announced that all signers: "DO promise and engage, to and with each other, that we will encourage the Use and Consumption of all Articles manufactured in any of the British American Colonies, and more especially in this Province; and that we will not . . . purchase . . . Articles from abroad."[53] A 1773 South Carolina subscription sounded remarkably similar to that of Boston. After reviewing a decade of oppressive parliamentary acts, persons collectively known as "We the undersigned" declared that they "DO hereby solemnly promise and agree, each for him or herself, that we will not, either directly or indirectly import, buy or sell, or any way encourage or countenance the importation, buying or selling, any teas. . . . And this we do, because we conceive, that the payment of . . . duties, will be acknowledging a power which the British Parliament hath assumed, and which we deny them to have under our excellent constitution."[54]

The subscription campaign caught the public interest. Numbers provide an index of political success. In 1767, the *Boston Evening-Post* reported that "the Subscription Rolls are daily filling up at the Town Clerk's Office."

Charlestown, Dedham, and Providence had launched efforts of their own, and there, too, the forms were "filling up fast."[55] The publisher of the *South-Carolina Gazette* established a central register where the separate subscriptions could be tabulated, and he urged "Gentlemen in the country possessed of these Forms . . . to transmit the names subscribed thereto, as frequently as possible."[56] The *Maryland Gazette* informed its readers that 840 people had already signed the local lists; many more were expected.[57]

One person's signature seems to have been as desirable as another's. In 1767, Boston town officials specifically urged "Persons of all Ranks" to come forward, and in Annapolis, Maryland, people circulating "our Association-Paper" predicted that colonists of "every Degree" would sign it.[58] The *South-Carolina Gazette* even reported that in New York, "The Sense of the People was taken by Subscription, and near 800 Names got, about 300 of the People without a single Shilling Property."[59]

Even more significant, the subscription movement actively involved women. It was as consumers participating in new interpretive communities that American women first gained a political voice. Although men may have pushed women to the margins of formal protest, so that they had to organize their own subscriptions, women made the most of this opportunity. In 1770, for example, a group of Boston women drew up an agreement "against drinking foreign TEA." One hundred twenty-six "young Ladies" announced: "We the Daughters of those Patriots who have and now do appear for the public Interest . . . do with Pleasure engage with them in denying ourselves the drinking of Foreign Tea, in hopes to frustrate a Plan that tends to deprive the whole Community of their all that is valuable in Life."[60] Another Boston subscription gained the signatures of 300 "Mistresses of their respective families." The next week, 110 more names appeared.[61] In 1774, the women of Charleston, South Carolina, formed an association and, according to the local newspaper, "are subscribing to it very fast."[62]

These innovative efforts to bring people into the boycott remind us that consumer-based actions were inherently more open than were the traditional political ones accessible only to white males with property. Peter Oliver, the Boston loyalist who later penned a caustic history of the Revolution, immediately spotted the radical thrust of the market protest. Recounting what he had witnessed during the late 1760s, Oliver claimed that agitators had circulated "A Subscription Paper . . . Enumerating a great Variety of Articles not to be imported from *England*, which they supposed would muster the Manufacturers in *England* into a national Mob to support their Interests. Among the various prohibited Articles, were *Silks, Velvets, Clocks, Watches, Coaches & Chariots*; & it was highly diverting, to see the names & marks, to the Subscription, of Porters & Washing Women."[63] Oliver ridiculed such activities. How could persons outside politics ever hope to have their opinions on important issues taken seriously? But the poor laborers of Boston—women as well as men—knew what they were doing. Their "names & marks" testify to their membership in a new volitional community that people of Oliver's status could never comprehend.

Subscription should be seen, therefore, as an instrument through which the colonists explored the limits of democratic participation. Appearing on the margins of mainstream political discourse, the popular lists raised the issue of political exclusivity.⁶⁴ Did the men and women who signed the papers, for example, necessarily represent the people? If they did not, then for whom did they speak?

These were the sorts of questions that "Cato" addressed in the *Pennsylvania Chronicle* in 1770. For him, the colonial political crisis was too important to be left in the hands of a minority pretending to speak for a majority. "This is a point," he wrote, "in which every freeholder of this province is highly interested, and in which every one of them has a right to a voice." He was irritated by inflated claims to political authority advanced by a select group of local "subscribers to the non-importation." These people assumed "an exclusive right to determine this matter." If they did possess such a privilege, Cato warned, "it follows that the subscribers to the non-importation have the sole right to determine a question of liberty, that most nearly concerns every freeman of this province. For if it is the only mode of opposition of any force, and those two or three hundred subscribers have a right to make the agreement void whenever they please, it is a plain inference that they have a right to decide on a point which affects the liberties of the people of this province." Cato wanted to open up the process. Votes, not signatures, reflected the popular will, and he trusted that "every freeman, whether he be farmer, merchant, or mechanick, will insist upon his right to a vote in so important an affair."⁶⁵

The question of political inclusion flared dramatically in New York on the eve of Independence, when a small group of wealthy merchants seized control of the local boycott. These men did not want to consult about politics or trade with people whom they regarded as social inferiors. Their expressions of public arrogance mocked new popular notions of an open, egalitarian commercial community. In a 1774 broadside, *To the Free and Loyal Inhabitants of the City and Colony of New-York*, "Brutus" spoke out for the political rights of ordinary men and women. "Nothing can be more flagrantly wrong," Brutus declared, "than the Assertion of some of our mercantile Dons, that the Mechanics have no Right to give their Sentiments about the Importation of *British* Commodities." The great merchants of New York failed to appreciate that ordinary colonists interpreted political events within ideological frameworks every bit as complex and compelling as those of their more privileged contemporaries. "For who," asked Brutus in the distinct language of eighteenth-century commercial capitalism, "is the Member of Community, that is absolutely independent of the rest? Or what particular Class among us, has an exclusive Right to decide a Question of general Concern?"⁶⁶

The key element of the developing argument was the rejection of *exclusiveness*. From Brutus's perspective, the common good was a public responsibility.

There was no celebration here—as one finds in the republican literature of that time—of the man of wealth and leisure, the independent property holder who rises above grubby commercial interests and contemplates with marvelous objectivity the general welfare. Legal standing did not define citizenship. After all, Brutus insisted, "We are all equally free." With equal freedom went equal responsibility. During the boycott movement, "Every Man saw, that between an Importation of Goods . . . and the Sacrifice of our inestimable Rights as Englishmen, there was no Medium." Political resistance within the consumer marketplace had to be open to people of all "Ranks." Otherwise it was an empty promise. Ignore those merchants, urged Brutus, "who dare to affirm . . . that the Mechanics, or in other Words, the Majority of the Community, are not to be consulted on a Point of universal, of dreadful Concern."[67]

During the summer of 1770, the New York boycott movement hotly debated the issue of democratic participation. After Parliament repealed the Townshend duties, thus dropping all taxes except that on tea, the major import merchants of the city agitated to renew trade as soon as possible. Delays in reestablishing English contacts might give competitors in Philadelphia or Boston a huge advantage. But however much the New York merchants wanted to turn a profit, they could not bring themselves unilaterally to break the local nonimportation agreement. What they needed at this decisive moment was authorization from the people, and this they determined to obtain through a public opinion poll of consumers—perhaps the first such effort conducted in America. If they could demonstrate with quantitative evidence that the public wanted to rescind the boycott, the merchants knew they would be safe. The tactic worked. Polling papers carried though the city wards revealed that a majority of the people of New York supported a greatly modified boycott that allowed the merchants to import virtually everything except British tea.

The radical leaders of New York found themselves confronted with a quandary that has haunted democratic theorists since ancient Greece. How does a minority respond when it is certain that the majority has made a mistake? The obvious ploy was to declare the poll a fraud, and over several months the supporters of a continued total boycott did just that. They hammered away at the merchants' sham democracy. The author of "A Protest" in the *New-York Mercury* argued that the reported numbers were not credible. "It appears from the Ward-Lists," the writer charged, "that only 794 Persons in this populous City, including all Ranks, and both Sexes; declared for the Affirmative of the Questions."[68] It is particularly significant for my argument that this writer assumed that a true canvass of colonial consumers—even one involving complex political issues—required inclusiveness, full participation by women as well as men, the poor as well as the rich.

"A Son of Liberty" also challenged the merchants' democratic claims. In the *New-York Advertiser* he ridiculed the assertion that "*a majority appeared for importation.*" The merchants had not even approached most of the men and women who composed the consumer public. A Son of Liberty observed that "there were not quite twelve hundred persons who signed for importing (notwithstanding the diligence and indefatigable industry of those who went about for the purpose), and I am well assured that they do not amount to above one third of the inhabitants of this city (not to mention the counties, who have an undoubted right to give their voices upon this very interesting and important subject)."[69]

During this contest, "A Citizen" produced a pointed defense of open, egalitarian procedures in a politicized consumer marketplace. To appreciate fully his contribution to the liberal discourse, we must remember that A Citizen was discussing civic responsibility within a commercial public sphere of quite recent invention—in other words, within a popular political arena that was just beginning to express itself apart from traditional institutions of governance. The merchant canvass of New York brought theory into contact with events, helping ordinary men and women better to appreciate the interdependence of liberty and commerce. "Will it excuse this City to the rest of the World," A Citizen asked, "if it should appear that a Majority of the Inhabitants concurred in desiring to break thro' the [nonimportation] Agreement?" He argued through interrogation, with hard questions leading to harder ones until the logic of the performance seemed irrefutable. "Supposing there is a Majority, (which is not admitted)," he inquired of the merchants,

was it fairly and properly obtained? Was that Opinion given and subscribed with due Deliberation, Knowledge and Freedom? Or were not a very considerable Number of the Subscribers, influenced and determined, by your Persuasions and Representations, or by submitting their Opinions to be guided by your Advice and superior Judgment? Can opinions so given and obtained, properly be called the Voice of the People, or given a Sanction to the Dissolution of an Agreement of such immense Weight and Importance?[70]

The breaking of the New York boycott in 1770 came to a curious conclusion that prefigured America's eventual separation from Great Britain. As in the larger imperial contest, the failure of local authorities to expand representation, to listen to a newly empowered "Voice of the People," ended in violence. When "Gentlemen" sought to rationalize the resumption of trade, they were confronted by a group of forty or fifty people who gathered at the "house of Mr. Jasper Drake, inn-keeper." The *New-York Mercury* reported that "they erected a flag, as a signal of the place appointed for their rendezvous, and after carousing and drinking very plentifully . . . they sallied out in the evening, . . . carrying with them music, colours and staffs, upon which were labels fixed with the inscription of, *Liberty and Non-importation.*" The mob marched through the streets "crying out, *No Importation.*" The leading merchants and their allies could not endure the provocation. The popular protest ended when "a Number of principal People . . . applied to an Alderman to go and stop those People, and take the Flag from them, upon which the Alderman headed a considerable Number with Canes and Clubs, and attempted to take their Colours, upon which a Scuffle ensued, and a few got hurt."[71]

Americans of different backgrounds and regions regularly insisted that without "virtue" their cause had no chance whatsoever. Virtue was the social glue that kept the newly formed liberal communities from fragmenting. Colonists who signed the subscriptions, supported the boycotts of British goods and marched the streets carrying banners proclaiming "Liberty and Non-Importation" assumed that their protests mobilized virtuous people.

Eighteenth-century virtue claims two distinguished genealogies. J. G. A Pocock traces it back to the Florentine world of Niccolò Machiavelli, arguing that the virtuous citizen was a man whose landed wealth enabled him to rise above the corrupting influences of commerce and thereby preserve the purity of republican government.[72] Such historians as Edmund S. Morgan associate eighteenth-century virtue with the so-called Protestant Ethic.[73] While both positions possess merit—indeed, political discourse on the eve of the Revolution seems to have drawn on both traditions—the virtue that resonated through the entire boycott movement was closer to what T. A. Horne provocatively labels "bourgeois virtue."[74]

When advocates of nonimportation spoke of virtue, they referred primarily to a personal attribute. A virtuous man or woman was one who voluntarily exercised self-restraint in the consumer marketplace. Such behavior represented a sacrifice. No one denied the desirability of the new manufactured items. But however appealing the British imports were, the virtuous person exercised self-control for the common good. It was in this spirit that the delegates to a New Haven boycott meeting in 1770 declared that "the non-importation agreement come into by the colonies in general, and by this in particular . . . were founded on free, virtuous, peaceable, manly and patriotic principles."[75] In *A Sermon on Tea*, published in Lancaster, Pennsylvania, an anonymous author argued that "if we have virtue enough to disuse every commodity on which they lay a tax," Parliament will soon tire "of cultivating the barren tree that produces no fruit."[76] And "Juris Prudens," writing in the *New-York Mercury*, urged all Americans: "let us import no Goods whatsoever from Great-Britain, and we shall be crowned Virtuous; we shall be free forever."[77]

This rather straightforward sense of market virtue that developed throughout the colonies before Independence had important implications for political mobilization. Anyone who regularly purchased manufactured goods from Great Britain could become virtuous simply by controlling consumption. The concept thus linked everyday experience and behavior with a broadly shared sense of the common good. What one did with one's money mattered very much to the entire community, for in this highly charged atmosphere, economic self-indulgence became a glaring public vice. Unlike Cincinnatus, the bourgeois patriot did not reach immediately for the sword. He first examined the household budget. "I laugh at a man that talks of facing cannon and red coats," explained a Boston writer in 1767, "who cannot conquer his foppish empty notions of grandeur. What is true grandeur, but a noble patriotic resolution of sacrificing every other consideration to the Love of our Country! And can he be a true lover of his country . . . who would sooner be seen strutting about the streets, clad in foreign fripperies, than to be nobly independent in russet grey!"[78] The *Boston Gazette* translated market virtue into a direct call to action: "Save your Money and you save your Country."[79] Wherever they lived, bourgeois Americans would instruct their "children . . . to practise verture and industry with good economy, which will naturally supply the individuals . . . with abundance, and enable them to improve in all kinds of learning and science and render them useful, respectable and independent."[80]

For all their insistence on voluntarism, the proponents of nonimportation developed a potentially coercive understanding of political obligation. To be sure, the individual consumer could exercise his or her free will and ignore appeals from those who supported the boycotts. But one thereby surrendered one's right to blame others for the destruction of political liberty. Membership in a commercial society implied responsibilities to the larger collectivity. As "Pro Aris Et Focis" wrote in 1769, "Our merchants have done worthily; but it is the body of the people, who must under GOD, finally save us. For while there are debauched consumers of foreign luxuries, there always will be, in this depraved state, mercenary creatures enough to import the *bane of their country*." The writer refused to let the vicious consumer sit complacently. Victory over Parliament required "the virtue of the people," all of them. "Nay, my fellowmen," warned Pro Aris, painting a vivid commercial portrait:

the servile emissaries and wicked minions of your inveterate foes have insultingly prophesied and blazed it abroad . . . that the mercantile endeavours would prove utterly abortive;—that no dependence was to be had upon the virtuous stability of the generality among us;—that the common people, or, as they distainfully term it, the herd, were sunk in luxury, intemperate and degrading vice;—and that hence, any *commercial plan* of political salvation would prove, only, an amusing dream—a transitory phantom.[81]

Within the framework of bourgeois virtue, organizers of local boycotts and subscription drives created a new political abstraction that would be of great significance in the coming of the American Revolution. The nonimportation movement constructed a "public," an imagined body of people who demonstrated virtue by renouncing British goods and thus earned the right to judge the behavior of the less virtuous. In the American colonies this may have been as close as people came to creating what Jürgen Habermas calls the "public sphere." For him, this imagined space was an arena in which intellectuals—writers who published largely in the pages of the newly founded urban journals of the eighteenth century—criticized the absolutist state. These independent critics addressed a growing audience of literate men and women in the name of the public. The public—an abstract body that never actually assembled—was composed of reasonable persons, individuals open to liberal argument and hostile to the arbitrary exercise of power.[82]

Despite charges of political oppression, Americans never really confronted absolutist authority—at any rate, nothing on the order of the ancien régime in France and Germany. British colonial government was notoriously weak. In this social and political setting American authors defined what was essentially a commercial public sphere. In newspapers and pamphlets, popular writers assumed separate, though entirely complementary voices. They spoke *for* as well as *to* a reasoning and virtuous public. The bourgeois audience invented by the commercial press was especially skilled at spotting fraudulent patriots. As a South Carolinian explained in 1770, "the non-Importers had long been endeavouring to discover who were true, and who Traitors to the Cause of American liberty, which nothing could so effectually discover as the present Measure: But, since the Sons of Liberty have got all their Names, and every Man who before wore a Mask, now appears with an uncovered Face, they begin to be not a little uneasy."[83]

When vicious consumers were caught with British manufactured goods, it was bourgeois virtue that held them accountable, often demanding full confession and restitution. A New York City merchant, Alexander Robertson, who violated the boycott, had to publish a broadside addressed specifically "To the PUBLICK." A chastened Robertson stated, "As I have justly incurred the Resentment of my Fellow Citizens, from my Behaviour, as set forth in an Advertisement, *of great Importance to the Publick*, assuring them that I am truly sorry for the Part I have acted; declared and promise that I never will again attempt an Act contrary to the true Interest and Resolutions of the People zealous in the Cause of *Virtue* and *Liberty*." He closed with a pathetic appeal to "the Publick in general to believe me."[84]

Such local conversations—however painful for the likes of Robertson—encouraged virtuous consumers to imagine even larger collectivities. The process was slow, halting, punctuated by self-doubt and mutual recrimination, but during the run-up to Independence, Americans living in scattered communities managed to reach out convincingly to distant strangers, to persons not directly known but assumed to share in the development of a new consumer marketplace. The initial boycott experiments of the 1760s persuaded the colonists of the need for broader, more effective alliances. They learned about each other through the weekly newspapers that were themselves both a product and a voice of expanding commerce.[85]

Often the imaginative spark arrived in the form of an invitation. The committees and associations—the local groups that presumed to speak for the public—received requests from other committees appealing for support. The "Gentlemen, Friends, and Fellow Citizens" of Philadelphia were called together in 1768 "to give your Advice and Opinion, what answer shall be returned to our Brethren of *Boston & N. York*, who desire to know whether we will unite with them, in stopping the Importation of Goods from *Great-*

Britain."[86] By voting in the affirmative, the nonimporters of Philadelphia expressed their trust in those about whom they knew very little. Soon after the New Englanders learned that Philadelphians and southerners had joined the boycott, the *Boston Gazette* announced excitedly, "We become one DETER-MINED PEOPLE: to pursue Industry and Oeconomy, and encourage our own Manufactures."[87]

Even as they condemned the perfidy of fallen boycotters living in other parts of America, colonists measured their own performance against that of distant strangers. In other words, bitter complaints and charges of betrayal were aspects of an imaginative process that was slowly forcing the colonists to think of themselves as Americans. The broader comparative perspective was apparent when the nonimporters of Philadelphia announced that almost no one else in America could equal their own exemplary virtue in the consumer marketplace. A 1770 broadside published in the City of Brotherly Love seemed intent on demonstrating the existence of a kind of negative union:

> Do not the Importers in that province [Maryland] expect the same quantities this Fall? Have not the Eastern-Governments most shamefully imported, notwithstanding their solemn declarations and resolves? Does not the conduct of the Bostonians sufficiently prove their perfidy, by re-shipping trunks and cases filled with rubbish, after gutting them of their British contents? In what manner have New-York and Rhode-Island behaved? Has Virginia ever entered into any agreement? Are not all the ports to the southward of South-Carolina open?[88]

Although defections angered the champions of liberty and nonimportation, we can appreciate that even in moments of extreme disappointment strangers scattered throughout the provinces had begun to situate themselves within a larger commercial and political union. To describe this mental process as incipient nationalism would suggest that we are anticipating independence long before the colonists did. The claim is rather that even when Americans most feared political fragmentation, they imagined themselves within a commercial and liberal discourse capable of sustaining self-conscious nationalism.[89]

New York's desertion in 1770 was such a moment. Residents of other colonies took the stunning decision to resume trade with Britain as a gratuitous insult to the "cause of American Liberty." A powerful continental association of virtuous consumers had been within reach, but at the instant of patriotic triumph the New York traders compromised "the union of the colonies."[90] Betrayal required explanation. "Why should [New Yorkers]," a South Carolinian asked, "endeavour to weaken that Phalanx which they were so eager to form?" Had they forgotten that patriotism involved acting "in mutual concert, for the good of the whole?" The New Yorkers had shown themselves lacking the necessary bourgeois virtue. According to one colonial newspaper, "The Common Cause of America [has] been most basely and traitorously deserted by a Number of Merchants, Traders, and others, of the City of New-

York . . . at a Time, when the Eyes of all the Colonies were more particularly fixed upon them: when their Virtue, to resist every Temptation, and to defeat every attempt of a prevailing Faction, was, relied on." The New Yorkers had certainly demonstrated themselves unworthy of alliance with "the virtuous people of PENNSYLVANIA [who had] received a cordial invitation to import, and . . . treated it just as it deserved."[91]

The collapse of nonimportation in 1770 left Americans in a sour mood. As they assessed the failure to wean themselves from British goods, they momentarily doubted their moral ability to create a truly virtuous state. Their self-deprecatory statements during this period seem to echo the anticommercial rhetoric of republican discourse, persuading some modern historians, at least, that preindustrial capitalism and the public good were in fact incompatible. What, inquired one newspaper essay, can the colonists learn from recent defection from the boycott?

That self-interest is irresistible.

That liberty and public good can stand no chance among men when self-interest is its rival.

That self-interest recommends the most underhanded schemes to every man's good conscience.[92]

"Cato" of New York agreed. "The late Conduct of the Merchants of New-York, Philadelphia, &c.," he explained, "sufficiently proves, that no Dependence is to be had upon any Combination or Agreement that can be entered into for the public Good, however well calculated to answer that End—*if it interfers with the private immediate Interest of Individuals.*"[93]

Such statements—and they were common—should not be interpreted as evidence that Americans rejected either preindustrial capitalism or the consumer marketplace. The renunciation of excess in the market made sense only in a society that took consumption for granted. The challenge for Revolutionary Americans was to negotiate between extreme self-indulgence and primitive simplicity. It involved mediation, not repudiation. As Max Weber explained in *The Protestant Ethic and the Spirit of Capitalism*, capitalism is not synonymous with greed. In fact, "capitalism *may* even be identical with the restraint, or at least a rational tempering, of this irrational impulse."[94]

In any case, the cries of the pessimists were unfounded. They misread the commercial changes sweeping American society and therefore underestimated the capacity of men and women to translate individual market behavior into mass political protest. The delegates to the First Continental Congress did not make that mistake. They appreciated the centrality of consumption in mobilizing persons of different regions and social backgrounds. On October 20, 1774, Congress authorized the Association, a broad network of local elected committees entrusted with the total enforcement of nonimportation. These bodies became in effect, "committees of public safety." At the moment of decision about ultimate political loyalties, the colonists' friends and neighbors were busy monitoring commercial behavior and enforcing bourgeois virtue in the name of the common good.[95] "We need only fight our Own selves," announced "A Carolinian" in 1774, "suppress for a while our Luxury and Corruption, and wield the Arms of Self Denial in our own Houses, to obtain the Victory. . . . And the Man who would not refuse himself a fine Coat, to save his Country, deserves to be hanged."[96]

We have traced a complex flow of ideas into actions, of shared assumptions about a commercial empire into forms of political resistance. This was most certainly not the only route from experience and ideology to revolution. Other, more celebrated political discourses helped Americans make sense out of rapidly changing social and economic conditions within the British empire. In this particular exploration, however, we have reconstituted a frame of reference that defined itself around participation in a newly established consumer marketplace. This focus powerfully illuminates how the great shaping forces of history—commercial capitalism, for example—impinged on the lives of ordinary men and women, compelling them to reimagine themselves within a larger polity. For consuming Americans, the mental process had unintended results: the creation of political instruments open to persons of "all ranks," the development of a concept of virtue that included any man or woman capable of economic self-restraint, and the formation of new interpretive communities based on shared, secular interests.

Notes

1. Gordon S. Wood, "Conspiracy and the Paranoid Style: Causality and Deceit in the Eighteenth Century," *William and Mary Quarterly*, 3d Ser., XXXIX (1982), 401–441; Bernard Bailyn, ed., *Pamphlets of the American Revolution, 1750–1776*, 1 (Cambridge, Mass., 1965), 20–90; James H. Hutson, "The Origins of The Paranoid Style in American Politics': Public Jealousy from the Age of Walpole to the Age of Jackson," in David D. Hall, John M. Murrin, and Thad W. Tate, eds., *Saints and Revolutionaries: Essays on Early American History* (New York, 1984), 332–372.

2. Hopkins, *The Rights of Colonies Examined* (Providence, R. I., 1765), in Bailyn, ed., *Pamphlets*, 512.

3. *Boston News-Letter*, Sept. 2, 1762.

4. This essay renders problematic accepted chronologies of the American Revolution, especially the temporal relation between causes and effects. I argue that colonists were exploring the radical political dimensions of a commercial discourse before they achieved Independence from Great Britain. Implicit in that interpretative move is the suggestion that the Revolution in itself cannot fully explain late 18th-century radical thought. For a masterly, although quite different, account of these materials see Wood, *The Radicalism of the American Revolution* (New York, 1992).

5. *Considerations Upon the Act of Parliament* . . . (Boston, 1764), 22. In his *The History of the Late Province of New-York*, 2 vols. (New York, 1829), I, 277, originally drafted in 1762, William Smith confirmed what British military officers had suspected: "Every man of industry and integrity has it in his power to live well, and many are the instances of persons who came here distressed by their poverty, who now enjoy easy and plentiful fortunes."

6. [Dickinson], *The Late Regulations, Respecting the British Colonies on the Continent*

of America Considered (Philadelphia, 1765), 23–24. The scholarly Dickinson footnoted his version of the narrative of commerce, citing Malachy Postlethwayt, *Universal Dictionary of Trade and Commerce* (London, 1766), who claimed that since Sir Walter Ralegh's time, English writers "have found an interest in *misrepresenting* or lessening the value" of the American colonies. During the 18th century, however, hostile commentators began alleging the Americans "were not *useful enough* to their mother country; that while we were loaded with taxes, they were absolutely free; that the *planters* lived like *princes,* while the inhabitants of England labored hard for a tolerable subsistence" ([Dickinson], *Late Regulations,* 23). To this, he added that especially heavy duties on Chesapeake tobacco in Great Britain were part of a "design to bring down the pride of these PRINCELY PLANTERS" (ibid., 23–24).

7. *The Power and Grandeur of Great-Britain, Founded on the Liberty of the Colonies, and the Mischiefs Attending the Taxing of Them* (New York, 1768), 5.

8. Ibid., 7–8.

9. [William Hicks], *The Nature and Extent of Parliamentary Power Considered ...* (Philadelphia, 1768), 18–20.

10. *New-London Gazette,* Jan. 20, 1769.

11. *Boston Evening-Post,* Jan. 2, 1769.

12. *Connecticut Journal, and New-Haven Post-Boy,* Oct. 11, 1771.

13. Ebenezer Baldwin, "An Appendix, Stating the Heavy Grievances the Colonies Labour Under ... ," in Samuel Sherwood, *A Sermon, Containing Scriptural Instructions to Civil Rulers* (New Haven, Conn., 1774), 50–51.

14. *New-York Gazette and Weekly Mercury,* July 4, 1774, repr. from *Pennsylvania Packet,* June 27, 1774.

15. David Ramsay, *The History of the American Revolution,* 2 vols. (Indianapolis, Ind., 1990; orig. pub. Philadelphia, 1789), I, 51.

16. Bailyn, *The Ideological Origins of the American Revolution* (Cambridge, Mass., 1967), vi.

17. J. G. A. Pocock, *The Machiavellian Moment: Florentine Political Thought and the Atlantic Republican Tradition* (Princeton, N.J., 1975), and "Virtue and Commerce in the Eighteenth Century," *Journal of Interdisciplinary History,* III (1972–1973), 119–134; Wood, *The Creation of the American Republic, 1776–1787* (Chapel Hill, N.C., 1969). For a useful review of the historiographic debate see *"The Creation of the American Republic, 1776–1787:* A Symposium of Views and Reviews," *WMQ,* 3d Ser., XLIV (1987), 549–640.

18. *Cato's Letters: or, Essays on Liberty, Civil and religious ... ,* 4 vols. (London, 1720), a collection of essays by the English writers Trenchard and Gordon, has become a virtual proof text for interpretations of early 18th-century American political ideology. Recent claims about the authors' anticommercial bias and their high republicanism cannot survive a close reading of their work. Trenchard and Gordon owed much to the insights of John Locke and, like many other political commentators of this period, were troubled by the excesses of commercial capitalism, not by capitalism itself. For an excellent discussion of a problematic republican canon see Ronald Hamowy, "Cato's Letters, John Locke, and the Republican Paradigm," *History of Political Thought,* XI (1990), 273–294. For the enthusiastic reception of "Cato's Letters" in America see Bailyn, *The Origins of American Politics* (New York, 1968), 3–58.

19. Appleby, *Capitalism and a New Social Order: The Republican Vision of the 1790s* (New York, 1984), and *Liberalism and Republicanism in the Historical Imagination* (Cambridge, Mass., 1992); Kramnick, *Republicanism and Bourgeois Radicalism: Political Ideology in Late Eighteenth-Century England and America* (Ithaca, N. Y., 1990). The most thoughtful review of pre-Revolutionary political thought remains James T. Kloppenberg, "The Virtues of Liberalism: Christianity, Republicanism, and Ethics in Early American Political Discourse," *Journal of American History,* LXXIV (1987), 9–33. Also useful are Pauline Maier, "The Transforming Impact of Independence, Reaffirmed: 1776 and the Defi-

nition of American Social Structure," in James A. Henretta et al., eds., *The Transformation of Early American History: Society, Authority, and Ideology* (New York, 1991), 194–217, and James Oakes, "From Republicanism to Liberalism: Ideological Change and the Crisis of the Old South," *American Quarterly*, XXXVII (1985), 568–569. For a splendid statement that may serve to end the increasingly arid debate over republicanism in American thought see Daniel T. Rodgers, "Republicanism: The Career of a Concept," *JAH*, LXXIX (1992), 11–38.

20. In an effort to reconstruct a popular political ideology on the eve of the Revolution, I have examined all the major colonial newspapers of this period as well as the familiar pamphlet and sermonic literature. I do not suggest that what lawyers, clergymen, and planters had to say about theories of governance was not important. Obviously, such figures played central roles in defining the continuing public debate. The weekly newspapers, however, reached a wider audience, and if they failed to entertain and enlighten their readers, they went out of business. The speed with which ideas were taken up, discussed, and frequently rejected in these journals was much faster than that of the pamphlets.

21. On the profound, although generally overlooked, philosophic implications of such interpretive fragmentation see David Harvey, *The Condition of Postmodernity: An Enquiry into the Origins of Cultural Change* (London, 1989), 113–118, and "Class Relations, Social Justice, and the Politics of Difference," paper delivered to Wissenschaftliche Jahrestagung der Deutschen Gesellschaft für Amerikastudien, Berlin, Germany, June 12, 1992.

22. Mayhew, *The Snare Broken. A Thanksgiving-Discourse* . . . (Boston, 1766), in Ellis Sandoz, ed., *Political Sermons of the American Founding Era, 1730–1805* (Indianapolis, Ind., 1991), 233–264, quotations on 239.

23. See Charles M. Andrews, *The Colonial Background of the American Revolution: Four Essays in American Colonial History* (New Haven, Conn., 1924), Jack P. Greene, *Peripheries and Center: Constitutional Development in the Extended Polities of the British Empire and the United States, 1607–1788* (Athens, Ga., 1986), and Richard L. Bushman, *King and People in Provincial Massachusetts* (Chapel Hill, N. C., 1985).

24. *Power and Grandeur of Great-Britain*, 3–4.

25. P. J. Marshall, "The British Empire in the Age of the American Revolution: Problems of Interpretation," in William M. Fowler, Jr., and Wallace Coyle, eds., *The American Revolution: Changing Perspectives* (Boston, 1979), 195–198.

26. *Conn. Journal*, Feb. 2, 1770. See also *Considerations upon the Act of Parliament* . . . (Boston, 1764).

27. *Boston Evening-Post*, Jan. 2, 1764. On this theme see *New-London Gaz.*, Dec. 16, 1763, *Boston News-Letter*, Sept. 2, 1762, and *Observations on Several Acts of Parliament* (Boston, 1769).

28. *Four Dissertations, on the Reciprocal Advantages of a Perpetual Union Between Great-Britain and Her American Colonies. Written for Mr. Sargent's Prize-Metal* (Philadelphia, 1766), 55–71.

29. *The Proceedings of the [Non-Importation Association] Committee Appointed to Examine into the Importation of Goods* . . . *from London* (Annapolis, Md., 1770), i–iii.

30. [Thomas Fitch], *Reasons Why The British Colonies in America, Should Not be Charged with Internal Taxes* . . . (New Haven, Conn., 1764), 21.

31. [Oxenbridge Thacher], *The Sentiments of a British American* (Boston, 1764), 13.

32. The most valuable summary of these mid-century economic developments is Neil McKendrick et al., *The Birth of a Consumer Society: The Commercialization of Eighteenth-Century England* (Bloomington, Ind., 1985). See also Roy Porter, *English Society in the Eighteenth Century* (London, 1982), 201–268, Paul Langford, *A Police and Commercial People: England, 1727–1783* (Oxford, 1989), 59–122, 461–518, and Carole Shammas, "How Self-Sufficient Was Early America?" *J. Interdis. Hist.*, XIII (1982–1983), 247–272. I have discussed these topics in greater detail in "An Empire of Goods: The Anglicization of Colonial America, 1690–1776," *Journal of British Studies*, XXV (1986), 467–499, and in

"The Meaning of 'Likeness': Portrait Painting in an Eighteenth-Century Consumer Society," *Word and Image*, VI (1990), 325–350.

33. Smith, *History of . . . New-York*, 277. See also "Autobiography of John Barnard," Massachusetts Historical Society, III, *Collections*, V (1986), 239–240, *Boston Evening-Post*, June 11, 1753, and *Power and Grandeur*, 5–6.

34. *Boston Gazette and Country Journal*, Aug. 28, 1769.

35. Shammas, *The Pre-Industrial Consumer in England and America* (Oxford, 1990); Lorena S. Walsh et al., "Toward a History of the Standard of Living in British North America," *WMQ*, 3d Ser., XLV (1988), 116–170; Jacob M. Price, "What Did Merchants Do? Reflections on British Overseas Trade, 1660–1790," *Journal of Economic History*, XLIX (1989), 267–284; Ralph Davis, "English Foreign Trade, 1700–1774," *Economic History Review*, 2d Ser., XV (1962), 285–303; and John J. McCusker and Russell R. Menard, *The Economy of British America, 1607–1789* (Chapel Hill, N. C., 1985), 277–294.

36. T. H. Breen, "The Meaning of Things: Consumption and Ideology in the Eighteenth Century," in John Brewer and Roy Porter, eds., *Consumption, Culture, and Society* (London, 1993), 249–259.

37. For the comparative dimensions of 18th-century commercial capitalism see the many excellent essays in Istvan Hont and Michael Ignatieff, eds., *Wealth and Virtue: The Shaping of Political Economy in the Scottish Enlightenment* (Cambridge, 1983). See also R. F. Foster, *Modern Ireland, 1600–1972* (London, 1988), 167–225; Declan O'Donovan, "The Money Bill Dispute of 1753," in Thomas Bartlett and D. W. Hayton, eds., *Penal Era and Golden Age: Essays in Irish History, 1690–1800* (Belfast, 1979), 55–87; Colin Jones, "Bourgeois Revolution Revivified: 1789 and Social Change," in Colin Lucas, ed., *Rewriting the French Revolution* (Oxford, 1991), 78–96; and Simon Schama, *The Embarrassment of Riches: An Interpretation of Dutch Culture in the Golden Age* (New York, 1987).

38. Shammas, "How Self-Sufficient Was Early America?" 247–272; McCusker and Menard, *Economy of British America*, 277–294; James T. Lemon, "Spatial Order: Households in Local Communities and Regions," in Jack P. Greene and J. R. Pole, eds., *Colonial British America: Essays in the New History of the Early Modern Era* (Baltimore, 1984), 86–122.

39. *Boston Gaz.*, Dec. 28, 1761. Unlike most of his contemporaries, Otis signed his newspaper essays. The best biography of Otis is John J. Waters, Jr., *The Otis Family in Provincial and Revolutionary Massachusetts* (Chapel Hill, N. C., 1968). There is a great need for a careful reexamination of Otis's political thought.

40. *Boston Evening-Post*, Dec. 7, 1767. See also ibid., Dec. 28, 1767.

41. Breen, " 'Baubles of Britain,' " 73–104.

42. Arthur Meier Schlesinger, *The Colonial Merchants and the American Revolution, 1763–1776*, Columbia University Studies in History, Economics, and Public Law, LXXVII, No. 182 (New York, 1918); Andrews, "The Boston Merchants and the Non-Importation Movement," *Transactions of the Colonial Society of Massachusetts*, XIX (1916–1917), 182–191; Edmund S. Morgan, "The Puritan Ethic and the American Revolution," *WMQ*, 3d Ser., XXIV (1967), 3–43; J. E. Crowley, *This Sheba, Self: The Conceptualization of Economic Life in Eighteenth-Century America* (Baltimore, 1974), 125–146; Gary B. Nash, *The Urban Crucible: Social Change, Political Consciousness, and the Origins of the American Revolution* (Cambridge, Mass., 1979), 321–378.

43. *The Following Address Was Read At A Meeting of the Merchants . . . , 25th of April, 1768* (Philadelphia, 1768).

44. [Dickinson], *Late Regulations*, 31.

45. [Thacher], *Sentiments of a British American*, 15.

46. *South-Carolina Gazette*, Oct. 26, 1769.

47. *Boston Chronicle*, Feb. 13, 1769.

48. See Judith N. Shklar, *American Citizenship: The Quest for Inclusion* (Cambridge, Mass., 1991).

49. *Pennsylvania Chronicle, and Universal Advertiser*, May 14, 1770.

50. *Debtor and Creditor, or A Discourse on the Following Words, Have Patience With Me, and I Will Pay Thee All* (Boston, 1762).

51. Breen, "An Empire of Goods," 467–499.

52. *New-York Mercury*; Sept. 10, 1770.

53. *Boston Evening-Post*; Nov. 2, 1767.

54. *S.-C. Gaz.*, Dec. 6, 1773.

55. *Boston Evening-Post*, Nov. 9, 23, Dec. 7, 1767.

56. *S.-C. Gaz.*, June 29, 1769.

57. *Maryland Gazette*, May 11, 1769. See Robert A. Gross, *The Minutemen and Their World* (New York, 1976), 49–52.

58. *Boston Gaz.*, Nov. 30, 1767; [Broadside], *Annapolis, May 23, 1769* (Annapolis, Md., 1769).

59. *S.-C. Gaz.*, [Supplement], Aug. 20, 1770.

60. *Boston Gaz.*, Feb. 5, 12, 19, 26, 26 [Supplement], 1770.

61. Ibid., Feb. 12, 1770.

62. *S.-C. Gaz.*, Sept. 19, 1774. For a misogynist critique of these organizing efforts see *Boston Evening-Post*, Feb. 7, 1774. See also Linda K. Kerber, *Women of the Republic: Intellect and Ideology in Revolutionary America* (Chapel Hill, N. C., 1980), 37–41; Laurel Thatcher Ulrich, " 'Daughters of Liberty': Religious Women in Revolutionary New England," in Ronald Hoffman and Peter J. Albert, eds., *Women in the Age of the American Revolution* (Charlottesville, Va., 1989), 211–243; Joan B. Landes, *Women and the Public Sphere in the Age of the French Revolution* (Ithaca, N. Y., 1988); and Breen, "Liberalism and Luxury: Eighteenth-Century American Women in a Revolutionary Political Discourse," Society of the Cincinnati Annual Lecture, Virginia Polytechnic Institute and State University, Apr. 20, 1992.

63. *Peter Oliver's Origin and Progress of the American Revolution: A Tory View*, ed. Douglass Adair and John A. Schutz (Stanford, Calif., 1961), 61.

64. On the "contagion of liberty" see Bailyn, *Ideological Origins*, 230–319.

65. *Pa. Chronicle*, June 4, 1770.

66. [Broadside], *To the Free and Loyal Inhabitants of the City and Colony of New-York . . .* (New York, 1774).

67. Ibid.

68. *N.-Y. Mercury*, Aug. 6, 1770. See also *New York or General Journal; The Advertiser*, Aug. 2, 1770.

69. *N. Y. or General Journal*, June 21, 1770.

70. Ibid.

71. Ibid., Sept. 27, 1770; *N.-Y. Mercury*, July 23, 1770; *New-London Gaz.*, July 20, 1770.

72. Pocock, *Machiavellian Moment*, 462–552.

73. Morgan, "Puritan Ethic," 3–43.

74. T. A. Horne, "Bourgeois Virtue, Property, and Moral Philosophy in America, 1750–1800," *Hist. Pol. Thought*, IV (1983), 317–340. See also Jeffrey C. Isaac, "Republicanism Vs. Liberalism? A Reconsideration," ibid., XI (1988), 349–377, and Kramnick, *Republicanism*, 260–288.

75. *N.-Y. Mercury*, Sept. 24, 1770.

76. (Lancaster, Pa., 1774).

77. *N.-Y. Mercury*, Aug. 6, 1770. See also *New-London Gaz.*, Nov. 2, 1770.

78. *Boston Evening-Post*, Dec. 7, 1767.

79. *Boston Gaz.*, Nov. 9, 1767.

80. *Conn. Journal*, Oct. 11, 1771.

81. *Boston Gaz.*, Sept. 11, 1769.

82. Habermas, *The Structural Transformation of the Public Sphere: An Inquiry into a Category of Bourgeois Society*, trans. Thomas Burger (Cambridge, Mass., 1989), 1–88. See

also Michael Warner, *The Letters of the Republic: Publication and the Public Sphere in Eighteenth-Century America* (Cambridge, Mass., 1990).

83. *S.-C. Gaz.*, [supplement], Aug. 20, 1770.

84. Robertson, *New-York, June 23, 1769. To the publick* (New York, 1769).

85. See Benedict Anderson, *Imagined Communities: Reflections on the Origin and Spread of Nationalism* (London, 1983), 80–148.

86. *The Following Address Was Read at a Meeting of the Merchants.*

87. *Boston Gaz.*, Nov. 23, 1767.

88. [Broadside], *To the Freeholders, Merchants, Tradesmen and Farmers, of the City and County of Philad.* (Philadelphia, 1770).

89. Breen, "A Ploughjogger's Complaint: Ideology and Nationalism in Anglo-American Context, 1740–1790," paper given at the annual meeting of the American Historical Association, Washington, D. C., Dec. 29, 1992. See also Anderson, *Imagined Communities*; Liah Greenfeld, *Nationalism: Five Roads to Modernity* (Cambridge, Mass., 1992), 397–484; Linda Colley, *Britons: Forging the Nation, 1707–1837* (New Haven, Conn., 1992); and Gerald Newman, *The Rise of English Nationalism: A Cultural History, 1740–1830* (New York, 1987).

90. *New-York Journal; or the General Advertiser*, Sept. 20, 1770.

91. *N.-Y. Mercury*, Sept. 24, 1770; *S.-C. Gaz.*, Aug. 14, 1770; *Connecticut Courant*, Sept. 10, 1770; *New-London Gaz.*, Oct. 5, 1770; *Massachusetts Spy*, Sept. 29, 1770.

92. *Conn. Courant*, Jan. 8, 1771.

93. *N.-Y. Journal*, Sept. 27, 1770; *New-London Gaz.*, Oct. 5, 1770.

94. Weber, *The Protestant Ethic and the Spirit of Capitalism*, trans. Talcott Parsons (New York, 1958), 17. See also Ignatieff, *The Needs of Strangers* (London, 1984), esp. chaps. 3, 4; Isaac, "Republicanism vs. Liberalism," 349–377; David E. Shi, *The Simple Life: Plain Living and High Thinking in American Culture* (New York, 1985); and John Sekora, *Luxury: The Concept in Western Thought, Eden to Smollet* (Baltimore, 1977).

95. Breen, " 'Baubles of Britain'," 97–104; Jerrilyn Greene Marston, *King and Congress: The Transfer of Political Legitimacy, 1774–1776* (Princeton, N. J., 1987); David Ammerman, *In the Common Cause: The American Response to the Coercive Acts of 1774* (Charlottesville, Va., 1974).

96. *S.-C. Gaz.*, June 27, 1774.

CHAPTER 8

Consumption in Early Modern Social Thought

Joyce Appleby

My subject is consumption—the desiring, acquiring and enjoying of goods and services which one has purchased—and I will concentrate upon my historical predecessors' investigation of consumption, examining what they have said about these activities, but especially what they failed to say, for my search of relevant texts took me to a void, an emptiness—at best, a hiatus or lacuna. I can pose the puzzle of this silence in several ways: why is it that consumption has rarely been examined thoroughly or dispassionately despite its centrality to economic life? Why is consumption uniformly construed negatively even though there is abounding evidence that consuming is pleasurable and popular and brings rare moments of satisfaction? Why, in the floodtide of Enlightenment enthusiasms for freedom—free speech, free inquiry, free labour, free trade, free contract—was free consumption never articulated as a social goal? Or put another way, why has the opportunity to consume been made dependent morally upon the opportunity to produce, but functionally upon the opportunity to purchase? I can think of no other human predisposition so essential to economic growth which has been so perversely treated. Why is it, to put the question in more total terms, that consumption, which is the linchpin of our modern social system, has never been the linchpin of our theories explaining modernity?

These questions take us back to the initial efforts to understand the emerging commercial economy. English men and women in the middle of the seventeenth century did not know that they had crossed a barrier which divided them from their own past and from every other contemporary society. Yet they had. Somewhere around 1650 the English moved beyond the threat of famine. It is true that chronic malnutrition lingered on for the bottom 20 per cent of the population, not completely disappearing for another century, but famine was gone. In the future there would be food shortages, skyrocketing grain prices, distress and dearth, but never again would elevated grain prices go hand in hand with rising mortality rates. Agricultural productivity combined with the purchasing power to bring food from other places in times of shortage had eliminated one of the four horses of the apocalypse from England's shores. A powerful reason for maintaining strict social order had unobtrusively disappeared, leaving behind a set of social prescriptions whose obsolescence had to be discovered one by one in the course of the next two centuries. It would be hard to exaggerate the importance of freedom from famine just as it is exceedingly difficult to follow all of the ways this material circumstance influenced behaviour and belief.

A second feature I would draw your attention to was the population growth which started again in Europe in the middle decades of the eighteenth century. The world's population had expanded and contracted over three millennia, but with eighteenth-century population growth a vital revolution was in the making. Unlike the old accordian-like pattern that had characterized previous European population fluctuations, the increase in people this time laid a new basis for future growth with each augmented cohort forming a kind of springboard from which world population still continues to soar. Food supplies were to be severely strained but instead of shrinking they expanded to sustain new levels of population. The twenty million Frenchmen Louis XIV ruled in 1700 became the forty million Frenchmen who couldn't be wrong in 1914. English population grew at an even faster clip. And in England's North American colonies—that catch basin of surplus people from northwestern Europe—the number of people doubled every twenty-five to twenty-six years.

Even more remarkable, the goods that people wanted grew apace—grew even faster than the number of people. A peculiar dynamic of the emerging world commerce had revealed itself most strikingly in England's first colony, that fragile outpost of European life established by the Virginia Company on the far side of the Atlantic. This settlement was explicitly tied to plans for extracting and producing vendible commodities. In 1617 John Rolfe successfully hybridized a tobacco strain which could compete with the much-esteemed Spanish orinoco. His leaf triggered a boom. Throughout the 1620s tobacco fetched between 1½ and 3 shillings a pound, a price high enough to encourage Virginia Company shareholders to pour money and men (and a few women) into their plantations. Cultivation spread along the tidal rivers emptying into the Chesapeake Bay. The volume of exports surged. When the inevitable bust of oversupply followed this boom of demand-driven expansion, prices dropped to as low as a penny a pound—a twenty-fourth of the price of good Virginia tobacco in the 1620s. However, at this cheap price a whole new crowd of consumers could and did begin to buy tobacco, or as we would say metaphorically, entered the market. Their demand in turn created an incentive to cut production costs in order to supply this larger body of consumers with cheap tobacco at a profit. Success at this endeavour sustained a slower expansion of tobacco cultivation for two centuries. A similar thing happened in

1634 with Dutch bulbs, only to be repeated over and over again with cutlery, calicos, printed pictures, blankets, pottery, pewter and pepper.[1]

When ordinary people joined their social superiors in the pursuit of the pleasures of consumption, their numbers changed the character of the enterprise. Retrospectively we can see that this boom and bust cycle unintentionally widened the market for new goods. Investors responded to the profits of the boom; ordinary people to the opportunity of the bust. This dynamic enabled commerce—a feature of human society as old as the Bible—to move out of the interstices of a traditional social order and impose its imperatives upon the culture as a whole. The enormous augmentation in the volume of goods when ordinary people became consumers meant enormous augmentations in the wealth and power of those nations and persons who participated successfully in supplying the new tastes.

We are of course used to hearing the litany of new products entering European markets from the sixteenth century onwards—first from the fabled East India trade, then from the homely shops of ingenious artisans, finally to be overtaken by the prodigious outputs of the marvellous machines of the factory age. Rattling off the names of new condiments, textiles and inventions has served as the incantation for summoning the spirits that presided over the rise of the west. These details of early modern enterprise have supplied the factual grist for the mill of material progress.

Told within the familiar narrative of the liberation of *homo faber*, man the maker, modern history presents no problems. There are no ruptures in the telling, if not the living, of this age so long as the stunning and devastating transformation of the world wrought by the cumulative revolutions of technology and human adaptations appear as the end-point of a plan which has design and meaning. But we, alas, live in a post-industrial era. We can't conceive of our own time as a mere coda. We've known civilization and its discontents too long to subscribe to the notion that the discontents are epiphenomenal. We have even begun to entertain doubts about the inevitability of the events in our past. We've lost faith that these transformations were either natural or evolutionary. Significantly, these doubts have enabled us to hear other voices from the past—the crazies who preferred occult mysteries to the plain and simple truths of nature; the atavists who harkened back to ancient prudence. Tuning into these alternative voices has unchained our imagination. We can begin to see that our history told as the history of progress might have served as the intellectual equivalent of whistling through the graveyard.

What was profoundly unsettling, even shattering about the cumulative gains in material culture which became manifest by the eighteenth century was that they made it evident that human beings were the makers of their world. There is no way to underestimate the reverberations of such a discovery; they resonate through every modern discourse. And if we are post-modern it is because we can now reflect upon these discourses in science, politics and literature from a perspective standing outside the engagement itself. We see how Hobbes's irreverences become the ingenious truths of Scottish moral philosophers, to be transmogrified once more into the social science disciplines of the first half of the twentieth century.

Here I am reminded of a passage in Louis Dumont's *From Mandeville to Marx*. After detailing the western conception of society as the interactions of rational, utility-maximizing, self-improving, materialistic individuals, Dumont commented that this was a radically aberrant world view shared by no other culture. Rather than ask why other people were taking so long to become like us, he suggested, we should turn our curiosity around and ask how 'this unique development that we call modern occurred at all.'[2] There has been a punitive arrogance in the west's refusal to see its cultural differences as differences and to characterize them instead as the end-point in a universal process. This grand explanation robbed the events of the indeterminacy essential to historical narrative and hence obscured the dynamics of change at work.

A peculiarly intense form of curiosity in western culture drew the countries of western Europe along the path of innovation which grew ever wider as the pathbreakers pushed against a comparatively weak attachment to customary practices. On this broad avenue of human inventiveness Europeans encountered themselves as the creators of their own social universe. But this discovery took place while the actual social arrangements of their world reflected traditional assumptions about divine punishments, fallen human nature and the inherent frailty of civil society. How was social order to be maintained when collective understandings were being undermined by the new Promethean powers at large in the world?

Consumption—the active seeking of personal gratification through material goods—was the force that had to be reckoned with. Like other social activities, consumption had first to be named before it could be discussed. I want to look at four responses to this new phenomenon, four sequential engagements with the idea of abundance and its social consequences: the Restoration pamphleteers on trade who first took note of new patterns of spending; the Augustans' revival of classical wisdom about luxury; the Scottish intellectuals' reaction to the classically inspired laments about corruption and finally Malthus's mordant rebuff to the enthusiasts of the French Revolution.

The first observers of England's material abundance had no trouble discerning the human impulse animating the lively round of goods that encompassed Europe and its colonies in a new trade system. I'll quote from a few:

> The Wants of the Mind are infinite, Man naturally Aspires, and as his Mind is elevated, his Senses grow more refined, and more capable of Delight; his Desires are inlarged, and his Wants increase with his Wishes, which is for everything that is rare, can gratifie his Senses, adorn his Body and promote the Ease, Pleasure and Pomp of Life.

From another

> the main spur to Trade, or rather to Industry and Ingenuity, is the exorbitant Ap-
> petites of Men which they will take pains to gratifie, and so be disposed to work,
> when nothing else will incline them to it; for did Men content themselves with bare
> Necessaries, we should have a poor World.[3]

Research done within the last two decades has confirmed the assertions of contemporaries that it was domestic consumption, not foreign trade, that sustained England's manufacturing expansion in the eighteenth century.[4] Simon Schama has made a similar case for Dutch economic development in his *The Embarrassment of Riches*.[5] However, these early investigators of consumption, writing in the 1680s and 1690s, did not lay the foundation for a theory of commercial sociability. Rather, it was the critics of material abundance who seized the discursive high ground in England, appealing to classical republican texts to stigmatize novelty as the harbinger of social unrest. Using the essay form to inveigh against the new consuming tastes, these Augustan moralists read the goods they saw in haberdashery shops and food stalls as dangerous signs of corruption and degeneration. Against the delights of consumption, they pitted predictions of social disintegration. The only antidote: frugality and simple living for the people, austere civic virtue in their leaders. These alone could provide the social underpinnings for the Constitution, itself England's sole preserver from the terrors of history, that zone of irrational behaviour which made up the realm of *fortuna*.[6]

Consumption, as I have described it, figured in the political discourse of eighteenth-century England under the rubric of luxury. Luxury was not a thing, but a concept. As John Sekora has pointed out, the Greek view of luxury was a secular and rational complement to the Hebrew view. Luxury for the Hebrews represented a complex of evils moving from the personal and inveterate propensities of man to the ethical tendencies of the nation which collectively succumbs to temptation. The gravest feature of the repeated lapses recorded in the Old Testament was the evidence of disobedience. When a people ignore the law of necessity they undermine the established hierarchy between law-giver and subject. Necessity sets limits and happiness consists in having the rational capacity to abide by those restraints. Luxury brings disorder because it destroys harmony and prevents the human being from fulfilling his or her nature.

In both Christian and classical thought the central unworthiness of human beings stemmed from their desiring things that were unnecessary, that is from their desire to consume. The control of this endemic envy, vanity, gluttony and lust required draconian laws and God's redeeming grace. Essayists, political figures, novelists, journalists—all contributed to an unrelenting, unrelieved depiction of the horrors awaiting England if the nation did not mend its luxurious ways. Luxury was not a personal indulgence; it was a national calamity, as the account of the ravages of luxury offered in the books of Samuel and Kings so powerfully demonstrated.

Hebraic tradition, which gave English Puritans so rich a rhetorical resource for vivifying sin, identified luxury with desire and desire with disobedience. Eve indulged in luxury when she unnecessarily ate the fruit of the tree of knowledge. The Israelites persisted in the most serious of human errors in their yearnings for things that they did not need nor had the right to claim. If represented graphically luxury, of course, is a woman—sometimes a powerful evoker of desire carrying the comb and mirror of cupidity and self-love; at other times an abject naked woman under attack from toads and snakes.

Depicted as a constant psychological drive, the attraction to luxury can never be more than suppressed, and the act of suppressing it constitutes the reason and justification for the minute control of the status, duties and privileges of all members of society. When in the *Republic*, Glaucon asked why the state should not provide for the citizens' wants as well as their needs, Socrates describes the inevitable engorgement of people that would follow this abandonment of the limits of necessity:

> Now will the city have to fill and swell with a multitude of callings which are not required by any natural want; such as the whole tribe of actors, of whom one large class have to do with forms and colours; another will be votaries of music—poets and their attendant trains of rhapsodists, players, dancers, contactors; also makers of diverse kinds of articles, including women's dresses. And we shall want more servants. Will not tutors be also in request, and nurses wet and dry, tirewomen and barbers, as well as confectioners and cooks; and swineherds too.[7]

In other words Athens will be visited by economic development.

It fell to Aristotle to explain how authority and necessity were linked. I must say it's ingenious. As nature shows that the household is subject to the father so most persons must be subject to the dominion of the legislator. The rulers embody reason which teaches restraint and it is a sign of luxury for slaves, women, servants, tradesmen, artisans, mechanics, the immature, the illiterate and the weak to want what they do not not need. In restraining them, the male leaders are demonstrating reason for the whole. From such an Aristotelian conception of order came the sumptuary laws common in Europe which elaborated specific standards of decorum and decoration under the doctrine of 'consumption by estates'. It was their obligation to maintain order among the predictably disorderly that saved the land-owning elite of England from the sting of the criticism about its luxurious consumption. While technically as prone to sin as others, the elite supplied security to the whole society through its vigilance in controlling servants, young people and women—that trilogy of categorical unfitness. To incriminate the guardians was to weaken the only dyke against the floodtide of riotous consumption.

Both the sentiment and the metaphor are reflected in Henry Fielding's reference to a 'vast torrent of Luxury which of late Years hath poured itself into the nation . . . almost totally changed the Manners, Customs, and Habits of the People, more especially of the lower Sort'. A political evil, luxury has inspired in the poor, he went on to explain, a desire for things they may not and cannot have, hence their wickedness, profligacy, idleness and dishonesty. Daniel Defoe less dramatically spoke of the decline of the Great Law of Subordination.[8] Shops bulging with cheeses, sweetmeats, coffee, tea, table linens, dry goods, gadgets, pictures and prints gave the lie to Fielding's assertion that the lower sort desired things they could not have. It was exactly their increasing ability to buy what was being made available in ever cheaper forms that created the crisis of social leadership.

What Sekora so nicely captures is the way that the human desire for the sensual pleasures of eating, entertainment, adornment and comfort, made manifest in actual consumption, became evidence for the need for strictly enforced hierarchies of authority in the home, the shop, the street, the town hall and the church. However, the disjuncture between the jeremiads on luxury and the actually visible, even conspicuous, behaviour of ordinary people cried out for clarification. As Bernard de Mandeville had earlier pointed out, English moralists were not confronting the fact that they were preaching truths which, if followed, would bankrupt the nation and undermine its greatness. The private vices of personal indulgence, Mandeville warned, amounted to the public benefit of national prosperity. Vice, not virtue, stoked the engine of commerce. Mandeville's goal, however, was to point up the hypocrisy in the outcry against luxury, not to endorse the abandonment of society to the consuming impulses of the least discerning members of society.

Roy Porter, writing on the English Enlightenment, has pointed to the strain of eudemonism running through the century's public commentary. Indeed he has characterized the English Enlightenment by its mildness. Not forced to overthrow an oppressive old regime like their neighbours across the Channel, prosperous Englishmen settled down to enjoying the affability afforded them by urban life. Sipping coffee, displaying new forms of politeness, relishing the wit of Addison and Steele, Porter's 'affluent, articulate and ambitious' Londoners, along with their provincial imitators, bent their minds to considering ways to make the world safe for egoism. Because the English had dealt with political tyranny in a previous century, they could address the more fundamental modern problem—the one connected with a recognition that society is a human product—of how individuals could pursue life, liberty, wealth and happiness while maintaining the social solidarity and order agreed upon by all as essential.[9]

If the optimistic men of Porter's English Enlightenment preferred *belles lettres* to comprehensive philosophies, the same cannot be said for the Scotsmen—Adam Ferguson, Thomas Reid, John Millar, Dugald Stewart, David Hume and Adam Smith—who moved the discussions about luxury and egoism onto an entirely different plane.[10] Classical republicanism had taught that men—and it was just men and only men of independent means—realized their full human potential when they participated in civic affairs. Supported by a substructure of labouring men and all women, this idealized citizen realized moral autonomy because of his independence from the necessities imposed by nature and through the interaction of a community of peers. A highly artificial construct, classical citizenship elevated the citizen above the crass, mundane, earthy and vulgar, and tested his fitness by his capacity to be virtuous. Commerce reeked of all the proscribed qualities, linking men and women together in new systems of interdependence while trading on physical needs, worldly tastes, undisciplined wants and preposterous yearnings. Where classical republican thought utterly failed was in explaining the economic changes transforming society. Without abandoning a concern with the moral dimension of the new market society, the Scots directed their attention to analysing the new forces at work.

Following Hume, Smith saw that in the esteemed primitive societies where men and women retained the whole of their produce, there was material equality, but lives of misery and want. In commercial societies with their flagrantly unequal distribution of wealth, the labouring poor prospered as well. This apparent paradox led Smith to examine the secret spring of British abundance—the organization of labour through the division of productive tasks. Fed with ever-renewed freshets of capital, the modern commercial system would escape the cycle of luxury, corruption and decline, because it had enlisted the self-improving energies of most members of society.

Of course Smith's description of how nations grow wealthy through commerce—ingeniously detailed as it was—would not have answered the moral question posed by republicanism had he and Hume before him not considered human morality from a new perspective, that of the great sympathies and sociability enlisted in commercial society. Smith gave to all human beings the propensity to truck and barter, as well as the incessant drive to improve their condition. From these promptings men were drawn to each other's company. Here in the market place, not the political assembly of classical times, modern men developed the capacity to reflect upon themselves in society, to excel by emulating virtue and shunning dishonour. In the concourses of commerce, men acquired their notion of probity and justice. As Thomas Paine wrote in *The Rights of Man*, economic life drew upon the naturally sociable and co-operative aspects of human nature. Commerce works 'to cordialize mankind,' Paine wrote, 'by rendering nations, as well as individuals, useful to each other.'[11]

It was also a feature of modern life that ordinary labourers were independent, feeding themselves through their wages and thereby participating in the system of natural liberty. By shifting investigations of human character from politics to economics, the Scots were including labouring people in their conceptual universe. Modern commerce had made it possible for all to be independent and thus cut the critical link in classical theory between independent citizens and the dependent, disenfranchised workers, leaving those categories to be redrawn on the basis of gender and race. Within the realm of independent men—wage-labourers, merchants, manufacturers and landlords—the natural operation of the invisible hand of the market could regulate affairs better than the legislator, thus adding to the freedom from servile dependency a freedom from overweening political authority. If commercial exchanges rather than government authority unified the nation, the talented few—the men of extraordinary virtue and rectitude—had no function which could justify their privileges. Indeed the whole concept of justification of privilege made its way into social discourse through the door marked utility.

Although it took him until Book IV to say it, Smith placed consumption at the heart of modern market society.

> Consumption is the sole end and purpose of all production and the interest of the producer ought to be attended to, only so far as it may be necessary for promoting that of the consumer. The maxim is so perfectly self-evident, that it would be absurd to attempt to prove it.[12]

Yet Smith was far from happy with the human propensity to consume, characterizing it variously as a fascination for 'baubles and trinkets,' a passion for accumulating objects of 'frivolous utility' and, worse, a vehicle for deception with the false promise that wealth will bring happiness. Money will at best 'keep off the summer shower', he said, 'but not the winter storm', thus leaving humans more exposed than before to anxiety, fear and sorrow, disease, danger and death.[13]

Probing for the causes of the avidity so evident in his society in the last months before his death, Smith concluded that it was envy and admiration for the rich and powerful and fearful contempt of the poor that drove men to seek wealth. And since in modern society with its striking inequality of condition the prods from above and beneath were omnipresent, the material wants of man would be insatiable. In reasoning thus, Adam Smith anticipated at least a part of Max Weber's celebrated line that 'A man does not "by nature" wish to earn more and more money, but simply to live as he is accustomed to live and to earn as much as is necessary for that purpose.'[14]

It was one of the strengths of the Scottish moral philosophers to build upon human nature as they found it and to discern the springs of moral action from the close observation of men in their own society. In the 'uniform, constant and uninterrupted effort of every man to better his condition' Smith found the greatest grounds for hope.[15] For this was the human disposition that prompted men to defer pleasure, to save, to compete and to shun prodigality.

Here the middle-class character of the Scottish ideal shows itself, but in fact no rigorous analysis of consumption was carried out. Rather it was sentimentalized. From the middle of the eighteenth century through to our own time a particular kind of consumption has been approved, that which was associated with respectable family life. In the eighteenth century the word 'comfort' began to figure as the happy mean between biting necessity and indulgent luxury. Working over a draft treaty sent to him from John Adams in 1787, Thomas Jefferson replaced the word 'necessities' with that of 'comforts.' The new American nation would establish commercial treaties on the basis of exchanging comforts, not necessities.[16] Mary Wollstonecraft elaborated the concept in her *Historical and Moral View of the Origin and Progress of the French Revolution* when she explained that the French people had never acquired an idea of that independent, comfortable situation in which contentment is sought rather than happiness, because the slaves of pleasure or power can be roused only by lively emotions and extravagant hopes. In fact she goes on to observe the French don't even have a word in their vocabulary to express comfort, 'that state of existence, in which reason renders serene and useful the days which passion would only cheat with flying dreams of happiness'.[17]

The urban conviviality which commercial prosperity introduced into the eighteenth-century Anglo-American world had narrowed to a family-based respectability in the nineteenth century. Increasingly the desire to better oneself became associated with the motive of providing for one's family. Novelists gave respectability a distinctly material embodiment in the cleanliness and cut of clothes, the privacy afforded in the home and the accoutrements required to support the round of domestic rituals. It is tempting to claim that the family was sentimentalized in order to supply the safe avenues for what otherwise might be riotous broadways of spending.

The passions which the French Revolution evoked challenged the benign optimism of those making their peace with Adam Smith's market society. Across the Channel it became apparent that competitive self-interest could translate quickly into violent clashes of interest. The discreet scepticism of David Hume flowered into the open irreverence of Thomas Paine, promulgated to ordinary people through mass printings. By making the economy rather than the polity the basic institution of the society, the Scots had left politics in something of a conceptual limbo. If labour created value instead of being God's curse on Adam, what was the position of the labourer? Even liberty and equality looked different when the economy rather than the polity became the preeminent social system. What need was there of the talented few whose extraordinary virtue and rectitude alone preserved the constitution if it was the economy that provided stability? And how firm was that stability? Commerce as the principal socializer lacked a certain disciplinary rigour.

These discursive speculations were shunted aside when economic commentators began groping for the certainties of science. The most striking reworking of consumption in modern social thought came from Thomas Malthus. Writing in the closing years of the eighteenth century, Malthus put forward a population theory which interpreted abundance as spurious and pernicious. He sidestepped the debate about human predispositions and socializing influences, arguing instead that human beings were ruled by a set of inexorable equations. Consumption was at the centre of his theory. Abundance created cheap food. In good times, men and women married early and had lots of children. Without the positive checks of war and disease (construed negatively in other discourses), human population would grow geometrically, swiftly outpacing the incremental increases of harvests which brought forth the surplus births. Would these unequal potentialities come into actual collision? Malthus was unequivocal about the immediate relevance of his mathematical discovery. 'The period when the number of men surpass their means of subsistence has long since arrived, has existed ever since we have had any histories of mankind, does exist at present, and will for ever continue to exist,' he wrote in the first essay which appeared in 1798.[18] Nor could deferred marriage and family limitations relieve this parlous human condition.

Malthus forestalled further speculation about the theoretical effects of material progress by consigning human beings to a new determinism, the one inflicted by nature. A proper understanding of the dynamics behind human procreation eliminated the troubling question of how to render social justice in an age of increasing abundance. Utopian dreamers like Condorcet and William Godwin could say that perverse social institutions accounted for the persistence of human misery in the presence of unparalleled wealth—Godwin had argued just this in his celebrated essay, *An Enquiry Concerning Political Justice*—but Malthus permanently reordered the debate. The crucial issue became whether men and women could regulate their numbers and thereby avoid the evils of population pressure. Malthus said, 'no,' and for the next thirty-eight years he refined his explanation of Nature's great catch-22 about plenty and poverty.

The possibility of easy living demonstrated to Malthus that it was only biting necessity that got human beings to exert themselves. Thus while the fear of famine was evil, it was only a partial evil, because it acted for a greater good. And, he stressed, not enough people knew about it. Instead of forming correspondence clubs to circulate radical tracts, working men should be taught their true situation. Malthus's words bear quoting:

> the mere knowledge of these truths, even if they didn't operate sufficiently to produce any marked change in the prudential habits of the poor with regard to marriage, would still have a most beneficial effect on their conduct in a political light, making them on all occasions less disposed to insubordination and turbulence.

Although the lower classes were clearly the focus of Malthus's attention, his principle was universal: 'Want has not infrequently given wings to the imagination of the poet, pointed the flowing periods of the historian, and added acuteness to the researches of the philosopher.'[19]

Malthus's sober strictures on the inevitable tendency of abundance (that is, more food) gave economics its label as the dismal science. In the hands of Ricardo the dreadful implications of omnipresent scarcity were worked out in the famous iron law of rents and declining rate of profits. Much that had remained open-ended in Smith was now closed. Demand, the activity closest to consumption, re-entered the picture as marginal utility, a concept which permitted all the passions of motivation from frivolity, vanity and boredom to ambition, avarice and need to be weighed on the same scale.

In ensuing decades the Malthusian principle of scarcity moved from economics to biology and then returned to sociology with powerful reverberations through all educated discourses in the nineteenth century. Human beings were folded back into nature. Physiology replaced original sin as the source of suffering. A uniform human nature and the stinginess of the physical environment controlled human destiny. Only familiarity keeps us from enjoying the irony that at a time when human productive powers were about to explode, competition for scarce resources became the centrepiece of theorizing in both biology and economics. The range of choices open to people had never been greater and yet it was positivism not poetry that dominated social thought. Variety and abundance became a permanent feature of western society, revealing the fecundity of human inventiveness, the insatiability of human curiosity, the splendour of human talents and the inaccuracy of aristocratic assumptions about ordinary peoples' abilities. Yet the reigning social theories assumed that human beings invariably sought gain through the equally invariant invisible hand of the market. Scholarly light narrowed to a laser beam directed at the workings of rational choice, utility maximization and competition for scarce resources while the rich diversity of human personality found no place in social theory.

The most consequential intellectual response to abundance was the awareness that human society was the product of human effort. To a large extent this is what is meant by secularization. Enveloped within the story of progress, this fact holds no terrors and few problems. Our proleptic histories assume that people want to rush into the future to enjoy their share of progressive improvement. In reality this encounter with unmitigated social responsibility was very troubling because it threw into high relief the issue of social justice, or more simply, how abundance was to be distributed. The classical discourse on luxury held the ground for a while, but it offered no intellectual tools for analysing economic developments. One of the responses to dramatic changes in the material world was the desire to explore the dynamic behind economic development. As William Reddy has noted, this extraordinary effort to understand the exchange economy ended up with a doctrine of indifference.[20] The existence of system was perceived—no mean feat—but once perceived it was declared best left alone. Those who spoke of the delights of the new material culture and the prospect of a more just distribution of them were drowned out by the new social scientists who gave human beings a nature so invariant that its inexorable workings determined social existence.

In this essay I have made consumption a generous concept, one that connects the social world of invention, taste and production with the personal world of sociability, experimentation and enjoyment. Why burden the concept of consumption with all this? Because in a commercial society consumption registers the range of human satisfactions; it leads to the creation of group affinities; it reveals the shifting patterns of human intentionality. What facets of human experience could be incorporated in a theory generous to consumption? I can think of three: self-indulgence, personal identity and privacy. Through consumption people indulge themselves, seeking gratification immediately and tangibly. Self-indulgence is a *terra incognita* in our social knowledge. Like sex in the nineteenth century, self-indulgence is so overly condemned that we can only approach it obliquely. We say that ordinary people—the masses—consume because they have been infected with artificial wants dreamed up by the international league of producers, or we treat it as a residual category—what people do when they are blocked from nobler activities like philanthropy, meaningful politics and becoming mature.

In addition to giving us access to the meaning of self-indulgence the study of consumption gives us a window on the elaboration of personal identity. Consumption offers people objects to incorporate into their lives and their presentation of self. This is as true of reading material as clothes and furnishings—purchasing and enjoying artefacts of material culture involves a constant expression of self. For this reason consumption opened up new avenues for rebellion. What were all those young women in the early nineteenth century doing when they eagerly consumed the literature of romance? They were seeking pleasure, learning about the world, finding models and exerting their own desires in the face of a clerical offensive against the reading of novels. Fashions set norms, but like statements, fashions point the way to their subversion. In every elaboration of a fresh style there is simultaneously created an armoury of defiant gestures. Perhaps not the grand stuff of revolutions, but splendidly innovative in the minor skirmishes of everyday insubordination.

Finally, consumption is instructive because the expanded world of goods enabled people to create privacy and embellish intimacy. Nothing so marked the eighteenth century as the building and refurbishing of residential space. And men and women seized this opportunity to shelter their informal, personal acts from outside scrutiny, first by simply adding partitions to close off rooms and subsequently by incorporating into their notion of privacy the daily acts of sleeping, eating, bathing, entertaining and reading, with appropriate rooms for each.

The novelty in consumption in the early modern period came from the inclusion of more and more people in the spending spree. Elite groups had always consumed and used consumption for self-gratification, establishing identity and creating privacy. Mass consumption was the driving force behind the new productive systems. Coming to terms with this reality impinged upon every social and political relation. Ordinary people had to brave the ridicule of others and buy beyond their station. Members of the elite had to give up many of the visual cues of their superiority. More important, they had to accept—however grudgingly—that ordinary people were self-activating agents, masters of their own dollars and shillings, if not their destiny. This dialectic of assertion, condemnation, indulgence, lamentation, insubordination and indignation remains an unexplored side of the democratization of society. Insisting upon the universality of the motive of gain has obscured the variety of human satisfactions sought through the market. It's not that our humanity requires commerce for its fulfilment, but rather that in a commercial society, a whole battery of new cultural means has been created to articulate a broader range of human intentions.

The economic development and social transformation which characterized the modern era depended upon changes in attitudes, habits and levels of consumption, and yet our social theorists from Smith through Malthus, Ricardo, Marx, Weber and Arthur Lafer have concentrated upon production. Their vocabulary has been drawn from the forbidding lexicon of control, discipline, struggle and competition. Through the course of two centuries, economic thought itself moved from the rhapsodizing of promoters through the moral outrage of Augustan classicism to the quantifiable factors of invariant responses and predictable outcomes.

Meanwhile back at the peddler's cart, the fair, the haberdashery, the milliners, the greengrocers, the market stall, the department store, the boutique, the discount house, the merchandise mart and the suburban mall, grown men and women, little children and their grandparents, have continued to consume, checked only by the limits of credit.

Notes

1. Sidney Mintz explores the complicated response to the popular consumption of New World commodities in *Sweetness and Power: The Place of Sugar in Modern History* (New York, 1985).

2. Louis Dumont, *From Mandeville to Marx* (Chicago, 1977), 6–7.

3. [Nicholas Barbon], *A Discourse of Trade* (London, 1690); [Dudley North], *Discourse upon Trade* (London, 1691), 14.

4. Neil McKendrick, 'Home demand and economic growth: a new view of the role of women and children in the Industrial Revolution,' in idem (ed.), *Historical Perspectives: Studies in English Thought and Society in Honour of J. H. Plumb* (London, 1974).

5. Simon Schama, *The Embarrassment of Riches* (New York, 1987), 298–335.

6. I am indebted to John Sekora, *Luxury: The Concept in Western Thought, Eden to Smollet* (Baltimore, 1977) for this discussion of consumption considered under the rubric of luxury. See also J. G. A. Pocock, *The Machiavellian Moment: Florentine Political Thought and the Atlantic Republican Tradition* (Princeton, 1975).

7. Sekora, *Luxury*, 44.

8. ibid., 5, 299.

9. Roy Porter, 'The English Enlightenment', in Roy Porter and Mikulá;aks Teich (eds), *The Enlightenment in National Context* (Cambridge, 1981), 1–18.

10. For a particularly insightful discussion of the Smithian tradition see Keith Tribe, 'The "histories" of economic discourse,' *Economy and Society*, vi (1977), 314–44. See also Isvan Hont and Michael Ignatieff, 'Needs and justice in the *Wealth of Nations*: an introductory

essay' and Nicholas Phillipson, 'Adam Smith as civic moralist,' in *Wealth and Virtue* (Cambridge, 1983). I am also indebted to the unpublished writing of Charles Nathanson.

11. Thomas Paine, *The Rights of Man* (London, 1791–2), 99.

12. Adam Smith, *An Inquiry into the Nature and Causes of the Wealth of Nations* (New York, 1937), 625.

13. Hont and Ignatieff, 'Needs and justice', 10.

14. Max Weber, *The Protestant Ethic and the Spirit of Capitalism* (New York, 1958), 60.

15. Smith, *Wealth of Nations*, 324–5.

16. Thomas Jefferson to John Adams, 27 November 1785, in Lester J. Cappon (ed.), *The Adams-Jefferson Letters: The Complete Correspondence between Thomas Jefferson and Abigail and John Adams*, vol. 1 (Chapel Hill, 1959), 103.

17. Mary Wollstonecraft, *An Historical and Moral View of the Origin and Progress of the French Revolution and the Effect it has Produced in Europe* (London, 1795), 511. I am indebted to Anne Mellor for this reference.

18. Thomas Robert Malthus, *An Essay on Population* (London, 1798), 54, as cited in Thomas Sowell, 'Malthus and the utilitarians,' *Canadian Journal of Economics and Political Science*, xxviii (1962), 272.

19. Malthus, *Essay*, 2nd edn, vol. 2 (London, 1803), 200.

20. William Reddy, *Money and Liberty in Modern Europe: A Critique of Historical Understanding* (Cambridge, 1987), 78–82.

PART III

Class, Gender, and Modernity, 1880–1940

Encountering Mass Culture at the Grassroots:
The Experience of Chicago Workers in the 1920s

Lizabeth Cohen

In 1929, the publishers of *True Story Magazine* ran full-page advertisements in the nation's major newspapers celebrating what they called "the American Economic Evolution." Claiming to be the recipient of thousands of personal stories written by American workers for the magazine's primarily working-class readership, they felt well placed to report that since World War I, shorter working hours, higher pay and easy credit had created an "economic millennium." Now that the nation's workers enjoyed an equal opportunity to consume, "a capital-labor war which has been going on now for upwards of three hundred years" had virtually ended. *True Story* claimed that twenty years ago, Jim Smith, who worked ten to twelve hours a day in a factory and then returned home "to his hovel and his woman and his brats," was likely to resort to strikes and violence when times got tough. Not so his modern-day counterpart. Today, the magazine asserted, Jim Smith drives home to the suburbs after a seven or eight hour day earning him three to seven times as much as before, which helps pay for the automobile, the house and a myriad of other possessions. Now an upstanding member of the middle class, Jim has learned moderation. Mass consumption had tamed his militance.[1] Advertising executives at the J. Walter Thompson Company shared *True Story Magazine's* confidence in the homogenizing power of mass culture. In an issue of their own in-house newsletter devoted to "the New National Market," they too claimed that due to standardized merchandise, automobiles, motion pictures and most recently the radio, the so-called "lines of demarcation" between social classes and between the city, the small town and the farm had become less clear.[2]

Sixty years later, historians are still making assumptions about the impact of mass culture that are similar to those of *True Story Magazine's* editors and J. Walter Thompson Company's executives. With not much more data

"Encountering Mass Culture at the Grassroots: The Experience of Chicago Workers in the 1920s" by Lizabeth Cohen from *American Quarterly* 41 (March 1989): 6–33. Copyright © 1989 The American Studies Association. Reprinted by permission of Johns Hopkins University Press.

about consumer attitudes and behavior in the 1920s than their predecessors had, they too assume that mass culture succeeded in integrating American workers into a mainstream, middle-class culture. When workers bought a victrola, went to the picture show, or switched on the radio, in some crucial way, the usual argument goes, they ceased living in an ethnic or working-class world. This common version of the "embourgeoisement thesis" credits a hegemonic mass culture with blurring class lines. When labor organizing occurred in the 1930s and 1940s, the view holds, it stemmed not from industrial workers' class consciousness but from their efforts to satisfy middle-class appetites.[3]

How can historians break free of the unproven assumptions of the era and reopen the question of how working-class audiences responded to the explosion of mass culture during the 1920s? Let me first acknowledge how difficult it is to know the extent to which workers participated in various forms of mass culture, and particularly the meanings they ascribed to their preferences. But I will suggest in this essay one strategy for discerning the impact of mass culture. Shifting the focus from the national scene, where data on audience reception is weak, to a particular locale rich in social history sources can yield new insights into the way that workers responded to mass culture. Chicago offers a particularly good case since it was the best documented city in the United States during the 1920s and 1930s. In this period, Chicago was a laboratory for sociologists, political scientists and social workers—and a multitude of their students. Their numerous studies of urban life, along with ethnic newspapers, oral histories, and other local sources, can serve social historians as revealing windows into working-class experience with mass culture. Chicago's industrial prominence, moreover, attracted a multiethnic and multiracial work force, which gives it all the more value as a case study.

In order to investigate how workers reacted to mass culture on the local level of Chicago, it is necessary to make concrete the abstraction "mass culture." This essay, therefore, will examine carefully how workers in Chicago responded to mass consumption, that is, the growth of chain stores peddling standard-brand goods; to motion picture shows in monumental movie palaces; and to the little box that seemed overnight to be winning a sacred spot at the family hearth, the radio.

While *True Story Magazine*'s Jim Smith may have bought his way into the middle class, in reality industrial workers did not enjoy nearly the prosperity that advertisers and sales promoters assumed they did. All Americans did not benefit equally from the mushrooming of national wealth taking place during the 1920s. After wartime, wages advanced modestly if at all in big manufacturing sectors, such as steel, meat-packing, and the clothing industry, particularly for the unskilled and semiskilled workers who predominated in this kind of work. And most disruptive of workers' ability to consume, unemployment remained high. Workers faced unemployment whenever the business cycle turned downward, and even more regularly, faced layoffs in slack seasons. So Chicago's average semiskilled worker did not have nearly as much money to spare for purchasing automobiles, washing machines and victrolas as manufacturers and advertisers had hoped.[4]

But people with commodities to sell worried little about workers' limited income. Instead, they trusted that an elaborate system of installment selling would allow all Americans to take part in the consumer revolution. "Buy now, pay later," first introduced in the automobile industry around 1915, suddenly exploded in the 1920s; by 1926, it was estimated that six billion dollars' worth of retail goods were sold annually by installment, about fifteen percent of all sales. "Enjoy while you pay," invited the manufacturers of everything from vacuum cleaners to literally the kitchen sink.[5]

But once again, popular beliefs of the time do not hold up to closer scrutiny: industrial workers were not engaging in installment buying in nearly the numbers that marketers assumed. Automobiles accounted for by far the greatest proportion of the nation's installment debt outstanding at any given time—over fifty percent. But while *True Story*'s Jim Smith may have driven home from the factory in his new automobile, industrial workers in Chicago were not likely to follow his example. One study of the standard of living of semiskilled workers in Chicago found that only three percent owned cars in 1924. Even at the end of the decade, in the less urbanized environment of nearby Joliet, only twenty four percent of lower income families owned an automobile, according to a *Chicago Tribune* survey. The few studies of consumer credit done at the time indicate that it was middle income people—not workers—who made installment buying such a rage during the 1920s, particularly the salaried and well-off who anticipated larger incomes in the future. Lower income people instead were saving at unprecedented rates, often to cushion themselves for the inevitable layoffs.[6]

When workers did buy on credit, they were most likely to purchase small items like phonographs. The question remains, however, whether buying a phonograph—or a washing machine—changed workers' cultural orientation. Those who believed in the homogenizing power of mass consumption claimed that the act of purchasing such a standardized product drew the consumer into a world of mainstream tastes and values. Sociologist John Dollard argued at the time, for example, that the victrola revolutionized a family's pattern of amusement because "what they listen to comes essentially from the outside, its character is cosmopolitan and national, and what the family does to create it as a family is very small indeed."[7] We get the impression of immigrant, wage-earning families sharing more in American, middle-class culture every time they rolled up the rug and danced to the Paul Whiteman orchestra.

But how workers themselves described what it meant to purchase a phonograph reveals a different picture. Typically, industrial workers in Chicago in the 1920s were first-or second-generation ethnic, from eastern or southern Europe. In story after story they related how buying a victrola helped keep Polish or Italian culture alive by allowing people to play foreign-language records, often at ethnic social gatherings. Rather than the phonograph drawing the family away from a more indigenous cultural world, as Dollard alleged, many people like Rena Domke remembered how in Little Sicily during those years neighbors "would sit in the evening and discuss all different things about Italy," and every Saturday night they pulled out a victrola "and they'd play all these Italian records and they would dance. . . . "[8] In fact, consumers of all nationalities displayed so much interest in purchasing foreign language records that in the 1920s Chicago became the center of an enormous foreign record industry, selling re-pressed recordings from Europe and new records by American immigrant artists. Even the small Mexican community in Chicago supported a shop which made phonographic records of Mexican music and distributed them all over the United States. And some American-born workers also used phonograph recordings in preserving their ties to regional culture. For example, Southerners—white and black—eased the trauma of moving north to cities like Chicago by supporting a record industry of hillbilly and "race records" geared specifically toward a Northern urban market with southern roots.[9] Thus, owning a phonograph might bring a worker closer to mainstream culture, but it did not have to. A commodity could just as easily help a person reinforce ethnic or working-class culture as lose it.

Of course, when the publishers of *True Story* spoke of a consumer revolution, they meant more than the wider distribution of luxury goods like the phonograph. The were referring to how the chain store—like A & P or Walgreen Drugs—and the nationally-advertised brands that they offered—like Lux Soap and Del Monte canned goods—were standardizing even the most routine purchasing. A distributor of packaged meat claimed, "Mass selling has become almost the universal rule in this country, a discovery of this decade of hardly less importance than the discovery of such forces as steam and electricity."[10] Doomed, everyone thought, were bulk or unmarked brands, and the small, inefficient neighborhood grocery, dry goods, or drug store that sold them. Americans wherever they lived, it was assumed, increasingly were entering stores that looked exactly alike to purchase the same items from a standard stock.

Closer examination of the consumer behavior of workers in a city like Chicago, however, suggests that workers were not patronizing chain stores. Rather, the chain store that purportedly was revolutionizing consumer behavior in the 1920s was mostly reaching the middle and upper classes. Two-thirds of the more than five hundred A & P and National Tea Stores in Chicago by 1928 were located in neighborhoods of above-average economic status (Table 1). An analysis of the location of chain stores in Chicago's suburbs reveals the same imbalance. By 1926, chains ran fifty three percent of the groceries in prosperous Oak Park, and thirty six percent in equally well-off Evanston. In contrast, in working-class Gary and Joliet, only one percent of the groceries were owned by chains. As late as 1929, the workers of Cicero found chain

Table 1. Location of chain grocery stores in Chicago, 1927–1929 by economic status of neighborhood

Chain store	Total no. stores	Total no. in census tracts with rental data	% stores in census tracts above men rental*
National Tea	535	530	66%
A & P	17	17	65%
Totals	552	547	65.5%

*using 1930 rental data where median monthly rental was $51.30.
Sources: Chicago Telephone Directory, Alphabetical and classified, 1927; *Polk's Directory of Chicago, 1928–29;* Charles S. Newcomb, *Street Address Guide by Census Area of Chicago, 1930* (Chicago: University of Chicago, 1933); "Economic Status of Families Based on Equivalent Monthly Rentals; Tracts Combined When Total Homes Are Less Than 300, But Homes With Value or Rental Unknown Were Omitted in Computing the Median," Data taken from Table 10, *Census Data of Chicago, 1930,* box 51, folder 8, Burgess Papers, University of Chicago Special Collections.

management in only five percent of this industrial town's 819 retail stores.[11] Chain store executives recognized that workers were too tied to local, often ethnic, merchants to abandon them, even for a small savings in price.[12] A West Side Chicago grocer explained: "People go to a place where they can order in their own language, be understood without repetition, and then exchange a few words of gossip of news."[13] Shopping at a particular neighborhood store was a matter of cultural loyalty. As one ethnic merchant put it, "The Polish business man is a part of your nation; he is your brother. Whether it is war, hunger, or trouble, he is always with you willing to help. . . . Therefore, buy from your people."[14]

No less important, the chain store's prices may have been cheaper, but it's "cash and carry" policy was too rigid for working people's limited budgets. Most workers depended on a system of credit at the store to make it from one payday to the next. In tough times, the loyal customer knew an understanding storekeeper would wait to be paid and still sell her food. So when an A & P opened not far from Little Sicily in Chicago, people ignored it. Instead, everyone continued to do business with the local grocer who warned, "Go to A & P they ain't going to give you credit like I give you credit here."[15] While middle-class consumers were carrying home more national brand, packaged goods in the 1920s, working-class people continued to buy in bulk—to fetch milk in their own containers, purchase hunks of soap, and scoop coffee, tea, sugar and flour out of barrels. What standard brands working-class families did buy, furthermore, they encountered through a trusted grocer, not an anonymous clerk at the A & P.[16]

When workers did buy mass-produced goods like ready-made clothing, they purchased them at stores such as Chicago's Goldblatt's Department Stores, which let customers consume on their own terms. Aware that their ethnic customers were accustomed to central marketplaces where individual vendors sold fish from one stall, shoes from another, the second-generation Gold-blatt brothers, sons of a Jewish grocer, adapted this approach to their stores. Under one roof they sold everything from food to jewelry, piling merchandise high on tables so people could handle the bargains.[17] The resulting atmosphere dismayed a University of Chicago undergraduate sociology student, more used to the elegance of Marshall Field's. To Betty Wright, Goldblatt's main floor was a mad "jumble of colors, sounds, and smells." Amidst the bedlam, she observed

> many women present with old shawls tied over their heads and bags or market baskets on their arms. They stopped at every counter that caught their eye, picked up the goods, handled it, enquired [sic] after the price, and then walked on with-out making any purchase. I have an idea that a good many of these women had no intention whatsoever of buying anything. They probably found Goldblatt's a pleasant place to spend an afternoon.

Most appalling to this student, "Customers seemed always ready to argue with the clerk about the price of an article and to try to 'jew them down.' "[18] Betty Wright did not appreciate that behind Goldblatt's respectable exterior facade thrived a European street market much treasured by ethnic Chicagoans.

Ethnic workers in a city like Chicago did not join what historian Daniel Boorstin has labeled "national consumption communities" nearly as quickly as many have thought. Even when they bought the inexpensive, mass-produced goods becoming increasingly available during the 1920s, contrary to the hopes of many contemporaries, a new suit of clothes did not change the man (or woman). Rather, as market researchers would finally realize in the 1950s when they developed the theory of "consumer reference groups," con-sumption involved the meeting of two worlds—the buyer's and the seller's—with purchasers bringing their own values to every exchange.[19] Gradually over the 1920s, workers came to share more in the new consumer goods, but in their own stores, in their own neighborhoods, and in their own way.

In the realm of consumption, workers could depend on the small-scale en-terprises in their communities to help them resist the homogenizing influences of mass culture. But how did ethnic, working-class culture fare against forms of mass culture—such as motion pictures and radio—which local communi-ties could not so easily control? Did the motion picture spectacle and a twist of the radio dial draw workers into mainstream mass culture more success-fully than the A & P?

Workers showed much more enthusiasm for motion pictures than chain stores. While movies had been around since early in the century, the number of theater seats in Chicago reached its highest level ever by the end of the 1920s. With an average of four performances daily at every theater, by 1929 Chicago had enough movie theater seats for one-half the city's population to attend in the course of a day; and workers made up their fair share—if not more—of that audience.[20] Despite the absence of exact attendance figures, there are consistent clues that picture shows enjoyed enormous popularity among workers throughout the twenties. As the decade began, a Bureau of Labor Statistics' survey of the cost-of-living of workingmen's families found Chicago workers spending more than half of their amusement budgets on movies.[21] Even those fighting destitution made the motion picture a priority; in 1924, more than two-thirds of the families receiving Mothers' Aid Assistance in Chicago attended regularly.[22]

But knowing that workers went to the movies is one thing, assessing how they reacted to particular pictures is another. Some historians have taken the tack of analyzing the content of motion pictures for evidence of their meaning to audiences; the fact that workers made up a large part of those audiences convinces these analysts that they took home particular messages decipherable from the films. But my investigations into the variety of ways that consumers encountered and perceived mass-produced goods suggests that people can have very different reactions to the same experience. Just as the meaning of mass consumption varied with the context in which people confronted it, so too the impact of the movies depended on where, with whom, and in what kind of environment workers went to the movies during the 1920s.[23]

Chicago's workers regularly patronized neighborhood movie theaters near their homes in the 1920s, not "The Chicago," "The Uptown," "The Granada" and the other monumental picture palaces built during the period, where many historians have assumed they flocked. Neighborhood theaters had evolved from the storefront nickelodeons prevalent in immigrant, working-class communities before the war. Due to stricter city regulations, neighborhood movie houses now were fewer in number, larger, cleaner, better ventilated and from five to twenty cents more expensive than in nickelodeon days. But still they were much simpler than the ornate movie palaces which seated several thousand at a time. For example, local theaters in a working-class community like South Chicago (next to U.S. Steel's enormous South Works plant) ranged in size from "Pete's International," which sat only 250—more when Pete made the kids double up in each seat for Sunday matinees—to the "Gayety" holding 750 to the "New Calumet" with room for almost a thousand.[24] Only rarely did workers pay at least twice as much admission, plus carfare, to see the picture palace show. Despite the fact that palaces often claimed to be "paradise for the common man," geographical plotting of Chicago's picture palaces reveals that most of them were nowhere near working-class neighborhoods: a few were downtown, the rest strategically placed in new shopping areas to attract the middle classes to the movies.[25] Going to the pictures was something workers did more easily and cheaply close to home. As a U.S. Steel employee explained, it was "a long way"—in many respects—from the steeltowns of Southeast Chicago to the South Side's fancy Tivoli Theater.[26]

For much of the decade, working-class patrons found the neighborhood theater not only more affordable but more welcoming, as the spirit of the community carried over into the local movie hall. Chicago workers may have savored the exotic on the screen, but they preferred encountering it in familiar company. The theater manager, who was often the owner and usually lived in the community, tailored his film selections to local tastes and changed them every few days to accommodate neighborhood people who attended frequently. Residents of Chicago's industrial neighborhoods rarely had to travel far to find pictures to their liking, which they viewed among the same neighbors and friends they had on the block.

When one entered a movie theater in a working-class neighborhood of Chicago, the ethnic character of the community quickly became evident. The language of the yelling and jeering that routinely gave sound to silent movies provided the first clue. "The old Italians used to go to these movies," recalled Ernest Dalle-Molle, "and when the good guys were chasing the bad guys in Italian—they'd say—Getem—catch them—out loud in the theater."[27] Stage events accompanying the films told more. In Back of the Yards near the packinghouses, at Schumacher's or the Davis Square Theater, viewers often saw a Polish play along with the silent film.[28] Everywhere, amateur nights offered "local talent" a moment in the limelight. At the Butler Theater in Little Sicily, which the community had rechristened the "Garlic Opera House," Italian music shared the stage with American films.[29] In the neighborhood theater, Hollywood and ethnic Chicago coexisted.

Neighborhood theaters so respected local culture that they reflected community prejudices as well as strengths. The Commercial Theater in South Chicago typified many neighborhood theaters in requiring Mexicans and blacks to sit in the balcony, while reserving the main floor for white ethnics who dominated the community's population.[30] One theater owner explained, "White people don't like to sit next to the colored or Mexicans. . . . We used to have trouble about the first four months, but not now. They go by themselves to their place."[31] Sometimes blacks and Mexicans were not even allowed into neighborhood theaters. In contrast, the more cosmopolitan picture palaces, like those owned by the largest chain in Chicago, Balaban & Katz, were instructed to let in whoever could pay.[32] Thus, the neighborhood theater reinforced the values of the community as powerfully as any on the screen. This is not to deny that working-class audiences were affected by the content of motion pictures, but to suggest that when people viewed movies in the familiar world of the neighborhood theater, identification with their local community was bolstered, and the subversive impact of the picture often constrained.

Thus, even if local communities did not control the production of motion pictures during the 1920s, they still managed for a good part of the decade to influence how residents received them. The independent, neighborhood theater in that way resembled the neighborhood store, harmonizing standardized products with local, particularly ethnic, culture.

Neighborhood stores and theaters buffered the potential disorientation of mass culture by allowing their patrons to consume within the intimacy of the community. Rather than disrupting the existing peer culture, that peer culture accommodated the new products. Shopping and theatergoing were easily mediated by the community because they were collective activities. Radio, on the other hand, entered the privacy of the home. At least potentially, what went out across the airwaves could transport listeners, as individuals, into a different world.

As it turned out, though, radio listening did not require workers to forsake their cultural communities any more than shopping or moviegoing did. Radio listening was far from the passive, atomized experience we are familiar with today. It was more active; many working people became interested in early radio as a hobby, and built their own crystal and vacuum tube sets. Radio retailers recognized that workers were particularly apt to build their own radios. "If the store is located in a community most of the inhabitants of which are workmen," a study of the radio industry showed, "there will be a large proportion of parts . . . ," in contrast to the more expensive, preassembled models stocked by the radio stores of fashionable districts. That radio appealed to the artisanal interests of Chicago's workers was evident in their neighborhoods in another way. As early as 1922, a Chicago radio journalist noted that "crude homemade aerials are on one roof in ten along the miles of bleak streets in the city's industrial zones."[33]

Even workers who bought increasingly affordable, ready-made radios spent evenings bent over their dial boards, working to get "the utmost possible DX" (distance), and then recording their triumphs in a radio log. Beginning in the fall of 1922, in fact, Chicago stations agreed not to broadcast at all after 7 p.m. on Monday evenings to allow the city's radio audience to tune in faraway stations otherwise blocked because they broadcasted on the same wavelengths as local stations. "Silent Nights" were religiously observed in other cities as well. In addition to distance, radio enthusiasts concerned themselves with technical challenges such as cutting down static, making "the short jumps," and operating receivers with one hand.[34]

Not only was radio listening active, but it was also far from isolating. By 1930 in Chicago, there was one radio for every two or three households in workers' neighborhoods, and people sat around in local shops or neighbors' parlors listening together (Table 2 and Table 3). Surveys showed that on average, four or five people listened to one set at any particular time; in eighty-five percent of homes, the entire family listened together. Communal radio listening mediated between local and mass culture much like the neighborhood store or theater.[35]

Even Chicago's working-class youth, whose parents feared they were abandoning the ethnic fold for more commercialized mass culture, were listening to the radio in the company of other second-generation ethnic peers at neigh-

Table 2. Radio ownership in five Chicago neighborhoods inhabited by industrial workers, 1930

Neighborhood	% Household owning radios
1. *Southeast Chicago* (Steel Mills)	53.00
East Side	69.37
South Chicago	55.90
Hegewisch	46.74
South Deering	40.00
2. *Back of The Yards* (Meatpacking)	46.07
Bridgeport	48.35
New City	43.78
3. *Old Immigrant Neighborhoods* (Small Factories & Garments)	37.41
West Town	41.33
Lower West Side	36.79
Near West Side	34.10
4. *Southwest Corridor* (Int'l. Harvester, West. Electr.)	55.42
North Lawndale	58.41
McKinley Park	55.03
South Lawndale	54.68
Brighton Park	53.55
5. *Black Belt*	46.44
Washington Park	61.58
Grand Blvd.	46.90
Douglas	30.85
Radio ownership in middle-class neighborhoods for comparison	
Avalon Park	83.96
Chatham	81.26
Greater Grand Crossing	76.04
Englewood	67.61

Source: Louis Wirth and Margaret Furez, eds., *Local Community Fact Book* (Chicago: Chicago Recreation Commission, 1938).

borhood clubs when not at home with their families. Known as "basement clubs," "social clubs," or "athletic clubs," these associations guided the cultural experimentation of young people from their mid-teens to mid-twenties. Here, in rented quarters away from parental eyes and ears, club members socialized to the constant blaring of the radio—the "prime requisite" of every club, according to one observer. The fact that young people were encountering mass culture like the radio within ethnic, neighborhood circles helped to minimize the disruption.[36]

But even more important to an investigation of the impact of the radio on workers' consciousness, early radio broadcasting had a distinctly grassroots orientation. To begin with, the technological limitations of early broadcasting ensured that small, nearby stations with low power dominated the ether waves. Furthermore, with no clear way of financing independent radio stations, it fell to existing institutions to subsidize radio operations. From the start, nonprofit ethnic, religious and labor groups put radio to their service. In 1925, twenty-eight percent of the 571 radio stations nationwide were owned

Table 3. United States census data on family ownership of radios, 1930

A. Radio ownership in Chicago and other U.S. community types. By race and ethnicity of families

Family Race and Ethnicity	Chicago	Urban	Rural Farm	Rural Non-Farm
Native White	74.2%	56.3%	24.0%	37.4%
For-born White	54.1%	46.2%	32.0%	35.1%
Black	42.6%	14.4%	.3%	3.0%
All Families	63.2%	50.0%	20.8%	33.7%

B. Percent radio-owning families in industrial suburbs of Cook County, 1930

City	Percent Families Reporting Radios
Berwyn	78.1%
Blue Island	73.7%
Calumet City	57.1%
Chicago Heights	53.5%
Cicero	65.4%
Harvey	66.7%
Melrose Park	57.8%
Cook County Overall	64.6%

Sources: United States Department of Commerce, Bureau of the Census, *Fifteenth Census of the United States: 1930, Population* (Washington, D.C.: U.S. Government Printing Office, 1933); "Families in Cook County with Radios (1930)," *Daily News Almanac and Year Book for 1933* (Chicago: Daily News, 1933), 801.

by educational institutions and churches, less than four percent by commercial broadcasting companies.[37] In Chicago, ethnic groups saw radio as a way of keeping their countrymen and women in touch with native culture. By 1926, several radio stations explicitly devoted to ethnic programming broadcasted in Chicago—WGES, WSBC, WEDC, and WCRW—while other stations carried "nationality hours." Through the radio, Chicago's huge foreign language-speaking population heard news from home, native music, and special broadcasts like Benito Mussolini's messages to Italians living in America.[38] One of the stations which sponsored a "Polish Hour" and an "Irish Hour" is also noteworthy for bringing another aspect of local, working-class culture to the radio. The Chicago Federation of Labor organized WCFL, "the Voice of Labor," to, in its own words, "help awaken the slumbering giant of labor." Having suffered a variety of defeats after World War I, most notable the failure to organize Chicago's steel mills and packing plants, the Federation seized radio in the 1920s as a new strategy for reaching the city's workers. "Labor News Flashes," "Chicago Federation of Labor Hour," and "Labor Talks with the International Ladies Garment Workers' Union" alternated with entertainment like "Earl Hoffman's Chez Pierre Orchestra" and "Musical Potpourri."[39]

Radio, therefore, brought familiar distractions into the homes of workers: talk, ethnic nationality hours, labor news, church services, and vaudeville-type musical entertainment with hometown—often ethnic—performers. More innovative forms of radio programming, such as situation comedy shows, dramatic series and soap operas, only developed later. And a survey commissioned by NBC in 1928 found that eighty percent of the radio audience regularly listened to these local, not to distant, stations.[40] Sometimes listeners even knew a singer or musician personally, since many stations' shoestring budgets forced them to rely on amateurs; whoever dropped in at the station had a chance to be heard. Well-known entertainers, moreover, shied away from radio at first, dissatisfied with the low pay but also uncomfortable performing without an audience and fearful of undercutting their box office attractiveness with free, on-air concerts. While tuning in a radio may have been a new experience, few surprises came "out of the ether."[41]

As a result, early radio in Chicago promoted ethnic, religious, and working-class affiliations rather than undermining them, as many advocates of mass culture had predicted. No doubt radio did expose some people to new cultural experiences—to different ethnic and religious traditions or new kinds of music. But most important, workers discovered that participating in radio, as in mass consumption and the movies, did not require repudiation of established social identities. Radio at mid-decade, dominated as it was by local, noncommercial broadcasting, offered little evidence that it was fulfilling the prediction of advocates and proving itself "the greatest leveler," capable of sweeping away "the mutual distrust and enmity of laborer and executive . . . business man and artist, scientist and cleric, the tenement dweller and the estate owner, the hovel and the mansion."[42]

By letting community institutions—ethnic stores, neighborhood theaters and local radio stations—mediate in the delivery of mass culture, workers avoided the kind of cultural reorientation that Madison Avenue had expected. Working-class families could buy phonographs or ready-made clothing, go regularly to the picture show, and be avid radio fans without feeling pressure to abandon their existing social affiliations.

While this pattern captures the experience of white ethnic workers in Chicago's factories, it does not characterize their black co-workers, who came North in huge numbers during and after World War I to work in mass production plants. Blacks developed a different, and complex, relationship to mass culture. Black much more than ethnic workers satisfied those who hoped a mass market would emerge during the twenties. Unlike ethnic workers, blacks did not reject chain stores and standard brands, nor try to harness radio to traditional goals. But blacks disappointed those who assumed an integrated, American culture would accompany uniformity in tastes. For ironically, by participating in mainstream commercial life—which black Chicagoans did more than their ethnic co-workers—blacks came to feel more independent and influential as a race, not more integrated into white middle-class society. Mass culture— chain stores, brand goods, popular music—

offered blacks the ingredients from which to construct a new, urban black culture.

Blacks' receptivity to mass culture grew out of a surprising source, a faith in black commercial endeavor not so very different from ethnic people's loyalty to ethnic businesses. During the 1920s, a consensus developed in Northern black communities that a separate "black economy" could provide the necessary glue to hold what was a new and fragile world together. If blacks could direct their producer, consumer and investment power toward a black marketplace by supporting "race businesses," the whole community would benefit. Less economic exploitation and more opportunity would come blacks' way. This was not a new idea. "Black capitalism" had been fundamental to Booker T. Washington's accommodationist, self-help philosophy at the turn of the century. What changed in the 1920s was that now blacks of all political persuasions—including the Garveyite nationalists and even the socialist-leaning "New Negro" crowd—shared a commitment to a separate black economy. In the face of racial segregation and discrimination, the black community would forge an alternative "Black Metropolis" which rejected white economic control without rejecting capitalism.[43]

At the center of the separate black economy stood "race businesses." Black consumers were told that when they patronized these enterprises, they bought black jobs, black entrepreneurship, and black independence along with goods and services, and bid farewell to white employment prejudice, insults and overcharging. "You don't know race respect if you don't buy from Negroes," sermonized one pastor.[44] Central to the nationalist program of Marcus Garvey's United Negro Improvement Association, not surprisingly, were commercial enterprises—a steamship line, hotel, printing plant, black doll factory, and chains of groceries, restaurants and laundries.[45]

But the "black economy" strategy was only moderately successful. Those black businesses which did best were geared solely to black needs, where there was a large Negro market with little white competition. For example, undertakers, barbers and beauticians faced few white contenders; black cosmetic companies even succeeded in selling hair products like Madame C. J. Walker's hair growth and straightening creams through nationwide chains.[46] And black-owned insurance companies whose salesmen knocked on doors up and down blocks of the Black Belt proved the greatest business triumph of all.[47] But insurmountable economic barriers kept other Negro entrepreneurs from competing viably. Black merchants and businessmen suffered from lack of experience, lack of capital (there were only two black banks in the city to provide loans, and these had limited resources), and an inability to offer customers the credit that ethnic storekeepers gave their own countrymen or Jewish businessmen in black areas gave black customers. The short supply of cash in black stores, moreover, kept wholesale orders small, retail prices high, and shelf stock low, all of which forced black customers to shop elsewhere.[48]

The poor showing of black business made black customers, even those deeply committed to a black economy, dependent on white business. But concern with black economic independence nonetheless left its mark. Within the white commercial world, blacks developed two preferences which they pursued when financially able: standard brand goods and chain stores. Blacks shopping in non-black stores felt that packaged goods protected them against unscrupulous storekeepers or clerks. Not sharing the ethnic worker's confidence in his compatriot grocer, the black consumer distrusted bulk goods. This reliance on brand names only grew, moreover, when black customers who could survive without credit increasingly chose to patronize chain stores, attracted to their claims of standardized products and prices.[49]

No less important, the chain store could be pressured to hire black clerks, while the Jewish, Greek or Italian store in a black neighborhood was usually family-run. If blacks could not own successful businesses, at least they should be able to work in them. By the mid- to late-1920s, consumer boycotts to force chains to hire blacks flourished in black neighborhoods. "Don't Spend Your Money Where You Can't Work" crusades sought black economic independence through employment rather than entrepreneurship. By 1930, consumers in Chicago's enormous South Side Black Belt had pressured local branches of The South Center Department Store, Sears Roebuck, A & P, Consumers' Market, Neisner's 5 Cents to a Dollar, Woolworth's, and Walgreen's Drugs to employ blacks, some almost exclusively.[50]

With strict limitations on where blacks could live and work in Chicago, consumption—both through race businesses and more mainline chains—became a major avenue through which blacks could assert their independence. But chain stores were not the only aspect of mass culture to contribute to the making of an urban, black identity. Blacks also played a role in shaping another major feature of mass culture in the twenties—jazz. In contrast to black commercial schemes which mimicked white examples or black consumption which contented itself largely with white products, here the trendsetting went the other way. Black folk culture, black inventiveness, black talent gave the twenties its distinctive image as the "Jazz Age" and dictated the character of mainstream American popular music for many years to come.

Chicago was the jazz capital of the nation during the 1920s. Here, in the middle of the Black Belt, mixed audiences in "Black and Tan" cabarets tapped to the beat of King Oliver, Louis Armstrong, Lil Hardin, "Fats" Waller, Freddy Keppard, Jelly Roll Morton and others. In segregated company, blacks relished Chicago's "hot jazz" at their own more modest clubs, black movie theaters, and semi-private house parties; whites, meanwhile, danced black dances like the Charleston to black bands playing in palatial ballrooms that prohibited Negro patronage.[51]

The Chicago jazzmen's music reached far beyond the city's night clubs. Blacks—and some whites—all over the country bought millions of blues and jazz phonograph recordings, known as "race records." At record stores on

Chicago's South Side, one store owner remembered, "Colored people would form a line twice around the block when the latest record of Bessie or Ma or Clara or Mamie come in."[52] With the exception of Negro-owned Black Swan Records, white recording companies like Paramount, Columbia, Okey and Victor were the ones to produce special lines for the Negro market. But because white companies depended on the profitable sales of race recordings as the phonograph business bottomed out with the rise of radio, they had little interest in interfering with the purest black sound. As far away as the rural south, blacks kept up with musicians from Chicago and New York by purchasing records from mail-order ads in the *Chicago Defender* or from Pullman porters travelling south.[53] The radio, too, helped bring black jazz to a broad audience. Chicago stations broadcasted Earl "Fatha" Hines with his band at the Grand Terrace Supper Club, and other groups performing at the Blackhawk Restaurant. Fletcher Henderson's Rainbow Orchestra played at New York's Savoy, but in time was heard in homes all over America.

Here again, then, mass culture in the form of commercial record companies and radio helped blacks develop and promote a unique, and increasingly national, black sound. And the dissemination of jazz not only contributed to black identity. It also helped shape the character of American popular music. True, white bands often reaped more financial profits from a "sweetened" and more "swinging" jazz than did its black creators in Chicago's Black Belt clubs (though black men—Duke Ellington, Fletcher Henderson and Don Redman—played an important role in turning the Chicago "hot" sound into the smoother, bigger, more tightly packaged "swing" that came out of New York.) And also true, by making a name for themselves in the music world, blacks fit right into white stereotypes of the "natural musician." Nonetheless, jazz gave black musicians and their fans recognition in the cultural mainstream, for expressing themselves in a language they knew was their own. Long before Motown, blacks were molding American popular music in their own image.

Black jazz recordings, or black employment in chain stores, became a vehicle for making a claim on mainstream society that racism had otherwise denied. When blacks patronized chain stores, they were asserting independence from local white society, not enslavement to cultural norms. No doubt their consumption of mass cultural products did give them interests in common with mainstream American society, and subjected them to the vagaries of the capitalist market. But with mass culture as raw material, blacks fashioned their own culture during the 1920s that made them feel no less black.

So it would seem that despite the expectations of mass culture promoters, chain stores, standard brands, motion pictures, and the radio did not absorb workers—white or black—into a middle-class, American culture. To some extent, people resisted aspects of mass culture, as ethnic workers did chain stores. But even when they indulged in Maxwell House Coffee, Rudolph Valentino and radio entertainment, these experiences did not uproot them since they were encountered under local, often ethnic, sponsorship. When a politically conscious, Communist worker asserted that "I had bought a jalopy in 1924, and it didn't change me. It just made it easier for me to function," he spoke for other workers who may not have been as self-conscious, but who like him were not made culturally middle-class by the new products they consumed.[54]

Beginning in the late 1920s and increasingly in the 1930s, local groups lost their ability to control the dissemination of mass culture. Sure of their hold over the middle-class market, chain stores more aggressively pursued ethnic, working-class markets, making it much harder for small merchants to survive. The elaboration of the Hollywood studio system and the costs of installing sound helped standardize moviegoing as well. Not only were neighborhood theaters increasingly taken over by chains, but the "talkies" themselves hushed the audience's interjections and replaced the ethnic troupes and amateur talent shows with taped shorts distributed nationally. Similarly, by the late 1920s, the local non-profit radio era also had ended. In the aftermath of the passage of the Federal Radio Act of 1927, national, commercial, network radio imposed order on what admittedly had been a chaotic scene, but at the expense of small, local stations. When Chicago's workers switched on the radio by 1930, they were likely to hear the A & P Gypsies and the Eveready Hour on stations that had almost all affiliated with either NBC or CBS, or had negotiated—like even Chicago's WCFL, "the Voice of Labor"—to carry some network shows. The Great Depression only reinforced this national commercial trend by undermining small distributors of all kinds.

Thus, grassroots control over mass culture did diminish during the thirties. But the extent to which this more national mass culture in the end succeeded in assimilating workers to middle-class values remains an open question. It is very likely that even though the structure of distributing mass culture did change by the 1930s, workers still did not fulfill the expectations of *True Story Magazine* editors and J. Walter Thompson Company executives. It is possible that workers maintained a distinctive sense of group identity even while participating, much the way blacks in the twenties did. Historical circumstances may have changed in such a way that workers continued to put mass culture to their own uses and remain a class apart. And increasingly over time, mass culture promoters—moviemakers, radio programmers, chain store operators and advertisers—would recognize this possibility, and gear products to particular audiences; the 1930s mark the emergence of the concept of a segmented mass market, which gradually displaced expectations of one homogeneous audience so prevalent in the 1920s.

Relatedly, we should not assume—as advocates of the embourgeoisement school do—that as workers shared more in a national commercial culture, they were necessarily depoliticized. In fact, there is much evidence to suggest that a more national mass culture helped unify workers previously divided along ethnic, racial and geographical lines, facilitating the national organizing drive of the CIO. A working population that shared a common cultural life offered new opportunities for unified political action; sit-down strikers who charted baseball scores and danced to popular music together and union newspapers which kept their readers informed about network radio programs testified to the intriguing connections between cultural and political unity. Extension of this study into the 1930s and beyond might reveal that, ironically, mass culture did more to create an integrated working-class culture than a classless American one. In taking this study beyond the 1920s, thus, it is imperative that investigators continue to pay careful attention to the context in which people encountered mass culture, in order not to let the mythical assumptions about mass culture's homogenizing powers prevail as they did in our popular images of the twenties.

Notes

1. True Story Magazine, *The American Economic Evolution*, vol. 1 (New York, 1930), 32–34, 67.

2. J. Walter Thompson Company, "Newsletter # 139," 1 July 1926, 157–59, RG 11, J. Walter Thompson Advertising Company Archives (JWT).

3. Stuart Ewen, *Captains of Consciousness: Advertising and the Social Roots of the Consumer Culture* (New York, 1976); Stuart and Elizabeth Ewen, *Channels of Desire: Mass Images and the Shaping of American Consciousness* (New York, 1982); Richard Wightman Fox and T. J. Jackson Lears, eds. *The Culture of Consumption* (New York, 1983). While this is also the general thrust of Roy Rosenzweig's argument, he does suggest that in bringing diverse groups of workers together, the movies unintentionally may have helped them mount a more unified political challenge in the 1930s. But they did not organize out of a working-class consciousness. Having shared in middle-class culture in the 1920s, they fought to sustain and expand their access to it, which was being endangered by the depression. Roy Rosenzweig, *"Eight Hours For What We Will": Workers and Leisure in Worcester, Massachusetts, 1870–1930* (New York, 1984).

Sociologists have also shared the assumptions of contemporary observers who were confident of the homogenizing power of mass culture. See Daniel Bell, *The End of Ideology* (New York, 1962); John Goldthorpe and David Lockwood, *The Affluent Worker in the Class Structure* (Cambridge, 1969). For criticism of the embourgeoisement thesis, see John Clarke, Chas Critcher and Richard Johnson, *Working Class Culture: Studies in History and Theory* (London, 1979) and James E. Cronin, *Labour and Society in Britain, 1918–1979* (London, 1984), 146–72.

Antonio Gramsci's theory of cultural hegemony applied to mass culture is more complex. If defined narrowly, it comes close to embourgeoisement in suggesting that by participating in mass culture, workers come to share values with the ruling elite and thereby reinforce its control. If defined more broadly, however, the theory allows for more diversity in responses to mass culture but nonetheless argues that if the experience does not make workers into revolutionaries, it still serves to legitimate elite rule. For a useful discussion of the strengths and weaknesses of Gramsci's theory of cultural hegemony, see T. J. Jackson Lears, "The Concept of Cultural l'egemony: Problems and Possibilities," *American Historical Review* 90 (June 1985): 567–93.

4. On the wages and unemployment of Chicago's factory workers, see my dissertation, "Learning to Live in the Welfare State: Industrial Workers in Chicago Between the Wars, 1919–1939" (Ph.D. diss., University of California, Berkeley, 1986), chap. 4, "Contested Loyalty at the Workplace."

5. Wilbur C. Plummer, "Social and Economic Consequences of Buying on the Installment Plan," "Supplement" vol. 129 of *The Annals of the American Academy of Political and Social Science* (Jan. 1927), 2; Edwin R. A. Seligman, *The Economics of Installment Selling: A Study in Consumers' Credit with Special Reference to the Automobile* (New York, 1927) cited in "Economics of Installment Selling," *Monthly Labor Review* 26 (Feb. 1928): 233.

6. Leila Houghteling, *The Income and Standard of Living of Unskilled Laborers in Chicago* (Chicago, 1927); Chicago Tribune, *Chicago Tribune Fact Book, 1928* (Chicago, 1928), 46; Frank Stricker, "Affluence for Whom?—Another Look at Prosperity and the Working Classes in the 1920's." *Labor History* 24 (Winter 1983): 30–32. Stricker estimates that even by 1929, a working-class family had no more than a thirty percent chance of owning a car.

7. John Dollard. "The Changing Functions of the American Family" (Ph.D. diss., University of Chicago, 1931), 137–38.

8. See the following transcripts of interviews from Italians in Chicago Project (IC), University of Illinois Chicago Circle (UICC): Rena Domke, 28 Apr. 1980, Chicago, 3; Mario Avignone, 12 July 1979, Chicago, 24; Thomas Perpoli, 26 June 1980, Chicago, 34; Theresa DeFalco, 28 Apr. 1980, Downers Grove, Ill., 17; Leonard Giuleano, 2 Jan. 1980, Chicago, 19; Rena Morandin, 22 July 1980, Chicago, 18; Ernest Dalle-Molle, 30 Apr. 1980, Downers Grove, Ill., 76; Edward Baldacci, 29 Apr. 1980, Chicago Heights, Ill., 17. For additional evidence of how Italians valued the phonograph as a way to enjoy their native culture, see Gaetano DeFilippis, "Social Life in an Immigrant Community" (c. 1930), 42, box 130, folder 2, Burgess Papers. University of Chicago Special Collections (UCSC); C. W. Jenkins, "Chicago's Pageant of Nations: Italians and their Contribution," *Chicago Evening Post*, 16 Nov. 1929. Chicago Foreign Language Press Survey (CFLPS), box 22, UCSC, Autobiography of an Italian Immigrant, n.d., 18, box 64, folder 24, Chicago Area Project Papers (CAP), Chicago Historical Society (CHS), Chicago.

9. Pekka Gronow, "Ethnic Recordings: An Introduction"; Richard K. Spottswood, "Commercial Ethnic Recordings in the United States," and idem., "The Sajewski Story: Eighty Years of Polish Music in Chicago," in *Ethnic Recordings in America: A Neglected Heritage*, American Folklife Center. Studies in American Folklife, no. 1 (Washington, D.C., 1982), 1–66, 133–73; Robert C. Jones and Louis R. Wilson. *The Mexican in Chicago* (Chicago, 1931), 7. I am grateful to an anonymous reviewer for *American Quarterly* for pointing out how similarly Southerners used phonograph recordings.

10. "Supreme Court of the District of Columbia in Equity No. 37623, United States of America Petitioner vs. Swift & Company. Armour & Company, Morris & Company, Wilson & Co., Inc., and The Cudahy Packing Co., et al., Defendants, On Petitions of Swift & Company, and Its Associate Defendants, and Armour & Company, and Its Associate Defendants, for Modification of Decree of February 27, 1920. Petitioning Defendants Statement of the Case," 1930, 14. For more on chain stores as a way of streamlining distribution to make it equal in efficiency to mass production, see *Chain Store Progress* 1 (Nov.–Dec. 1929), *Chain Store Progress* 2 (Jan. 1930).

For basic information on the development of chain stores, see James L. Palmer. "Economic and Social Aspects of Chain Stores," *Journal of Business of the University of Chicago* 2 (1929): 172–290; Paul H. Nystrom, *Economic Principles of Consumption* (New York, 1929), 518–22; Nystrom, *Chain Stores* (Washington, D.C., 1930); Walter S. Hayward. "The Chain Store and Distribution," *Social Science Review* 115 (Sept. 1924): 220–25.

For details on Chicago's chain stores, see Ernest Hugh Shideler, "The Chain Store: A Study of the Ecological Organization of a Modern City" (Ph.D. diss., University of Chicago, 1927); Committee on Business Research, "Study Sales of Groceries in Chicago," *Chicago Commerce*, 14 Apr. 1928, 15; "Analyze Variety Store Sales Here," *Chicago Commerce*, 1 Sept. 1928, 23; Einer Bjorkland and James L. Palmer. *A Study of the Prices of Chain and Independent Grocers in Chicago* (Chicago, 1930); Ernest Frederic Witte, "Organization, Management, and Control of Chain Drug Stores" (Ph.D. diss., University of Chicago,

1932); Robert Greenwell Knight, "A Study of the Organization and Control Methods of Walgreen Company's Chain of Drug Stores" (M.A. thesis, University of Chicago, 1925).

11. "How Strong Are the Chain Groceries in the Leading Cities?" *J. Walter Thompson News Bulletin* (June 1926): 14–21, RG 11, JWT; United States Department of Commerce, Bureau of the Census, *Fifteenth Census of the United States: 1930, Volume 1, Retail Distribution* (Washington, D.C., 1934), 662.

12. Ling Me Chen, "The Development of Chain Stores in the United States" (M.A. thesis, University of Chicago, 1929), 12, 102; William J. Baxter, "The Future of the Chain Store," *Chicago Commerce*, 29 Oct. 1928, 24; "The Science of Chain Store Locations," *Chain Store Progress* 1 (Mar. 1929): 5; Stanley Resor, "What Do These Changes Mean?" *J. Walter Thompson News Bulletin* 104 (Dec. 1923): 12–13, JWT.

A 1927–28 study of chain store locations in Atlanta found a situation much like Chicago's. Forty-five chain stores served the 8,634 families in the "best" areas of town—one store for every 191 families—while in the "third best" and "poorest" areas combined, the same number of chains served 33,323 families, one store for every 740 families. Guy C. Smith, "Selective Selling Decreases Costs: Market Analysis Enables Seller to Choose His Customer, Saving Costly Distribution Wastes," *Chicago Commerce*, 14 Apr. 1928, 24.

13. Quoted in Paul S. Taylor, *Mexican Labor in the United States, Chicago and the Calumet Region*, vol. 7 in the University of California Publications in Economics (Berkeley, 1932), 169.

14. *Dziennik Zjednoczenia*, 28 Nov. 1932, quoted in Joseph Chalasinski, "Polish and Parochial School Among Polish Immigrants in America: A Study of a Polish Neighborhood in South Chicago," n.d., 20, box 33, folder 2, CAP Papers.

Among Mexican immigrants, who came to Chicago in increasing numbers during the 1920s, loyalty to Mexico entered into the selection of stores to patronize. It was not enough that a merchant be Mexican, but he had to also remain a Mexican citizen. One storekeeper complained, "I have a store in the Mexican district. If I become a citizen of the United States the Mexicans won't trade with me, because they wouldn't think I was fair to them or loyal to my country. I read the papers and I would like to vote, but I must not become a citizen. I have to have the Mexican trade to make a living." Quoted in Edward Hayden, "Immigration, the Second Generation, and Juvenile Delinquency," n.d., 10, box 131, folder 3, Burgess Papers.

On a practical level, patrons felt that they could best trust their own merchants; butchers of other "races" would certainly put a heavier thumb on the scale. R. D. McCleary, "General Survey of Attitudes Involved in the Formation of a Youth Council on the Near-West Side," n.d., 2, box 101, folder 10, CAP Papers.

15. Paul Penio, 30 June 1980, Itasca, Ill., IC, UICC, 17.

16. Sidney Sorkin, "A Ride Down Roosevelt Road, 1920–1940," *Chicago Jewish Historical Society News* (Oct. 1979): 6; The Chicago Tribune, "Consumer Survey: An Investigation into the Shopping Habits of 2205 Chicago Housewives, October 1929," mimeographed. A Study of one hundred working-class Chicagoans found that in 1927 "curiously enough, canned goods and American inventions—the cheaper ways of filling an empty stomach . . . —seem to have invaded the ranks but little." Laura Friedman, "A Study of One Hundred Unemployed Families in Chicago, January 1927 to June 1932" (M.A. thesis, University of Chicago, 1933), 112.

Sophonisba Breckinridge spoke with a Croatian woman who pointed out that in her neighborhood store she could ask the grocer about new things she saw but did not know how to use, whereas elsewhere she could not ask and so would not buy. Sophonisba Breckinridge, *New Homes for Old* (New York, 1921), 123.

17. JoEllen Goodman and Barbara Marsh, "The Goldblatt's Story: From Poverty to Retailing Riches to Ch. 11 Disgrace," *Crain's Chicago Business* 4 (19–25 Oct. 1981): 17–27; "Four Boys and a Store," 30 June 1960, mimeographed press release.

18. Betty Wright, Paper for Sociology 264, Mar. 1931, 4–6, box 156, folder 2, Burgess

Papers. William Ireland noted that the Wieboldt's Store on Milwaukee Avenue lost its lower-class customers to Iverson's—across the street—when it changed its merchandising techniques to attract middle-class customers. " 'The lower-class' Poles will only trade where the store puts out on the sidewalk baskets of wares through which customers can rummage." William Rutherford Ireland, "Young American Poles" (written as M.A. thesis, University of Chicago, 1932, but not submitted), 26.

19. Louis E. Boone, *Classics in Consumer Behavior: Selected Readings Together With the Authors' Own Retrospective Comments* (Tulsa, 1977).

20. Alice Miller Mitchell, *Children and Movies* (Chicago, 1929), 66.

21. "Cost of Living in the United States—Clothing and Miscellaneous Expenditures," *Monthly Labor Review* 9 (Nov. 1919): 16.

22. Mary F. Bogue, *Administration of Mothers' Aid in Ten Localities with Special Reference to Health, Housing, Education and Recreation*, Children's Bureau Publication No. 184 (Washington, D.C., 1928), 90.

At the end of the decade, one study showed wage earner families spending a greater percentage of income on picture shows than families of either clerks or professionals: the $22.56 a year they put toward movies equalled that expended by clerks with a third more income and was twice as much as professionals spent who were earning salaries almost four times higher. President's Research Committee, *Recent Social Trends in the United States*, vol. 2 (New York, 1933; reprinted Westport, Conn., 1970), 895.

23. For a study that analyzes film content for insight into audience response, see Lary May's fascinating *Screening Out the Past: The Birth of Mass Culture and the Motion Picture Industry, With a new Preface* (Chicago, 1983).

24. "Trip to Calumet Theatre Brings Back Memories," *Daily Calumet*, 23 Nov. 1981; "South Chicago Was Home to Many Theaters," *Daily Calumet*, 25 Apr. 1983; Felipe Salazar and Rodolfo Camacho, "The Gayety: A Theatre's Struggle for Survival," Project for Metro History Fair, n.d., manuscript; "Southeast Chicago Theatres Filled Entertainment Need." *Daily Calumet*, 3 Jan. 1983; "Theaters Plentiful on the Southeast Side," *Daily Calumet*, 10 Jan. 1983.

25. Douglas Gomery, "Movie Audiences, Urban Geography, and the History of the American Film," *The Velvet Light Trap Review of Cinema* 19 (Spring 1982): 23–29.

26. Interview with Jim Fitzgibbon, 16 July 1981, Chicago, Oral History Collection, Southeast Chicago Historical Project (SECHP), 14.

27. Interview with Ernest Dalle-Molle, 30 Apr. 1980, Chicago, IC, UICC, 76.

28. Robert A. Slayton, " 'Our Own Destiny': The Development of Community in Back of the Yards" (Ph.D. diss., Northwestern University, 1982), 59–60.

29. For a description of amateur night, see "Fitzgibbons Was Important Part of Southeast Historical Project," *Daily Calumet*, 13 June 1983. On the "Garlic Opera House," see Harvey Warren Zorbaugh. *The Gold Coast and the Slum: A Sociological Study of Chicago's Near North Side* (Chicago, 1929), 164–65.

30. Student paper, n.a., n.d. but c. 1930, box 154, folder 5, Burgess Papers; for more evidence of the discrimination blacks encountered at movie theaters, see The Chicago Commission on Race Relations, *The Negro in Chicago: A Study of Race Relations And A Race Riot* (Chicago, 1922), 318–20.

31. Quoted in Taylor, *Mexican Labor*, 232.

32. Barney Balaban and Sam Katz, *The Fundamental Principles of Balaban and Katz Theatre Management* (Chicago, 1926), 15, 17–20.

33. Hiram L. Jome, *Economics of the Radio Industry* (Chicago, 1925), 11–117. For more on home assembly of radios by workers, see Provenzano, 17 Mar. 1980, Brookfield, Ill., IC, UICC, 24–25; Thomas Perpoli, 26 June 1980, Chicago, IC, UICC, 59; Anita Edgar Jones, "Conditions Surrounding Mexicans in Chicago" (Ph.D. diss., University of Chicago, 1928), 85. On abundance of aerials, see *Radio Broadcast* (Oct. 1922), quoted in Erik Barnouw, *A Tower in Babel: A History of Broadcasting in the United States*, vol. 1-to 1933

(New York, 1966), 88. Also, Paul F. Cressey, "Survey of McKinley Park Community," 20 Oct. 1925, 1, box 129, folder 7, Burgess Papers.

34. For an amusing picture of "DX fishing," see Bruce Bliven, "The Legion Family and the Radio: What We Hear When We Tune In," *Century Magazine* 108 (Oct. 1924): 811–18; on Chicago's "silent night" see Barnouw, *Tower in Babel*, 93; on technical challenges see "Merry Jests and Songs Mark Radio Party," *Chicago Commerce*, 5 Apr. 1924, 17; "Radio Marvels Will Be Seen at Show," *Chicago Commerce*, 2 Oct. 1926, 9.

35. Daniel Starch. "A Study of Radio Broadcasting Made for the National Broadcasting Company, Inc.," 1928, 23, box 8, folder 4, Edgar James Papers, Wisconsin State Historical Society (WSHS); American Telephone and Telegraph Company, "The Use of Radio Broadcasting as a Publicity Medium," 1926, mimeographed, 4, box 1, folder 8, Edgar James Papers, WSHS; Clifford Kirkpatrick, *Report of a Research into the Attitudes and Habits of Radio Listeners* (St. Paul, 1933), 26; Malcolm Willey and Stuart A. Rice, *Communication Agencies and Social Life* (One of a Series of Monographs Prepared Under the Direction of the President's Research Committee on Social Trends) (New York, 1933), 202; Provenzano, IC, UICC, 25.

36. For more discussion of youths' attraction to mass culture, see my "Learning to Live in the Welfare State," 190–95. For vivid descriptions of club life, see Isadore Zelig, "A Study of the 'Basement' Social Clubs of Lawndale District," Paper for Sociology 270, 1928, box 142, folder 3, Burgess Papers; S. Kerson Weinberg, "Jewish Youth in the Lawndale Community: A Sociological Study," Paper for Sociology 269, n.d., 50–79; box 139, folder 3, Burgess Papers; Meyer Levin, *The Old Bunch* (New York, 1937), 3–9, 18–26, 121–39; Ireland, "Young American Poles," 72–75;"The Regan's Colts and the Sherman Park District" and "The Neighborhood," 1924, box 2, folder 10, McDowell Papers, CHS; Guy De-Fillipis, "Club Dances," 1935, box 191, folder 7, CAP Papers: Robert Sayler, "A Study of Behavior Problems of Boys in Lower North Community," n.d., 24–27; box 135, folder 4, Burgess Papers; William J. Demsey, "Gangs in the Calumet Park District," Paper for Sociology 270, c. 1928, box 148, folder 5, Burgess Papers; Donald Pierson, "Autobiographies of Teenagers of Czechoslovakian Backgrounds from Cicero and Berwyn," 1931, box 134, folder 5, Burgess Papers.

37. Willey and Rice, *Communication Agencies and Social Life*, 196, 200.

38. Bruce Linton, "A History of Chicago Radio Station Programming, 1921–1931, with Emphasis on Stations WMAQ and WGN" (Ph.D. diss., Northwestern University, 1953), 155; Mark Newman, "On the Air with Jack L. Cooper: The Beginning of Black-Appeal Radio," *Chicago History* 12 (Summer 1983): 53–54;*Chicago Tribune Picture Book of Radio* (Chicago, 1928), 75–86; *WGN: A Pictorial History* (Chicago, 1961), 28; *Poles of Chicago, 1837–1937: A History of One Century of Polish Contribution to the City of Chicago* (Chicago, 1937), 240; Martha E. Gross, "The 'Jolly Girls' Club: Report and Diary," Mar. 1933, 28, box 158, folder 5, Burgess Papers; Joseph Kisciunas, "Lithuanian Chicago" (M.A. thesis, DePaul University, 1935), 40; Interview with Margaret Sabella, 29 Mar. 1980, Chicago, IC, UICC, 8; from the CFLPS, UCSC:"Colonial Activities," *Chicago Italian Chamber of Commerce*, May 1929, 17, and "Radio Concert of Polish Songstress," *Dziennik Zjednoczenia*, 5 Aug. 1922; *Immaculate Conception, B.V.M. Parish, South Chicago, Diamond Jubilee: 1882–1957*, n.p.: Peter C. Marzio, ed., *A Nation of Nation: The People Who Came to America as Seen Through Objects and Documents Exhibited at the Smithsonian Institution* (New York, 1976), 443.

39. Edward Nockels to Trade Union Secretaries, 23 Dec. 1926, box 15, folder 106, Fitzpatrick Papers, CHS; William J. H. Strong, "Report on Radiocasting for the Special Committee, Mssrs. Fitzpatrick, Nockels and Olander, of the Chicago Federation of Labor and the Illinois Federation of Labor, November 5th, 1925," 1, box 14, folder 100, Fitzpatrick Papers; "The Aims, Objects and History of WCFL." *WCFL Radio Magazine* 1 (Spring 1928), 58–59; Erlign Sejr Jorgensen, "Radio Station WCFL: A Study in Labor Union Broadcasting" (M.A. thesis, University of Wisconsin, 1949).

40. Starch, "Study of Radio Broadcasting," 28.

41. Willey and Rice, *Communication Agencies and Social Life*, 195–99; Linton, "History of Chicago Radio Station Programming," 61–62, 121; Barnouw, *Tower in Babel*, 99–101; Arthur Frank Wertheim, *Radio Comedy* (New York, 1979); Christopher H. Sterling and John M. Kittross, *Stay Tuned: A Concise History of American Broadcasting* (Belmont, Calif., 1978), 71–78.

42. N. Goldsmith and Austin C. Lescarboura, *This Thing Called Broadcasting* (New York, 1930), 296.

43. On the philosophy of a separate black economy, see Allan Spear, *Black Chicago: The Making of a Negro Ghetto, 1890–1920* (Chicago, 1967), 111–18, 192–200 and M. S. Stuart, *An Economic Detour: A History of Insurance in the Lives of American Negroes* (New York, 1940), xvii–xxv, 101. P. W. Chavers devoted his life to the establishment of a viable black economy in Chicago. Madrue Chavers-Wright, *The Guarantee—P. W. Chavers: Banker, Entrepreneur, Philanthropist in Chicago's Black Belt of the Twenties* (New York, 1985).

44. St. Clair Drake and Horace R. Cayton, *Black Metropolis: A Study of Negro Life in a Northern City* (New York, 1945), 430.

45. Edmund David Cronon, *Black Moses: The Story of Marcus Garvey and the Universal Negro Improvement Association* (Madison, 1968), 50–61, 174–75.

46. On black businesses which flourished in Chicago and in the nation in general, with special attention to successful trades like undertaking, barber and beauty shops, cosmetics and newspapers, see Drake and Cayton, *Black Metropolis*, 433–36, 456–62; Spear, *Black Chicago*, 112–15, 184–85; Chicago Commission on Race Relations, *The Negro in Chicago*, 140–41; Thomas E. Hunter, "Problems of Colored Chicago," 1930, box 154, folder 4, Burgess Papers; Camille Cohen-Jones, "Your Cab Company: How a Colored Man Organized a Cab Company in Chicago," *The Crisis* 34 (Mar. 1927): 5–6; Abram L. Harris, *The Negro as Capitalist: A Study of Banking and Business among American Negroes.* (Philadelphia, 1936), 170–72; J. H. Harmon, Jr., "The Negro as a Local Business Man," *The Journal of Negro History* 14 (Apr. 1929): 137–38, 140–41, 144–51; Gunnar Myrdal, *American Dilemma: The Negro Problem and Modern Democracy*, vol. 1 (New York, 1944), 309–10, 317; Jervis Anderson, *This Was Harlem, 1900–1950* (New York, 1981), 92–98.

47. Although black companies faced aggressive competition from mainline insurance companies, they exploited the fact that white firms charged blacks higher premiums and rarely hired black agents. Leo M. Bryant, "Negro Insurance Companies in Chicago" (M.A. thesis, University of Chicago, 1934), 1–80; Hylan Garnet Lewis, "Social Differentiation in the Negro Community" (M.A. thesis, University of Chicago, 1936), 98–101; Robert C. Puth, "Supreme Life: The History of a Negro Life Insurance Company" (Ph.D. diss., Northwestern University, 1967), 1–93; Spear, *Black Chicago*, 181–83; C. G. Woodson, "The Insurance Business Among Negroes," *The Journal of Negro History* 14 (Apr. 1929): 202–26; Harry H. Pace, "The Possibilities of Negro Insurance," *Opportunity* 8 (Sept. 1930): 266–69; Stuart, *Economic Detour*, 35–62, 72–108.

48. For discussion of the difficulties that black businessmen faced, see Drake and Cayton, *Black Metropolis*, 438–56; Hunter, "Problems of Colored Chicago," 12; Spear, *Black Chicago*, 183–84; Paul K. Edwards, *The Southern Urban Negro As a Consumer* (New York, 1932), 126, 135–39; Harris, *Negro as Capitalist*, 54–55, 172; Myrdal, *American Dilemma*, vol. 1, 307–12; Harmon, "Negro As a Local Business Man," 131, 140, 142, 144–45, 147, 152–55.

49. Edwards, *Southern Urban Negro As Consumer*, 153–66, 209–13. Several years after this study was published, Edwards expanded his investigation into urban black consumption habits to include the North. He concluded that Northern Negroes showed the same predisposition to brand names as Southern urbanites. Also see Raymond A. Bauer and Scott M. Cunningham, *Studies in the Negro Market* (Cambridge, Mass., (1970), 11–14 and Raymond A. Bauer, Scott M. Cunningham, and Lawrence H. Wortzel, "The Marketing

Dilemma of Negroes," *Journal of Marketing* 29 (July 1965), reprinted in Boone, *Classics in Consumer Behavior*, 353–64.

50. St. Clair Drake, "Churches and Voluntary Associations in the Chicago Negro Community," Report of Official Project 465–54–3–386 Conducted Under the Auspices of the Works Projects Administration, 1940, mimeographed, 247; Oliver Cromwell Cox, "The Negroes Use of Their Buying Power in Chicago As a Means of Securing Employment," Prepared for Professor Millis, University of Chicago, 1933, cited extensively in Drake, "Churches and Voluntary Associations," 230, 247–51; T. Arnold Hill, "Picketing for Jobs," *Opportunity* 8 (July 1930): 216; Stephen Breszka, "And Lo! It Worked: A Tale of Color Harmony," *Opportunity* 11 (Nov. 1933): 242–44, 350; "Butler Stores Cheat," *The Messenger* 7 (Apr. 1925), 156; Wright, Paper for Sociology 264, Mar. 1931, 7, Burgess Papers; Elizabeth Balanoff, "A History of the Black Community of Gary, Indiana, 1906–1940" (Ph.D. diss., University of Chicago, 1974), 200–02; John L. Tilley, *A Brief History of the Negro in Chicago, 1779–1933 (From Jean Baptiste DeSaible—To "A Century of Progress")* (Chicago, 1933), 16–18, 25–26; Hunter. "Problems of Colored Chicago," 10, Burgess Papers.

51. Of course, the Afro-American influence on American popular music did not begin in the 1920s, but in this decade its impact on mainstream music was particularly formative. The sources on jazz are voluminous. On black jazz in Chicago, see particularly Thomas Joseph Hennessey, "From Jazz to Swing: Black Jazz Musicians and Their Music, 1917–1935" (Ph.D. diss., Northwestern University, 1973); Robert L. Brubacker, *Making Music Chicago Style* (Chicago, 1985), 16–25, 148–55; Louis Armstrong. *Swing That Music* (New York, 1936); Demsey J. Travis, *An Autobiography of Black Jazz* (Chicago, 1983).

52. Marshall W. Stearns, *The Story of Jazz* (New York, 1956), 167–68.

53. A survey of a 1929 out-of-town edition of the *Chicago Defender* revealed that 18.7 percent of the 1070 advertisements were for race records. Edwards, *Southern Urban Negro as Consumer*, 185. For information on race records, see Lawrence W. Levine, *Black Culture and Black Consciousness: Afro-American Folk Thought From Slavery To Freedom* (New York, 1977), 224, 231; LeRois Jones, *Blues People: The Negro Experience in White America and The Music That Developed From It* (New York, 1963), 99–103, 128–29; Stearns, *Story of Jazz*, 167–68, 190; Barnouw, *Tower in Babel*, 128–31.

54. Steve Nelson, James R. Barrett and Rob Ruck, *Steve Nelson: American Radical* (Pittsburgh, 1981), 68.

CHAPTER 10

Familiar Sounds of Change: Music and the Growth of Mass Culture

George Sanchez

Just south of Los Angeles' central Plaza lay the area known throughout the city as the main arena for activities of leisure in the Mexican community of the 1920s. Sundays were not only a big day for religious practice; they also were big business days for the area's movie theatres, gambling dens, and pool halls—all of which dominated the streets to the south. The constant sound of Mexican music—music that ranged from traditional Mexican ballads to newly recorded *corridos* depicting life in Los Angeles—was everywhere. A burgeoning Mexican music industry flourished in the central and eastern sections of the city during the 1920s, largely hidden from the Anglo majority.

The diminished role of organized religion in the day-to-day life of Mexican immigrants was coupled with increased participation in secular activities. In Mexico, most public events in rural villages were organized by the Catholic Church, with few other opportunities outside the family for diversion. Los Angeles, however, offered abundant entertainment of all sorts. These amusements were generally part of a rapidly growing market in leisure which targeted working-class families during the 1920s. Money spent on leisure-time activities easily outstripped donations to the Church, revealing much about the cultural changes occurring in the Mexican immigrant community.[1] Chicano entrepreneurs responded to the emerging ethnic mass market in cultural forms, even though that market was often dominated by outside advertising and controlled primarily by non-Mexicans. Still, the presence of a growing ethnic market in Los Angeles provided room for many traditional practices to continue, some flourishing in the new environment, but most being transformed in the process.

This chapter will explore the intersection between the growing mass market in cultural forms found in Los Angeles and the leisure-time activities of Mexican immigrants. The various actors who helped shape the creation of a market aimed at providing Mexican immigrants with products, services, and activities that somehow connected with the ethnic self-identification and collective culture will be identified. The complicated nature of this exchange can best be described, however, by looking at one particular arena of cultural interaction. Music, specifically the creation of a Spanish-language music industry and market in Los Angeles, provides one of the best windows for viewing this nexus of cultural transformation in detail.

The Plaza itself continued to cater to single males, offering pool halls, dance rooms, bars, and a small red-light district. Protestant reformers, therefore, consistently viewed Plaza residents as prime targets for moral rejuvenation. In addition, many small, immigrant-owned eateries were located in the area which catered to a male clientele often unable or unwilling to cook for themselves.

A description of a dancing club frequented by single males during this period indicates the extent of the intermingling between sexes and nationalities in the Plaza, a situation which concerned reformers. Located on Main Street, the club "Latino" was open every night except Sunday from 7:30 p.m. to 1 a.m., although it did most of its business on Saturday night. Inside and out, the hall was illuminated by red, white, and green lights, the colors of the Mexican flag. Entrance to the club cost 25 cents, and tickets were 10 cents apiece to dance with women. The female employees were mostly immigrant Mexicans or Mexican Americans, although Anglo-American, Italian, Filipino, Chinese, and Japanese women also were available. The band, however, was made up of black musicians and played only American pieces. Mexican immigrant men, dressed in working-class garb, danced "Mexican style" to the American songs; a ticket was required for every dance; and the women partners earned 5 cents per dance. In one corner of the dance floor a Mexican woman sold sandwiches, tacos, pastries, and coffee.[2]

As Los Angeles Mexicans moved away from the Plaza and the community became more familial in structure, different diversions predominated. Some customs were carried over to marriage from single life. For example, a federal survey reported that three-quarters of Mexican families in Los Angeles continued to spend an average of $14 a year for tobacco. Almost two-thirds read the newspaper on a regular basis. Increasingly Mexican families began to purchase other forms of entertainment which could be enjoyed by all ages and in the confines of one's home. Over one-third of the families in the Los Angeles study owned radios, often buying the equipment "on time" for an average of $27 a year. A smaller number (3%) owned phonographs, and only 4 percent owned musical instruments. Expenditures for vacations, social entertainment (other than movies), and hobbies were rare.[3]

During the 1920s, many American manufacturers and retailers discovered a fairly lucrative market in the local Mexican immigrant community. Despite the clamor for Mexican immigration restrictions, these producers understood that Los Angeles contained a large and growing population of Spanish-speaking immigrants. By 1930, some national products were advertised in the Spanish-language press, and increasingly large distributors sponsored programs in Spanish on the radio.[4] Among products heavily advertised in *La Opinión* during this period were cigarettes, medicinal remedies, and recordings to help immigrants learn the English language.

Even more widespread were appeals to Mexican shoppers by certain downtown department stores. In 1929, for example, the Third Street Store advertised in *La Opinión* by asking, "Why are we the store for Mexicans?" The answer stressed the appeal of special merchandise, prices, and service. Located near the Plaza, offering generous credit, the store had apparently already become a favorite in the Mexican community.[5] This kind of ethnic appeal fostered competition among some of downtown Los Angeles' largest retailers. Another department store even offered free "Cinco de Mayo" pennants to any Mexican who purchased its merchandise.[6]

Many of the mass-produced consumer goods in the 1920s were specifically marketed with an appeal to youth. This appeal had profound consequences for Mexican immigrant families. Older children who entered the work force often earned enough to become more autonomous. Adolescents and young adults were often the first to introduce a Mexican family to certain foods, clothing, or activities that were incompatible with traditional Mexican customs. For example, younger Mexican women began to use cosmetics and wear nylon stockings. Young men were more likely to seek out new leisure-time activities, such as American sports or the movie houses. Second-generation youth were often the first in their families to see a motion picture. At times, experimentation led to intergenerational conflict, with much tension revolving around consumer purchases and the control of earned income.

Despite some initial reservations, most Mexican parents joined other Americans in the 1920s in a love affair with motion pictures. Ninety percent of all families in the Los Angeles survey spent money on the movies, averaging $22 a year per family. In San Diego, a government committee investigating local economic conditions observed that "as in American families, movie tickets were an essential feature of these Mexican families' spending ways except under pressure of a special need for economy." In addition, the committee presumed that some working children retained a portion of their wages to spend on movie tickets.[7]

The movie industry in Los Angeles aided Mexicans in retaining old values, but also played a role in cultural change. On the one hand, films produced in Mexico made their way into the many theatres in the downtown area in the late 1920s catering to the Mexican immigrant population. These supplemented American- and European-made silent films which were aimed by their promoters at an often illiterate immigrant population. Sound was not introduced until 1929, so that throughout the decade of the 1920s, movies stressed visual images and presented few language barriers for the non-English speaker.

Since their inception in the nickelodeons of eastern seaboard cities, American films consistently contained storylines intentionally made for the immigrant masses.[8] Messages tended to be largely populist and democratic in tone. Plots stressed the commonality of all Americans. The children of Mexican immigrants were especially intrigued by the open sexuality depicted on the screen. The experience of sitting alone in a darkened theatre and identifying with screen characters, as Lary May has argued, could feel quite liberating.[9]

What made American-made films even more appealing was the appearance of actors and actresses who were Mexican by nationality. Although Ramón Navarro and Lupe Vélez were introduced to audiences in the early twenties, the arrival of Dolores del Río in 1925 brought Mexican immigrants flocking to the box office. The attraction was not simply the desire to support a compatriot; it was also generated by the close proximity of the movie industry. *La Opinión*, for example, the city's leading Spanish-language periodical, regularly followed the Hollywood scene, paying particular attention to the city's rising Latin stars. As citizens of Mexico themselves, the newspaper's editors were quick to condemn stars who distanced themselves from their national origins, while praising others, like del Río, who showed interest in preserving their Mexican identity.[10]

While the motion-picture industry displayed one aspect of the impact of consumerism on immigrant cultural adaptation, opportunities for other entrepreneurs to make an ethnic appeal emerged during this period. Ethnic marketing, usually considered a recent phenomena, in fact has long-standing roots in this era. While huge American corporations consolidated their hold on a national mass market of goods during the 1920s, much room was left for local entrepreneurs to seek sub-markets that catered to the interests and desires of particular groups. In many ways, the standardization of messages brought about by large-scale advertising created new avenues for ethnic entrepreneurs. Since few national advertising agencies were located in Los Angeles or in the American Southwest, little attention was paid by national corporations to distinctly regional appeals. This void was filled by Mexican and non-Mexican entrepreneurs who realized that money could be made by servicing the large and growing Mexican population in the city.

As early as 1916, small Mexican-owned businesses advertised in Spanish-language newspapers.[11] These establishments were generally store-front operations which allegedly provided items that were "typically Mexican." El Progreso Restaurant on North Main Street, for example, claimed that it cooked food in the "truly Mexican style." Similar restaurants were frequented by the large Mexican male population around the Plaza. Other businesses attempted to bring Mexican products into the Los Angeles market directly. La Tienda Mexicana, on San Fernando Street, carried herbs and cooking supplies which were generally unavailable elsewhere. Down the street, a clothing store, the

Sastrería Mexicana, was less successful in its appeal to ethnic taste in dress.[12] It was one thing to continue to put Mexican food in your stomach and quite another to continue to dress in "traditional" Mexican garb on the streets of Los Angeles.

By 1920, large, well-financed operations dominated the Mexican retail business. Their advertisements regularly appeared in the city's Spanish-language periodicals for the next two decades. Farmacia Hidalgo, run by G. Salazar and located at 362 North Main street, declared that it was the only store "positively of the Mexican community." Farmacia Ruiz was founded by a influential Mexican expatriate and quickly gained much status in the immigrant community. Over the next ten years, it was frequented by several candidates for the Mexican presidency, most notably José Vasconcelos.[13] Mauricio Calderón, another emigrant from Mexico, would soon dominate the Spanish-language music industry in Los Angeles. During this decade he established the Repertorio Musical Mexicana, an outlet for phonographs and Spanish-language records, which he claimed was "the only Mexican house of Mexican music for Mexicans." Finally, two theatres, the Teatro Novel and the Teatro Hidalgo, located on Spring and Main streets respectively, were already in operation in 1920, offering both silent films imported from Mexico as well as live entertainment.

A host of rival Mexican-owned firms gave these early businesses much competition. Advertisements usually stressed that their particular establishment was the most "genuinely Mexican" of the group. The Farmacia Hidalgo went so far as to place an Aztec eagle on some of its products to insure "authenticity." A new and important enterprise was the Librería Lozano, providing Spanish-language books to the literate Mexican community and owned by Ignacio Lozano, the editor of *La Opinión*. Not surprisingly, Lozano heavily advertised in his own paper.

In addition, the 1920s witnessed the emergence of Mexican professionals who also targeted their fellow countrymen for patronage. A small, but significant group of doctors, dentists, and lawyers from Mexico set up shop in Los Angeles, and their advertisements stressed that their training had been conducted in the finest Mexican universities.[14]

Mexican entrepreneurs, however, were not the only individuals in Los Angeles who appealed to the Mexican consumer; non-Mexicans also tried to capitalize on the growing ethnic clientele. Leading this effort was the medical profession, particularly women doctors and physicians from other ethnic groups not likely to develop a following within a highly male-dominated, Anglo Protestant profession.[15] Most of these physicians were located near the Plaza area, particularly along Main Street, an area which provided direct access to the immigrant population. Female physicians held special appeal as specialists for women, capitalizing on the sense of propriety among immigrant women. "Doctora" Augusta Stone, for example, advertised as a specialist for "las señoras," and was among the first to use the phrase "Habla Español" in her advertisements. Dr. Luigi Gardini, an Italian American physician, also advertised in Spanish-language newspapers in 1916. Asian American physicians, however, were the largest group of non-Mexican professionals to appeal to Mexican immigrants, largely stressing their training in herbal medicine, an area not unfamiliar to rural Mexicans. Among them was Dr. Chee, who characterized himself as "Doctor Chino" in 1920, and Dr. Y. Kim, who boasted the combination of a Yale degree and a speciality in Oriental herbal treatments.

The growth and increasing economic stability of the Mexican immigrant community in Los Angeles made these appeals profitable. While the Mexican middle class remained small and relatively insignificant, the large working-class community was quickly developing east of the Los Angeles River. Lack of capital and professional training in the Mexican community made it difficult for most Mexicans to take direct economic advantage of this growth. Yet their cumulative purchasing power did allow for the growth of certain enterprises which catered to the unique backgrounds of Mexican immigrants, while creating new modes of ethnic expression.

One of the most important of these enterprises was music. Although the musical legacies of different regions in Mexico were significant, traditions were both reinforced and transformed in the environment of Los Angeles. As a diverse collection of immigrant musicians arrived from central and northern Mexico, often via south Texas, they stimulated the growth of a recording industry and burgeoning radio network that offered fertile ground for musical innovation.

Of 1,746 Mexican immigrants who began the naturalization procedure, 110 were musicians (6.3% of the total), making them the second largest occupational group in the sample, well behind the category of "common laborer."[16] Although 80 percent of the musicians did not complete the process, their ample presence among those who initiated the naturalization process indicates their willingness to remain in the United States. Unlike working-class musicians of Mexican descent in Texas, it appears that many Los Angeles-based musicians were willing to consider changing their citizenship.[17] If, as Manuel Peña has claimed, musicians do function as "organic intellectuals" for the working class, challenging American cultural hegemony while expressing the frustrations and hopes of their social group, then the experiences of Los Angeles musicians indicate a complex, if not contradictory, relationship with American cultural values.[18]

Compared with the larger sample of Mexican immigrants, musicians were more likely to have been born in the larger cities of the central plateau in Mexico, particularly Guadalajara and Mexico City. Over 25 percent of Mexican musicians in Los Angeles came from these two cities alone, compared with 10 percent of the entire sample. Other towns in central Mexico, such as Zacatecas, Guanajuato, Puebla, and San Luis Potosí, were also well represented in the musical community. Unlike the larger sample, northern states were generally underrepresented among musicians, except for the state of Sonora, which accounted for 9 percent of the performers. In central Mexico, the states of Jalisco and Guanajuato and the Federal District alone produced over 41 percent of all Mexican musicians in Los Angeles.[19]

The musical traditions brought to the United States from these locales were varied. The mobility within Mexico caused by economic upheaval and violence related to the revolution had pushed many rural residents, including folk musicians, to seek shelter in towns and cities. There, previously isolated folk music traditions from various locations were brought together, and musicians also encountered the more European musical tastes of the urban upper classes. One study of street musicians in Mexico City during the 1920s, for example, found twelve different regional styles performing simultaneously on the corners and in the marketplaces of the capital. One could hear mariachis from Jalisco, *canciones norteñas* from Chihuahua, troubadors from Yucatán, *bandas jarochas* from Veracruz, and marimba groups from Chiapas and Oaxaca.[20]

If there was one particular musical style which stood out from the rest in popularity during this period, it was certainly the *corrido*. A prominent student of this genre has called the *corrido* "an integral part of Mexican life" and the creative period after 1910 its "most glorious epoch."[21] During the Mexican Revolution, almost every important event, and most political leaders and rebels, became the subjects of one or more *corridos*. Pedro J. González, who later emerged as the most well-known Mexican musician in Los Angeles, remembered composing *corridos* with seven other soldiers fighting with Pancho Villa in secluded mountain hideouts during lulls between battles. None was a trained musician, but each used the opportunity to criticize each other jokingly for past misfortunes or to immortalize some heroic deed through song.[22] As these *corridos* made their way into Mexico's urban centers, they were codified and transformed from folk expression to popular songs.[23]

The *corrido's* continued popularity during the 1920s in areas far away from its folk origins can be explained by particular characteristics of its style which made it appealing as an urban art form. First, the urban *corrido*, like the *canción ranchera*, embodied what was a traditional music style from the countryside, while adapting it to a more commercially oriented atmosphere. It reminded those who had migrated from rural areas of their provincial roots, and gave urban dwellers a connection to the agrarian ideal which was seen as typically Mexican.[24] Second, most *corridos* appealed to a Mexican's nationalist fervor at a time when the pride of Mexican people, places, and events was flourishing. Several observers have identified the period between 1910 and 1940 as one of "national romanticism" in Mexican cultural affairs, extending beyond music to literature and mural painting. *Corridos* produced in the United States often exalted "Mexicanism" at the expense of American culture, but even those composed within Mexico paid inordinate attention to promoting Mexican cultural identity.[25]

Finally, the *corrido* was an exceptionally flexible musical genre which encouraged adapting composition to new situations and surroundings. Melodies, for the most part, were standardized or based on traditional patterns, while text was expected to be continuously improvised. A vehicle for narration, the *corrido* always intended to tell a story to its listeners, one that would not necessarily be news but rather would "interpret, celebrate, and ultimately dignify events already thoroughly familiar to the *corrido* audience."[26] As such, *corrido* musicians were expected to decipher the new surroundings in which Mexican immigrants found themselves while living in Los Angeles. Its relation to the working-class Mexican immigrant audience in Los Angeles was therefore critical to its continued popularity. As one L.A.-based composer explained, "The *corrido* is a narrative viewed through the eyes of the people—its subject almost always follows the truth."[27] This adaptive style was particularly well suited for the rapidly expanding Los Angeles Mexican community of the 1920s and the ever-complex nature of intercultural exchange in the city.

The first commercial recording of a *corrido* in the United States was "El Lavaplatos." Performed in Los Angeles on May 11, 1926, by Los Hermanos Bañuelos as a duet with guitar accompaniment, the song was apparently originally written by Pedro J. González.[28] The *corrido* describes a Mexican immigrant who dreams of making a fortune in the United States but, instead, is beset with economic misfortune. Finally, after being forced to take a job as a dishwasher, the narrator bemoans: "Goodbye dreams of my life, goodbye movie stars, I am going back to my beloved homeland, much poorer than when I came."[29]

Most Mexican composers and musicians had firsthand knowledge of working-class life in Los Angeles; not only were they products of working-class homes, but most continued in some form of blue-collar occupation while struggling to survive as musicians. Pedro J. González, for example, worked as a longshoreman on the San Pedro docks before being "discovered," and the two musicians who played with him, Victor and Jesus Sánchez, were farmworkers.[30] The vast majority of Mexican musicians never were able to support themselves as full-time artists. One composer of *corridos*, for example, worked in a cement plant, a lumber yard, an oil refinery, the railroad, the telephone company, agricultural fields, and at the Biltmore Hotel while composing songs during the 1920s and 1930s.[31] Several who applied for American citizenship listed additional occupations with authorities.[32] A similar situation existed among Texas *conjunto* musicians. According to Manuel Peña, they "played and earned just enough to satisfy a few—not all—of their economic needs. There simply were not enough dances during a week for full-time employment: Saturday and Sunday were practically the only days for celebrating."[33]

Los Angeles during the 1920s, however, presented more possibilities for earning a livelihood as a musician than any other location outside of Mexico City, or perhaps San Antonio. To begin with, the Los Angeles metropolitan area contained a huge Spanish-speaking population, second only to Mexico City itself. By 1930 the Chicano population in the city of Los Angeles was larger than any other in the United States. The potential audience for Mexican music was enormous. Since most of these residents were recent migrants from Mexico, they often longed for tunes from their homeland. Others had come from south Texas, where the Spanish-language musical tradition was strong and widespread.[34] In fact, one writer claimed in 1932 that more Mexican music had been composed in the United States than in Mexico.[35]

One stimulus to the Mexican music industry was the explosion of Chicano theatre in Los Angeles during the 1920s. Over thirty Chicano playwrights moved to the city during the decade, producing shows ranging from melodrama to vaudeville. The Spanish-speaking population of the region was able to support five major theatre houses from 1918 until the early 1930s: Teatro Hidalgo, Teatro México, Teatro Capitol, Teatro Zendejas (later Novel), and Teatro Principal. In addition to these five which featured programs that changed daily, at least seventeen other theatres housed Spanish-speaking professional companies on a more irregular basis.[36]

Many of these theatres alternated vaudevillian-style shows with Mexican- or Hollywood-made silent films (three shows a day, four on weekends) during the 1920s. Both live performances and silent movies required musical accompaniment. Theatres, therefore, provided relatively stable employment to a diverse collection of musicians throughout the 1920s. The lack of formal training among many of the musicians did not necessarily hamper them, since playing on the streets often helped them prepare for the spontaneity and improvisation required for this type of performance.

The presence of a large number of middle-class Mexican expatriates also created a market for formally trained musicians who could read music. They performed for a type of theater which featured drama from Spain with orchestral accompaniment, similar to the more refined entertainment among the middle classes in Mexico City. While never enjoying the mass appeal of movies and vaudeville, this European-style performance did provide employment for other musicians from Mexico.[37]

A more disparate, yet still lucrative market for Mexican musicians existed among the streets and informal gatherings of Los Angeles. During Mexican patriotic festivals and the Christmas season, musicians had larger audiences, more exposure, and greater potential for earnings. From these "auditions," Mexican groups were often recruited to play for weddings and other ethnic festivities. Moreover, a market for "traditional" Mexican music also existed among some Anglo residents of Los Angeles, often to provide a nostalgic backdrop to the distinctive "Spanish" past of the city. Pedro J. González, for example, often entertained at parties conducted by city officials and the police department.[38] Another *corrido* composer, Jesus Osorio, was able to make a living as a singer combining work in Olvera Street booths, private gatherings, and in the small theatres and cabarets along Main Street.[39]

The emergence of Hollywood as the leading movie-making capital in the United States during the 1920s stimulated a flourishing recording industry in the city that began to rival New York's. Both these developments boded well for Mexican musicians in Los Angeles, although prejudice, union discrimination, and the lack of formal training kept many out of regular employment in the entertainment industries in the western part of town. Still, by providing the music in English-speaking theatres or working as studio musicians, some were able to break into the larger music business in Los Angeles.[40] Even the possibility of such employment—"the dream of a life in Hollywood"—was enough to attract some performers from south of the border.

Thus musicians from Mexico flocked to Los Angeles during the 1920s, becoming a significant segment of the Mexican cultural renaissance of that decade. Unlike the Harlem Renaissance, where black writers and entertainers were often sponsored by white patrons, this Chicano/Mexicano renaissance was largely supported by Mexican immigrants themselves and existed far out of the sight of the majority of Angelinos. The presence of large numbers of Mexican musicians in the city not only preserved the sights and sounds familiar to Mexican immigrants; it also created an environment of cultural experimentation where traditional music was blended with new methods. In short, musicians often served as social interpreters who translated and reflected the cultural adaptations that were taking place among the Mexican immigrant population as a whole.[41] In fact, one astute observer of *corridos* in Los Angeles recognized that this music often served to "sing what they cannot say":

Mexicans are so intimidated by the government officials, even by social workers, and so timid on account of the language difficulty that it is almost unheard of for a Mexican to express his opinion to an American. Here, however, he is speaking to his own group and an emotional outlet is offered in the writing of *corridos* on the subject so well known to every Mexican. He is reasonably sure that only Mexicans will ever hear his *corrido*.[42]

Despite their economic and cultural connection to the greater immigrant population. Mexican musicians displayed different patterns of migration and settlement. As a group, they were among the first of the migrants to see the advantages of settling in Los Angeles, with many arriving in the city around World War I or in the early 1920s. Moreover, they usually arrived as adults, crossing the border at an average age of twenty-four years during the 1910s and an average of thirty-two years during the 1920s. The profession was also dominated traditionally by men. Only four of the 110 musicians in my sample were women, and two of these listed their occupation as singers. One study conducted in 1939, for example, found no *corrido* written by a woman in the music shops of Los Angeles.[43] Few avenues of opportunity were available to women in the Spanish-language music industry in Los Angeles, although several women—including the singer Lydia Mendoza—did make names for themselves during the 1930s.

By necessity, most Mexican musicians lived west of the river, even after many of their people began to venture into East Los Angeles. The recording and film industry was located in the western part of the city, and Mexican cultural life continued to be centered around the plaza and downtown areas of the city until the 1940s. Most Spanish-language theatres were located on Main Street, and opportunities for steady income depended on the patronage of the audiences that gathered around the Placita or in downtown restaurants. During the 1930s when so-called "Latin" music clubs were established, they too were located in the downtown area until after World War II. Lalo Guerrero, who arrived in Los Angeles in 1937, remembered that not until economic opportunities around the Plaza declined did many Mexican musicians decide to move to East Los Angeles:

> Since the clubs in the westside started dying off . . . the musicians that had not wanted to come to East L.A., because they thought it was a step down, . . . were practically forced to come back because there was not too much happening on the westside, 'cause the latin scene had passed.[44]

The data confirm this pattern of residence for musicians: 60 percent in the naturalization sample lived around the downtown area, including 20 percent that resided near the Plaza. This compares with less than 39 percent of the overall sample who lived downtown, and 9 percent whose residence was located in the Plaza area.[45] Steady income and the opening up of the electric railway into East Los Angeles gave some musicians the opportunity to move to Belvedere or some of the other communities east of the river. Pedro J. González, for example, moved to Belvedere after residing close to the Plaza.[46]

This residential pattern is an indication that life as a musician did not usually provide the glamour and security which many associated with the entertainment field. Even the advent in the 1920s of an ethnic mass market centered in Los Angeles, which prompted American recording companies and local entrepreneurs to search for Mexican musical talent, meant only short-lived economic returns. Rapid exploitation of the talents of musicians brought quick profits to upstart recording companies but left most Chicano performers—even those who developed a loyal following—with limited resources to show for their newfound fame.

When Los Hermanos Bañuelos first recorded "El Lavaplatos," they ushered in the commercial recording of Mexican music. Already, several large American recording companies such as Vocalion, Okeh (a subsidiary of Columbia), Decca, and Bluebird (RCA) had begun to produce "race" records, featuring black folk music. These companies now realized the potential ethnic market among Mexicans, and sought out Chicano musicians and singers from Texas to California. Many of the early recording sessions took place in temporary studios located in Los Angeles hotels, where a steady stream of performers were expected to produce a finished product in one or two "takes."[47]

To most musicians, the $15 or $20 they earned per record seemed substantial for a few hours' work, especially when compared with the wages they earned as laborers or the limited income from playing on the streets. Yet these tiny sums were a pittance relative to the hundreds or thousands of dollars any single recording could earn, even with records selling for 35 cents apiece. Musicians rarely earned sufficient income to feel secure as recording artists. Offering only "contracts" that were usually verbal agreements consisting of no royalties or other subsidiary rights, the recording companies profited handsomely from this enterprise.[48] Similar contractual agreements were made with Chicano artists as late as the 1940s, even though the pay scale had moved up to $50 a side or $100 per record.[49]

Local ethnic middlemen played an important role in identifying talented musicians and putting them in contact with recording companies. In Los Angeles, one important liason was Mauricio Calderón, owner of the music store Repertorio Musical Mexicana, established on Main Street around 1920 to feature records and phonographs produced by Columbia Records. According to Pedro J. González, Calderón was in charge of everything in Los Angeles that related to Mexican music. He recruited talented musicians by advertising in the Spanish-language press, and kept an ear out for the latest musical trends among the city's performers and audiences. Not only did Calderón make money by serving as a go-between between American companies and the Mexican artists, but he also held a monopoly on the area-wide distribution of these recordings through his store. A standard practice of the time for such businesses was to sell phonographs as well as records, and stores such as Calderón's profited as well from these items. In fact, Calderón's store, located at 418 North Main Street near the Plaza, regularly promoted itself by using a loudspeaker mounted in front on the store playing the latest *corrido*. A small group of men regularly stood in front of the store, listening intently and enjoying the music. Another popular promotion tactic was to give away records with the purchase of a Victrola.[50]

American laws prohibited the importation of records from Mexico, a fact which greatly stimulated the recording industry in Los Angeles. In addition, Mexican companies were not allowed to record in the United States. These restrictions severely crippled the music industry in Mexico, while creating a vast economic opportunity for American companies and ethnic entrepreneurs. When Mexican recordings were finally admitted during the 1950s, interest in immigrant and native-born Spanish-language talent evaporated quickly, and many Chicano musicians were left without an outlet in the recording world. In fact, some labels which had showcased Mexican artists, such as Imperial, began concentrating on black rhythm and blues artists, such as Fats Domino and T-Bone Walker.[51]

During the 1920s and 1930s, however, a vibrant environment for Mexican music existed in Los Angeles. Another factor in creating this cultural explosion was the advent of the radio. During the 1920s, commercial radio was still in an experimental era where corporate sponsors and station managers tried to discover how best to make radio broadcasting profitable and enlightening. For most of the decade, the radio was seen as a way of uplifting the masses, of bringing elite American culture into the homes of common laborers.[52] By the end of the decade, however, advertising and corporate economic interests dominated the air-waves. This transformation created a market for Spanish-language broadcasts. Although many Anglo Americans continued to believe that only English should be heard on the nation's airwaves, the goal of reaching Spanish-speaking consumers silenced their opposition.

American radio programmers scheduled Spanish-language broadcasts during "dead" airtime—early morning, late night, or weekend periods which had proven to be unprofitable for English programs. Pedro J. González remembers first broadcasting from 4 to 6 a.m. on Station KELW out of Burbank. He often scheduled live music, including many amateur musicians and singers from the community.[53] While Anglo Americans were rarely listening at this hour, many Mexican immigrants tuned into González's broadcasts while they prepared for early morning work shifts. González's daily shows provided day laborers important information about jobs as well as cherished enjoyment to workers who toiled all day.[54]

Corporate radio sponsors in the mid-1920s were quick to understand the profitability of ethnic programs. Large advertisers such as Folgers Coffee used airtime to push their product in the Spanish-speaking market. More often, local businesses appealed to Mexican immigrants to frequent their establishments. In Los Angeles, radio broadcasting soon became a highly competitive industry. By selling blocks of airtime to foreign-language brokers, marginally profitable stations could capture a ready-made market. During the late 1920s, the hours dedicated to Spanish-language broadcasts multiplied. González's program was expanded until 7 a.m., and additional hours were added at lunchtime and in the early evening. Chicano brokers such as Mauricio Calderón profited handsomely as they negotiated with stations, paying them a flat rate during cheap broadcasting time, which they then sold to businesses advertisements.[55]

Key to the success of Spanish-language broadcasting was its appeal to the thousands of working-class Mexican immigrants within the reach of a station's radio signal. Radio, unlike *La Opinión* and other periodicals, reached Mexican immigrants whether or not they could read. In addition, the content of radio programming focused less on the tastes of the expatriate middle class and more on those of the masses. A 1941 analysis of Spanish-language programming found that over 88 percent of on-air time (outside of advertisements) was dedicated to music, with only 4 percent used for news.[56] Programming was dominated by "traditional" music from the Mexican countryside, rather than the orchestral, more "refined" sounds of the Mexican capital and other large urban centers. "The corrido, the shouts, and all that stuff was popular" with working people, remembered González. Although some bemoaned the commercialization of the *corrido* tradition and its removal from its "folk tradition," most Mexican immigrants found this transformation to their liking because it fit well with their own adaptations to urban living.[57]

The potential power generated by this mass appeal was so substantial that it not only threatened the cultural hegemony of the Mexican middle class in Los Angeles but also worried local Anglo-American officials. González himself was the target of District Attorney Buron Fitts, who in 1934 had the musician arrested on trumped-up charges. Earlier, Fitts had attempted to force González off the air by getting federal authorities to rescind his broadcasting license. Along with other government authorities, Fitts believed that only English should be heard on the radio and that only American citizens should have the right to broadcast. As a result, many radio stations curtailed their Spanish-language programs during the early 1930s, often because of the continued harassment directed at ethnic broadcasters and the imposition of more stringent rules for radio licensing.[58]

These restrictions in the United States encouraged the growth of Spanish-language broadcasting in Mexico. Although many American stations continued to reserve Spanish-language blocks, entrepreneurs based just across the border capitalized on the potential market on both sides by constructing powerful radio towers capable of reaching far-flung audiences. Increasingly, individuals unable to be heard on American-based stations moved their operations to Mexico. It proved much harder for American authorities to control the airwaves than the recording industry Mexican immigrants could now listen to radio programming from Mexico itself, ironically often featuring music performed by U.S.-based Mexicans.[59]

The economic crisis of the 1930s curtailed much of Mexican cultural activity in Los Angeles. First, deportation and repatriation campaigns pushed almost one-third of the Mexican community back to Mexico, effectively restricting the market for Spanish-language advertising campaigns. Second, the enthusiasm of American companies for investing in "experimental" markets that did not insure a steady flow of income understandably cooled. The Mexican immigrant community itself had fewer resources to support cultural activities, given its precarious economic situation. Since expenditures on leisure-time activities were the first to be reduced during times of need, many families cut back drastically on attendance at musical events or the purchase of radios and phonographs. Many theatres in the community shut down during the Great Depression.[60]

Movies and other forms of cheap, cross-cultural entertainment continued to thrive in Depression-era Los Angeles. Simply because of the economics of scale, Hollywood was able to continue to produce entertainment accessible to families at every economic level. In addition, the introduction of sound to motion pictures made it more difficult to sustain a steady Spanish-language audience with Mexican imports, since the Mexican film industry had difficulty throughout the transition of the 1930s.[61] English talking-pictures, on the other hand, had a wider, and therefore more secure audience. The advent of sound coincided with the rise of the second generation of Mexicans in this country, more likely to be as fluent in English as in Spanish. Increasingly, changing demographics and limited economic resources stunted the growth of the ethnic market. A new era in Mexican/Chicano cultural activity began.

Although commercial activity was slowed during the Depression, Mexican cultural life did not die out in Los Angeles. Indeed, aspects of cultural life were altered dramatically, reflecting the changing composition and nature of the Mexican/Chicano community. Musical activity, for example, became less dependent on *corrido* story-telling (which required the ability to understand Spanish lyrics) and more concentrated in dance clubs. La Bamba night club, at Macy and Spring streets, and La Casa Olvera, adjacent to Olvera Street, were only two of many small clubs which opened during the decade. Dancing, of course, did not require a working knowledge of Spanish, and had appeal well beyond the Mexican immigrant population.[62]

Second-generation youth, in particular, flooded the dance clubs during the 1930s. Social commentators of the period commented on the "dance craze" that had seemingly overtaken adolescents and young adults in Mexican American families. One such nineteen-year-old, known only as Alfredo to his interviewer, boastfully explained this "craze":

> I love to dance better than anything else in the world. It is something that gets in your blood. Lots of boys are that way. I go to five dances a week. I can't wait for Saturday night because all the time I am thinking of the dance. It is in my system. I could get a job playing my trumpet in an orchestra but then I couldn't dance. I quit school because I got plenty of everything they teach, but dancing.[63]

This new "dance craze" did not often sit well with Mexican immigrant parents. Even when participation was closely chaperoned in school clubs and community centers, public dancing seemed to offend the sensibilities of decency among older Mexicans. Increasingly, however, it became difficult for parents to withstand the effect of peer pressure on their children, as evidenced by the words of one mother in the early 1930s:

> Juanita has joined a club and now she wants to learn to dance. That is what comes of these clubs. It is wrong to dance and my Juanita wants to do it because the others do. Because everybody does it does not make it right. I know the things I was taught as a girl and right and wrong cannot change.[64]

Although the vast majority of musicians and clientele in each of these establishments were Mexican, the music demonstrated a wide variety of American and Latin American styles. Cuban music was especially popular in the latter half of the decade, with many orchestras specializing in the mambo. The Cuban style was popular throughout Latin America, and this trend filtered into Los Angeles through traveling bands and musicians. Regular groups that played in these clubs all included Mexican songs in their repertoire.[65] In addition, English-language music increasingly became popular among American-born youth. Many Mexican immigrants bemoaned this turn of events, as evidenced by the comments of one unnamed señora:

> The old Spanish songs are sung only be the old people. The young ones can sing the "Boop-da-oop" like you hear on the radio but they can't sing more than one verse of *La Cruz*. Do you know *La Cruz*? It is very beautiful. It is about our Lord carrying the cross. It is sad. In Mexico we would all sing for hours while someone played a guitar. But here, there are the drums and the saxophones.[66]

Undoubtedly, a more eclectic and diverse musical life than in former decades emerged among the Mexican/Chicano community in Los Angeles. In fact, Los Angeles probably offered a richer environment for such leisure-time activity than any other city in the American Southwest.

This diversity of choice in musical styles and taste not only created a more experimental environment for musicians themselves but also reflected developments in Chicano culture as a whole. Clearly, the control of the individual over his or her own cultural choices paralleled the growth of an ethnic consumer market. In a consumer society, each Mexican immigrant alone, or in conjunction with family, embraced cultural change—consciously or unconsciously—through the purchase of material goods or by participation in certain functions. Neither the Mexican elite nor the Anglo American reformers intent on Americanization could completely determine the character of these private decisions. Instead, an unsteady relationship between American corporations, local businesses, Mexican entrepreneurs, and the largely working-class community itself influenced the range of cultural practices and consumer items available in the Spanish-language market. If appeals to Mexican nationalism could be used to sell a product, then so be it. Although barriers to the ethnic market were constructed by local officials, particularly during the Great Depression, change in economic circumstances and in cultural tastes of the population had the most important impact.

Appeal to the tastes of youth also created subtle power shifts within the Chicano community. In Mexico, few outlets were available to young people for influencing cultural practices in an individual village or even one's own family. The American metropolis, on the other hand, gave Mexican youth an opportunity to exercise more cultural prerogatives merely by purchasing certain products or going to the movies. Rebellion against family often went hand in hand with a shift toward more American habits. This pattern was stimulated by the extent to which adolescents and unmarried sons and daughters worked and retained some of their own income. As the second generation came to dominate the Chicano population by the late 1930s, their tastes redefined the community's cultural practices and future directions of cultural adaptation.

Behind the vast American commercial network lay an enterprising group of ethnic entrepreneurs who served as conduits between the Mexican immigrant population and the corporate world. These individuals were often the first to recognize cultural changes and spending patterns among the immigrant population. Individuals such as Mauricio Calderón and Pedro J. González were able to promote Mexican music in entirely new forms in Los Angeles because they had daily contact with ordinary members of the Los Angeles Mexican community. Although they found tangible financial rewards in their efforts, they also served an important role in redefining Mexican culture in an American urban environment.

Notes

1. The Heller Committee for Research in Social Economics of the University of California and Constantine Panunzio, *How Mexicans Earn and Live: A Study of the Incomes and Expenditures of One Hundred Mexican Families in San Diego, California*, Cost of Living Studies, 5 (Berkeley: Univ. of California Press, 1933), 49–52, 63–64.

2. "Observaciones—Los Salones de Baile," Observations of Luis Felipe Recinos, Los Angeles, Calif., 15 April 1927, Manuel Gamio collection, Bancroft Library, University of California, Berkeley.

3. U.S. Department of Labor, Bureau of Labor Statistics, "Mexican Families in Los Angeles," *Money Disbursements of Wage Earners and Clerical Workers in Five Cities in the Pacific Region, 1934–36*, Bulletin 639 (Washington, D.C.: GPO, 1939), 108–9, 231. For similar figures from San Diego, see Heller Committee and Panunzio, *Earn and Live*, 50–52.

4. See *Ballad of an Unsung Hero*, Cinewest/KPBS, 1983.

5. *La Opinión*, 10 May 1929.

6. *La Opinión*, 3 May 1927.

7. U.S. Department of Labor, *Money Disbursements*, 231; Heller Committee and Panunzio, *Earn and Live*, 50, 71.

8. See Lary May, *Screening Out the Past: The Birth of Mass Culture and the Motion Picture Industry* (Chicago: Univ. of Chicago Press, 1980), and Kathy Peiss, *Cheap Amusements: Working Women and Leisure in Turn-of-the-Century New York* (Philadelphia: Temple Univ. Press, 1986), 139–62.

9. May, *Screening*, 152–58.

10. Larry Carr, *More Fabulous Faces: The Evolution and Metamorphosis of Dolores Del Río, Myrna Loy, Carole Lombard, Bette Davis, and Katharine Hepburn* (Garden City, N.Y.: Doubleday, 1979), 1–51; De Witt Bodeen, "Dolores Del Río: Was the First Mexican of Family to Act in Hollywood," *Films in Review* 18 (1967), 266–83; José Gómez-Sicre, "Dolores Del Río," *Américas* 19 (1967), 8–17.

11. From content analysis of advertisements in Spanish-language newspapers in Los Angeles from 1916 to 1935. *El Heraldo de México*, 3 May 1916, 2 May 1920, and 13 Sept. 1925, and *La Opinión*, 6 April 1930 and 5 May 1935.

12. *El Heraldo de México*, 3 May 1916.

13. See "Juan B. Ruiz," interview by Eustace L. Williams, 6 May 1937, Racial Minorities Survey, Federal Writers Project collection, University of California, Los Angeles.

14. *La Opinión*, 6 April 1930 and 5 May 1935.

15. See Regina Markell Morantz-Sanchez, *Sympathy and Science: Women Physicians in American Medicine* (New York: Oxford Univ. Press, 1985); Mary Roth Walsh, *"Doctors Wanted: No Women Need Apply": Sexual Barriers in the Medical Profession, 1835–1975*

(New Haven: Yale Univ. Press, 1977); and Gloria Melnick Moldow, *Women Doctors in Gilded-Age Washington:Race, Gender, and Professionalization* (Urbana: Univ. of Illinois Press, 1987).

16. From Naturalization documents, National Archives, Laguna Niguel, California. The occupational structure of this Mexican immigrant sample will be discussed in full in the next chapter.

17. Take for example the words of conjunto musician Narciso Martínez, who explained: "No puedo ser americano, porque mi papá y mamá eran mexicanos" ("I cannot consider myself American, because my father and mother were Mexicans"). Manuel Peña, *The Texas-Mexican Conjunto: History of a Working-Class Music* (Austin: Univ. of Texas Press, 1985), 54–55.

18. Peña, *Conjunto*, 146–48; Tim Patterson, "Notes on the Historical Application of Marxist Cultural Theory," *Science & Society* 39 (1975), 257–91. The notion of "organic intellectuals" comes from Antonio Gramsci's theory of cultural hegemony, which can be found in *Selections from the Prison Notebooks*, Quintin Hoare and Geoffrey Newell Smith, eds. and trans. (New York: International, 1971).

19. Analysis of Naturalization documents, National Archives, Laguna Niguel, California.

20. Daniel Castañeda, "La música y la revolución mexicana." *Boletín Latín-Americano de Música* 5 (1941), 447–48; Claes af Geijerstam, *Popular Music in Mexico* (Albuquerque: Univ. of New Mexico Press, 1976), 88–91.

21. Merle E. Simmons, *The Mexican Corrido as a Source for Interpretive Study of Modern Mexico (1870–1950)* (Bloomington: Indiana Univ. Press, 1957), 7, 34. See also Vicente T. Mendoza, *El corrido mexicano* (México, D.F.: Fondo de Cultura Economíca, 1974), xv, who calls the years between 1910 and 1929 the "Golden Age" of the corrido.

22. Pedro J. González, *Translated Transcripts* (Cinewest/KPBS, 1983), 75–77.

23. Geijerstam, *Popular Music*, 49–58. For traditional songs from one particular region in central Mexico, see Juan Diego Razo Oliva, *Rebeldes populares del Bajío (Hazanas, tragedias y corridos, 1910–1927)* (Mexico City: Editorial Katun, S.A., 1983).

24. Geijerstam, *Popular Music*, 68–69.

25. Ibid., 83–88; Américo Paredes, "The Ancestry of Mexico's Corridos: A Matter of Definitions," *Journal of American Folklore* 76 (1963), 233. For a collection of folk songs composed by Mexicans in conflict with Anglo Texans, see Américo Paredes, *A Texas-Mexican Cancionero: Folksongs of the Lower Border* (Urbana: Univ. of Illinois Press, 1976), particularly part II.

26. John Holmes McDowell, "The Corrido of Greater Mexico as Discourse, Music and Event," in *"And Other Neighborly Names": Social Process and Cultural Image in Texas Folklore*, Richard Bauman and Roger D. Abrahams, eds. (Austin: Univ. of Texas Press, 1981), 47, 73; Geijerstam, 52–53, 56; Merle E. Simmons, "The Ancestry of Mexico Corridos," *Journal of American Folklore* 76 (1963), 3.

27. Quoted in Nellie Foster, "The *Corrido*: A Mexican Culture Trait Persisting in Southern California" (Master's thesis, University of Southern California, 1939), 7.

28. Peña, *Conjunto*, 40, according to Library of Congress informant Richard Spottswood; Pedro J. González, videocassette tape interviews for *Ballad of an Unsung Hero* (San Diego: Cinewest/KPBS, 1983), 2:12 to 2:19. There is some dispute over whether this recording was indeed the first, since Pedro González remembers recording sessions he participated in as early as 1924. See González, *Transcripts*, 72–74. There is also a dispute over whether, indeed, Gonzalez was the original composer. In 1939, a recording of "El Lavaplatos" was discovered in Los Angeles which claimed that the music and words had been written by Jesus Ororio. See Foster, "*Corrido*," 24.

29. "El Lavaplatos" (The Dishwasher) from Philip Sonnichsen, *Texas-Mexican Border Music, Vols. 2 & 3: Corridos Parts 1 & 2* (Arhoolie Records, 1975), 9. For more lyrics, see the beginning of Chapter 7.

30. González, *Transcripts*, 82–85, 96–98, 217–19, 227–30.

31. Foster, "*Corrido*," 30.

32. Naturalization documents, National Archives, Laguna Niguel, California.

33. Peña, *Conjunto*, 58.

34. See ibid., esp. chap. 1.

35. J. Xavier Mondragón, "El Desarrollo de la Canción Mexicana en Estados Unidos," *La Opinión*, 27 March 1932.

36. Nicolás Kanellos, "An Overview of Hispanic Theatre in the United States," in *Hispanic Theatre in the United States*, Nicolás Kanellos, ed. (Houston: Arte Público Press, 1984), 9; Nicolás Kanellos, "Two Centuries of Hispanic Theatre in the Southwest," *Revista Chicano-Riqueña* 11 (1983), 27–35. Tomás Ybarra-Frausto, "I Can Still Hear the Applause: La Farándula Chicana: Carpas y Tandas de Variedad," in *Hispanic Theatre*, 56.

37. González, *Transcripts*, 221.

38. Ibid., 246–49.

39. Foster, "*Corrido*," 26.

40. Pedro J. González remembers being asked to play for the studios in *Transcripts*, 96–98.

41. In this fashion, Chicano musicians in Los Angeles resembled their counterparts in Texas. See Peña, *Conjunto*, 146–48.

42. Ibid., 49–50.

43. Foster, *Corrido*, 19.

44. Quoted in Stephen Joseph Loza, "The Musical Life of the Mexican Chicano People in Los Angeles, 1945–1985: A Study in Maintenance, Change, and Adaptation" (Ph.D. diss., University of California, Los Angeles, 1985, 110–11.

45. Analysis of Naturalization documents, National Archives, Laguna Niguel, California.

46. González, *Transcripts*, 124–25.

47. Peña, *Conjunto*, 39–41.

48. Ibid., 42; exceedingly rare was González's claim that he made $50 a recording and began receiving royalties in the 1930s. Since he was considered the top Mexican artist by 1930, this claim is understandable. González, *Transcript*, 118, 234, 240.

49. According to Lalo Guerrero, in Loza, "Musical Life," 118.

50. González, *Transcript*, 74; Foster, "*Corrido*," 22–23. The only other musical outlet I have discovered that advertised in the Spanish-language press was La Platt Music Company. For go-betweens in San Antonio, see Peña, *Conjunto* 40.

51. Loza, "Musical Life," 105, 117–20.

52. Roland Marchand, *Advertising the American Dream: Making Way for Modernity, 1920–1940* (Berkeley: Univ. of California Press, 1985), 89–94.

53. González, *Transcript*, 99; Felix F. Gutiérrez and Jorge Reina Schement *Spanish-Language Radio in the Southwestern United States* (Austin: Center for Mexican American Studies, Univ. of Texas, 1979), 5.

54. González, *Transcript*, 102–6.

55. Gutiérrez and Schement, *Spanish-Language Radio*, 5–7; Gonzalez, *Transcript*, 98–99.

56. Gutiérrez and Schement, *Spanish-Language Radio*, 7.

57. Foster, "*Corrido*," 20–22; González, *Transcript*, 114–15; see also 249–51 for a description of rural jestering with pig.

58. González, *Transcript*, 101–9, 119–37; Gene Fowler and Bill Crawford *Border Radio* (Austin: Texas Monthly Press, 1987), 207–8.

59. See Fowler and Crawford, *Border Radio*, esp. 162, 247.

60. Kanellos, "Overview," 10, and "Two Centuries," 36.

61. See Carl J. Mora, *Mexican Cinema: Reflections of a Society, 1896–1980* (Berkeley Univ. of California Press, 1982), 25–51, for a description of this present transition in the Mexican film industry.

62. Loza, "Musical Life," 102–4.

63. Mary Lanigan, "Second Generation Mexicans in Belvedere" (Master's thesis, University of Southern California, 1932), 58.

64. Ibid., 62.

65. Ibid., 103–5.

66. Ibid., 22.

CHAPTER 11

From Scarcity to Abundance:
The Immigrant as Consumer

Andrew Heinze

The chasm between a past of inveterate want and a future of potential comfort profoundly shaped the perspective of immigrants to the United States between the 1870s and 1914, when the First World War ended the great migration of over 20 million Europeans to America. Louis Borgenicht, a Galician Jew who came to New York City in 1888 and shortly afterward launched a successful career in the garment industry, expressed clearly the revolutionary change of condition that was inherent in immigration to the United States. "Even at his wealthiest, my father lived in very much the same fashion as his tenth-generation grandfather," Borgenicht observed—"I have shifted my mode of living more in fifty years than my ancestors [had] in a thousand."[1]

No transition was more dramatic than the movement from a material life that was nearly medieval to one that thrived on modern mass production. The psychological adaptation of the immigrant to American society was defined largely by this enormous leap in material circumstances and possibilities. Because of an overriding desire to become established in the United States, eastern European Jews responded especially quickly to the condition of mass consumption. They recognized that, as consumers, they could begin to move toward the goal of fitting into American society.

In the sphere of consumption, virtually all newcomers to America discovered an opportunity for social advancement that often eluded them in the domain of production. By contrasting the status of urban immigrants as consumers to their position as laborers, a comprehensive study of industrial workers in the United States published by the British Board of Trade in 1911 emphasized this fact. In the workplace, the differences between newcomers and citizens were often accentuated, as immigrants typically were pushed into, and congregated in, the least tolerable kinds of labor. Through the marketplace, however, newcomers had the opportunity almost immediately to adopt basic forms of American life. The report explained that "the industrial status" of most southern and eastern Europeans was "different from and lower than" that of most Americans. But, the position of immigrants "as measured by the command of material comforts" began "at once to be relatively 'American' in standard." Consequently, even among the poorest groups of urban workers the term "American" was found to have a meaning that was "definable and real."[2]

The significance of emulating the American consumer was highlighted by the impoverishment of those millions who had come from eastern and southern Europe between 1880 and 1914. The shifting source of immigration to the United States directly reflected economic changes across the Atlantic. As the German economy expanded in the last decades of the nineteenth century, the number of German immigrants to the United States, which neared one-and-a-half million between 1881 and 1890, dropped to one-half million, at the most, between 1891 and 1900. At the same time, the deterioration of economic opportunities in the largely agricultural societies of eastern and southern Europe stimulated a titanic increase of people from Italy, Austria-Hungary, Russia, and from Poland, which had been divided and annexed by Russia, Austria-Hungary, and Prussia in the late eighteenth century. Between 1881 and 1890, approximately 926,116 people arrived from these lands; between 1891 and 1900, the number jumped to about 1,846,610; between 1901 and 1910, roughly 5,788,449 flooded into the United States.[3] In all, about ten million had left for the United States between 1880 and 1914. The one characteristic unifying these diverse peoples was poverty. Not only did they arrive, on the average, with virtually no capital, but they had known a meagerness of material existence that was fast becoming outmoded in the more industrial regions to the north and west of Europe.

The regions that supplied so many emigrants had an aspect that contrasted sharply with the setting of urban consumption in the United States. The people of southern Italy conceived of their society as having two major groups—those who ate white bread and those who ate black bread. This point of view clarified the deep division between the gentry and the peasantry, for whom white bread symbolized an unattainable style of life. The peasants of southern Italy lived in abysmal homes that were often no more than hovels made of interwoven sticks or straw and daub. Some inhabited caves. In the cities, particularly Naples, several families of impoverished workers typically cohabited in underground apartments that made the tenements of New York City seem luxurious. The average diet was as poor as the water supply, consisting mainly of corn meal, pasta, rice, beans, and bread. Meat was esteemed a "rich man's food."[4]

The impoverishment of eastern Europe was accentuated by the fact that, until 1863, masses of Russian peasants were serfs. Designed to turn peasants into urban factory workers, the abolition of serfdom actually provided little relief from the unrelenting pressure of poverty. Many laborers continued to be tied to land that they did not own, and factory operatives ended up with extremely low wages. In Lithuania and Poland, the regions of northwestern Russia that provided a large proportion of immigrants to America, life on the land had become increasingly untenable after the breakdown of the traditional agricultural order. Descriptions of Lithuanian life prior to World War I were portraits of drabness and want. The average diet revolved around cottage cheese and sour cream, beet soup, onions, cabbage, potatoes, and rye or raisin bread. Rolls and pastries were unusual, as were most vegetables and fruits. Fresh milk was rarely enjoyed, and butter, considered a luxury, was made to sell rather than to eat. Tea and coffee were rare, the main drink thus being water. As forks were used only by the rich, peasants relied on handmade wooden spoons and other small utensils. Their clothing and interior furnishings were simple and nondescript.[5]

Estranged from the land, the Jews of eastern Europe endured material conditions that differed somewhat from those of the surrounding peasantry. Working primarily as artisans and merchants, Jews had much greater familiarity with urban refinements, and their autonomous, communal institutions helped the poorest among them to enjoy the special foods of the Sabbath and holidays. Dispersed throughout the Russian Pale of Settlement—the stretch of land between the Baltic and Black Seas that confined most Jews—the eastern edges of Austria-Hungary, and Rumania, they varied in their customs and tastes. Yet, their culture was remarkably uniform, and their experience of material scarcity was quite consistent.

Despite the effort of Jews to punctuate the year with religious celebrations that included luxurious foods, gabardine, cashmere, or silk garments, and handcrafted silverware, the want of daily life in eastern Europe was ineluctable, often demanding that the holiday diet be hedged, the clothes be well-worn, and the tableware inherited. In fact, the Jewish perception of luxuries as an important part of regular celebrations made for a trying tension between expectation and reality. Echoing the impact of deprivation, some Jewish immigrants recalled in detail the most minute elements of the daily diet—a piece of bread, an apple, or a cookie that persisted in memory despite the passage of years.[6]

The cities of eastern Europe often lacked the most basic commodities and conveniences enjoyed by the poor in American cities. In the 1880s and 1890s, the women of Minsk chopped their own wood for the oven, walked distances to draw well water, and washed the family's clothes in the river with the aid of a wooden hammer and board. In the winter, washing had to be done through a hole in the ice.[7] Lacking domestic appliances, the vast majority of urban families were also burdened by a limited selection of garments. Until 1912, residents of the Galician city of Shniatyn had neither shoe stores nor retailers of ready-made clothes.[8] The confinement of the consumer in the largest cities of the Pale was conveyed by a description of a Jewish marketplace in Warsaw in 1898: "All kinds of old clothes, and some new ones of the worst quality are sold by auction in the wooden shanties ... sometimes a pair of high-boots constitutes the whole of their stock-in-trade, and a whole day is sometimes uselessly devoted to getting rid of them."[9]

The embrace of material scarcity on the consciousness of Jews extended to their attitude toward living space. Disproportionately urban, the Jews of eastern Europe suffered acutely from the miasma of overcrowded housing. In 1900, a traveling correspondent for the New York *Yiddishes Tageblatt*, America's first successful daily newspaper printed in Yiddish, described as indescribable "the want, the misery, the wretchedness" of the poor in Kazmierz, the Jewish suburb of Cracow, "where half-a-dozen families . . . live together in one cellar with bad food and scanty light."[10]

The journalist's impassioned chronicle was well corroborated by detailed reports of living conditions in the Jewish Pale of Settlement during the first decade of the twentieth century. The majority of artisans' homes was described by one investigator as being "small, crowded, and poverty-stricken."[11] This terse description was amplified by an inspector of the United States Immigration Service who visited the homes of urban Jews in the Pale during the summer of 1906. In one cellar room, twelve feet underground, three families totaling seventeen people were found living together. For several families to cohabit one room was "a common sight."[12] These city residents were so conditioned by the fact of material scarcity that they calculated joint "ownership" of a single room in terms of fractions as minute as one thirty-second. In one case, three families claimed twenty-eight thirty-seconds ownership of a room, one individual with a one thirty-second share had to live elsewhere, and the remaining parts were viewed by their "owner" as an investment.[13]

Even families that were comparatively comfortable lacked the stimulation provided by a variety of domestic furnishing and personal possessions. Marc Chagall, the most renowned of the Jewish artists to emerge from the Pale, recalled what to his eyes was a painful lack of adornment in his childhood home of Vitebsk, where "there wasn't a single painting, not a single engraving on the walls of the rooms." Until the age of nineteen, Chagall had "never seen drawings or paintings."[14] The painter's recollection was significant partly because, by prevailing standards, his family was not poor. In the homes of comparatively comfortable Jewish families, the dearth of possessions was often relieved only by the presence of religious and ceremonial objects, such as pictures of great rabbis, Jewish shrines, and Jewish philanthropists, a *yortsayt*, or memorial tablet for relatives, a charity box, brass candlesticks, a finely wrought spice box, a wine beaker, a menorah, a silver-plated ornamental box to hold etrog, the Mediterranean citrus fruit used for the celebration of Sukkot, and perhaps a set of silver goblets and a special snuff box for use on Sabbath and holidays.[15] The lack of secular commodities in the homes of all but the affluent bred monotony. "No dolls, no books, no games," recalled Mary Antin of her childhood in a moderately well-off family in Polotsk—"the days drew themselves out too long sometimes, so that I sat at the window thinking what should happen next."[16]

The desire to escape a world of deprivation figured prominently in the constellation of motives that moved people from Europe to America after 1880. In 1911, a report of the United States Immigration Commission stated that "the chief motive behind the movement" to the new world was "a laudable ambition for better things" than the emigrants possessed at home.[17] As had been the case throughout the nineteenth century, letters brimming with optimism about American prosperity passed from the recently arrived to their relatives back in the old country, and this personal correspondence constituted one of the most powerful catalysts of immigration.[18]

In the era of exodus from eastern and southern Europe, however, the content and impact of letters home changed in a subtle way. During the middle of the nineteenth century, the rhetorical enthusiasm of land-hungry newcomers from central and northern Europe dwelled on the agricultural dimension of American prosperity—the abundance of inexpensive land, superfluous crops, and light taxation of the farmer.[19] At the end of the century, the factory-bound arrivals from eastern and southern Europe focused more on the scale of wages and the urban refinements of the new society. Moreover, the formidable gap in material condition separating the impoverished newcomer from the American at this time made for many analogies between the status of the average worker in the United States and the nobleman in Poland or Italy. An American consular official reported in 1904 that "the greatest influence in promoting emigration" came from relatives and friends in the United States who wrote "glowing accounts of the enormous wages received, food such as the nobility [ate] at home, and houses grandly furnished."[20] Historians of the immigration of Italian and Slavic peasants have found these newcomers to have been motivated by a fierce commitment to the pragmatic goal of accumulating money and material possessions, both of which served as tangible signs that they had transcended the degradation of their material and social condition in Europe.[21]

The vision of America as a place of bounty had a unique significance for Jews because of the circumstances behind their immigration. Although the eastern European Jews responded to similar pressures of population growth, economic disruption, and political persecution that had motivated most immigrants to the United States, they contended as well with special, and potentially catastrophic, problems. Since the beginning of the nineteenth century, the dramatic growth of Europe's population had aggravated the economic frustration of multitudes of peasants who had lost the ability to make a living from farmlands that were quickly being consolidated by powerful landlords.

By the second half of the century, the Jews of eastern Europe were also unsettled by the joint pressure of overpopulation and economic dislocation. Around 1800, Russian Jews numbered approximately one million. Fifty years later, they were three and a quarter million. By 1900, nearly five and a half million Jews lived in the Russian Empire. As the Jewish population grew, economic opportunities dwindled. Since the abolition of serfdom in 1863, the customarily Jewish occupations of provisioning and administering the estates of noblemen were subverted, and the role of Jews as small-scale moneylenders and merchants was further undercut after 1880 by the growth of large-scale industry, which relied on major banks for credit and on the railroads for the shipment of goods.

Throughout the nineteenth century, the burgeoning number of Russian Jews had migrated within the Empire in search of new opportunities, but this alternative had inherent limits that would eventually make emigration inevitable. Flowing out of the densely populated provinces of Lithuania and Poland into the areas of "New Russia" around the Black Sea, the migrants rapidly achieved roughly the same ratio to the Gentile population that existed in the older regions of settlement. Further expansion was precluded by the boundaries of the Pale of Settlement.[22]

Physically cramped to the point of frustration, many Jews needed only an upsurge of anti-Semitism to convince them that the future in Russia would be increasingly dismal. The decline in the security of the eastern European Jews accompanied the decline in the eighteenth century of the Kingdom of Poland, most of which came into the possession of Russia. Under the Tsars, the insecurity of the Jews was accentuated by policies that both inadvertently and deliberately undermined their political autonomy and economic privileges. After the assassination of Tsar Alexander II in 1881, the group's position turned from a state of insecurity to one of virtual siege. Led by high ranking, anti-Semitic officials and sustained by deeply rooted suspicions and animosities among the Russian folk, the government began systematically to bar Jews from customary occupations, to limit sharply their enrollment in universities, and to incite pogroms that destroyed millions of dollars worth of Jewish property as well as thousands of lives. Although other ethnic and religious minorities in the Empire, notably the Lithuanians and Poles, suffered persecution that helped produce waves of emigration, the plight of Russian Jews between 1881 and 1914 was unparalleled in scope and intensity.[23]

The two million Jews who left eastern Europe for the United States in this period—nearly one-quarter of whom fled deteriorating conditions in Rumania and Austria-Hungary—held a deep desire for freedom that lent special importance to the vision of abundance inspiring the majority of impoverished newcomers. More than for other groups of immigrants, America represented for Jews a promised land, a mysterious place of redemption from the accumulated iniquities of the past. As a form of relief from the harrowing conditions of scarcity, the anticipation and experience of material abundance in the United States enriched the perception of the new world as a source of liberation and promise.

Since the publication in 1817 of a Yiddish edition of Joachim Heinrich Campe's *The Discovery of America*, which attained great popularity in eastern Europe, the United States had acquired a mystique among Jews.[24] As larger numbers of Polish Jews started to emigrate to America in the 1870s, the images of American prosperity conveyed through letters and return visits to the homeland took on greater clarity, deepening the country's appeal. In the summer of 1880, a thirty-eight-year-old Polish Jew living on East Houston Street was interviewed by a reporter for the *New York Tribune* about the conditions and attitude of the small community of immigrants. In answer to the question of whether the Polish Jews sought to return to Jerusalem, the man stated, "we are satisfied here; indeed, among us America is known as 'the new Jerusalem.' "[25]

The vision of American abundance intertwined with the vision of America as a haven. Interpreting American life in intensely spiritual terms, Jewish newcomers tended to view their new material existence as an integral part of the New Jerusalem. While acknowledging that the life of the Jewish garment worker was difficult, Abraham Cahan, the socialist editor of the New York *Forward* and the conscience of the city's Yiddish-speaking community, recalled that most Jewish newcomers perceived their new living conditions as justification for the claim that "America was paradise."[26]

The cultural heritage of the newcomers had prepared the ground for such an attitude. Although Judaism had not systematically formulated a description of Paradise, a conception arose among eastern Europeans that the sublime world of redemption might be full of milk and honey, a splendid banquet for the sake of the righteous. The tradition of Hasidism that flourished in eastern Europe in the eighteenth and nineteenth centuries encouraged the idea of a mystical union of the act of eating and spiritual liberation. One older version of Paradise was contained in an Aramaic poem pertaining to the holiday of Shavuoth. In the time of the Messiah, the poem foretold, meat, fish, and wine would be enjoyed at a special banquet, and God would set forth jars of wine that were made during the six days of Creation and sealed until the occasion of redemption.[27]

The concept of the afterlife that prevailed among the Jewish folk of eastern Europe, and that influenced the vision of American abundance, was articulated by Isaac Loeb Peretz, the brilliant writer of Yiddish short stories whose simplicity of style managed to evoke the popular imagination of Polish and Russian Jewry. One of Peretz's best stories, first published in 1894 in the New York *Arbeter Tsaytung*, was "Bontshe the Silent," the tale of a physically and spiritually downtrodden Jew who finds himself transported to the Other World.

The story of Bontshe played on the profound tension between the impoverishment of the Jews and their grand vision of redemption. Having endured in apparently noble silence a life of constant abuse and poverty, Bontshe arrives in the divine kingdom to receive his final Judgment. Surrounded by little angels with gold-filigreed wings and silver slippers, the subdued "hero" is received with a gold easychair and a gold crown with inlaid gems, and he is escorted into the Court of Virtue, the floor of which (Bontshe is too awestruck to lift up his head) is composed of alabaster and diamonds. A review by the divine court ends so favorably that Bontshe is offered everything he desires from the glorious realm of the Afterlife. In Peretz's satirical conclusion, the hero turns out to be an anti-hero, his lifelong silence having reflected not noble forbearance but an utter lack of spirit. Bontshe answers the court meekly that he would like every morning to have a hot baked roll with fresh butter![28]

Although written as a commentary on the degrading aspects of Jewish life in eastern Europe, "Bontshe the Silent" gave form to the evocative sense of Paradise harbored by impoverished Jewish immigrants. Unlike Bontshe, these people had not been beaten down into passivity by deprivation—they were able not only to envision the splendor of redemption but also to imagine and pursue the prospect of a satisfying standard of material existence. A more realistic, poignant expression of the yearning for a worldly paradise was given by Kate Simon, in her recollection of immigration to New York from Warsaw just after World War I. "My life was filled with images of raisins and chocolate, cookies and dolls, white slippers and pink hair bows, all waiting for me in a big box called America," she wrote of her last days in Poland. Her rich mental image of a promised land had been formed from the stories of comfort and luxury told by adults expecting to emigrate.[29]

If the new potential for consumption completed the Jews' notion of America as a promised land, it served also as a starting point toward a goal that was more immediate for them than for other newcomers—the goal of fitting into American society. There was a strong desire among the peasants of eastern and southern Europe to make money quickly in the United States in order to buy land and raise their social position in the old country. Consequently, most groups of immigrants included a greatly disproportionate number of young males who originally viewed America as a means to an end rather than as an end in itself. Of the most populous groups of newcomers, the Italians exemplified the tendency to return home. More than two million Italians arrived in the United States between 1899 and 1910, over three-fourths of them males, largely "birds of passage" aiming to return home with American wages. During the period 1897–1906, more than one-half of the immigrants repatriated, and, from 1907–1911, almost three-fourths returned to Italy.[30]

By contrast, few Jews returned to Russia, Poland, Galicia, or Rumania. Statistics for the period 1908–1914 showed only 7 percent re-emigrating, compared to 31 percent of immigrants in general. Furthermore, Jewish immigration consisted of families rather than single men, including almost twice as many women as the groups from southern and eastern Europe contained. The reason for these striking differences was clear: Jews intended to stay.[31]

The unique attitude of Jews toward America motivated them to view items of consumption as foundation stones of American identity. A study of the cultural adjustment of American immigrants conducted by sociologists Robert Park and Herbert Miller in 1921 described six personality "types" that characterized the majority of immigrants. Of the six, two were formulated by immigrants themselves and thus arose directly from the milieu of urban communities rather than from the observation of social scientists. These two stereotypes were the "allrightnik" and the "cafone," deriving from the Jewish and the Italian immigrants respectively. In the contrast between the "allright-nik" and the "cafone," the significance of being a consumer in the American way emerged most clearly.

Reflecting the old-world orientation of many non-Jewish immigrants, the "cafone" represented the Italian who sought only to make money in America in order to gain a higher position in the native community in Italy. As a result of his singleminded focus on a future in the old world, the "cafone" cared nei-ther about adopting American ways nor about fitting into the settled group of Italians in the United States. Standing in diametrical opposition to the "ca-fone," the "allrightnik" reflected the deep tendency of Jewish immigrants to view themselves in the light of potential roles and social position in America, rather than in the European birth-place. The "allrightnik" stood for the suc-cessful Jewish immigrant who adopted American habits, particularly habits of consumption, so thoroughly as to blend into the group of cosmopolitan Jews who had attained a high degree of cultural assimilation.[32]

The cultural flexibility and cosmopolitan outlook of Jewish newcomers made it easier to understand and adopt American habits of consumption. Unlike the majority of immigrants, who had been raised within the narrow confines of vil-lage life, Jews had an almost proverbial versatility stemming from a history of migration within and beyond national borders. Mendele Moykher-Sforim, the "grandfather" of modern Yiddish literature, evinced the breadth, as he satirized the depth, of perspective of the most ignorant shtetl Jews of the mid-nineteenth century, whose conversation behind the old stove of the synagogue ranged be-yond domestic secrets to "the politics of Istanbul, the Sultan, the Austrian Kaiser, high finance, Rothschild's fortune compared with the wealth of the great aristocrats and the other magnates . . . and so on and so forth."[33] The cultural flexibility of the Jews was characterized by a traveler who had spent enough time in Russia to recognize that the Russian had "great facility in language" but that the Russian Jew was "the most versatile man in the empire."[34]

In the American setting, viewed overwhelmingly as the best available to Jews, the cultural adaptability of Jewish newcomers made for the rapid adop-tion of American ways. Perhaps the surest sign of quick cultural change was the commitment to learning English. David Blaustein, a Russian immigrant who gained a reputation as a social worker on the Lower East Side, where he served as a director of the Educational Alliance, noted that, in Russia, the vast majority of Jews made no effort to learn the dominant language, whereas in America "they feel they are welcome, and with high hopes" they set at once to learning English with the aim of lessening "as far as possible the gulf between them and native-born Americans."[35]

The intensity of Jewish motivation to fit into American society by learning English underlay the success of Alexander Harkavy's "briefenshteller," hand-books written by the Yiddish lexicographer to instruct newcomers in the forms of American correspondence. The popularity of the first two "letter writers" in the 1890s prompted the issue of an expanded third edition in 1902. Although the English model in the handbook was at times rigid and melodramatic, the volume guided the newcomer through virtually every social situation that would warrant a verbal exchange, from complaints to a wholesaler about defective merchandise, to apologies for late payment of rent, from greetings and invitations relating to holidays, rites of passage, concerts, meetings, and telegrams to letters containing passionate expressions of love as well as delicate phrases of distaste. Harkavy's letter-writer also included extensive lessons on English pronunciation—with a special section of words most likely to be mispronounced by the speaker of Yiddish—as well as exercises in spelling, punctuation, diction, and penmanship.[36]

As a result of such efforts to master the language, many eastern Europeans gained access to the thoroughfare of urban American society. A survey of readers of the Yiddish press in New York City, which was undertaken after 1914 but probably reflected tendencies among Jews in earlier years as well, found that almost two-thirds of the randomly sampled readers could and did read English-language newspapers. They patronized the Yiddish press out of desire, rather than from necessity.[37]

The English language was an essential avenue into American culture, but it was time-consuming and often difficult to adopt. In contrast, habits of consumption constituted the most easily accessible element of the new society. New clothes, foods, and furnishings were as tangible as syntax was abstract and as obtainable as idioms were elusive.

In responding to the environment of consumption in urban America, Jewish newcomers shared with other immigrants a general sense of wonder and enthusiasm. The simplest changes in lifestyle, such as increasing the size of meals, were accepted with little hesitation by virtually all newcomers. The prevalence of high-protein foods, like meat, milk, and eggs, and the abundance of food in general made for a sharp and immediate change in daily life, not only for newcomers from the poverty-stricken regions of eastern and southern Europe but even for western Europeans like the Germans.[38] In good part, the craving for old world dishes reflected the fact that these foods could suddenly be afforded in America.[39]

First impressions of mass-marketed products like clothes and furniture were also universal. Many newcomers must have experienced the amazement of David Levinsky, the protagonist of Abraham Cahan's novel *The Rise of David Levinsky*, which first appeared in 1917. Newly arrived in New York City from a Lithuanian shtetl, Levinsky sees an evicted family sitting on the sidewalk with its belongings. He is shocked to discover that the furniture of these poor people would have properly belonged to a prosperous family in Russia. "But then," Levinsky reminded himself, "anything was to be expected of a country where the poorest devil wore a hat and a starched coller."[40]

Although the prospect of consumption in America attracted people of various origins, Jews adopted the ways of the American consumer more quickly, largely because of their dedication to the new society. One of the surest signs of the comparative sophistication of Jewish consumption was the flourishing retail business established in the neighborhoods of these eastern Europeans. The Jewish districts of the American city prior to 1914 offered immigrants a range of products that would have been inconceivable in the ramshackle shtetls and urban ghettos of the eastern European Jews. The streets of the Lower East Side of New York inspired Henry James to speak of the "new style of poverty" in the American city, a social phenomenon of the first order that eluded most observers who were preoccupied with the environmental problems of the Lower East Side. As the great novelist walked through the area in 1904, after a twenty-two-year sojourn in Europe, he was surprised and impressed by "the blaze of the shops addressed to the New Jerusalem wants and the splendor with which these were taken for granted." Not oblivious to the sordid aspects of the crowded Jewish neighborhoods, James nonetheless considered the massive striving of the people for a more refined existence to be "the larger harmony" that united the energies of immigrants who had become urban consumers in America.[41]

The development of the Lower East Side as an emporium for immigrants betrayed the mythic image of the area as a monument to poverty. The dense Jewish section of lower Manhattan has been perceived as a prototype of urban poverty in the United States, and the Jewish population that lived there continues to be broadly described as impoverished.[42] Notorious for its crowded housing, the Lower East Side did have residents who lived in a deplorable condition. Nonetheless, the rapid flowering of retail commerce in the district would have been impossible without a population that upheld standards of consumption.

The ability to cultivate such standards had everything to do with the bustling activity of eastern European Jews. By the late 1880s, when the number of Jewish newcomers in the area approached 100,000, the influence of the Jews' traditional familiarity with commerce began to be felt. The saloons and rundown shops that had marked the Lower East Side as a slum gave way steadily to groceries, cafés, and restaurants, and to clothing, jewelry, and furniture stores.[43] Particularly after the depression of 1893–1897 had ended, the signs of material sophisitication came clearly to the surface of the community. Reviewing the retail boom of 1901, the *Yiddishes Tageblatt* concluded that the flourishing of business provided "the best proof of the great buying power of the people."[44] Visitors to the Lower East Side frequently commented on the quality of the food sold on the streets as well as in groceries and butcher stores, on the fine appearance of Jewish children, and on Jewish standards of domestic furnishing.[45] In 1902, the *Tageblatt* justifiably boasted about the regenerative power of Jewish consumers and merchants on the downtown community.

In clothing the East Side beats all other worker neighborhoods and it does not stand behind the most beautiful business areas. The Jewish quarter is the best customer for silk and velvet, and also for gold and diamonds. . . . Furniture stores have multiplied and grown big and beautiful. The most beautiful furniture is sold on the East Side, and pianos have become a fashion in Jewish homes."[46]

The newspaper went further, suggesting that Jews were becoming more definitely American by raising their material standards. This point was made by linking the popular concept of "greening oneself out" ("oysgrinen zich"), which meant becoming more like an American, to sophistication in the area of consumption. Purporting to give "Clear Evidence How Jews Green Themselves Out Very Quickly in this Land," the paper dwelled on the change in attitudes toward housing that had occurred over the previous decade. In the early 1890s, many Jewish newcomers lived in small "room and bed-room" apartments rented for eight or ten dollars a month. A three-room place in a modern building was a distinct luxury. But, within a few years, many of the old tenements had been demolished, and the newcomers became accustomed to four- and five-room apartments with more conveniences. As the pace of modernization quickened, rents rose, but the supply was met by demand as newcomers entered the cycle of heightening tastes. By 1902, there had been a burst of construction of buildings with five- and six-room apartments and the latest conveniences. Bathrooms had become a commonplace, and electricity and elevators were not unusual. "The same people who had earlier been proud of living in three rooms," the *Tageblatt* stated, "began to be ashamed of their living situation and they opted for the new houses."[47]

The phenomenon of continually rising expectations was officially documented by the New York City Tenement House Department, which reported that, by 1914, the city housed around 1,500,000 tenants in over 22,000 buildings constructed since the passage of the New York Tenement House Law in 1901, which required much better lighting and ventilation, and a bathroom inside each apartment. As the pressing demand of consumers for better housing suggested, the standards of 1900 were well outmoded by the end of the decade.[48] A changing sense of desirable housing inevitably spurred desires for newer furnishings as well. Recalling her childhood in New York City around the turn of the century, a Jewish immigrant from Serbia explained that belongings that had been "perfectly acceptable" in one apartment became "impossible" in a different dwelling.[49]

Adjusting to the idea that luxuries could regularly be converted into necessities, newcomers found themselves involved in what appeared to be an endless cycle of acquisition. A Jewish version of the American notion of "keeping up with the Joneses" gave expression to the new view of material standards. "If the Browns next door hang up expensive lace curtains," a social commentator declared, replacing "Jones" with a name more common to American Jews, "we are discontented until lace curtains have gone up to our windows, no matter how much smaller our income may be than that of the Browns."[50] In eastern Europe, the concept of a continually rising standard of material life would have had little foundation. In urban America, however, it found sustenance.

With subtle yet irresistible force, new habits of consumption triggered a profound change in perspective among the majority of newcomers. Acquiring the American perspective of abundance, Jews learned that aspirations need not be tailored to means. By the start of the twentieth century, the Yiddish press could focus on the topic of "Families That Live Better than They Earn." Although many Jews saved money fastidiously, an equal number apparently lived well beyond their means as a result of credit, particularly the installment plan. Exemplifying this phenomenon was a family that had a combined income of twenty-three dollars a week from three wage-earning members, but that spent twice that amount in order to have a new suit "every two months" and diamonds "as big as icicles."[51] Although most Jews were not spendthrifts, they had to balance the pressure to save money against the imperative of increasing their standard of living.

The installment plan relieved the potential conflict between saving and spending. Despite the desire to identify with urban Americans through consumption, Jews shouldered a double burden of saving. They needed to accumulate money for the sake of relatives in Europe, most of whom required financial aid, and many of whom also wanted to emigrate to the United States. In addition, they needed savings for investment in business and real estate, two important avenues of economic success, and for education, a prerequisite for the social advance of the young in America. The economic and educational success of the newcomers and their children demonstrated the ability to save money in the hope of achieving long-term goals.[52] Saving money for investment in the future, however, did not preclude American habits of consumption.

The practice of installment buying initiated newcomers into the possibilities of immediate acquisition and familiarized them with the impatient optimism that characterized the American consumer. One immigrant suggested the impact of installment buying upon Jews by entitling a chapter of her memoirs "Buy Now, Pay Later—Mama Discovers an American Custom."[53] On the Lower East Side, items as various as children's treats, wedding dresses, and cemetery plots were available on the installment plan in the 1880s and 1890s.[54] Musician Samuel Chotzinoff remembered how luxuries bought on credit relieved the tense existence of his mother, who had to run a large household with small earnings. A percentage of the family's income was regularly devoted to "the never-ending succession" of domestic furnishings and personal possessions that his mother "could not resist buying" on installment.[55]

Encouraged by the activity of installment peddlers, young couples and families were particularly impressed by the possibility of instantly furnishing a new apartment with elegant-looking parlor sets and with dining room and bedroom pieces that contained the promise of a comfortable life. Abraham Cahan recalled that, when he married in 1885, he and his wife moved into an apartment furnished on the installment plan. The "three new rooms with brand-new furniture" passed even the stern scrutiny of the Russian intellectuals who composed Cahan's circle of friends. They gave the home high approval, judging the furniture to be "just fine."[56]

The availability of consumer credit was viewed not only in pragmatic terms, as a means of expediting consumption, but also as the outward sign of the dynamic state of demand that seemed to animate American society. Thomas Eyges, a Russian Jewish anarchist who immigrated from England to America in 1902, was prompted by his first law class—on the topic of contracts—to comprehend intellectually the general sense of wonder about American abundance which he had held for over a decade in the new society. Once his law professor made the opening comment that the underlying principle of American economic life was the assumption that everybody is honest, Eyges felt that he suddenly understood how such a young nation could become the richest in the world. "The extension of credit to everybody," he reflected, on the practice of selling luxuries on installment, was "the key to success," enabling virtually everyone to imagine material abundance and to realize that spending could be a legitimate way to confront the future.[57]

In 1914, as Europe verged on a war that would both assure the economic superiority of the United States in the world and herald the end of free immigration for Jews, an editorial in the *Yiddishes Tageblatt* made it clear that Jewish immigrants had developed the American perception of material abundance as a precious legacy. "Who can deny that [America] is more fruitful," began the argument under the title "A Great America— the Land of Tomorrow," which continued, "that her inhabitants eat better, dress more beautifully and live more comfortably than does the average population of other lands?"[58] Capping a generation of feverish immigration, this patriotic message reflected the psychological adaptation of eastern European Jews to the phenomenon of American abundance.

Though critical to the adaptation of immigrants, acceptance of the ever-rising American standard of living conflicted with traditional Jewish culture. In the old world, Jewish identity depended upon a venerable distinction between the holy and the mundane spheres of existence. To augment that distinction, Jews had cultivated a unique concept of material luxury, one that would be undermined by American abundance.

Notes

1. Louis Borgenicht, *The Happiest Man: The Life of Louis Borgenicht* (New York, 1942), p. 368.

2. British Board of Trade, *Report on the Cost of Living in American Towns* (London, 1911), pp. xxxix–xl.

3. Leonard Dinnerstein and David M. Reimers, *Ethnic Americans: A History of Immigration and Assimilation* (New York, 1975), pp. 164–165.

4. George E. Pozzeta, "The Italians of New York City, 1890–1914" (Ph.D. thesis, University of North Carolina, 1971), pp. 17–19, 177–179.

5. For a detailed description of conditions in Lithuania, see Peter Paul Jonitis, *The Acculturation of the Lithuanians of Chester, Pennsylvania* (New York, 1985), pp. 4–65. This book is a reprint of the author's Ph.D. thesis, University of Pennsylvania, 1951.

6. Carole Malkin, *The Journeys of David Toback* (New York, n.d.), pp. 213–214. The book was first published in 1981.

7. Morris R. Cohen, *A Dreamer's Journey* (Boston, 1949), pp. 17–19; Marcus E. Ravage, *An American in the Making* (New York, 1917), p. 82.

8. Joachim Schoenfeld, *Shtetl Memoirs: Jewish Life in Galicia Under the Austro-Hungarian Empire and in the Reborn Poland, 1898–1939* (Hoboken, N.J., 1985), p. 33.

9. New York *Jewish Daily News*, August 2, 1898. The *Jewish Daily News* was the English page of the *Yiddishes Tageblatt*. It appeared for about a decade after 1897 and was reinstituted in 1914. As an aid to the reader, this source will be identified by its English title throughout the book.

10. *Ibid.*, April 28, 1900.

11. Isaac M. Rubinow, *Economic Conditions of the Jews in Russia* (New York, 1975), p. 526. The book was first published in 1907.

12. Philip Cowen, *Memories of an American Jew* (New York, 1932), p. 231.

13. *Ibid.*

14. Quoted from Sidney Alexander, *Chagall* (New York, 1978), p. 42.

15. Benjamin L. Gordon, *Between Two Worlds: The Memoirs of a Physician* (New York, 1952), p. 12, for a specific recollection of the home of a petty grain merchant in Lithuania during the 1880s.

16. Mary Antin, *The Promised Land* (Boston, 1969), p. 100. This well-written account of the immigration of a Jewish family from Russia to America first appeared in 1912.

17. United States Immigration Commission, *Reports* (Washington, D.C., 1911), vol. 4, *Emigration Conditions in Europe*, p. 56.

18. Marcus Lee Hansen, *The Atlantic Migration 1607–1860* (New York, 1961), pp. 157–158. The book was first published in 1940; Maldwyn Allen Jones. *American Immigration* (Chicago, 1960), p. 100.

19. Hansen, *Atlantic Migration*, pp. 157–158.

20. United States Immigration Commission, *Emigration Conditions in Europe*, p. 57.

21. Ewa Morawska, " 'For Bread with Butter': Life-Worlds of Peasant Immigrants from East Central Europe, 1880–1914," *Journal of Social History* (Spring 1984), 17:388–389, 392. For an expanded version of this work, see Ewa Morawska, *'For Bread with Butter': Life-Worlds of East Central Europeans in Johnstown, Pennsylvania, 1890–1940* (New York, 1985). Robert Anthony Orsi, *The Madonna of 115th Street: Faith and Community in Italian Harlem, 1880–1950* (New Haven, 1985), pp. 156–162.

22. Salo W. Baron, *The Russian Jew Under Tsars and Soviets* (New York, 1976), pp. 68–69; Howard Morley Sachar, *The Course of Modern Jewish History* (New York, 1982), p. 188. The first editions of these standard texts of Jewish history in the modern era appeared in 1964 and 1958 respectively.

23. Hans Rogger, *Russia in the Age of Modernization and Revolution, 1881–1917* (New York, 1983), p. 199; Baron, *Russian Jew Under Tsars and Soviets*, pp. 43–62.

24. Bernard Weinryb, "Eastern European Immigration to the United States," *Jewish Quarterly Review* (April 1955), 45:501.

25. *New York Tribune*, July 11, 1880.

26. Leon Stein, Abraham P. Conan, and Lynn Davison, eds., *The Education of Abraham Cahan* (Philadelphia, 1969), p. 400.

27. *Encyclopedia Judaica* (Jerusalem, 1972), 2:337–339; 13:78–86; L. Jacobs, "Eating as an Act of Worship in Hasidic Thought," in Siegfried Stein and Raphael Loewe, *Studies in Jewish Religious and Intellectual History* (Tuscaloosa, Ala., 1979), 157–161. The verses

evoking the aura of the divine banquet are from "Akdamut," a mystical poem composed in Aramaic by a European rabbi of the eleventh century. This version of the poem was described by a reporter for the *New York Tribune*, whose story on the celebration of Shavuoth by Jewish newcomers appeared on May 31, 1903.

28. Isaac Loeb Peretz, *Alle Verk* (Buenos Aires, 1944), 6:98–106.

29. Kate Simon, *Bronx Primitive* (New York, 1982), p. 18.

30. Humbert S. Nelli, *The Italians in Chicago* (New York, 1970), pp. 42–47.

31. C. Bezalel Sherman, *The Jew Within American Society* (Detroit, 1965), pp. 60–61.

32. Robert E. Park and Herbert A. Miller, *Old World Traits Transplanted* (New York, 1921), p. 101.

33. Mendele Moykher-Sforim, "The Travels of Benjamin the Third," in Joachim Neugroschel, ed., *The Shtetl* (New York, 1979), p. 182.

34. *New York Tribune*, March 29, 1903.

35. Miriam Blaustein, ed., *Memoirs of David Blaustein* (New York, 1913), p. 60.

36. *Harkavy's American Letter Writer and Speller, English and Yiddish* (New York, 1902).

37. Mordecai Soltes. *The Yiddish Press: An Americanizing Agency* (New York, 1925), p. 44.

38. Dorothee Schneider, " 'For Whom Are All the Good Things in Life?': German-American Housewives Discuss Their Budgets," in Hartmut Keil and John B. Jentz, eds., *German Workers in Industrial Chicago, 1850–1910* (DeKalb, Ill., 1983), p. 152.

39. Nelli, *Italians in Chicago*, p. 119.

40. Abraham Cahan, *The Rise of David Levinsky* (New York, 1960), p. 95. The book was first published in 1917.

41. Henry James, *The American Scene* (London, 1907), pp. 135–136.

42. The Lower East Side as a prototype of urban poverty appears in Anthony Sutcliffe, ed., *Metropolis, 1890–1940* (Cambridge, 1984), p. 24, which draws on the depiction of Irving Howe, *World of Our Fathers* (New York, 1976), p. 88. The almost chronic tendency to preface the phrase "Jewish immigrants" with the adjective "poor" can be observed in the symposium "A Reexamination of a Classic Work in American Jewish History: Moses Rischin's The Promised City, Twenty Years Later," *American Jewish History*, (December 1983), 73:141. Moses Rischin, however, originally noticed the marked improvement in standards of consumption on the Lower East Side, *The Promised City, New York's Jews, 1870–1914* (Cambridge, Mass. 1977), p. 92. The book was first published in 1962.

43. For a chronicle of change on the Lower East Side since the 1880s, see New York *Yiddishes Tageblatt*, March 20, 1910.

44. *Tageblatt*, December 31, 1901.

45. Two vivid accounts of food on the Lower East Side are found in the *New York Tribune*, August 20, 1899, and *Jewish Daily News*, February 11, 1900. A visit of college students to the Lower East Side in 1904 is recalled by Philip Cowen, founder and publisher of the *American Hebrew*, in *Memories of an American Jew* (New York, 1932), p. 298. For the high opinion held by social workers of Jewish tastes, see Charles Bernheimer, *Russian Jew in the United States* (Philadelphia, 1905), p. 35, and Mary Simkhovitch, *The City Worker's World in America* (New York, 1917), pp. 12–13.

46. *Tageblatt*, July 4, 1902.

47. *Ibid.*

48. New York City Tenement House Department, *Seventh Report of the Tenement House Department of the City of New York* (New York, 1915), pp. 8–9.

49. Marie Jastrow, *A Time to Remember: Growing Up in New York Before the Great War* (New York, 1979), p. 149.

50. *Jewish Daily News*, April 23, 1900.

51. New York *Forward*, December 1, 1904.

52. On Jewish economic advancement, see Thomas Kessner, *The Golden Door: Italian*

and Jewish Immigrant Mobility in New York City, 1880–1915 (New York, 1977); see Moses Rischin, *The Promised City New York's Jews, 1870–1914* (Cambridge, Mass. 1977), pp 51–75, 92–93, 199–200 for discussions of activity in business, real estate, and education; the theme of education as a means of advancement is addressed by Leonard Dinnerstein, "Education and the Advancement of American Jews," in Bernard J. Weiss, *American Education and the European Immigrant, 1840–1940* (Urbana, Ill., 1982), pp. 44–60; good primary references to Jewish investment in real estate are Isaac Markens, *The Hebrews in America* (New York, 1975), p. 157, first published in 1888; Riis, *How the Other Half Lives*, p. 94; Charles S. Bernheimer, ed., *Russian Jew in the United States* (Philadelphia, 1905), pp. 46, 354–55; *New York Tribune*, June 25, 1905; *Jewish Daily News*, January 1, 1906.

53. Jastrow, *A Time to Remember*, p. 147.

54. *Yiddishes Tageblatt*, January 1, 1889, for advertisement of H. Silberman and Son, January 18, 1892, for advertisement of Mt. Neboh Cemetery, and January 15, 1892 for advertisement of B. Zeller; Stein, et al., *Education of Abraham Cahan*, pp. 219, 261; Samuel Chotzinoff, *A Lost Paradise* (New York, 1955), p. 75.

55. Chotzinoff, *Lost Paradise*, p. 122, also pp. 113, 124.

56. Stein et al., *Education of Abraham Cahan*, p. 306.

57. Thomas B. Eyges, *Beyond the Horizon: The Story of a Radical Emigrant* (Boston, 1944), p. 140.

58. *Tageblatt*, July 3, 1914.

CHAPTER 12

Consuming Brotherhood: Men's Culture, Style and Recreation as Consumer Culture, 1880–1930

Mark A. Swiencicki

In her exploration of the historical relationship between American men and cosmetics, Kathy Peiss outlines how the late-nineteenth and early twentieth-century discourse of heterosexual masculinity denied and covered up men's cosmetics use by defining men's numerous grooming products as toiletries rather than cosmetics or beauty products. This denial of the feminine "other" lurking within men was so sustained and successful that it became a "self-evident statement" of twentieth-century culture that "real men" do not use cosmetics.[1]

A parallel, self-evident statement of American culture and research would be that pre-Depression, American men were not major consumers since most buying and shopping were done by women. While such an idea is nearly ubiquitous in American popular culture, sociology, and women's history, my examination of the leisure activities of white American men between 1890 and 1930 suggests that such men were indeed a very large and important consuming constituency. Moreover, the advertisements in numerous men's and general interest magazines of the period show that such men were highly courted by early twentieth-century advertisers. However, most of this consumption and consumerism has been shielded from view since the terms "consumer" and "consumer goods" have been constructed in such a profoundly gendered fashion. Thus after documenting the degree to which pre-Depression men were: 1) engaged in consumption and consumer activity, and 2) explicitly courted by magazine advertising, I will examine how and why such information has been overlooked by most scholars of gendered consumption and advertising.

The Elision of the Male Consumer

Over the past decade, a rich literature on the relationship between gender, shopping, and consumer culture has emerged within U.S. cultural history,

"Consuming Brotherhood: Men's Culture, Style and Recreation as Consumer Culture, 1880–1930" by Mark A. Swiencicki from *Journal of Social History* 31 (Summer 1998). Reprinted by permission of the *Journal of Social History*.

women's history, and historical sociology.[2] Although such scholars have done a remarkable job of investigating the impact of consumerism on women and femininity, American men's experiences with consumption and consumerism have been left virtually unexplored. In fact, the consensus among the above disciplines holds that until the Great Depression: 1) American women were the "primary" consumers (i.e., purchasers); 2) most consumption (i.e., utilizing goods) occurred within, or on behalf of the home and family; and 3) male consumption was a marginal activity at best.

The characteristic focus on women, shopping, department stores, and domestic consumption overlooks male consumption and consumerism for a number of reasons. First, the emphasis on the acquisition of goods rather than on their ultimate consumption has overemphasized women's role in the consumption process. Since women have historically done most of the family's shopping they are seen as "consumers" of articles they never use themselves. Women's control of the home did lead to a control over the purchasing of domestic goods, but this did not translate into a control over the larger process of consumption itself. Second, because consumer items are usually conceptualized as those articles acquired in retail outlets and used in the home, most scholars overlook the extensive consumer activity that pre-Depression men engaged in outside of the home. Third, because the analysis of gendered consumerism virtually never looks at spending on consumer *services*, it misses one of the most important types of male consumer activity. Finally, scholars' lack of attention to male consumption reflects and perpetuates the myth that women consumed and men produced. By portraying consumption and consumerism as largely alien to pre-1930s American men, the literature unwittingly reinforces the stereotype of consumption as "feminine."

Because the history and scope of male consumerism have been so dramatically understudied and undertheorized, new research into gendered consumption needs to address the following questions: 1) how much did pre-Depression American men consume; and 2) to what extent did their consumption of goods and services transform them into consumers (i.e., active seekers of goods and services)?

To address the first question, I examine the 1890 U.S. Census of Manufacturers to estimate the value of each sex's personal consumption of individual and recreational goods. My analysis suggests that the monetary value of men's consumption may have been about twice as large as women's. To address the second question, I focus on how men of 1880–1930 spent their leisure time outside of the house and the nature of the goods consumed there. I find that men actively incorporated lavish consumption and consumerism into their daily lives via banquets, drinking parties, fraternities, well-equipped men's clubs and sporting activities, and by visiting male-only brothels, saloons, dime museums, pool halls, variety theaters and minstrelsy shows. Finally, I theorize *how* scholars came to view consumption as "feminine," and *why* the evidence of past male consumption that has been uncovered by labor and men's historians has not been integrated into the standard literature on the intersection of gender and consumerism.

Because the terms shopping, consumption, and consumerism are conflated so often, a few conceptual definitions would be useful here.[3] I define "consumption," "consume" and "consuming" as the mere use of manufactured goods or services, whereas a "consumer" is one who acquires such goods or services by exchanging money. Accordingly, consumers need not be shoppers since many goods and services can be acquired for money without visiting retail outlets (i.e., haircuts, shaves, fraternal inners and paraphernalia, tickets to professional sporting events and theaters, drinks, men's club and gym facilities, etc.). Finally, "consumerism" will refer to the social process whereby individuals exchange money for the goods and services that they use or buy. Armed with such definitions, it becomes possible to assess more critically the degree to which pre-Depression white men were involved in consumption and consumer activity.

Literature Review

Most of the literature which explicitly focuses on the interaction of gender and consumption in pre-1930's America can be divided into two camps: that which studies gendered consumption vs. that which focuses on gendered consumer activity. A major difference between the two is that while the consumption research comments on male (and female) consumption, the consumer research largely focuses on women's involvement with shopping, department stores, the control of the home, and the process by which women were structurally and ideologically transformed into consumers.

In the consumption research tradition would be scholars such as Horowitz, Cross, Breazeale and Ehrenreich, who either explicitly or implicitly characterize pre-Depression consumption as a principally "feminine" or "domestic" activity. For example, Horowitz describes the housewife as society's "proxy consumer," and asserts that industrialization transformed the home "from the center of production to the center of **consumption**" (emphasis added).[4] Similarly, Cross argues that "[male] consumption was inevitably more passive, and . . . bound more closely to the wage earning experience" (i.e., buying rounds of drinks), and that the basis for a "consumerist freedom" lay in the "division between male providers and female domestic consumers."[5]

Two rare feminist studies of American masculinity and consumption also characterize consumption as an historically "feminine" activity, to be contrasted with what they depict as a "new" male consumerism. Kenon Breazeale's analysis of *Esquire* magazine's 1933 campaign to portray masculine consumption as both glamorous and manly unequivocally declares that "*Esquire's* editorial staff sought to constitute consumption as a **new** arena for masculine privilege" (emphasis added). Likewise, Barbara Ehrenreich's examination of 1950's masculinity and consumption asserts that "[n]ew products for men, like toiletries and sports clothes, appeared in the fifties" (emphasis added), yet such goods have been widely enjoyed by middle-class American men since at least the late 1880s.[6] Admittedly, the above two studies concern themselves more with the changing discourse on masculine consumption than with male consumption itself. Nevertheless, their description of male consumption as a "new" activity or "arena for masculine privilege" implicitly characterizes consumption as a predominantly "feminine" prerogative or activity until well into the twentieth century. Consequently, they too indirectly reinforce the dichotomy of productive males and consuming females.[7]

This notion of a division between productive males and consuming females is also reinforced by those feminist scholars within the gendered consumerism research tradition who have most closely examined the gendered dimensions of shopping and consumerism. For instance, Bowlby's study of consumerism and femininity calls it an "empirical fact" that "women at the time of Marx and increasingly over the next 50 years were the principal consumers." Similarly, Abelson's remarkable history of Victorian shoplifting declares that "[a]lthough men were certainly not excluded from consumption choices and often were active participants, women were the primary consumers." Finally, Damon-Moore feminizes and domesticates consumption by defining "consuming" as "choosing and buying commercial products and using them in the home . . . [which] in turn, rested on the capacity of adults, particularly male adults, to earn money."[8]

This conceptualization of consumption as shopping, buying things, and then using them at home is problematic since it largely limits our understanding of the consumption process to knowledge about how *retail* goods were acquired and used in the home—thus overlooking most non-domestic consumption, and nearly all spending on consumer *services*. This domestication of consumption is profoundly gendered. Because late-Victorian and early twentieth-century men spent so much time and money outside of their homes, it is important to examine their non-domestic consumption of consumer goods and services. It is also important to include services since recent economic research shows that early twentieth-century consumer spending on "consumer services . . . form[ed] a consistently rising share of all consumer spending after 1900 . . . [and] surpasse[d] even the proportional weight of *perishables* before 1920."[9] And, because entertainment, amusements, and recreational services comprised an important part of the consumer service revolution, the examination of men's involvement with consumer services and non-domestic consumer goods promises a more accurate picture of the relationship between men and consumerism than has been achieved to date.

The Contributions of Labor, Men's, and Urban History

Some scholars have described the consuming activities of pre-1930s American men, but their findings have not been integrated into the consumption literature. Numerous labor and men's historians have noticed the link between men's culture and consumption, and various turn-of-the-century budgetary studies of working-class families discuss working men's consumption. However, these findings have not been connected to the gender and consumption literature for a number of reasons.

First, their findings have been framed as part of a discussion about class rather than gender. American labor historians such as Kingsdale, Rosenzweig, and Roediger have perceptively examined how and why late-Victorian working-class men spent their time and money in male-only places such as saloons, union halls, and minstrelsy shows, but they tend to view working-class male recreation and sociability as more of a class issue than a highly **gendered** class issue.[10] Consequently, their work is rarely cited by the gender and consumption scholars.

Second, the relatively new field of men's history has also begun to document the link between late nineteenth-century men's culture and consumption, but its practitioners do not address their findings to the pre-existing literature on gender and consumption either. For example, Rotundo describes some of the surprising consumption that occurred in late-Victorian men's clubs, body building, sports, and fraternal organizations, and Carnes' and Clawson's books on fraternal organizations reveal the lavish, theatrical consumption that accompanied most fraternal rituals and interaction. Kimmel's history of American manhood links turn-of-the-century masculinity to the consumption of health food, sporting goods and adventure fiction.[11] But since the above scholars do not specifically focus on the issue of consumption itself, few of their findings have made their way into the gendered consumption literature.

A useful but untapped source of information on pre-Depression male consumption and consumerism in America would be the various social histories of urban entertainment and public amusements. Scholars such as Erenberg, Nasaw, Chauncey and Gilfoyle do a remarkable job of describing life in the late nineteenth-century male-only districts where men spent money on brothels, saloons, dime museums, concert saloons, variety shows, minstrel shows, billiards and gambling.[12] Chauncey's 1994 book on the emergence of gay culture in New York City is doubly insightful in that it also reveals the degree to which gay male life revolved around the City's commercial entertainment. However, because male consumption and consumerism are theoretically regarded as not significant, the rich evidence uncovered by labor, men's, gay and urban historians goes unnoticed. Finally, although these historians tend to study men's commodified activities to understand particular subcultures (i.e., gay, bachelor, working class, or urban, etc.) rather than to understand the gendered nature of consumption, their important findings do suggest the need to rethink the relationship between masculinity and consumption and consumerism.

Modern Masculinities and Consumerism

Although modern male consumerism is generally overlooked, a few scholars have examined how various recent masculinities were constructed around consumerism. For example, Ehrenreich's 1983 book insightfully examines how American masculinity became increasingly orientated around hedonistic consumerism from the 1950s on. Barthel's 1988 book describes how the (middle-class) "new" man which appeared in the United States in the 1980s was largely concerned with hedonistic style and consumer goods. Similarly, Mort's 1996 book on male shopping and style in Britain traces how these activities became increasingly important to many British men between the 1950s and the 1980s.[13] However, because neither of these scholars connects this consumerism to the long history of male consumerism, their work tends to be ahistorical. Thus this paper aims to historicize such male consumerism by demonstrating that the present-day male love of style, recreation, and consumer goods goes back more than a century.

Quantifying Male Consumption

Surprisingly, the firm consensus among scholars that pre-1930's male consumption was marginal has been held without the benefit of much empirical evidence. The only empirical evidence cited to my knowledge is the turn-of-the-century marketing industry's estimates that women comprised between 75–90 percent of the consumer market at various points between 1896 and 1932.[14] However, these estimates are problematic precisely because they refer to those who marketers believed were **purchasing** goods rather than to those who were ultimately **consuming** them. For the study of consumption itself, the question of who acquired the goods may be irrelevant.

Furthermore, many of the commodities and services that men consumed such as lodge paraphernalia, uniforms, work-out gear, haircuts, shaves, and theater and saloon spending were not included in what the marketers of the day thought of as "consumer goods" since these expenditures did not ideologically conform to their idea of what consumer goods were (i.e., retail goods purchased by women). The terms "consumption" and "consumerism" are socially constructed concepts; much as the term housework came to refer to the work women do rather than to all non-market household work. What men consumed was almost by definition not "consumption" since it was understood that women were the "consumers."[15]

To estimate each sex's consumption of personal and recreational commodities I analyze the 1890 Census of Manufactures to determine the approximate monetary value of the goods consumed by each sex. The Census of Manufactures was chosen because this is the only document which provides a reliable aggregate level accounting of the physical commodities consumed by each sex. Although the Census reflects gross domestic product rather than actual consumption, we know that virtually all of these commodities were consumed by Americans because the U.S. exported few personal or recreational consumer goods in 1890. Moreover, since imports comprised only 6–8 percent of the market in 1890, the Census provides a good approximation of goods consumption in general.[16]

The year 1890 was chosen because it marks a point when the majority of clothing and commodities began to be purchased in the market rather than made at home.[17] Moreover, between 1870 and 1890 enormous increases in the consumption of recreational goods such as toys, games, athletic goods, and fancy articles had already occurred.[18] Most importantly, though, 1890 is a critical base year: much later and we would get into a period that many regard as a pivotal cultural shift in gender and consumption (the early 20th century); much earlier and too much of the economic output would have been produced at home. Finally, the 1890 Census predates the crushing depression which followed the Panic of 1893.

Methods and Data

To date there are evidently no statistics or estimates of the ratio of male to female consumption of non-work commodities. While such estimates could be fairly accurately acquired today through consumer spending surveys, this method is obviously not applicable to the 1890s. However, because men's and women's styles of dressing, recreating, and socializing were so dramatically different from each other during the 1890s, a number of experimental and inferential methods can be used to estimate the probable consumption ratio between the sexes.

The 1890 Census data lend themselves to the reliable estimation of sex-consumption ratios for clothing since they specify most clothing as male or female. Thus, in cases such as "furnishing goods, men's" or "clothing, women's," I attributed 100 percent of the consumption of these goods to the specified sex. For those clothing goods which could be utilized by either sex, such as woolen, worsted and cotton goods, I used the more detailed commodity breakdowns and descriptions to estimate ratios. For example, the Census of Manufactures (COM) subdivides woolen and worsted goods into the sex-specific categories of "men's wear," "women's wear," "shawls," and "jeans."[19]

For goods not identified by the Census as belonging to a particular sex (i.e., watches, shoes, hats, cosmetics, furs, sporting goods, tobacco and alcohol), I used the historical literature *and* the newspaper and magazine advertisements of the day to: 1) decide **whether** each sex consumed such a good, and 2) estimate the percentage of the good each sex would have probably consumed. Historical studies of Victorian fashion, jewelry, music, sports, fitness, and leisure were used to estimate each sexes' consumption of various goods, and since magazine and newspaper advertisements provide additional information as to who uses each good, I consulted them also before arriving at my final estimates. However, because advertisements can shape social practice as well as reflect it, consumption ratios were never assessed solely on the basis of the ads, but only in conjunction with the historical literature on each particular item.

214   *Mark A. Swiencicki*

Table 1 includes only the ready-made commodities utilized by males and females in the direct satisfaction of their own expressive and recreational needs and desires. Expressive goods are items such as clothing, jewelry, body-building equipment, or cosmetics which would allow individuals to define or embellish their presentation of self. Recreational goods are commodities which would normally be consumed during periods of relaxation when one is not engaging in domestic, industrial, or commercial labor. Included here are items such as alcohol, tobacco, sporting goods, and musical instruments. Specifically excluded are goods that mix leisure with work, such as sewing equipment and newspapers. Commodities used to produce goods or services for others (i.e., work tools, hardware, cooking/laundry utensils, baby supplies, curtains, furniture, etc.) are also excluded from this study since they primarily constitute implements of industrial or domestic labor. Consequently, the value of goods consumed in the industrial workplace or business office was **not** coded as "male" consumption, just as the goods women used to care for their families cannot be viewed as "female" consumption. Thus, by concentrating on the

Table 1. Value and type of personal and recreational goods consumed by each sex in 1890

Commodity	Value in millions	%Model % Female consumption	Value-male consumption	Value-female consumption
1. All men's clothing, furnishings & tailored goods	446.2	100/0	446.2	0.0
2. Liquor & alcohol	289.8	80/20	231.8	58.0
3. Boots & shoes	274.1	50/50	137.1	137.1
4. Tobacco & pipes	197.4	95/5	187.5	9.9
5. All women's clothing, millinery & custom work	182.5	0/100	0.0	182.5
6. Hosiery & knit goods	67.2	50/50	33.6	33.6
7. Hats/caps/gloves/mittens	52.7	50/50	26.4	26.4
8. Musical instruments/materials	36.9	50/50	18.5	18.5
9. Jewelry	34.8	15/50	5.2	29.6
10. Unisex woolen, worsteds & silk goods	34.5	50/50	17.3	17.3
11. Fur goods	20.5	50/50	10.3	10.3
12. Umbrellas & canes	13.8	50/50	6.9	6.9
13. Corsets	12.4	5/95	0.6	11.8
14. Watches	6.0	50/50	3.0	3.0
15. Perfumery & cosmetics	4.6	30/70	1.4	3.2
16. Billiard tables/materials	2.8	95/5	2.7	0.14
17. Sporting goods	2.7	60/40	1.6	1.1
18. Pocket books	2.2	0/100	0.0	2.2
Total Value in millions	1,681.1		1130.0 (67.2%)	551.5 (32.8%)

Source: U.S. Bureau of the Census, *Abstract of the Eleventh Census & Report on Manufacturing Industries in the United States at the Eleven Census* vol. VI: 3.
Note: Total figures are off by $0.4 million due to rounding error.

consumption of individuals (rather than that of workers, parents or wives), this analysis controls for the proxy consumption that women undertook for their families by excluding consumption not undertaken for one's own use.

What is most striking about Table 1 is that the value of men's clothing (category #1) is nearly 2.5 times larger than that of women's clothing (category #5). In other words, 71 percent of all ready-made clothing was consumed by males in 1890—probably because they had to dress for both work and their extensive social lives.[20] These figures are especially reliable since clothing was one of the few items that both the manufacturers and the Census Bureau specifically divided into male and female product. Moreover, because the figures for women's clothing include the thriving dressmaking industry that fell between ready-made and home-made dresses, they represent a good portion of the total clothing worn by women, as well.

Although such figures do not reflect the dresses made by middle-class women at home, such dresses cannot be counted as consumer goods precisely because they were produced at home rather than purchased in the market. In this case, women were producers rather than consumers. However, the raw materials purchased to make such dresses were consumer goods. Because working-class women generally relied on ready-made clothing by 1890 (see endnote 5), women as a group probably made no more than about one third of their clothing at home (worth $91.3 million if store bought). Thus, assuming that the raw materials for the homemade third of women's clothing cost about 40 percent of what the finished products would cost, women would have only spent about $36.5 million on materials such as thread, silk, buttons and fabric. This means that even after this sum is added to net female consumption, women's total consumption would only rise by 1.4 percentage points (32.8%–34.2%). In 1890 the market clearly reserved most of its clothing resources and commodities for men rather than for women.

Since men bought most of their clothes off the rack, and the value of clothing comprises such a large proportion of the commodities in Table 1 (37%), overall statistics might exaggerate men's place in the commercial nexus. However, even after excluding all men's and women's clothing from the analysis (categories #1 & 5), men still consumed about 65 percent of the value of all commodities (as opposed to 67 percent when clothing is included). Thus, since the ratio of male-to-female consumption in both cases is virtually identical, this suggests that late-Victorian men probably did consume about twice the value of personal/recreational commodities as women (see Table 1). Moreover, even if these estimates somehow missed a third of all female consumption, the adjusted female portion would still comprise only 44 percent of all consumption. Consequently, any talk about late-Victorian consumption being "principally" or even largely feminine would not appear to be empirically sustainable. In fact, considering that the above estimates do not even reflect men's substantial expenditures on non-retail goods and consumer services such as fraternal paraphernalia, entertainment costs, barber shops, and tickets to professional sporting events, the size and value of late-Victorian male consumption seems clearly dominant compared with that of women.[21]

Although the list of commodities analyzed does not shed much light on the qualitative aspects of male consumption, a few observations are in order here. While a number of male consumption activities such as smoking and drinking are intuitively obvious, others may surprise the modern reader. For instance, the amount of opulent and stylish fur that late-Victorian men wore contradicts most current assumptions about Victorian male asceticism. More striking is the fact that men openly used so many cosmetics. According to historian Fenja Gunn, "Victorian m[e]n could blatantly use cosmetics devices . . . [while] women of the day had to disguise any attempts at self-improvement."[22] Indeed, the historical record shows that late-Victorian men used everything from shaving soaps, aftershave lotions, pomade oils, and hair dyes, to cosmetics for training one's mustache. And if the contemporary advertisements reflect social practice, then late-Victorian men also consumed skin beautifiers, hair restorers, and cosmetic vaporizers.[23] In effect, the "[n]ew products for men, like toiletries and sports clothes" which Barbara Ehrenreich attributed to the 1950s were already in use by the late-Victorian era (see below, discussion of sports clothing). At any rate, the above analysis clearly suggests that late-Victorian white men were hardly the stridently ascetic beings that separate spheres historians presumed them to be.

Historical budget studies provide further evidence that late-Victorian male consumption was enormous (compared with that of women). For example, Louise More's 1907 study of the spending habits of 200 working-class families in New York City from 1903–5 indicates that the lion's share of most families' disposable income went to husbands. Using More's figures, it would appear that about 11 percent of the average working family's disposable income went to the husband's drinking, while another 16 percent was reserved for his personal spending money.[24] Thus working-class men appear to have spent about 27 percent of their family's disposable income on drinking and socializing alone, and even more if one includes the money spent on lodge and benefit society dues ($5–$120 per family annually).[25] In light of the striking disparity between men's and women's personal spending money, then, one can only conclude that non-rural, late-Victorian white men must have been a major consuming constituency.

At this point, some readers might ask why it matters who ultimately consumed most goods if they were purchased by women. Women's consumerism is an important way in which women exercised agency in a highly constraining gender order.[26] Nonetheless, the next several sections of this paper show that pre-Depression white men consumed many commodities that were not purchased by women, and that many, if not most, of their homo-social leisure activities and organizations revolved around consumption itself, since consumerism was an important social activity for men.

Middle-Class Men's Consumption, 1880–1920

New Sports, New Equipment, New Clothes

The literature on sports and masculinity has largely viewed late-Victorian sports as a vehicle for mediating the crisis of masculinity which occurred among white-collar workers by promoting competition, militarism, character development, and a "strenuous" masculinity.[27] Current scholars point out that late-Victorian gender reactionaries such as Henry James and Ernest Thompson Seton (founder of the Boy Scouts of America) promoted sports and fitness as an antidote to the "damnable feminization" and "over-civilization" besetting America's newly sedentary middle classes.[28] While most reactionaries were primarily opposed to what they saw as the growing "effeminacy" of middle-and upper middle-class American men, some implicitly linked the problem to consumer society itself by stating that athletics substituted "hardiness for effeminacy, and dexterity for luxurious indolence."[29]

Although it seems undeniable that late-Victorian sports helped white-collar men who no longer owned property or directly ran factories to rejuvenate their flagging sense of masculinity, the capacity of sports to promote consumption and consumer activity has received less attention from historians and sociologists of sport. Exclusive sports like golf, yachting, and tennis have been linked with the conspicuous consumption of the rich, and the indulgent lifestyle of the sporting underworld has been noted, but no one has focused on the ability of sports to promote wide scale, comprehensive consumption among ordinary middle-class men.[30] Thus, in the following section I argue that since so many late-Victorian sports entailed expensive equipment, showy uniforms, fashionable fitness wear, sneakers, and playing and spectator fees, they appear to have promoted festive middle-class male consumption as much as they reinforced an apparently compromised white-collar masculinity.

Body building is a perfect example of the capacity of athletics to promote consumerism. As the muscular ideal for men became increasingly prevalent in the late nineteenth century, "countless men and boys from good families began exercising as never before . . . [amidst] images of bulging muscles and naked virility."[31] One study of magazine articles revealed that the most frequently emphasized traits of heroes in the 1890s were their impressive size and strength.[32] What is most notable about such a pursuit, though, is the degree to which its practice depended upon consumer goods. According to Harvey Green's history of health, fitness and sport in America, at least ten different pieces of work-out equipment were available to the body builder by the 1890s. Enthusiasts would often purchase equipment such as gymnastic crowns, indian clubs, parlor gymnasiums, parlor rowers, health lifts, dumbbells, rings, weight machines, pulleys, and trapezes, or join expensive urban gymnasiums.[33] Of course, middle-class boys and men who merely owned sneakers, shorts and a T-shirt could simply work out at the local YMCA for a fee, but this still constituted a form of consumer activity.[34] Therefore, since body building required access to so much commodified equipment, its practitioners were transformed *defacto* into consumers.

Numerous other sports and athletic recreations of the period required a similarly high level of consumption as well. Enthusiasts of tennis, golf, croquet, badminton, and ping pong not only had to purchase expensive rackets, balls, or accoutrements, but also had to pay to use the tennis courts and golf courses since there were no public sports facilities at the time. Moreover, the norms of respectability required bourgeois devotees of the above sports to purchase special workout clothes or uniforms.[35] Indeed, an article published in 1901 by the influential physical educator Dudley A. Sargent complained that fashion accounted for the rise and fall of many sports, rather than the other way around.[36]

Baseball is another example of a typically "male" activity which promoted middle-class consumption.[37] In general, late nineteenth-century sports participation was a "pay-to-play" proposition. While working-class men sometimes played baseball in vacant sandlots, baseball diamonds for more organized games had to be rented by the game or purchased by wealthy baseball enthusiasts. And as baseball developed into a spectator sport in the second half of the nineteenth century, admission was charged at professional games. Therefore, the baseball fan of 1890 would have to pay fifty cents to see a National League game, a fee which excluded most working men.[38] Besides admission, many fans also gambled and purchased the liquor that was sold at many stadiums after 1881, and from the late 1880s on, fans could buy ten-cent guide books introducing them to Spalding's growing line of sporting goods products.[39] Thus, in view of the fact that baseball's spectators were largely middle-class and male, one could say that baseball was not just a sport but was also an outlet for middle-class male consumption.[40]

Perhaps the clearest example of the ability of sports to promote conspicuous male consumption are the exclusive athletic clubs in late nineteenth-century urban areas. In the New York City area alone, membership in the leading clubs numbered in the thousands, and there were many more such clubs in cities such as Boston, New Orleans, and San Francisco.[41] The best clubs in New York had most of the following: running tracks, gymnasiums, swimming pools, club rooms, dining rooms, bowling alleys, billiard parlors, rifle ranges, Russian and Turkish baths, sleeping rooms, ballrooms, theaters, and the latest in exercise equipment.[42] However, the clubs in Boston, New Orleans, and San Francisco "rivaled the New York clubs in terms of facilities and membership" and sometimes "sponsored exotic and extravagant shows" such as the detailed reconstruction of Greek and Roman games.[43]

For the late-Victorian middle and upper classes, then, engaging in sports and athletics meant engaging in consumption. In fact, since participating in many sports and fitness activities entailed multiple levels of consumption (i.e., equipment, sports clothing, sneakers, tickets, and rental or club fees), such activities transformed their participants into not merely consumers, but *comprehensive* consumers at that. And, while many non-working-class women did engage in sporting and fitness activities, their involvement (and subsequent consumption) was limited by the variety of sports and the amount of free time that was available to them.[44] Early sports, then, both facilitated and stimulated festive middle- and upper-class male consumption and consumer activity.

Spare no Amenities: Fraternities and Bachelor Club Consumption

Because late-Victorian society was so patriarchal, the canon of respectable bourgeois manliness demanded both property and marriage. Normally, this meant that young middle-class men would leave home for a time to study and then begin their professional lives in the commercial or urban areas of the country. Cut off from their families and most young women, such men often formed informal mutual support systems such as clubs, fraternities, literary and secret societies, and lodges.[45] According to historian Anthony Rotundo's study of Victorian male youth culture, such homosocial organizations "grew up like weeds throughout the nineteenth century ... [and] flourished in any place with a concentration of young men—cities, towns, colleges."[46]

These clubs and organizations centered their social activities around domestic and leisure consumption. For example, such organizations rarely got together without enjoying a meal, and many held "elaborate banquets," frequent drinking parties, and purchased libraries for the use of group members.[47] Other organizations, such as the Naomi Bachelor Club of Stockton, California, and the Owl's Club of Tucson, Arizona, were noted for their lavish amenities and furnishings. For example, the Naomi Bachelor Club contained a hat rack, crystal tumblers, fancy colored shelf papers, "dainty bits of Dresden china," a piano, camera, and ice distilled water on draught.[48] And the Owl's Club, a bachelor home/club set up in Tucson in 1886 by a group of Easterners who sought "comfortable living quarters, and fine food," "decorat[ed] their quarters with paintings, fine furnishings ... beautiful ornaments ... [and] hired a housekeeper, and a Chinese cook" to serve "elegant, multi-course meals." Moreover, "any visitor to the Owl's Club provided an excuse for an elegant dinner party ... [consisting of] several courses of oysters and other delicacies ... pints of wine ... dessert and champagne."[49]

Even groups organized around the lofty goal of studying art and literature, such as the many intellectual clubs of late-Victorian Boston and New York, surrounded themselves with the amenities of bourgeois life. For example, St. Botolph's Club, a "poor man's club" for intellectuals founded in 1879 in Boston, served "wine, liquors and cigars and whatever [wa]s necessary to eat or drink in social Clubs" and featured an art gallery, a Chickering grand piano, public utilities, and baseball matches with other clubs. And the Club of Odd Volumes, a Boston intellectual club founded in 1887, had an outing "[i]n their very first year of existence" in which they:

were met by a horse drawn barge . . . inspected the library and collection of art [of the Hollingsworth estate in Mattapan] and were regaled with a supper consisting . . . of "bivalves, deliciously cooked, salads palatable and creams most delicate, while crystal sparkled occasionally from a quiet corner with its tempting contents."[50]

Fraternal lodges and secret societies comprised one of the most important bases for male socializing in late nineteenth-century America.[51] According to the *Cyclopedia of Fraternities*, 40 percent of all males over 20 years of age held membership in at least one secret society in 1896.[52] While fraternal lodges are not usually associated with rampant consumerism, the rituals and entertainment of many fraternities were so dependent upon lavish consumption that they acted as another important stimulant to middle-class male consumption.

In her path breaking study of freemasonry in the United States, Lynn Dumenil studied the case history of Live Oak (masonic) Lodge No. 61 in Oakland, California.[53] Dumenil's study is of more than local importance since fraternal orders universally subscribed to the masonic practice of initiations and symbolic dramas.[54] To begin with, in order to join Live Oak Lodge between 1880 and 1920, a man would have to pay annual dues of between $6–12, an initiation fee of between $50–100, and considerably more for the additional degrees of membership. Initiations and ceremonial rituals were quite ornate, and routinely required such goods as top hats, jewels, special seats, lambskin aprons, horses, glittering swords, drill corps uniforms, sashes, plumes, knight's dress, double-barred crosses, white gloves, embroidered banners, and numerous medals and regalia.[55] In fact, the demand for lodge regalia was so extensive that numerous companies existed in the late nineteenth century to meet such a demand.[56]

Such festive consumption was hardly limited to the freemasons, since the Improved Order of Red Men (one of the largest fraternal orders of the late-nineteenth century) made extensive use of bows and arrows, knives, tomahawks, ropes, tents, shepherd's robes, sandals and gongs during their ceremonies.[57] Moreover, many lodges served alcoholic beverages, and/or customary "sumptuous dinners," while others adjourned to nearby taverns and restaurants after meeting.[58] Indeed, an 1897 article in the *North American Review* estimated that the average lodge member spent $50 a year on dues and insurance, and $200 over the course of his life on initiation fees, uniforms, ritualistic paraphernalia, banquets, travel, and gifts for retiring officers.[59] However, since the "secrets" of the fraternal order were protected by a "pledge more binding in its nature than perhaps any known to man," such consumption evaded the moral scrutiny and condemnation of a patriarchal society that vociferously condemned the "extravagant" spending of its women.[60]

In sum, although most of the above late nineteenth-century men's organizations certainly amounted to more than mere excuses for consuming goods together, such groups did provide middle- and upper middle-class Victorian men with excellent opportunities to consume and spend outside of the purview of women. Such lavish consumption was organized and carried out without the services of women shoppers (although women probably cooked or cleaned at many of these clubs). Thinking of women as society's "proxy consumer" elides the enormous consumer activity that middle-class white men engaged in directly.

Working-Class Male Consumption, 1880–1930

For at least the past century, the American working class appears to have taken considerable pleasure and pride in the flamboyant and ostentatious display of goods. Working-class families generally rejected the simple furniture styles of the middle class for plush Victorian furniture, and working women in turn-of-the-century New York took great pains to adorn their apartments with cheap lace curtains, bric-a-brac, gaudily colored religious prints, portraits, and advertising posters.[61] Moreover, when it came to fashion, numerous European visitors to the U.S. reported that the American workers of the 1890s preferred stylish and flamboyant dress rather than the quality and durability prized by British workers.[62] As the next section will show, the working-class taste for showy consumption was not limited to women, but was shared by urban working men, and to a lesser extent, African American men.

B'hoys, Bloods, Mashers and Dudes: A Stylish New Working Class

During the second half of the nineteenth century three major developments occurred which transformed the way gender was performed by working-class people: 1) young people began to receive their own pay checks, 2) fashion became mass-produced and readily available, and 3) dazzling commercial entertainment areas sprouted up in the major urban areas. Young working women began to militantly assert their own brand of class and gender pride by boldly rejecting middle-class styles of femininity in favor of gaudy colors, outrageous accessories, and (relatively) low skirts and dresses which accentuated their hips and thighs.[63] By the 1890s this style became common in the urban areas, as "rowdy" and "factory girls" rebelliously appropriated the cultural style of the prostitute (i.e, cosmetics, sleeveless dresses, gaudy colors) for their own use.[64]

Meanwhile, young working men also used fashion to express their new personas. For example, in mid nineteenth-century New York City, B'hoys, or dandified street toughs, began to prowl the Bowery in search of women, fights, commercial entertainment and alcohol.[65] According to the Knickerbocker socialite Abram Dayton, "[t]hese 'B'hoys' ... were the most consummate dandies of the day," and paraded about with lavishly greased, long front locks, black, straight, broad-brimmed hats, turned-down shirt collars, black frockcoats with skirts below the knee, embroidered shirts, tight pantaloons, ever present cigars, and "a profusion of jewelry as varied and costly as the b'hoy could procure."[66] Similarly, urban street gangs such as New York's largely Irish "Dead Rabbits" also "promenad[ed] in distinctive dress . . . [during] their leisure hours," and Walt Whitman described the manual workers seated in the pit of a Broadway theater as "well dress'd . . . young and middle-aged men."[67]

By the 1880s, then, a flamboyantly consumerist working-class strand of masculinity emerged as large numbers of working (and lower middle-class) men began adopting behavior that had previously been confined to the old sporting crowd and theatrical world of gamblers, libertines and dandies. Such men adopted a sexually assertive style, and according to contemporary observers "hover[ed] everywhere, from the marketplace to the meetinghouse, and from the promenade to the theater."[68] Some described the masher as a "barber-and-tailor-shop decoration," and the novelist Theodore Dreiser noted that the masher prized "[g]ood clothes . . . without which he was nothing," and had a "keen desire for the feminine . . . [and] an insatiable love of variable pleasure."[69] Furthermore, such working-class male dandy-ism was not limited to white men, since the *New York Tribune* reported in 1895 that on African Broadway:

> [there is a] daily promenade of gayly dressed girls and *sprig* young colored men. . . . The favorite dress of the young men "in style" is a glossy silk hat, patent leathers, a black suit with a sack coat of remarkable shortness, and a figured waist-coat. Paste diamonds are *de riguer*.

Most importantly, though, these African American men were not part of New York's black elite, who lived on 53rd Street and dressed like bourgeois whites, but rather had "only a dollar or two standing between them and starvation most of the time."[70]

This is not to say that all working-class men dressed like the masher, B'Hoy, or stylish African American. Working-class dandies, or "dudes," seem to have primarily inhabited the major urban areas, and appear to have been a relatively youthful lot. However, since the masher's presence has been described as ubiquitous in the large cities, we can infer that the stylish, working-class young man was hardly a rare sight in the 1890s.[71] Thus, because a significant number of late-Victorian working-class men expressed their masculinity through stylish clothing, fashion, jewelry, and smart hairstyles, it would appear that the working-class taste for ostentatious consumption was not limited to women and girls. This no doubt helps explain the high proportion of male expenditure on clothing and personal goods seen in the census figures.

Fraternal Lodges, Cellar Clubs, Saloons, Burlesque

While masher fashion may have had less appeal for older or married working-class men, such men could satisfy their taste for spectacle and extravagant consumption by joining a fraternal order. Since working-class men made up 25 percent of the masonic lodges, and up to 50 percent of many non-masonic fraternal orders in 1891, we can assume that they comprised between 30–35 percent of the 6,000,000 fraternity members in 1896.[72] In other words, nearly two million working-class men may have taken part in the rituals and ceremonies of the fraternal order in 1896 alone.[73]

Besides spending money on initiation and the three to four required levels of rank, working-class lodge members also had to purchase the uniforms and regalia that corresponded with each rank.[74] Furthermore, many of the more working-class lodges created special elaborately costumed Uniformed Ranks to march in public parades as drill corps. Such drill teams and parade units were typically outfitted with helmets, gauntlets, epaulets, chevrons, ribbons, ornaments, and swords, rifles, or axes, and the official *Pythian Manual* of 1887 specified that drill corps officers must wear:

> black silk folding chapeau trimmed with two black ostrich plumes . . . a gold chapeau tassel on each peak . . . a black silk rosette . . . surmounted by a strap with gold embroidery . . . a silver bullion lily . . . a gold emblematic button . . . [and] black silk ribbon sashing . . . showing the gilt ornament on the right side.[75]

The Knights of Pythias were hardly unique, since orders such as the Independent Order of Odd Fellows, the Foresters, and the Knights of Columbus established showy public drill teams of their own which "offered men who were attracted by elaborate regalia . . . an opportunity to indulge their fantasies to the limit."[76]

It would seem that a major difference between the middle- and working-class fraternal orders was their willingness to display fancy costumes and consumer styles in public. While the middle-class masonic orders discretely conducted private dress-up and dinner parties, working-class lodges preferred to publicly display their ornate drill uniforms and paraphernalia, and by implication, their consumer prowess itself. Such flamboyant displays suggest that working-class men linked the public display of consumption with class and gender pride.

Besides lodges, working-class men spent their free time on an assortment of other commodified recreational activities. For example, working-class saloon goers not only bought one another drinks in the saloons; they also spent money there on lunch, billiards, prostitutes, and sports betting.[77] Billiard games alone cost a nickel a game per player.[78] Moreover, working men in urban areas often hung out at special billiard halls and attended bawdy burlesque and minstrel shows.[79] Even young working men without money had commodified amusements since most Catholic temperance societies provided free non-drinking alternatives to the saloon. Indeed, their "well-appointed clubrooms [had] . . . newspapers, domino sets, gymnasiums, card tables, libraries, and even pool tables." And these clubs usually offered concerts, minstrel shows, excursions, coffee parties, and sports teams, while some even had paramilitary auxiliaries with elaborate uniforms and drilling routines.[80] In effect, temperance societies subsidized working men's recreational consumption. Regardless of who paid the bill for their recreational commodities, working-class men in the urban areas engaged in recreational consumption.

Young, single, working-class men who were not involved in lodges or temperance halls often created their own organizations to meet their social and recreational needs. In the 1890s young men's clubs appeared "in greater numbers than ever before." According to Herbert Asbury, these clubs arose largely due to the "patronage of the political associations," and were a "feature of life in the congested tenement districts."[81] It is unclear how many of these clubs existed in the 1890s, but in the 1920s the New York area had about 500 such clubs, and in 1934 between six to ten thousand youths in the East Side of Manhattan alone were connected to cellar clubs.[82]

Typically, these clubs were set up in basements, the upper floors of storefronts, in halls, the back rooms of saloons, or wherever the rent was cheapest.[83] Organized as pleasure, athletic, or cellar clubs, they provided young men who lived in extremely crowded tenements with a private place to be with their friends or to entertain women. Although few of these social clubs attained the affluence of the average middle-class men's club, the young working men who ran them labored to make them as attractive and domestic as possible. For example, such clubs were painted and often equipped with sofas, fake fireplaces, colored light bulbs, and showers. Many of the better off clubs had individual mail boxes, dishes, silverware, ice boxes, pianos, heavy brocade drapes, large mirrors, and libraries, while some featured laundry facilities.[84] Moreover, club members did not merely eat in their clubs, but occasionally threw stag or drinking parties, and rented strip teasers or prostitutes as entertainment.[85] Thus, like the middle-class bachelors and university students referred to earlier, young working men created social clubs which simultaneously provided the comforts of home *and* allowed them to engage in commodified recreation.

Trans-Classed Male Pursuits

Male-Only Entertainment

Because working- and middle-class men so rarely socialized together in the late nineteenth century, their consumption patterns have been discussed in separate sections. However, one popular urban pastime did successfully draw men of both classes: the male-only entertainment and amusement industry. Male-only entertainment consisted of establishments such as concert saloons, cheap variety theaters, gambling halls, brothels, peep shows, dime museums, and the "red light" districts found in "[e]very major metropolitan and even some good-sized towns."[86] Most importantly, though, all were off limits to most women, and most attracted both working- and middle-class men.

Concert saloons and cheap variety theaters were barrooms or taverns which offered free or cheap entertainment in adjacent back rooms, halls, or theaters. Generally located near mining camps, urban areas, and in red light districts, such establishments combined singing, dancing, drinking, gambling, and risque "girly" entertainment with prostitution.[87] The entertainment consisted of local performers singing and dancing, acrobats, scantily clad female vocalists, absurd farces, and variety, burlesque, and minstrel shows.[88] However, since the only women normally present were waitresses, performers, or prostitutes, such establishments have been described by historians and contemporary observers as drawing exclusively male audiences.[89]

Another point historians agree upon is that these concert saloons and variety theaters were not exclusively working class in clientele, but usually drew roughly equal numbers of working- and middle-class men. Nasaw attributes this to the fact that such shows were neither cheap, located near most working-class neighborhoods, nor conducted in the native languages of most immigrants. Others point out that many of the patrons were out of town middle-aged men.[90] Finally, numerous contemporary observers have remarked on how such places drew men from such diverse backgrounds as roughs, laborers, mechanics, salesmen, accountants, judges, politicians and businessmen.[91] Thus, while some of these places did cater to "a more thoroughly upper-class or working-class clientele," most provided a rare venue for men of different social classes to congregate and spend money together.[92]

Besides the thousands of concert saloons and variety theaters which existed in the late nineteenth-century urban areas, men seeking commodified, homosocial thrills could also go to the peep shows, dime museums, gambling halls, or the red light districts found in most urban areas. At a peep show, or a dime museum, men would pay a dime to view such oddities as freaks, scantily clad women, or female genitalia preserved in glass containers.[93] And because "[v]ariety, burlesque, minstrelsy, and the saloon shaded down to the whorehouse and dance halls of the red-light districts," most of the above establishments were conveniently located in the same area of the city.[94] Thus such areas can best be characterized as male entertainment districts.

Because such male entertainment districts were usually seen as places of vice by respectable society, many middle-class men who were particularly concerned with their respectability avoided such places. However, they too could publicly recreate at exclusively male clubs since "in the nineteenth century, every hotel and major restaurant . . . had its own luxuriously appointed men's cafe."[95] As women's historians have noted, the downtown areas of most cities had traditionally been the location for men's clubs and cafes.[96] In fact, some towns, such as Nashville, Tennessee, even had a downtown men's quarter which featured sport, gambling and liquor places, seven men's furnishing/clothing stores, three tobacco shops, a number of barber shops, and the Nashville Athletic Club which contained Russian and Turkish baths and choice exercise equipment. Due to the presence of so many gambling and amusement facilities, several loan offices were even located there to provide cash to men who needed more money. Finally, the quarter was fairly upscale, since it was populated mostly by white collar workers and professionals who worked nearby, and was only ruined by the state-wide prohibition legislation of 1909.[97] Male consumption of such services thus provided an important form of male-only consumer activity that studies of consumerism that assume women are the "typical" consumer necessarily overlook.

Men's Fiction

Although the above examination of men's consumption largely focuses on public, or group, forms of male consumption, late-Victorian men obviously engaged in commodified amusements at home as well. Studies of nineteenth-century American reading habits indicate that working- and middle-class boys and young men made up a large share of the huge market for lowbrow adventure and dime novel fiction.[98] The primary consumers of such literature were usually boys and young men.[99] Thus an 1879 *Atlantic* article suggested that while all sorts of working people came into the bookstores for dime novels, "the most ardent class of patron . . . are boys."[100] Alternatively, William Wallace Cook's editor disputed this point and advised him not to make the hero too juvenile since, "[t]he stories in the Ten Cent Library are not read by boys alone but usually by young men."[101]

Whereas working-class boys and men usually read stories dealing with the lives of mechanics and factory life,[102] middle-class boys and men preferred stories which dealt with outdoors adventure or individual self improvement. For example, western novels and wilderness adventure such as Jack London's *Call of the Wild* were very popular among young men, as were books about manly heroes such as Paul Bunyan, John Henry, Davey Crockett and Daniel Boone.[103] More mature men could enjoy the hundreds of rags-to-riches books about social mobility by authors such as Horatio Alger. And although women also read a large share of the lowbrow press, such as romance and working women's novels, it is important to acknowledge men's reading since most recent scholarly attention has focused on women's reading.[104]

Men's Consumption as a Distinct Process of Distribution

It would appear that the recognition of late-Victorian and early twentieth-century male consumption and consumerism may have been obstructed by the manner in which men consumed many goods. Unlike women, who purchased most goods directly from grocers, dry goods, and department stores, men could obtain many of their consumer goods through non-retail outlets such as saloons (drinks, tobacco, billiards), lodges (uniforms, rings, paraphernalia), clubs (books, fancy amenities, trips), athletic clubs and associations (uniforms, equipment, supplies), barbershops (shaves, haircuts), and dime theaters and minstrel shows (tickets and liquor).

This is not to say that men did not do a fair amount of shopping, for even the large department stores devoted quite a few sections to men's products. For example, as early as 1894 Macy's department store (in New York City) offered a wide selection of men's and boy's clothing and hats, lawn mowers, chest weights, a cigar department, and a "complete" line of fishing tackle and accessories. Men's products were so lucrative that in the middle of the crushing 1896 depression Macy's opened up a six story annex "devoted principally to merchandise of special interest to men and boys: clothing, furnishings, and shoes . . . harness[es] and 'horse goods,' sporting goods, and bicycles."[105]

It is important to note, however, that extensive men's shopping at department stores between 1890 and 1930 generally only happened when the stores located their men's sections close to an exit.[106] As a trouble-shooting study of a department store in 1920 found, "men preferred to shop quickly and objected to walking through the main aisles which would bring them into the areas filled with women."[107] Other industry observers noted that men preferred shopping in specialty stores rather than in department stores.[108] Thus, pre-Depression men appeared to be willing to shop as long as they could do so under gender-segregated conditions.

Because men often acquired consumer goods in a different manner from women (i.e., as services or at specialty stores), a large degree of their consumption escaped the public scrutiny of turn-of-the-century marketers, critics and gender reactionaries. And while working-class saloon going and gambling were criticized by middle-class reformers and religious figures,[109] to the extent that male consumption avoided being excessively identified with the working class it generally escaped public comment or criticism.

In sum, the above examination of men's leisure activities, modes of expression, and homo-social culture suggests that many, if not most, of the leisure activities and social organizations of pre-Depression, non-rural, American white men revolved around the consumption of goods. One might even say that such men were engaged in group, or "organizational" consumption (i.e., as clubs, lodges, athletic teams, etc.). At any rate, it is hard to imagine many men's leisure activities that did not involve substantial amounts of consumption. Thus, the remaining question is: if pre-Depression men were such a major consuming constituency, why have consumption and consumerism been characterized as so decidedly feminine?

The Social Construction of the Concepts "Consumerism" and "Consumer Goods"

Victoria de Grazia's 1996 essay on the changing meanings of the term consumption suggests an approach.[110] In the pre-industrial era, consumption had originally meant "to waste," "to devour," or "to use up." As knowledge about the national wealth became increasingly necessary, though, political arithmeticians began to distinguish between the manufacturing and the use of goods via the antonymic concepts of "production" and "consumption." However, because during the industrial revolution all human activity came to be evaluated in terms of its economic productivity, the labor market became the ideal-typical site of production, whereas the home became "the" site for consumption. And because consumption was never conceptualized as a discrete problem (as production was), the household became "in theory a mere receptacle for commodities."[111] Therefore, since women were left with the job of shopping and caring for the family, it became increasingly common to view women as "consumers."

While the nineteenth-century division of labor and its nascent breadwinner ideology did encourage people to associate men with productive wage labor, and women with domestic consumption, these two forces alone do not appear entirely responsible for the turn-of-the-century tendency to define women as "consumers" and "consumption" as a thoroughly feminine activity. Such a development seems to be more the product of a national, public discourse of heterosexual masculinity and its corollary campaign by early-twentieth century marketers and consumption promoters to convince the public that consumption was a woman's true vocation, and that consumers, in turn, were women.

As Kathy Peiss found in her study of makeup and gender, the century-old discourse of heterosexual masculinity strenuously denied the male use of cosmetics by calling men's grooming products toiletries rather than cosmetics. Consequently, toiletries and cosmetics developed as separate industries, with the former being sold by barbershops, soap makers and razor manufacturers, and the latter by beauty shops, perfumeries and pharmaceutical companies.[112] A very similar process took place with consumer goods, in which whatever commodities that women purchased and controlled were considered to be "consumer goods," whereas whatever goods or services that men purchased generally fell under the category of "expenditures" rather than consumer goods. For example, the turn-of-the-century studies of working-class family budgets typically refer to the things that men spent money on, such as tobacco, alcohol, clubs, and lodge dues and paraphernalia, as "expenditures" or "sundries" rather than as consumer goods. Thus Horowitz reproduces 1875/1918 budget studies which list working-class husbands' expenditures on tobacco, liquor, carfare, lodges, clubs, and societies, but creates no indexed category for "men as consumers" nor specifically discusses the subject of male consumption.[113] On the other hand, the category "women-as-consumers" is indexed on ten separate pages, and women's consumption is discussed throughout the book.

Similarly, because sports and athletics have been so heavily promoted by the discourse of heterosexual masculinity, the commodities that men used while engaging in these activities (i.e., balls, uniforms, running shoes, gyms, rackets and golf clubs) have generally been viewed as props in the rituals of militaristic training rather than as products which transform their participants into consumers (surely they are both). An ideological thread running from the cult of strenuous masculinity to the recent sociology of sports points to sports as primarily a training ground for hegemonic and/or militaristic masculinity (see endnote 27).

Nor have the male commercial entertainment and red-light districts often been viewed as sites or forms of consumer culture. Such activities have long been viewed by moralists and scholars as components of an underworld, vice-laden, or "bachelor" subculture (see above section on labor, men's, and urban history). Yet if such commercial entertainment and services are not a part of consumer culture, than what is consumer culture after all? Like the toiletries vs. cosmetics dichotomy, then, the gendered view of consumerism magically transforms the leisure activities of most pre-Depression American men into something other than consumer activity.

Gender and the Advertising Subject of 1895–1930

According to the accepted wisdom on gender and advertising, the target of advertisers in the early twentieth century was almost always female. Marchand's study of American advertising between 1920 and 1940 suggests that "the overwhelmingly male advertising elite [perceived] that it was engaged primarily in talking to masses of women," and Bowlby describes early advertising as a "seduction of women by men, in which women would be addressed as yielding objects to the powerful male subject forming . . . their desires."[114] According to Damon-Moore, the marketing establishment had grown so attached to the compelling idea of the female consumer that they refused to advertise in any magazine that primarily attempted to appeal to men as consumers.[115] Although these three studies do marshal up considerable evidence to support their arguments, all are methodologically flawed in that nearly all the ads they cite are taken from either women's or general interest magazines, thereby overlooking the important data found in early men's magazines.

For example, Marchand draws 28% of his sample of advertisements from women's magazines, 55% from general interest or literary magazines read by both sexes, 8% from the business periodical *Fortune*, and the remaining 9% from advertising journals which relied heavily on women's magazine advertisements for much of their revenue (i.e., *Printer's Ink*).[116] Excluded from his study are the numerous sports and recreation magazines which were targeted to consuming males. In effect, his sampling methodology is *a priori* disposed to support the argument that women were overwhelmingly the main target of advertisers. Moreover, because the male-targeted ads that Marchand does reprint are mostly for expensive commodities such as automobiles and life insurance, the reader is left with the impression that men were rarely portrayed as consumers of smaller ticket items by magazine advertisers.

To demonstrate that pre-Depression men were commonly appealed to as consumers in their own right, the following section examines the advertisements in magazines such as *Outing, Forest & Stream*, and *Field & Stream* in the period between 1895 and 1925. I show that such ads were explicitly targeted to male consumers, and then discuss why such advertisements have not received much scholarly attention.

Although the above magazines printed ads which were directed toward men as early as 1895, it is not until around 1905 that such ads became both copious and explicitly designed to appeal to men.[117] For instance, the March 18, 1905 issue of *Forest & Stream* carried an ad for "Club Cocktails" which showed two men enjoying cocktails together at a restaurant table, and another ad for "Pond's Extract" which claimed to be strong enough for a man's pain (pp. vi, vii).

The April 1906 issue of *Outing Magazine* featured more than twenty-seven ads which were obviously intended for men, such as racing tires, tobacco, beer, and camping, fishing, and hunting supplies, and most of the ads were explicitly targeted to men. For example, one "Postum Coffee" ad featured a man hanging from a coffee cup and recommended itself to "those who appreciate strength and health" (p. 129), while a "Gillette Razor Blade" ad described itself as made of a "steel of neolithic hardness" (p. 135). Another ad praised "President Suspenders" for allowing men the freedom to move about without worrying about losing their pants (p. 142), and an ad for "Deviled Ham" described itself as ideal "for the hungry (male) camper and fisherman" (p. 161). Numerous ads for underwear, men's hosiery, and coat shirts showed happy men wearing their products (pp. 157, 180, 187), while tire ads often showed excited men "racing" down a hill in a sports car (p. 143). Two more memorable ads, though, were one for "Makaroff Cigarets," which was marketed "To Men Who Are Accustomed To Cutting Coupons" (p. 165), and another for "Grapenuts Cereal" which featured a close up of a huge, muscular, male bicep (p. 199).

By 1916, *Field & Stream* magazine had at least 30 pages of advertisements per monthly issue which sold everything from hunting, fishing and camping equipment to foods, tobacco, beer, razor blades, clothing, phonographs, cameras, boats and automobiles. Many of these ads were quite gendered, as in the case of the June 1916 inside cover-page ad for "Fatima Cigarettes," which were allegedly chosen by "men who win success by clear thinking," and a May 1916 ad for a fishing book which declared that "Every Red-Blooded Man Should Read this Book" (p. 103). More remarkable, though, was a July 1916 "Gillette Razor Blade" ad which urged men to shave their underarms on a regular basis for hygiene and comfort (p. 323), and a "Piper Chewing Tobacco" ad which offered overtaxed (male) brainworkers "poise and soothing, helpful comfort" (June 1916, p. 223). Such ads carried over into the 1920s, where one could see ads for hairdressing lotions, stomach-shrinking girdles for the man who found his "waistline too big," and numerous ads for "Justrite" and "Coleman" camp stoves which portrayed men cooking breakfast for their families and fellow male campers.[118]

Male-targeted ads were hardly limited to men's magazines, though, since general interest magazines such as the *Saturday Evening Post* (*SEP*) could have a surprisingly large number of its ads targeted to male consumers. Thus the July 7, 1906 *SEP* contained twenty ads explicitly targeted to man, five ads explicitly targeted to women, while the remainder of the ads made neither a pictorial nor editorial reference to either sex.[119] As for the July 4, 1925 issue, 39% of all ads were targeted to men, 16% were targeted to women, and the rest (42%) referred to neither sex. In other words, male consumers were targeted between 2.5 to 5 times more heavily than were female consumers. Therefore, if these issues are even moderately representative of the rest of the 1900–1930 issues, then it would appear that the ads in the *SEP* may have targeted male consumers more than they did female consumers.

Although the above study of advertising is not extensive enough to allow for sweeping generalizations about the degree to which each sex was targeted by advertisers, it does uncover enough evidence to suggest that early twentieth-century advertisers were not addressing a primarily female audience. Thus an important question becomes why have so many scholars missed such data and gone on to describe the advertising (and consuming) audience as "feminine"?

In the case of scholars such as Marchand and Bowlby, one can only assume that the notion of the pre-Depression consumer as feminine had become so entrenched ideologically that little need was felt to fully examine men's role as consumers. After all, a mountain of evidence in the form of early twentieth-century marketing journals, magazine articles, and recent women's history collectively testified to the "fact" that women were society's main consumers until some point in the mid-twentieth century. Consequently, the remaining problem is to trace the process whereby women were ideologically transformed into society's consumers.

The Campaign to Transform Women into "the Consumers"

The publicizing of the idea that consuming was women's work, and that consumers were, in turn, women, can be traced back to three groups of people who made money by selling goods to early twentieth-century women: advertisers, marketers, and women's magazine editors. When marketers noticed that a majority of department store and dry goods shoppers were female they attempted to capitalize on this observation by: 1) trying to convince certain manufacturers and retailers that appealing to women was the surest way to sell their goods, and 2) developing a gendered advertising which portrayed consumers as women and played upon their duties as the family's purchasing agent.

In order to attract clients and business, marketers of the goods that women often bought (i.e., clothing, foodstuffs, detergents, makeup, etc.) began running articles and advertisements in trade journals and general interest magazines which claimed that the best way to sell goods was by marketing them directly to women. Between 1900 and 1910 numerous articles appeared in the *Saturday Evening Post* which noted how much women purchased and offered advice on how to boost sales by manipulating women into buying.[120] The Emerson B. Knight market research firm ran an ad in *Printer's Ink* which boldly claimed that "[t]he proper study of mankind is *man* . . . but the proper study of markets is *women*."[121] Christine Frederick even published a full-length book in 1929 on the subject for the industry entitled *Selling Mrs. Consumer.*[122]

While many advertisers and marketers sought to convince the public that shopping and consumption were women's work, women's magazine editors and publishers directed a similar campaign toward the marketing industry. Since women's magazines could best boost profits by increasing advertising revenue, they aggressively sought to sell their space by running ads of their own which extolled the power of the female consumer in marketing journals such as *Printer's Ink (PI)*. In the 1920s and 30s, hundreds of women's magazine advertisements appeared in *PI* which claimed that women purchased most goods in America and that such magazines reached the largest number of consumers in America. For example, one advertisement for the *Farmer's Wife* magazine claimed that American farm women "actually buy or influence a majority of the food, clothing and household equipment in America," and an ad for a consortium of Canadian women's magazines claimed that their magazines "reach an average of 1 in 4 of all homes in Canada."[123]

Sometimes, these ads would specifically appeal to the ego of male advertisers and marketers. For instance, *Redbook* magazine ran a series of provocative 1933 ads in which they superimposed the shadow of a man over a nude women in a bathtub accompanied by the following text, "the influence of the male in determining the purchases of the female is conceivable even in personal matters of beauty culture." *McCall's* even ran a 1937 ad in *Advertising Age* stating that "categorically . . . man is always the producer . . . woman, the consumer."[124] Because so much of the 1920s and early 1930s advertising space in marketing journals was paid for by women's magazines, then, advertisers and marketers were constantly "reminded" of the enormity and importance of the female consumer.

The articles and editorials in women's magazines also played an important role in linking femininity with consumerism. The *Ladies' Home Journal (LHJ)* was the first periodical in the United States to explicitly discuss, represent, and editorialize about gender roles to a large, national audience.[125] In fact, Edward Bok's monthly editorial page (from 1890 on) consisted of a vigorous, condescending campaign to define women's roles for them. Not surprisingly, one of his longest and most emphatic editorials deals with the relationship between gender and shopping. As Bok declares, while for women:

> shopping . . . is a sort of regular diet . . . a man takes shopping only in one way—just as he does house-hunting or hiring a servant. And if a man is at all reasonable, one shopping tour is about all he wants in a lifetime.[126]

Thus, the *LHJ* officially declares that shoppers are women, and that shopping is a decidedly unmasculine activity. More importantly, though, by consistently portraying the shoppers in its advertisements as women, and by carrying numerous articles on women's work as consumers, the *LHJ* worked hard to advance the "twin notions that women were the primary consumers for their families and in the culture at large, and that women were primarily consumers."[127]

In sum, a sort of joint-partnership existed between the trade journals which marketed women's goods (i.e., *Dry Goods Economist, Printer's Ink*) and the publishers of women's magazines to promote the idea that the best way to sell goods was by appealing to female shoppers. Consequently, future research needs to be done on why the publishers of men's magazines did not attempt to sell themselves to the marketing journals before the 1930s in the way that women's magazines had always done so. For example, the first men's magazine to market its consuming audience to *Printer's Ink* was *Esquire*, which ran two remarkable ads in 1933 which announced to the marketing world that "Esquire Has Made a Study of Men" and has "Sort[ed] Out Those Men Who Spend."[128] It is interesting to note that if pre-1930s men's magazines had sold their audiences to marketing journals as women's magazines had been doing since the late 1890s, then consumerism would probably not have been defined as a primarily feminine enterprise.[129]

Conclusion

The evidence presented in this paper suggests that American men consumed about twice as many recreational and leisure goods as women and spent about 30 percent of the family's disposable income in doing so. It also suggests that male consumption and consumerism were neither marginal nor dependent upon women. Non-rural, late-Victorian, white men appear to have spent considerable free time consuming numerous goods and services. It would be inaccurate, though, to think of either men or women as the "primary" consumers. Rather, it makes more sense to think of men as the primary consumers of certain goods and services (i.e., commercialized leisure, entertainment, and recreation) and women as the "primary" consumers of domestic and family goods. Unfortunately, the latter category has received the bulk of scholarly attention.

While it is clear that pre-Depression white men were major consumers, little is known about their actual attitudes and feelings about shopping and consumerism. An examination of the diaries, memoirs, and letters of pre-Depression men would probably reveal when men began to think of themselves as "consumers." Such research would also help determine whether there were so few turn-of-the-century male kleptomaniacs merely because men spent less time in department stores or because they felt ambiguous about shopping in the first place?[130] Finally, a more extensive content analysis of early twentieth-century advertisements would help reveal the degree to which marketers courted each sex. This would provide additional evidence of the degree to which pre-Depression men participated in consumer culture.

This article takes issue with the way historians and sociologists have viewed late nineteenth- and early twentieth-century consumption and shows how studies that view consumption and consumerism as women's work inevitably obscure the actual extent of pre-Depression male consumption. This is not simply a matter for historians, though, as a good deal of the current sociological research on contemporary consumption and consumerism in the United States still views consumerism as a feminine activity. The fact that only minor attention is paid to contemporary male consumers suggests that sociologists still associate consumerism with women. And because no one has produced any figures which indicate that women actually do outspend or outconsume today's men, the disinterest in current male consumerism reinforces the notion that consumption and consumerism are basically feminine activities. Until the male consumer becomes an object of widespread study, consumerism and consumption will remain associated with women and femininity, and the ideology of separate spheres will continue to distort history and sociology's view of women, men, and consumerism.

Notes

1. Kathy Peiss, "Of Makeup and Men: The Gendering of Cosmetics," paper presented at "The Material Culture of Gender Conference" (Winterthur Museum, November 1989), p. 2.

2. Books dealing with the history of gendered consumption include Elaine S. Abelson, *When Ladies Go A-Thieving: Middle-Class Shoplifters in the Victorian Department Store* (New York, 1989); Susan Porter Benson, *Counter Cultures: Saleswomen, Managers and Customers in American Department Stores* (Chicago, 1986); Rachel Bowlby, *Just Looking: Consumer Culture in Dreiser, Gissing and Zola* (New York, 1985); Gary Cross, *Time and Money: The Making of Consumer Culture* (New York, 1993); Barbara Ehrenreich, *The Hearts of Men* (Garden City, 1983); Stuart Ewen and Elizabeth Ewen, *Channels of Desire: Mass Images and the Shaping of American Consciousness* (Minneapolis, 1992); Daniel Horowitz, *The Morality of Spending: Attitudes toward the Consumer in America, 1875–1940* (Baltimore, 1985); Roland Marchand, *Advertising the American Dream: Making Way for Modernity, 1920–1940* (Berkeley, 1985); Jackson Lears, *Fables of Abundance: A Cultural History of Advertising in America* (New York, 1994); while articles include Kenon Breazeale, "In Spite of Women: *Esquire* Magazine and the Construction of the Male Consumer," *Signs: Journal of Women in Culture and Society* 20 (1994): 1–22; and Rudi Laermans, "Learning to Consume: Early Department Stores and the Shaping of the Modern Consumer Culture (1860–1914)," *Theory, Culture & Society* 10 (1993): 79–102.

3. For instance, Weinbaum and Bridges refer to consumption as "purchasing goods and services for household members"; Batya Weinbaum and Amy Bridges, "The Other Side of the Paycheck: Monopoly Capital and the Structure of Consumption," in Zillah R. Eisenstein ed., *Capitalist Patriarchy and the Case for Socialist Feminism* (New York, 1979), pp. 190–205, 193.

4. Horowitz, *The Morality of Spending*, pp. 70, 79, xxiii.

5. Cross, *Time and Money*, pp. 167–8.

6. Breazeale, "In Spite of Women," p. 1; Ehrenreich, *The Hearts of Men*, p. 49.

7. Although numerous women's historians have exposed the inaccuracy of the producer/consumer dichotomy by showing how economically productive domestic labor was during the eighteenth and nineteenth centuries (i.e., Laura Thatcher Ulrich, *Good Wives: Image and Reality in the Lives of Women in Northern New England, 1650–1750* [New York, 1982]; Julie Matthaei, *An Economic History of Women in America: Women's Work, the Sexual Division of Labor, and the Development of Capitalism* [New York, 1982]), such a dichotomy still permeates the literature on gendered consumption.

8. Bowlby, *Just Looking*, p. 27; Abelson, *When Ladies Go A-Thieving*, p. 28; Helen Damon-Moore, *Magazines for the Millions: Gender and Commerce in the Ladies' Home Journal and the Saturday Evening Post 1880–1910* (Albany, 1994), p. 4.

9. Eric Lampard. "Introductory Essay," in William R. Taylor, ed., *Inventing Times Square: Commerce and Culture at the Crossroads of the World* (New York, 1991), pp. 16–35.

10. Jon Kingsdale, "The 'Poor Man's Club': Social Functions of the Urban Working-Class Saloon," in Elizabeth Pleck and Joseph Pleck eds., *The American Man* (Englewood Cliffs, 1980), pp. 255–83; David Roediger. *The Wages of Whiteness: Race and the Making of the American Working Class* (New York, 1991); Roy Rosenzweig, *Eight Hours for What We Will: Workers and Leisure in an Industrial City, 1870–1920* (New York, 1983).

11. Anthony E. Rotundo, *American Manhood: Transformations in Masculinity from the Revolution to the Modern Era* (New York 1993); Mark Carnes, *Secret Rituals and Manhood in Victorian America* (New Haven 1989); Mary Ann Clawson, *Constructing Brotherhood: Class, Gender, and Fraternalism* (Princeton 1989); Michael S. Kimmel, *Manhood in America: A Cultural History* (New York, 1996).

12. Lewis A. Erenberg, *Steppin' Out: New York Nightlife and the Transformation of American Culture, 1890–1930* (Westport, 1981); David Nasaw, *Going Out: The Rise and Fall of Public Amusements* (New York, 1993); George Chauncey, *Gay New York: Gender, Urban Culture, and the Making of the Gay Male World 1890–1940* (New York, 1994); Timothy J. Gilfoyle, *City of Eros: New York City, Prostitution, and the Commercialization of Sex, 1790–1920* (New York, 1992).

13. Ehrenrich, *The Hearts of Men: Diane Barthel, Putting on Appearances: Gender and Advertising* (Philadelphia, 1988); Frank Mott, *Cultures of Consumption: Masculinities and Social Space in Late Twentieth-Century Britain* (London, 1996).

14. See Marchand, *Advertising the American Dream*, p. 66; Abelson, *When Ladies Go A-Thieving*, p. 223 n.77; Damon-Moore, *Magazines for the Millions*, p. 178.

15. Thus the perceived invariance of women doing "housework" across time and cultures; caring for chickens or hauling wood was "housework" if women did it, chopping wood was not if men did it.

16. For the data on 1890 imports and exports see William Howard Shaw, *Value of Commodity Output since 1869* (New York, 1947).

17. The home manufacture of men's garments virtually ceased by 1879 (Claudia B. Kidwell and Margaret C. Christman, *Suiting Everyone: The Democratization of Clothing in America* [Washington, 1974], p. 111), and the industrial poor relied almost totally on ready-made clothing (Ewen and Ewen, *Channels of Desire*, pp. 118, 123). Only middle-class women continued making some clothing until the end of the century (Abelson, *When Ladies Go A-Thieving*, p. 39; Lois Banner, *American Beauty* [New York, 1983], p. 32).

18. U.S. Bureau of the Census, *A Compendium of the Ninth Census* (New York, 1976; first published 1870), pp. 800–11; U.S. Bureau of the Census, *Abstract of the Eleventh Census* (Washington, 1890), pp. 143–57.

19. U.S. Bureau of the Census, *Abstract of the Eleventh* Census, pp. 148, 146. U.S. Bureau of the Census, *Report on Manufacturing Industries in the United States at the Eleventh Census* vol. VI: 3 (Washington, D.C., 1890), p. 46.

20. From here on, all statements about male or female consumption will refer to the monetary *value* of the goods consumed rather than to their numerical value.

21. See Kathy Peiss, *Cheap Amusements: Working Women and Leisure in Turn-of-the-Century New York* (Philadelphia, 1986); and Matthaei, *An Economic History of Women.*

22. Fenja Gunn, *The Artificial Face: A History of Cosmetics* (New York, 1973), p. 136.

23. On men's cosmetics use, see Gunn, *The Artificial Face*, p. 136; and Leonard de. Vries, *Victorian Advertisements*, ext by James Laver (Philadelphia, comp. 1968), pp. 40, 41–65, 105.

24. These figures were calculated as follows: 1) More lists drinking within the home as consuming 14.1% of the average family's sundries; Louise Bolard More, *Wage Earners' Budgets: A Study of Standards and Cost of Living in New York City* (New York, 1971, first published in 1907), p. 96. Assuming husbands drank about four-fifths of the home's alcohol (see Appendix, #2), they would have consumed about 11.3% of the family's total sundries (i.e., 4/5 x 14.1% = 11.3%), especially since drink consumption was reported as zero in most families in which the husband was dead or absent (pp. 96–7). 2) More reports that "spending money" was basically reserved for husbands and children (p. 99), with husbands receiving $4641.96 and children only $861.50 (pp. 100–1). Therefore, about 15.7% of the family's sundries would have gone to the husband for his personal spending money (i.e., .84 x 18.7% = 15.7%).

25. More, *Wage Earner's Budgets*, p. 43.

26. See Matthaei, *An Economic History of Women*; and Susan Levine, "Worker's Wives: Gender, Class and Consumerism in the 1920s United States," *Gender & History* 3 (1991): 45–64.

27. See Gerald Franklin Roberts, "The Strenuous Life: The Cult of Manliness in the Era of Theodore Roosevelt," unpublished Ph.D. dissertation, Michigan State University, 1970; Melvin Adelman, *A Sporting Time: New York City and the Rise of Modern Athletics, 1820–70* (Chicago, 1986); Elliot J. Gorn, *The Manly Art: Bare-Knuckle Prize Fighting in America* (Ithaca, 1986); Todd Crosset, "Masculinity, Sexuality, and the Development of Early Modern Sport," in Michael A. Messner and Donald F. Sabo eds., *Sport, Men and the Gender Order: Critical Feminist Perspectives* (Champaign, 1990), pp. 45–54; Steven A. Reiss, *City Games: The Evolution of American Urban Society and the Rise of Sports* (Urbana, 1989); Michael S. Kimmel, "Baseball and the Reconstitution of American Masculinity, 1880–1920," in Messner and Sabo eds., *Sport, Men, and the Gender Order*, pp. 55–66; Kimmel, *Manhood in America.*

28. Gorn, *The Manly Art*, p. 192; Kimmel, "Baseball and the Reconstitution," p. 58; J. P. Hantover, "The Boy Scouts and the Validation of Masculinity," in Pleck and Pleck eds., *The American Man*, p. 293; Riess, *City Games*, p. 61; Adelman, *A Sporting Time*, pp. 283–84.

29. Adelman, *A Sporting Time*, p. 284; Kimmel, "Baseball and the Reconstitution," p. 58.

30. On the conspicuous consumption of elite sports see Donald J. Mrozek, *Sports and the American Mentality, 1880–1910* (Knoxville, 1983); for the indulgent sporting underworld lifestyle see Gorn, *The Manly Art*. And although Kimmel's 1996 chapter on masculinity as recreation acknowledges considerable late-Victorian men's consumption via sports and fitness activities, he views such consumption as the therapeutic ingesting of the "symbols and props" of a pre-crisis masculinity rather than something men might also do for the sheer joy of consumption itself; Kimmel, *Manhood in America*, pp. 118–27, 155.

31. Harvey Green. *Fit for America: Health, Fitness, Sport, and American Society* (New York, 1986), p. 187; Rotundo, *American Manhood*, pp. 223–24.

32. Theodore P. Greene, *America's Heroes: The Changing Models of Success in American Magazines* (New York, 1970), pp. 127–31, 258–62.

33. Green, *Fit for America*, pp. 190–202; David I. Macleod, *Building Character in the American Boy: The Boy Scouts, YMCA, and their Forerunners, 1870–1920* (Madison, 1983), p. 75.

34. Macleod, *Building Character*, p. 75.

35. Roberta J. Park, "Healthy, Moral, and Strong: Educational Views of Exercise and Athletics in Nineteenth-Century America," in Kathryn Grover ed., *Fitness in American Culture: Images of Health, Sport, and the Body, 1830–1940* (Amherst, 1990), pp. 124–50; Green, *Fit for America*, pp. 186–94; John Durant and Otto Bettmann, *Pictorial History of American Sports: From Colonial Times to the Present* (New York, 1952), pp. 61–100.

36. Dudley Allen Sargent, "Ideals in Physical Education," *Mind and Body* 8 (1901): 221–26, 223.

37. By typically "male" activity I mean not "male-only" activities, but any activity in which males typically engaged or were associated with.

38. On baseball diamond costs see Ted Vincent, *The Rise and Fall of American Sport: Mudville's Revenge* (Lincoln, 1994), p. 65; and Benjamin G. Rader, *American Sports: From the Age of Folk Games to the Age of Spectators* (Englewood Cliffs, 1983), p. 110. For admission fees see Vincent, *The Rise and Fall*, p. 122; and Mrozek, *Sport and the American Mentality*, p. 110.

39. For liquor consumption see Rader, *American Sports*, p. 111; and for sports paraphernalia see Stephen Hardy, " 'Adopted by All the Leading Clubs': Sporting Goods and the Shaping of Leisure, 1800–1900," in Richard Butsch ed., *For Fun and Profit: The Transformation of Leisure into Consumption* (Philadelphia, 1990), 71–104, 82.

40. For spectator class status see Rotundo, *American Manhood*, p. 239; and Vincent, *The Rise and Fall*, p. 122.

41. Vincent, *The Rise and Fall*, pp. 67–68.

42. Vincent, *The Rise and Fall*, p. 68; Rader, *American Sports*, pp. 56–57.

43. Rader, *American Sports*, pp. 57–58.

44. See Mrozek, *Sport and the American Mentality*, 112–17; Green, *Fit for America*, 225–26; Margaret Marsh, "Suburban Men and Domestic Masculinity, 1870–1915," in Mark C. Carnes and Clyde Griffen eds., *Meanings for Manhood: Constructions of Masculinity in Victorian America* (Chicago, 1990), pp. 111–27, 124–25.

45. Rotundo, *American Manhood*, p. 61–62.

46. Rotundo, *American Manhood*, p. 63.

47. Rotundo, *American Manhood*, pp. 64–68, 143.

48. Louis Sullivan, *From Female to Male: The Life of Jack Bee Garland* (Boston, 1990), pp. 38–42.

49. Dawn Moore Santiago, "The Owls Club of Tucson," *Journal of Arizona History* 33 (1992): 241–68, 241–43, 261.

50. Alexander W. Williams, *A Social History of the Greater Boston Clubs* (Barre, 1970), pp. 31–3, 44.

51. Mary Ann Clawson, "Fraternal Orders and Class Formation in the Nineteenth-Century United States," *Comparative Studies in Society and History* 27 (1985): 672–95. Carnes, *Secret Rituals and Manhood*.

52. Albert C. Stevens, comp. and ed., *The Cyclopaedia of Fraternities* (Detroit, 1966, first published 1907), p. xvi.

53. Lynn Dumenil, *Freemasonry and American Culture 1880–1930* (Princeton, 1984).

54. Clifford Putney, "Service Over Secrecy: How Lodge-Style Fraternalism Yielded Popularity to Men's Service Clubs," *Journal of Popular Culture* 27 (1993): 179–90, 180.

55. Dumenil, *Freemasonry and American Culture*, pp. 13, 15–23, 114.

56. Putney, "Service over Secrecy," p. 181.

57. Carnes, *Secret Rituals and Manhood*, pp. 41–9.

158. Dumenil, *Freemasonry and American Culture*, p. 24.

59. Carnes, *Secret Rituals and Manhood*, p. 4. Annual expenditures on working-class lodges appear to have been somewhat lower, since the 200 families in More's budget study spent only $5–$26 per year on lodges; More, *Wage Earner's Budgets*, p. 43.

60. W. S. Harwood, "Secret Societies in America," *North American Review* 164 (1897):

617–23, 617. A notable exception to the discrete nature of middle-class fraternal consumption would be the Shriners, who were notorious for their lavish parades, red fezes, and exaggerated titles—see Clawson, "Fraternal Orders and Class," p. 232.

61. Margaret F. Byington, *Homestead: The Households of a Mill Town* (Pittsburgh, 1974; first published 1910), pp. 84–86; Lizbeth A. Cohen, "Embellishing a Life of Labor: An Interpretation of the Material Culture of American Working-Class Homes, 1885–1915," *Journal of American Culture* 3 (1980): 752–75; Peiss, *Cheap Amusements*, pp. 24–25.

62. Peter R. Shergold, *Working-Class Life: The "American Standard" in Comparative Perspective* (Pittsburgh, 1982), pp. 204–6.

63. Banner, *American Beauty*, pp. 74–75; Christine Stansell, *City of Women: Sex and Class in New York 1789–1860* (Chicago, 1986), p. 94.

64. Banner, *American Beauty*, p. 75; Peiss, *Cheap Amusements*, pp. 63–65.

65. Stansell, *City of Women*, pp. 90–91; Roediger, *The Wages of Whiteness*, p. 99.

66. Abram C. Dayton, *The Last Days of Knickerbocker Life in New York* (New York, 1897), pp. 217–18.

67. Gorn, *The Manly Art*, p. 134; Whitman cited by Nasaw, *Going Out*, p. 10.

68. Cited by Banner, *American Beauty*, p. 239.

69. John L. Jennings, *Theatrical and Circus Life* (St. Louis, 1882), p. 55; Theodore Dreiser, *Sister Carrie: An Authoritative Text, Backgrounds, and Sources of Criticism*, Donald Pizer ed. (New York, 1970; first published 1900), p. 3.

70. Cited by Jervis Anderson, "That was New York: Harlem," Part I, "The Journey Uptown," *New Yorker* 29 (June 1981): 38–69, 44, 43–44, 58.

71. Banner, *American Beauty*, p. 239.

72. Dumenil, *Freemasonry and American Culture*, p. 12–13; Clawson, *Constructing Brotherhood*, pp. 95, 97; Stevens, *The Cyclopaedia of Fraternities*, p. v.

73. One might wonder how so many working-class men could afford to join lodges, but since lodges offered many working people their only opportunity to obtain sickness and death benefits, lodge membership was often more of a necessity than a luxury; Clawson, "Fraternal Orders and Class," 673.

74. Clawson, *Constructing Brotherhood*, p. 181; Stevens, *The Cyclopaedia of Fraternities*, p. 264.

75. Clawson, *Constructing Brotherhood*, p. 235; Jno Van Valkenberg, *The Knights of Pythias Complete Manual and Textbook* (Canton, 1887), p. 113.

76. Clawson, *Constructing Brotherhood*, p. 235; Christopher J. Kauffman, *Faith and Fraternalism: The History of the Knights of Columbus 1882–1992* (New York, 1982), pp. 56, 80; Clawson, *Constructing Brotherhood*, p. 234.

77. On non-alcoholic saloon spending, see Kingsdale, "The 'Poor Man's Club,' " pp. 261–62, 267; Rosenzweig, *Eight Hours for What We Will*, pp. 53–56; Gorn, *The Manly Art*, pp. 99, 133; and Chauncey, *Gay New York*, p. 42.

78. Riess, *City Games*, p. 73.

79. Peiss, *Cheap Thrills*, pp. 141–42; Gorn, *The Manly Art*, pp. 133–34; Roediger, *The Wages of Whiteness*, pp. 120–21.

80. Rosenzweig, *Eight Hours for What We Will*, p. 106.

81. Herbert Asbury, *The Gangs of New York: An Informal History of the Underworld* (New York, 1927), p. 269.

82. John Mariano, *The Second Generation of Italians in New York City* (Boston, 1921), p. 140; Suzanne Wasserman, "Cafes, Clubs, Corners and Candy Stores: Youth Leisure-Culture in New York City's Lower East Side during the 1930s," *Journal of American Culture* 14 (1991): 43–48, 46.

83. Asbury, *The Gangs of New York*, pp. 269–70; Wasserman, "Cafes, Clubs, Corners," p. 46.

84. Wasserman, "Cafes, Clubs, Corners," p. 47; Randy D. McBee, " 'He Likes Women More Than He Likes Drink and That is Quite Unusual': Working-Class Male Culture, Social

Clubs, and the Dilemma of Heterosociality in the United States, 1890s–1930s," unpublished Ph.D. dissertation, University of Missouri, 1996, p. 4, 11.

85. Frederic Milton Thrasher, *The Gang: A Study of 1,313 Gangs in Chicago* (Chicago, 1927), pp. 234–35; McBee, "He Likes Women," pp. 17, 19.

86. Erenberg, *Steppin' Out*, p. 21.

87. Nasaw, *Going Out*, p. 13; Erenberg, *Steppin' Out*, pp. 18–21.

88. Robert W. Synder, *The Voice of the City: Vaudeville and Popular Culture in New York* (New York, 1989), p. 8; Nasaw, *Going Out*, p. 14.

89. Erenberg, *Steppin' Out*, p. 18; Synder, *The Voice of the City*, p. 12; Nasaw, *Going Out*, p. 13.

90. Nasaw, *Going Out* p. 14; Synder, *The Voice of the City*, p. 10.

91. Synder, *The Voice of the City*, p. 10; Nasaw, *Going Out*, p. 14.

92. Synder, *The Voice of the City*, p. 10.

93. On the proliferation and particulars of such establishments, see Nasaw, *Going Out*, pp. 13, 18.

94. Erenberg, *Steppin' Out*, p. 18.

95. Erenberg, *Steppin' Out*, p. 18.

96. Laermans, "Learning to Consume," p. 89.

97. See Philip Thomason, "The Men's Quarter of Downtown Nashville," *Tennessee Historical Quarterly* 41 (1982): 48–66.

98. Henry Nash Smith, *Democracy and the Novel: Popular Resistance to Classic American Writers* (Oxford, 1978).

99. Michael Denning, *Dime Novels and Working-Class Culture in America* (New York, 1987), pp. 29–30.

100. W. H. Bishop, "Story-Paper Literature," *Atlantic Monthly* 44 (1879): 383–393, 384.

101. William Wallace Cook [John Milton Edwards, pseud.], *The Fiction Factory* (Ridgewood, 1912), p. 35.

102. Denning, *Dime Novels*, chps. 5–6.

103. Kimmel, *Manhood in America*, pp. 120, 141–3.

104. See Denning, *Dime Novels*, pp. 171–203, and the chapters on women's novels.

105. Ralph M. Hower, *The History of Macy's of New York, 1859–1919; Chapters in the Evolution of a Department Store* (Cambridge, MA, 1943), pp. 161, 235, 285.

106. Robert W. Twyman, *The History of Marshall Field & Co.* (Philadelphia, 1954), p. 121.

107. *National Clothier* 6 (September 1920), p. 90.

108. Dameron, *Men's Wear Merchandising*, pp. 38, 131.

109. See Horowitz, *The Morality of Spending*, p. xviii; Rosenzweig, *Eight Hours*, pp. 94–95; Victorian de Grazia, "Changing Consumption Regimes" & "Establishing the Modern Consumer Household," in Victoria de Grazia (with Ellen Furlough) ed., *The Sex of Things: Gender and Consumption in Historical Perspective* (Berkeley, 1996), pp. 11–24, 151–61, 155.

110. de Grazia, "Changing Consumption Regimes," pp. 11–24.

111. de Grazia, "Changing Consumption Regimes," p. 16.

112. Kathy Peiss, "Of Makeup and Men," pp. 1–6.

113. Horowitz, *The Morality of Spending*, 15, 55, 178.

114. Marchand, *Advertising the American Dream*, p. 66; Bowlby, *Just Looking*, p. 20.

115. Damon-Moore, *Magazines for the Millions*, pp. 116–17.

116. I separate Marchand's magazines into "women's," "general interest," and "business" magazines based upon the periodical segmentation which appears in the back of each *Printer's Ink* of the period.

117. For example, the January 12, 1895 *Forest & Stream* carried a tobacco ad with the copy, "Yale Mixture: The Gentlemen's Smoke."

118. *Field & Stream*, May 1925, pp. 130, 101, 69.

119. Ads were only counted as targeted to a particular sex when accompanied by a drawing or photo of one particular sex, *or* if the copy specifically mentioned that the product was for men or women. All other goods were recorded as "gender-neutral" commodities (i.e., stoves, tools, foodstuffs, etc.). The first July issues of 1906 & 1925 were sampled to avoid the bias of self selection.

120. Helen Damon-Moore, *Magazines for the Millions*, p. 178.

121. *Printer's Ink*, November 7 1929, p. 133.

122. Christine Frederick, *Selling Mrs. Consumer* (New York, 1929).

123. *Printer's Ink* (January 19, 1922): 60; *Printer's Ink* (January 19, 1922): 94.

124. *Printer's Ink* (November 2, 1933): 42; *Advertising Age* (July 12, 1937): 14–15.

125. Damon-Moore, *Magazines for the Millions*, pp. 81, 106.

126. *Ladies Home Journal* (editorial by Edward Bok) vol. 9 (1892): 12.

127. Damon-Moore, *Magazines for the Millions*, p. 98.

128. *Printer's Ink* (September 7): 5; (August 24): 5.

129. Here many scholars might point out that the concept of a "men's magazine" did not arise until *Esquire* came along; yet this does not explain why magazines like *Field & Stream* did not promote its audience more aggressively.

130. On the low male rate of kleptomania, see Abelman, *When Ladies Go A-Thieving*.

CHAPTER 13

"Don't Buy Where You Can't Work"

Cheryl Greenberg

Harlem's unionizing efforts coincided with another sort of jobs campaign: one to win clerical positions for qualified blacks in white-owned Harlem businesses. If some unions came to understand the advantages of including blacks and treating them as equals, most employers did not. Hiring blacks for menial tasks or threatening to replace white workers with lower-paid blacks served many private employers well, and the Depression saw no shift in their thinking comparable with that of many unions.

In the absence of laws barring racial discrimination in private industry, black political action became the critical force in securing positions, particularly skilled and white-collar, for qualified black workers. Numerous Harlem organizations devoted their energies to this struggle, relying on the activism of the Harlem community. Many considerations made this an attractive issue. Non-manual employment would grant higher status to the entire community. The displacement of black workers by white all over the city intensified black frustration with the inequality of economic opportunity and generated greater sympathy for a "buy black" or "hire black" solution. The energies of middle-class blacks who had lost their white-collar and skilled jobs to whites galvanized black organizations and the wider community. Perhaps the unskilled also hoped to receive jobs from middle-class blacks once the latter had won white-collar employment and opened businesses. Certainly the absence of blacks in these positions was visible to the entire black community. Thus, challenging discrimination in white-collar work captured the imagination of thousands of blacks, including those who could not benefit from it personally. This effort became known as the "Don't Buy Where You Can't Work" campaign, which used mass protests and boycotts as its most important weapons. The story of this campaign offers an example of how the varied political expressions of the community came together in a broad movement. It also suggests the strengths and limits of such alliances in this era.

With a population already organized in disparate and diverse groups, Harlem needed only a focus to unify protest action. Aldon Morris found in his study of the roots of the modern civil rights movement that political efforts were most successful in communities or "movement centers" that already contained organized groups, generally church-centered. Existing networks could then be used to organize a broad-based and unified campaign in the local community. Harlem in the Depression was such a "movement center." Church-based programs, fraternal and women's groups, and political and social organizations already existed, and many individuals held membership in several simultaneously. Thus Harlem leaders had a network in place and could work (theoretically) in unison when the "Don't Buy Where You Can't Work" campaigns spread across the country to Harlem. The New York effort was aided further by the presence of a charismatic minister, Adam Clayton Powell, Jr., who managed for a time to unify the diverse strands of the movement.[1]

But while this campaign tapped the talents of existing groups and fostered new connections, it also gave voice to those who dissented from the mainstream effort. The community agreed on the broad goal of increased employment for black Harlemites, but disagreed on other goals, and on the means to achieve them. More radical activists, impatient for additional and more dramatic victories, first splintered the moderate movement. Later they moved the mainstream toward more radical positions. If black leaders organized and galvanized the Harlem community, the community in turn pushed black leaders to move farther and more energetically than established organizations are often wont to do.

Black leaders sought to create one coherent movement, but the diversity of Harlem's population proved an obstacle. The problems facing the black community were deep and intractable. To make a significant impact on the practices of white employers, black political efforts had to be both strong in numbers and unified in tactics and goals. Yet the diversity of the backgrounds of the participants often meant conflicting political beliefs and aspirations. Thus, while coalitions of the various black organizations provided numerical strength, they could not always coordinate strategy, since constituent groups viewed the problem of discrimination from different perspectives and often sought different goals. Bitter sectarian battles often raged, focusing energies inward rather than on white employers. At first, therefore, the "Don't Buy" movement was unable to press for change as vigorously as necessary, nor could it maintain a presence effective enough to prevent employers from backsliding once gains had been won.

Ultimately, though, as with most successful political movements, diversity provided the movement's real strength. A coalition allowed for broader community participation because individuals with differing needs and outlooks could find a home within a movement that embraced varied positions. Because the several member organizations served different constituencies, joint efforts spread information to all segments of black society.

Sometimes the programs of one group inadvertently strengthened others. While vocal extremists most dramatically publicized the struggle, for example, their tactics frightened some who, though mobilized by the radicals' exhortations, joined with the more moderate groups within the coalition. Much of the movement's successes can in fact be attributed to the diversity of coalition membership; the agitation of the more radical organizations convinced those at whom the protest efforts were directed of the need to negotiate with centrist groups to forestall the possibility of facing more radical demands. In sum, diversity offered great possibilities and imposed severe limits on the development of political organization and coalition-building in the Harlem community.

An ever-changing coalition, the "Don't Buy" campaign sought to boycott stores in Harlem that refused to hire blacks in white-collar positions. It took almost a decade for Harlem activists to organize a sufficiently wide, yet sufficiently unified campaign to win such jobs. Because it sought to place already trained and educated blacks in white-collar employment in existing white stores rather than to establish training programs or community-owned cooperatives, the movement could be viewed as having primarily middle-class goals, yet it galvanized the poor as well as the middle class to action.

Building a Base

As with unionizing, the drive to place blacks in white stores began in the 1920s. In 1925 the *Amsterdam News* urged the use of consumer pressure to increase the number of local jobs for blacks. The New York Urban League, the NAACP, and the Harlem branch of the State Employment Service had been fighting for such goals for years, albeit through quiet negotiation, not mass action. The NYUL, for example, through its Cooperative Committee on Employment, wrote letters to merchants in 1926 and surveyed 300 Harlem stores on their attitude toward hiring blacks. Little was accomplished. The Negro League for Equal Political and Civic Rights surveyed Harlem businesses the next year with the aim of selecting three or four that refused to hire blacks and trying to "correct this inequality. A peaceful but forceful manner will be carried out to induce the proprietors . . . to change their methods. Failing, the combined strength of the League will be brought to bear to the end that the places under watch will feel the loss of patronage without which they cannot function." It appears the Negro League's "combined strength" was not enough to persuade any owners.[2]

The onset of the Depression impelled some further action. In a 1930 speech to the New York Urban League, Joseph Bibb, the editor of the *Chicago Whip*, described that city's "Don't Buy Where You Can't Work" campaign and suggested that a similar effort be launched in New York. He reminded his listeners that whites owned most of the businesses in Chicago's black neighborhoods, just as they did in Harlem. Through a combination of boycotts, picketing, and meetings with white business leaders, blacks in Chicago had secured jobs—white-collar jobs—in several local businesses. While this proposal had been made before, this time many Harlem political groups and coalitions explicitly endorsed the idea. Still, little progress was made for the first few years.[3]

In the forefront of the early efforts to encourage local stores to hire blacks was "a group of serious and determined women" organized as the Harlem Housewives League. By 1931, less than a year after its inception, the group claimed over a thousand members, meeting every Monday night in the NYUL building. Its leaders, by and large, were better off, prominent in the community, and had long been politically active. A. Philip Randolph's wife Lucille, for example, was the group's vice-president, and Bessaye Bearden, journalist and activist, served as publicity chairman. The women visited the Atlantic and Pacific Tea Company (A&P), Woolworth's, and "other chain stores having branches throughout Harlem," and requested that the management hire blacks as "clerks, messengers, etc. in proportion to the amount of money spent in those stores by Negroes in Harlem." When Blumstein's, a large local department store, hired a black doorman and elevator operator, the Housewives League thanked the owner "for this recognition of the purchasing power of Negroes." The group encouraged all Harlem wives to shop only at stores that belonged to the Colored Merchants' Association or that hired blacks. Even more than the Urban League, which at least urged businesses to allow blacks access to better-quality jobs, the Housewives League accepted the given limits on black occupational mobility. It demanded only that employers hire more blacks; it made no efforts to ensure blacks would be hired for non-menial jobs. The League did not believe it had the resources to wage such a battle.[4]

Adam Clayton Powell, Sr., headed Harlem's Citizen's Committee on More and Better Jobs, which, in addition to collecting food and clothing for the poor, tried to organize a drive to boycott stores refusing to hire black employees. Other churches and political organizations did the same. Through its "New Economic Program," the NAACP negotiated with white merchants in black neighborhoods like Harlem to hire black clerks. Still, these early Depression programs could devote little energy to the cause of white-collar employment. Because of the lack of relief funds, most gave priority to the requirements of the desperately needy.

These efforts indicated a general recognition of the employment discrimination problem, but without a broad base, none posed enough of an economic threat to have any impact on white employers. Nor was there a sufficiently high level of awareness in the community of the potential for black action to establish such a base. As James Allen, president of the local branch of the NAACP, complained, "I don't know any section in New York City that is harder hit by unemployment than Harlem and I don't know of any section that is doing so little about it."[5] Harlemites were devoting their energies to "making do" in the sudden hard times.

Internal differences also slowed the movement's progress, for each group involved in the effort to increase black employment sought different and often contradictory goals. Much of the impetus for the struggle had come from blacks who believed that integration into the larger world of economic opportunities offered the only hope for black workers, but black nationalists joined the effort to further their own cause. Black nationalism cut across class lines. Many middle-class and professional blacks joined with Garveyites in advocating the creation of a separate economy, since a commitment to "buy black" meant more business for them.

Thus, early in the Depression, a few black merchants launched their own version of a jobs campaign. An advertisement for an African-American clothing store in the *American and West Indian News* featured the headline, "American Negroes Competing Against Jews in Haberdashery World." The rest of the advertisement described the black-owned store, its goods, prices, and service, and made no further mention of Jews. Rather, the plea for race solidarity allowed merchants to use the campaign to boost sales, announcing

> a drive for more and better business ... a profit sharing plan that will not only help to reduce expenses but also decrease unemployment. Colored businessmen invariably employ colored help. Each of us CAN and WILL add from 1 to 10 employees, if you will support us. We are doing our utmost to give you low prices, correct weight, and superior service, in return for your patronage. Think it over. Trade with Negro stores or only with those that employ colored help.

These merchants designed a "Race Loyalty" button for blacks "not ashamed of their Negro ancestry" to be worn by those who agreed to shop only at such stores. The button proclaimed: "I hereby pledge myself to buy from Race Enterprises whenever and wherever practicable (or from stores employing Negro help) thereby helping to create MORE and BETTER jobs right here in Harlem." As August Meier and Elliott Rudwick point out, for black businessmen the campaign was "essentially petit bourgeois" in nature. It sought to increase their sales and profits rather than to alter the structure of black employment opportunities.

Not all black leaders supported these "buy black" attempts. E. Franklin Frazier, for instance, insisted black shopkeepers simply wanted Harlem to "be reserved as their field of exploitation." Nevertheless, this drive to support black businesses as the best hope for black employment did enjoy ample and continued support in the community. The Reverend John Johnson of St. Martin's Protestant Episcopal Church preached: "If you want to do something for the Negro race today ... you can start right here. ... We must spend our money among our own people."[6]

A further barrier to united action was the disagreement within the community over whether boycotts (and later, pickets) were an appropriate or effective solution, especially in light of the ongoing debate over black nationalism versus integration into the larger work force. The *Amsterdam News* editorialized that even if every store in Harlem hired black help, thousands more would remain unemployed if they could not find jobs elsewhere in the city. Why antagonize white employers with boycotts and protests, and possibly jeopardize that much larger pool of jobs by provoking a white backlash? The *News* feared an intensification of segregation outside Harlem in retaliation. Most white Harlem stores also advertised heavily in the *Amsterdam News*, which may help explain that paper's position.

Black businessmen had their own reservations about a "Don't Buy" campaign. While they supported the drive to patronize black stores, several felt less happy with the concurrent effort to persuade white employers to hire black help. They feared white stores would then woo still more black business away from their own establishments.[7]

The Socialist party and the Negro Labor Committee opposed the jobs campaign because they believed it conflicted with their primary goal of integrating blacks into the AFL (and later the CIO). They feared the campaign would antagonize unions because it ignored union hiring agreements and negotiated directly with employers. They also worried that employers might seize the opportunity to hire blacks at subunion wages or as strikebreakers, and that the effort would generally divert energy and attention from their trade union struggle. The words of some campaign advocates justified that fear. In a defense of the boycott effort, Vera Johns noted that white store owners did not hire blacks out of love but rather "because it is found that the colored worker can do better work and may be paid a lesser wage." Even in the campaign for economic equality, at least some accepted unequal pay scales for white and black.[8]

Another group conspicuously absent from the action was Harlem's Communist party. Seeking the solidarity of the working class, black and white, the party feared increased racial antagonism as a result of a campaign that might cause white workers to be fired to make room for black. Instead, it sought to redirect protest energies towards class-oriented problems, such as blue-collar unemployment and inadequate relief—problems local boycotts and pickets could not solve but that required a far broader organizing base. Also, until the Popular Front period, party members were reluctant to work with organizations that sought solutions within the capitalist system. When the jobs campaign did become active after 1933, the party organized a parallel movement called the Committee Against Discrimination of Negro Workers on Jobs. This awkwardly titled group demanded the hiring of blacks in Harlem stores without firing whites. By 1935, the "Don't Buy" campaign was having such success that the party did join the picket line for a time.

Interestingly, the NYUL and NAACP had doubts about the jobs campaign for similar reasons. The Urban League feared the potential for increased racial antagonism in the jobs campaign would jeopardize the tenuous cooperation it had established with white employers elsewhere in the city. Yet rather than stay aloof from the "Don't Buy" effort, the NYUL sponsored letter-writing campaigns and used personal connections to promote black hiring in white-owned shops. For example, in its attempts to place blacks in department stores, white League members sought to persuade white store owners of the advantages of hiring black help. Next, NYUL leaders would "cultivate a top industrialist" and ask him to persuade others. The League also sponsored Vocational Opportunity Campaigns reminding blacks of existing opportunities and urging whites to provide more.[9]

When asked what his organization had done for black employment, James Hubert, executive director of the NYUL, replied:

A. The Urban League has written numerous letters and has had one conference. . . . It has cooperated with other organizations . . .
Q. What has the league done by way of protesting publicly?
A. That is not the Urban League's method of procedure—not through protest. . . . [That] may be the way to get what you want, but it is not our method.

The NYUL trod a difficult road in the Depression, determined to remain visibly active in black efforts to improve economic opportunity, yet struggling to maintain its good relations with the white business and professional community. The League recognized the growing black activism and sought to use it as leverage but feared it could alienate the League's white allies. The resulting schizophrenia prompted pronouncements such as this one in 1933:

There is no doubt that this prolonged unemployment period has had its effects upon the political and social ideology of the Negro. . . . Throughout the country Negroes are expressing continued dissatisfaction with an industrial system fraught with such dire unemployment. . . . It should not be concluded, however, that the whole Negro group has become "radical." . . . [Negro business and professional leaders are] in the main, very conservative . . . [while Socialists and Communists are followed] largely by sections of the working classes, students and the so-called intellectuals.[10]

Similarly, the NAACP diverged in two important ways from the jobs campaign. First, it sought city-wide opportunities for blacks, focusing on questions of segregation as well as employment. Second, the NAACP preferred different methods than direct street action. The organization challenged the status quo of segregation, for example, by taking discriminatory public facilities to court, since such segregation was illegal in New York. NAACP efforts apparently had an impact on such practices: "Of late, law suits have compelled many . . . to alter their policy," commented the Federal Writers' Project. Still, because the organization's major thrust was litigation, few in the black community had any deep or active involvement with it. In job discrimination cases the NAACP generally became involved when the discrimination was obvious, as in the struggle to integrate the work force on the Eighth Avenue subway or to place black nurses in municipal hospitals, and worked behind the scenes rather than joining in visible public actions.[11]

The majority of black leaders, however, supported the boycott efforts. By 1934 they were able to begin organizing a formal campaign as New Deal programs freed them somewhat from meeting the immediate needs of the hungry. Furthermore, grass-roots community activism had been building, as Harlemites took to the streets in ever-increasing numbers to protest evictions or to demand equal treatment from relief and municipal agencies. Each episode of activism inspired more. The unwillingness of moderate groups like the NAACP to embrace more activist or confrontational tactics left those who clamored for mass action to form their own organizations and thus dominate the early jobs campaign. The impatience of many in the black community, their frustration at the seeming foot-dragging of the NAACP, the Urban League, and others, had helped spur new mass movements for black jobs in Chicago, Baltimore, Detroit, Washington, D.C., and elsewhere, and would do so in Harlem as well.

In February of 1934, Effa Manley called a meeting of "progressive women" to discuss the employment situation on 125th Street. After surveying the problem, she requested help from local black ministers. First to respond was the Reverend John Johnson of Saint Martin's Protestant Episcopal Church. He and Fred Moore, publisher of the *New York Age,* called a mass meeting to form the Citizens' League for Fair Play. As the Reverend William Imes told it:

> The next step was to bring the matter before the group of the Special Citizens' League. It was not . . . [our] desire to form another organization. We were already in too many. [If Johnson would agree to run it] there are some of us in other churches, lodges, labor unions and the like who will be very glad to combat this particular effort to displace colored people or discourage colored people from seeking employment. . . . A great many organizations came in. The thing was rather new and got some publicity. . . . Finally it seemed that nothing short of the actual demonstration in the form of picketing would do.[12]

Participants included eighteen churches and forty-four other Harlem groups, including women's, political, fraternal, and social clubs; and business organizations. Street-corner orators like Ira Kemp, Georgia-born president of the African Patriotic League, and Arthur Reid from Barbados, both black nationalists from the Garvey movement who had been preaching their versions of black separatism from soapboxes, joined with the more traditional activists of the black churches, the *New York Age,* the Unity Democratic Club, a Fusion-Republican club, the Cosmopolitan Social and Tennis Club, Young West Indian Congress, Premier Literary Circle, and the New York Chapter of the UNIA to promote black employment—evidence of the diversity of the Harlem groups involved in political action.[13]

Sufi Abdul Hamid and his Negro Industrial Clerical Alliance worked along-side the coalition. Hamid, who claimed Egyptian ancestry (but who was actu-ally native-born) and dressed dramatically in flowing robes and turban, had come from the successful Chicago campaign a year before. There he and his followers had won 300 jobs in two months with the use of pickets requesting blacks not to shop at stores that practiced systematic racism in hiring. It was this early success that prompted the *Chicago Whip* and others to join the struggle there. But his anti-white slogans and black separatist arguments alien-ated many in Chicago, as they would in Harlem, and led the *Whip* to launch a parallel campaign rather than join his efforts. Now, through street corner speeches in Harlem, Sufi Hamid carried on the rhetoric and tactics that had worked in Chicago.

Division on the goals of the jobs campaign had not disappeared with the formation of the Citizens' League for Fair Play. The nationalist political beliefs of Hamid, Kemp, and Reid could not be reconciled easily with the more tradi-tional views of those in the coalition eager to expand the range of opportuni-ties available to blacks in the larger work force. Furthermore, the participants were not always ideologically self-consistent. The fact that the Reverend John Johnson also preached "buy black" sermons and that the *Amsterdam News* first recommended putting pressure on white Harlem store owners but later opposed this strategy indicate that the boundaries between the people who be-lieved in integration and those who sought black nationalist goals were often quite fluid. Personal disagreements played their part in creating internal ten-sions as well. Clashes between Hamid's group and the UNIA, for example, had become so fierce in 1932 that police temporarily barred both from street speaking.[14]

All agreed on the primary goal of black employment in a period of intense hardship. In an interview with the *Amsterdam News,* Kemp explained his ac-tivism: "Harlem in 1932 was in a sorry condition. The depression and dis-crimination against Negroes and the suffering that was the lot of these people forced me to action." But the consensus between the nationalists and the mod-erates reached no further. This created severe internal tensions that eventually led to the dissolution of the coalition.

The First Campaign

The Citizens' League for Fair Play chose as its first target Blumstein's on 125th Street, Harlem's largest department store. The Reverend Mr. Johnson preached to his congregants: "I want our meeting this morning to begin a 12 day campaign to persuade Blumstein's department store where 140 persons work (with 16 colored menials) to hire colored girls as sales clerks."[15]

The coalition began with traditional tactics. Approaching Mr. Blumstein, CLFP representatives reminded him of the volume of black patronage and requested that he hire blacks. He replied that he did in fact have several blacks in his employ. All worked in menial positions, however, and Blumstein refused to hire black clerks. He promised to consider the possibility of doing so in the fall, when new positions became available, but insisted that currently he had a sufficient number of workers.

The CLFP found this unacceptable. Churches raised money to print thousands of leaflets advertising a protest parade, and the League set up a picket line in front of the store. The Reverend Mr. Imes testified at a hearing:

> . . . The Reverend Johnson and I were there, just as many other clergymen were there and numbers of men and women from various organizations and leagues. The real demonstration went on for a number of weeks. . . .
>
> Q. Is it not a fact that some of our most respected and qualified citizens in Harlem took part? . . . There has been propaganda . . . it is done by the lower element.
>
> A. In all these troubles there have been cross sections of people involved. You will find society people, religious people, atheists, you will find cross sections of each community interested in these problems.

Carrying signs that read "Don't Buy Where You Can't Work," picketers pleaded with would-be shoppers to take their business elsewhere. League leaflets requested "all self-respecting people of Harlem to REFUSE TO TRADE WITH L. M. BLUMSTEIN . . . Refuse to Buy There!" At times the pickets became disruptive. Several shoppers reported that picketers seized their bags and destroyed the purchases inside or yelled derogatory remarks. Some picketers pulled patrons' hair. While boycotts were a time-honored tactic for otherwise powerless black communities, pickets were newer, reflecting the shift toward broad-based, visible political strategies. The numbers of participants were impressive. Between 400 and 1,500 attended any given weekly meeting, and the "honor roll" of picketers included 58 men and 83 women who marched regularly.

Blumstein bowed to the pressure and the threat of lost revenue, particularly acute in a depression, and agreed to hire fifteen black women as clerks immediately "to offset any loss of good will," and twenty more in the fall. Yet his difficulties were not over. As he explained to an interviewer in 1935, "the store naturally picked the most attractive personalities among the Negro girls." He meant that Blumstein's selected only light-skinned women. Kemp and Reid, the black nationalists of the picket committee, protested vigorously. They argued that light and mulatto women received employment, "while black ones did all the [picket] work." Again, Blumstein agreed. As he told the story, "This [complaint] was remedied, and Reverend Johnson seemed satisfied." The CLFP called off the picket. Other local stores, fearing pickets and loss of sales themselves, also promised to hire black clerks. Woolworth's, for example, agreed to hire thirty-five.[16]

It is not surprising that Reid, a West Indian and a follower of Garvey, made an issue out of color. In the West Indies color distinctions among blacks determined social status and economic class to a large extent. The lighter one's skin, the higher one's status. This suggests that to Kemp and Reid, the issue was one of class as well as race—lower-class (dark) blacks worked for change, while upper-class (light-skinned) blacks benefited. This charge of class bias was valid, in part. By seeking only to obtain white-collar positions, the campaign mainly helped blacks with middle-class skills, since they were most likely to be qualified for such jobs. Nevertheless, in a sense it was unfair to blame the CLFP for fulfilling its explicitly stated goal of placing white-collar workers in appropriate (middle-class) jobs. Moreover, Kemp and Reid did not acknowledge that, as with other ethnic and minority groups, the potential for unskilled job opportunities would increase once educated and skilled blacks rose in the economic world and established business with their own labor needs.

Although the association of lighter skin with higher class had no legal basis in American society, Reid's charge did have resonance for native-born dark-skinned blacks. Historically, many slave masters and, later, white employers demonstrated a bias toward lighter-skinned blacks (as Blumstein had), so economic level, social status, and color did overlap to some extent. Presumably, Reid hoped his charges of bias would win him the allegiance of the dark-skinned, the West Indians, and the poor.

Kemp's and Reid's accusation of color discrimination also represented an attempt to change the jobs campaign into a nationalist movement represented by "true" (dark-skinned) blacks, equating dark skin with race pride. In the spirit of Marcus Garvey, Kemp and Reid told a *New York Age* reporter they were "black people, not Negroes." Ultimately, they hoped blacks would fill all Harlem jobs, creating an all-black, independent economy there. Finally, Kemp and Reid broke from the CLFP to organize a more strongly nationalist Harlem Labor Union, Incorporated. Most members were young and from the West Indies. When Kemp died two years later, Reid continued to run it.

The separation from the Citizens' League was also the result of a more personal power struggle. In part, the color issue was a screen for the struggle to control job allocation. Reid's picket line was sustained by men and women who joined it to gain employment. Since under the terms of the League agreement Blumstein's was not obligated to hire his people, Reid felt his power base was threatened and he left the coalition. Despite the Blumstein's victory, then, the color issue and internal dissension splintered the Citizens' League.[17]

Sufi Abdul Hamid was no more satisfied with the Blumstein's settlement than were Kemp and Reid. He wanted Blumstein's and other white-owned stores to hire more black clerks—and members of his own group—and to guarantee job security. According to Mr. Snyder, manager of the 125th Street store of the W. T. Grant Company chain, he "was approached by Abdul Hamid who wanted the manager to place some of his followers in jobs in the store." The interviewer concluded: "It appears that Hamid was not interested in the employment of Negroes generally but only those who were his 'disciples.' "[18] This claim would be leveled again. Both Kemp's group and the Negro Industrial Clerical Alliance reinstated their picket lines at Blumstein's. Hamid demanded Blumstein hire seventy-five blacks, with a provision against arbitrary firing. The Alliance also picketed Beck's Shoe Store on 125th Street with similar demands. The *New York Age*, until this point a staunch supporter of the jobs campaign, lamented the behavior of the two groups. It described Reid's organization in the article "Renegade 'Boycott Committee' Runs Wild, Assaults Shoppers":

> Intimidating store-keepers, assaulting shoppers and by a campaign of maliciousness with no regard as to the results of their vicious tactics, a group of members of the Citizens' League . . . have broken away from the parent body, constituted themselves a separate group . . . and are demanding complete control of the allocating of jobs to Negroes in 125th street stores. With propaganda against Negroes of light complexion, they are charging that the girls employed by L. M. Blumstein's Department Store are not dark enough to suit them and have even gone so far as to demand of employers that light colored clerks be fired and men and women associated with their organization be hired in their stead. . . . Their tactics are said to be the same as those used by racketeers.

These pickets became disruptive—or effective—enough for the merchants to seek redress from the city government. According to the president of the Board of Aldermen in September of 1934.

> I have had considerable complaint during the last few weeks from merchants throughout the northern end of the Harlem in the colored section, complaining that several colored organizations are picketing their places of business.
>
> The first effort is an attempt to compel the employment of colored persons, then, where colored persons are employed, some of the organizations object to the light or dark color of the employees, and attempt to dictate to the storekeepers first as to the kind of colored employees, then the positions in which they are to be placed, and they finally wish to dictate the personnel themselves.

The merchants claimed they were "perfectly willing to employ a fair percentage of colored people provided they are competent to fill the positions, but they do not feel called upon to appoint to positions certain personnel dictated by various groups, nor to create unnecessary positions to which colored help may be employed, nor to discharge one set of colored help and substitute another." This claim is disingenuous, as the merchants demonstrated very little "perfect willingness" to hire black clerks from the Citizens' League picket, either. White store owners complained that black clerks were poorly trained, and that both black and white patronage fell after black clerks were employed. They also admitted, however, that the newly hired clerks "learned readily enough."[19]

Hamid was arrested for disorderly conduct and otherwise hindered by police several times, but he continued the picket until the A. S. Beck Shoe Company received a court injunction. On October 31, 1934, New York's Supreme Court ruled that picketing was illegal because there was no labor dispute. By this time, the Citizens' League had disavowed the increasingly confrontational actions of the pickets, and the black press almost universally condemned it. John Johnson reported he was unhappy with "the uncontrollable forces [the] movement had unleashed." All the opponents of black nationalism rushed to assert the superiority of their approach and heap criticism on Hamid, Kemp, and Reid. James Hubert lambasted the "soapbox orators who . . . heckle and vilify publicly anyone and every other organization that is attempting to deal with the problems at hand . . . a most disgusting scene."[20]

Hamid reorganized his picketers into the AfroAmerican Federation of Labor, reasoning that a union picket would be considered legal. The state Supreme Court ruled otherwise, recognizing that a title did not make a union. Hamid left the business of organizing in 1935 to marry "policy queen" Madame Stephanie St. Claire and found the Temple of Tranquillity on Morningside Drive, which operated a cooperative vegetable market and a garage. He died in a plane crash in 1938 during an attempt to rise (literally) higher than Father Divine, whom he perceived as his foremost rival.[21]

Without the broad-based picket, the hard-won triumphs of the Citizens' League evaporated. Other stores on 125th Street that had agreed to hire blacks never did. Blumstein's kept the first fifteen black women on staff, but never hired the promised twenty in the fall. Without a continuing, visible presence, the League could not force store owners to keep their agreement. Meeting in early 1935, the League found half of the blacks who had won clerical jobs in 1934 had been laid off. Without the legal right to picket, the Citizens' League collapsed. Alternative strategies, such as leafleting or using church pulpits to publicize the boycotts, were certainly still possible, but the League would not or did not adopt them. In view of the large numbers of participants in church activities and the centrality of churches in the campaign, the lack of enthusiasm for continuing the boycott through church efforts is puzzling. Nor did the churches join the ongoing efforts of the NAACP and the Urban League to improve job opportunities by quieter means. Perhaps the Depression gave Harlem activists more than enough else to do. Perhaps the prospects for success were still too discouraging, once the courts took the side of the white merchants. Certainly the Citizens' League was not alone in failing to find viable alternative tactics in the face of the ban. Picket and boycott activities dwindled all over the country as a result of similar court rulings.[22]

In any event, by 1935, conditions were little better for skilled and educated blacks than they had been two years previously.

Q. In regard to the retail stores in New York, could you tell me whether it is a
   general custom to abstain from employing Negro clerks?
A. Yes, unless the girl is very light in complexion . . .
Q. Does this apply to Harlem

Interjection: Yes, even in Harlem
Interjection: Some stores
Interjection: Kress stores
Chairman: Order!

The fact was that any improvements that had come resulted from the pickets. Little hope remained for continued improvement so long as boycotts and pickets were not used, as Cecilia Saunders' testimony before the Mayor's Commission on Conditions in Harlem suggests:

Q. You are familiar with the employment of Negroes in the stores on 125th Street. When did that begin?
A. Less than a year ago.
Q. Did the employment of Negroes precede or come after the picketing on 125th Street?
A. After the picketing.
Q. The merchants to your knowledge, had they done anything before the picketing began in order to give the Negro consideration by way of employment?
A. I never heard that they had.[23]

More radical groups in Washington, D.C., Atlanta, and elsewhere defied court orders and continued pickets, despite arrests. Some Harlem groups did so as well. Both the Harlem Labor Union (HLU) and the Negro Industrial Clerical Alliance continued their work after the dissolution of the Citizens' League and turned the drive for black jobs increasingly into an explicitly anti-white campaign, often targeting particular white ethnic groups. Certainly such a tactic was effective in achieving their nationalist political goals; by stirring up the people against a group of whites who were also tradespeople in the area, the two groups encouraged patronage of black-owned stores. Thus, for example, the HLU used the anti-Italian fervor that swept Harlem after Italy invaded Ethiopia to urge a boycott of Italian and white pushcarts in Harlem in favor of black ones. Hundreds of blacks joined these protests and demonstrations.[24]

Their strongest invective, however, was reserved for Jews. Jewish store owners in Harlem, having helped form the Harlem Merchants' Association at the time of the initial pickets, first complained of Hamid's anti-Semitism in 1934. They accused him of repeating Nazi propaganda, and called him "Black Hitler." The *Amsterdam News*, the *New York Age*, and others corroborated these claims, and reported anti-Semitic remarks he had made. He was brought to municipal court in 1935 on charges of disorderly conduct and "instigating a race war." He denied the charges and was released with a warning.

Equally anti-Semitic was the Harlem Labor Union, which, according to the Eighth Avenue merchants, relied to a large extent on Nazi propaganda and some of Garvey's teachings to protect "Jewish control" of black economic life.

These merchants reported to the police commissioner that the Harlem Labor Union representatives "used the[ir] platform to vilify the Jewish race and in their addresses have used such expressions as . . . 'The Jews are the exploiters of the colored people' . . . 'Harlem's worst enemies are the Jews' . . . 'Jews and leprosy are synonymous.' " A Federal Writers' Project researcher concluded that the HLU "assumed the character of a 'crusade against Jewish merchants' " and that Sufi Hamid preached anti-Semitism and race hatred. In a rare show of agreement, both the Harlem Merchants' Association and the Communist party protested Hamid's and the HLU's rhetoric.[25] The party opposed the anti-Semitism as divisive and a barrier to the goal of uniting the working class of all races and religions. It opposed such bigotry also because so many party members were Jewish.

While anti-Semitism was only part of the broader anti-white rhetoric, Jews did make the most visible target. The majority of store owners were Jewish, since the Jews had settled in Harlem before the blacks, and remained in their stores after they moved from their apartments. Therefore, anti-white feeling could easily be translated into anti-Semitism. The relationship between blacks and Jews was tense in other economic areas as well (at the Bronx "slave market," for example, most of the housewives hiring domestic workers were Jewish), which undoubtedly encouraged anti-Jewish sentiment in the jobs campaign.

The issue of anti-Semitism polarized the activist black community, with the groups from the original Citizens' League and black trade unionists protesting such tactics, while supporters of Hamid, Kemp, and Reid denied all charges of anti-Semitism. Claude McKay came to Hamid's defense: "No one was more astonished than the Sufi himself when he was accused of organizing an anti-Semitic movement. . . . There was never any anti-Semitism in Harlem and there still is none, in spite of the stupid and vicious propaganda which endeavored to create an anti-Semitic issue out of the legitimate movement of Negroes to improve their social condition. . . . In fact, it is that reactionary attitude that is increasing anti-Jewish feeling." Even this defense, then, conceded the presence of anti-Semitism in Harlem, but denied that Hamid or Kemp was the source. Other defenders viewed anti-Semitism, or anti-white feeling in general, more benignly as simply part of the struggle for black nationalism. Once again, differences in political aspirations prevented the formation of a workable jobs coalition in Harlem.

Questions of corruption and self-interest served to further widen the division between the nationalists and the more moderate, integrationist groups. The remaining members of the League argued that the Harlem Labor Union and the Negro Industrial Clerical Alliance were undermining the campaign for black clerical jobs by using political means for personal ends, fighting for the employment only of workers who supported them. Sufi Hamid promised all who joined the Alliance a clerical job, but membership dues were $1 each month even if no job was obtained. Store managers like Mr. Snyder of Grant's were not the only ones to charge Hamid with exploiting the situation for his own benefit. Several black employees reported threats of violence from him if they refused to join his "union," even if they already belonged to another. There is also some evidence of bribery of store owners. According to Bernard Deutch, president of the Board of Aldermen: "There has sprung up a racket whereby some of those colored leaders are forcing small storekeepers who employ no help at all to pay a certain sum each week in lieu of employing unnecessary help."[26]

Kemp and Reid's Harlem Labor Union was reported to be equally corrupt. "This organization," reported the *Amsterdam News*, "is racketeering of the most vicious type. It not only lines the pocket of its leader, but plays up the most ancient of prejudices—race hatred." The HLU's arch-enemy, the Negro Labor Committee, called the HLU "a terroristic campaign in Harlem against Jews, against whites and against the legitimate trade union movement. The leaders of this Incorporated union have literally terrorized many merchants into not only giving employment to members of this alleged union at the expense of both Negro and white union men, but they have also been known to extract money from certain Harlem merchants as insurance against a picket line." Given the NLC's position as competitor, one might suspect it of hyperbole, except that independent investigations by the city and testimony by several merchants corroborated these complaints. The owner of the Owl Shoe Company on 125th Street told Frank Crosswaith that the HLU tried to organize his two black workers in June of 1939. They refused. The HLU picketed and "indulged in dangerous anti-white propaganda." The owner, frightened, signed a contract with the HLU that made no change in work conditions, and agreed to pay $2 a month to the union to prevent another picket. Whether or not the pickets were as "dangerous" as he claimed, certainly they did not win benefits for the staff.

Occasionally these practices flew in the face of the explicitly nationalist commitment of the HLU, calling the sincerity of that position into question. Had the HLU's intent honestly been to promote black employment, it would not have picketed establishments where blacks were already employed, demanding they be fired and that HLU members be hired in their place. In 1933, the owner of Orkin's Dress Shop, fearing that the Blumstein's pickets might soon extend to his store, hired blacks until they made up half his work force. The Harlem Labor Union established a picket line there two years later that demanded a 50 percent black staff. Realizing its error, the HLU quickly changed its signs to 75 percent and demanded that present employees be fired in favor of picketers. The HLU justified its action by arguing that since the clerks had not picketed to win their jobs in the first place, the hard-working HLU members deserved first fruits of the picket committee's success.[27]

Apparently, Reid's organization sometimes seemed more committed to furthering the fortunes of its members and leaders than to furthering the cause of black nationalism. In fact, Reid did not deny that inproprieties occurred. In a defense of Sufi Hamid's racketeering practices and presumably by implication, his own, he explained to an interviewer that while Hamid and his colleagues did use organization money to support themselves,

> [a]n agitator must eat to live, and no matter how noble the cause, petty graft will occur and no one could have grown rich on the amount of money involved. As for the rough tactics which his group employed, such methods were not out of keeping with the necessities of organizing reluctant workers. . . . The fact that Sufi put pressure on employers to fire Negroes and hire members of his own group was a natural corollary to his desire to strengthen the union. . . . Furthermore, many of the Negroes who found employment on 125 Street during the months following the Blumstein affair, were light skinned Negroes who had been employed for the sole purpose of forestalling future boycotts. . . . It was this tactic on the part of the employers which forced Sufi to agitate for the dismissal of the newly hired Negroes.[28]

Accusations of corruption aside, it was clear the Alliance and the HLU had very different organizing styles from that of the League, as Reid's statement hints. Even when anti-white rhetoric was not explicit, the methods used by these groups to integrate white-owned stores also set them apart from the moderate non-nationalists in Harlem. In general, the Harlem Labor Union used more confrontational tactics. It successfully tapped the anger and frustration of black working people who had been consistently denied fair treatment by unions and employers. In an interview, an organizer working for the HLU in 1938 described the strategy used to integrate Harlem's butcher shops. He entered shops when many black women were inside purchasing meat and inquired loudly why no black butchers worked there. The women would murmur assent—their husbands and sons were unemployed. The butcher would reply that the AFL butchers' union already had a contract there. " 'I'd say to hell with the AFL, they are downtown and we are in Harlem and they can't help you if we throw a picket line around the place.' . . . We finally put in Negro butchers all over Harlem. . . . You see we could always depend on the Harlem people [to support us] because they were mad, hungry and hemmed-in."[29]

Not surprisingly, Crosswaith's Negro Labor Committee often came into conflict with the HLU. Each group defended its own unionizing efforts, and condemned the other's. "Because of the so-called closed shop contracts with the CIO local 1125," Reid claimed, "several stores on 125th Street cannot put Negro girls to work [because the union denied blacks membership]." He criticized Crosswaith for not fighting such discrimination. Since, as Reid saw it, Harlem's black merchants could not afford to pay the prevailing union wage, the HLU signed contracts to employ blacks at lower pay. When the Moving Van Drivers' Locals 805 and 807 tried to standardize city pay rates by raising prices and wages in Harlem, the HLU organized twenty-eight black van operators into the Harlem Movers' Association, and signed a contract at lower rates. The HLU justified such contracts on grounds that it saved Harlemites money and provided more jobs for black drivers. Crosswaith fired back that it was not enough merely to win employment for blacks: "We worked for 245 years during slavery, but we got nothing for our work." By contrast, he argued, "The NLC has been responsible, not only for much of the increase in employment among Negro workers in this area, but especially in raising the wages and working standards of those workers." With less overt rancor, Crosswaith described his differences with the HLU's approach in his testimony before the Mayor's Commission: "Perhaps the only difference is that others have been putting emphasis on getting jobs for Negroes. That is not the essential solution. I am concerned with what the Negroes will get for work they do."[30]

Part of the antipathy can be accounted for by the opposing goals of the two groups. Since the Harlem Labor Union was committed to black nationalism, it opposed the unionizing drive of the *Amsterdam News* workers; Kemp and Reid believed it inappropriate for blacks to strike against employers of the same color. Here self-interest coincided with nationalism rather than undermining it. The NLC, the HLU's competition, had launched the strike.

The Negro Labor Committee, on the other hand, supported the *Amsterdam News* strike as part of the struggle to improve working conditions. The NLC sought the integration of blacks into the larger work force, both because its socialist leanings led it to seek unity of the working class, and because Harlem could not employ all the blacks who lived there, even were it an all-black economy. Crosswaith believed blacks' economic future lay in a strong, unionized work force that extended beyond the confines of Harlem. Until these sectarian fights could be resolved, the jobs campaign would remain stalled.

The antagonism between the two, of course, came also from competition, as they sought to organize the same workers for their own group. In this, the NLC seemed marginally more successful in winning better contracts for its members. To cite one example: since they were already members of the HLU, the seven black workers at Bishop's Dress Shop could not join with the eight white workers there in a CIO union drive. The white CIO-won salaries rose and their hours declined, but Reid could not win the same concessions for his members. After a prolonged struggle, the black employees succeeded in switching their affiliation and received the higher salaries.[31]

While this bitter infighting plagued the campaign, the NUL and the NAACP continued with their own behind-the-scenes efforts to win better opportunities for black workers. Though the NAACP's most important efforts remained focused on litigation, the organization had become more activist as the Great Depression wore on, pushing government agencies and trade unions to accept qualified blacks, as well as fighting lynching and segregation. Like the NUL it also demanded that employers and unions not only hire qualified blacks, but train them. Both groups' style of letter-writing and quiet pressure did not require or utilize mass movements, but their successes were nonetheless significant.[32]

Black leaders and groups involved in direct action did not find these low-key methods satisfactory. Yet confrontational and often corrupt activities seemed to mainstream black leaders to have dominated the public protests. The Citizens' League, the Negro Alliance, and the HLU had aroused the energies and expectations of many in the Harlem community, but only the nationalists had succeeded in sustaining their momentum. Black leaders supporting non-nationalist solutions watched their control over Harlem's political energies weaken. The HLU's successes challenged them to reclaim the initiative, and the model of several integrationist organizations like the Negro Labor Committee showed them how. Especially as more unions accepted black workers, these black leaders came to agree with the NLC's views. As Adam Clayton Powell, Jr., wrote in 1937, "The HLU can never achieve any success for the Negro worker," as it did not demand union wage levels and actually campaigned against legitimate unions. "For anyone to strive to build a nationalist movement in America among Negroes is to commit racial suicide," he insisted. The NLC's success getting unions throughout the city to accept black members challenged black leaders to think of the jobs campaign more broadly.

The Communist party also inspired centrist black leaders to broaden their goals. During the Popular Front period, the party's new policies resembled those of the Negro Labor Committee and the Citizens' League, but embraced the wider city. Although the party had initially opposed the "Don't Buy Where You Can't Work" campaign, seeing it as disruptive to working-class unity and a tool for capitalists, the Popular Front strategy forced the party to re-evaluate. In order to keep credibility in the community and with liberal black organizations, it had to participate in some fashion.[33]

The Communist party developed a strategy appropriate for its seemingly contradictory position of support for Harlem cooperative action and encouragement of black and white working-class unity. It demanded the hiring of blacks in Harlem establishments without firing whites. It encouraged job actions at large chain stores and public utilities rather than at small family stores where racial antagonism might intensify and undermine class unity. Under the banner of the Committee Against Discrimination of Negro Workers on Jobs, the party led a boycott and picket of the Empire Cafeteria on 125th Street and Lenox Avenue.

Toilers of Harlem! Negro and White
DEMONSTRATE AGAINST DISCRIMINATION!

For jobs for Negroes in Empire Cafeteria and for Unemployment Relief. Wed., September 5, 7 P.M. at 126 Street and Lenox . . .

Negro and White, demonstrate and picket for the following demands:

1. No dismissal of white workers
2. Hiring of additional Negro workers with equal pay
3. No reduction in pay

Again sectarian lines blurred: Sufi Hamid's Alliance and the UNIA participated in this picket because it sought black jobs. The cafeteria hired four black workers without letting any white workers go.

The Joint Conference Against Discriminatory Practices, a Communist-led organization that concentrated primarily on relief policies, also set up (illegal) pickets. At one Saturday demonstration in front of Weisbecker's Market at 125th Street and Eighth Avenue, the Joint Conference was joined by the Elks, the African Patriotic Union, and the Communist party. They demanded (but did not win) a 25 percent reduction in prices as well as the hiring of black clerks. These efforts, confrontational as they were (the Empire picket turned into a mêlée when a protester hurled a rock through the window) did bring both political awareness and jobs to Harlem. As Charles Franklin reluctantly granted: "However illegitimate or racketeering Hamid's organization may have been, it was at least striking at those very frightful conditions in its attempts to get employment for Negroes and to improve working conditions for those already employed." The same could be said for each illegal protest.[34]

Rebuilding: The Second Campaign

The successes of the Communist party and of the Negro Labor Committee made their broad approach realistic and attractive to Harlem's mainstream black leaders disgusted with Hamid's and Kemp's tactics. Ironically, the extremism of Hamid, Kemp, and Reid also strengthened the integrationist organizations. Alerted to the campaign by vocal radicals, many Harlemites joined the struggle for white-collar jobs. The general opposition to confrontational or extreme tactics led many of these newcomers to embrace the more moderate positions in the jobs coalition. Thus, support for the center swelled, as evidenced by rising numbers of participants in the protests and demonstrations led by moderate groups.

All these challenges persuaded black leaders like Powell that they needed to regain the ascendancy in the jobs campaign. The time also seemed appropriate. The Harlem riot of 1935 had raised the specter of further violence if economic changes were not made. As the Mayor's Commission on Conditions in Harlem warned, "The blame [for the riot] belongs to a society that tolerates . . . unemployment, discrimination in industry and the public utilities. . . . As long as these conditions remain, the public order can not and will not be safe." The riot had also heightened municipal officials' awareness of the plight of blacks in the Depression. Meanwhile, the New Deal broadened and legitimized the involvement of government in economic affairs. The blue ribbon commission appointed by Mayor LaGuardia to study Harlem's conditions and recommend policy changes, the speed-up of construction of several schools and low-cost apartment blocks in Harlem, the new responsiveness of city agencies to complaints of discrimination, and the appointment of a statewide panel to investigate conditions of the "urban colored population," all attest to this change in atmosphere. Despite continuing racism, the conscience—or self-interest—of New York's political leaders had been aroused. The opportunity for winning over white store-owners in such a climate appeared far more favorable than in 1933. Even the Urban League apparently reconsidered. James Hubert backed off from earlier positions critical of the boycott efforts, although he still distanced himself from the more confrontational tactics of the HLU.

Q. Do you favor that organizations of Negroes should boycott, especially the 125th Street stores?

A. I favor any method on the part of any group or individual so long as it is lawful. . . .

Q. A newspaper attributes to you the statement that you do not favor such methods. . . .

A. I do not recall making such a statement. . . . I question how far one could go in the use of force . . . you have seen the results obtained. Most of the good has already been lost.

The successes of both nationalist and integrationist efforts, the emergence of a CIO supportive of black issues, and the improvement of the political climate in terms of race relations heightened Harlemites' sense of their community's potential power. They were ready to mobilize. Yet the legal ban on picketing remained a barrier to further effective action by law-abiding groups until 1938. In that year the United States Supreme Court ruled in *New Negro Alliance vs. Sanitary Grocery Company* that because blacks suffered employment discrimination solely because of their race, they could in turn make special employment demands based on race and could therefore picket.

The law had always played an important, though not definitive, role in charting the course of the "Don't Buy" coalition. The Citizens' League had won victories with its pickets, victories that evaporated when the courts denied the right to picket on the basis of race. Yet the court decision alone did not destroy the Citizens' League. The end of the picket line did not have to mean an end to the coalition's progress; other solutions could have been tried. The disputes among the constituent groups over League tactics were more to blame for its collapse.

Nor did the right to picket in itself necessarily ensure further gains. The Negro Alliance, the HLU, and the Communist party continued picket activities illegally after 1934. When stopped by police, they tried impromptu sit-ins, persisting despite frequent arrests.[35] Yet these groups only won small isolated victories until joined by a larger coalition.

The importance of the New Negro Alliance case was that it allowed moderate integrationist groups to reassert control over the jobs campaign. In 1935 the Citizens' League had abandoned the effort rather than resort to illegal picketing or new tactics. By doing so, it lost control of the campaign. Its constituent groups soon realized their error. By then, Hamid, Kemp, and Reid had established energetic, visible picket lines that could not be countered by subtle or private maneuvering. The Supreme Court decision restored to the main-stream groups an effective way to unite with like-minded organizations and re-enter (and dominate) the struggle. The Communist party also cooperated in this, hoping both to solidify the legitimacy of its Popular Front strategy and to keep its political vision in the forefront of the jobs campaign.

Adam Clayton Powell, Jr., of the Abyssinian Baptist Church held a mass meeting on March 12, 1938, to form the Greater New York Coordinating Committee for Employment, co-chaired by Powell and William Imes of Saint James Presbyterian Church. Soon after its formation, the committee claimed to enjoy the support of over 200 organizations and 170,000 members—over three times the number in the original Citizens' League. It had the cooperation of the New York Urban League, the NAACP, the Joint Conference Against Discriminatory Practices, the Harlem YMCA, A. Philip Randolph, and the Communist party. As Powell described it, "It was honest because it was poor."[36]

It is likely that the Communist party helped organize and participate in the Coordinating Committee to regain the initiative on fighting job discrimination from the moderate NAACP and NUL on the one side and the nationalists on the other. Communist-organized transport unions continued to discriminate against blacks, another motive for the party to move in this direction. Thus the committee was not simply a non-ideological compromise coalition, which explains why bitter sectarian and turf battles continued even after the committee's founding. Reid, for example, a fervid anti-Communist, refused to associate his group with the committee, which in turn missed no opportunity to criticize the HLU.

Staunch unionist Frank Crosswaith also opposed the Coordinating Committee. Despite the committee's efforts not to conflict with unions, he believed "the legitimate labor movement in this area appears to be the main target. . . . Perhaps the C.P. will get some notoriety out of another race riot in Harlem, but the Negro groups will suffer [;] so will the growing trade union movement up here." The visibility of the Communist party in the committee dismayed anti-Communist Crosswaith, which helps explain his dissatisfaction. More-over, he took the committee's activities as a personal affront. The whole effort implicitly criticized other groups working for black employment, including the NLC and organized labor. Its successes infuriated him.[37]

Much of the strength of the committee came from black educated and skilled workers, formerly of the middle class, who had lost their jobs in the De-pression. Now in menial jobs or unemployed, they helped provide the energy and commitment necessary for political mobilization. Still, this was undeni-ably a movement of the working class, peopled by domestics, laborers, and service workers. Not only did participants and eyewitnesses make this claim, sheer numbers require it to be true. The black middle class was too small to have generated this size protest alone.

The presence of Adam Clayton Powell, Jr., as leader of the coalition also helped explain the committee's energy and huge numbers. Son of a dynamic and influential minister, minister in his own right of one of the largest and most prestigious churches in Harlem, leader of numerous community efforts on behalf of the poor and the unemployed, and a dynamic and charismatic speaker, Powell symbolized for thousands the noble struggle for equality in Harlem. His presence, like that of Martin Luther King, Jr., in the later civil rights movement, helped unify and direct the campaign.

The Coordinating Committee embraced many of the goals of the Citizens' League, the Negro Labor Committee, and the Communist party; it sought to employ blacks in white-owned stores without displacing whites or undermining legitimate unions, and it worked to integrate public utilities outside Harlem. It tried all of the usual tactics: negotiations, conferences, cooperative agreements. This time, success came much more easily. With such a large constituency, and with the legal right to picket restored, its requests carried clout. The extremism of Hamid and Reid made white store-owners eager to negotiate with the committee, whose demands seemed more reasonable in comparison. In fact, the successes of 1938 might not have been possible earlier, without the conflicts and the extremism that ultimately promoted united action among blacks and put pressure on merchants to negotiate with moderates. Almost immediately the Coordinating Committee won its first victories. The A&P hired a black manager; a local jewelry company hired six black typists.

The committee also employed creative tactics, especially to tackle large public utilities that could not be reached with boycotts and pickets. To persuade the energy companies to hire blacks in non-menial positions, the Coordinating Committee turned Harlem dark once a week by asking families to use candles instead of electricity on Tuesday nights, and it led hundreds in "billpayers' parades" to the gas company offices each month to pay their bills in pennies. Other tactics included asking all Harlemites to request a (legal) out-of-turn gas meter inspection simultaneously and to refuse to pay gas bills until the inspection was completed. Prior to the campaign, at Consolidated Gas, of 10,000 employees, 213 were black, working as porters. New York Edison, also with 10,000, employed just sixty-five blacks, and only as messengers, porters, and janitors. After the campaign, the newly merged Consolidated Edison hired four blacks in non-menial positions, promoted four more, and promised that "an appreciable percentage of all new Consolidated Edison employees would be Negroes." Adam Clayton Powell, Jr., hailed these successes as "the first victory in our campaign for white-collar jobs for Negroes in industry."

The Coordinating Committee then turned to the New York Telephone Company, which had refused to hire black repairmen or operators. Here it employed several strategies at once. Direct negotiations with the company made clear the community's position, while threats of retaliatory action made the company receptive to compromise. For example, the committee threatened that Harlemites would make operator-assisted telephone calls rather than dial directly, which would increase each operator's workload by close to 70 percent, and would jam the phone lines at the moment Wall Street reported its daily figures. The cumulative effects of these pressures compelled the telephone company to re-examine its position. Quickly, it hired black clerical staff. Even these tactics were not enough, however, to force the company to hire black operators. Ultimately it took further pressure from several black groups and government agencies and the exigencies of the war to get black operators on staff.[38]

When necessary, the committee carried out the threat to picket. At the end of April 1938, each firm in Harlem not yet employing blacks received this letter from the committee, signed by Adam Clayton Powell, Jr., and the other officers:

Dear Sir:
The Coordinating Committee for Employment representing over 200 organizations in Harlem decided unanimously . . . to begin picketing each store in Harlem which does not employ Negroes. . . .
If we do not receive an answer to this letter by Friday at 2:00 your store will be picketed beginning this Saturday and every Saturday thereafter.[39]

After four months of negotiation with the Uptown Chamber of Commerce, the two groups reached an agreement, which stated:

To effect a fair and equitable settlement of the Negro employment problem as it affects Harlem retail establishments, the Uptown Chamber of Commerce . . . and the Greater New York Coordinating Committee for Employment . . . agree . . .
That stores not already employing between 33 and [h] percent and 40 percent colored workers in so-called white collar positions agree to do so as speedily as possible by making replacements with qualified Negroes as white employees resign or are discharged for cause. . . .
[In family-owned stores] the owners agree to engage a qualified Negro for the first new job created in their establishment.
That the stores agree not to limit the opportunities of Negro workers for advancement, . . . nor shall colored workers be discriminated against in the matter of wages.
That when stores operate under a closed shop agreement with a recognized union the owners or managers agree to use their influence with union officials to the end that Negroes may be admitted to membership. In short, there will be no pretense at denying Negroes employment in union stores on the subterfuge that to hire them would be in violation of existing union contracts. . . .
[Chain stores] will not adopt a policy of discrimination against Negroes employed in their stores located out of Harlem.

The "Memorandum of Agreement," as it was called, further required employers not to discriminate in the event of forced layoffs, and to submit all disputes to a joint arbitration committee made up of the two organizations.

For its part, the Coordinating Committee agreed that:

at no time will it demand the replacement of a white worker with a Negro except [when that worker was hired in direct violation of the agreement]. . . .

That resort to picketing, boycotts and other mass demonstrations against stores shall not be made [unless the store violates an Arbitration Committee decision].

The Coordinating Committee agrees to encourage campaigns among the masses to increase the colored trade of all cooperating stores. . . .

The Coordinating Committee agrees to use every possible means to prevent independent action against stores subscribing to this agreement by colored groups not associated with the Coordinating Committee.[40]

Within two months of the memorandum, 300 blacks had white-collar jobs in Harlem. Every large store on 125th Street had at least one black employee. The Chamber of Commerce reported higher sales by 1940, although this was probably due to the increased prosperity brought about by war preparations.

As for the "colored groups not associated with the Coordinating Committee," that is, the Harlem Labor Union, trouble with that organization finally eased after an agreement that Reid would join the Coordinating Committee and cease picketing stores already unionized by the AFL or CIO. He violated that agreement numerous times until District Attorney Thomas E. Dewey prosecuted him as a racketeer in 1939. Although the charges were ultimately dropped, he left the Union, and it lost its militant and nationalist character soon thereafter. (Kemp had left the group to run for New York Assembly in 1938 on a more mainstream platform. He lost by only a few votes, and died a few days later.)[41]

Powell and the Coordinating Committee turned next to the World's Fair, which was to be held in New York City in 1939. He asked the World's Fair Corporation to ensure the availability of non-menial jobs for blacks. When polite requests failed, blacks moved their pickets downtown for the first time, to the Fair's headquarters in the Empire State Building. Bill Robinson and chorus girls from Ethel Waters' shows joined the hundreds of lower-class and middle-class demonstrators. After two months of such efforts, Fair organizers yielded, promising positions for several hundred black clerks and other workers.[42]

The Lessons of the Campaigns

The jobs campaign had meant different things to different segments of the Harlem community. To middle-class black leaders it represented an opportunity for white-collar blacks to acquire appropriate jobs. To black merchants it meant an increase in black business; to black nationalists it was a step toward a black state; to others it offered an opportunity to build a power base among the unemployed. To Socialists, Communists, and black trade unionists it diverted attention from the struggle of black workers to integrate existing unions unless the two efforts went hand in hand. This disunity of purpose and internal competition hampered the campaign and divided public opinion. Not until the members of the coalition agreed on both tactics (legal pickets, support for unions, and negotiations) and goals (the hiring of blacks without the firing of whites) did the campaign achieve success.

The 1935 riot in Harlem alerted the white community to the economic discrimination practiced against blacks and the need for some response, however small, to avert further violence. This new willingness to cooperate helped contribute to the jobs campaign's success, but any success would have been impossible without the activist participation of Harlem blacks. The campaign allowed them to take whatever control they could of their economic future through political action and the forging of alliances in the community. In the "Don't Buy" campaign, every individual in Harlem made real choices about whether and how to become involved in the efforts to bring better employment opportunities—an empowering experience. The struggle to gain white-collar employment could not have solved Harlem's economic problems even if all the movement's programs had been implemented. Its real contribution was the political mobilization of Harlem. The campaign allowed the black community to test its strengths, refine its arguments, and try out its struggle for equal opportunity in a narrow setting that offered African-Americans some hope of having an impact.

The success of the Coordinating Committee and the jobs campaign brought new goals. Having black clerks in Harlem stores did not solve the unemployment problem, as there were not enough jobs in that community for everyone. Nor were enough Harlem men and women sufficiently educated or skilled to take advantage of such employment opportunities had they been offered. The problems were more deeply rooted. By 1944, the majority of salespeople in Harlem were black, yet Harlem's economic troubles persisted. The huge number of unemployed black workers willing to accept lower wages in order to obtain a job challenged unions to join with blacks rather than to exclude them. In this case blacks may have been unemployed because of their race, but unemployment was the issue that had to be addressed.

Furthermore, the campaign, by picketing exclusively in Harlem, did not persuade stores not located there to end their discriminatory policies. That would require new, broader, and bolder strategies—cooperation between black groups and organized labor, a recognition of working-class needs, and the expansion of the campaign beyond Harlem's boundaries.

In recognition of this, the Coordinating Committee, the Communist party, the Urban League, the NAACP, and the Negro Labor Committee had begun to move out of the black community to integrate the public utilities, working with the trade union movement and focusing on training and apprenticeship programs as well as on white-collar and skilled jobs. Cooperating this way had brought success with New York Telephone, Consolidated Edison, and the World's Fair; these groups went on in the next decade to use the techniques of the "Don't Buy" campaign to integrate more of the transit system's labor force, several large insurance companies, and department stores.[43]

While black nationalism retained some community support, its strength had diminished with the victories of the churches and the unions, and it would not rise again with such popular force until the late 1950s. On the other hand, the Communist party, having strengthened its base in the black community with its staunch support for black economic opportunity, then lost it with the Nazi-Soviet pact, the end of the Popular Front, and the increased virulence of Red-baiting in the 1940s. This left the moderates in the dominant position, something demonstrated by their most popular spokesperson, the younger Powell, as he swept into city office in 1941 and Congress shortly thereafter.

The Depression saw an expansion of black political action in Harlem that had begun earlier, instigated by changes both internal and external to the black community. African-Americans had undertaken numerous efforts in earlier years to gain improvements for their race. But the economic desperation of the Depression and the new willingness of government, unions, and employers to respond to organized grievances and to threats of violence or riot marked this period as a particularly active one for political organizing. This expansion brought thousands into the political process who had not participated before, and activism essentially burst the confines of traditional politics. While existing party organizations and black groups participated actively in these political efforts, many people also sought different political vehicles. Thus, the new energy had many outlets: the reinvigorated traditional parties, mass rallies, union drives, black nationalist and integrationist organizations, churches, and newly formed political groups. The boundaries between these new and on-going structures were remarkably fluid. Not only did much of the leadership of these organizations overlap, but individual Harlemites joined with different groups, depending on the issue at hand. Class and race intersected with and reinforced each other, as did black nationalism and a commitment to improve Harlem's economic opportunity structure.

Yet conflicts among and within groups at times weakened these efforts, as when self-interest overwhelmed a commitment to nationalism, or sectarian battles vitiated programs and actions to bring about jointly supported goals. Internal struggles over class and nationalist visions and between moderate and radical perspectives provided a spectrum of opportunity for involvement, but also worked against farther-reaching structural change. Even if these internal conflicts had disappeared, the external limits on black economic advancement: racism, lack of training, the Depression, and entrenched economic and political practices preferential to white or middle-class groups, were still too great to be overcome at that time.

Despite its limitations, however, black mass action in the Depression also revealed the tremendous potential of such efforts. Harlemites struggled in this decade to alter the power relations of society, and while they did not succeed in that, they solidified a political base and experimented with tactics that would prove critical in the years to come.

While certainly not all the problems of coalition-building in a diverse population had been resolved, these political programs set the stage for more dramatic and sweeping efforts, such as the 1941 March on Washington Movement led by A. Philip Randolph, and ultimately the modern civil rights movement. All over the country, black efforts had produced improved job opportunities for the black middle class, and helped galvanize mass action on other fronts, such as housing and the distribution of relief. They also furthered the involvement of blacks in organized party politics, making possible the ascendancy of such elected leaders as Adam Powell in New York and William Dawson in Chicago.[44]

There were significant differences between this campaign and the modern civil rights movement, however. The efforts of the 1930s sought primarily to improve black employment opportunities. Black organizations used racial equality and nondiscriminatory legislation as the tools for pursuing better opportunities, but the jobs themselves were the goal. For the modern civil rights movement, equality was the central focus.

The tactics of the two eras also differed. In the 1930s the moderates obeyed the law and ceased all activities when they saw that continued action would violate a legal court injunction. In the 1950s and 1960s, however, intentional civil disobedience was the centerpiece of moderate efforts. The reason for these opposing approaches reflects the two movements' different goals. While a jobs campaign fought for opportunities within an existing structure, civil rights was by definition a struggle against unjust laws. The civil rights movement's moral force came from actively challenging the legal basis of racist social structures. Finally, unlike the civil rights movement, the jobs campaign did not persuade many whites to actively pursue black equality.[45]

Yet the victories of the civil rights movement could not have been won without the groundwork laid by these earlier efforts. The New Deal decade made the value of political organizing particularly visible. The Depression alerted the white public to the plight of those who suffered, bringing black problems into the open and ensuring that they received a sympathetic hearing. The political struggles for equal opportunity that emerged in such an environment laid an indispensable foundation for future efforts. When the time was right, new coalitions would draw on tactics first employed in unionizing and "Don't Buy" campaigns in Harlem and elsewhere, thereby fighting more effectively for equality in the decades following the Great Depression.

Notes

1. The movement has been known variously as "Don't Buy Where You Can't Work," "Don't Buy from Where You Can't Work," and "Buy Where You Work." I have used Powell's term. Aldon Morris, *The Origins of the Civil Rights Movement* (New York, 1984).

2. NYUL: Ira Reid, NYUL, "Annual Report, Industrial Department, 1926," 1 November 1927, p. 3, National Urban League papers, series 5, box 10, Library of Congress Manuscript Collection, Washington, D.C.; "League of Equal Political and Civic Rights to Tackle Em-

ployment Problem," *March of Events* 1 (January 1928): 12–13; NYUL et al., "Employment Mass Meeting," Transcript, 24 April 1930, pp. 3–4, 10–11, NUL papers, series 7, box 21.

3. NYUL et al., "Employment Mass Meeting," pp. 4, 10–11; Guichard Parris and Lester Brooks, *Blacks in the City: A History of the National Urban League* (Boston, 1971), p. 208. In Chicago, blacks owned 3 of 45 groceries, 4 of 15 service establishments, and 8 of 49 furniture stores on State Street. Gary Hunter, " 'Don't Buy from Where You Can't Work': Black Urban Boycott Movements During the Depression, 1929–1941" (Ph.D. dissertation, University of Michigan, 1977), p. 52. For a good discussion of the Chicago efforts, see Hunter.

4. Harlem Housewives League, "The Harlem Housewives League," Report [1931?], pp. 1–2, NUL papers, series 4, box. 32.

5. NYUL et al., "Employment Mass Meeting," pp. 2–4, 9, quotation, p. 10; "Relief for Harlem," *Dunbar News*, 17 December 1930, p. 1. NAACP: Hunter, p. 48.

6. *Harlem Business Men's Bulletin* 1 (March 1931): 1–3. Advertisement: *American and West Indian News*, 19 January 1929, p. 5, Black Newspapers collection, box 1, Schomburg Archives, New York City. August Meier and Elliott Rudwick, "The Origins of Nonviolent Direct Action in Afro-American Protest: A Note on Historical Discontinuities," in Meier and Rudwick, eds., *Along the Color Line* (New York, 1976), pp. 346, 380. E. Franklin Frazier, "Some Effects of the Depression on the Negro in Northern Cities," *Science and Society* 2 (Fall 1938): 496. Johnson: sermon given 8 April 1934, printed in John Johnson, *Harlem, the War and Other Addresses* (New York, 1942), pp. 62, 68.

7. William Muraskin, "The Harlem Boycott of 1934 and Its Aftermath" (M.A. thesis, Columbia University, 1966), pp. 11–12; Melville Weiss, " 'Don't Buy Where You Can't Work': An Analysis of Consumer Action Against Employment Discrimination in Harlem, 1934–1940" (M.A. thesis, Columbia University, 1941), p. 61. The *Crisis* presented a debate on the merits of picketing and boycotting that raises many of these points. Vera Johns (pro), George Schuyler (con), "To Boycott or Not to Boycott," *Crisis* 41 (September 1934): 258–60, 274. Businessmen: Melville Weiss, p. 62.

8. Johns and Schuyler, p. 274. The NLC did not participate in the coalition until the end of the decade.

9. Mark Naison, "Communism and Black Nationalism in the Depression: The Case of Harlem," *Journal of Ethnic Studies* 2 (Summer 1974): 26–29; NYUL, "Newsletter," 12 November 1940, p. 2, NUL papers, series 4, box 33; Nancy Weiss, *National Urban League: 1910–1940* (New York, 1974), pp. 306–7. League strategy: Ira de Augustine Reid and T. Arnold Hill, "The Forgotten Tenth," Pamphlet, May 1933, p. 6, Columbia University Social Work Library, New York City. The league used similar tactics in other black areas.

10. James Hubert, testimony before Mayor's Commission on Conditions in Harlem, 20 April 1935, Mayor LaGuardia papers, new box 3770, Municipal Archives, New York City. "Conservative" quotation: Reid and Hill, p. 55.

11. Quotation: WPA Federal Writers' Project, *New York Panorama* (New York, 1938), p. 148. NAACP Minutes, William Pickens' papers, box 16, Schomburg Archives; Harvard Sitkoff, *A New Deal for Blacks* (New York, 1978), p. 249.

12. William Imes, Testimony before Mayor's Commission on Conditions in Harlem [1935], LaGuardia papers, new box 3770; "Blumstein's to Hire Negro Clerks," *New York Age*, 4 August 1934, p. 9. The *Age* reports Manley's group as the Harlem Women's Association, while Hunter places her in the Harlem Housewives League.

13. The history and activities of the Citizens' League are discussed in Muraskin; Melville Weiss; Hunter, as well as in the primary sources cited here. Names of participating groups taken from Citizens' League for Fair Play flyer advocating Blumstein's boycott, Schomburg Archives. The NAACP considered a shift toward more activist tactics in 1933, but decided instead to continue its focus on the judicial process. Hunter, p. 63.

14. Hunter, pp. 85–89, for Hamid (in Chicago known as Bishop Conshankin). The *Defender* and the Urban League refused to participate in the Chicago efforts. Ultimately, Chicago blacks won 10,261 jobs: Hunter, p. 299. Hunter claims it was Hamid who prompted

the organization of Harlem's Citizens' League; Effa Manley, shocked at the ferocity of Hamid's rhetoric, asked Reverend Johnson to organize a "respectable" jobs campaign. Hunter, p. 183. Hamid: Wilbur Young, Federal Writers' Program, New York City, "Activities of Bishop Amiru Al-Mu-Minin Sufi A. Hamid," n.d., pp. 1–2, papers of the WPA, Federal Writers' Program. "Negroes of New York," box 1, Schomburg Archives; Claude McKay, *Harlem: Negro Metropolis* (New York, 1940), pp. 185–85; Charles Franklin, *The Negro Labor Unionist of New York* (New York, 1936), p. 135; Muraskin, pp. 1–4. "Ira Kemp Insists He Will Send One Harlemite to Congress," *Amsterdam News*, 13 November 1937, Crosswaith papers, additions, box 2, Schomburg Archives. Clashes: *New York Age*, 13 August 1932. Hamid's group was sometimes called the Negro Industrial *and* Clerical Alliance.

15. Kemp: "Kemp Insists." John Johnson, sermon given 4 August 1934, in *Harlem, the War and Other Addresses*, pp. 62, 68. Note that the issue was identified as that of women obtaining jobs.

16. Imes testimony; Franklin, p. 130; Mayor's Commission on Conditions in Harlem, L. M. Blumstein, Interview [1935], p. 1, LaGuardia papers, box 33; Federal Writers' program, New York City [Ottley and Weatherby?], "I Too Sing America," n.d., p. 2, WPA, Federal Writers' Program, "Negroes of New York," box 4; Roi Ottley and William Weatherby, *The Negro in New York: An Informal Social History, 1626–1940* (New York, 1967; reprinted from the Federal Writers' Project ed.), pp. 281–82; Roi Ottley, *New World A-Coming* (Boston, 1943), pp. 114–15; Charles Lawrence, "Negro Organizations in Crisis: Depression, New Deal, World War II" (Ph.D. dissertation, Columbia University, 1952), pp. 284–85; Muraskin, pp. 9–11, 13; Melville Weiss, pp. 58–59; Mark Naison, *Communists in Harlem During the Depression* (Urbana, Ill., 1983), pp. 115–19. The progress of the pickets can be followed in the *New York Age*. See, for example: "Blumstein's Bans Negro Clerks," 26 May 1934, p. 1; "Negro Clerks for 125th Street Store," 9 June 1934, p. 1 (Koch's Department Store); "Pickets to Continue Activity in Front of L. M. Blumstein Co. Store," 16 June 1934, p. 1; "Blumstein's Said to Be Weakening as Citizens' Committed Pushes Boycott," 23 June 1934, p. 1; "Harlem's Campaign for Jobs Gets Added Support," 30 June 1934, p. 1; "Push Fight on Blumstein's," 7 July 1934, pp. 1–2; " 'Blumstein's Must Go!' Shouted by 500 Harlemites at Meeting for Citizens' League," 16 July 1934, pp. 1, 3; "Blumstein's Patrons Assaulted," 21 July 1934, p. 1; "Parade and Mass Meeting Set to Climax Boycott Against the Blumstein 125th Street Store," 28 July 1934, p. 1; "Blumstein's to Hire Negro Clerks," 4 August 1934, pp. 1, 9; "Honor Roll of Pickets in 125th Street Boycott," 4 August 1934, p. 9.

17. Larry Greene, "Harlem in the Great Depression: 1928–1936" (Ph.D. dissertation, Columbia University, 1979), pp. 459, 462. Slave masters did not favor lighter-skinned slaves for aesthetic reasons only; often these slaves were in fact the master's children. "Negroes" quotation: "Renegade 'Boycott Committee' Runs Wild, Assaults Shoppers," *New York Age*, 22 September 1934, p. 1. HLU: "Kemp Insists"; Muraskin, pp. 49, 51–52. Incorporated in 1936. Power: Melville Weiss, pp. 70–71. For a defense of Hamid, Kemp, and Reid on the color issue, see Muraskin, pp. 39–41, 43 ("there is ample reason for assuming total sincerity on their [Kemp's and Reid's] part" because Reid was West Indian and a Garveyite, and Kemp dark and a Garveyite.)

18. Mr. Snyder, Interview, 22 April 1935, by R. J. McBride. LaGuardia papers, new box 33. Also see "Citizens' League for Fair Play to Continue Employment Fight," *New York Age*, 11 August 1934, pp. 1, 3, about Hamid; and "Picket Weisbecker's Store," *New York Age*, 25 August 1934, p. 1, about Kemp and Reid.

19. Bernard Deutsch, President, Board of Aldermen, to Mayor LaGuardia, 25 September 1934, LaGuardia papers, box 658. Merchants' claims: Myrtle Pollard, "Harlem As It Is" (B.B.A. thesis, City College of New York, 1936), p. 22 (interview with Mr. Blumstein and Mr. Berler, president of Koch's Department Store, July and August, 1935). "Renegade 'Boycott Committee' Runs Wild," p. 1.

20. "Racial Picketing Barred," *New York Times*, 1 November 1934, p. 12. The article noted it was the nation's first such decision. Similar decisions would be handed down in other cities, including Cleveland, Baltimore, and Newark. Hubert to Eunice Carter, 16 April 1935, LaGuardia papers, new box 3529. Muraskin, p. 48; Greene, pp. 455, 471; Ira Reid, "The Negro in the American Economic System," Report, 1 August 1940, p. 149, Carnegie-Myrdal study, Reid, vol. 1, Schomburg Archives; Melville Weiss, pp. 64–66; Franklin, p. 134. Johnson: Muraskin, p. 48. Rev. Imes called it "an unfortunate altercation among the elements that originally composed [the League]." Imes testimony.

21. "Plane Crash Kills Sufi Hamid," *New York Age*. 6 August 1938, p. 1; "Plane Crash Fatal to 'Harlem Hitler,' " *New York Times*. 1 August 1938, p. 1; Melville Weiss, pp. 75–77, 80; Franklin, pp. 131, 140–41; McKay, *Harlem*, pp. 133, 201; Muraskin, pp. 14–17, 33–38; Young, pp. 3–8. The Lerner Company brought the suit against Hamid's group.

22. Melville Weiss, p. 78; "I Too Sing America," p. 3; Greene, p. 472. Elsewhere: Hunter, pp. 120–21, 142.

23. Both quotations: Cecilia Saunders. Testimony before Mayor's Commission on Conditions in Harlem, 13 April 1935, LaGuardia papers, new box 3770.

24. Melville Weiss, p. 87. Elsewhere: Hunter, pp. 142, 146.

25. Hamid in court: McKay, *Harlem*, pp. 210–11. Hamid and anti-Semitism: Muraskin, p. 18; "Plane Crash Kills Sufi Hamid"; Ottley, p. 118; McKay, *Harlem*, p. 200; Hunter, p. 189. Complaints: see, for example, *Amsterdam News*, 29 September 1934, and 13 October 1934; *Jewish Day*, 22 September 1934; "Shopkeepers Are Heard," *New York Times*, 26 September 1934, p. 44 HLU: Ottley, pp. 119, 121–23; Charles Segal, representative of a committee of Eighth Avenue merchants, to Police Commissioner Lewis Valentine, 27 July 1938, LaGuardia papers, box 89. The speeches in question took place in "public addresses on Eighth Avenue between West 115th Street and West 116th Street" in 1938. Mayor La-Guardia responded with a sympathetic letter. Harlem Merchants' Association: merchants between 110th and 155th Streets, between St. Nicholas and Third Avenues. It claimed a membership of over 500, few of whom were black. Imes testimony. Crusade: "I Too Sing America," pp. 3, 4, 6. Communists and merchants: McKay, *Harlem*, pp. 195–96; Naison, *Communists*, pp. 102, 121–22.

26. The Sufi's defense: McKay, *Harlem*, pp. 198, 208. Bribery and pressure: Deutsch to LaGuardia; Franklin, p. 138; Ottley, p. 117.

27. "Job for Dewey" (editorial), *Amsterdam News*, 9 October 1937, p. 14. NLC and Owl Shoe Co.: [Crosswaith?] "Harlem Labor Union," notes, n.d., Negro Labor Committee papers box 28, Schomburg Archives; Deutsch to LaGuardia; Muraskin, pp. 46–48; Melville Weiss, pp. 71–72; Franklin, p. 138 (testimony from employees threatened by Hamid).

28. Arthur Reid, Interview with Muraskin, n.d., in Muraskin, pp. 32–33.

29. HLU organizer, Interview with Lawrence, 15 April 1943, in Lawrence, pp. 288–89.

30. Reid: Wendell Malliet, "Big Job Drive Seems Headed for the Rocks,"*Amsterdam News*, 29 October 1938, p. 11; Melville Weiss, p. 92. Crosswaith: Malliet, p. 11; Frank Crosswaith, Testimony before Mayor's Commission on Conditions in Harlem [1935], p. 46, LaGuardia papers, new box 3770.

31. Malliet, p. 11; Melville Weiss, p. 110.

32. Sitkoff, p. 249; NAACP minutes, n.d., William Pickens' papers, box 16; Naison, *Communists*, p. 59.

33. Naison, *Communists*, pp. 102, 108. Quotation: Adam Clayton Powell, Jr., "Soapbox," *Amsterdam News*, 30 October 1937, p. 13. James Ford's speech delivered at meeting of Joint Conference Against Discriminatory Practices, Abyssinian Baptist Church, New York, New York, 23 October 1935, pp. 4–7, LaGuardia papers, box 35 (quoted in Chapter 4), was referring specifically to participation in the "Don't Buy" campaign.

34. At Weisbecker's also the police stopped the picket line. "Open Fight on Weisbecker's," *Amsterdam News*, 15 June 1935 June 1935 (clipping), LaGuardia papers, new box 3538. Empire Cafeteria: "1,500 in Harlem Protest," *New York Times*, 1 September

1934, p. 17 (306 Lenox Ave.); Naison, *Communists*, pp. 100, 120, 122; Naison, "Communism," pp. 27–29; Alliance and UNIA: Melville Weiss, p. 67; Lawrence, p. 287; James Ford and Louis Sass, "Development of Work in the Harlem Section," *Communist* 14 (April, 1935): 313. Empire handbill: in LaGuardia papers, new box 3538. Franklin, p. 139.

35. Mayor's Commission: quoted in Alain Locke, "Harlem, Dark Weather-Vane," *Survey Graphic* 25 (August 1936): 460. Myrdal, p. 313; McKay, *Marlem*, pp. 210–11, 228; Hunter, pp. 131–42; Hubert, Testimony; Muraskin, p. 53; "Open Fight on Weisbecker's." The New Negro Alliance was a group of young students and lawyers in Washington, D.C., including William Hastie and Thurgood Marshall, who organized in 1933 to ensure equal access to government programs and private employment.

36. Sydney French, Federal Writers' Program, New York City, "Biographical Sketch of Rev. A. C. Powell, Jr.," 1939, pp. 3, 17, WPA, Federal Writers' Program, "Negroes of New York," box 1; Melville Weiss, p. 95; Neil Hickey and Ed Edwin, *Adam Clayton Powell and the Politics of Race* (New York, 1965), p. 53; Adam Clayton Powell, Jr., *Marching Blacks: An Interpretive History of the Rise of the Black Common Man* (New York, 1945), pp. 93, 96. Poor: Powell, *Marching Blacks*, p. 98; French, "Biographical Sketch," p. 96. The number of members was undoubtedly inflated, but certainly participation was enormous. Members: Matthew Eder, Secretary, Uptown Chamber of Commerce, to Mayor LaGuardia, 20 July 1938, p. 1, LaGuardia papers, box 89; Charles Collier, Jr., New York Urban League, "Report of Industrial Secretary for Board Meeting, May 11, 1938," pp. 3, 4 NUL papers, series 4, box 33. Chicago moderates organized similarly in the Council of Negro Organizations. It claimed 100,000 members, and also launched mass demonstrations and pickets after the *New Alliance* decision. Often working with the Negro Labor Relations League, a group of younger blacks committed to improving black employment opportunities, black Chicagoans won important victories such as the placement of black managers in the local newspapers. Hunter, pp. 270–71. These efforts across the country were not isolated or separate; just as the *Whip's* editor helped spark Harlem's efforts, Powell's address to the NLRL in 1938 spurred Chicago blacks to rejoin the struggle.

37. Crosswaith to LaGuardia, 30 April 1938, LaGuardia papers, box 89; Melville Weiss, p. 101.

38. "Consolidated Gas Co. to Put 4 Negroes to Work As Clerks," *New York Age*, 7 May 1938, p. 1; Alyse Abrams, Federal Writers' Program, New York City, "Rev. Adam Clayton Powell, Jr." [1939?], p. 1, WPA, Federal Writers' Program, "Negroes of New York," box 1; Melville Weiss, pp. 97–99; "I Too Sing America," p. 17; Ottley and Weatherby, pp. 268, 288; Ottley, p. 228–29; Hickey and Edwin, p. 54; Reid, "The Negro in the American Economic System," p. 154; Miriam Carpenter II, "Some Aspects of the Depression on Negroes" (Master's thesis, Columbia University, 1937), pp. 50–51; N.Y.S. Temporary Commission on the Condition of the Urban Colored Population, *Second Report*, Legislative Document #69 (Albany, 1939), p. 64. Powell quotation: "Negroes Win Jobs with Utility in Harlem When Anti-Bias Group Threatens Boycott," *New York Times*, 29 April 1938, p. 8. "Job Discrimination on Negroes Charged," *New York Times*, 2 November 1938, p. 25; NUL, "Number Please? Employment of Negro Workers in the Telephone Industry in 44 Cities," Report, January 1946, p. 5, Columbia University Social Work Library. For more information on phone company, see Venus Green, "The Impact of Technology upon Women's Work in the Telephone Industry, 1880–1980" (Ph.D. dissertation, Columbia University, 1990). There is no evidence the jamming threat was carried out.

39. Copy of this letter (on Abyssinian Baptist Church letterhead), dated 28 April 1938, sent to Mayor LaGuardia from Frank Crosswaith, LaGuardia papers, box 89. Pickets also reported in "Negroes Win Jobs."

40. "Memorandum of Understanding Between the Uptown Chamber of Commerce and the Greater New York Co-ordinating Committee for Employment, in Relation to the Employment of Negroes in Harlem Stores," 20 July 1938, LaGuardia papers, box 89, and NUL papers, series 4, box 6. See also "Negroes Win Help in Fight for Jobs," *New York Times*, 28

August 1938, Section IV, p. 10; "Merchants Sign Employment Pact," *New York Age*, 16 July 1938, pp. 1, 5.

41. Employees: NYUL, "Annual Report, 1938," New York Public Library; Melville Weiss, p. 102. HLU: "Harlem Emerges as Stronghold of Trade Unionism," *New York Post*, 13 May 1938, p. 6; Melville Weiss, pp. 104, 106–8, 111–14. Complaints continued to trickle into the Attorney General's office until 1946. In that year, Crosswaith was called to testify at an investigation into the HLU. The problems may have continued still longer, but no information is available for later dates. Negro Labor Committee, "HLU."

42. Powell, *Marching Blacks*, p. 101; Hunter, p. 278. This was less than a total victory, though, as most of the jobs did not in fact go to clerks but to unskilled workers.

43. Hickey and Edwin, p. 60; Powell, *Marching Blacks*, p. 99; Meier and Rudwick, p. 32; NYUL, "Executive Board Minutes," 17 December 1937, pp. 2–3, Arthur Schomburg papers, box 16, Schomburg Archives. By the middle of the 1940s, blacks held clerical and sales positions in Alexander's, Macy's, Lane Bryant, Lord and Taylor, Bloomingdale's, and B. Altman. LeRoy Jeffries, NUL, "Integration of Negroes in Department Stores," Report, July 1946, Columbia University Social Work Library.

44. Hunter, p. 285.

45. For an eloquent argument that black political action in the New Deal period did bring changes in race relations, presaging the modern civil rights movement, see Sitkoff.

Consumerism Since World War II

The 'Work' Ethic and 'Leisure' Activity:
The Hot Rod in Post-War America

H. F. Moorhouse

Some Orthodoxies in the Study of 'Work'

In post-war America full employment and the changes associated with a general rise in real incomes caused a number of analysts to ponder the nature of work, its meanings, and its effects on the individual. Quite often the targets of this attention were workers in the automobile industry, and it was in this period that labour in automobile factories (this labour very narrowly conceived) was elevated to an iconic status, such that labour on the track or line became, somehow, the explicit or implicit model of what most modern work is like, or would soon be like, and in which major guidelines for investigation were provided such as repetition, boredom, degradation, de-skilling, and so on, all spun round a central thread of alienation.[1] Such studies helped establish an orthodox tradition in the social analysis of work which is still dominant today, given added weight, if not much more depth, by a renewed Marxist interest in the labour process in the last decade.[2]

One of the largest of these post-war studies was carried out by Kornhauser. His book, pregnantly titled *The Mental Health of the Industrial Worker*, emerged out of interviews with over four hundred male Detroit workers and their spouses carried out in 1953–4.[3] Kornhauser, like so many other students had no doubts that 'work' was synonymous with job, or of its significance for the individual:

> clearly work not only serves to produce goods and services, it also performs essential psychologistical functions. It operates as a great stabilising, integration, ego satisfying, central influence in the pattern of each person's life. If the job fails to fulfil these needs of the personality, it is problematic whether men can find adequate substitutes to provide a sense of significance and achievement, purpose and justification for their lives.[4]

Such confident proclamations underpin many other, much more recent, studies of work, its meanings, and effects, but Kornhauser departed somewhat from the orthodox tradition in that he at least tried to establish whether his workers found 'compensations' in other aspects of their lives for what he believed to be their routinised work. However, his search led him to conclude that only 10–15% of his sample were engaged in hobbies or pastimes which:

are of genuine current significance in their lives as sources of pride and enjoyment.[5]

The destructive effects of modern work were not, it seemed, checked by other activity. Kornhauser, despite his excursion, was able to swing back into the path of orthodox analysis by deploying more assumptions. He exemplifies an approach to the study of work which is both quick to assume the crucial existential significance of some conceptually unclear 'work', and also demands that, if *other* activities are to enter into consideration as possible sources of pride, fulfillment, identify formation, and affirmation, they must pass the most stringent scrutiny as to their *moral* worth. The dismissive use of terms like 'hobby', 'pastime', 'amusements' is indicative here, and Kornhauser's analysis abounds with phrases like '*serious* reading', '*shallow* routine pastimes', '*genuine* self-expression,' '*challenging* quests for knowledge', and the like, where an undisclosed and undiscussed moral evaluation merges with what purports to be detached appraisal, and operates so as to exclude various categories of action as being unworthy sources of meanings, purpose, and self-definition. So Kornhauser excluded that considerable percentage of auto-workers who insisted that all their spare time was devoted to house, car or garden. He excluded those who referred to gambling or drinking, and the 20% who alluded to sports (including hunting). All these were joined by those who said visiting or TV-watching was their main leisure activity. Kornhauser's residue was composed only of the boat-builders, violin-makers, and short-story writers. Such value judgements, concealed in commonsense concepts and taken-for-granted connections, reek of the power of the 'work ethic' which may, or may not, have penetrated the minds of most workers but is certainly lodged, as a moral ideal, in much of what purports to be the analysis of work and its meanings.

This criticism of Kornhauser's book is intended to reveal a quite widespread set of assumptions which underpin most orthodox study in this field, and which serve to simplify the real puzzle of issues which lie around work, its meanings and effects. The most important of these assumptions are that:
(1) 'work' is paid labour;
(2) it is just this work that is the crucible in which social identity is forged;
(3) the dominant values of capitalist society did, and do, without much equivocation, stress just this work as the critical area in which male life is played out.
Feminist critiques, it is true, have shaken this set of assumptions somewhat, but still the weight of their objections have not forced most analysts to really think what they mean by the concept 'work', and to assess the variety of values surrounding that term. Recently, a critique has been developing within, as it were, the sociology of work itself.[6] In their books Rose and Pahl both point

to the fallacy of treating 'work' as equivalent to the regular paid labour of, usually, men and both point out that what are all too often claimed to be 'new' attitudes or 'departures' from 'old' values invariably rest on comparisons with an implied or idealised past based on no or inadequate evidence as to exactly what such attitudes or values were in earlier periods.

Rose concentrates on the issue of whether some 'work ethic' *ever* affected the behavior of most workers. This scepticism is most refreshing, but his analysis does tend to dwindle in force because his attention is directed at paid labour and so other activities, other labour, does not attract the careful scrutiny he applies to the meanings of 'work' as conventionally understood. Indeed, he is led to argue that a 'work ethic' cannot now represent truly bourgeois values since modern economic performance depends on avid consumption. The activities of the modern sales effort:

> reinforce a broader hedonistic frame of mind which is directly at odds with the bourgeois doctrine of deferred gratification.[7]

and he refers to:

> an immensely competent advertising and promotion industry whose creative elite possess every skill needed to reassure people of their personal right to self-indulgence, to frequent escape from social obligation, and work commitments, to an undue concern with time, or from worries over budgeting.[8]

In such quotes Rose reveals that he has not entirely escaped the frameworks imposed by the assumptions of the dominant tradition. He certainly simplifies the accomplishments of the groups in modern capitalism who work with and on culture and symbols, *and* assumes they produce an undifferentiated, one-dimensional ideology of easy indulgence in leisure time.

Pahl's text concentrates on discussing the various types of work that were and are done in society, and makes a useful distinction between employment (paid labour) and work, which is conceived of as a very broad category encompassing all productive activities (paid and unpaid), reproductive activity, and some consumption. Such a broadening of the key term has great implications for orthodox study, for if 'work' is the place where 'man makes himself' and if, 'work' is an unclear concept, with many dimensions, then it is by no means clear which *work* is to be afforded centrality in identity creation, or perhaps all are important, or perhaps relative weights change through time or through a life. Each work may have its own ideologies and preferred meanings which can vary through time and space. Pahl catches part of what is at issue here in his concluding remarks that:

> the work ethic is alive and well: people enjoy working and there is plenty to do. Often they may not particularly enjoy their employment.[9]

However, Pahl does concentrate on examining the work done and tends to neglect questions of meanings and associated ideologies, and occasionally suggests that the existential significance of various types of work can be illuminated by quantitative measures, whereas what is of the essence here is the varying quality of labour times. Moreover, Pahl's stress that work (in all its forms) is a strategy of households directed to a project of 'getting by' and 'cosiness' means that he both neglects independent, individual work strategies, as he recognises,[10] and tends to adopt too instrumental a view of what work is done for. So he has little to say about work in relation to expressive needs, self-presentation, and symbolic display. He does appreciate that such labour is done and is promoted in society:

> the development of consumption as a form of work is, perhaps, the dominant new element that capitalism has imposed on household work strategies.[11]

but he does not investigate the qualitative significance of such work and relegates mention of it to footnotes or throwaway lines. And, as with Rose, Pahl tends to assume that advertising and marketing always link to 'new' needs and 'new' commodities.

So, even these important new critiques of the orthodox tradition do not really touch on all of the important issues involved in recasting the study of work. In particular, if there are many *types* of *work*, and the meanings of each can vary, then there is a great need to focus on the way people learn about work and are socialised to various meanings. For there is no intrinsic meaning to any piece of labour. Meanings have to be attached, sustained, promulgated and learned. Now most analyses, and, again, Kornhauser's is a typical example, rather vaguely assume that the dominant values of capitalist society do present some 'work ethic' which is both smooth and unequivocal in tone, and paramount in the messages emanating from the major institutions of society.

Neither of these assumptions is obviously correct and, at a bare minimum, students of the meanings of work need to be alive to a diversity of dominant sources presenting rather different messages about work. They need to be aware also that while dominant values will provide a good deal of input, albeit in a more complex and contradictory fashion than is often suggested, other sources exist with their own institutional supports which will mediate and mix with dominant views. Specifically, class, gender, and ethnic cultures will make complex inputs, as will quite precise occupational ideologies formed in varying workplaces which will have both formal and informal expressions: from union rule books to workgroup norms. Acceptance of even this point makes it clear that the meanings of work are not likely to be neat and simple, or form some uncomplicated 'ethic' but rather likely to be jumbled and variegated, so that any individual has a whole range of types and levels of meanings on which to draw, and with which to understand or appreciate the labour they are doing at any particular moment. The notion of 'a work ethic' as central to the experience of work—even when this is understood as paid labour—simplifies this issue since it picks out only a few of the heterogenous meanings which circle around labour and promotes these as 'the most important'.

One of the fullest descriptions of the work ethic is provided by Rodgers when considering nineteenth-century America:

The central premise of the work ethic was that work was the core of moral life.
Work made men useful in a world of economic scarcity. It staved off the doubts
and temptations that preyed on idleness, it opened the way to deserved wealth and
status, it allowed one to put the impress of mind and skill on the material world.[12]

This formulation is preferable to most, if only because Rodgers understands
that worry about the dangers of sheer idleness form part of dominant ideologies
about work. In all too many analyses the 'work ethic' has been slimmed down
to equate to a craft ethic or professional ethic—work as a vocation—in which,
it is argued, the job should yield a sense of mastery, control over materials and
techniques, command of technology, an engagement of hand *and* brain in solv-
ing problems and so on. This then becomes linked to another aspect, as alluded
to by Rodgers, that the job should allow the opportunity for development in
personality, *and*, though the rather imprecise connections are usually quickly
skated over here, an opportunity for advance and mobility in material terms.

The problem with this kind of formulation of the 'work ethic' is that it
posits far too simple a relation between objective task and subjective perception: the most routinised and paced paid labour requires some worker's
knowledge to be applied if the task is to be done in the optimum way, and
thus virtually *all* jobs provide the raw material for workers to regard themselves as 'skilled', even if this is not institutionalised. Pride can be obtained
from doing *any* job, even the most menial, well, in the eyes of bosses or other
workers. The respect of significant others in the workplace can be what is
sought and valued, and this does not depend on the abstract quality of the
task to be done.[13] Or work can gain meanings by being defined as a sacrifice,
through which the individual yields himself or herself to unpleasant tasks or
routine in order to meet obligations to others—usually wife, husband or children, and so gain respect.[14]

However, and more crucially, the tendency to align 'a work ethic' with a
craft job ethic has meant that there are numerous meanings around work
which have received—from history, sociology, or Marxism—little attention.
Even Rodgers' formulation misses a lot of these. The meanings of work which
circulate around its role in marking passages in the life cycle—adulthood, retirement—is a good example. Others concern meanings which arise out of the
job's location in quite particular contexts: thus purpose and identity can be
summoned out of working for a well-known firm, or in a glamorous location,
or from being linked with broad ideological notions of 'scientific progress', or
from being associated with a desirable product.[15] Car workers call on all of
these to locate their work and infuse it with meaning. Nor has work as an area
for the experience and display of sheer strength, endurance and courage been
much discussed, yet, for males at least, such values are of some importance
and by no means nestle easily with the craft ideal. Much hard, routine, labour
is infused with meaning because it allows a physical confrontation. Life in any
industrial concern is fraught with danger. Many labour processes routinely
produce potentially dangerous incidents. The radical response to this is to

analyse why such processes have come to be in the service of profit maximisation, but much less analysed is the response of workers to such recurrent situations, and the way danger and bravery, drawing on notions of masculinity, become important in the meanings surrounding work.[16] Men can gain pride, respect, confirm identity, by pitting themselves against fear or furnace.

So, and while the others I have mentioned certainly do not exhaust the stock, there are many ideologies which lurk around work and which provide meanings, and only some of these are caught in orthodox appeals to the power of some 'work ethic.' Clearly then the actual position confronting the student of work is extremely complex, for there are many types of *work* in a capitalist society and many ethics or ideologies about work. The task has to be to trace the ethics that apply to different kinds of work, for only if some activities can be shown to be intrinsically trivial and devoid of ideological justifications, should they be written-off by social analysis as inadequate sources of pride, identity, and social understanding. In the rest of this paper I want to consider these matters by looking at the automobile *in use* (where it is usually ignored), at the automobile as an object in consumption. I have adopted this strategy to try to indicate what meanings are evoked there, what values, beliefs, and cultural injunctions surround the motor car in this area of life and what, if anything, this suggests to us about the definition of work, and the social location of the 'work ethic'. The aspect of the automobile in use I want to consider is its incarnation as 'hot rod', but I must stress this is only an example of a host of other automobile-related 'leisure' subcultures which could be scrutinised, all of which have their own institutions, literature, heroes, calendars, and their own ideologies which often seem to draw on what is called the 'work ethic' but which, in hobbies, enthusiasms, interests, and passions, are not related to paid labour. So the hot-rod subculture is far from unique or odd.

The Hot-Rod Subculture

In 1947 *Fortune* magazine estimated that while real incomes had risen by 40% in the 1940–7 period, discretionary spending was up 160%.[17] In the next decade credit for the purchase of automobiles rose by 800%, and in the 1950s general consumer indebtedness rose three times as fast as personal incomes.[18] By 1955 around one-third of spending units in the *lowest* quintile of incomes owned a car,[19] and by 1958 5.9 million teenagers had a licence to drive and around one and a half million teenagers owned cars.[20] In short, the years after the war were that period of affluence when most Americans became comfortable and well-off compared to their parents or to pre-war standards. The automobile was the symbol of this change and came to a new peak as commodity *and* as a cultural symbol.

In just this period the 'hot rod' became significant in the lives of a large number of (mainly young) Americans. A culture was created around the term with definite values, interests, a special vocabulary, and a variety of informal and formal institutions: used car lots, races, clubs, events, speed-shops, maga-zines, local and national associations. The term was used for abuse and admi-ration in the news media of the time, while the cinema, radio, TV, and books drew on the culture for background and for symbolism, refining and spread-ing its messages.[21]

The main theme of the culture was the modification of 'Detroit iron', the 'lead barges' which were the American production car. There was both a tech-nical and an aesthetic aspect to such modification. The aura which hung around the culture, and its presentation in the media certainly was that of a 'hot' car, a speedy vehicle engaged in racing, often illegally on public high-ways. But, in fact, engineering and ornamentation, the desire to go faster and the wish to look sharper, were combined or separated in all manner of ways to provide a variety of sub-cultures, styles, and specialisms. And, of course, like any other activity, there was a continuum of commitment: from simply bolting a few shop-bought accessories onto your car, to creating, through one's own labour over many months, a streamlined dry-lake special.[22] The horizontal and vertical dimensions of attachment to the hot-rod culture provided many niches for individual placement and many permitted the exercise of skilled manual labour and intense mental work of design, costing, and racing.

The ethos of this culture, expressed through the specialist magazines and books of post-war America, is not one of redolent passivity but rather of ur-gent prescriptions to labour, to strive, to plan, to exercise skill, to compete, to succeed, to risk: themes like those supposedly typical of some traditional 'work ethic' but now directed to unpaid time.

The main myth of the culture is of buying a junked Ford for a few dollars, of reclaiming various parts from it, and with these and some other standard and custom accessories reassembling, via a great deal of hard and skilled labour, a high performance vehicle.

Jaderquist's manual *The New How To Build Hot Rods*, first published in 1957 and through to its sixth printing by 1977 is, like other books, full of pic-tures revealing how to do it yourself. The emphasis is on study, problem solv-ing, initiative, making do and saving money by 'knuckle scraping' and 'back breaking' in an overall tone that would have heartened Benjamin Franklin:

> Tools, remember, are only extensions of your hands, arms and fingers. Unless the original will and muscle is there, the finest tools in the world are useless.[23]

In Horsley's *Hot Rod It: And Run For Fun* of 1957 the bias of the text and photography is on the never-ending business of understanding the machine, especially the engine, in theory and practice. This kind of theme coexists with messages which stress, not occupational success, but, say, that working on your hot rod after paid labour is a source of satisfaction whatever your occu-pation, or that all rodders form a special community of interest, or that there is a relation between your rod and personal style and identity. Mass-produced automobiles, it is held, are standardised as the result of an inevitable compro-mise: they are, therefore, nobody's 'dream machine', whereas:

Your rod expresses you in more than just looks. Its quality of workmanship and roadability, as well as its power advertise your status and power as a rodder. You want to be able to point to your car with pride and say, 'want to take a ride'.[24]

In this chapter I want to focus on *Hot Rod* magazine, the pivot of this sub-culture.[25] My material is drawn from reading each monthly issue of this magazine from January 1948 to December 1960. This periodical took a very active role in trying to control and shape the nature of 'hot rodding'. For, in post-war America, this term referred to two distinct activities. In its common and mass-media usage it pointed to a highly visible, relatively affluent, teenage lifestyle which seemed to turn on drive-ins, noise, jalopies held together with chewing gum, and 'dragging the strip'. The phrase *also* denoted a much less visible, less publicised, technical and achievement-oriented amateur sport of automobile racing against the clock which had developed on the dry lakes of California from the 1920s and which had its own organisations. This small group of often older men (especially as war veterans returned) felt threatened by the mass-media use of the term, and the moral panics that ensued. This group feared that threatened action by legislators and authorities against the street-racing teenagers might curtail their rather serious and all-American activity. They met with police, civic officials, and parent–teachers' associations to put their views, and *Hot Rod* was set up, in large measure, as a voice for respectable rodding. Its publishers and early writers were all lakes enthusiasts.

The magazine was first published in January 1948 with a print run of 5,000 copies, by 1950 200,000 copies were produced each month, and by 1956 it was promoted as the world's top-selling automobile magazine with half a million copies sold each month and a claimed readership of well over a million.[26] In short, this magazine was a great commercial success and soon outran its initial constituency. As sales spread across the USA, and as the lake-beds of California cracked under increasing use, it was in the van of creating a new participant and spectator sport—drag racing—which became what, it asserted, real hot rodders did and wanted to do. It had very close links with the National Hot Rod Association, founded in 1951, which was, and is, the major organisation in the big sport of drag racing which, in the mid 1970s, ran events catering for four and a half million spectators and half a million (mostly amateur) competitors.[27]

This kind of ephemeral literature which hangs around free-time pursuits is rarely examined *but* on the numbers of readers alone I think I can stake some claim as to the worth of looking at this magazine as an important vehicle of value transmission. If that is granted, and we might well think that such material may be read with much *closer* attention than a lot of other literary items which are given much greater prominence in social analysis, then I will add that *Hot Rod* is but one example of a host of other special interest magazines which did, and do, exist and in which 'leisure' is presented as a very serious matter indeed.[28] If, as I have argued, students of the meaning of work need to trace the actual type and diffusion of ideas about a variety of types of work, then it might be as well if analysts laid to one side of the texts of Franklin,

Alger and Weber, and picked up other examples of this type of the popular literature of contemporary capitalism.

To help in this process I want to review the messages, themes, values, and ideas that this magazine promoted and repeated. In fact there were a variety, but a large part of its message was taken up with the ideologies of activity, involvement, enthusiasm, craftmanship, learning by doing, experimental development, display, and creativity, all of these circulating around the motor car in unpaid time. I have traced this message as it related to mechanical labour, but it could as easily be illustrated in other aspects of hot-rod activity, about fuel for example:

on page sixteen is the first of twelve enlightening articles on fuel and carburation.[29]

Or driving, for many articles urged that, whether on the strips or streets, a true hot rodder should be a top class driver: knowledgeable, cool, able to marry mental awareness to manual dexterity to foresee and forestall danger. So what follows is but one facet of an ideology covering many other rod-related activities. Hot Rod's conception of its younger readers was that they were a group of normal males who, being American, were attracted to mechanics, tinkering, competition, and the search for success. Because these combined speed and the automobile, readers were always on the brink of lawlessness. They could succumb to temptation. They must not be allowed to be idle. They must have the right path constantly set before them. They required leadership, organisation, and a sympathetic control. The magazine tried to accomplish this in part via the individuals and cars it featured as the measures of success in this 'leisure' pursuit and in part by its overall ideological tone.

This magazine does not present hot rodding as an activity for the idle or for the spectator; it is not about triviality or passiveness or easy hedonism. The bottom line is that nothing good comes easy:

Stuart has been developing the same engine, a 1934 Ford for the last eight years. He has constantly improved it and hopes to improve it even more in the future. At one lakes meet a rod went through the block, shattering a four by eight inch hole in the side of the engine. He salvaged the pieces, welded them together and welded that piece into the hole. Performance was not altered.[30]

Almost every month there is a story about someone who works several hours a day, 300 days a year, on their rod. Nor can it or should it be a matter of money. In 1949 when the editor asked for snapshots of readers' cars to be sent to the journal for publication he remarked:

By the term 'good car' we do not necessarily mean one that has thousands of dollars sunk into it. Most of us cannot afford that. We do mean a car that reflects good workmanship and ingenuity.[31]

The hot rodders' project is presented as a serious one. Indeed the magazine argued it was just this that distinguished the true hot rod ('the million of us') from the 'shot rod', i.e. those cars which have only the surface appearance of what an ignorant public think is a hot rod, owned by people who 'do not burn the midnight oil', whereas:

> A real hot rod is a car that is lending itself to experimental development for the betterment of safety, operation and performance, not merely a stripped down or highly decorated car of any make, type of description or one driven by a teenager.[32]

These kind of messages spill out of the numerous technical articles about engines, components, fuels, etc.; through DIY pictorial strips; in the assessments of featured cars; in stories of individual achievement; in the technical question and answer section; on the readers' letters pages; and in the editorials. So in January 1951 when the magazine tries to get a hot rod (with a truck engine) into the Indianapolis 500 track race, it muses:

> Whether it qualifies or not, the car will still long be remembered as a tribute to American ingenuity and the average man's desire to build something of his own design, with his own hands.[33]

The emphasis was not simply on working with metal but on theoretical understanding, scientific knowledge, and designing skill:

> In many cases you can improvise, but when you can't, take it easy. Save your muscles for the gym and use your head in the garage.[34]

An outline of some typical articles may indicate what I mean. In November 1948 the magazine printed the first part in a series of 'Building a Hot Rod'. The titles of the successive monthly articles were:
(1) Glossary of terms
(2) Classification and selection
(3) Running gear part I
(4) Running gear part II
(5) Power plant part I
(6) Power plant part II
(7) Power plant part III
(8) Power plant part IV
(9) Roadster completion
If this does not give the flavour, then consider the subheadings of the Power Plant Part I article:[35]
(1) Disassembly of engine
(2) Inspecting and reboring block
(3) Increase in power output
(4) Reasons for porting and relieving
(5) Methods of porting
(6) Methods of relieving
And so it goes on through the years with articles on 'Crankshaft stroking: more engine torque and how to get it'[36] one month and 'Do a better valve job'[37] another. Such knowledge was not regarded as important in its own right. What mattered was its application. The magazine had a particular philosophy both on the reasons for American economic success and on the importance of applying and testing knowledge in a practical, down-to-earth way. It argued that the true American genius was to translate and improve on a basic invention and:

American youth is the most advanced among the nations of the world in mechanical know-how, the attribute which has kept this country foremost in progress. Building cars, studying engines and learning basic mechanics, the essence of hot rod activity, is one of the greatest contributing factors to such progress.[38]

This is a theme constantly stressed in the Korean War period. In 1951 an editorial reflected that hot rodders were doing the job in the motor pools at the war front and in the training camps:

We take pride in the fact that we possess great mechanical know-how. In a measure, the very essence of American armed might rests in our ability to maintain technological superiority over the rest of the world.[39]

The mass media was proud of this but was quick to condemn 'the schools of experience' in which this pre-eminence had its birth. It was not a natural trait nor could it be learned from textbooks, rather:

young Americans must learn to do by *doing*, there is no substitute or shortcut for actual experience.[40]

This stress on learning by practice and not via books, was a repeated theme in the magazine and was underlined as a characteristic, indeed crucial, American trait. In general, the magazine was sceptical about 'experts with slide-rules' who could impose restraints on invention and imagination. In 1952 it reported how two rodders were trying to create a car capable of 300 miles an hour. Many said this is impossible:

But it is an accepted fact that hot rodders don't always *know* what can't be done, so they go ahead and *do* the impossible anyway.[41]

The hot rodder was the practically-oriented underdog who could exasperate theorists and could match Detroit. The Motorama car show of 1954 provided an opportunity to show that:

backyard built cars and the people who build them are capable of matching or surpassing the world's finest.[42]

When individuals were featured it was as enthusiasts or mechanics, their paid occupations were either not mentioned or mentioned in passing—they were not significant. What mattered was their absorption in the activity, the technical details of their car, their sweat, and dedication to their task. The theme of this kind of article was on the unity of mental and manual labour. So when the magazine featured Fred Iges' roadster in February 1950, after plenty of technical data, the article ran:

Using a 1925 Model T body, Fred filled and smoothed all the contours and added many original ideas to the lines of the car. The turtle back was welded to the back of the body and leaded in smooth. The deck lid is made of sheet aluminum to save weight, and the joined edges have been filled with a special cold solder. A metal worker by profession, Fred has done all of the body in his backyard garage. Faced with the problem of getting short louvres punched in the curved edges of the hood and side panels, Fred manufactured his own jig and dies and stamped the louvres himself. Power behind the dies was provided by use of a heavy hammer.[43]

This is a fair example of featured individuals. A craft-like approach to the task, attention to the smallest, apparently insignificant detail, was often held up as the route to success in building or racing, and was sometimes contrasted with attitudes found in paid labour. In 1948 an industrial designer praised hot rodding as:

> it encourages the development in our youngsters of the art of mechanical artisanship. This artisanship is seldom found in the auto-brotherhood. There is so much sloppy work performed in the great majority of garages that it becomes a rarity to see a mechanic who is proud of his work.[44]

Or in 1959:

> Incompetency among mechanics in garages and new car agencies has become a major problem for today's motorists.[45]

Akton Millar, dry-lakes veteran and elected official in hot rodders' associations presented a concentrated statement of the magazine's ethos in his article, 'Hot rods, I love 'em' in 1951. He never mentions his paid occupation, except to joke about being an infantry private in the war, but talks about his first hot rod:

> Working nights and Sundays, I spent approximately four months building my car and enjoying every minute of it while I learned many new angles to car construction which cannot be found in a book.

And goes on:

> I have always felt that successful participation in hot rod activities, as in any other form of activity is based on the age-old law of compensation in that the amount of effort one puts forward on a project determines the degree of education, fellowship and satisfaction which he may expect to enjoy in return. I have seen boys come into the organisation, compete in one or two meets and drop out because they found the competition too tough or the financial demands too great. Others work hard, sacrifice time and money, and remain in year after year eagerly awaiting the next event and the challenge it has to offer. One can compare the sport to a ladder; some take one step, others ten or more. But one thing is certain in all cases: the boys learn that there is a relationship between man and machine which cannot be found in any other sport. Words cannot describe the rewarding satisfaction of doing things with one's own hands, then seeing, hearing and feeling the gratifying results of hard labour and sacrifice. Nor can mere words ever convey the sensation that the hot rodder experiences when he gets behind the wheel of 200 plus horsepower and begins a run against the clock with the knowledge that he is about to demonstrate the union of speed and acceleration as personified in a hot rod of his own making.

Moreover:

> Progress within the Association makes it necessary for one to change ideas, methods and styles constantly if he wishes to keep pace with the top men.[46]

Generally *Hot Rod* was not averse to intellectual reflections or musings about what the activity 'signified' or 'meant', and such analysis often suggested to hot rodders that what they were involved in was a reworking of old values in new contexts. In 1951 it reprinted an article by Balsey (a postgraduate student of David Riesman's) from an academic journal (the only contemporary academic piece on this subculture),[47] and a year later it published a long article by Dr P. E. Siegle—once on the staff at the University of Illinois but then consultant psychologist to the Maremont Automotive Products Corporation. His article—'Psychological components of the hot rodder'[48]—related the sub-culture to a wider American culture which stressed initiative, competition, and free enterprise. It was about the :

> opportunity to make more and better things. The ideal dream is that of a man alone with his raw materials, using his ingenuity and know-how along with his industriousness to produce a better *thing*.

And Siegle goes on:

> There is an almost mystic quality to the picture of the young American boy working from scratch in the shop hoping to build a better hot rod. It fits with the American shibboleth of recognition for the ability to pull oneself up by the boot-straps. Hard work and luck are key ideas in the American success story.

Hot rodding allowed this. Indeed it was perhaps *more* in tune with the older virtues than was the modern 'conspicuous consumption' society where status came from the acquisition of goods and which was, anyway, frustrating and anxiety-provoking since competition was not clear-cut. Siegle also explained to his readers that rodding allowed an outlet for aggressions, and the achievement of mastery over machines, in a society where the relevance of older standards of personal success were by no means clear-cut. In Siegle's portrayal the hot-rod movement involved a more vital working out of basic cultural values than a rather flabby 'normal' life now allowed. Everyone would benefit:

> from the opportunities the hot rod provides for the expansion of mechanical expression (which is really the heartbeat of the American socio-economic system). It's good for today's youth to have a place, either at home or in the community at large, where he can learn to build and use the ingenuity so prized by Americans.

And, Siegle ended, activity surrounding the hot rod was:

> creative, educative, competitive, constructive, and masculine all of which are desirable elements in furthering the best in the American way of life.

I could give many other examples of the inspirational message of this magazine, only one of a number centering around car knowledge, modification and maintenance. Indeed, as readership increased, those in control obviously realised that it was being purchased by large numbers of people who were not hot rodders in any pure sense (about 30,000 the journal estimated). In 1953 the magazine added the logo 'The automotive how-to-do-it-magazine' under its main title on the front page, and the magazine began to broaden the definition of what could be considered a 'hot rodder' so as to cover all 'the mechanically minded' or 'motor minded Joes' as the publication put it.[49] These were people, so it said, who wanted to know more about the automobile than was available in other publications and who wanted to get a better performance out of their stock models. The magazine was often scathing about the so-called technical details printed in the mass media or in the advertisements of the Detroit companies. It sneered at the ordinary motorist who believed that because his speedometer registered 120 miles per hour he was actually *doing* 120 miles an hour. The magazine proclaimed itself as being for the insider, the knowledgeable, and so while the technical articles, and question and answer pages changed somewhat in the mid 1950s, so that a lot more attention was given to technical details of new cars and new engines, still, the DIY ethos and urgings to learn and to strive, to improve, to work on your car and make it better looking and better performing, were paramount in this magazine as it spoke to its million and more readers each month.

Discussion

The hot-rod subculture of post-war America can be dismissed as a trivial topic, one to be shunned by the serious minded, of little moment to the analysis of work and its meanings. However, if it is granted that 'work' is a multifaceted activity, and that the meanings of work are not to be encompassed by invoking the power of some immutable 'work ethic,' then there is a real necessity to consider exactly what social sources are promulgating what ideas about what work at any particular period, and so the literature that surrounds popular pursuits is significant. The, more or less, unexamined activities and ideological material of gardening, angling, cooking, do-it-yourself, boating, motoring, home-computing, sport and so on, all have plenty to say about labour and identity, skill and self, craft and commitment.

Of course, there are powerful arguments which suggest that in the post-war period a basic cultural shift occurred with a devaluation of paid labour as a significant area of life, with people's prized images becoming focussed on the weekend-self or holiday-self,[50] but regardless of such hypotheses about the varying importance of pieces of life, true students of work would still need to consider the social organization of a lot of enthusiasms and interests, and the kinds of ideologies which surround them.

My review of the themes contained in the specialist literature of a particular subculture indicate that the weight of its messages stood very close to the mélange known as 'the work ethic'. The desire of the lakes enthusiasts to safeguard their sport, or at least a sport, and the mutation of some of them into a creative elite who also sought to protect a bundle of economic opportunities which grew up around the sport, meant that hot-rod literature rang with a serious tone. Its fire was trained on idleness, time was to be filled with skilled activity, and success seeking. The journal addressed its readers through an idiom stressing excelling through effort, progress by trial and error, advance via defeat, and learning from mistakes. Benjamin Franklin's nostrums that 'there are no gains without pains' or 'God helps those who help themselves' echoed again and again in subcultural argot and were pursued in action by the magazine through its influence over the local and national organisations.

Hot Rod did not seek to challenge commonsense categories of 'work' or 'leisure'. Its language was, in the main, quite conventional. It spoke of hot rodding as 'a hobby', as 'tinkering,' as an 'avocation'. However, as the quote by Akton Millar cited earlier indicates, *Hot Rod* often tripped over the definitional problems more sophisticated analysis has now come to. In August 1950 the magazine featured the 'Recuperated Coupe':

> The entire process consumed many hours in time and considerable expense in parts, but like many other car builders he took great pride in his work and enjoyed the work he was doing.[51]

Or another featured car is:

> a real tribute to the craftsmanship that makes car building a great hobby.[52]

This, unrecognised, conceptual confusion (mirroring orthodox social analysis) carried out into mass-media surveys of the subculture. *Hot Rod* was instrumental in presenting its version of the activity in a well-selling novel, a number of low-budget films, and in popular radio and TV shows of the 1950s.[53] A *Life* cover story in 1957 (heralded with suspicion by *Hot Rod*) did speak of illegal street races but also told its readers:

> These cars are usually hand built with much ingenuity and affectionate care by avid teenagers.

Life featured the 'Dream Boat' of 24-year-old Norman Grabowski, much admired in the Los Angeles drive-ins:

> By working for five years on a poultry farm and as an extra for the movies Grabowski has earned the money it cost to hand make his machine—$8,000[54]

So a wider audience was made aware of the craftsmanship and expertise ethos of the hot-rod world.

Of course, the levels of achievement reported and honoured in the magazine were symbolic, not representative of the average level of effort or achievement in the subculture as the slightly apologetic tone of readers' letters about *their* cars indicates.[55] The specialist literature and its echoes in the mass media presented a mythological version of the hot-rod endeavour: stating what should be done if you wanted to reach the pinnacle. It was an optimistic version too. Nothing is said about botched jobs, or cars that look aesthetically awful, or perform badly as a result of home tinkering. There is little about racing accidents (when that racing is legal) while disasters—engines blowing, cars turning over—are presented as challenges, as opportunities for progress, not as being physically or financially crippling. The ethos is positive and exuberant, with little time to dwell on failure except as a stepping stone. The route to success, status, and self-satisfaction, is still labour, and practical, manual labour at that, but the appeal here is to something much higher than working for wages. Often the magazine suggested that the purpose of conventional work can be merely to provide the wherewithal for this finer pursuit.

However, in general the magazine, and most other hot-rod literature, had very little to say about paid labour. Sometimes, but by no means always, the employment of featured rodders is mentioned, but such references carry about the same significance as their home town. Of the jobs that are mentioned in this random and peripheral fashion, a high proportion (though not *that* high, given the place of automobile work of *all* kinds in the American economy at the time) are in automobile-related employment, and the vast majority are in skilled manual or petit-bourgeois occupations.

Hot Rod's search for respectability for the enthusiasm did lead it to some-times suggest that 'know-how' could lead onto employment. In 1952 it reprinted a NHRA pamphlet—*The Hot Rod Story*—whose author argued:

> That hot-rodding provides an incomparable proving ground for amateur experi-mentation and research is not open to question. That out of such activity—be it classified as a sport, hobby, or avocation—may arise some of our foremost engi-neers or designers of tomorrow is a reasonable speculation.[56]

Or in 1953, in reply to a decision by the National Automobile Dealers Associ-ation not to sell to hot rodders, the editor proclaimed:

> The thinking men of Detroit's industry are increasingly aware that from such en-thusiasm and enterprise can come the skilled manpower pool necessary to keep American wheels rolling.[57]

This theme was reinforced, as the magazine's circulation expanded, by regular full-page advertisements which also suggested that the hobby could be turned into employment. From the mid 1950s the Army and the Air Force regularly sought 'men with mechanical skill', while correspondence courses counselled:

> If you eat, sleep and live cars
> TURN YOUR HOBBY INTO A CAREER
> Get America's big-time, big-future
> AUTO MECHANICS, DIESEL COURSES
> at *home*, in your spare time.[58]

Then too the development of a paid elite of racers (greeted none-too-enthusiasti-cally by *Hot Rod*) suggested another way that personal interest and paid em-ployment could be combined, in advance to professional ranks. And the hot-rod literature does sometimes suggest that any rodder's ideal would be to marry hobby and payment. Bill Kenz, a racer and speed shop owner, remarked in 1951:

> When cars are a man's hobby as well as a livelihood, there is always something new and interesting coming up . . . there's *never* a dull day.[59]

Don Garlits, who metamorphised from Florida street-racing to world cham-pion professional drag racer, recalls that when he left school in 1950 he took up a book-keeping job:

it was just taken for granted—including by myself—that I'd get a job of that kind. It was awful. Working conditions were all right. It simply boiled down to my dislike of the day-in, day-out drudgery of working with invoices and receipts, bills of lading. It was an utter drag.[60]

Hot-rod expertise gave the chance of a career to:

the kid who wasn't very good at schoolwork, especially all that English, but who could speak to engines. He could rest his fingertips on the hood of any car and detect its illness.[61]

However, this is not painted as an easy, simple, or always desirable option. It requires total dedication, single-mindedness, perseverance, and luck. There is a stress on the costs of professional success—injury, loss of friends, broken marriages, loss of family life.[62] Moreover, it is not presented as necessarily that enjoyable as in Prudhommes weary description of drag racing:

Six seconds sometimes feels like a lifetime—especially when you look out the side and there's a car right next to you. There are so many things that can happen. Tyre vibrations. The car gets out of shape. While the car is out of shape and while the tyres are shaking, not only are you concerned about beating the guy next to you, especially in a big race like Indy., but you're thinking *'I've got to fix that before the next round'*. There must be a million thoughts that go through your mind driving the six second run. Then people look at me at the end of the day and say 'Boy you sure look tired'. Doggone right. I have thought about every thought in the world.[63]

The stars of any subculture are important in the production of meanings as they serve both as the embodiment of ideological principles and allow lower-level practitioners to relate their immediate experience to mediated experience through similarities of circumstance and event. Stars exist at a higher but essentially parallel plane. However, heroes are not necessarily portrayed as entirely successful. In the hot-rod literature there is more than a hint that the drive required to reach professional status could involve failure as a human being.[64] *Hot Rod*'s stress was on an *amateur* ethos. It was quick to point out that professionalism could bring a displacement of goals so that running for fun could shift down into earning a living. For example, in October 1950 replying to letters asking why the times achieved by rodders were not filed as world records the editor stressed that hot rodding was a strictly amateur activity:

As long as the boys are running for the fun of it, rather than for the almighty dollar, the sport will remain a hobby and recreation. Main objective in entering any sport is for relaxation and the attainment of self-satisfaction.[65]

The professional elite were regarded both as craftsmen with mysterious secrets,[66] but also as having sacrificed some spontaneity and enjoyment. Amateur endeavour was not only seen as more authentic experience, untainted by an instrumentalism which could lead to scandals and cheating, but could be combined with calls to high standards of morality, attention to unwritten rules, and, indeed, financial *sacrifice*, much more than could be expected from any mere job.

In all, the hot-rod literature tends to be silent about any paid labour which is not connected to automobiles, and while reference to the possibility of moves into rod-related jobs can be found, they are by no means a major element in the specialist literature. In this, and in its incorrigible stress on the importance of manual labour (albeit founded on contemplation and study) *Hot Rod* presented a highly romantic vision of work and what it was for. The rodder was enjoined to see himself (and herself—women did feature) in the roles of craftsman, inventor, the independent artisan, and as practical dreamer, whose garage improvements and drag-strip experiments were, the magazine constantly asserted, monitored by Detroit and which paid off in the form of improved cars for everyone. As well, the literature stressed the experience to be gained through racing. This gave to life a rare quality of excitement, found when you were out there, at the edge, wheel-to-wheel, in competition. The magazine enjoined that fine workmanship and controlled aggression could be fused, in a way which allowed masculinity to be tested, celebrated and displayed. And unlike the confusion of much of the rest of life, racing on the lakes or strips offered plain measure of success and failure. There were clear victories, intelligible defeats, comprehensive standards of personal achievement and progress, laid down by the exact second hand of a timing device or the finishing line. So complex cultural imperatives of all kinds surrounding 'work' could be easily understood, obeyed, and applied in the drag race.

My example of the hot-rod literature is designed to show that injunctions to strive, to create, to study, and achieve are around in plenty in 'leisure' activities, and most people are touched by them in some part of their life. What is revealed when we look at the hot-rod subculture of the 1940s and 1950s are directives in its literature, and the carrying out in practice, of personally-chosen projects, not connected to paid labour: 'work' as hobby, as relaxation, as fascination, as something *you really want to do* rather than being forced to do. About feeling *good* by working hard. This I am sure is true of the literature of many other activities, but I would argue, is especially significant in automobile pursuits. The automobile is a machine, it is technology: and people confront it, handle, know, master, and enjoy it in a way which is often very satisfying; as it was for the hot rodders. And the automobile is important as a symbol as well as a product. Words which are 'naturally' associated with it— mobility, freedom, pace, progress, competition—have parallels in other, apparently more 'important' areas of culture, and metaphors, allusions, if not direct substitutions from one cultural sphere to the other, are plentiful.

The assumptions which underlie a lot of social analysis define many areas of life as unimportant. The orthodox tradition of the study of 'work' and its meanings has largely ignored 'leisure', and when it has noticed it there has been a depiction in broad-brush strokes like 'trivialisation', 'passive response', 'incorporation by the mass media', 'hedonism' and so on. Such categorisations flatten out the varied contours of non-paid activity, avoid issues of the relative quality of time, and ignore ambiguities inherent in the way life has developed in capitalist society.

Special interests and specialist literature with its 'insiders' views, 'expert' opinion, assurance of 'community', and assertions of authenticity, abound in modern capitalism but have been neglected by social analysis. In *Hot Rod*, as in much other literature, social identities were offered, arcane language was explained, mysteries of craft were laid bare, tasks were invested with purpose, each reader was addressed as part of a wide movement, and everyone was held to be implicated in 'scientific progress' and 'technological advance'. Those who operate as the cultural entrepreneurs of unpaid time,[67] working through unexamined texts and disregarded organisations, do draw on grander and long-established cultural themes, in order to explain and promote their activities, and make them respectable, but, in so doing, they can alter accents, replace essences, and shuffle significances, so that older messages ring out in new areas of life. Part of what they seek to do is to really rework the 'work ethic', locate it to unpaid labours and so, quite possibly, make it **more** psychologically meaningful for the bulk of the population than in earlier periods of capitalist society. Until social analysis gives such moral entrepreneurs and the transformations they achieve a lot more attention, then, I suggest, we will not know very much about the various meanings of a variety of types of work, and their differing significance for the individual.

Notes

1. The following were all influential: C. Walker and R. Guest, *The Man on The Assembly Line* (Cambridge, Mass., Harvard University Press, 1952); E. Chinoy, *Automobile Workers and the American Dream* (Garden City, NY, Doubleday, 1955); R. Blauner, *Alienation and Freedom* (University of Chicago Press, 1964). They are often much more sophisticated in tone than a continuing genre of exposés of the 'nature' of car 'work.' See, for example, H. Beynon, *Working For Ford* (London, Allen Lane, 1973), and S. Kamata, *Japan in The Passing Lane* (London, Allen and Unwin, 1983).

2. Sparked off by: H. Braverman, *Labor and Monopoly Capital* (New York, Monthly Review Press, 1974). Braverman expressly ignored the subjective perception of 'work,' a convenient device which has served his myriad followers well in prolonging the 'labour process debate.'

3. A. Kornhauser, *The Mental Health of the American Worker* (London, 1965).

4. *Ibid*. p. 7.

5. *Ibid*. p. 199.

6. M. Rose, *Re-Working The Work Ethic* (London, Batsford, 1985); R. E. Pahl, *Divisions of Labour* (Oxford, Blackwell, 1984); H. F. Moorhouse, 'American automobiles and workers' dreams,' in K. Thompson, ed., *Work, Employment and Unemployment* (Milton Keynes, Open University Press, 1984).

7. Rose, *Re-Working*, p. 19.

8. *Ibid*. p. 105.

9. Pahl, *Divisions*, p. 336.

10. *Ibid*, p. 329. Thus I do not think I could fit the work on hot rods I discuss in the text into Pahl's 'Preliminary typology of work' on his p. 125.

11. Pahl, *Divisions*, p. 106 fn.

12. D. Rodgers, *The Work Ethic in Industrial America 1850–1920* (London, University of Chicago Press, 1978), p. 14.

13. See the neglected book by K. Kusterer, *Know How on the Job* (Colorado, Westview, 1978).

14. R. Sennett and J. Cobb, *The Hidden Injuries of Class* (Cambridge University Press, 1972), though I doubt that most workers do 'suffer' in the way this book suggests. Rather 'sacrifice' *does* provide purpose.

15. And see the interesting hypotheses about the cognitive style intrinsic to automobile production in P. Berger *et al.*, *The Homeless Mind* (London, Penguin, 1974) pp. 32–43.

16. See the extended discussion of this, and its effects in dividing workers on gender lines, in C. Cockburn, *Brothers* (London, Pluto, 1983).

17. *Fortune*, 36:5 (November 1947).

18. M. Dubofksy *et al.*, *The United States in the Twentieth Century* (London, Prentice Hall, 1978), p. 427.

19. R. P. Smith, *Consumer Demands for Cars in the U.S.A.* (Cambridge University Press, 1975), Appendix A, Table 3.

20. J. Bernard, 'Teenage culture: an overview,' *The Annals of the American Academy of Political and Social Science*, vol. 338 (November 1961), p. 4.

21. The position of *Hot Rod* and the NHRA (National Hot Rod Association) at the centre of the subculture has meant that their version of its history tends to be that which prevails in the few accounts which are available. As well as items indicated below, introductions to the hot-rod culture are contained in J. Storer, 'Coach-building in customizing,' in S. Murray, ed., *Petersens Creative Customizing* (Los Angeles, Petersen, 1978), pp. 4–13; W. Parks, *Drag Racing: Yesterday and Today* (New York, Trident, 1966); R. Denny, *The Astonished Muse* (University of Chicago Press, 1957), ch. 7; R. Boyle, *Sport: Mirror of American Life* (Boston, Little Brown, 1963), ch. 4; L. Levine, *Ford: The Dust and the Glory* (London, Collier-Macmillan, 1968), ch. 16. E. Lawrence, 'Gow jobs,' *Colliers*, July 26 1941 and 'Hot rods,' *Life*, 5 November 1945, are early mass-media accounts.

22. See the typology set out by G. Balsley, 'The hot rod culture,' *American Quarterly*, 2:1 (Spring 1950).

23. E. Jaderquist, *The New How to Build Hot Rods* (New York, Arco, 6th printing 1977), p. 33.

24. F. Horsley, *Hot Rod It—and Run For Fun* (Englewood Cliffs, Prentice Hall, 1957), p. 151.

25. *Hot Rods* interventions in the subculture are discussed in detail in: H. F. Moorhouse, 'Organising the hot rods,' *British Journal of Sports History*, 3:1 (May 1986), and H. F. Moorhouse, 'Racing for a sign: defining the "hot rod" 1945–1960', *Journal of Popular Culture* 20:2 (Fall 1986).

26. *Hot Rod* (afterwards *HR*) 1:10 (1948); 3:5 (1950), 2:1 and 2 (1958).

27. S. Alexander, 'All over in 6 seconds,' *Road and Track*, August 1974, pp. 73–78.

28. Pahl, *Divisions*, p. 102 fn notes the development in Britain of DIY magazines from 1959 onwards but does *not* investigate the ideologies they promoted.

29. *HR* 1:2 (1948)

30. *Ibid.* 1:4(1948).

31. *Ibid.* 2:3 (1949).

32. *Ibid.* 2:12 (1949).

33. *Ibid.* 4:6 (1951).

34. *Ibid.* 6:12 (1953).

35. *Ibid.* 2:3 (1949).

36. *Ibid.* 4:9 (1957).

37. *Ibid.* 7:2 (1954).

38. *Ibid.* 4:7 (1951).

39. *Ibid.* 4:9 (1951).

40. *Ibid.* 4:9 (1951).

41. *Ibid.* 6:5 (1953).

42. *Ibid.* 7:1 (1954).

43. *Ibid.* 3:2 (1950).

44. *Ibid.* 1:11 (1948).

45. *Ibid.* 11:2 (1959); J. P. Viken, 'The sport of drag racing and the search for satisfaction, meaning and self' (unpublished Ph.D. thesis, University of Minnesota, 1978), pp. 80–81 notes that the hot rodders he observed were better at mending cars than 'professional' mechanics at the local garage.

46. *HR* 4:3 (1951).

47. Balsley, 'Hot rod culture,' reprinted in *HR* 4:7 (1951).

48. *HR* 5:8 (1952).

49. I discuss how *Hot Rod* worked on the term 'hot rod' to try to encompass more and more of the 'motor-minded' in H. F. Moorhouse, 'Racing for a sign.'

50. C. W. Mills, *White Collar* (New York, Oxford University Press, 1951), chs. 10–11; T. Burns, 'The Study of consumer behavior,' *Archives Européenes de sociologie*, 7 (1966). See my discussion in H. F. Moorhouse, 'American automobiles and workers' dreams,' in K. Thompson, ed., *Work, Employment and Unemployment* (Milton Keynes, Open University Press, 1984); S. Ewen, *Captains of Consciousness* (New York, McGraw Hill, 1976) sees the roots of 'consumer culture' in the 1920s but the flowering as a post-war phenomenon.

51. *HR* 3:8 (1950).

52. *HR* 4:5 (1951).

53. H. Felsen, *Hot Rod* (New York, Dutton, 1950) is the novel. TV and radio shows include 'Dragnet,' 'Life with Riley,' 'Public Defender,' and 'The Bob Cummings Show.' In all of these, according to *Hot Rod*, the shows' central characters were made to appreciate the serious nature of the hot rod enterprise.

54. 'The drag racing rage,' *Life*, April 29 1957, p. 78.

55. Of course, one of the assumptions in much of the literature about 'work' as paid labour is to assume that every skilled worker was actually a good or competent craftsman. This is one of the ways in which social analysis has presented an idealised view of 'work' in the past.

56. *HR* 5:3 (1952).

57. *Ibid.* 6:5 (1953).

58. *Ibid.* 8:1 (1955).

59. *Ibid.* 4:9 (1951).

60. D. Garlits and B. Yates, *King of the Dragsters* (London, Chilton, 1967), pp. 18–19.

61. B. Ottum, 'Is there life after hot rodding?' *Sports Illustrated* (March 1981), pp. 40–41.

62. Exemplified in the title and text of T. Madigan, *The Loner: The Story of a Drag Racer* (Englewood Cliffs, Prentice Hall, 1974).

63. H. Higdon, *Six Seconds to Glory: Don Prudhommes Greatest Drag Race* (New York, Putnams, 1975), p. 95.

64. Close to that 'Reader's Digest philosophy' which Mills, *White Collar*, p. 283, regarded as important in post-war America. Serious study of the 'stars' of any unpaid activity is virtually non-existent.

65. *HR* 3:10 (1950).

66. See an example: 'Losinski, what are your secrets?' in *HR* 6:12 (1953).

67. By 1960 Petersen, the owner of *Hot Rod* could appear on the front page of the *Wall Street Journal* in a series about 'the new millionaires and how they made their fortunes,' serving, perhaps, as an inspiration to the entrepreneurial elite. This story, though, does not really emphasise his 'work,' but cleverness in spotting gaps in the market and, indeed, his 'high-living.' 'Road to riches,' *Wall Street Journal*, 22 July 1960.

CHAPTER 15

The Commodity Gap:
Consumerism and the Modern Home

Elaine Tyler May

As a normal part of life, thrift now is an un-American.
—WILLIAM H. WHYTE, JR., 1956[1]

No man who owns his own house and lot can be a Communist. He has too much to
do.
—WILLIAM J. LEVITT
Developer of Levittown, 1948[2]

The sexually charged, child-centered family took its place at the center of
the postwar American dream. The most tangible symbol of that dream was
the home—the locale of the good life, the evidence of democratic abundance.
Let us return briefly to Moscow in 1959, where Vice President Richard M.
Nixon articulated the essence of American superiority by describing the
consumer-oriented suburban home. It is important to keep in mind that the
ideal home Nixon described was one that obliterated class distinctions and accentuated gender distinctions. The "model home" he extolled was not a mansion but a modest ranch-style structure, "within the price range of the average
U.S. worker," complete with modern appliances that would "make easier the
life of our housewives." For Nixon, the most important feature of the suburban home was its availability to Americans of all classes.

"Let us start with some of the things in this exhibit," he began. "You will
see a house, a car, a television set—each the newest and most modern of its
type we produce. But can only the rich in the United States afford such things?
If this were the case, we would have to include in our definition of rich the
millions of America's wage earners." Nixon felt certain that the possibility of
home ownership would diffuse the most dangerous potential of class conflict.
As he explained to Soviet Premier Nikita Khrushchev, "Our steel workers, as
you know, are on strike. But any steel worker could buy this house. They earn
$3 an hour. This house costs about $100 a month to buy on a contract running twenty-five to thirty years." Khrushchev countered, "We have steel

workers and we have peasants who also can afford to spend $14,000 for a house." But for Nixon, home ownership represented even more than a comfortable way of life; it was the validation of the free enterprise system.[3]

Nixon's frame of reference was the family: "There are 44 million families in the United States. Twenty-five million of [them] live in houses or apartments that have as much or more floor space than the one you see in this exhibit. Thirty-one million families own their own homes and the land on which they are built. America's 44 million families own a total of 56 million cars, 50 million television sets and 143 million radio sets. And they buy an average of nine dresses and suits and 14 pairs of shoes per family per year."

Nixon then described other miracles of domestic technology. Pointing to a television screen, he said, "We can see here what is happening in other parts of the home." Khrushchev, scorning the American obsession with gadgets, chided, "This is probably always out of order. . . . Don't you have a machine that puts food into the mouth and pushes it down? Many things you've shown us are interesting but they are not needed in life. . . . They are merely gadgets." Yet both leaders took the consumer gap seriously. The Soviet premier continued, "[N]ewly built Russian houses have all this equipment right now. Moreover, all you have to do to get a house is to be born in the Soviet Union. So I have a right to a house. In America if you don't have a dollar, you have the right to sleep on the pavement. Yet you say that we are slaves of communism."

Khrushchev further accused Americans of building houses to last only twenty years, so builders could continually sell new ones. "We build firmly," said the Soviet leader, "We build for our children and grandchildren." But Nixon argued that after twenty years, the older home or kitchen would be obsolete. Linking consumer aspirations to scientific expertise, he explained that the American system is designed to take advantage of new inventions and new techniques. Unimpressed, Khrushchev replied, "This theory does not hold water." But for Nixon the theory did hold water, for it reflected his belief in the potential for individualism and upward mobility.

The metaphor that prevailed throughout the debate was that of a race. But it was not the arms race or the space race; it was the consumer race—centered on the home. Khrushchev estimated that it would take only seven years before the U.S.S.R. would reach the American standard of living. Already in eight years, grain and milk output had nearly doubled, and television sets were up from 67,000 to a million. The terms of the cold war were set in these figures. Nixon was willing to concede Russian successes in the space race, but he argued that domestic consumer goods were the most meaningful measure of American superiority over the Soviet Union: "There are some instances where you may be ahead of us, for example in the development of the thrust of your rockets for the investigation of outer space; there may be some instances in which we are ahead of you—in color television, for instance." Not to be outdone, Khrushchev claimed, "No, we are up with you on this, too." Nixon remarked, "We welcome this kind of competition because when we engage in it, no one loses, everyone wins." Thus, the commodity gap took precedence over the missile gap.

In Nixon's vision, the suburban ideal of home ownership would diffuse two potentially disruptive forces: women and workers. In appliance-laden houses across the country, working-class as well as business-class breadwinners could fulfill the new American work-to-consume ethic. Home ownership would lessen class consciousness among workers, who would set their sights toward the middle-class ideal. The family home would be the place where a man could display his success through the accumulation of consumer goods. Women, in turn, would reap rewards for domesticity by surrounding themselves with commodities. Presumably, they would remain content as housewives because appliances would ease their burdens. For both men and women, home ownership would reinforce aspirations for upward mobility and diffuse the potential for social unrest.

Nixon was not the only one who believed that the American preoccupation with procurement would be a safeguard against the threat of class warfare and communism. Mayor Joseph Darst of St. Louis, for example, wrote to the city's board of aldermen in 1951 that if everyone had good housing, "no one in the United States would need to worry today about the threat of communism in this country. Communists love American slums. Our clearance of these slums and erection of adequate housing is one of the most effective answers we can give communism locally."[4]

For those who agreed that economic optimism was essential to keep the free enterprise system alive and well, there were reasons to rejoice. The postwar years witnessed a huge increase in discretionary spending power, an increase that surpassed gains in income or prices. Between 1947 and 1961, the number of families rose 28 percent, national income increased over 60 percent, and the group with discretionary income (those with money for nonnecessities) doubled. Rather than putting this money aside for a rainy day, Americans were inclined to spend it. A 1946 Gallup poll indicated that in spite of persistent pockets of poverty and fears of another depression, the desire to spend was much stronger than the desire to save. This is not to say that the concern for future security was tossed to the wind; on the contrary, security remained a high priority. Americans were only slightly more hopeful about the economic future in 1945 than they had been in 1937 at the depth of the depression. Fears of another depression were widespread, and one-third of the population was still in poverty.[5] But the increase in income for the middle and working classes, combined with new governmental supports, encouraged Americans to invest their money in purchases. Social security no doubt eased their fears of poverty in old age, and veterans' mortgages facilitated expenditures for home ownership. Americans responded with guarded optimism by making purchases that would strengthen their sense of security. In the postwar years, investing in one's own home, along with the trappings that would presumably enhance family life, was seen as the best way to plan for the future.

Instead of rampant spending for personal luxury items, Americans were likely to spend their money at home. In the five years after World War II, consumer spending increased 60 percent, but the amount spent on household furnishings and appliances rose 240 percent. In the same five years, purchases for food rose only 33 percent, and for clothing a mere 20 percent. From the depression onward, the trend in spending was striking. Between 1935 and 1950, the money income of Americans increased 50 percent. But this increase was not divided evenly among purchasing categories. Expenditures for food and drink increased only 30 percent; for clothing, 53 percent; for personal care, 69 percent; and for education, 73 percent. These increases were modest compared to the increased expenditures for household operation (108 percent), recreation (185 percent), and automobiles (205 percent). In the four years following the end of the war, Americans purchased 21.4 million cars, 20 million refrigerators, 5.5 million stoves, and 11.6 million televisions and moved into over 1 million new housing units each year. The same patterns extended into the 1950s, a decade in which prosperity continued to spread.[6]

The locale for this consumer-oriented family life was suburbia. The suburban home caught the imaginations as well as the purse strings of postwar Americans. A study of the psychology of spending noted, "The impact of suburbia on consumer behavior can hardly be overstated. . . . Young people chose to marry early, to have several children in the early years of marriage, to live in . . . nice neighborhoods, and to have cars, washing machines, refrigerators, television sets, and several other appliances at the same time." Americans channeled their spending accordingly. With the exception of the very poor, those of ample as well as modest means exhibited a great deal of conformity in their consumption attitudes and behavior. Spending patterns reflected widely shared beliefs about the good life, which seemed within reach of many, even those of the lower middle and working classes.[7]

Consumer patterns, then, reflected one more aspect of containment behavior as the nation's affluent majority poured their income into homes and family pursuits. The old version of the virtuous home was a much more ascetic one. Still, the values associated with domestic spending upheld traditional American concerns with pragmatism and morality, rather than opulence and luxury. Purchasing for the home helped alleviate traditional American uneasiness with consumption: the fear that spending would lead to decadence. Family-centered spending reassured Americans that affluence would strengthen the American way of life. The goods purchased by middle-class consumers, like a modern refrigerator or a house in the suburbs, were intended to foster traditional values.[8]

Pragmatism and family enrichment were the keys to virtuous consumerism. The commodities that people bought were intended to reinforce home life and uphold traditional gender roles. After all, American women were housewives; their lives were functional, not merely ornamental. In general, male breadwinners were expected to provide the income for household goods, and their wives were expected to purchase them. Public opinion polls taken after the war indicate that both men and women were generally opposed to employment for women, and believed that a woman who ran a home had a "more interesting time" than did a woman with a full-time job. There were, however, circumstances when employment for women was approved—especially if the income it generated fostered family life. For example, one poll showed that postwar women and men believed that if a young couple could not marry because the man was not earning enough to support them both, "the girl should take a job so they can get married right away."[9] By and large, however, employment for married women was to be avoided. Given these prevailing attitudes, it is no wonder that Nixon continually interchanged the words "woman" and "housewife" as he extolled the American way of life at the Moscow exhibition.

Yet that equation should be examined closely, since not all married women were full-time homemakers during the 1950s. In fact, the postwar years brought more wives into the paid labor force than ever before. Americans felt a great deal of ambivalence toward women's employment—a legacy of the depression and the war. On the one hand, it was unfortunate if a wife had to hold a job; on the other hand, it was considered far worse if the family was unable to purchase what were believed to be necessities for the home.

During these years, the very definition of household needs changed to include many more consumer items. Since it was the homemaker's responsibility to purchase these items, women sought employment, ironically, to promote their role as consumers. The economic importance of women's role as consumers cannot be overstated, for it kept American industry rolling and sustained jobs for the nation's male providers. Nearly the entire increase in the gross national product in the mid-1950s was due to increased spending on consumer durables and residential construction.[10] Many employed wives considered their jobs secondary to their role as consumers and in tune with the ethic of togetherness and subordination that characterized their marital relationships. This was one legacy that depression-bred daughters inherited: women sought employment to bolster the family budget but not to disrupt domestic power relationships. As long as their employment provided a secondary source of income and did not undermine the authority of the male breadwinner, it was acceptable to the family.[11]

The house and commodity boom also had tremendous propaganda value, for it was those affluent homes, complete with breadwinner and homemaker, that provided evidence of the superiority of the American way of life. Since much of the cold war was waged in propaganda battles, this vision of domesticity was a powerful weapon. Although they may have been unwitting soldiers, women who marched off to the nation's shopping centers to equip their new homes joined the ranks of American cold warriors. As newscaster and noted cold warrior George Putnam said in 1947, shopping centers were "concrete expressions of the practical idealism that built America . . . plenty of free parking for all those cars that we capitalists seem to acquire. Who can help but contrast [them] with what you'd find under communism?"[12]

Consumers no doubt had less global concerns in mind. They had saved their money for specific purposes. During the war, a survey of bank depositors indicated that 43 percent were eager to spend their money on "future needs," and half of those specified purchases for the home. Leading architects helped give tangible form to these desires by publishing plans for "dream houses" in leading magazines like the *Ladies Home Journal.* Construction companies also fed consumer longings by selling scrapbooks for saving ideas for future houses, with sections divided into the various rooms of the home. The Andersen Window Company, for example, which was well aware of the potential market, distributed 350,000 personally embossed scrapbooks before the end of the war. By June 1944, appliances topped the list of the most desired consumer items. When asked what they hoped to purchase in the postwar years, Americans listed washing machines first, then electric irons, refrigerators, stoves, toasters, radios, vacuum cleaners, electric fans, and hot water heaters. Advertisers claimed that these items constituted the American way of life that the soldiers were fighting for.[13]

The pent-up desires for homes and appliances represented something more than mere fantasies of luxurious living. The need for wartime housing was great. Dislocated war workers needed $100 million worth of new housing, which prompted a construction boom during the war. By 1943, residential real estate buying reached levels unknown since the 1920s. But wartime building was inadequate to meet the increasing need. The housing shortage reached crisis proportions after the war. In 1945, 98 percent of American cities reported shortages of houses, and over 90 percent reported shortages of apartments. By 1947, 6 million families were doubling up with relatives or friends. The housing industry gained tremendous momentum after the war in the face of these immediate needs, and took advantage of the conversion of production technology for peacetime use.[14]

Supply and demand came together to foster and explosion in residential housing after the war. But the expansion did not take place equally in all types of housing. Largely as a result of governmental policies, massive suburban developments of single-family houses took precedence over apartments and inner-city dwellings. The Servicemen's Readjustment Act of 1944 (the GI Bill of Rights) created a Veteran's Administration (VA) program of guaranteed mortgage insurance, expanding the Federal Housing Authority (FHA) program dating back to 1934. The new programs, which provided federal insurance for loans to veterans, encouraged private investors to enter the housing mortgage market. In addition, the tax benefits for homeowners became substantial in the 1940s. The government also financed large suburban tracts, such as those built by William Levitt. With all these incentives for building and purchasing suburban residences, it soon became cheaper to buy than to rent. Veterans could buy homes in Levittown, for example, with a thirty-year mortgage and no down payment, by spending only $56 per month. At the same time, the average apartment rental in many cities was $93. As a result of all these inducements, housing starts went from 114,000 in 1944 to an all-time high of 1,692,000 in 1950.[15]

Postwar policies fostered the construction of the vast majority of new housing in the suburbs. The cold war made a profound contribution to suburban sprawl. In 1951, the *Bulletin of Atomic Scientists* devoted an issue to "defense through decentralization" that argued in favor of depopulating the urban core to avoid a concentration of residences or industries in a potential target area for a nuclear attack. Joining this effort was the American Road Builders Association, a lobbying group second only to the munitions industry. As a result of these pressures, Congress passed the Interstate Highway Act in 1956, which provided $100 billion to cover 90 percent of the cost for 41,000 miles of national highways. When President Dwight D. Eisenhower signed the bill into law, he stated one of the major reasons for the new highway system: "[In] case of atomic attack on our key cities, the road net must permit quick evacuation of target areas."[16]

Many people believed that the suburbs also provided protection against labor unrest, which might lead to class warfare and its presumed inevitable result, communism. The report of a 1948 meeting of a San Francisco businessman's association, chaired by the ex-president of the National Association of Home Builders, argued for the dispersion of industry outside central cities: "Conditions under which employees live, as well as work, vitally influence management-labor relations. Generally, large aggregations of labor in one big [central-city] plant are more subject to outside disrupting influences, and have less happy relations with management, than in smaller [suburban] plants."[17]

The suburban growth that resulted from these policies was neither universal nor inevitable; in Europe, centralization rather than decentralization was predominant. In the United States, the FHA and VA mortgage policies, the highway system, the financing of sewers, the support for suburban developments such as Levittown, and the placing of public housing in the center of urban ghettos, facilitated the dispersal of the white middle class into the suburbs and contributed to the decay of the inner cities. Furthermore, blacks were excluded from the suburbs by de facto segregation and the FHA's redlining policies, more than by poverty.[18]

In 1946, as a result of all these supports for home ownership, for the first time a majority of the nation's families lived in homes they owned. Over the next 15 years, 12 million more families became homeowners. By the 1950s, most of those who purchased homes did so to buy a better house or move into a better neighborhood. Loans available to homeowners favored purchase over repair, which further spurred the movement of the population into newly constructed suburban developments. Between 1950 and 1970, the suburban population doubled, from 36 million to 74 million; 83 percent of the nation's growth during those years took place in the suburbs.[19]

Although the suburbs were clearly designated for whites only, they offered a picture of domestic comfort available to those with modest incomes. These homes represented the American way of life, democratic and affordable, that Nixon would extoll in Moscow. Confirming Nixon's assertion of the American desire for change and newness, upgrading was a widespread motive for spending. The nation's consumers continually replaced, improved, or expanded their homes, appliances, and cars, long before those items had worn out. Federal policies, combined with increased affluence, made it possible for white Americans of moderate means to indulge their desires for newness and mobility.[20]

These federal programs did more than simply spur a trend toward home ownership in the expanding suburbs. Policies that reflected and encouraged the American domestic ideology fostered and reinforced a particular kind of family life. In effect, these federal programs provided subsidies and incentives for couples to marry and have several children. Houses were designed to accommodate families with small children. Builders and architects assumed that men would be away at work during the day and houses would be occupied by full-time homemaker-mothers. In the first Levittown, a standardized suburban development built by William Levitt, 17,400 houses accommodated 82,000 residents. The structures were mass produced and inexpensive, with a flexible interior design that was easily expandable if the family increased in size. Kitchens were near the front entrance, so mothers could keep an eye on their children as they cooked. Living rooms featured picture windows facing the backyard, also to facilitate the supervision of children. Appliances were included in the purchase price. The one-story design gave the home an informal look and was practical for families with young children, since there were no stairs, which could be dangerous. As young parents of the baby boom moved into these homes, it is no wonder that the first Levittown quickly earned the nicknames "Fertility Valley" and "The Rabbit Hutch."[21]

By stimulating these particular kinds of suburban housing developments and providing subsidies to homeowners, the federal government effectively underwrote the baby boom, along with the lifestyle and community arrangements that fostered traditional gender roles in the home. The government, along with the National Association of Home Builders, provided plans in the 1950s for smaller, inexpensive ranch-style homes that would allow for openness, adequate room for appliances and other consumer goods, and the easy supervision of children. Appliances were not intended to enable housewives to have more free time to pursue their own interests, but rather to achieve higher standards of cleanliness and efficiency, while allowing more time for child care. The suburban home was planned as a self-contained universe. Technological advances made housework efficient and professional; lawn mowers and cake mixes guaranteed a perfect result. In addition, homes were designed for enjoyment, fun, and togetherness. Family members would not need to go out for recreation or amusements, since they had swing sets, playrooms, and backyards with barbecues at home.[22]

Leisure pursuits encouraged a further infatuation with commodities. One of the most powerful of all postwar entertainments—the television set—sat squarely in people's living rooms. By the 1950s, televisions were selling at a rate of over five million a year. Television also fostered the classless ideal. Commercials extended the reach of advertising into people's homes, as did the abundant lifestyles portrayed on the screen. As historian George Lipsitz noted, situation comedies in the postwar years, especially those aimed at ethnic or working-class audiences, eased the transition from a depression-bred psychology of scarcity to an acceptance of spending. In shows like "I Remember Mama" or "The Honeymooners," the dramas of daily life revolved around the purchase of consumer goods for the home. Characters in these programs urged each other to buy on installment, "live above our means—the American way," and spend rather than save. Commodities would solve the problem of the discontented housewife, foster pride in the provider whose job offered few intrinsic rewards, and allow children to "fit in" with their peers. Consumerism provided a means for assimilation into the American way of life: classless, homogeneous, and family centered.[23]

The desire for the single-family home as a refuge against a chaotic world was not a postwar creation. Indeed, it dates back to housing reformers of the nineteenth century who first articulated the suburban family ideal. But it achieved new vigor in the postwar years, largely because the ideal was now within reach of most middle-class and many working-class Americans. In its modern manifestation, the suburban ranch-style home was to blend in with nature. As historian Clifford Edward Clark, Jr. observed, "the ranch house . . . was . . . seen as creating a unity with nature, but it was a unity that pictured nature as a tamed and open environment. . . . The 1950s design standards conceived of the natural world in a simplified and controlled way that eliminated anything that was wild or irregular."[24]

The contained, natural style, enhanced by modern technology and design, offered a sense of security as well as privatized abundance. The natural look was more personal and even sensual than the formalized structures of public life and business. And although most ranch-style tract homes were relatively small, standardized one-story structures, the flexible interior space allowed for individuality—something increasingly lacking in the highly organized and bureaucratic world of work.[25]

Who purchased these homes, and did they satisfy their owners' needs and desires? According to surveys at the time, about half those who purchased houses in 1949 and 1950 were white World War II veterans in their mid-thirties with young children. The second half were about ten years older; their housing needs or financial resources had changed, prompting them to buy larger homes in the suburbs. Both groups were parents of the baby-boom generation. The second group included Americans of the age and circumstances of the respondents to the Kelly Longitudinal Study (KLS). The residents of Levittown, however, were more likely to belong to the first group: younger, less affluent, and largely working class. In his study of Levittown, Herbert Gans found that most of the residents claimed to be satisfied with their living arrangements.[26]

Nevertheless, there were frustrations. As with expectations for exciting sexuality or fulfilling child rearing, the suburban ideal often promised more than it delivered. Many home owners wished for more space but had to make do with smaller houses because of financial constraints. If spaciousness was an elusive goal for many suburbanites, so was the life of the happy housewife. Women in Levittown often complained about feeling trapped and isolated, facing endless chores of housekeeping and tending to children. For them, suburban life was not a life of fun and leisure but of exhausting work and isolation. In addition, since houses and neighborhoods were created with young children in mind, adolescents often chafed against the small rooms, lack of privacy, constant supervision, and absence of stores and restaurants in their neighborhoods. And although parents frequently mentioned the benefits of togetherness and the ability to spend more time with their families, the time-consuming commute for the men, and for the 25 percent of suburban women who were employed, actually reduced the amount of time available for families to share. Nevertheless, most homeowners expressed contentment with their residences, largely because they were significantly more spacious and comfortable than their previous dwellings, even if they did not measure up to one's "dream house."[27] Once again, postwar Americans lowered their expectations and expressed satisfaction with their suburban lot.

Although these suburban tracts have borne the brunt of scorn for their lack of individuality and mass-produced sameness, they did offer a modicum of comfort and convenience to growing families of modest means. Most of the contract-built houses, like those in Levittown, had central heating, indoor plumbing, telephones, automatic stoves, refrigerators, and washing machines—conveniences that most middle-class Americans would not like to sacrifice. Yet these isolated enclaves also weakened extended-family ties, promoted homogeneity in neighborhoods, intensified racial segregation, encouraged conformity, and fostered a style of life based on traditional gender roles in the home.[28]

With the exception of avant-garde intellectuals and a small number of politically active feminists, few Americans articulated viable alternatives to the suburban lifestyle. Those who complained that life did not fit the ideal, like overworked housewives in Levittown, generally tried to alleviate their miseries with more money or goods. The ideal itself was rarely called into question, at least not publicly. Nevertheless, it was difficult to achieve, even for those who could afford it. These were by and large affluent middle-class Americans, well educated and ambitious, who believed in the American dream and belonged to the postwar consensus. The men worked in a highly organized and bureaucratized economy, the women focused their energies on the home, and together they sought personal fulfillment in their families, surrounded by children and consumer goods. They entered marriage with a utopian vision that included happiness as well as security. Did the "good life" in consumer-laden houses fulfill their expectations? The responses of the couples in the KLS provide some answers.

These men and women were among the comfortable group of white middle-class Americans able to take advantage of the fruits of prosperity. Eighty-five percent had a family income of over $5,000 a year, although only 13 percent earned over $15,000. Most had never been heavily in debt; 98 percent had never received any kind of public assistance and only 30 percent had received aid from relatives or friends. Their purchasing habits reflected a national pattern: personal extravagance was rare, but consumption for family enrichment was a high priority. They exhibited a desire for consumer goods combined with a concern for future financial security. About 70 percent of the sample spent between $1,000 and $3,000 in housing expenses per year; 63 percent had one car and 33 percent had two cars. Slightly more than half had purchased their cars new.[29]

Reflecting the values of the time, which linked status to consumer purchases as well as to occupational level, Kelly rated the "prestige value" of the cars each family owned. He determined that 45 percent fell into the "low prestige" category; 30 percent, the middle; and 22 percent, the high. Only 3 percent owned cars in the "super-high prestige" range, such as a Cadillac. Most said they had one or two thousand dollars to spend per year above basic needs and rarely, if ever, purchased anything on the installment plan. These, then, were well-to-do but conservative people, not extravagant consumers.[30]

Like the rest of the middle class, the KLS respondents sought an expansive, affluent life within the security of their suburban homes. They spent their money in ways that would achieve that goal. The most important spending priority for 60 percent of the respondents was future financial security; for 23 percent, it was "increasing day-to-day living for family members"; and for 15 percent, it was "providing special opportunities for children." Clearly, security and family-oriented pursuits, not personal luxuries, were their major concerns.[31]

These women and men reveal how deeply domestic aspirations were rooted in the postwar success ethic. The increasing emphasis on familial rewards as validation for work found expression in the popular literature as well. Elizabeth Long's study of best-selling novels in the decade after World War II reveals a dramatic shift. In 1945, popular novels celebrated a vision of entrepreneurial success. But by 1955, themes had shifted toward more personal rewards. Heroes now made choices between work and leisure, family and the public world. They were more likely to accommodate themselves to the job and accept a secure place in the organizational hierarchy. According to Long, in these later novels the individual depends on others for happiness, and on the organization merely for a job. She called this theme the "corporate suburban" model, in contrast to the entrepreneurial model that prevailed a decade earlier.

A typical mid-fifties best seller was Sloan Wilson's *The Man in the Grey Flannel Suit*, in which the protagonist is the new type of corporate hero who accommodates himself to bureaucratic constraints and wants to get ahead without sacrificing his family. Success is defined not by being at the top, but by having a secure, balanced life. In all these novels, successful career women were portrayed as "selfish," female ambition was associated with sexual promiscuity. Suffering was the final lot for most such women in these stories.[32]

Husbands in the KLS sample reflected the values expressed in these novels. The family, rather than the workplace, was the arena in which men demonstrated their achievement. Work appeared relatively meaningless without the family to give purpose to their efforts. When the men responded to an open-ended question asking what marriage had brought them which they could not have gained if they had remained single, many referred to the motivation it provided them to work hard and succeed. One husband wrote that his marriage gave him "the incentive to succeed and save for the future of my family." Others mentioned "greater incentive to succeed in business career," "feeling of accomplishment," "a family to work for," and "greater financial security." Echoing Nixon's remarks, many of these husbands wanted to make life better for their wives. In return, they expected to be appreciated. One husband complained that the "chief weakness of our marriage seems to be her failure to feel any . . . accomplishment from mutual efforts—particularly the family increases in net worth—house and car, furniture, insurance and bank accounts."[33]

What is interesting about all these responses, particularly their frequency of occurrence, is that these husbands claimed that they would have had neither the motivation nor the success without marriage. Clearly, the provider role itself—and an economically dependent wife's recognition and appreciation of it—often offered a greater source of satisfaction than the actual work a man performed. Men were likely to place this aspect of their role in the center of their feelings of marital satisfaction. Ten husbands mentioned a better financial position as a benefit of marriage, another 13 listed security and stability, and 11 others included social position; 43 said marriage gave them a sense of purpose and responsibility. Together, these responses made up the third largest category of answers to the question of what marriage gave them that they would not have had without it, following closely after love and children.

The potential tragedy in this situation was that in spite of widespread prosperity, the provider role was a heavy burden, and not all men could be successful at it. Nor was the status of family breadwinner always adequate compensation for an otherwise monotonous or dissatisfying job. Just as material goods could contribute to marital harmony or even compensate for unhappiness to some extent, the failure to achieve or appreciate the fruits of prosperity could cause tension. One case illustrates how this could happen. Charlotte Oster complained that her aspirations for the good life were continually thwarted by her husband Brad's failure to achieve what she thought was an appropriate standard of living. "Having been forced to buy, after three wartime evictions, in a section which was not quite up to the social standards we were used to, we found it hard to accept the choice of friends of our oldest daughter ... It has been very hard to keep her within the boundaries of what we consider the proper social standards."

Charlotte's dissatisfaction was not lost on Brad, who was acutely aware of his inability to provide adequately for a wholesome family environment. Charlotte noted that he "is often upset because he thinks he hasn't provided for us as well as he would like to, and considers himself rather a failure." Nevertheless, she said that marriage brought her "four wonderful children, a home of our own, and always something better to look forward to and strive for." In the last section of the survey, in which respondents were asked to add anything that had not already been covered, Charlotte wrote the saga of their marriage:

> We were married during the depression years on a shoestring, my husband lost his job soon after, and went into business for himself, also with no capital. Though he was excellent in his field (photography), he didn't have the drive necessary to sell himself, and we had very meager living for several years, til he got a factory job during the war. Though he did well, he liked having his own independence, and after quitting at several factory jobs because he didn't like the unfairness or domination, he started another business with a partner, in aerial photography. Then a series of unfortunate setbacks began ... eviction ... hurricane damage to his place ... injuries ... now my husband is back working for another aerial concern, but he dislikes the work, feels he is too old to start at the bottom in another line, and therefore is inwardly upset a good deal of the time. ... I have always felt that he shouldn't cater to his feeling of having to be independent, and that he should take any kind of a good job with a steady pay ... which would give us all a much stronger feeling of security.

Charlotte's words demonstrate the centrality of the provider role and the difficulties it could create when it conflicted with a man's effort to achieve independence and personal fulfillment through work. The Osters' marriage lasted until 1961, when the couple divorced.[34]

Although some husbands in the sample were content to be "organization men" as long as they could bring home the fruits of material success, others shared with Brad Oster a need for autonomy at work. But like him, they were likely to find that this need placed in jeopardy their ability to be good providers, which, in turn, created marital friction. In a similar case, Maureen Gilford complained, "My husband is a tireless worker but insists on working *in his own business* and has made so many changes, it has been a constant struggle for 18½ years with just one short period of success. I don't feel my standards are the cause of his hard work. So he is always tired and has little time for enjoyment. I feel badly about this, preferring that he get a modest *but steady salary* and work for someone else. It has made me pinch pennies for years. Also, I have to work *hard* to increase our income and have little time for my own use. Too much housework, *too much work* altogether."

Maureen longed for more leisure, more planned activities together, and more regular hours for her husband. "He is always tired and overworked." She said he had some emotional disturbances from worry about business and too many job changes. "I wish he had *more time* for the children and for himself." George Gilford wrote little in his report. He said marriage brought him "a good way of life." He sacrificed "nothing material," and rated his marriage as generally satisfying, although he, too, worried about providing for his family's needs, particularly a college education for both his children. Nevertheless, the fulfillment of the provider role would not necessarily satisfy George's need for meaningful work.[35]

The men in these cases faced the double anguish of failure to earn an adequate living in work they enjoyed and failure to be successful providers. For others, the breadwinner role, if performed successfully, might offer compensation for dissatisfaction at work. For women, marriage offered the possibility of material comforts and social standing—something a single woman earning a meager wage was not likely to achieve. Women also might gain some measure of autonomy in their domestic responsibilities—something that neither they nor their husbands were likely to find easily in the paid labor force. In addition, as wives of productive breadwinners, women might be able to gain the trappings of success unavailable to them in the work and public arenas. Suburban houses, after all, were not built with single working women in mind.

Some women focused their personal ambitions vicariously on their husband's careers. One husband noted that this contributed to his own drive: "Being somewhat lazy to begin with," he wrote, "the family and my wife's ambition have made me more eager to succeed businesswise and financially." Other wives were explicit about the centrality of material possessions to their marital and family satisfaction. One equated marriage with keeping up with the Joneses: "We feel that our possessions are as good if not better than our neighbors as they are different, antique as to modern, and we hold that thought to us dearly."[36]

Another woman, Lucille Windam, elaborated on this theme more fully, offering a shopping list of name-brand consumer items as evidence of a successful marriage. Yet her testimony also provides a glimpse of the difficulties that might arise even if—or perhaps because—one lived fully in accord with the domestic consumer ethic. She wrote,

One fortunate thing which is important in our marriage is our fortunate change in income bracket. When we were married my husband earned $30 a week. We rented a five room flat . . . had a baby, etc. Now we have five children and an income of over $25,000 a year. We own our 8 room house—also a nice house on a lake. We have a sailboat, a Cris Craft, several small boats. We own our own riding horse which we keep at home. Our oldest child goes to a prep school. We have a Hammond organ in our home. . . . Our two sons at home own expensive instruments. We have and carry a lot of life insurance. Unless some disaster hits us, we see our way clear to educate all our children thru prep-school and college.

It is important to note the kind of consumerism Lucille mentioned: all the goods were geared toward home, family leisure, education, and recreation. She did not mention diamonds, mink coats, or other personal luxuries. Yet, here again is the potential hazard of domestic consumerism becoming the center of personal identity, for this woman's pride in her shopping-list definition of marital success was tempered by the complaint she added, almost as an afterthought: "My reaction to all this is that my husband doesn't seem content to save. He continually seeks something new to own; he doesn't keep his interest in any one thing very long." Her final remark is most telling, since it reflects the connection between success, consumerism, and domestic power relations: "He has terrific drive and aggressiveness, and I feel he tries to own all of us in the family too much." It is clear from Lucille's bitter words that the domestic consumer ethic, even at its most opulent, might be rife with tension. For her, family-oriented consumerism was the measure of successful married life and provided some compensation for her obvious disappointment in her relationship with her husband. For her husband, ambition and drive for power were expressed through his acquisition of goods and his total domination at home. Together they created an imperfect domestic relationship; nevertheless, that relationship clearly offered them both enough reasons for staying married.

Consumerism and children were the rewards that made the marriage worthwhile for Lucille Windam. In dedicating herself to the task of raising her children, she gained a sense of achievement that she believed she would not have found elsewhere. Her husband's ample income made her homemaking career possible. Even though she felt he was "overbearing, expects too much of me, and is inconsiderate of me," she appreciated his "ability to do almost anything he tries, his popularity, and his generosity to me financially." That financial generosity meant that she could devote herself to her children and provide them with all the finest things that money could buy: "I've worked hard at making my marriage work—for my own and for my children's sake. . . . Certainly—materially—I never could attain the things I have now. Of course, the children are a great satisfaction. My job seems to swamp me sometimes but I am really very fond of my family and I do try to treat each as a special individual so each personality is important and each child can have every advantage we can possibly give them. I can't imagine my life without children. I have no special talents so as a career person I'm sure I would not be a great success. As a mother and homemaker, I feel I am quite successful." Although she blamed her lack of "talent," rather than the lack of viable opportunities, she turned her creative efforts toward homemaking with the dedication and high standards of a professional.

Yet this domestic success was gained at a price: "Because of the size of our family, we have very little personal fun—I mean no clubs or activities. I used to be very active in PTA, church (taught Sunday school), and garden club, but my last two children now 4 and 2 years old changed all this. I just stay home with them and taxi my oldest boys around. Our oldest boy, almost 15, is away at prep school, but in our rural community I have to drive someone somewhere every day. I expect to get back into community life when my younger children are in school all day. I feel quite stale as though I don't use my mind enough." Still, she claimed to be satisfied with her marriage, in spite of a "stale" mind and an "overbearing inconsiderate" husband. The children, apparently, made it all worth it; the affluence made it all possible.

Ronald Windam also claimed to be satisfied with their life together. He took pride in his role as provider. He wrote that marriage had brought him "stability, a family which I very much admire and enjoy doing my best to provide for." As for sacrifices, he wrote, "There is nothing other than Utopia, and a little give and take in sexual relationship. Other than that, there has been no sacrifice." Like so many of their peers, Ronald and Lucille Windam resigned themselves to their disappointments and looked on the bright side. Although their affluent suburban lifestyle fell short of their dreams, they were determined to make the best of it.[37]

Consumerism in the postwar years went far beyond the mere purchases of goods and services. It included important cultural values, demonstrated success and social mobility, and defined lifestyles. It also provided the most vivid symbol of the American way of life: the affluent suburban home. There can be no doubt that the gender roles associated with domestic consumerism—homemaker and breadwinner—were central to the identity of many women and men at the time. It is also evident, however, that along with the ideology of sexual containment, postwar domestic consumerism required conformity to strict gender assumptions that were fraught with potential tensions and frustrations. Suburban homes filled with material possessions could not always compensate for the dissatisfactions inherent in the domestic arrangements consumerism was intended to enhance and reinforce. In fact, those very domestic arrangements, although idealized and coveted at the time, were the source of countless miseries. As one looks through the "window of vulnerability" in the cold war era, one sees families inside their suburban homes struggling to achieve the postwar dream of abundance and security. Many men and women made heroic efforts to live according to the ideal of domestic containment. Some were able to carve out meaningful and rewarding lives within its limits. For others, the rewards remained elusive.

Notes

1. William H. Whyte, Jr., "Budgetism: Opiate of the Middle Class," *Fortune*, May 1956, p. 133.

2. Quoted in Kenneth Jackson, *Crabgrass Frontier: The Suburbanization of the United States* (New York: Oxford University Press, 1985), p. 231.

3. Quotes from the debate in Moscow are from "The Two Worlds: A Day-Long Debate," *New York Times*, 25 July 1959, pp. 1 and 3; "When Nixon Took On Khrushchev," a report on the meeting, and the text of Nixon's address at the opening of the American National Ex-

hibition in Moscow on 24 July 1959, printed in "Setting Russia Straight on Facts about the U.S.," *U.S. News and World Report,* 3 August 1959, pp. 36–39 and 70–72; and "Encounter," *Newsweek,* 3 August 1959, pp. 15–19.

4. Letter to board of aldermen from Mayor Joseph Darst, 13 December 1951, Raymond Tucker Papers, Box 104, Special Collections, Olin Library, Washington University, St. Louis, Mo.

5. George H. Gallup, *The Gallup Poll, Public Opinion 1935–1971,* vol. 1, 1935–1948 (New York: Random House, 1972), p. 594; Hadley Cantril, ed., *Public Opinion, 1935–1946* (Princeton, N.J.: Princeton University Press, 1951), pp. 829 and 831; and Susan Hartmann, *The Home Front and Beyond: American Women in the 1940s* (Boston: Twayne Publishers, 1982), p. 8.

6. George Katona, *The Mass Consumption Society,* pp. 14–15, and *The Powerful Consumer: Psychological Studies of the American Economy,* pp. 9–32 (New York: McGraw-Hill Book Co., 1964 and 1960, respectively). U.S. Bureau of the Census, *Historical Statistics of the United States, Colonial Times to 1970* (Washington, D.C.: U.S. Government Printing Office, 1975), part 1, pp. 49 and 316–20; Hartmann, *The Home Front and Beyond,* p. 8.

7. Katona, *The Powerful Consumer,* p. 27.

8. *See* Daniel Horowitz, *The Morality of Spending* (Baltimore, Md.: Johns Hopkins University Press, 1985), esp. chap. 8, for shifting ideas on spending in the 1930s.

9. Cantril, *Public Opinion,* pp. 1047–1048.

10. Katona, *The Powerful Consumer,* pp. 46, 156.

11. *See* Winifred D. Wandersee, *Women's Work and Family Values, 1920–1940* (Cambridge, Mass.: Harvard University Press, 1981), for a discussion of changing material expectations and the role of women's employment in family support. On the depression's legacy of employment for women, *see* S. Bennett and Glen Elder, Jr., "Women's Work in the Family Economy," *Journal of Family History* 4 (Summer 1979), pp. 153–76.

12. George Putnam, newscast in the documentary film by The Archives Project, *The Atomic Cafe,* 1982, Thorn Emi Video.

13. National Association of Savings Banks survey, and Office of Civilian Requirements survey, cited in John Morton Blum, *V Was For Victory: Politics and American Culture During World War II* (New York: Harcourt Brace Jovanovich, 1976), pp. 100–101; Clifford Edward Clark, *The American Family Home, 1800–1960* (Chapel Hill: University of North Carolina Press, 1986), p. 195.

14. Ibid., pp. 102–103.

15. Jackson, *Crabgrass Frontier,* pp. 231–32.

16. Clark, *The American Family Home,* p. 213; Jackson, *Crabgrass Frontier,* p. 249.

17. "Should-Must Cities Decentralize?" *Commonwealth,* 31 May 1948, quoted in John H. Mollenkopf, "The Postwar Politics of Urban Development," William K. Tabb and Larry Sawyers, eds., *Marxism and the Metropolis* (New York: Oxford University Press, 1978), p. 131.

18. Jackson, *Crabgrass Frontier,* pp. 11, 190–93, 203–18, and 283–95.

19. Clark, *The American Family Home,* pp. 221–33; Jackson, *Crabgrass Frontier,* chaps. 11 and 12.

20. Katona *The Mass Consumption Society,* pp. 14–18 and 265–73.

21. Jackson, *Crabgrass Frontier,* p. 235.

22. Clark, *The American Family Home,* p. 219.

23. Stuart Ewen, *Captains of Consciousness: Advertising and the Social Roots of the Consumer Culture* (New York: McGraw-Hill Book Co., 1976); George Lipsitz, "The Meaning of Memory: Family, Class and Ethnicity in Early Network Television Programs," *Cultural Anthropology* 1 (November 1986), pp. 355–87.

24. Clark, *The American Family Home,* pp. 198, 210–213, 236.

25. Ibid., pp. 210–13.

26. Herbert Gans, *The Levittowners: The Ways of Life and Politics in a New Suburban Community* (New York: Pantheon, 1967), pp. 163–65.

27. Ibid., pp. 153–55 and 206–12; Clark, *The American Family Home*, pp. 224–43.

28. Jackson, *Crabgrass Frontier*, pp. 235–43.

29. Calculated from D43C61, D45C34, D45C36, D45C35, pertaining to income and debts, KLS.

30. Calculated from D43C62, D43C57, D43C56, D43C55, D43C53, pertaining to expenditures for housing, cars, and installment buying, KLS.

31. Calculated from items D43C63–D43C67, pertaining to factors most important in determining the way extra money was spent, KLS.

32. Elizabeth Long, *The American Dream and the Popular Novel* (Boston: Routledge & Kegan Paul, 1985), pp. 52–76. *See also* Sloan Wilson, *The Man in the Grey Flannel Suit* (New York: Simon & Schuster, 1955).

33. Cases 224, 250, 24, 237, 244, 72, KLS.

34. Case 153, KLS. The reader is again reminded that the names of the KLS respondents used in this chapter are the author's invention and that the KLS identified respondents only by case number. For a provocative discussion of the tensions in the male provider role which illuminates issues raised in this case, *see* Barbara Ehrenreich, *The Hearts of Men* (Garden City, N.Y.: Doubleday & Co., 1983).

35. Case 109, KLS.

36. Cases 244 and 75, KLS.

37. Case 62, KLS.

CHAPTER 16

The Revolution Will Be Marketed:
American Corporations and
Black Consumers During the 1960s

Robert E. Weems, Jr.

The Black Freedom Movement of the 1950s and 1960s captured the attention of millions. Yet, the African-American experience during this period included more than boycotts, "sit-ins," "freedom rides," and massive protest marches. With the wartime and postwar migration from the South, African-Americans were transformed from a predominantly rural people into a predominantly urban people by 1960. As African-Americans streamed into American cities, or what American corporations call "major markets," U.S. businesses sought to influence the consumption patterns of these increasingly important black consumers. This article will survey the dynamics of the relationship between U.S. corporations and African-American consumers during the 1960s.

Before the 1960s, American corporations generally ignored African-American consumers. Most black-oriented radio stations, for example, experienced difficulties attracting advertising from large corporations; most had to demonstrate to prospective corporate advertisers the potential profitability of advertising aimed at black consumers. The establishment of the National Negro Network, Inc. (NNN) in 1954 represented one such effort.[1] The NNN was a nationwide consortium of forty two black-oriented radio stations formed to attract "blue-chip" corporate advertising. To assist this campaign, the NNN produced a daytime serial entitled "Ruby Valentine" that aired on the network's affiliates. In promoting "Ruby Valentine" to potential corporate advertisers, the NNN's promotional material declared:

> Now . . . for the first time in advertising history . . . a single coordinated program can take you to the heart of the 16 billion dollar American Negro Market. This new selling concept offers an advertiser a rich sales frontier virtually uncultivated by national advertising.[2]

"The Revolution Will Be Marketed: American Corporations and Black Consumers During the 1960s" by Robert E. Weems, Jr. from *Radical History Review* 59 (Spring 1994). Reprinted with the permission of Cambridge University Press.

By the early sixties, as African-Americans proliferated in U.S. cities, American corporations no longer had to be convinced of the profitability of seeking black customers. This is borne out by such advertising trade journals as *Sponsor, Advertising Age*, and *Broadcasting*, all of which began featuring articles about the "Negro Market" and its growing importance to corporate marketers.[3] For instance, *Sponsor*'s October 1962 special edition pertaining to black American consumers summed up the new reality as follows:

"I could have become President. I needed only five percent more votes in the Negro areas. I could have gotten them if I had campaigned harder."

That's how Richard Nixon earlier this year crystallized the lesson of history's closest presidential race. It's a meaningful lesson not only for politicians, but for marketers and advertising strategists. Reason: the Negro today is the last big uncommitted force in the battle for the consumer dollar. His $27 billion income is new wealth; it is spent generously, but where it will gain the most value. There are 19 million of these new buyers today, and in major markets across the nation they can now force the outright success or failure of mass marketing campaigns.[4]

Sponsor's observations concerning African-Americans' growing economic clout graphically illustrated the intensity of post-World War II black migration. For example, between 1940 and 1960, the black urban population in the West grew by nearly 700 percent. In the northeast and north-central regions of the country, the percentage of African-American population increase appeared less dramatic. Still, the numerical increase of blacks in these areas was staggering. In 1940, approximately 2,495,000 African-Americans resided in northeast and north-central urban areas. By 1960, this figure had grown to 6,193,000 (see Table 1). Moreover, the number of African-Americans living in southern cities also increased significantly (see Table 2).

This significant black migration to northern, southern, and western cities represented not only a change of address for the migrants, but a distinct improvement in their occupational status. Between 1940 and 1960, the percent-

Table 1. African-Americans residing in urban areas outside the South, 1940–1960

	Northeast	North central	West
1940	1,234,000	1,261,000	143,000
1950	1,897,000	2,082,000	513,000
1960	2,896,000	3,297,000	1,000,000

Source: Daniel O. Price, *Changing Characteristics of The Negro Population: A 1960 Census Monograph* (Washington, D.C.: Bureau of the Census, 1969), 246–247. The Northeast region of the U.S. included Maine, Vermont, New Hampshire, Rhode Island, Connecticut, Massachusetts, New York, New Jersey, and Pennsylvania. The North Central region included Ohio, Michigan, Indiana, Illinois, Wisconsin, Minnesota, Iowa, Missouri, North Dakota, South Dakota, Nebraska, and Kansas. The West included Montana, Wyoming, Colorado, New Mexico, Idaho, Utah, Arizona, Washington, Oregon, Nevada, and California.

Table 2. African-Americans residing in selected southern cities, 1940–1960

	1940	1950	1960
Miami, FL	54,000	62,000	102,000
Baltimore, MD	166,000	225,000	326,000
Atlanta, GA	105,000	121,000	186,000
Memphis, TN	121,000	151,000	184,000
Jackson, MS	24,000	40,000	52,000
New Orleans, LA	149,000	182,000	234,000
Houston, TX	86,000	125,000	215,000
Mobile, AL	29,000	46,000	66,000

Source: U.S. Bureau of the Census, *U.S. Census of Population: 1960, Selected Area Reports, Standard Metropolitan Statistical Areas* (Washington, D.C.: U.S. Government Printing Office, 1963), 41, 153, 173, 189, 194, 197, 203, 218.

age of African-Americans in (relatively low-paying) southern agriculture work declined dramatically (see Table 3). Moreover, as fewer and fewer blacks worked in agriculture, the larger society—especially corporate America— slowly began to change its perception of African-Americans. By the early 1960s, blacks, once viewed as poor, rural workers with a minimum of disposable income, were seen as a market whose annual purchasing power exceeded that of Canada.[5]

Although 1960 census data demonstrated African-American gains in income and their strategic proliferation in major markets,[6] many corporations, who had previously ignored the African-American consumer market, were at a loss as to how to reach black shoppers. Consequently, advertising trade journals throughout the 1960s assisted these corporations by featuring numerous "how-to" articles concerning selling to African-Americans. An 9 October 1961 article in *Sponsor* entitled "Know-How Is Key To Selling Negro Today," epitomized this trend.

Sponsor advised its readers that the key to success in marketing to African-Americans could be summer up in three words: recognition, identification, and invitation. Specifically, prospective corporate advertisers were told:

Table 3. Percentage of African-Americans involved in Southern agriculture, 1940–1960 (male/female)

	1940	1950	1960
Farmers & farm managers:	25.9/3.8	19.3/2.5	7.1/1.0
Farm laborers and foreman:	23.816.6	14.5/11.4	11.7/4.8
TOTAL:	49.7/20.4	33.8/13.9	18.5/5.8

Source: Daniel O. Price, *Changing Charateristics of the Negro Population: A 1960 Census Monograph* (Washington, D.C.: United States Bureau of the Census, 1969), 119.

The Negro needs to be recognized as a person. The very fact that an advertiser will undertake a special campaign (for) the Negro is interpreted as a form of recognition to the Negro. And that advertiser immediately stands to gain an important competitive edge over the advertisers who has not taken this step . . . identification is equally important. Can the Negro identify with your product? Can the Negro identify with the ad that promises "lovelier, whiter hands with ABC soap?" Because of the Negro's history of suppression his need to be "invited" to try the product appears to be a strong one indeed. True, he may use it without invitation, but this power of a special invitation to him, alone, can be considerable.[7]

Armed with insights about the psyche of black Americans, and market research data that demonstrated that blacks listened to radio more frequently than whites,[8] corporate marketers increasingly used radio advertising to reach African-American consumers. Between 1961 and 1966, American corporations, according to *Broadcasting* (another advertising trade journal), increased their advertising budget for black-oriented radio stations three-fold.[9] American corporations maximized their advertising campaigns on black-oriented radio stations by encouraging African-American radio personalities (disc jockeys) to directly market their products.[10] Because black disc jockeys were celebrities in their own right, they were ideal potential allies for white-owned businesses seeking to make inroads in a new market. The following example illustrates this special relationship.

In 1965, Proctor & Gamble had become increasingly concerned that only 5 percent of its redeemable coupons were being used by black consumers. To counteract this situation, Proctor launched a major campaign in Chicago, one of its major urban markets, to increase the number of blacks using Tide detergent, Comet cleanser, and Ivory soap. In October, Proctor & Gamble sent out 260,000 letters to Chicago blacks signed by popular radio personality "Daddy-O-Daylie" of jazz radio WAAF. These letters, besides soliciting entries for a "smart shopper sweepstakes," included three five-cents-off coupons, one each for Tide, Comet, and Ivory. To reinforce these letters, Proctor bought 240 advertising spots on WAAF to be delivered by "Daddy-O." Daylie, known as "the musical host who loves you the most," ended his pitch to black Chicago female consumers by stating: "so moms, don't just sit there and stare, grab your coupons and roar to the store."[11]

While national, regional, and local white businesses were accelerating their use of black-oriented radio to reach black consumers, these same companies sought as much information as possible concerning the nuances of the "Negro Market." But American racism and the legacy of racial segregation left most white businesspersons ill-equipped to understand African-American life. Consequently, many white companies had to rely upon the services of black consultants, the most influential being John H. Johnson, publisher of *Ebony* magazine, and D. Parke Gibson, president of D. Parke Gibson Associates, Inc.

Johnson had long been interested in making corporate America aware of the potential profits associated with black consumers. As early as 1947, Johnson's

Ebony asserted that major corporations were missing lucrative opportunities by ignoring the African-American market.[12] It should be noted, however, that Johnson's observations were based upon self-interest. From the moment of its founding in 1945, *Ebony* failed to secure substantial advertising from large corporations.[13]

Nevertheless, by the early 1960s, *Ebony* had established itself as a major American magazine and John H. Johnson stood as one of the country's top executives. Moreover, Johnson's success as a publisher appeared to have been based upon his ability to gauge the mood and interests of his readers.[14] Consequently, to white corporate leaders seeking insights about black consumers, Johnson appeared to be an ideal ally. In his autobiography, *Succeeding Against The Odds*, Johnson described his consulting role to corporate America as follows:

> In the decade of the long hot summers, I held the unofficial position of special ambassador to American Whites. . . . Enlightened self-interest: that was my theme. I asked corporate leaders to act not for Blacks, not for civil rights, but for their corporations and themselves. For it was true then and it's true now that if you increase the income of Blacks and Hispanics and poor Whites, you increase the profits of corporate America. And if you decrease the income of the disadvantaged, you decrease income and potential income of American corporations. . . . What it all boiled down to was that equal opportunity was good business.[15]

Johnson's advice to corporate America deserves closer examination. His theme of "enlightened self-interest" suggests a major reinterpretation of the 1960s. If corporate leaders took Johnson's message to heart, it can plausibly be argued that some of the gains associated with the Civil Rights Movement were based upon "conservative," rather than "liberal" impulses.

For example, during the sixties, the Congress of Racial Equality (CORE) stood in the forefront of the movement to force American corporations to use African-American models in their print and television advertising. To CORE and other civil rights organizations, this was a "social" issue.[16] However, when U.S. businesses realized that using black models increased black purchases of their products without alienating white consumers,[17] corporations gladly utilized black models in print media and on television. Johnson's concern about the "enlightened self-interest" (profits) of large white corporations appeared intimately connected with his concern about *Ebony*'s financial well-being. Once he convinced corporate leaders that it was "good business" to reach more black consumers, these same corporations had to find a vehicle to do just that. Although Johnson's autobiography claims that he did not directly approach white corporate leaders about advertising in *Ebony* during the 1960s,[18] *Ebony*'s advertising revenue nearly tripled between 1962 and 1969 (see Table 4).

While Johnson urged corporate America to take a greater interest in selling to African-American consumers, D. Parke Gibson advised corporate America on how to most effectively reach black consumers. Gibson's company, estab-

Table 4. Advertising revenue *Ebony* magazine, 1962–1969

1962	3,630,804
1963	5,129,921
1964	5,641,895
1965	5,495,537
1966	7,020,279
1967	6,895,379
1968	8,551,463
1969	9,965,898

Source: "Records of *Ebony* magazine," Publishers Information Bureau, Inc./Magazine Publishers of America, New York, New York.

lished in 1960, specialized in market research and public relations consulting.[19] Gibson and his associates subsequently offered their services to a myriad of companies, including Avon Products, Inc., Coca Cola USA, Columbia Pictures, Greyhound, and the R. J. Reynolds Tobacco Company.[20] Moreover, Gibson published two books about the African-American consumer market, *The $30 Billion Dollar Negro*(1969), and *$70 Billion In the Black* (1978).

An example of the advice Gibson's company gave its corporate clients appeared in the 25 July 1966 issue of *Sponsor*. Elsie Archer, director of the company's Women's Interest Bureau, published a brief article entitled "How To Sell Today's Negro Woman." Among other things, Archer offered the following insights about the black female consumer:

> She wants advertising and marketing people to understand that her needs and desires are often different. For example, she does not want a blue-eyed suburban housewife telling her to use a particular product when she is faced with urban living. Particularly in the area of personal care products, advertisers should use extreme caution to avoid pricking the high sensitivity of the Negro woman. . . . One last word—never, never, under any circumstances refer to the Negro woman as "Negress or Negresses," a phrase guaranteed to produce an unfavorable reaction.[21]

About the same time Archer instructed corporate America on how to best reach African-American female consumers, the black community was in the throes of a dramatic shift in political orientation. Despite corporate America's increasing recognition of black consumers, as well as the passage of the Civil Rights Act of 1964 and the Voting Rights Act of 1965, a significant proportion of African-Americans remained frustrated and angry about continuing racial injustice in the United States. The Watts Rebellion of 1965, along with the immediate popularity of the term "Black Power" in 1966, reflected a growing militancy toward, and mistrust of, white society.

The appearance of overt black nationalist sentiment during the mid 1960s initially confused corporate executives. During the early 1960s, they had been led to believe that African-Americans were preoccupied with trying to assimilate into mainstream U.S. society. For example, the 4 October 1963 issue of *Sales Management* featured an article entitled "The Negro Market: Growing, Changing, Challenging," which not only surveyed what the author believed were the basic characteristics of black consumers, but sought to project their activities into the immediate future. Considering what *actually* happened, the following prognostication turned out to be way off the mark: "Negroes will de-emphasize race consciousness and differences, and focus attention on social and cultural similarities compatible with the concept and practice of an integrated society."[22]

Despite their initial confusion, corporate marketers quickly adjusted their marketing campaigns aimed at African-American consumers. Early 1960s' ad campaigns that sought to promote the image of an integrated society[23] were replaced with attempts to exploit blacks' growing sense of racial pride. The development of the "soul market" illustrates corporate America's attempt to adapt to African-American consumers' political and cultural reorientation. Corporate marketers co-opted growing black pride by extolling the virtues of African-American life and culture. Moreover, such things as "Soul Music" and "Soul Food" were promoted for both black and white consumption. From a business point of view, the "soul market" appeared to be especially profitable. Not only would corporate America reach African-Americans, but also faddish whites wanting to be viewed as "hip." Nonetheless, as the following excerpt from a June 1969 article in *Sales Management* suggested, corporations seeking to exploit the "soul market" had to demonstrate some knowledge of African-American consumers and their cultural world:

> A few weeks ago, 800 people sat down to a $100-a-plate "authentic Soul Food" supper in the Grand Ballroom of New York City's stately Waldorf-Astoria Hotel. After sampling the fried chicken, corn bread, collard greens, and sweet potato pie, TV star Bill Cosby, the charity affair's co-chairman, announced over the public address system that his meal had left an authentic grease ring around his mouth all right, but, he complained, "this is not how real Soul Food tastes." The Waldorf's flop with Soul is par for the course in the long, sad history of white encounters with virtually everything Negro. . . . Now unless they are plugging into today's Soul scene, many a marketer risks yet another blunder with the nation's 23 million blacks—and a sizable number of whites too.[24]

To help themselves "plug" into the Soul scene, corporate America, once again, relied upon the expertise of black consultants. The black-owned Vince Cullers *Advertising Agency* of Chicago surfaced as the leading consultant to companies seeking to make their advertisements convey "Soul." Cullers' most noteworthy creation was a print advertisement used by the Lorrilard Corporation to promote its Newport cigarette brand. A young bearded black man, wearing a dashiki, stood next to a huge pack of Newport cigarettes. The copy read: "Bold Cold Newport . . . a whole new bag of menthol smoking."[25]

About the same time corporate American desired to make its existing products attractive to "soul brothers and sisters," some white-owned companies sought to expand their black customer base by developing consumer items exclusively for African-Americans. This trend centered around the production of black personal care products. During the "Jim Crow" era, African-American entrepreneurs had monopolized the production of hair and skin products for blacks. An examination of advertisements in black newspapers during the early to mid twentieth century reveals myriad such products.[26] White corporations, because of their general disregard for black consumers, had little interest in getting a share of the black personal care products market. However, as the African-American standard of living rose during the 1960s, and as market research revealed that blacks spent a significant proportion of money on personal care products, some white-owned companies made a concerted effort to produce these goods.[27]

Because whites were unaware of how blacks took care of their hair and skin, corporations turned once again to consultants to provide vital information. One such individual was Marvin K. Cook, a black chemist whose May 1970 article in the trade journal *Drug and Cosmetic Industry* revealed the actual formulas for a variety of black personal care products.[28]

Some white companies relied upon their own efforts to enter the black personal care products market. For example, before the National Toiletries Company decided to start its "Libra" cosmetic line for black women in 1969, it conducted an exhaustive preliminary market research campaign that included ten hour interviews.[29]

By the beginning of the 1970s, African-Americans were recognized as an increasingly important consumer market. Indeed, American corporations took the advice offered by trade journals and black consultants, and actively wooed prospective African-American customers. Yet, continuing racial strife clearly indicates that blacks, while desired as shoppers, are often less desired by whites as classmates, co-workers, and neighbors. Moreover, African-Americans' current annual collective spending power of between $250–300 billion has not halted the steady decline of urban black America. These ongoing problems suggest that black consumers, despite their recognized importance to the U.S. economy, cannot *buy* substantive respect and power from American corporations.[30]

Notes

1. "NNN: Negro Radio's Network," *Sponsor* (20 September 1954), 54. It is important to note that the overwhelming majority of these black-oriented radio stations were owned by white entrepreneurs. See William Barlow, "Commercial and Noncommercial Radio" in *Split Image: Africa-Americans In The Mass Media*, ed. Jannette L. Dates and William Barlow (Washington, D.C.: Howard University Press, 1990), 209, 214.

2. "NNN: Negro Radio's Network," *Sponsor* (20 September 1954), 46.

3. A crosssection of such articles included: C. H. Hall, "Advertisers' Guide To Marketing, 1960 Negro Market," *Printer's Ink* (30 October 1959), 246–47; "Marketing To The Negro

Consumer; Special Report," *Sales Management* (4 March 1960), 36–44; "Tapping The Negro Market; Association Formed To Promote Its Value," *Broadcasting* (8 August 1960), 52; "Know-How Is Key To Selling Negro Market Today," *Sponsor Negro Issue* (9 October 1961), 9–10; H. C. Russell, "Ads Alone Won't Win Negro Market," *Advertising Age* (21 October 1963), 3; "Is There A U.S. Negro Market? *Yes* Can It Be Reached As Easily As Any Other Market? *No,*" *Sponsor* (17 August 1964), 32.

4. "The 1963 Market Opportunity," *Sponsor Negro Issue* (22 October 1962), 7.

5. "Know-How Is Key to Selling Negro Today," *Sponsor Negro Issue* (9 October 1961), 9.

6. "Past Decade Saw the Market Zoom," *Sponsor Negro Issue* (9 October 1961), 11–12, 33, 37.

7. "Know-How Is Key To Selling Negro Today," *Sponsor Negro Issue* (9 October 1961), 26–27.

8. "Negro Radio's Prosperous Market," *Sponsor Negro Issue*, (26 September 1960), 47; "Radio: Major Medium For Reaching Negroes," *Sponsor* (17 August 1964), 37.

9. "Advertiser Interest In Negroes Zooms," *Broadcasting* (7 November 1966), 76.

10. "Know-How Is Key To Selling Negro Market Today," *Sponsor Negro Issue* (9 October 1961), 27; "Is There A U.S. Negro Market? *Yes* Can It Be Reached As Easily As Any Other Market? *No*" *Sponsor* (17 August 1964), 32; Negro Radio's 1965 on); "Negro Radio's 1965-Style New Sound," *Sponsor* (26 July 1965), 57.

11. "P&G Signs Chicago's Daddy-O To Help Swing Negro Market," *Advertising Age* (11 October 1965), 2, 90; Barlow, "Commercial and Noncommercial Radio," 217. Daylie's notoriety extended beyond Chicago. Barlow cited jazz legend Dizzy Gillespie's assertion that Daddy-O Daylie created much of the "hip" vocabulary used by post-World War II bebop musicians.

12. John H. Johnson and Lerone Bennent Jr., *Succeeding Against The Odds* (New York: Warner Books, 1980), 229.

13. Ibid., 173, 179–80.

14. Ibid., 156–57, 287.

15. Ibid., 277–80.

16. Maurine Christopher, "CORE Seeks More Integrated Ads; Core Invites 14 Major Advertisers To Discuss Using Negroes In Ads," *Advertising Age* (9 September 1963), 1, 128; Maurine Christopher, "CORE Intensifies Drive For Negroes In Ads; Zeroes In On Pepsi-Cola Co.," *Advertising Age* (9 November 1964), 3, 71; "Boycott By Negroes?," *Printer's Ink* (23 August 1963), 5–6.

17. "Same Ad, Intelligently Done, Can Sell To Both Whites, Negroes: Bullock" *Advertising Age* (12 June 1961), 23; "Integrated Ads Not Offensive To Whites, Dallas Group Told," *Advertising Age* (14 October 1968), 31; "Use Of Negro Models In Ads Won't Reduce Sales To Whites, Johnson Advises Workshop," *Advertising Age* (9 December 1968), 24; "Use Of Black Models In Ads Doesn't Alter Sales Patterns, BofA [Bureau of Advertising] Reports," *Advertising Age* (9 November 1970), 52; Lester Guest, "How Negro Models Affect Company Image," *Journal of Advertising Research* (10 April 1970): 29–33.

18. Johnson and Bennett, *Succeeding Against The Odds*, 27.

19. D. Parke Gibson, "Advertising and The Dual Society: Challenge Of The Seventies," *Mediascope* 13 (August 1969): 63.

20. Ibid.

21. Elsie Archer, "How To Sell Today's Negro Woman," *Sponsor* (25 July 1966), 49.

22. Lawrence E. Black, "The Negro Market: Growing, Changing, Challenging," *Sales Management* (4 October 1963), 46.

23. Black advisors to American corporations appeared partially responsible for this development. See "Don't Contrive Integrated Ads, (John H.) Johnson Advises," *Advertising Age* (23 September 1963), 1, 111; "Help Negro In Image Effort Via Ads, [Roy] Wilkens Asks," *Advertising Age* (11 November 1963), 1, 112.

24. "The Soul Market In Black And White," *Sales Management* (1 June 1969), 37.

25. Ibid., 40.

26. The Chicago *Defender*, among other African-American newspapers, featured a vast number of advertisements for personal care products (hair and skin) during this period. Most of the companies providing these products were small black-owned firms.

27. "Negro Radio's Prosperous Market," *Sponsor* (26 September 1960), 9; Raymond A. Bauer and Scott M. Cunningham, "The Negro Market," *Journal of Advertising Research* 10 (April, 1970): 10–11.

28. Marvin K. Cook, "Modern Negro Cosmetics II," *Drug & Cosmetic Industry* 106 (May 1970): 42–44.

29. "Libra: New Line Of Negro Cosmetics," *Drug & Cosmetic Industry* 105 (December 1969): 45.

30. David H. Swinton, "The Economic Status Of African-Americans: Permanent Poverty and Inequality," in *The State of Black America, 1991* (New York: National Urban League Inc., 1991), 28.

CHAPTER 17

All Work and No Play. It Doesn't Pay

Juliet B. Schor

Here's some advice for companies in search of a better bottom line: Send your workers home early.

Sound silly? It certainly does to most executives. If anything, they say, hours will have to rise. According to a survey by *Fortune* magazine, for instance, 77 percent of American executives believe that "large U.S. companies will have to push their managers harder" to achieve global success.

This belief in "working long" strongly affects the economy and individual businesses. Why do we have a "jobless recovery?" Because, in part, employers are using record levels of overtime instead of hiring new workers. Why are many companies—both failing and profitable—slashing their work forces by thousands? Because, in part, they believe the road to profit is to be lean and mean, to push their employees harder and longer.

"Working long" is hardly new. While earlier eras were interested in the promise of shorter working hours, for the past 20 years job time has been rising. After World War II, the United States had the shortest work time of all advanced industrial countries. Today, our hours are topped only by Japan. While the average working American put in 1,786 hours on the job in 1969, by 1989 annual work time had risen to 1,924 hours—adding almost a 13th month of work to the year.

It is time to critically examine this 20-year trend, and the assumptions behind it. Is it true that longer hours improve the bottom line? Or, conversely, is it true that shorter hours are unacceptably expensive? If history is any guide, the answers are no and no. At the least, corporate fears about the costs of shorter work time are unfounded. During the shift after 1910 from a 10- to an 8-hour day, for instance, workers produced more per hour. Why? Because the 10-hour day simply proved too tiring for maximum productivity.

Generally, as the workday has gotten shorter over the past 100 years, the efficiency of work has increased. For example, studies of American and British companies in the 1970s—when there was still some management interest in shorter hours—have reached a compellingly consistent conclusion: Shrinking the 40-hour work week by up to five hours without shrinking pay leads to less absenteeism, less turnover, less personal business on company time and lower costs.

These results still hold true today. Last summer, when New York Life Insurance gave its employees Friday afternoons off, its chief executive reported that the work was made up during the rest of the week. His experience was not atypical: The rise in hourly productivity from a shorter day often fully makes up for the reduction in hours.

Frequently, in fact, the shorter day *more* than makes up for the lost time. When the Kellogg Company adopted a 6-hour day in the 1930's, workers packed more cereal than they had in an 8-hour shift. The Kellogg experience is hardly unique. Late 19th-century estimates showed that, for three-fourths of all companies, reducing daily hours not only raised productivity per hour, but also each worker's total daily production.

Aside from productivity, shorter hours can soothe the growing problems of stress, burnout and disrupted personal lives that long hours incur. This is no small advantage. The International Labor Organization recently reported that three of four Americans describe their jobs as stressful, and believe that work pressure is increasing. And, according to a 1991 Gallup poll, 43 percent of working parents experience "a great deal" or "quite a lot" of conflict between work and family, and more than 75 percent say their personal life bears the burden.

Of course, the shorter workday is only one way to reduce work time. Another option is job sharing, which combines the diverse strengths of two people, offers flexibility in total weekly hours without the use of overtime, and can dramatically reduce absenteeism. Other alternatives include permanent part-time employment and employee trade-offs of income for free time.

Reducing work time—particularly through job sharing, permanent part-time employment and longer vacations—can also ease our growing problem with jobs. It is no coincidence that, as work time has increased since the 1970's, unemployment and underemployment have doubled. Given the dim outlook for national and global growth in demand, reducing work time may now be the only feasible way to generate significant numbers of jobs.

But convincing Corporate America to offer these options won't be easy. For 20 years, "working smart" has been confused, more and more, with "working long." But this confusion is not inevitable. Early this century, the value of shorter hours was widely appreciated. It is time to regain that appreciation.

CHAPTER 18

When High Wage Jobs Are Gone, Who Will Buy What We Make?

Kim Moody

For decades many unionized workers in the U.S. believed that their relatively high wages were the backbone of America's mass consumption economy. We buy what we make.

But what happens when the high wage jobs are gone? Who will buy the U.S. economy's still growing output of goods and services if the majority of working people get too poor? Isn't business shooting itself in the foot?

Clearly, business doesn't see it this way.

They are looking abroad to elite markets and fighting overseas competition in the U.S. market by cutting costs. And this, they believe, requires whole new ways of working—cheaper.

They want fewer workers per company, not more; lower-paid workers, not high-cost ones; and more economically insecure workers willing to work harder.

Whether they call it "high performance work organization," "agile manufacturing," or "lean production," it calls for cheaper, more flexible, even disposable, labor.

Big corporations are "downsizing" by over 3,000 jobs each business day, with no end in sight.

Small businesses, which account for most new jobs these days in the U.S., pay about one-third less in wages and benefits.

Full-time jobs are going the way of steady jobs. Last year, Labor Secretary Robert Reich noted that 90% of the new jobs were part-time. Part-timers now fill over 21 million jobs.

Temporary jobs are displacing regular employment, making the temp agency Manpower, Inc. the biggest employer in the U.S. Employment at personnel supply agencies rose from 543,000 in 1980 to 1,665,000 in 1992.

Kim Moody, "When High Wage Jobs Are Gone, Who Will Buy What We Make?" from *Labor Notes* (June 1994). Reprinted by permission of Kim Moody.

Joining The Have-Nots

In this kind of labor market, there can be only one result. Worker incomes are falling. [There has been an] enormous shift from high-wage to low-wage jobs for production and non-supervisory workers.

As a result, the U.S. is becoming a nation of haves and have-nots. The majority of Americans are getting poorer each year.

- Real average family income fell by 6% from 1989 through 1992.
- Average family net worth (homes, cars, savings, investments) fell by 12% from 1988 through 1991.
- The official poverty rate rose from 12.8% in 1989 to 14.5% in 1992, bringing the total to 37 million people. For Blacks it rose from 30.7% to about 33% and for Latinos from 26.2% to about 29% in this period.

On the other hand, a minority of Americans are getting richer. The shift to low-wage, short term jobs has meant a massive redirection of wealth away from wages to business income and away from workers to the rich.

CEO salaries increased by 15 times from 1960 to 1992, while worker pay grew only four times. By 1993, CEOs made 149 times what workers made on average.

As outrageous as CEO compensation has become, it is the growth of incomes on investment that is making the rich richer.

[While] real wages fell by 10% between 1980 and 1993, income on interest rose by 60% and that on dividends by 120%.

The wealthiest 10% of U.S. families control about 90% of the stocks, bonds, trusts, and business assets that produce interest and dividends, so naturally they benefit when these incomes rise faster due to cost-cutting and corporate reorganization.

The share of U.S. income of the top 20% of U.S. families rose from 41.7% in 1979 to 44.2% in 1991. This may sound small, but it represents a transfer of over $100 billion in household income from the majority to the wealthy.

The bottom 60% of U.S. households own—together—only 3% of all personal wealth. In this have-not majority, nearly a third are people of color and a fifth are female-headed households.

Obviously, the wealthy have a very deep personal stake in the shift to low-wage disposable workers.

But they still need to sell the consumer goods and services that spin out of their low-wage, high performance factories and offices. Not even rich Americans can buy them all. Who can?

Global Consumer Elite

Some of these goods and services are bought by the bloated globe-trotting business elite that runs the international production systems, world-wide financial markets, and global retail chains.

As it is with capital goods, energy, and raw materials, business is the greatest consumer of airline flights, hotel rooms, cellular phones, computers, financial services, and telecommunications equipment and services.

But beyond such business expenses are the world-wide sales of final consumer goods made to the elites who benefit from poverty the world around.

Last year, in the heat of the debate over GATT, World Bank economists Herman Daly and Robert Goodland expressed concern about how free trade was pushing down worker incomes in the industrial countries while at the same time creating a greater flow of goods between countries of the world's industrial North and those of the less developed South or Third World.

They characterized this trade as one between "Northern capitalists" and "Southern elites," many of whom are business partners. In order to sustain this growing trade, Daly and Goodland argued, both elites needed to get continuously richer.

And so they have, forming a global consumer elite.

The global consumer elite includes managers, certain types of professionals, government officials, financial speculators, and other well-paid hangers-on able to buy Western-style consumer goods.

Income distribution in the poor nations of the South is even more unequal than in the U.S. The top 20% of individuals earn 67.5% of all income in Brazil, 63% in Chile, and 56% in Mexico.

Clearly, many in this 20%, which represents some 900 million people in poorer countries, are able to join in the upscale consumer binge sponsored by the transnational producers and distributors of pricey items. In effect, they are able to stand in as major consumers for millions of U.S. workers with declining incomes.

The Solution

This global consumer elite is today's solution to the problem of who will buy what we make. It is one of the reasons, along with cheaper internationalized production, why open markets in the Third World and free trade (GATT, NAFTA, European Union) in general are so important to Northern capitalists.

Right now, U.S. government and business leaders are focusing on growing economies in Asia and Latin America as a source of sales. As Commerce Secretary Ronald Brown recently noted, "In the last decade, American exports to emerging markets nearly tripled."

Will this export-driven, global consumer strategy work? The answer is, for now it will work for some and not for others. Capitalists make their production and marketing decisions separately as firms and then compete with one another for market share. They tend to adopt similar strategies to stay competitive, but they don't worry much about the overall social or economic consequences.

So Toyota produces more and more upscale Lexus models and loads up the Corolla. Bennetton opens stores in Latin America and Asia rather than downtown Detroit, L.A.'s South Central, or New York's lower-east side. U.S. workers can buy inexpensive Asian-made clothes at K-Mart, while designer houses sell world-wide.

The dismal conclusion for workers in the U.S. and other industrial countries is that capital is not shooting itself in the foot, it is shooting workers in the back and getting away with it.

The slide to have-not status will continue for the majority if it is not forcefully opposed and alternatives fought for.

Partners in Poverty?

Tragically, many unions are buying into this trend, not by what they say or want, but by what they do.

There is a myth in the making that unions are winning job security in exchange for becoming partners in the workplace of tomorrow. The AFL-CIO's recent report, *A New American Workplace: A Labor Perspective* spins a version of this yarn.

Some recent contracts, such as that between the UAW and the Big Three last year and the CWA and NYNEX earlier this year, do include important protections for those currently employed—at least for the life of the contract. By U.S. standards, these are some of the best contracts.

But the "partnership" involved is one that encourages the company to continue stripping jobs and shuffling workers around. The CWA calls it "rightsizing" rather than downsizing, but it still means dumping thousands of jobs with the union's blessing.

Jobs will be lost by attrition, not by layoffs. But the company has the right to restructure and re-engineer as it wishes. Major geographic reorganizations often make it difficult or impractical for workers to follow their job in spite of the transfer rights in the contract, as is the case with the 1993 UAW contract at GM.

In addition, there are buyouts and early retirement schemes to grease the process. At the end of each such agreement, however, the negotiations start with fewer union members and lower morale.

Not only does this approach weaken the union over time, it clears the way for the further elimination and fragmentation of work in society as a whole, as it forces more workers into a labor market where choices are narrowing.

This "partnership" amounts to an abandonment of the next generation of workers. It is a partnership with poverty.

Alternative Partnership

The alternative does not lie in the hope there is a "right" corporate size down the road that will protect us. Nor does it lie in some fantasy about everyone becoming a high-paid, high tech nomad through more and better training. These are corporate-sponsored, dog-eat-dog ideas that will simply pit each against all on the slippery slopes of today's labor market.

New Directions activist Tom Laney said, "What we need is a partnership with the poor." Laney was talking about a partnership that creates good jobs rather than destroying them, one that starts worker income going up and brings the wealthy down to earth.

Labor needs to start drawing the line on the fragmentation of employment. The Teamsters did this in their April strike against increased part-timing in the freight industry. There could have been tens of thousands fewer full-timers earning full wages and more part-timers making $9 an hour. The Teamsters said no, the future was at stake.

But we also need an alternative that can create new jobs. Business won't do it. Government won't do it. Labor must.

Work time is labor's main tool for creating jobs. Right now, most unions ignore this tool. Worse, they allow massive overtime to kill jobs—once again in the name of competitiveness. The average workweek in manufacturing is now 42.2 hours, the longest since World War II. For auto workers, it's 47.5 hours.

Dave Yettaw, president of UAW Local 599 in Flint, Michigan, notes ironically, "In some situations, because of overtime, our members are working six weeks in a month." That is, they are working 240 hours a month instead of the 160 they would with a 40-hour week.

Reducing the real hours of work would make a difference.

The UAW estimates that if Big Three workers put in a 40-hour week, there would be 59,000 more auto jobs—almost as many as GM plans to eliminate by 1996.

The limitation of the work week to 40 hours in January 1994 would have created almost 800,000 new full-time manufacturing jobs at current levels of production. The *shortening* of the work week could create millions of new full-time jobs. This would create a concrete link between organized labor and the poor and underemployed.

This, in turn, would create more favorable conditions to organize the unorganized and fight for real increases in worker income.

Productivity and profits are up by all accounts. Now is the time for unions to turn the heat up.

CHAPTER 19

The Green Consumer

John Elkington, Julia Hailes, and Joel Makower

You probably don't realize it, but every week you make dozens of decisions that directly affect the environment of the planet Earth. At work, at home, and at play, whether shopping for life's basic necessities, taking a vacation, or cleaning the house, the choices you make are a never-ending series of votes for or against the environment.

Buy a burger, fries, and a soda and you are probably worsening the already critical landfill crisis. Take your car in for repairs and you may be contributing to the gradual warming of the earth and increasing your chances of getting skin cancer. Do your laundry and you may be fouling America's lakes and rivers, perhaps your own drinking water. Discard your trash and you may be polluting the air, water, and soil, and helping to deplete the earth's natural resources.

But the products and services you buy need not be so destructive to the environment. By choosing carefully, you can have a positive impact on the environment without significantly compromising your way of life. That's what being a Green Consumer is all about.

It wasn't very long ago that being a Green Consumer was a contradiction in terms. To truly care for the environment, it was said, you had to drastically reduce your purchases of everything—food, clothing, appliances, and other "lifestyle" items—to a bare minimum. That approach simply doesn't work in our increasingly convenience-and consumption-oriented society. No one wants to go back to a less-comfortable, less-convenient way of life.

And yet most Americans do care about the state of the earth. Increasingly, according to surveys, people say that their concern for environmental issues is affecting the way they shop. More than half of the 1,000 adults in a 1989 survey conducted by the Michael Peters Group, an international marketing firm, said they chose not to buy a product in the last year because of concern that it or its packaging might harm the environment. Just over three-fourths said they would be willing to pay as much as 5 percent more for a product packaged with recyclable or biodegradable materials. Sixty-one percent of those in another survey said they were "much" or "somewhat" more inclined to patronize a store or restaurant that showed its concern over the environment by doing such things as reducing its use of plastic containers and utensils, and by recycling other waste materials.

Such concern notwithstanding, there's no question that the jump from environmental concern to environmental consumerism is easier said than done. As is true with so many other parts of our lives—dieting comes quickly to mind—one's good intentions don't always translate readily into effective action. In the case of being a Green Consumer, the problem stems in part from a lack of understanding about how your purchasing decisions can affect the environment, and about what qualities make your purchases "green."

In addition, a green product ideally should not trade price, quality, nutrition, or convenience for environmental quality.

The Many Shades of Green

Meeting all these requirements is no small task, although a growing number of companies large and small are finding ways to meet the challenges. There are hundreds of green products introduced each year, with thousands more coming in the foreseeable future.

Unfortunately, few of these products are perfectly green. Most incorporate some improvements in packaging or contents, but do not necessarily meet all of the criteria listed above. One big problem is that there is considerable disagreement even among dedicated environmentalists about whether some purportedly green products truly are less harmful to the environment. For example, is biodegradable plastic a suitable alternative to nonbiodegradable plastic? Some people strongly object to biodegradable plastic because it does not completely break down into benign materials when disposed of in landfills. Others applaud the use of biodegradable plastic, pointing to the fact that while not a perfect solution, it is at least one step better than the nonbiodegradable variety. . . . Is it better to do something imperfect now or wait for perfect solutions to come later on? The answer is for you to decide.

Equally frustrating is that there are no nationally accepted standards or coding systems for determining what products are environmentally sound. There are no agreed-upon definitions of when something may rightfully be labeled as "biodegradable," "degradable," "recyclable," or "made from recycled materials," among the more common terms now being used on product labels. And there are even less-specific labeling terms, such as "not harmful to the environment" or "environment-friendly."

The result is a mixed bag of green products. There are some environmentally harmful products wrapped in green packaging. Some green products don't clearly state their greenness, while other products claiming to be green are not. To make matters worse, several of the corporations producing green products are among the world's biggest polluters. In short, it's a confusing world, with many shades of green.

The Power of Green Consumerism

In the chapters that follow, we will attempt to lead you through this sometimes murky world of Green Consumerism. We have tried to present the different sides to some controversial issues, but it will be up to you to make the final decisions.

While those decisions won't always be easy to make, we urge that it is better to do something than nothing. While perfect solutions are still lacking, there are many companies making some attempt to improve the environmental quality of their products. Your support of these progressive companies and products will be heard loud and clear in the executive suites of the nation's largest companies, and will encourage other companies to follow these leaders.

You may be surprised at how easy it is to make your voice heard in the marketplace. The marketplace is not a democracy; you don't need a majority opinion to make change. Indeed, it takes only a fairly small portion of shoppers—as few as one person in ten—changing buying habits for companies to stand up and take notice. For example, if 10 percent of consumers decided not to buy napkins, paper towels, and other paper goods that contain bleach (which pollutes the water supply when disposed of), you can be sure that the nation's leading paper products companies would seriously consider making unbleached products widely available. Such changes in corporate behavior are brought about by the behavior of individuals, one purchase at a time.

There are other things you can do to make your voice heard even louder. Consider the supermarket, one of the front lines in the battle for a better environment. A simple request to the manager of your local supermarket—or better yet, a call or letter to the regional manager or corporate headquarters—stating your preference for environmentally safe products will encourage them to stock such items. You may also suggest that the store offer shelf labeling, with signs (green, of course) highlighting green products. Stores in other countries have already heeded their customers' wishes. In Canada and several European countries, for example, supermarkets distribute their own green product lines.

Persuade one major company to change its tack and others are likely to follow. McDonald's decision to abandon the use of CFCs in fast-food cartons in the United States was one of the environmental milestones of 1987. The threat that consumers might boycott Big Macs was surely a factor influencing the company's decision. Competitors promptly started talking to their carton suppliers, explaining: "We don't want to be left behind."

There are other victories. For example, at its customers' urging, Wal-Mart, the national discount store chain, launched a national advertising campaign featuring full-page newspaper ads challenging its suppliers to provide products packaged in environmentally sound ways. Procter & Gamble, the huge packaged-goods company, has responded to customer outcry about the trash produced by Pampers, its disposable diaper, by launching a recycling experiment in Washington State. The company also is test-marketing household cleaners in concentrated form, packaged in plastic pouches, permitting customers to refill empty bottles by adding water instead of purchasing a new container. In Canada, Cascade-Dominion, one of the country's leading producers of foam egg cartons made from a material that harms the ozone layer, cited consumer pressure as the key motivator when it announced plans to close its foam egg carton plant and switch all production to pulp egg cartons.

The bandwagon effect will be inevitable: as markets and product manufacturers get the message that Americans want their products green, the trickle of green products will turn into a flood.

Please understand that buying green products alone won't solve the huge environmental problems facing our nation and our world. Many of the problems are beyond our individual control. Acid rain, for example, comes largely from antiquated power plants emitting sulfur dioxide and nitrogen oxides; solutions to this and other environmental problems must come principally from businesses and governments working together.

But there are many environmental problems that you *can* do something about. Being a Green Consumer is a good and effective start—your own personal message to Mother Earth that you are grateful for her many gifts.

How the American Way of Life Is Destroying the Earth

Per-person daily household trash produced in Calcutta, India: 1.12 pounds; in New York City: 3.96 pounds

Barrels of oil wasted annually because the federal government has not raised efficiency standards for cars by 1 mile per gallon: 420,000

Amount of oil the U.S. would have to import to meet present demand if the average fuel efficiency of all cars on U.S. roads averaged 42 MPG: none

Pounds of agricultural pesticides applied each year in California: 80 million pounds

Portion of the 35,000 pesticides introduced since 1945 tested for potential health effects: 10 percent

Plastic beverage bottles Americans go through every hour: 2.5 million

Styrofoam cups thrown away each year in the U.S.: 25 billion

Americans living in areas with levels of air pollutants the federal government considers harmful: 110 million

Trees wasted each week by Sunday newspapers not being recycled: 500,000

Homes that could be heated by the wood and paper thrown away each year: 5 million homes for 200 years

Scrap tires generated by American drivers in 1988: 246.9 million

Plastic containers dumped overboard daily by commercial fishing fleets: 640,000

Northern fur seals drowned each year by lost plastic fishing net: 500,000

Estimated number of sea birds, marine mammals, and fur seals killed each year as a result of eating or being strangled by plastics: 1 million, 100,000, and 50,000, respectively

Gallons of water that can be contaminated by a single quart of motor oil: up to 2 million

Grazing area required to produce a single all-beef hamburger: 55 square feet

PART V

Critiques and Celebrations

Delectable Materialism:
Second Thoughts on Consumer Culture

Michael Schudson

On 31 January 1990, when McDonald's opened in Moscow, Soviet citizens seemed stunned by the politeness of the people behind the cash registers who smiled and said, "May I help you?" They were delighted at the efficiency of the service despite a wait of two hours, and many took home their logo-laden McDonald's refuse as souvenirs. Tongue in cheek, the *New York Times* wrote of hope-starved Soviet consumers won over to "delectable materialism." The *Washington Post*, similarly jocular, painted a portrait of a factory worker standing beneath the golden arches and said of him, "He had seen the future—and it tasted good."[1]

In the waning days of the Cold War, American journalists poked fun at the Soviet passion for American consumer goods because they could not consider consumerism in the United States without depreciating it. It takes an immigrant or outsider to speak of American abundance in beatific terms. Boris Yeltsin, back home from a nine-day American tour in the fall of 1989, was effusive about the extraordinary wealth of American life: "Their supermarkets have 30,000 food items," he told supporters. "You can't imagine it. It makes the people feel secure." Yeltsin urged that "at least 100 million Soviets must pass through the American school of supermarkets," to understand the American system. "The leaders must be first."[2]

The late Henry Fairlie, a British immigrant to America, waxed eloquent about his adopted country in a celebratory Fourth of July essay. The United States is the first country, he said, in which he felt free. He cited his experience, in 1965, on his first morning in America, when the wife of the English friend he was staying with "took me, not to the Washington Monument, but to a supermarket—just to stare." What the supermarket, the cafeteria, and various gadgets told Fairlie was that "convenience is liberating" and that the chief conveniences of American life were democratic. "Like the Franklin stove or the Ford Model T, these amenities were meant for all." And Fairlie, like Yeltsin later, held that "there is a meaning to the material progress of America . . . beyond the physical benefits which it bestows."[3]

This celebratory attitude toward American materialism is rarely shared by homegrown journalists and intellectuals. They view American materialism skeptically and critically. In part, they draw on the anticapitalism of the left and the antibourgeois values of the aristocratic right. Even more, they trade on a distaste for consumerism that is as close to the heart of the American tradition as consumerism itself. President Jimmy Carter, for instance, found in his own tradition of evangelical Protestantism the anxiety that "too many of us now worship self-indulgence and consumption" and he affirmed that "owning things and consuming things does not satisfy our longing for meaning."[4] Here Carter provided an echo of Franklin Roosevelt's rhetoric. Roosevelt criticized Americans' "obeisance to Mammon" and sought to bring people out of "an era of selfishness." It was time, he urged, to "put faith in spiritual values above every material consideration."[5]

Of course, Americans have often celebrated material abundance and even worshiped it; at the same time, American tradition has a long-standing distrust of material goods. I am not about to endorse the idolatry of goods, but the primary task of this essay is to hold up for examination the view that attachment to material goods is pathological. For most intellectuals and social critics, this position is much more congenial than hearty praise of an acquisitive society. In its many variants, it offers an opening attempt to construct an ethics of consumption. But it is as often a reflexlike rejection of consumption as encomiums to abundance and free markets are an uncritical embrace of consumption. My critique of the critics of material goods, then, is an effort to clear the way for a more balanced assessment of consumerism.

Critics of Consumer Culture

Criticism of advertising and consumer culture today emerges not so much from a single source as from at least five distinguishable traditions of criticism. Three of these lie within bourgeois culture and two lie outside it, critical not only of the distinctive institutions of advertising and consumer culture but of middle-class society and capitalism in general. Teasing out and examining these strands of thought may help clarify the conflicted relationship to the world of goods that social critics, intellectuals, and others share today.

Most criticism of consumer culture shares a few basic assumptions, which should be questioned at the outset. The critiques of consumer culture all object, as Emerson did, that things are in the saddle and ride us. They all seem to hold that if we could live the simple life, where things satisfy natural, biological needs and little more, we could properly devote attentions to justice or

comradeship or aesthetic pleasures. We could then bask in the spiritual satisfactions the natural world can provide. But "the simple life" expresses only
one view of the good life, and not self-evidently the best.

The advocates of the simple life presume that we can neatly separate *necessary* from *artificial* needs and wants, and they hold that we should attach our
desires to the former alone. But what is necessary to sustain human life? This
is not an easy question. Its answer certainly does not lie in biology alone.
People in all societies are biological and social at once. The infant's first suck-
ing at the breast is an act both biological and social, both nourishing and attaching. From that point on, the infant will want to be not only a *living* person
but also a living *person*, a socially creditable member of a society. Human biological functions, like eating, are culturally coded and socially organized. It is
important in all human societies that people eat like human beings, not like
animals. This requires adherence to social conventions for eating that differ
from one culture to the next. In the American middle class, a person must eat
a certain quantity of food so that it cannot be said that the person "eats like a
horse," on the one hand, or "eats like a bird," on the other. More important
still, one must retain a certain reserve about eating so as to acknowledge that
the activity is one of eating a meal, not one of simply consuming food. Without that reserve, a person can be accused of "eating like a pig" or failing to engage in the social activity of eating altogether by "inhaling" food.

In Alexander Solzhenitsyn's *One Day in the Life of Ivan Denisovich,* pris-
oners in the Soviet labor camp are fed only a thin gruel with some fish heads
and tails thrown in. Ivan Denisovich, weak from malnutrition and overwork,
nonetheless organizes his own ritual for eating. He takes off his cap before he
eats. He refuses to eat fish eyes. In a subsociety intended to animalize prison-
ers, Ivan retains his humanity by continuing to eat meals rather than simply
consuming food. Even in the poorest societies, human needs and desires are
culturally constituted and socially defined. Human needs are for inclusion as
well as for survival, for meaning as well as for existence. And consumer goods,
as Mary Douglas and Baron Isherwood argued and as most scholars who
think on these matters have now fully accepted, are for modern societies central elements in the establishment and circulation of meaning.[6]

But what, then, is required to live a social and socially creditable life? And
how much? This will differ from one society to the next. The requirements of
personhood differ across societies as both philosopher of modern capitalism
Adam Smith and capitalism's most severe critic, Karl Marx, understood. Smith
defined "human necessaries" as "not only the commodities which are indis-
pensably necessary for the support of life, but whatever the custom of the
country renders it indecent for creditable people, even of the lowest order, to
be without."[7] He observed that a linen shirt is not "strictly speaking" a necessary of life but that, in most of Europe in his day, "a creditable day-labourer
would be ashamed to appear in public without a linen shirt, the want of which
would be supposed to denote that disgraceful degree of poverty, which, it is

presumed, no body can well fall into without extreme bad conduct."[8] Similarly, Smith judged leather shoes a necessity in England for men and women but for men only in Scotland and for neither in France.

Marx, like Smith, understood human needs to be socially and historically produced. In *Capital*, he distinguishes between two kinds of consumer goods, necessities and luxuries, but he does not assume that necessities are either biological or natural. True articles of luxury are items that only the capitalist class consumes. A consumer necessity is something that is in general and habitual use among the working class—such as tobacco—whether or not it is physiologically essential to life.[9] Like Smith, Marx fully appreciated that human needs are social and relative. In *Wage-Labour and Capital*, he wrote that an owner may find a small house adequate so long as other houses in the same neighborhood are the same size. Then someone builds a palace and "the house shrinks from a little house to a hut. . . . Our desires and pleasures spring from society; we measure them, therefore, by society and not by the objects which serve for their satisfaction. Because they are of a social nature, they are of a relative nature."[10]

For Marx, the frightening invention of capitalism is not the creation of artificial or new needs but the emergence of a concept that there is such a thing as purely physical or biological need. Other social systems had treated human beings as social entities, not biological machines. Only capitalism conceived of people as raw material and only capitalists dared calculate the minimum amount it would take to keep workers alive and healthy enough to work in factories and reproduce in families the next generation of laborers.[11]

Criticism of consumer culture may adopt more of this dehumanized understanding of the relation of persons and things than it realizes. It seems to me fundamental, in grappling with the ethics of consumption, to begin from that area of agreement between Adam Smith and Karl Marx—that human life is by definition social and cultural, that human needs are relative across societies, and that what counts as necessary in a given society has to be defined somehow in relation to what the poorest members of society require for creditable social standing. In the United States, for instance, this almost certainly means a television. It may even mean an automobile, except, perhaps, for residents of New York City and a few other places where public transportation is a passable alternative. The driver's license may be as close to a badge of full social membership as this society has.

Keeping in mind the fundamental socialness of human needs and insisting that we cannot get around a degree of relativism even in trying to define *basic* needs (but I will return to just how this relativism is constrained), let me turn to the five critiques of consumer culture in American social thought. I will first take up three bourgeois objections to consumer culture. Some critics, whom I shall call Puritans, attack people's attitudes toward material goods in pursuit of spirituality; some critics, whom I shall call Quakers, attack features of the goods themselves in pursuit of simplicity; and some, whom I shall label republicans, in pursuit of civic virtue attack the consequences of possession, notably complacency and the loss of civic engagement.[12]

The Puritan Critique

The Puritan critique worries about whether people invest an appropriate amount of meaning in goods. By Puritan, I refer to the conviction, symbolized by the sturdy and sober New England colonists, that people should invest less meaning in worldly possessions than in spiritual pursuits. In this view, pleasure should be subordinated to duty, the flesh to the spirit, and temporal concerns to religious obligations. Yet Puritan critics do not necessarily agree about what an appropriate degree of meaning investment in material possessions might be. Some critics have suggested that contemporary American attitudes toward goods are not crassly materialist enough, that people find goods insufficient without investing surplus meaning in them. British critic Raymond Williams writes that advertising is the very proof that people in modern capitalist societies are not materialist—because the job of the ad is to convey added value to the product itself. "If we were sensibly materialist, in that part of our living in which we use things, we should find most advertising to be of an insane irrelevance. Beer would be enough for us, without the additional promise that in drinking it we show ourselves to be manly, young in heart, or neighbourly."[13] Advertising, then, is magic, and it magically associates extra, non-essential meaning with perfectly ordinary, serviceable goods. For Williams, the trouble with contemporary attitudes toward goods is that goods, in themselves, are undervalued but, in their associations, are overspiritualized. In adopting this view, Williams accepts that there is such a thing as "goods in themselves." He implies that drinking beer is no more than consuming a beverage rather than, among other things, a rich expressive display of comradeship (a remarkably Puritanical assumption for someone coming from pub-strewn Britain).

In contrast, the late American historian and critic Christopher Lasch has argued that people underspiritualize goods. In *The Minimal Self*, Lasch complains that manufactured goods are inferior to handmade goods in that they cannot serve as "transitional" objects, that is, objects that bridge the gap between the individual's inner self and the social world.[14] He borrows here from psychoanalyst D. W. Winnicott's view that children often use physical objects to represent or stand in for the mother, even in the absence of the mother. Far from being regressive, this behavior helps the child develop autonomy from the mother. For Lasch, handcrafted goods have the mark of human activity upon them, while commodities are elements in a prefabricated dream world that cannot aid us in gaining a sense of mastery over our experience. Lasch is able to maintain this view only because he traces the beginnings of American consumer culture to the 1920s rather than recognizing, as many social historians now do, its eighteenth-century origins.[15] In *The True and Only Heaven*, Lasch again writes with admiration of craftsmanship or, at least, with resentment of intellectuals who fail to appreciate manual labor as he does.[16] But his larger point is that contemporary attitudes toward goods are more satanized than spiritualized, that we are possessed by our possessions, that we are, in a word, addicted. In his earlier work, *The Culture of Narcissism*, Lasch held that consumers are "perpetually unsatisfied, restless, anxious, and bored." Capitalism shapes in them "an unappeasable appetite" for new goods and new experiences.[17] This is not, Lasch emphasizes, conventional hedonism but something worse—a compulsion, an addiction, a sickness linked intrinsically to consumer capitalism.

So the heart of the Puritan critique is a utilitarian valuation of goods. Goods should serve practical human needs (or human social relationships, in Lasch's view). They should be valued for their capacity to fulfill human needs but they should not be ends of desire in themselves. The concept of needs here tends to be very limited. Certainly the Puritan critique is suspicious of the aesthetic dimension of human experience and has no place for someone who takes pleasure in the feel or look of a consumer good. It may be, as James Agee once wrote, that the sense of beauty is a class privilege—that only the comfortable have the leisure to contemplate the beautiful. But this is an argument for economic improvement or redistribution, not an argument that an aesthetic sense is unrelated to the good life. The original Puritans found offensive dancing, music, theater, nonreproductive sexuality, and other material and bodily pleasures. They at least had the virtue of consistency.

There are implicitly empirical claims in the notion that people overspiritualize or underspiritualize goods, with little proffered evidence one way or the other. Is Williams right to suppose people do not find most advertising "insanely irrelevant?" My reading of the evidence is that people ignore the vast amount of advertising they see and distrust much of the little advertising they take in.[18] Is Lasch correct that mass-produced goods fail as transitional objects? I see no evidence, certainly not from my own children, that mass-produced blankets are inferior to grandma-made Afghans as "transitional objects." I wished that my preschool daughter was as attached to the quilt my wife made or the afghan my grandmother made as to the cotton blanket we got from J. C. Penny, but she was not. Do I overspiritualize goods in this desire? Does my daughter underspiritualize? And what is the appropriate standard?

Of course, the preference for the handcrafted good may also betray an indifference to the burden of the laborer who does the handcrafting. In 1900, the American housewife did a great deal of handcrafting, spending more than forty hours a week in preparing meals. In 1975, the average housewife spent ten hours in food preparation and about one hour a week, rather than seven, doing laundry.[19] Is this to be regarded as progress and liberation? Or must we conclude that it represents the underspiritualization of food and clothing?

The Quaker Critique

The Quaker critique is less concerned with how people feel about goods than with objectionable features of the products themselves, usually their wastefulness or extravagance. Christopher Lasch, whose multifarious critiques of consumer culture fit into almost all of my categories, took up the old complaint that modern industry is dictated by "planned obsolescence" or Sloanism, the annual model change that Alfred P. Sloan introduced to General Motors more than half a century ago to coax people to buy new cars even when they have serviceable old ones.[20] Here critics take changes in products to be not only useless but also manipulative, aimed only at pointless product differentiation to which people will attribute unfounded meaning. The fashion industry is a regular target of such criticism, as it was for the Quakers themselves in their adherence to plain dress.

Critics, however, have too easily generalized from a few salient examples. Does Sloanism actually guide American industry? Does it even guide the automobile industry? While General Motors was developing the annual model change, other companies were producing washing machines, radios, single-family homes, bicycles, phonographs, and bathroom fixtures that were designed to last, and did last, for years. Sloanism is an aspect of the American economy, but it is more a marketing strategy for a particular set of conditions than a deep cultural force.

In the case of automobiles, consumers were not happily holding onto their cars for years until Sloan found a way to introduce wasteful fashion to utilitarian transport vehicles. Before Sloan dreamt of the annual model change, the used-car market was large and growing; people were obviously "buying up" as they could afford to, reproducing in the automobile an objective correlative of already existing systems of class and status distinction. They were resisting the implications of Henry Ford's one-model, one-price policy. So were many of Detroit's auto makers, for reasons no more calculating. Many of Detroit's entrepreneurs were building more expensive cars, pricing themselves out of the lucrative mass market, and ultimately bankrupting themselves in a status-driven effort to manufacture cars of a sort appropriate to their own station, or desired station, in Detroit society.[21] They went too far up-market while Henry Ford controlled the lower end of the market and Alfred P. Sloan looked to the middle.

The fashion consciousness Sloan helped institutionalize was the General Motors solution to a perceived problem for the industry—the expanding market in used cars.[22] Sloan himself understood General Motors to be using the annual model change to adapt to the existing trends of American life, notably the practice of trading up. "Middle-income buyers," he later wrote, "assisted by the trade-in and installment financing, created the demand, not for basic transportation, but for progress in new cars, for comfort, convenience, power, and style."[23] The problem for the industry was that the cars were in fact well made and lasted a long time. The annual model change may indeed be wasteful, but "planned obsolescence," as critics still call it, does not characterize most of American industry and it was in its origins as much a response to the desire of consumers to be fashionable as a cause of fashion consciousness.

Still, we can concede that some kinds of consumption are more practical, less ostentatious, and less wasteful than others and, by that measure, more morally defensible—perhaps a bicycle is better than a car. But what about a plain car rather than a fancy one? Volkswagen advertising used to be morally smug, emphasizing that the VW was plain, even ugly, simple, graceless, and unchanging year after year. Did this make the VW a more ethically satisfying choice of car? Or had VW just found a way to turn Puritan and Quaker sentiment into a marketing ploy?

What is the appropriate level of aesthetic interest a consumer good should evoke? What is the appropriate level of workmanship and luxury for products? How should we weigh the Cadillac against the subcompact Chevy? The former may use up more resources and be less fuel efficient but it may also be a better—and safer—car. Some practical and spartan products may not only be aesthetically unappealing but ecologically unsound. Paper plates and towels may be easier to use and dispose of than china and cloth towels that are designed for regular reuse, but they are wasteful.

Not that wastefulness is always easy to measure. Polyester has long been abused in some circles—because it is artificial and, so go the rationalizations, it does not last like cotton. But polyester manufacturers have pointed out that polyester takes less energy to produce and to maintain (it never needs ironing) than cotton and, over the lifetime of a garment, absorbs less of the earth's total energy and resources. A product that never needs ironing saves not only electricity but also human, almost invariably female, labor. Today polyester can even be manufactured from recycled soda bottles.[24] A similar case has been made for disposable diapers and other products that appear to be wasteful but, relatively speaking, may not be.[25]

The Quaker critique tends to suggest that consumption that is more practical, less ostentatious, and less wasteful is better. Goods should not be pointlessly differentiated. They should not be made useful, efficient, speedy, or convenient beyond some consensual standard of what level of usefulness is normative; they should not be multiplied if they can be made durable for sharing or personal reuse. They should husband the earth's resources with care. People should, as they produce and consume, have human posterity in view.

But what is the standard of appropriate convenience and who is to set it? In 1930 only one-half of American households boasted flush toilets while in 1980 more than 98 percent did.[26] In 1980, indoor plumbing was surely a necessity in Adam Smith's terms—it was required to be a socially creditable person, but clearly it was not "physically" necessary and surely it was quite wasteful of limited water supplies. On what grounds is the Boeing 747 acceptable but the Concorde wasteful? In my house, the electric blender is considered acceptable but not the electric can opener, the electric toothbrush but not the electric blanket. But on what grounds are such decisions made? How do we arrive at a baseline for consensus—and, if we cannot (and I think that we cannot), then what is the character of the moral objection to excessive consumption? The distinction between necessary and superfluous consumption is, as historian Lorna Weatherill suggests, "deeply misleading." The notion of luxury simply "does not provide a firm basis for examining the meaning of consumer behaviour."[27]

The Republican Critique

The last of the bourgeois objections to consumption, the republican perspective, is concerned not with attitudes toward goods nor with the wastefulness of goods themselves but with the corrupting influence on public life of a goods orientation in private life. This is perhaps the most trenchant and resonant of the critiques. In the republican vision, a goods orientation or consumerist orientation is debilitating in three ways. First, it is passive. People consume themselves, Stuart Ewen has written, "into social and political passivity."[28] Satisfaction with goods produces acquiescence in politics. People who transfer their passive orientation toward goods to the world of politics expect political life to be prefabricated and expect to participate in it simply by making a choice between predetermined alternatives. This idea of politics reduces a voting booth to a vending machine.

Second, a goods orientation gives priority to possession rather than to production as a defining feature of personal identity. In a consumer society, "lifestyle" surpasses a person's work life as the defining feature of existence. Republicans take this to be not only a misunderstanding of what human beings are but also a politically conservative misunderstanding that diverts attention from the task of making our work lives more vital and democratic.

Third, a goods orientation is privatizing. People abandon the town square for the front porch, and then later the front porch for the backyard or the television room. The town pump gives way to the commercial laundry or Laundromat, the Laundromat to the home washer and dryer. People seek comfort increasingly inside their domiciles, and their domiciles increasingly house only members of a nuclear family, not an extended family, servants, or boarders.

Is a consumerist orientation to goods necessarily passive? H. F. Moorhouse makes a strong argument to the contrary, as have many others who emphasize the "active" involvement of audiences in their consumption activities. Moorhouse examines the consumption of automobiles in the United States. He writes of the appropriation by young people of Detroit-made cars in the "hot rod" culture of the 1940s. Teenagers did not passively accept the automobile but decorated, redesigned, and even reengineered Detroit cars for their own purposes in racing (often illegally). The ethos of hot rod culture was not passivity but a commitment "to labour, to strive, to plan, to exercise skill, to compete, to succeed, to risk."[29] One does not have to look back to the 1940s, of course, to find people actively engaged with the things they consume, developing expert knowledge about goods they like even to the point of becoming manufacturers themselves. This may involve redesigning products for their own purposes or even directly entering the world of production, like women romance novel readers who turn to writing and publishing romances themselves.[30]

I do not mean to protest too much here. Certainly even active forms of watching baseball are, with respect to physical activity, more passive than the most passive ways of playing the game (the daydreaming elementary school right fielder at least stands erect and trots on and off the field). But it is important to note that there are degrees of activity in consumption just as there are degrees of disengagement in labor. A youngster may watch as a coach demonstrates a gymnastics routine or how to field a ground ball; watching of this sort is not likely to be passive at all.

The role of work in human identity is scarcely self-evident. Why must we assume that it is the defining feature of human identity? Many sociological studies of labor take it for granted that only in labor can "real" satisfaction in life be attained; all other satisfactions have to be regarded as substitutes, more or less unsatisfying, more or less illusory.[31] But why treat consumption, a priori, as peripheral to key matters of human fulfillment? Moorhouse holds that there is no empirical rationale for privileging workplaces as "the crucial sites of human experience and self understanding."[32] I agree. Labor and occupation are very important but it is some kind of metaphysics that makes labor the defining feature of human life.

As for the privatizing character of consumerism, this too is contestable. When are private satisfactions in consumer goods too private? When backyard swimming pools replace the community pools? When purchased books weaken public libraries? When a washer and dryer replaces the commercial Laundromat or commercial laundry, themselves replacements for hard domestic labor and household servants? When radio and television replace movies, theaters, and concerts, themselves rather recent commercial replacements for quilting bees and barbecues and social visiting on the front porch?

But the most serious riposte to republican critics is this: the rise of consumer culture has been a building block of a participatory, active, democratic society, not a barrier to it. Political activism in the years leading up to the American Revolution was organized around consumer identity and the nonimportation of British consumer goods. The anti-importation movement, as David Shi has suggested, was in part encouraged by the ethic of republican simplicity; the battle against Britain was seen also as a war for moral regeneration. Many colonial leaders saw frugality and patriotism linked closely together. Samuel Adams, though the owner of a brewery, was indifferent to his own economic well-being and took pride in the frugality and simplicity of his living while he devoted himself to political affairs.[33] But anti-importation was not a protest against commercial culture so much as an effort to regulate life within it. The rapidly growing consumer culture and improving living standards were widely welcomed. The anti-importation movement provided, as T. H. Breen has argued, a basis for the democratization of political protest. While traditional political action was available only to propertied white males, consumer-based protest could be much more widely shared. Basing protest on consumer identity was a radically egalitarian move and a novel one: "No previous popular rebellion had organized itself so centrally around the consumer."[34]

This is not a unique instance. Lizabeth Cohen has suggested that the growth of a national mass culture "helped unify workers previously divided along ethnic, racial, and geographic lines" in the 1920s and 1930s, and so contributed to the Congress of Industrial Organizations (CIO) organizing efforts.[35] Organizing around a consumer issue proved a potent force: ethnic working-class opposition to Prohibition, she argues, brought workers a new unity as Democrats and a new openness to state actions as solutions to their problems.[36] In the 1960s, political protesters certainly did not all use marijuana, but a common culture of protest was forged in part by a shared appreciation of rock music and the democratic aura of both rock and pot. It is clear, at the very least, that consumer culture cuts two ways in its effects on political protest and popular militance. Perhaps critics are right that consumerism may sometimes take people out of the public square, but clearly there are also powerful historical instances where consumer culture has provided the avenue and the engine for entrance into public life.

Antibourgeois Critiques

I will discuss more quickly the nonbourgeois or antibourgeois objections to consumer culture since, in a variety of ways, they have been bootlegged into the bourgeois self-criticism. The Marxist or socialist objection to consumer culture is that, however beneficent the economic system may appear from the side of consumption, it rests on the exploitation of workers in the capitalist system of production. Indeed, Ewen and Lasch have separately argued that the point of consumer society is to distract the minds and bodies of workers, to serve as an opiate of the people, submerging dissatisfaction with life in the exploitative workplace. "The tired worker," Lasch writes, "instead of attempting to change the conditions of his work, seeks renewal in brightening his immediate surroundings with new goods and services." Advertising, Lasch complains, "upholds consumption as an alternative to protest or rebellion."[37]

Twenty years ago, Lasch's hyperventilating prose seemed persuasive, at least for those already critical of American materialism. But he offers no evidence that the baubles of consumerism buy off discontent or that, if they do, we are nonetheless safe in dismissing them as baubles. A questionable assumption in his argument is that the satisfactions of the consumer world are illusory. Ordinarily, they are quite real. The critics may see goods as distractions, but they can also be seen as authentic sources of both utility and meaning. Moreover, as I have just suggested, they may be as often motivation for political activity as a substitute for it. The current social transformation of Eastern Europe, galvanized by economic aspirations as well as by political hope, is the most recent case in point.

The aristocratic objection to consumer society is primarily aesthetic. Where the socialist critique of consumer culture is a critique of exploitation on behalf of the goal of equality, the aristocratic or elitist objection to consumer society is an attack on ugliness in defense of culture. Mass-produced goods are ugly. The trouble with this critique is its anti-democratic bias; the attack on mass-produced goods is often a thinly veiled attack on the masses themselves. Mass-produced goods may be judged ugly by some, but they are often significantly cheaper than handcrafted products. The evidence of this is not only before our eyes but available in the historical record. For instance, carpets were once available only to the wealthy; the power loom made them available to most citizens. Ready-to-wear clothing was available by the mid-nineteenth century to working-class people who could not have afforded items of such quality before.[38] A great amount of homemade wear was shoddy and ill-fitting.[39]

Again, the problem is one of standards and relativism. We cannot just smuggle in an assurance that we know what valid culture is: no one does. Worse, as economist Fred C. Hirsch argued, aesthetics are intrinsically implicated in hierarchical relations when "positional" goods like parks, vacation spots, and restaurants are found beautiful in part because of their exclusiveness, spaciousness, quiet, and seclusion—in short, because of the absence of other people.[40] Valuing what is exclusive, we call it fine or beautiful and so incorporate social distinction into our very definition of quality. Some of our terms of praise call attention specifically to scarcity, and scarcity becomes linguistically equated with quality—*rare, unique, one of a kind*. The problem of not having aesthetic standards on which we could all agree is compounded by the problem of having too readily at hand aesthetic standards that are intrinsically antidemocratic.[41]

Conclusion

Historian Daniel Horowitz, in his study of social science discussions about consumerism at the turn of the century, comes to a curiously modest conclusion. His book is critical of the "moralism" of the critiques of profligacy and self-indulgence he analyzed, but he says in the end that his work is "a critique of a view of consumption that I still hold to a considerable extent."[42] He lists what he takes to be pieces of an alternative and more positive view of consumption, including studies that demonstrate people's complex incorporations of commercial goods into their own lives. People make these goods serve their individual needs and, even when they use the goods in standard fashion, take them quite pragmatically, not attributing to them any of the spiritual or romantic qualities that advertising seeks to build up. He concludes of these and other arguments, "No one has yet pulled these scattered pieces of evidence and different modes of interpretation into a coherent counterargument."[43]

This remains true a decade later. What has changed, however, is the world scene, particularly the economic collapse and political disintegration of the Soviet Union and Eastern Europe. Communism's collapse does not justify capitalism's remarkable failures, at least in the United States, to provide citizens with basic needs of affordable shelter, health care, and economic security. But it does make more apparent the need to scrutinize the criticisms of consumer culture that have flourished among relatively affluent intellectuals in Western societies. It is time to criticize, as Michael Walzer has, the mistake of "rational leftism" in its critique of consumption, "as if it were not a good thing for ordinary men and women to possess useful and beautiful objects (as the rich and the powerful have always done)." When owning things becomes the exclusive aim of living, then something is clearly amiss, "but we need to mark off that moment from all previous moments of innocent desire and acquisition."[44]

There may be no way out for us yet. We may be stuck in our intellectual life as in our culture with ambivalence about goods. Albert O. Hirschman finds this ambivalence in Adam Smith himself.[45] David Shi finds it throughout American history: "From colonial days, the image of America as a spiritual commonwealth and a republic of virtue has survived alongside the more tantalizing vision of America as a cornucopia of economic opportunities and consumer delights."[46] Neil Harris finds even in Sinclair Lewis, that great critic of crass American values, an ambivalence about the commercial world: "Merchandising, then, occupied a curiously ambiguous place in Lewis' scheme of things: on the one hand, testimony to the commercialization of American culture, the triumph of mass-produced objects over personality; and on the other, evidence of taste, culture, artistic accomplishment, and sophistication. Buying could be either an act of subservience to manufacturers and advertisers or a demonstration of individuality."[47] Horowitz insists that it is inevitably and necessarily both.[48]

It is time to face up to that ambivalence en route to a political and moral position beyond the snickering, joking, and hypocritical posturing of most criticism of consumer culture. This does not mean we should forgo criticism of consumer culture, especially at a moment of growing concerns about environmental and ecological catastrophe and the distribution of consumption not only among rich and poor people within a society but among rich and poor nations within a world system. It is more difficult to take for granted, as Adam Smith did, that a clearly demarcated national society is the correct social world within which necessity and luxury are to be defined. We do need to think today of consumption in a global context. Issues such as "dumping" of products in the Third World, international agreements on fishing and whaling, or international policy on the production of ozone-depleting products all lift our moral horizons to the global level.

At the same time, the implications of a global vision are difficult to fathom. To live as well in Phoenix as one might in New York for a middle-income person requires air-conditioning, just as for a resident of Boston to live as well as a resident of Los Angeles requires substantial investment in fuel during the winter. If Americans all agreed to move to the more temperate climates of the country, we could save enormously in world energy resources. If we required everyone to live within a certain distance of their place of employment, we could also save enormously on gasoline. But people have investments in locale, even in a global age. It is one thing to question the political legitimacy of, say, Jewish settlers in the West Bank, whose presence, less than a generation old, has divided Israelis from the outset, but it is quite another thing to question the ecological legitimacy of the entire population of southern California, northern New York state, or Minnesota. Without any practical policy suggestions to justify massive redistributions of population and resources it is hard to know just where a global consumer ethic might end.

But a global consumer ethic should begin, and it should begin afresh. Freeing ourselves from biblical or republican or Marxist moralisms, we should recognize that there is dignity and rationality in people's desire for material goods. We should then seek to reconstruct an understanding of the moral and political value of consumption that we and others can decently live with.

What might that understanding look like? What principles might it be founded on? I have raised a host of questions about various existing standards of moral condemnation and I have suggested that the standards most frequently appealed to are inconsistent and ill considered. But I do not mean to say that *no* standards can be established.

Amartya Sen offers some guidance in his emphasis on human "capabilities." He writes of the same Adam Smith passage I cited earlier that Smith's example of the leather shoes is not an argument for moral relativism. It is only an argument that leather shoes may or may not be a human necessity. What particular consumer goods mean will vary from one society to another and one era to another. But what remains constant is the goal that people should have goods sufficient so that they will not be ashamed in society. Societies should be organized so that no one falls below a level that provides access to the consumer goods required for social credit and self-respect. The protection of human dignity or, more broadly, the ensuring of human "capability to function" is not relative.

If societies should be organized so that all inhabitants (or all citizens—there are important debates here about who counts as a society member) possess a "capability to function," this may suggest a moral and political baseline concerning consumption. It has to do most of all with the distribution of goods across classes. If some few consume so much bread that there are not enough crumbs left for others to have the capability to function, the society has failed.

Just what this means, practically, is an intensely difficult problem, on two grounds. First, to a large extent, people understand their own capacity to function locally, not nationally or globally. People's social reference groups, modern mass media notwithstanding, are the people they see face-to-face on a daily basis or the people they feel closely connected with by kinship or social location. These are the people who truly matter to their capacity to function. Think of the hundreds of tales, in novels, short stories, and films, of the young couple from different ethnic groups, religions, or social classes meeting each other's families for the first time. The young people anxiously fret that their parents will embarrass them—either because their material possessions are too humble and shabby or, on the other hand, because they are too extravagant and ostentatious. We still live in a multitude of differentiated social worlds and the goods that make a person creditable in one may be meaningless or even discrediting in the next.

Second, we have increasingly and paradoxically an opposite problem: that we have more and more information about how the other half lives, an other half from across the street or half way around the world. There is a sense, more than ever before, that we are all part of a single reference group. Humanity as a whole is not of daily concern to most people, but people in the developed regions of the world certainly have easy access to information about people all over the globe. We also know that we are globally connected more than ever and that economic and political decisions in one corner of the world influence daily life in other corners—the worldwide sensitivity to oil prices is a good example. Whatever people's particular religious or cosmological views may be, there is certainly a growing veneer, at least, of universalism. No one is an island, no one stands alone, as the John Donne-based song says, "each man's joy is joy to me, each man's grief is my own." Whether from universalistic ethical principles of traditional religions, from Enlightenment liberalism, or from growing awareness of the interdependence of people in a global economy on a planet with finite resources, it grows hard *not* to imagine that the whole of humanity is *my* reference group, *my* community.

On the one hand, then, there is the persistent localness of reference groups and the consequently local definition of what package of goods is required for the human capability to function. On the other hand, there is the growing globalness of human consciousness that compels universalistic standards. The former would seem to suggest a nearly boundless relativism, the latter a set of universal standards that would imply a redistribution so radical that even saints might hesitate to recommend it.

Somewhere in between the radically relativist and the hopelessly universal, there may be some standards, flexible but not spineless, for judging consumption. When we find a way to define them, they may resemble some of the standards I have found wanting here. It seems to me there is something to save from the heritage of Puritanism, which recognizes possession as an inappropriate aim of life, however valuable a means; from Quakerism, which recognizes the vanity of goods and, in a modern ecologized variant, moves from objecting to the vanity of goods before God to the wastefulness of goods before a resource-scarce and unequal world; from republicanism, which scouts out dangers of private satisfaction in the face of public squalor—not that private satisfaction in itself is wrong but that it can dangerously remove people from pitching in to maintain our public household, our common life; from a Marxist or socialist vision, which sees that for every act of consumption there is an act of production and that a calculus that weighs the moral worth of the consumption of goods must take into account the human dignity of the work that went into their production; and from aesthetic elitism, which, without making beauty a class privilege or craftsmanship a religious cult, honors both utilitarian and aesthetic standards of grace and durability, form and function.

Certainly people should live by some set of moral rules for consumption—and, in any event, we do. How much and what we consume can have moral consequences. Increasing awareness of environmental deterioration and ecological and economic interconnectedness makes this more apparent than ever before. At the same time, I do not see any likelihood of establishing a calculus that will enable us to reach agreement about whether our own or anyone else's uses of products are justified. Coming to agreement on such matters is more likely to be worked out in the thick of politics than in any clear-cut philosophical guidelines.

Notes

1. Frances X. Clines, "Moscow McDonald's Opens: Milkshakes and Human Kindness," *New York Times*, 1 February 1990, 13; and Michael Dobbs, *Washington Post*, 1 February 1990, A1.

2. Associated Press, *San Diego Union*, 24 September 1989, A24.

3. Henry Fairlie, "Why I Love America," *New Republic*, 4 July 1983, 12–17.

4. "A Crisis of Confidence," *Weekly Compilation of Presidential Documents* 15 (15 July 1979): 1235–41.

5. From several different public addresses, cited in David Shi, *The Simple Life: Plain Living and High Thinking in American Culture* (New York: Oxford University Press, 1985), 233.

6. Mary Douglas and Baron Isherwood, *The World of Goods* (New York: Basic Books, 1979).

7. Adam Smith, *The Wealth of Nations* (New York: Modern Library, 1937 [1776]), 821.

8 Smith, *The Wealth of Nations*, 822.

9. Karl Marx, *Capital*, vol. 2 (London: Penguin Books, 1978 [1885]), 479.

10. Marx, "Wage-Labour and Capital" in *Karl Marx: Selected Writings*, ed. David McLellan (Oxford: Oxford University Press, 1977), 259.

11. Marx, "Economic and Philosophic Manuscripts of 1844" in *The Marx-Engels Reader*, 2d ed., ed. Robert Tucker (New York: W. W. Norton, 1978), 94–96.

12. I borrow these labels, very loosely, from Shi, *The Simple Life*, and Neil Harris, "The Drama of Consumer Desire" in *Yankee Enterprise*, ed. Otto Mayr and Robert C. Post (Washington, D.C.: Smithsonian Institution Press, 1981), 189–216.

13. Raymond Williams, *Problems in Materialism and Culture: Selected Essays* (London: Verso, 1980), 185.

14. Christopher Lasch, *The Minimal Self: Psychic Survival in Troubled Times* (New York: W. W. Norton, 1984), 193–95.

15. See Lasch, *The Minimal Self*, 28. The key work that dates consumer culture to the eighteenth century is *Birth of a Consumer Society: The Commercialization of Eighteenth-Century England*, ed. Neil McKendrick, John Brewer, and J. H. Plumb (Bloomington: Indiana University Press, 1982).

16. Christopher Lasch, *The True and Only Heaven: Progress and Its Critics* (New York: W. W. Norton, 1991).

17. Christopher Lasch, *The Culture of Narcissism: American Life in an Age of Diminishing Expectations* (New York: W. W. Norton, 1978), 72.

18. For a full discussion, see Michael Schudson, *Advertising, the Uneasy Persuasion: Its Dubious Impact on American Society* (New York: Basic Books, 1984).

19. Stanley Lebergott, *Pursuing Happiness: American Consumers in the Twentieth Century* (Princeton, N.J.: Princeton University Press, 1993), 51.

20. Lasch, *The True and Only Heaven*, 63, 110, 520.

21. Donald Finlay Davis, *Conspicuous Production: Automobiles and Elites in Detroit, 1899–1933* (Philadelphia: Temple University Press, 1988).

22. John B. Rae, *The American Automobile Industry* (Boston: Twayne Publishers, 1984), 62.

23. Alfred P. Sloan, *My Years with General Motors*, ed. John McDonald with Catharine Stevens (Garden City, N.Y.: Doubleday, 1964), 163.

24. Martha M. Hamilton, "It's Not Your Father's Leisure Suit," *Washington Post National Weekly Edition*, 15–21 April 1996, 19.

25. Maura Dolan, "Disposable Articles of Faith," *Los Angeles Times*, 12 March 1991, 1; Reid Lifset and Marian Chertow, "Changing the Waste Makers," *The American Prospect* 3 (Fall 1990): 83–88.

26. Lebergott, *Pursuing Happiness*, 102.

27. Lorna Weatherill, "The Meaning of Consumer Behavior in Late Seventeenth-and Early Eighteenth-Century England" in *Consumption and the World of Goods*, ed. John Brewer and Roy Porter (London: Routledge, 1993), 207.

28. Stuart Ewen, *Captains of Consciousness: Advertising and the Social Roots of the Consumer Culture* (New York: McGraw-Hill, 1976), 204.

29. H. F. Moorhouse, "American Automobiles and Workers' Dreams," *Sociological Review* 31 (August 1983): 411.

30. Janice A. Radway, *Reading the Romance: Women, Patriarchy and Popular Literature* (Chapel Hill: University of North Carolina Press, 1984).

31. H. F. Moorhouse attributes this view to Ely Chinoy in his classic study of American automobile workers, Moorhouse, "American Automobiles," 405.

32. Moorhouse, "American Automobiles," 407.

33. Shi, *The Simple Life*, 56, 60.

34. T. H. Breen, "Narrative of Commercial Life: Consumption, Ideology, and Community on the Eve of the American Revolution," *William and Mary Quarterly* 3d ser., 50 (1993): 486.

35. Lizabeth Cohen, "Encountering Mass Culture at the Grassroots: The Experience of Chicago Workers in the 1920s" in *Popular Culture and Political Change in Modern America*, ed. Ronald Edsforth and Larry Bennett (Albany: State University of New York Press, 1991), 99.

36. Lizabeth Cohen, *Making a New Deal: Industrial Workers in Chicago, 1919–1939* (Cambridge and New York: Cambridge University Press, 1990), 364–65.

37. Lasch, *The Culture of Narcissism*, 138.

38. Stuart M. Blumin, *The Emergence of the Middle Class: Social Experience in the American City, 1760–1900* (Cambridge and New York: Cambridge University Press, 1989), 140–41.

39. Daniel J. Boorstin, *The Americans: The Democratic Experience* (New York: Random House, 1973), 97.

40. Fred C. Hirsch, *Social Limits to Growth* (Cambridge, Mass.: Harvard University Press, 1976).

41. These issues are developed in comprehensive fashion in the work of Pierre Bourdieu, notably, in *Distinction: A Social Critique of the Judgement of Taste*, trans. Richard Nice (Cambridge, Mass., and London: Harvard University Press, 1984).

42. Daniel Horowitz, *The Morality of Spending: Attitudes toward the Consumer Society in America, 1675–1940* (Baltimore: Johns Hopkins University Press, 1985), xi. For a recent positive assessment of mass consumption, focusing on the resourcefulness of immigrants (Jewish immigrants, in this case) in making use of consumer goods to help themselves assimilate to American society, see Andrew R. Heinze, *Adapting to Abundance: Jewish Immigrants, Mass Consumption, and the Search for American Identity* (New York: Columbia University Press, 1990).

43. Horowitz, *The Morality of Spending*, 169.

44. Michael Walzer, "Only Connect," *New Republic*, 13 August 1990, 34.

45. Albert O. Hirschman, *Shifting Involvements: Private Interest and Public Action* (Princeton, N.J.: Princeton University Press, 1982), 48–50.

46. Shi, *The Simple Life*, 277.

47. Harris, "The Drama of Consumer Desire," 210.

48. Horowitz, *The Morality of Spending*, xii.

CHAPTER 21

The Tyranny of Choice

Steven Waldman

Why did I nearly start crying the last time I went to buy socks? I'd stopped in a store called Sox Appeal, the perfect place, one might imagine, to spend a pleasant few minutes acquiring a pair of white athletic socks. After a brief visit to the men's dress sock department—dallying with more than 300 varieties, among them products embroidered with bikini-clad women, neckties, flowers, Rocky and Bullwinkle, and elegant logos such as "The Gold Bullion Collection: Imported" and "D'zin Pour Homme"—I finally made it into the athletics section. Here, the product-option high was even headier. Past the "Hypercolor" socks that change hue, combination "sport-and-dress" white socks, and "EarthCare" environmentally safe socks (which, unfortunately, boast of decomposing easily) were hosiery for every sport: racquetball, running, walking, cycling, hiking, basketball, and aerobics. I needed help.

"What if I play racquetball occasionally and run occasionally and walk sometimes, but don't want to get a different sock for each one?" I asked the saleswoman. She wrinkled her nose: "It's really a matter of personal preference." Did she have any standard-issue white tube socks? The nose-wrinkle again. "Well, yeah, you *could* get those, but . . . " I started reading the backs of the boxes, elaborately illustrated with architects' renderings of the stress points in the "Cushion-Engineered (TM) Zone Defense." After briefly contemplating the implications of the Cross-Training Sock—"Shock-Woven elastic arch brace contours to arch, providing additional support and normal articulation of the bones in the foot, while keeping sock migration minimal"—I spent another five minutes studying shapes (anklet, crew, or quarter) and manufacturers, and grabbed a Cross Trainer, two walkers, and, in an environmental guilt-spasm, one pair of the EarthCare.

Since that day, the sock metaphor has crept constantly into my mind—and not just when I'm buying consumer products. At work I pick through dozens

"The Tyranny of Choice" by Steven Waldman from *New Republic* (January 27, 1992). Reprinted by permission of Steven Waldman.

of options on my cafeteria insurance benefits plan. At the doctor's I'm offered several possible treatments for a neck problem and no real way to decide. At the video rental store I end up renting four movies even though I'll watch only one. Choices proliferate everywhere. My mental "tilt" light flashes continuously. I keep thinking that the more choices there are, the more wrong choices there are—and the higher the odds I'll make a mistake.

The topic of how much freedom freedom brings has fascinated philosophers throughout the ages. But when Sartre urged man to embrace and acknowledge his own power to choose, he did not have in mind figuring out the difference between hair conditioner, rejuvenator, reconstructor, and clarifier. So far, public debate on choice has been limited to just two realms: abortion and, more recently, public schools. But we're in the midst of a choice explosion that is much further reaching.

Think it over. A typical supermarket in 1976 had 9,000 products; today it has more than 30,000. The average produce section in 1975 carried sixty-five items; this summer it carried 285. (Kiwi has hit the top 20 list.) A Cosmetic Center outside Washington carries about 1,500 types and sizes of hair care products. The median household got six TV stations in 1975. Thanks to deregulation of the cable TV industry, that family now has more than thirty channels. The number of FM radio stations has doubled since 1970. A new religious denomination forms every week. (The 1980s brought us major additions such as the Evangelical Presbyterian Church and smaller groups such as the Semjase Silver Star Center, which follows the Twelve Bids from Patule that were given by extraterrestrial Space Brothers to Edmund "Billy" Meier.) In 1955 only 4 percent of the adult population had left the faith of their childhood. By 1985 one-third had. In 1980, 564 mutual funds existed. This year there are 3,347.

There has been a sharp rise in the number of people choosing new faces. More than twice as many cosmetic surgery operations were performed in the 1980s than in the 1970s, estimates the American Academy of Cosmetic Surgery. In the past decade a new periodical was born every day. Some have perished, but the survivors include: *Elvis International Forum, Smart Kids* (recent cover headline: "Should Babies Learn to Read?"), *American Handgunner, Triathlete, Harley Women, Log Home Living, Musclecar Classics*, and (my favorite) *Contemporary Urology*.

The growth of variety predates this recession, will continue after it, and, to a large extent, has persisted during it. *New Product News* reports that despite the depressed economy 21 percent more new products were introduced in supermarkets and drug stores in 1991 than the year before. Obvious benefits abound, of course, and not just for people with money. Telephone deregulation has made it cheaper to stay in touch with faraway friends; periodical proliferation meant I had *Fantasy Baseball* magazine to help me prepare for Rotisserie draft day; increased social tolerance has allowed more people (including me) to marry outside their faith or ethnic group; low sodium orange juice means people with high blood pressure can drink it (and it has increased juice sales); more cosmetics mean black women have shades that match their complexions. And so on. And in the words of Morris Cohen, a professor at the Wharton Business School: "If you're overwhelmed by the sock store, don't go there anymore." The beauty of the free market, he explains, is that each individual can select which options to exploit and which to ignore.

But Cohen's rational approach fails to account for how the mind actually processes all this variety. In fact, choice can be profoundly debilitating. It forces us to squander our time, weakens our connections to people and places, and can even poison our sense of contentedness. What follows is a simple checklist—take your pick—of the drawbacks of our new way of choosing.

Choice Erodes Commitment

The same psychological dynamic that has led to a decline in brand loyalty can operate on more important decisions. The more options we have, the more tenuous our commitment becomes to each one. The compulsion to take inventory of one's wants and continually upgrade to a better deal can help explain everything from the rise of the pathological channel switcher who can never watch one TV show straight through to staggering divorce rates and employer-employee disloyalty. Baseball players have never had as many career options as they do now. As a result, sportswriter Thomas Boswell notes, the slightest sign of trouble leads the player or team to try someplace or someone better, producing many "insincere love affairs and very few committed marriages." Sound familiar? Yes, even the infamous male commitment problem results in part from the same thinking. I recently married a wonderful woman, but only after several years of embarrassingly tortured contemplation of what kind of "options" I might be foreclosing. There are, after all, 9,538,000 unmarried females aged 24–39, each with the potential to be more "perfect" than the one before.

Choice Takes Too Much Time

Taken individually, most choices are manageable and, for some sector of the population, a pleasure. Stereo buffs love being able to select the finest woofers. But spend the optimal amount of time on each decision and pretty soon you run out of life. It's not surprising, then, that people feel more rushed than they used to. John P. Robinson, a professor of sociology at the University of Maryland who studied time diaries in 1965, 1975, and 1985, believes we feel harried partly because so much of our free time is absorbed by the process of deciding what to do with it. For all consumers, some time is simply wasted, not in figuring out which options suit them best but rather which distinctions matter. Before you can compare breakfast cereals' bran content you have to figure out if bran is really healthful. Should one care if a hair dryer has higher wattage? Are disposable diapers really worse for the environment than cloth? Being an educated consumer is a full-time job. You need to subscribe to several consumer magazines to do it properly. But which magazine to choose?

Choice Awakens Us to Our Failings

Choice-making lays claim to an expanding portion of our mental energy because the perceived consequences of making the wrong selection keep growing. Under cafeteria insurance plans, if you choose to forgo the dismemberment benefits in favor of extra teeth cleanings, you have no one to blame after an accident but yourself. Each time I checked off a box on my benefit election form I flashed forward to some weepy scene when I had to explain to my wife why I had decided to consign us to poverty and despair. When the company dictated my dental plan I could at least curse the Bosses for their gross disregard of dental self-esteem and go about adapting to the situation. Arbitrariness had its comforts.

Similarly, before the mid-1970s, people had little choice about how to invest their money. If inflation eroded their savings accounts, they were at least suffering, along with others, from the cruelty of an irresistible outside force. Today the availability of hundreds of possible investment "products" means everyone is fully capable of doing much worse than her neighbor. The wealthy try to solve that problem by spending still more money to hire financial advisers, only to confront a new set of worries about whether they have selected the best one. For the financially strapped, the anxiety can grow even more intense: the fewer dollars you have the more consequential each mistake becomes. Even when the stakes are small, we live in constant fear of being a Bad Consumer, which in a consumer-oriented society translates roughly into "sucker."

Choice Leads to Inept Consumption

The more choice available, the more information a consumer must have to make a sensible selection. When overload occurs, many simply abandon the posture of rational Super-Consumer. Warning labels on products have become so common that many shoppers simply ignore them all, including the important ones. Several friends have confessed that the selection of car models—591 and rising—has become so dizzying that they tossed aside *Consumer Reports* and relied entirely on the recommendation of a friend. Some become so paralyzed by the quest for the better deal that they postpone decisions indefinitely, while others become so preoccupied with absorbing the new features touted by a manufacturer that they forget to consider the basics. After all the fretting over the migration patterns of the socks, I took them home and found them to be quite fluffy and supportive, but the wrong size.

Consumers may be better informed than they were two decades ago, but salespeople have more tools with which to fight back. I spent three days studying up for a trip to Circuit City to buy a CD player. Despite having read several magazine and newspaper articles, I was, within minutes, putty in the salesman's hands. When I asked for a particular model, he rolled his eyes and laughed, "You must have gotten that from *Consumer Reports.*" With a simple well-timed chuckle he made me doubt my entire research regimen. He then battered me with a flurry of techno-terms and finally moved in for the kill by giving me an audio comparison test between two different systems that sounded exactly alike. My resistance was exhausted, so I bought the system he suggested, which, of course, cost more than I had intended to spend.

Choice Causes Political Alienation

Voters don't necessarily have more choices than they used to—an increase in primaries and referenda having been offset by the influence of incumbency and money—but the *way* voters choose has changed dramatically. As a result of the weakening of political parties, voting behavior now closely resembles the consumption of products. The biggest political group is not Democrats or Republicans, but "independents," shopper-equivalents who've dropped brand loyalty in favor of product-by-product analysis. Last century two-thirds of voters went straight party line; in 1980 two-thirds split tickets. In theory, this means voters carefully weigh the candidate's policies, character, and history. In reality, it's nearly impossible to sort through a candidate's "stands" on the "issues" from a blizzard of untrustworthy ads, a newspaper editorial, or a blip on the TV news. Was he the one who wants a revolving loan fund for worker retraining or the one who gives flag burners early parole? No wonder voters, like shoppers, act impulsively or vote according to the wisdom of their favorite interest group. Many who vote for ballot initiatives or lower offices simply follow the recommendation of the local newspaper, which is like buying a car on the word of the local auto columnist. When I was voting absentee in New York I selected judicial candidates on the basis of gender and race since I knew little else about them. The ultimate political choice overload came in California in 1990, when voters received a 222-page ballot pamphlet to help them decide among twenty-eight initiatives.

Candidates have responded to the rise of the consumer-voter by turning to marketing professionals who've only made the voters' dilemma worse. In the 1950s political consultants were advertising men who selected a candidate attribute and then sold it, the way an automaker might remind consumers of a large car's natural advantages, like spaciousness and safety. Political consulting has evolved, though. Candidates now rely heavily on market researchers—i.e., the pollsters—trying less to determine what part of their essence they should highlight than what they should become to match voters' desires. Sometimes that means candidates become more responsive to public thinking, but more often it means politicians forget to consult (or have) their own core beliefs. Witness the breathtaking spectacle of pro-life pols who once assailed the supreme immorality of baby-killing quickly becoming pro-choice because of the supreme importance of polls. This "politics as consumption" (in the phrase of University of Rochester professor Robert Westbrook) seems to produce more gelatinous politicians—precisely the sort that voters have the hardest time judging.

Choice Erodes the Self

In theory, choice enables an individual to select the car, money market fund, or spouse that expresses herself most precisely. But if choice is self-definition, more choices mean more possible definitions. Kenneth Gergen, a professor of psychology at Swarthmore, argues in his new book, *The Saturated Self*, that the postmodern personality becomes "populated" with growing numbers of "selves" as it's bombarded by an ever increasing number of potential relationships from TV, travel, telephones, faxes, computers, etc. From an insecure sense of self, you then spiral toward what Gergen calls "multiphrenia," in which the besieged, populated self frantically flails about trying to take advantage of the sea of choices. This condition may never merit its own telethon, but as choices increase so do the odds that multiphrenia will strike, leaving the scars of perpetual self-doubt. It's why the people who work hardest to improve their appearance never seem to feel much better than before they sampled the offerings of the Self-Perfection Industry (exercise videos, customized makeup, cosmetic surgery, health food). They become like politicians with their own private pollsters; the quest to re-create virtually supplants whatever person was once there.

Choice Reduces Social Bonding

The proliferation of choice helps cause, and results from, another trend—social fragmentation. Together they ensure that Americans share fewer and fewer common experiences. A yuppie diet bears less and less resemblance to that of a lower-income family. I don't even know who's on the Wheaties box anymore because my cereal is located about ninety feet down the aisle. As marketers divide us into increasingly narrow segments, we inevitably see ourselves that way too. When there was one movie theater in a neighborhood, everyone sat under the same roof and watched the same film. Video rental stores enable you to be a movie junkie without ever having to sit next to another human being.

Three decades ago, even when everyone was sitting in their own homes they were at least all watching "Gunsmoke." Today's viewing public scatters to its particular demographic niche on the cable dial.

Even the spiritual realm has evolved like a supermarket. "It has become a consumer-oriented, highly fragmented religious marketplace," says David Roozen, director of the Hartford Seminary for Social and Religious Research. In a buyer's market, the individual can select the religious institution with which he or she is most comfortable. But as each generation discards the nasty (or difficult) parts of the faith, religious traditions decay. Moreover, instead of integrating people of different backgrounds under the same theological roof, denominations sprout to appeal to smaller groups of like-minded people. (If, for example, you decide the followers of the teachings of Billy Meier's Space Brothers aren't your kind of people, you can turn to the Universe Society Church, which observes the wisdom of Fahsz, an extraterrestrial contacted by someone named Hal Wilcox.) The comedian Emo Philips tells a joke about discovering similarities in religious backgrounds with someone he just met. "I said [are you] Protestant or Catholic? He said, 'Protestant.' I said, 'Me Too! What franchise?' He says, 'Baptist,' I said, 'Me too! Northern Baptist or Southern Baptist?' He says, 'Southern Baptist.' I said, 'Me Too!' " The two go back and forth in this vein. Finally, Emo asks, " 'Northern conservative fundamentalist Baptist Great Lakes Region Council of 1879 or Northern conservative fundamentalist Baptist Great Lakes Region Council of 1912?' And he says 'Northern conservative fundamentalist Baptist Great Lakes Region Council of 1912.' And I said, 'Die Heretic!' "

How can we adapt to this world of choice? Some steps are being taken for us. The Food and Drug Administration recently announced rules to standardize product labels that should simplify our task in the supermarket. Some school districts have required uniforms in order to curb the clothing competition that has led to killings over sneakers. Regulatory agencies could further help by simply banning products they consider unsafe, rather than slapping on warning labels that force us to perform quickie risk assessment studies. The market itself will develop some innovations to help us cope. "Price clubs" have sprouted up in which customers shop at huge warehouses stocked with just a few brands, but very low prices. Bicycle stores now offer "hybrids" for those who can't decide between mountain, city, touring, and racing. But the general trend remains overwhelmingly toward market fragmentation.

Dealing with an abundance of choices mostly requires a mental reorientation. Choice overload helped me finally understand what was so offensive about the stereotypical yuppie obsession with "quality," of which I have often been guilty. It's not that some coffee beans aren't, in fact, more flavorful than others, it's that people who spend so much of their lives thinking about small differences become small people.

Imagine instead a world in which we used our choice brain lobes for the most important decisions and acted more arbitrarily on the rest. Perhaps you might select a brand name and buy all its products for the next four years, scheduling Choice Day during non-presidential election years. Or you might embrace the liberating powers of TV commercials. As everyone knows, ads brainwash us into choosing products through insidious appeals to sex or other animal urges. But sometimes it feels good to let an ad take us by the hand. A few years ago I had an epiphany while deciding what to eat for dinner. I looked in the refrigerator, thought about nearby restaurants and markets, and grew puzzled. Just then an ad came on the TV for Burger King, featuring a luscious Whopper with fake charcoal stripes painted with perfect symmetry across the juicy meat. I put on my coat and immediately walked, zombielike, to the nearby Burger King and ordered a Whopper. I found it exhilarating, because I knew it wasn't the behavior of a rational economic player, and that it didn't matter.

As the Twelve Steppers say, we must acknowledge our powerlessness. We cannot knowledgeably make even a fraction of the appropriate choices available. Say it out loud. Today I will make several wrong choices. Now, whether you've selected an inferior vacuum cleaner, bought the large soda when the jumbo was a better deal, or accidentally prayed to the wrong god—forgive yourself. If we took some joy in being bad choosers, or at least placed less value on being stellar consumers of unimportant things, we would be training ourselves to accept a few extra drops of imperfection in our lives. Somehow, that would seem more like progress than having the choice between polypropylene arch brace contours and a solar-powered argyle.

CHAPTER 22

The Pleasures of Eating

Wendell Berry

Many times, after I have finished a lecture on the decline of American farming and rural life, someone in the audience has asked, "What can city people do?"

"Eat responsibly," I have usually answered. Of course, I have tried to explain what I meant by that, but afterwards I have invariably felt that there was more to be said than I had been able to say. Now I would like to attempt a better explanation.

I begin with the proposition that eating is an agricultural act. Eating ends the annual drama of the food economy that begins with planting and birth. Most eaters, however, are no longer aware that this is true. They think of food as an agricultural product, perhaps, but they do not think of themselves as participants in agriculture. They think of themselves as "consumers." If they think beyond that, they recognize that they are passive consumers. They buy what they want—or what they have been persuaded to want—within the limits of what they can get. They pay, mostly without protest, what they are charged. And they mostly ignore certain critical questions about the quality and the cost of what they are sold: How fresh is it? How pure or clean is it, how free of dangerous chemicals? How far was it transported, and what did transportation add to the cost? How much did manufacturing or packaging or advertising add to the cost? When the food product has been manufactured or "processed" or "precooked," how has that affected its quality or price or nutritional value?

Most urban shoppers would tell you that food is produced on farms. But most of them do not know what farms, or what kinds of farms, or where the farms are, or what knowledge or skills are involved in farming. They apparently have little doubt that farms will continue to produce, but they do not know how or over what obstacles. For them, then, food is pretty much an abstract idea—something they do not know or imagine—until it appears on the grocery shelf or on the table.

The specialization of production induces specialization of consumption. Patrons of the entertainment industry, for example, entertain themselves less and less and have become more and more passively dependent on commercial suppliers. This is certainly true also of patrons of the food industry, who have tended more and more to be *mere* consumers—passive, uncritical, and dependent. Indeed, this sort of consumption may be said to be one of the chief goals of industrial production. The food industrialists have by now persuaded millions of consumers to prefer food that is already prepared. They will grow, deliver, and cook your food for you and (just like your mother) beg you to eat it. That they do not yet offer to insert it, prechewed, into your mouth is only because they have found no profitable way to do so. We may rest assured that they would be glad to find such a way. The ideal industrial food consumer would be strapped to a table with a tube running from the food factory directly into his or her stomach.

Perhaps I exaggerate, but not by much. The industrial eater is, in fact, one who does not know that eating is an agricultural act, who no longer knows or imagines the connections between eating and the land, and who is therefore necessarily passive and uncritical—in short, a victim. When food, in the minds of eaters, is no longer associated with farming and with the land, then the eaters are suffering a kind of cultural amnesia that is misleading and dangerous. The current version of the "dream home" of the future involves "effortless" shopping from a list of available goods on a television monitor and heating precooked food by remote control. Of course, this implies and depends on, a perfect ignorance of the history of the food that is consumed. It requires that the citizenry should give up their hereditary and sensible aversion to buying a pig in a poke. It wishes to make the selling of pigs in pokes an honorable and glamorous activity. The dreamer in this dream home will perforce know nothing about the kind or quality of this food, or where it came from, or how it was produced and prepared, or what ingredients, additives, and residues it contains—unless, that is, the dreamer undertakes a close and constant study of the food industry, in which case he or she might as well wake up and play an active and responsible part in the economy of food.

There is, then, a politics of food that, like any politics, involves our freedom. We still (sometimes) remember that we cannot be free if our minds and voices are controlled by someone else. But we have neglected to understand that we cannot be free if our food and its sources are controlled by someone else. The condition of the passive consumer of food is not a democratic condition. One reason to eat responsibly is to live free.

But if there is a food politics, there are also a food esthetics and a food ethics, neither of which is dissociated from politics. Like industrial sex, industrial eating has become a degraded, poor, and paltry thing. Our kitchens and other eating places more and more resemble filling stations, as our homes more and more resemble motels. "Life is not very interesting," we seem to have decided. "Let its satisfactions be minimal, perfunctory, and fast." We hurry through our meals to go to work and hurry through our work in order to "recreate" ourselves in the evenings and on weekends and vacations. And then we hurry, with the greatest possible speed and noise and violence, through our recreation—for what? To eat the billionth hamburger at some fast-food joint hellbent on increasing the "quality" of our life? And all this is carried out in a remarkable obliviousness to the causes and effects, the possibilities and the purposes, of the life of the body in this world.

One will find this obliviousness represented in virgin purity in the advertisements of the food industry, in which food wears as much makeup as the actors. If one gained one's whole knowledge of food from these advertisements (as some presumably do), one would not know that the various edibles were ever living creatures, or that they all come from the soil, or that they were produced by work. The passive American consumer, sitting down to a meal of pre-prepared or fast food, confronts a platter covered with inert, anonymous substances that have been processed, dyed, breaded, sauced, gravied, ground, pulped, strained, blended, prettified, and sanitized beyond resemblance to any part of any creature that ever lived. The products of nature and agriculture have been made, to all appearances, the products of industry. Both eater and eaten are thus in exile from biological reality. And the result is a kind of solitude, unprecedented in human experience, in which the eater may think of eating as, first, a purely commercial transaction between him and a supplier and then as a purely appetitive transaction between him and his food.

And this peculiar specialization of the act of eating is, again, of obvious benefit to the food industry, which has good reasons to obscure the connection between food and farming. It would not do for the consumer to know that the hamburger she is eating came from a steer who spent much of his life standing deep in his own excrement in a feedlot, helping to pollute the local streams, or that the calf that yielded the veal cutlet on her plate spent its life in a box in which it did not have room to turn around. And, though her sympathy for the slaw might be less tender, she should not be encouraged to meditate on the hygienic and biological implications of mile-square fields of cabbage, for vegetables grown in huge monocultures are dependent on toxic chemicals—just as animals in close confinement are dependent on antibiotics and other drugs.

The consumer, that is to say, must be kept from discovering that, in the food industry—as in any other industry—the overriding concerns are not quality and health, but volume and price. For decades now the entire industrial food economy, from the large farms and feedlots to the chains of supermarkets and fast-food restaurants, has been obsessed with volume. It has relentlessly increased scale in order to increase volume in order (presumably) to reduce costs. But as scale increases, diversity declines; as diversity declines, so does health; as health declines, the dependence on drugs and chemicals necessarily increases. As capital replaces labor, it does so by substituting machines, drugs, and chemicals for human workers and for the natural health and fertility of the soil. The food is produced by any means or any shortcut that will increase profits. And the business of the cosmeticians of advertising is to persuade the consumer that food so produced is good, tasty, healthful, and a guarantee of marital fidelity and long life.

It is possible, then, to be liberated from the husbandry and wifery of the old household food economy. But one can be thus liberated only by entering a trap (unless one sees ignorance and helplessness as the signs of privilege, as many people apparently do). The trap is the ideal of industrialism: a walled city surrounded by valves that let merchandise in but no consciousness out. How does one escape this trap? Only voluntarily, the same way that one went in: by restoring one's consciousness of what is involved in eating; by reclaiming responsibility for one's own part in the food economy. One might begin with the illuminating principle of Sir Albert Howard's *The Soil and Health*, that we should understand "the whole problem of health in soil, plant, animal, and man as one great subject." Eaters, that is, must understand that eating takes place inescapably in the world, that it is inescapably an agricultural act, and that how we eat determines, to a considerable extent, how the world is used. This is a simple way of describing a relationship that is inexpressibly complex. To eat responsibly is to understand and enact, so far as one can, this complex relationship. What can one do? Here is a list, probably not definitive;

1. Participate in food production to the extent that you can. If you have a yard or even just a porch box or a pot in a sunny window, grow something to eat in it. Make a little compost of your kitchen scraps and use it for fertilizer. Only by growing some food for yourself can you become acquainted with the beautiful energy cycle that revolves from soil to seed to flower to fruit to food to offal to decay, and around again. You will be fully responsible for any food that you grow for yourself, and you will know all about it. You will appreciate it fully, having known it all its life.

2. Prepare your own food. This means reviving in your own mind and life the arts of kitchen and household. This should enable you to eat more cheaply, and it will give you a measure of "quality control": you will have some reliable knowledge of what has been added to the food you eat.

3. Learn the origins of the food you buy, and buy the food that is produced closest to your home. The idea that every locality should be, as much as possible, the source of its own food makes several kinds of sense. The locally produced food supply is the most secure, the freshest, and the easiest for local consumers to know about and to influence.

4. Whenever possible, deal directly with a local farmer, gardener, or orchardist. All the reasons listed for the previous suggestion apply here. In addition, by such dealing you eliminate the whole pack of merchants, transporters, processors, packagers, and advertisers who thrive at the expense of both producers and consumers.

5. Learn, in self-defense, as much as you can of the economy and technology of industrial food production. What is added to food that is not food, and what do you pay for these additions?
6. Learn what is involved in the *best* farming and gardening.
7. Learn as much as you can, by direct observation and experience if possible, of the life histories of the food species.

The last suggestion seems particularly important to me. Many people are now as much estranged from the lives of domestic plants and animals (except for flowers and dogs and cats) as they are from the lives of the wild ones. This is regrettable, for these domestic creatures are in diverse ways attractive; there is much pleasure in knowing them. And farming, animal husbandry, horticulture, and gardening, at their best, are complex and comely arts; there is much pleasure in knowing them, too.

It follows that there is great *dis*pleasure in knowing about a food economy that degrades and abuses those arts and those plants and animals and the soil from which they come. For anyone who does know something of the modern history of food, eating away from home can be a chore. My own inclination is to eat seafood instead of red meat or poultry when I am traveling. Though I am by no means a vegetarian, I dislike the thought that some animal has been made miserable in order to feed me. If I am going to eat meat, I want it to be from an animal that has lived a pleasant, uncrowded life outdoors, on bountiful pasture, with good water nearby and trees for shade. And I am getting almost as fussy about food plants. I like to eat vegetables and fruits that I know have lived happily and healthily in good soil, not the products of the huge, bechemicaled factory-fields that I have seen, for example, in the Central Valley of California. The industrial farm is said to have been patterned on the factory production line. In practice, it looks more like a concentration camp.

The pleasure of eating should be an *extensive* pleasure, not that of the mere gourmet. People who know the garden in which their vegetables have grown and know that the garden is healthy will remember the beauty of the growing plants, perhaps in the dewy first light of morning when gardens are at their best. Such a memory involves itself with the food and is one of the pleasures of eating. The knowledge of the good health of the garden relieves and frees and comforts the eater. The same goes for eating meat. The thought of the good pasture and of the calf contentedly grazing flavors the steak. Some, I know, will think it bloodthirsty or worse to eat a fellow creature you have known all its life. On the contrary, I think it means that you eat with understanding and with gratitude. A significant part of the pleasure of eating is in one's accurate consciousness of the lives and the world from which food comes. The pleasure of eating, then, may be the best available standard of our health. And this pleasure, I think, is pretty fully available to the urban consumer who will make the necessary effort.

I mentioned earlier the politics, esthetics, and ethics of food. But to speak of the pleasure of eating is to go beyond those categories. Eating with the fullest pleasure—pleasure, that is, that does not depend on ignorance—is perhaps the profoundest enactment of our connection with the world. In this pleasure we experience and celebrate our dependence and our gratitude, for we are living from mystery, from creatures we did not make and powers we cannot comprehend. When I think of the meaning of food, I always remember these lines by the poet William Carlos William, which seem to me merely honest:

> There is nothing to eat,
>   seek it where you will,
>   but the body of the Lord.
> The blessed plants
>   and the sea, yield it
>   to the imagination
> intact.

CHAPTER 23

Coming Up for Air:
Consumer Culture in Historical Perspective

Jean-Christophe Agnew

Then, the mariners were afraid and cried every man unto his god, and cast forth the wares that were in the ship into the sea to lighten them.

Taking this dramatic passage from the Book of Jonah for his epigraph, the historian Simon Schama opens the second part of his recent book, *The Embarrassment of Riches*, with a fascinating discussion of "Feasting, Fasting, and Timely Atonement" among the Dutch of the Golden Age. For Schama the tale of the terrified sailors jettisoning their cargo neatly captures the sense of foreboding that haunted Holland's otherwise complacent bourgeois culture during the sixteenth and seventeenth centuries. Masters of banking and trade and for a time rulers of the sea, the Dutch nonetheless displayed a nagging ambivalence toward the commodities that served as both the source and signature of their affluence. Was not the very visibility of their wealth, they wondered, an invitation to disaster? Were so many goods not an omen of evils yet to come? This, then, was their "embarrassment."

The terms of embarrassment could run both ways, of course. Like the polished, auratic skull of a Dutch vanity painting, such anguished spiritual reflection on the comforts of commerce could just as easily deepen the lustre of the material objects upon which it ostensibly stood in judgment. Here Schama is scarcely the first historian to remark on the material and symbolic density with which the Dutch infused the prints and paintings of their commodity-world. Still, few scholars can rival his own dazzling interpretations of the cultural meanings the Dutch attached to such otherwise prosaic items as pipes, soap, and herring. And among Schama's readings, none is more impressive than the extended explication of a series of popular engravings of beached whales with which he begins his analysis of the complex attitudes the Dutch brought to the consumption of their own "riches."

Beached whales. An unpromising beginning, one might think, for a discussion of Dutch domestic possessions, but Schama manages to sort out the meanings of these prints in a fashion that gently but firmly leads the reader from the whale-ridden shores of the North Sea shore into the quiet interiors of the Northern Renaissance, which is to say, into the hearts and hearths of the Dutch. In fact, by the time Schama's reading is complete, the prints have been made to yield up almost as much wealth as the whales themselves. We learn, for example, of the Dutch fascination with mapping and measurement and of their hunger for news of the odd and miraculous; we read as well of their commercial interest in beached whales and of their corresponding fear of them as auguries of national misfortune and providential reminders of the vanity of worldly goods.[1]

The surplus of meaning that Schama finds at play in these marine images is truly remarkable; it is almost as if—in contemporary American terms—the *National Geographic*, the *National Review*, and the *National Enquirer* were condensed into a single tabloid image. The whales have not just been thought about; they have been thought through and through. "Metaphorical compression," Schama calls this process and then shows how Dutch engravers used the technique to navigate their own commercial route between the conflicting public demands for allegory, inventory, and reportage—demands that were driving "the first mass consumers' art market in European history."[2] As to the whales, he writes, "[t]he great leviathans, their sonar scrambled by the North sea, were migrating not only from Atlantic to Arctic, but from the realm of myth and morality to that of matter and commodity, sometimes becoming stranded on the submarine slopes of Dutch cultural contradiction."[3]

Description doesn't get much thicker than this. Between the tactility of the imagery and the surfeit of its significance, Schama's panorama of Dutch culture teems with art and artifacts that are larger, not to say longer, than life. Indeed, so dense and nuanced is Schama's treatment of the Dutch world of goods that one must occasionally remind oneself that his is an interpretation of Dutch culture, not of Dutch *consumer* culture. And the reminder is that much more necessary for the ease with which one could fit. *The Embarrassment of Riches* together with a number of other important recent studies that have challenged virtually every aspect of our understanding of the development of consumer culture in the West. If we cannot now speak about contemporary consumer culture without at least nodding toward sixteenth and seventeenth century Europe, then that reflex alone attests to the impact of the new scholarship. It would seem appropriate, then, to offer a preliminary review and assessment of a body of work that has—within a period of a few years—compelled so many historians to revise their familiar notions about culture, commodities, consumers, and their historical relationships.

1

Now while there is no single interpretive paradigm or point of departure from which to chart this sea-change in our present thinking about consumer

culture, one might for convenience's sake invoke two influential strands of critical thought that have set the boundaries to the debate and, at the same time,
defined its moral and political charge. The first strand is English and extends
from Thomas Carlyle's caustic denunciations of advertising puffery through
George Orwell's even grimmer ruminations, a century later, on the "sodden"
ideological messages of the British boys' weeklies.[4] The second strand of thinking is continental and extends from Marx's discussion of commodity fetishism
to the work of Georg Lukacs, Walter Benjamin, and the Frankfurt School.
These two traditions of criticism differ in important respects, but they both
picture western history and culture—time and space—as invaded and colonized by commodities and commodity-relations. Orwell epitomizes this state
of affairs most vividly and mockingly in the fictional figure of George Bowling,
a pitiable, petit bourgeois antihero who squanders his modest racetrack win-
nings upon a futile pilgrimage to the lost fishpond of his youth, only to find a
rubbish-heap upon which a new housing development is to grow. "What's the
good of trying to revisit the scenes of your boyhood?" the indignant Bowling
concludes. "They don't exist. Coming up for air! But there isn't any air. The
dustbin we're in reaches up to the stratosphere."[5]

This is a familiar refrain. On the other side of the Atlantic, we hear the same
plaintive message in Stuart Ewen's recent attack on "the politics of style in
contemporary culture." Ewen's title, *All Consuming Images*, itself registers the
deep, almost platonic distaste he feels for the ubiquitous productions—the
modern hoardings—of the culture industry. To him the politics of style means
the "dominance of surface over substance," yet he also discovers, to his dis-
may, that such surfaces can run disturbingly deep. Having asked his undergraduate students to write on the question of style, for example, Ewen is ap-
palled to discover just how thoroughly the vagaries of fashion have entered
into their constructions of self; there, in the memoirs his inner-city students
have written, the ordinary and sometimes extraordinary claims of their own
lives insert themselves, when they do not actually lose themselves, in the far
more insistent and accelerated half-lives of contemporary commodities. It
could be said that for these students history also appears as an embarrassment
of riches, but if so, it is an embarrassment prompted less by the fear of sudden
reversal than by the spectre of imminent obsolescence. Styles may be recycled,
but the goods themselves are soon jettisoned; sneakers to die for today become
artifacts to reminisce about tomorrow.[6] And though "the long-term ecological
implications of this trajectory may be disastrous," Ewen adds that "from a
strictly merchandising point of view, it is *the air we breathe*."[7] History has
been thus doubly lost, buried under the weight of shoddy goods and repressed
beneath the surface of a shopworn consciousness.

Aesthetic revulsion and political despair converge in Ewen's work, but in
that respect so too do the Orwellian and Marxian strands of cultural criticism
to which I have alluded. To the English concern with the designers of consciousness, Ewen adds the continental concern with the design itself, with the

peculiar ways in which the commodity has captured and colonized American culture in the image of its own relations—in the image, that is, of images. Even more than his earlier book, Stuart Ewen's *All Consuming Images* conjures up the presence of a horizonless ideological flatland, an impoverished consumerist dystopia whose mirage-like surfaces leave the radical political imagination no way out. For all its gestures in the direction of post-modernism, then, Ewen's latest work harks back to an older tradition of criticism—not just to George Orwell's ideas but to Georg Lukacs' notion of reification, to Max Horkheimer's and Theodor Adorno's portrait of the culture industry as mass deception, and, not least of all, to Herbert Marcuse's concept of ideological one-dimensionality.[8] In fact, it is this unwaveringly pessimistic view of the massive *totality* of contemporary consumer culture that makes Ewen's work such a convenient signpost (and foil) from which to measure the intellectual and political distance traveled by the most recent generation of writers on consumer culture.

This is not to say that the initial steps away from the pessimistic reading of consumer culture were particularly easy ones. They weren't, and a fair sense of the difficulties encountered along the way may be had by a glance at a collection of essays that appeared in 1983 under the title *The Culture of Consumption*.[9] The contributors to this volume, myself included, advertised their work as attempting to rehistoricize and retheorize American consumer culture. "Historians have taken the world of goods for granted," I wrote at the time. "More precisely, they have taken that world as the outcome of other historical developments—industrial capitalism, for example—that are felt to be more compelling."[10] Consumer culture deserved a more considered historical treatment, we felt, if not on its own terms than in its own time. This meant, among other things, backdating the emergence of consumer culture in America to the 1880s and linking that birth in turn to the social formation of a professional-managerial class. Not all the authors approached this story in the same way, but whether our frameworks were Weberian, Marxist, or Durkheimian, the story we did tell remained in many respects a familiar one, marked by the shift from a producer-ethic to a consumer-ethic, from a salvationist ideal to a therapeutic ideal, and from local performances to mass-mediated spectacles. And though the editors acknowledged that conspiratorial theories of mass deception were inaccurate, people being "not that passive," the collection itself remained an unashamedly supply-side enterprise: a study of the producers, stylists, and critics of a hegemonic consumer ideal and not an inquiry into "patterns of consumption" or the "lives of ordinary consumers."[11] Despite the distance we tried to put between ourselves and the pessimistic critiques of a Ewen or a Marcuse, our contributions were understandably received as revisions and extensions of the Frankfurt School's central insights and assumptions.[12] One-dimensional man, and he was quite plainly a man, had emerged weightless and famished as early as the turn of the century. Or so the collection seemed to suggest.

Of course I caricature *The Culture of Consumption* here, but then I am scarcely the first to do so, and such caricatures can and do serve to inspire corrective impulses among other scholars. And, in that respect, it seems fair to say that we now stand corrected.[13] The narrative, interpretations, and methods laid out in our volume—not to mention those laid out in Stuart Ewen's work—have all been challenged in the intervening years. Not only do we now have before us outstanding histories of early modern material culture and promotion, of nineteenth-century popular culture and recreation, and of twentieth-century advertising and working-class consumption, but we have as well a variety of intriguing approaches to consumer culture growing out of other disciplines. These would include new sociological and anthropological studies of tastes, goods, and their uses; literary studies of reader response; and cultural studies of genre formation and of the symbolic or semiotic order of consumption.[14] We have, to borrow again from Simon Schama, an embarrassment of riches, and in accordance with Schama's own formulation of Dutch ambivalence in the Golden Age, I would like to convey some of my excitement and pleasure in this newfound wealth and, at the same time, some of my lingering doubts and questions.

Exciting as this body of work may be, however, it would be tedious to review it all. Instead, I shall select and group works according to the triple challenge I see them posing to the conventional understanding of the history of consumption: First, their challenge to the received narrative of consumption in the Euro-American world; second, their challenge to the perceived causes and conditions of that history; and third, their challenge to the judgments on consumer culture—moral, aesthetic, and political—that have for so long underwritten and overdetermined our perspectives on the subject. At the risk of anticipating my argument, let me also summarize briefly what I see as the results of these challenges. First, historians have shifted the birth of western consumer culture to the early modern period and deferred the arrival of mass consumer culture to the mid-twentieth century. Second, they have rejected the Weberian dichotomies between Puritanism and Romanticism and, correspondingly, between saving and spending and, in some instances, they have also abandoned the classic Marxist distinction between use-value and symbolic value. Finally, they have revalued the political and moral dimensions of fantasy, fetishism, dream, and wish—the keywords of consumer mystification as it has heretofore been understood. As a result, the productionist, supply-side, and hegemonic interpretation of consumer culture has been shaken, if not overthrown, leaving one-dimensional man marooned on a small and ever shrinking island of history.

2

Let me return, then, to the first of the challenges I have enumerated: the challenge to the received narrative or periodization of consumer culture, for the question of narrative entails, as it almost always does, virtually every other question a historian might bring to a subject. As it happens, the recent back-dating (as I have called it) of consumer culture to the early modern period is a by-product of a much earlier debate over the origins of industrial capitalism in the West, a debate in which historians tended to divide over the relative roles of commerce and class—or of exchange and production. Yet even within the ranks of those who favored the market as the prime motor of development, historians fell into two camps: the globalists or world-systems advocates, who looked to the international wheels of commerce as the vehicle of capitalist de-velopment, and the nationalists, who looked to indigenous demand as the driving force. The world-systems advocates were associated with the work of Fernand Braudel and Immanuel Wallerstein, and it was upon their example and that of John Nef and Werner Sombart that the historical sociologist, Chandra Mukerji, relocated the origins of "modern materialism," as she called it, in fifteenth- and sixteenth-century Europe.[15] As the title of her book, *From Graven Images*, suggests, she saw the international commerce in prints, maps, and calicoes as both modeling and diffusing a new and intense orientation to-ward material objects. A "hedonistic culture of mass consumption" she called this new worldview and contrasted it with the now classic, Weberian portrait of an ascetic, savings-minded Reformation.[16] Mukerji, it should be added, did not so much discard Weber's psychohistorical sequence of savings and spend-ing, asceticism and hedonism, as telescope it in time. As a result, she trans-formed a story of anguished cultural and temperamental change from one ethic to another into a portrait of complementary and mutually energizing traits. Early modern capitalists saved *and* spent, and, in doing so, ushered in modernity.

Standing not so much against as with the internationalists were the nation-alists, historians like Joan Thirsk, D. E. C. Eversley, Jan de Vries, and most re-cently, Simon Schama, all of whom stressed the impact of home demand upon commercial and industrial development.[17] In Holland, for example, where the North Sea appears to have played the role of a merciless Calvinist Providence, Schama painted a complex, Breugelian panorama of a "perennial combat be-tween acquisitiveness and asceticism" within the society and within the minds of the Dutch.[18] As skeptical of Weber as Mukerji was, Schama likewise found in this internal fusion of opposite impulses a motive force powerful enough to move the Dutch economy ahead of its rivals.[19]

For Braudel, though, the "right string to pull to start the engine" of capital-ism was always demand, and it has been to the demand-side of the capitalist marketplace that current revisionists have devoted most of their attention.[20] Among these efforts by far the most influential revisionist manifesto appeared in the essays that Neil McKendrick wrote for the book he co-authored with John Brewer and J. H. Plumb in 1982: *The Birth of a Consumer Society*, subtitled *The Commercialization of Eighteenth-Century England*. Building upon the earlier studies of home demand by Thirsk, Plumb himself, and oth-ers, McKendrick announced the discovery of "a consumer revolution in eighteenth-century England." He agreed with Braudel's belief that "there is always a potential consumer society ready to be awakened in any society," but insisted that for the eighteenth century, only England presented the right mix of ingredients: a fluid social structure, rising wages, an emulative bourgeoisie and its servants, a showcase capital city, and an intellectual environment increasingly hospitable to the public benefits of private vices.[21]

All that seemed missing from this heady stew of latent hedonism was a chef to stir it up, an entrepreneur sufficiently to alert to the possibilities before him; thus McKendrick's interest in Josiah Wedgwood, the pottery king. The choice of Wedgwood, however, was not an immediately obvious one, since his historical reputation to that point had been as a pioneer of large-scale craft production, industrial discipline, and the division of labor. Indeed, what made McKendrick's argument that much more persuasive was the ease with which he was able to transfer Wedgwood's achievement as an entrepreneur from the supply side to the demand side of England's commercialization. Despite or, more accurately, because of his many aristocratic connections, Josiah Wedgwood had made himself into a promotional wizard, able, as McKendrick put it, to "milk the effects of social emulation and emulative spending" among England's middling ranks.[22] Economists have traditionally referred to such imitative or bandwagon phenomena as "Veblen effects," but having described what he considered "one of the most brilliant and sustained campaigns in the history of consumer exploitation," McKendrick wondered whether such behavior were not better labeled as "Wedgwood effects."[23]

Wedgwood thus stood in for a variety of merchandising pioneers whose bold promotional campaigns released an unprecedented wave of bourgeois spending that spread across the kingdom and, as production and distribution caught up with demand, eventually spilled over into Britain's colonies. In other words, "by creating new wants and provoking new needs," these orchestrators of desire were able "to create new demand which would not have become economically operational without the requisite entrepreneurial skills to conjure it into existence."[24] Imaginative as these businessmen were, though, and bold as McKendrick's view of them may have been, his argument as a whole bore the marks of the original historical debate that had given it birth, namely the argument over the origins of England's industrial revolution. It was Wedgwood—the entrepreneur—and not his consumers, who pulled the strings of demand. In fact, had McKendrick not been so visibly impressed by Wedgwood's indisputable brilliance as a promoter, the strikingly magical and manipulative metaphors ("exploiting," "milking," "conjuring") with which he formulated his revisionist account could have been as easily assimilated to the kind of conspiratorial or hypodermic theory of mass culture before which even the most devoted hegemonic theorist might balk.[25] To put it another way, McKendrick's story of the birth of a consumer society in eighteenth-century England left us with an unforgettable portrait of its enterprising midwife but with only the faintest sketch of the infant itself. We were still in important respects fixed on the supply side of the ledger, with the mechanics of demand-stimulation now included in the costs of production.

As we shall see, McKendrick's work, like that of his central figure Wedgwood, had important reverberations on the other side of the Atlantic. But perhaps one of the most thoughtful and provocative responses to it came some five years later from within Britain itself and in the form of a book with the deliberately Weberian title, *The Romantic Ethic and the Spirit of Modern Consumerism*. Written by an historical sociologist, Colin Campbell, *The Romantic Ethic* accepted McKendrick's reperiodization of western consumerism while seeking to remedy its cultural or demand-side shortcomings. Drawing on a number of disciplines, including (interestingly) the philosophy of mind, Campbell dismissed what he called McKendrick's "instinctivist, manipulationist, Veblenesque" approach to the consumer revolution as an inadequate explanation for a pattern of consumption that eighteenth-century critics themselves labeled as manic and addictive.²⁶ Purchasing power, he argued, could not of itself generate new propensities to consume, just as marketing brainstorms could not explain the new willingness of entrepreneurs to shift resources toward promotion. Fashion and its democratization were less the answer to the question of consumer culture's birth than the problem to be resolved: the problem, that is, of explaining both the rapid multiplication and the equally rapid extinction of wants. In other words, how might one account for the almost Proustian cycle of anticipatory pleasure and consummatory disappointment upon which the Wedgwoods of the eighteenth century so skillfully played?²⁷

Twentieth-century economists, from Werner Sombart to Tibor Scitovsky and Albert O. Hirschman, have long wrestled with the problem of consumer disappointment or "exit," but it was Campbell's special contribution to imbue this seemingly timeless puzzle of evanescent demand with the kind of historicity—of timeboundedness—that McKendrick's work had conferred upon the strategies of its manipulation.²⁸ Consumer letdown and the longing that disappointment nourished were indeed consequences of manipulation, but of a manipulation, Campbell insisted, in which consumers pulled their own strings. How and why, then, had England's middling orders learned to do this? This was the question Campbell set for himself, and for us.

Though the argument of *The Romantic Ethic* is far too complex and nuanced to recapitulate adequately here, it may reasonably be said to hang on a distinction Campbell drew between "traditional" and "modern hedonism." Traditional hedonism orients itself toward the material attributes of objects as means to relieve discomfort, he argued, whereas "modern, autonomous, and self-illusory hedonism" orients itself toward the imagined associations of objects as means to cultivate a "state of enjoyable discomfort."²⁹ Modern hedonism operated in a twilight zone of longing best typified in the experience of window-shopping.³⁰ Its peculiar, daydreamlike fusion of the pleasures of fantasy and reality inserted itself into that ever-expanding moment or "hiatus" between actual production and consumption (or between desire and consummation), which is to say, the moment of circulation or exchange. By Campbell's lights, modern (i.e., eighteenth-century) hedonism collapsed the Weberian dichotomy and sequence between deferred and immediate gratification—savings and spending—into a single, iterable experience of unquenchable desire. Like Veblen and, in a measure, like the anthropologist Mary Douglas, Campbell treated the symbolic values of consumer objects as their use-value, but unlike them he defined those communicative uses as fundamentally private, covert, and inconspicuous. Where Veblen and Douglas had treated acquisitions as forms of direct address, Campbell regarded them as—at best—soliloquies. The modern consumer or hedonist, he argued, "is continually withdrawing from reality as fast as he encounters it, ever-casting his daydreams forward in time, attaching them to objects of desire, and then subsequently 'unhooking' them from these objects as and when they are attained and experienced."[31] This was the dialectic of demand that Campbell saw entering, "irreversibly," into eighteenth-century, English commercial culture.

But if this was how bourgeois Britons stimulated their own demand, one may still ask why. Here Campbell, who might otherwise have been expected to join Mukerji and Schama in jettisoning once and for all Weber's theoretical legacy, unexpectedly and quite ingeniously proposed (under Weberian auspices) a theory of an "other Protestant ethic." Specifically, he located an alternative and, once again, complementary, intellectual tradition within the Reformation, a tradition running parallel to Weber's inner-worldly asceticism but rejecting its emotional economies. Campbell thus traced a genealogy of feeling extending from Dutch Arminian ministers through increasingly secular Latitudinarian, Sentimentalist, and Romantic writers of the eighteenth century. Their cumulative impact was to legitimize the kind of affective self-indulgence at play in the new consumerism.[32]

As with Weber's own genealogy of asceticism, Campbell's party of feeling was perhaps the most ideational and therefore least compelling feature of his causal argument. But his case for the Other Protestant Ethic was not a purely intellectualist one. Much as Caroline Bynum has argued in relation to the fasting practices of Catholic women during the Middle Ages, so Campbell suggested the intimate, if not dialectical, relation between the control and the exploration of appetite and feeling. As he put the relation, "both the delaying of gratification and the suppression of emotion work together to create a rich and powerful, imaginative inner life within the individual, the necessary prerequisite for a 'romantic' personality," and, one need only add, for a modern consumer.[33]

With this move, it is possible to say that Colin Campbell had not so much reconstructed the Protestant Ethic as deconstructed it: demonstrating, albeit deductively, how that superfluity of feeling which asceticism was in earnest to displace could become, by the very power of its own repressive mechanisms, the sentimentality it eventually came to embrace.[34] But to acknowledge, as Campbell did, this "social irony" is to recognize its familiarity as well. Americanists, for example, will make out in this dialectic of discipline and desire many of the features of Daniel Bell's theory of the cultural contradictions of capitalism, of Ann Douglas's theory of the feminization of American culture, and of Jackson Lears's theory of the shift from salvation to self-realization—all of whom critically link the cultural fascination with intense and expressive feeling to the onset of an anti-puritanical consumerism.[35] Unlike Bell, Douglas, and Lears, however, Campbell rejected any formulation of these dichotomies as contradictions, much less as a sequence of declension. There was for him no lamentable fall out of Calvinist discipline into the symbolically impoverished world of consumerism. To the contrary, he saw an almost Hegelian leap in the imaginative possibilities—a new emotional "recipe-knowledge" so to speak—available to the West as a result of the centuries-long "rationalization of plea-sure." For Campbell, the historical irony of Sixties counter-culture was not its moral sellout to contemporary consumerism but its moral indebtedness to a centuries-old tradition of hedonistic longing—not *Thirtysomething*, in other words, but two-hundred-thirtysomething.[36]

3

Already, then, we can see how an historical reperiodization of consumer cul-ture has brought with it a reconceptualization of its causes and a revaluation of its moral and political consequences. Still, to backdate origins in this fash-ion is to leave out just those men and women whose class, race, or religion placed them outside the orbit of Reformation rhetoric and Wedgwood adver-tisements. What, for example, of the so-called counter-cultures of America's native and ethnic working classes? If consumer culture as middle-class phe-nomenon dates from eighteenth-century England, if not fifteenth-century Flor-ence and sixteenth-century Holland, what of consumer culture as a mass phe-nomenon? At what point did the "masses" effectively enter and thereby constitute a recognizable consumer culture? In what way did they do so, and with what consequences?

For a population as heterogeneous and polyglot as America's working men and women, no definitive answer and certainly no definitive point of entry seems possible. But glancing over the extraordinarily rich and detailed studies of working-class leisure that have appeared over the past decade, we are en-couraged to look to the 1930s and 1940s as a pivotal historical moment when commodity culture achieved sufficient breadth and density as to define the ground—if not the atmosphere—within which a shaken society was to be re-stored and reconstructed. Before then it seems more useful to speak of the presence of an urban, commercial culture spanning the century between 1830 and 1930. By that I mean a fully commercialized yet distinctively local or re-gional network of cultural production and exchange, with goods, services, and performances organized in a fashion closer to cottage industry than to mass production.[37] By that I also mean a commercial culture with (at least) two quite distinct dimensions and market-orientations. The first dimension would encompass the high-profile, English-speaking forms of amusement—from theater to vaudeville—that flourished in nineteenth-century America. Until the syndication and eventually the broadcasting of these forms after the turn of the century, these leisure commodities remained typically local, syncretic, male, rowdy, and often contested forms of cultural expression. As Lawrence Levine has recently shown, impresarios served up scenes from Shakespeare along with entre-acte gymnastics and farcical finales, all open of course to the vigorous commentary of the audiences.[38] Fragmented and satirical as these performances seem to us, they are nonetheless distinguishable from our own time's deeply ironic ventures into cultural pastiche. Where a critic like Fredric Jameson regards the plagiarized or cannibalized texts of post-modernism as grim reminders of cultural dispossession, Levine treats the motley offerings of nineteenth-century theater as evidence of the insistently proprietary claims that urban folk made upon their stage.[39]

The second dimension of working-class consumerism moved in many respects away from this mixed (if still Anglicized) public sphere and toward a realm of ethnic separateness and insularity. As Roy Rosenzweig has shown in relation to leisure goods and services and as Lizabeth Cohen has argued more recently in relation to consumer durables, immigrant workers and their families entered hesitantly, if at all, into the developing infrastructure of bourgeois consumption—the sanitized "dream worlds" of the movie palace, department and chain stores.[40] And when new goods and services were purchased, they were often incorporated into imported, inherited, or in other ways alternative systems of meaning. As a consequence, even imitative or emulative consumption stood at an oblique angle to mainstream consumer culture by virtue of the different reference points of respectability and fashionability to which these Veblen—or Wedgwood—effects were aligned.[41]

Again, the arguments and examples of these studies are too complex to summarize here, but, taken together, they tell a story of a staggered working-class entry into the world of "rationalized pleasure," an entry delayed and deferred by the constraints of income, race, ethnicity, gender, and their corresponding cultural meanings. But as it is also a story retold with every new migration to American shores, the narrative of this encounter with organized leisure bears a striking resemblance to Herbert Gutman's now classic account of immigrant workers' repeated encounters with (and resistance to) the world of rationalized labor.[42] And like Gutman, these historians reject the received image of the blue-collar consumer's passive immersion in a ready-made mass leisure experience; working-class consumption was less a form of cultural suicide than a model of cultural awakening, a case of native and immigrant workers actively appropriating and transforming leisure goods to suit their pleasures and purposes. So active in fact were these working men and women in shaping the conventions and content of urban commercial culture that when television—a

truly mass medium—finally did appear, its promoters looked to earlier vernacular forms (from variety to vaudeville) and to conspicuously blue-collar
themes to draw a mass audience. Describing television as the "central discursive medium in American culture" in the post-World War Two period, George
Lipsitz has suggested that the industry's dream of entering every household
drove the producers of the early family sitcoms to piece together a working-
class "realism" in their shows, a realism whose awkward and refractory social
content the industry itself could not fully control.[43] Determined to confer legitimacy and credibility upon the prospect of post-war consumerism, television
was compelled to dramatize the very social tensions and contradictions for
which consumption was being offered up as a resolution. The result of these
grudging concessions to the "real," Lipsitz concludes, was the opening up of
these half-hour parables of consumption to the possibility of "oppositional or
negotiated readings" by their blue-collar audiences.[44] Even at the high point of
consumerism's Happy Days, then, the culture industry inadvertently infused
its products with the same malaise the products were supposed to resolve. If
the industry did indeed operate as an ideological hypodermic needle, as some
mass culture critics insisted, its solution appeared to carry unanticipated and
unwanted antibodies.

As this capsule summary of George Lipsitz's argument indicates, I hope,
mass consumer culture has offered scholars an especially fertile field in which
to nurture a new and hybrid form of cultural history born of the marriage between American social and labor history on the one hand and literary and cultural theory on the other. Lipsitz himself has acknowledged the intellectual influence of Mikhail Bakhtin's notion of the "dialogic imagination," Stuart
Hall's notion of the "ideological effect," and Fredric Jameson's notion of reification as models for his own analysis of post-war television, and these same
theoretical influences are everywhere visible as more and more historians come
to look upon the boundaries between high and low cultural commodities as
themselves politically contested conventions.[45] Now there have been many interesting developments springing out of this cross-fertilization between history
and cultural studies, but one of the most intriguing (and arguable) has been the
political redemption of consumer choices once airily dismissed as forms of
working-class escapism and wish-fulfillment. This recuperation of blue-collar
consumer fantasy proceeds, though, on quite different premises from those
upon which Colin Campbell has reinterpreted and reclaimed the bourgeois
daydream. Whereas Campbell treats the middle-class longing after goods as a
characteristically private, almost Rousseauan reverie that has been wishfully
freed of all obstacles and discomforts, the interpreters of working-class consumption have stressed the social dimension of that consumption and the
class, gender, and generational tensions with which its fantasies are invariably
laced.

Perhaps one of the most impressive and innovative instances of such an interpretation is Michael Denning's recent study of the nineteenth-century dime

novel, *Mechanic Accents*. There he argues against those literalist and co-optative readings of the novels that take the genre's formulaic happy endings as parables of working-class assimilation and incorporation into an Algeresque or bourgeois scheme of upward mobility. Instead he argues for a subversive, allegorical reading of the dime novel that takes its seemingly harmonious endings as covert enactments of class expropriation and redistribution.[46] For him, then, class functions less as a set of boundaries structuring the production of cultural commodities than as a set of accents inflecting their consumption. And since those inflections run through and through commodities in a manner that keeps them forever open to political reclamation, commodities thereby become both objects and sites of symbolic struggle; overtly, as in the tradition of working-class dandyism stretching from the Bowery B'hoys and Gals of 1840s New York to the Zoot Suiters of 1940s Los Angeles;[47] but covertly also, in, say, the licensed pleasures that Janice Radway and Anne Snitow see women claiming from Harlequin Romances, or in the more explicit generational and gender negotiation of sexual pleasure and freedom that Kathy Peiss and John Kasson have found at play in turn-of-the-century New York City.[48]

To the extent, then, that pleasures publicly enjoyed, if not flaunted, cease to be a bourgeois, male prerogative and become instead an object of competitive claims, the pleasure principle itself has been politicized. From this perspective a world of increasingly libidinized goods would seem to present as many opportunities for aggressive as for repressive desublimation. The ghost of the Frankfurt School thus returns unbidden to the interpretation of consumer culture, but this time in the guise of Herbert Marcuse's deepest utopian longings.[49] The resemblance is striking. However different may be the starting points of these historical ventures into the alternative dream-worlds of middle-class and working-class consumers, they all seem to converge upon the same endpoint: the counter-culture of the 1960s and its ambiguous aftermath. Is that surprising?

Is it really surprising that a generation of scholars raised on mass culture and, many of them, involved in the movements of the Sixties should chafe against a tradition of inquiry into mass consumer culture hobbled between the stark alternatives of celebration and revulsion? And is it any more surprising that the fantasy life long associated with commodity-consumption should at this moment receive another look and, with it, another historical and political valuation? I think not. Recent cultural studies on the Left reveal a discernible restlessness with the old categories of consumer culture, a restlessness that springs from something more, I suspect, then, the hunger for novelty. Rather, it seems to grow out of the conviction that mass culture, mass consumer culture—whatever its origins—can no longer be discussed as if its presence were still an open question, a matter of choice. One way to dispose of that sense of moral or political option, then, is to push the boundaries of consumer culture backward in time, making the moment of its birth coeval with that of capitalism itself; another strategy is to push its boundaries outward in space so as to encompass all contemporary experience.⁵⁰ Consumer culture thus dissolves historically and analytically into the success of its own inexorable proliferation. Under this dispensation, it might be claimed, as an indignant George Bowling did some sixty years ago and as an impatient Michael Denning did only recently, that "We have come to the end of 'mass culture'; the debates and positions which have named 'mass culture' as an other have been superseded. There is no mass culture out there; it is the very element in which we all breathe."⁵¹ After this long hunt for the leviathan of consumer culture, it is ironic indeed to discover that we are all, like Jonah and Orwell, inside the whale—inside the whale and thus unable in any intelligible sense to take its outward, historical measure.⁵² Perhaps that is why one notes a preference within recent cultural studies for metaphors of mapping, as if the task remaining for the historian lay in the careful, detailed charting of this ever-expanding universe of goods—complete, of course, with its fissures and fault lines of class, race, gender, and ethnicity. Obviously, there is a world of political difference between these critics' careful mapping of the 'politics of value' and the glib, zip-code demographics served up in current micro-marketing manuals. But there is at the same time an uncanny structural and figurative resemblance in the world-picture each tendency presents of a totalizing yet reassuringly segmented culture of consumption.⁵³ Redrawn in this way, the globe appears as a crazy quilt of desire which, depending on one's agenda, may be mobilized to produce a hegemonic bloc or a marketing coup: a Rainbow Coalition or a pot of gold.

Yet another indication of the way in which the world of goods has expanded to fill the available analytical space—to become, as it were, the air we breathe—has been the gradual marginalization of labor and production in many recent cultural studies. What began after 1968 as a legitimate effort to correct the labor metaphysic of classical and Marxist political economy and to restore the symbolic dimension of consumption has given way to a blanket dismissal of such categories as subsistence, use-value, and labor.⁵⁴ The word "production" survives largely as a figure of speech, a metaphor used to evoke the active powers at play in the symbolic uses to which a produced and purchased good may be put. Consumers invariably reread, reconfigure, and recontextualize their purchases, and, in doing so, reproduce, recreate, and refashion themselves. Not surprisingly, terms like "fashion," "fiction," and "fabrication" have all acquired such strong connotations with manual or craft labor—a kind of mental inscription upon the material world—as to displace many of their earlier associations with semblance, illusion, and deceit. In this manner consumption becomes "cultural work," productive of "cultural capital," and grist for cultural "resistance."⁵⁵ From the ashes of the dead author (or producer) arises the heroic figure of the restless reader (or consumer), for it is in the sphere of consumption, as the anthropologist Daniel Miller has recently argued, that "the strategies of recontextualization are at their most advanced." Consumption, Miller has announced, "is now at the vanguard of history."⁵⁶

All that remains for this customized Marxism to perform, then, are the last rites on itself.

Daniel Miller's approach, it should be said, is far more Hegelian than Marxist. For him consumption belongs not to the mysteries of commodity fetishism, as Georg Lukacs and his followers insisted, but to "the full project of objectification in which the subject becomes at home with itself in its otherness."[57] This is a lot to swallow, to be sure, but whatever one's doubts at the prospect of a Hegelian epiphany in the Housewares department of K-Mart, it is worth noting how closely Miller's notion of consumption as the act of a homemaking (as distinct from the homeless) mind conforms to the arguments of several other sociologists and anthropologists.[58] Even more significantly, for our purposes, Miller's approach to consumption recalls some of the most influential writing in the historiography of consumer culture, namely, Warren Susman's now classic essays on America in the 1930s and 1940s.[59] In those pieces Susman illustrated in brilliantly eclectic fashion the essentially conservative and domesticating role played by consumer culture during those years of crisis. Deliberately ignoring the political and labor orientations that had dominated the interpretation of the depression and the homefront, he instead held up every artifact of consumer culture he could lay his eye upon—from Disney films to the 1939 World's Fair—in order to show how variously yet how deeply they all had suggested, not to say constructed, a sense of belonging.[60] In a way, Susman's argument was about mass cultural commodities as belongings, as cultural properties so powerfully and personally evocative as to have invented the "American Way of Life" in their image.

Susman's interpretation of consumer culture, it is safe to say, has permanently altered our understanding of the larger history of the Thirties and Forties in America. By showing this mass experience of homecoming to have been achieved in the sphere of consumption, Susman established a turning point not just in history but for historiography as well. It seems appropriate, then, to close this review and assessment with some further reflections about this "moment" and its mementos. With luck we might be able to get outside the whale and take stock—in Melvillian, if not Orwellian fashion—of the riches and limits of Warren Susman's legacy.

4

Susman was interested in what he called "middle-class America," but many of the recent studies of working-class consumption likewise look to the mass culture of the 1930s and 1940s as a pivotal orientation for the working class as well. By the end of the Depression, historians seem to agree, the insularity and autonomy of urban, commercial culture had greatly diminished. Local groups, according to Lizabeth Cohen, had also "lost their ability to control the dissemination of mass culture." Chain stores at last displaced local shops;

talkies "hushed" noisy movie audiences; and radio now broadcasted network fare in place of the chaotic local programming that had typified the 1920s.[61] Mass culture had finally arrived, and though the culture industry was prepared to segment its markets, it nonetheless serviced them out of the same national infrastructure.

Having acknowledged this institutional transformation, however, these same historians have been quick to point out that American working men and women were not thereby incorporated into a system of middle-class values or, for that matter, into a pattern of labor quietism. Quite the reverse in fact. As Roy Rosenzweig suggests toward the end of his study of Worcester's working class and as Ronald Edsforth argues throughout his study of Flint's blue-collar households, the pervasive promise of American consumerism inspired the labor militance of the 1930s and after.[62] Whether it was the car described in Robert and Helen Lynd's study of Middletown or the fully applianced, nuclear household pictured in Thomas Bell's labor novel of 1941, *Out of this Furnace*, the working-class dream of consumption became, according to this argument, the business-class's nightmare of production as pickets and sitdowns spread throughout the industrial heartland. "Even in the depths of the Great Depression," Edsforth writes, "most working people did not give up the dream of a new way of life." "Instead," he adds, quoting Susman, " 'Many who might have chosen the socialist way went instead with the hope of the culture of abundance.' "[63]

What then is at stake here if consumerism only fueled the militance it was designed to quench? As I see it, it is not so much the issue of mass absorption into a monolithic consumer culture, for working men and women doubtless continued to dream, to 'think,' and to use their goods with different accents. What is at work in this struggle, however, and what deserves further scrutiny is an implicit cultural reformulation of working-class consumer expectations as political or protopolitical entitlements. And that is news, for if to this image of depression-born, consumption-fueled labor militance, we add the thesis— first intimated by Susman but most recently developed by Robert Westbrook— that war mobilization likewise operated on conspicuously private, consumptionist themes, then we may very well be describing a process whereby private desires reconstructed notions of public rights and obligations—reconstructed them, that is, in the image of the objects upon which those desires happened to be cathected.[64] As one wartime G.I. was reported to have said, "I am in this damn mess as much to help keep the custom of drinking Cokes as I am to preserve the million other benefits our country blesses its citizens with."[65]

There is something admittedly disarming about a confession of this sort, but disarming in a more troubling sense than might appear at first. For it is one thing to pursue the politics of consumption, to struggle over and through the meaning of goods; it is quite another thing to pursue the consumption of politics, to form one's political thought and practice upon the model of commodity-exchange. Depressions and wars are by definition moments of crisis, moments when a society is potentially open to radical definitions of its political, social, and economic foundations. And what the history of twentieth-century consumption is telling us is that a far-reaching ideological redefinition of polity and society did begin to take hold during the 1930s and 1940s: the promotion of the social contract of cold-war liberalism, which is to say a state sponsored guarantee of private consumption. But, more importantly, we are also being told that this redefinition of rights and obligations articulated itself in the seemingly innocuous language of soft drinks, arms, and household appliances, and that it therefore occurred, as Colin Campbell might put it, privately, imaginatively, and inconspicuously—in short, without discussion.

This is not to suggest, however, that Franklin D. Roosevelt was the first political leader to exploit the symbolic dimensions of goods. Embargoes, boycotts, and fasts all have long and honorable traditions. We need only think of the courtly endorsement of black cloth during the Middle Ages, or the traditional references to England and roast beef, or, for that matter to the Swadeshi movement in India.[66] Closer to home, one thinks as well of Timothy Breen's innovative study of the nonimportation movement before the American Revolution. One thinks of it in particular because in many ways Breen's argument about nation-building in the 1760s and 1770s seems to rehearse Warren Susman's own interpretation of national rebuilding in the 1930s and 1940s.[67] It seems fitting, then, to close this discussion of the historiography of consumer culture by comparing Susman's and Breen's accounts, for by their juxtaposition, we are enabled to throw the central questions of periodization, causality, and judgment into greatest relief.

The two accounts resemble one another because they both attempt to interpret different, critical moments in the history of American nationalism as structurally and symbolically conditioned by consumer goods. But in other respects, Breen's argument is also an imaginative extension of Neil McKendrick's eighteenth-century consumer revolution to American shores. By 1775, Breen points out, the American colonists were absorbing some nine thousand different commodities, most of them British, with the result that the colonists were becoming gradually and visibly Anglicized. "The colonists belonged to an empire of goods," he concludes, and "loyalty depended on commerce . . . and not upon coercion."[68] Drawing here on symbolic anthropology rather than Antonio Gramsci, Breen suggests that commodities were the most widely shared "semiotic order" in the colonies and that the patriots did not hesitate to conscript this system of signs when constitutional crises erupted in the 1760s and 1770s. Without knowing it, then, British parliamentarians, effectively "transformed private consumer acts into public political statements."[69] Nonimportation agreements further politicized these goods, such that the "artefacts of a consumer culture took on a new symbolic meaning." In other words, the "confrontation with British imports was extending the political horizons of ordinary people," extending them in a way that would make it "possible for the colonists to imagine a new nation."[70] For the colonists British imports suddenly became, as Mary Douglas might put it, "good for thinking."[71]

Perhaps. But one may still wonder about the thought or systems of thought these goods were drafted to express. For it is just as plausible to argue that the rich, differentiated, and conspicuously British language of goods was just that which nonimportation deliberately and extravagantly negated. And the rhetoric of denial—the rhetoric, that is, of nonimportation—operated in considerable measure at a distance from the "language" of those commodities, for it sprang directly out of the evangelical and republican traditions that the patriots deployed exactly in order to defamiliarize those commodities around which British loyalties were suspected to have formed.[72] Indeed, one could argue that nonimportation Anglicized imported goods as never before, stripping them of any domestic cultural accretion that might have adhered to them. Moreover, when one recalls that Americans promptly rushed back to their British goods after the Revolution, one realizes that the coordinates of loyalty and citizenship lay not in the sphere of goods—and certainly not in anything that could be called a consumer culture—but rather in other spheres: religion, ideology, and so on. As I've already suggested, then, there is an important historical and theoretical distinction to be drawn between the politicization of commodities and the commodification of politics, between a concept of citizenship framed around religion and republicanism and a concept of citizenship framed around an "American Way of Life," especially when that way of life is defined as a shifting ensemble of cultural and material commodities. Only the latter concept, one would think, indicates the presence of a "consumer culture."

Still, when one is told that the colonists' experiences with British goods expanded their political horizons and enabled them to imagine a new polity, it is easy to telescope the historical differences between the 1770s and the 1930s and imagine for oneself a trajectory of consumer culture lofting upwards from Timothy Breen's eighteenth-century colonies through Daniel Boorstin's nineteenth-century "consumption communities" to Warren Susman's twentieth-century "Adlerian Age of Adjustment."[73] More to the point, one is tempted to think of the cognitive effects of consumption in much the same way that Thomas Haskell has elsewhere urged us to think of the cognitive effects of commerce, which is to say as a practice that has historically expanded our perceived horizons of human efficacy and moral responsibility.[74] Now, were goods that good to think?

I don't think so. True, commodities have and will continue to be used to construct and communicate the meaning of social relationships and, if Colin Campbell is right, to order and indulge our affective response to them.[75] But there is nothing in the literature that I have reviewed here to support the view that commodity consumption has enhanced our appreciation of the remote consequences of our acts or has clarified our responsibilities for them. A political unconscious, an allegorized desire, a subversive reverie of plenitude—all may provide the commodified ground for alternative or oppositional readings of consumer culture. But the distance between that ground and the groundwork required to translate such longings into organized practice seems vast indeed. Like Simon Schama's whales, it seems infinitely more likely that in the migration back from matter and commodity to myth and morality, one would find oneself stranded on the "submarine slope . . . of cultural contradiction."

Even less charitably, one could argue that it is precisely because the meanings of commodities are so fluid and recontextualizable that questions of responsibility and accountability remain submerged within them. Whatever the personal meanings that the American G.I. may have attached to the custom of Coke-drinking that he fought for in World War Two, they probably did not include the conviction that he was also fighting for the Coca-Cola company. How, then, might it be said that his political horizons were thereby extended and his concept of citizenship thereby clarified by Coke?

And how, finally, might it be said that the soldier's sense of citizenship was thereby intensified? How does brand loyalty mediate civic loyalty? The question arises because, as Ronald Edsforth and others have pointed out, there has been a strong chronological parallel between consumer booms and anti-communist campaigns in this country since the 1920s.[76] To many historians, such a connection merely confirms their suspicion that employers are always ready to promote moral panics in order to defeat the demands of a militant and organized labor force. But the connection between appeals to the Good Life and appeals against the Evil Empire also lends weight to Michael Walzer's thesis that a market-modeled liberalism must of necessity draw on other, non-liberal traditions and fears in order to inspire a loyalty that reaches beyond the marketplace.[77] As the G.I.'s invocation of Coke suggests, commodities can be used—ironically, nostalgically, militantly—to put the state in its place; but they are next to useless when deciding what to put in place of the state.

If such reflections seem a trifle abstract, one need only consider the recent turn of events in Eastern Europe to see how directly they bear upon the future its citizens are forging for themselves. There, people are being encouraged to treat the language of commodities as the vernacular of civil society and the Esperanto of European unity, so it seems reasonable to wonder what language will be employed to reconceive the polity. No fullfledged consumer culture exists in Eastern Europe, of course, but the images of such a culture are familiar to virtually everyone and have been for some time. They *are* the horizon, and it is easy to imagine that if Hobbes were to rewrite his thoughts on the social contract in such a context, he too would surely recast his infamous cover-portrait of Leviathan as a construct of commodities rather than of people. So much for the "recipe-knowledge" of consumer culture: whatever else such knowledge may yield up, it seems as likely to obscure as to clarify our social and political consciousness.

And, I might add, historical consciousness as well. The last decade of research has boldly challenged and immeasurably enriched our picture of consumer culture, but the very richness of that work—the thickness of its description and the detail of its maps—has at times submerged important questions of periodization, of power, and, if you will, of principle—questions that historians can ill afford to ignore. Only last year, for example, the National Archives in Washington, D.C. received $600,000 from the Philip Morris Companies in return for an agreement permitting the firm to stage a two-year, $30 million television and print advertising campaign that invites the public to "join Philip Morris and the National Archives" in celebrating the bicentennial of the Bill of Rights.[78] Were it not for the awkward spectre of death that presently haunts Marlboro country, one could scarcely imagine an objection being raised to such a quid pro quo. Yet it is precisely the controversy over tobacco, with all of its rich, polysemous, and contestatory symbolism, that distracts us from the implications of an arrangement that would further elide the difference between a bill of rights and a bill of goods. The privatization of civil rights and obligations is a problem that reaches far beyond Eastern Europe, and neither the history nor the historiography of consumer culture has done much to help us think about it.[79] It is for that reason that I have laid such stress on questions of historicity, causality, and politics in my remarks. We need more studies of consumer culture, to be sure, but we need breathing-space as well—a chance to reconnoitre a subject that otherwise threatens to engulf us all: to leave us, that is, inside the whale.

Notes

1. Simon Schama, *The Embarrassment of Riches: An Interpretation of Dutch Culture in the Golden Age* (New York: Knopf, 1987), 130–144.

2. *Ibid.*, 143, 318.

3. *Ibid.*, 140.

4. George Orwell, "Boys' Weeklies" [1939], *A Collection of Essays* (New York: Harcourt Brace Jovanovich, 1981), 308–9.

5. George Orwell, *Coming Up for Air* [1939] (London: Secker & Warburg, 1948), 220.

6. "Kids are Dying for Designer Duds," *New Haven Register*, November 12, 1989; "A Growing Urban Fear: Thieves Who Kill for 'Cool' Clothing," *New York Times*, February 6, 1990.

7. Stuart Ewen, *Al Consuming Images: The Politics of Style in Contemporary Culture* (New York: Basic Books, 1988), 271, 52.

8. Georg Lukacs, *History and Class Consciousness* (Cambridge: MIT Press, 1971); Max Horkheimer and Theodor W. Adorno, "The Culture Industry: Enlightenment as Mass Deception," *Dialectic of Enlightenment*, John Cumming, tr. (New York: Seabury Press, 1972), 120–167; Herbert Marcuse, *One-Dimensional Man.* (Boston: Beacon Press, 1964).

9. Richard Wightman Fox and T. J. Jackson Lears, eds., *The Culture of Consumption: Critical Essays in American History, 1880–1980* (New York: Pantheon, 1983).

10. Jean-Christophe Agnew, "The Consuming Vision of Henry James," *Culture of Consumption*, 68–9; Neil McKendrick had ventured a similar complaint a year before in his introduction to *The Birth of a Consumer Society: The Commercialization of Eighteenth-Century England* (Bloomington: Indiana University Press, 1982), 5–6.

11. Fox and Lears (eds.), *Culture of Consumption*, x.

12. The work of William Leiss, a student of Herbert Marcuse (and Herbert Gutman), influenced my essay, for example.

13. It should be said that a few works have kept pretty much to the chronological scheme of *The Culture of Consumption*, among them: Daniel Horowitz, *The Morality of Spending: Attitudes toward the Consumer Society in America, 1875–1940* (Baltimore: Johns Hopkins University Press, 1985); Simon J. Bronner, ed., *Consuming Visions: Accumulation and Display of Goods in America, 1880–1920* (New York: Norton, 1989); Susan Strasser, *Satisfaction Guaranteed: The Making of the American Mass Market* (New York: Pantheon, 1989).

14. Some of these works will be discussed in this essay; for a more complete bibliography, see Horowitz, *Morality of Spending*, 187–201, as well as Charles F. McGovern, "The Emergence of Consumer History," paper presented at the Organization of American Historians Meeting in Reno, Nevada, March, 1988.

15. Chandra Mukerji, *From Graven Images: Patterns of Modern Materialism* (New York: Columbia University Press, 1983), 22–29.

16. *Ibid.*, 2; this portrait, it should be said, has been colored as well by the hand of R. H. Tawney; though Weber's work focused on the Puritan sense of "calling," his name has come to be associated with anything remotely to do with Protestant asceticism.

17. Joan Thirsk, *Economic Policy and Projects: The Development of a Consumer Society in Early Modern England* (Oxford: Oxford University Press, 1978); D. E. C. Eversley, "The Home Market and Home Demand, 1750–1780," in *Land, Labour, and Population in the Industrial Revolution*, E. L. Jones and E. E. Mingay, eds. (London: Edward Arnold, 1967), 206–259; Jan de Vries, "Peasant Demand Patterns and Economic Development: Friesland 1550–1750," in *European Peasants and their Markets: Essays in Agrarian History*, William N. Parker and Eric L. Jones, eds. (Princeton: Princeton University Press, 1976), 205–238; Neil McKendrick, "Home Demand and Economic Growth: A New View of the Role of Women and Children in the Industrial Revolution," *Historical Perspectives: Studies in English Thought and Society*, Neil McKendrick, ed. (London: Europa, 1974), 152–210.

18. Schama, *Embarrassment of Riches*, 338.

19. *Ibid.*, 298.

20. Fernand Braudel, *The Wheels of Commerce*, Sian Reynolds, tr. (New York: Harper and Row, 1982), 177.

21. *Ibid.*; both McKendrick and Schama resurrect Mandevillian ideas in their work; see *Birth of a Consumer Society*, 15–19, 51–3; *Embarrassment of Riches*, 297, 321, 467–8; Mandeville, it should be noted, was a Dutch emigré to England.

22. McKendrick, *Birth of Consumer Society*, 72.

23. *Ibid.*, 103, 140–1.

24. *Ibid.*, 71.

25. For such metaphors, see *ibid.*, 13, 42, 43, 71 and *passim*.

26. Colin Campbell, *The Romantic Ethic and the Spirit of Modern Consumerism* (Oxford: Blackwell, 1987), 42–3.

27. *Ibid.*, 36–57.

28. Tibor Skitovsky, *The Joyless Economy: An Inquiry into Human Satisfaction and Dissatisfaction* (New York: Oxford University Press, 1976); Albert O. Hirschman, *Shifting Involvements: Private Interests and Public Action* (Princeton: Princeton University Press, 1982).

29. Campbell, *Romantic Ethic*, 77–95, esp. 86.

30. Compare Agnew, "Consuming Vision," 73.

31. Campbell, *Romantic Ethic*, 86–7.

32. *Ibid.*, chaps 6, 7.

33. *Ibid.*, 222; see also Caroline Walker Bynum, *Holy Feast and Holy Fast: The Religious Significance of Food to Medieval Women* (Berkeley: University of California Press, 1987).

34. For a different kind of deconstruction of capitalist asceticism, see Walter Benn Michaels, *The Gold Standard and the Logic of Naturalism* (Berkeley: University of California Press, 1987), chap. 5; see also my discussion of Adam Smith in *Worlds Apart: The Mar-*

ket and the Theater in Anglo-American Thought, 1550–1750 (Cambridge: Cambridge University Press, 1986), 177–188.

35. See Daniel Bell, *The Cultural Contradictions of Capitalism* (New York: Harper and Row, 1978); Ann Douglas, *The Feminization of American Culture* (New York: Avon, 1977); T. J. Jackson Lears, "From Salvation to Self-Realization: Advertising and the Therapeutic Roots of the Consumer Culture, 1880–1930," in Fox and Lears, eds., *Culture of Consumption*, 3–38.

36. Campbell, *Romantic Ethic*, 217–18; Bell makes much the same point but with a different judgment, *Cultural Contradictions*, 73–74.

37. I am indebted to Lawrence Senelick for this sense of cottage industry.

38. Lawrence Levine, "William Shakespeare in America," *Highbrow Lowbrow: The Emergence of Cultural Hierarchy in America* (Cambridge, Mass.: Harvard University Press, 1988), 13–81.

39. Fredric Jameson, "Postmodernism and Consumer Society," in *The Anti-Aesthetic: Essays in Postmodernist Culture*, Hal Foster, ed. (Port Townsend, Wash.: Bay Press, 1983), 113–14; still, it could be said that Levine glosses the extent to which nineteenth-century plebeian playfulness toward Shakespeare might have been mocking a campaign for cultural sacralization that was already underway.

40. Roy Rosenzweig, *"Eight Hours for What We Will": Workers and Leisure in an Industrial City, 1870–1920* (Cambridge: Cambridge University Press, 1983); Lizabeth Cohen, "Encountering Mass Culture at the Grass Roots: The Experience of Chicago Workers in the 1920s," *American Quarterly*, 41 (March 1989), 6–33; "Embellishing a Life of Labor: An Interpretation of the Material Culture of American Working-Class Homes, 1885–1915," *Journal of American Culture*, 3 (Winter 1980), 752–775; on the limited reach of such new retailing institutions as catalogues and chain stores, see Strasser, *Satisfaction Guaranteed*, 219, 249. Though a good deal has been written on cultural production in black communities, correspondingly little has been done on consumer goods and their consumption.

41. For a theoretical treatment of the ways in which goods may be "singularized" or "decommoditized" by their incorporation into other personal, familial, or cultural frameworks of meaning, see Igor Kopytoff, "The Cultural Biography of Things: Commoditization as Process," in *The Social Life of Things: Commodities in Cultural Perspectives*, Arjun Appadurai, ed. (Cambridge: Cambridge University Press, 1986), 64–91.

42. Herbert G. Gutman, "Work, Culture and Society in Industrializing America, 1815–1919," *Work, Culture and Society in Industrializing America* (New York: Knopf, 1976), 3–78.

43. See George Lipsitz, "The Meaning of Memory: Family, Class, and Ethnicity in Early Network Television" and "Why Remember Mama? The Changing Face of Women's Narrative," *Time Passages: Collective Memory and Popular Culture* (Minneapolis: University of Minnesota Press, 1990), 39–96.

44. *Ibid.*, 69.

45. M. M. Bakhtin, *The Dialogic Imagination*, Michael Holquist, ed., Caryl Emerson and Michael Holquist, trs. (Austin: University of Texas Press, 1981); Stuart Hall, "Culture, the Media, and the 'Ideological Effect,' " in *Mass Communication and Society*, James Curran, Michael Gurevitch, Janet Woollacott, eds. (Beverly Hills: Sage, 1979); "Notes on 'deconstructing the popular,' " in *People's History and Socialist Theory*, Ralph Samuel, ed. (London: Routledge and Kegan Paul, 1981); Fredric Jameson, "Reification and Utopia in Mass Culture," *Social Text*, 1 (1979), 130–148; for a more recent formulation of this challenge to cultural boundaries—in relation to the status of middlebrow culture—see Andrew Ross, "Introduction" and "Reading the Rosenberg Letters," *No Respect: Intellectuals and Popular Culture* (New York: Routledge, 1989), 1–41.

46. Michael Denning, *Mechanic Accents: Dime Novels and Working-Class Culture in America* (London, Verso, 1987), 200–213.

47. Christine Stansell, *City of Women: Sex and Class in New York, 1789–1860* (New York: Knopf, 1986), 90–100; Mauricio Mazon, *Zoot Suit Riots* (Austin: University of Texas Press, 1984).

48. Janice A. Radway, *Reading the Romance: Women, Patriarchy, and Popular Literature* (Chapel Hill: University of North Carolina Press, 1984); Ann Barr Snitow, "Mass Market Romance: Pornography for Women is Different," *Radical History Review*, 20 (Spring/Summer 1979), 141–161; Kathy Peiss, *Cheap Amusements: Working Women and Leisure in Turn-of-the-Century New York* (Philadelphia: Temple University Press, 1986); John Kasson, *Amusing the Million: Coney Island at the Turn of the Century* (New York: Hill and Wang, 1978).

49. Herbert Marcuse, *Eros and Civilization: A Philosophical Inquiry into Freud* (Boston: Beacon, 1955); Richard King, *The Party of Eros: Radical Social Thought and the Realm of Freedom* (Chapel Hill: University of North Carolina Press, 1972), Chap. 4; see also Fredric Jameson, "Pleasure: A Political Issue," in *Formations of Pleasure* (London: Routledge and Kegan Paul, 1983), 1–14; *Powers of Desire: The Politics of Sexuality*, Ann Snitow, Christine Stansell, Sharon Thompson, eds. (New York: Monthly Review Press, 1983).

50. See note 45; both Fredric Jameson and Stuart Hall have challenged the distinction drawn between 'authentic' popular culture and mass consumer culture; James Clifford has made similar arguments to anthropologists in *The Predicament of Culture: Twentieth-Century Ethnography, Literature, and Art* (Cambridge, Mass.: Harvard University Press, 1988); see also the inaugural issue of the journal *Public Culture* (1988).

51. Michael Denning, "The End of Mass Culture," *International Labor and Working-Class History*, 37 (Spring 1990), 17.

52. George Orwell, "Inside the Whale," [1940] in *Collected Essays* (London: Secker and Warburg, 1961), 118–159.

53. See Arjun Appadurai, "Commodities and the Politics of Value," in *Social Life of Things*, 3–63; John Clarke, Stuart Hall, Tony Jefferson, Brian Roberts, "Subcultures, Culture, and Class," in *Resistance Through Rituals: Youth Cultures in Post-War Britain*, Stuart Hall and Tony Jefferson, eds. (London: Hutchinson, 1976), 9–74; for the family resemblance between the two tendencies, compare Pierre Bourdieu, *Distinction: A Sociological Critique of the Judgment of Taste*, Richard Nice, tr. (Cambridge, Mass.: Harvard University Press, 1984) and Michael J. Weiss, *The Clustering of America* (New York: Harper and Row, 1988); for a different criticism of the mapping metaphor, see Janice Radway's comment on Michael Denning's article, "The End of Mass Culture," entitled "Maps and the Construction of Boundaries," *International Labor and Working-Class Newsletter*, 37 (Spring 1990), 19–26.

54. The change can be best appreciated in Jean Baudrillard, *Selected Writings*, Mark Poster, ed. (Stanford: Stanford University Press, 1988); but compare as well Marshall Sahlins's *Stone Age Economics* (Chicago: Aldine, 1972) with his *Culture and Practical Reason* (Chicago: University of Chicago Press, 1976).

55. On the concept of "cultural capital," see Bourdieu, *Distinction, passim*; Daniel Miller, *Material Culture and Mass Consumption* (Oxford: Blackwell, 1987), 176, 106.

56. Miller, *Material Culture*, 213.

57. *Ibid.*, 192.

58. See, for example, Appadurai, ed., *Social Life of Things*; Mihaly Csikszentmihalyi and Eugene Rochberg-Halton, *The Meaning of Things: Domestic Symbols and the Self* (Cambridge: Cambridge University Press, 1981); Grant McCracken *Culture and Consumption: New Approaches to the Symbolic Character of Consumer Goods and Activities* (Bloomington: Indiana University Press, 1988).

59. Warren I. Susman, "The Culture of the Thirties," "Culture and Commitment," "The People's Fair: Cultural Contradictons of a Consumer Society," in *Culture as History: The Transformation of American Society in the Twentieth Century* (New York: Pantheon, 1984), 151–229.

60. Orwell's "Inside the Whale" runs like a thread through Susman's "The Culture of the Thirties"; see also Roland Marchand, *Advertising the American Dream: Making Way for Modernity, 1920–1940* (Berkeley: University of California Press, 1985); Richard Pells, *Radical Visions and American Dreams: Cultural and Social Thought in the Depression Years* (New York: Harper and Row, 1973).

61. Cohen, "Encountering Mass Culture," 26.

62. Rosenzweig, *Eight Hours*, 226–8; Ronald Edsforth, *Class Conflict and Cultural Consensus: The Making of a Mass Consumer Society in Flint, Michigan* (New Brunswick: Rutgers University Press, 1987).

63. Edsforth, *Class Conflict*, 224.

64. "Commodities are symbols of belonging," Michael Walzer has written; "standing and identity are distributed through the market, sold for cash on the line (but available also to speculators who establish credit). On the other hand, in a democratic society, the most basic definitions and self-definitions can't be put up for purchase in this way. For citizenship entails what we might call 'belongingness'—not merely the sense, but the practical reality, of being at home in (this part of) the social world. This is a condition that can be renounced but never traded; it is not alienable in the marketplace"; *Spheres of Justice: A Defense of Pluralism and Equality* (New York: Basic Books, 1983), 106. See also Robert Westbrook, " 'I Want a Girl Just Like the Girl that Married Harry James': American Women and the Problem of Political Obligation in World War Two," paper presented at the American Historical Association Meeting in Cincinnati, Ohio, December 1988; "Fighting for the Family: Private Interests and Public Obligation in World War Two," paper presented at the Organization of American Historians meeting in St. Louis, Missouri, April 1989.

65. Quoted in E. J. Kahn, *The Big Drink: The Story of Coca Cola* (New York: Random House, 1960), 13, and in Richard Ruisel, "Coca-Cola au pays des buveurs de vin," *L'Histoire*, 94 (November 1986), 24. Such a response can easily be interpreted as a backhanded commentary on the more abstract and pretentious themes of morale-building, but to focus entirely on the symbolism that the response deflates is to ignore that symbolism—namely, Coca-Cola—which is thereby inflated; compare Paul Fussell, *Wartime: Understanding and Behavior in the Second World War* (New York: Oxford, 1989), 90.

66. See Jane Schneider, "Peacocks and Penguins: The Political Economy of European Cloth and Colors," *American Ethnologist*, 5 (August 1978), 413–447; C. A. Bayley, "The Origins of Swadeshi (Home Industry): Cloth and Indian Society, 1700–1930," in Appadurai, ed., *Social Life of Things*, 285–321.

67. T. H. Breen, "An Empire of Goods: The Anglicization of Colonial America, 1690–1776," *Journal of British Studies*, 25 (October 1986), 467–499; " 'Baubles of Britain': The American and Consumer Revolutions of the Eighteenth Century," *Past and Present*, 119 (May 1988), 73–104.

68. Breen, "Baubles of Britain," 86.

69. *Ibid.*, 88.

70. *Ibid.*, 93, 104.

71. Mary Douglas and Baron Isherwood, *The World of Goods: Towards an Anthropology of Consumption* (New York: Norton, 1979), 62; the phrase is of course a deliberate echo of earlier structuralist formulations by Claude Levi-Strauss and Stanley Tambiah.

72. The term is Breen's, "Baubles of Britain," 91.

73. Daniel Boorstin, *The Democratic Experience* (New York: Random House, 1973), 89–114, but esp. 145–8; Susman, "Culture and Commitment," *Cultural History*, 202.

74. Thomas Haskell, "Capitalism and the Origins of Humanitarian Sensibility, Parts I and II," *American Historical Review*, 90 (April 1985), 339–361; (June 1985), 547–566.

75. See, for example, Fred Hirsch's discussion of "positional goods" in *Social Limits to Growth* (Cambridge, Mass.: Harvard University Press, 1978); Bourdieu, *Distinction*; Roger S. Mason, *Conspicuous Consumption: A Study of Exceptional Consumer Behavior* (Farnborough, Hampshire: Gower, 1981).

76. Edsforth, *Class Conflict*, 216 and *passim*; see also George Lipsitz, *Class and Culture in Cold War America: "A Rainbow at Midnight"* (South Hadley: J. F. Bergin, 1982), chap. 8; Paul Boyer, *By the Bomb's Early Light: American Thought and Culture at the Dawn of the Atomic Age* (New York: Pantheon, 1985); Elaine Tyler May, *Homeward Bound: American Families in the Cold War Era* (New York: Basic Books, 1988).

77. See Michael Walzer, *Obligations: Essays on Disobedience, War, and Citizenship* (Cambridge, Mass.: Harvard University Press, 1970).

78. *New Haven Register*, December 4, 1989.

79. On privatization and questions of civic accountability, see Sheldon S. Wolin, *The Presence of the Past: Essays on the State and the Constitution* (Baltimore: Johns Hopkins University Press, 1989), 25–27, and more generally, Alan Wolfe, *Whose Keeper? Social Science and Moral Obligation* (Berkeley: University of California Press, 1989).

Bibliographic Essay

Lawrence B. Glickman

Classics

Starting in the late nineteenth century and for most of this century, books analyzing American consumer society were enormously popular; many became best sellers. Edward Bellamy viewed the possibilities of consumption positively; his utopian novel, *Looking Backward, 2000–1887* (1887; New York: Penguin, 1982), was one of the best sellers of the nineteenth century. The pioneering work which established the terms of modern consumer criticism is, however, Thorstein Veblen's *The Theory of the Leisure Class: An Economic Study in the Evolution of Institutions* (New York: MacMillan, 1899). Another influential novel, written in the mode of muckraking journalism, set off Progressive Era regulation of food and drugs: Upton Sinclair's *The Jungle* (New York: Doubleday, 1906). Economist Simon Nelson Patten described a shift from scarcity to abundance as a good thing for America's morals as well as its pocketbook. His most important work is *The New Basis of Civilization* (New York: Macmillan, 1907). For a pioneering attempt to merge psychological research with marketing, see Walter Dill Scott's *The Theory and Practice of Advertising* (Boston: Maynard, 1914). A popular guide to advertisers is Christine Frederick's *Selling Mrs. Consumer* (New York: The Business Bourse, 1929). For one of the most influential books of the first half of the twentieth century, revealing the extent to which consumer culture was changing the landscape of small-town America, see Helen and Robert Lynd's *Middletown: A Study in American Culture* (New York: Harcourt Brace, 1929).

Maud Nathan, a pioneering leader of the consumer movement, described the early years of the National Consumers League in *The Story of an Epoch-*

Many of the books cited here contain useful bibliographies. For an excellent cyberbibliography of the years 1877–1920 see David Blanke, "H-SHGAPE Bibliographical Essays: Consumer Culture During The Gilded Age and Progressive Era." (www.h-net.msu.edu/~shgape/bibs/consumer.html) Another useful more sociologically-focused bibliography is Don Slater, "Bibliography: Consumer Culture and Leisure." (www.gold.ac.uk/slater/consumer/biblioa.htm).

Making Movement (Garden City, N.Y.: Doubleday, Page and Company, 1926). Several authors drew attention to consumer issues and the investigative studies by the founders of two of most significant consumer organizations of the twentieth century, Consumers Research and Consumers Union, gained a wide readership. The writings include: Stuart Chase, *The Tragedy of Waste* (New York: Macmillan, 1929); Stuart Chase and F. J. Schlink, *Your Money's Worth: A Study in the Waste of the Consumer's Dollar* (New York: Macmillan, 1927); Arthur Kallet and F. J. Schlink, *100,000,000 Guinea Pigs: Dangers in Everyday Foods, Drugs, and Cosmetics* (New York: Vanguard, 1937); J. B. Matthews, *Guinea Pigs No More* (New York: Covici Friede, 1936); and, M. C. Phillips, *Skin Deep—The Truth About Beauty Aids, Safe and Harmful* (New York: Vanguard Press, 1934).

A number of participants described the very active consumer movement of the Depression decade and World War II years. In *The Decline and Rise of the Consumer: A Philosophy of Consumer Cooperation* (New York: Appleton, 1936), Horace Kallen argued that consumption was deeply woven into the fabric of American history. The title is significant because it suggests that the consumer society did not emerge suddenly in the twentieth century. Helen Sorenson described the proliferation of consumer organizations during the New Deal in *The Consumer Movement: What It Is and What It Means* (New York: Harper and Brothers, 1941). See also Persia Campbell's *Consumer Representation in the New Deal* (New York: Columbia University Press, 1940); Joseph Gaer's *Consumers All: The Problem of Consumer Protection* (New York: Harcourt, Brace and Company, 1940); and, Caroline Ware's *The Consumer Goes to War* (New York: Funk and Wagnalls, 1942).

Three best sellers from the 1950s and 1960s, each of which challenged the benefits of unlimited private consumption and pointed to the malfeasance of those who produced consumer goods are: Vance Packard's *The Status Seekers* (New York: McKay, 1959); John Kenneth Galbraith's *The Affluent Society* (Boston: Houghton Mifflin, 1958); and, Ralph Nader's *Unsafe at Any Speed: The Designed-In Dangers of the American Automobile* (New York: Grossman, 1965). For a collection of criticisms of popular culture in postwar America, refer to *Mass Culture: The Popular Arts in America*, edited by Bernard Rosenberg and David Manning White (Glencoe, Ill.: Free Press, 1957).

Two probing examinations by thoughtful social scientists include: David Riesman's *Abundance for What?* (1964; New Brunswick: Transaction, 1993); and, Tibor Scitovsky's *The Joyless Economy: The Psychology of Human Satisfaction and Consumer Dissatisfaction* (1972; New York: Oxford University Press, 1992).

One of the few older works to examine consumer society from an explicitly historical perspective is David Potter's *People of Plenty: Economic Abundance and the American Character* (Chicago: University of Chicago Press, 1954).

Collected Essays

The immensely influential volume, *The Culture of Consumption: Critical Essays in American History 1880–1980*, edited by Richard Wightman Fox and T. J. Jackson Lears (New York: Pantheon, 1983), shows how much light can be shed on American history through the study of consumption. Other important historical essays are contained in *Consuming Visions: Accumulation and Display of Goods in America 1880–1920*, edited by Simon J. Bronner (New York: Norton, 1989); *For Fun and Profit: The Transformation of Leisure into Consumption*, edited by Richard Butsch (Philadelphia: Temple University Press, 1990); *The Sex of Things: Gender and Consumption in Historical Perspective*, edited by Victoria de Grazia with Ellen Furlough (Berkeley: University of California Press, 1996); *His and Hers: Gender, Consumption, and Technology*, edited by Roger Horowitz and Arwen Mohun (Charlottesville: University Press of Virginia, 1998); *Consumption and American Culture*, edited by David Nye et al. (Amsterdam: VU University Press, 1991); *Consumers Against Capitalism?: Consumer Cooperation in Europe and North America, 1840–1990*, edited by Ellen Furlough and Carl Strikewerda (Lanham, Md.: Rowman and Littlefield, 1997); *Consuming Desires: Consumption, Culture, and the Pursuit of Happiness*, edited by Roger Rosenblatt (Washington D.C.: Island Press, 1999); and, *Getting and Spending: European and American Consumption in the Twentieth Century*, edited by Susan Strasser, Charles McGovern, and Mathias Judt (New York: Cambridge University Press, 1998). Four journals have produced special issues on consumption: "The History of Consumer Culture," *Maryland Historian* 19 (Spring–Summer 1988); "Consumption," *Culture and History* 7 (1990); "The Culture of Consuming," *Critical Review* 8 (Fall 1994); and "Class and Consumption," *International Labor and Working-Class History* 55 (Spring 1999).

Other important collections include: *In The Marketplace: Consumerism in America*, edited by Frank Browning et al. (San Francisco: Canfield Press, 1972); *The Consumer Society*, edited by Neva R. Goodwin, Frank Ackerman, and David Kiron (Washington D.C.: Island Press, 1997); *The Consumer*, compiled by Gerald Leinwand (New York: Washington Square Press, 1970); *The Consuming Public*, edited by Grant S. McClellan (New York: H. W. Wilson Company, 1968); *Acknowledging Consumption: A Review of New Studies*, edited by Daniel Miller (London: Routledge, 1995); and *The Consumer Revolution: Redressing The Balance*, edited by Robin John (London: Hodder and Stoughton, 1994).

A useful collection of recent evaluations of consumer society is *Ethics of Consumption: The Good Life, Justice, and Global Stewardship*, edited by David A. Crocker and Toby Linden (Lanham, Md.: Rowman and Littlefield, 1998).

Frameworks and Definitions

Most of the important theories about consumer society and languages of consumer analysis have been produced by nonhistorians. However, a number of historians have offered significant ways of thinking about consumption. Daniel Boorstin coined the phrase "consumption communities" in *The Americans: The Democratic Experience* (New York: Random House, 1973). Boorstin also placed the quest for novelty at the heart of the consumer experience. "We expect new heroes every season, a literary masterpiece every month, a dramatic spectacular every week, a rare sensation every night," he wrote in *The Image: A Guide to Pseudo-Events in America* (1960; New York: Atheneum: 1987). Daniel Horowitz drew a distinction between traditional and modern moralism in the discourse on consumer society and called for a "reciprocal model . . . that emphasizes the power of the economic system and elites to set the framework of consumer culture but does not forget the ability of people, within limits, to shape the meaning of their consumption patterns" in *The Morality of Spending: Attitudes toward the Consumer Society in America, 1875–1940* (1985; Chicago: Ivan Dee, 1992). The perception by social theorists that consumer society would create new possibilities for human happiness can be read about in, Daniel M. Fox's *The Discovery of Abundance: Simon N. Patten and the Transformation of Social Theory* (Ithaca: Cornell University Press, 1967).

In *Culture as History: The Transformation of American Society in the Twentieth Century* (New York: Pantheon, 1984), Warren I. Susman placed mass culture in a political framework. T. J. Jackson Lears pointed to the significance of a therapeutic worldview in the development of consumer society in *No Place of Grace: Antimodernism and the Transformation of American Culture, 1880–1920* (New York: Pantheon, 1981). Christopher Lasch placed consumption at the center of modernity in many forcefully argued, controversial, brilliant—if wrongheaded—works including, *The Culture of Narcissism: American Life in an Age of Diminishing Expectations* (New York: Norton, 1979); *The True and Only Heaven: Progress and Its Critics* (New York: Norton, 1991) and "The Culture of Consumption," in *Encyclopedia of American Social History*, edited by Mary Kupiec Cayton, Elliot J. Gorn, and Peter W. Williams (New York: Scribner, 1993), 2:1381–90. In a difficult but rewarding work, James Livingston placed consumption in a broad philosophical and economic context: *Pragmatism and the Political Economy of Cultural Revolution, 1850–1940* (Chapel Hill: University of North Carolina, 1994). David E. Nye persuasively placed consumption at the center of history and technology in *Consuming Power: A Social History of American Energies* (Cambridge: MIT Press, 1998). In *Why the American Century?* (Chicago: University of Chicago Press, 1998), Olivier Zunz examined the ways in which the American "sense of achievement became increasingly tied to success within complex organizations and through full participation in consumption." For a fine overview that emphasizes the business and marketing dimension, see Susan Strasser, "Consumption," in *Encyclopedia of the United States in the Twentieth Century*, edited by Stanley I. Kutler et al. (New York: Scribners, 1996), 3: 1017–1035. A robust defense of consumer society can be found in James B. Twitchell, *Lead Us into Temptation: The Triumph of American Materialism* (New York: Columbia University Press, 1999).

Important review essays include: Gary Cross's "Consumer History and the Dilemmas of Working-Class History," *Labour History Review* 62 (Winter 1997): 261–74; Michael Denning's "The End of Mass Culture," *International Labor and Working-Class History* 37 (Spring 1990): 4–18; Mary Louise Roberts' "Gender, Consumption, and Commodity Culture," *American History Review* 103 (June 1998): 817–44; Peter N. Stearns' "Stages of Consumerism: Recent Work on the Issues of Periodization," *Journal of Modern History* 69 (March 1997): 102–17; and, Lisa Tiersten's "Redefining Consumer Culture: Recent Literature on Consumption and the Bourgeoisie in Western Europe," *Radical History Review* 57 (Fall 1993): 117–59.

Anthropologists, literary critics, and sociologists have been particularly important in providing frameworks for the study of consumption. Among the most influential writings are: *The Social Life of Things: Commodities in Cultural Perspective*, edited by Arjun Appadurai (New York: Cambridge University Press, 1986); Jean Baudrillard's *The Consumer Society: Myths and Structures* (Thousand Oaks, Calif.: Sage, 1997); Zygmunt Bauman's *Work, Consumerism and the New poor* (Buckingham, U.K.: Open University Press, 1998); Daniel Bell's *The Cultural Contradictions of Capitalism* (New York: Basic Books, 1976); Pierre Bourdieu's *Distinction: A Social Critique of the Judgement of Taste* (London: Routledge, 1984); Colin Campbell's *The Romantic Ethic and the Spirit of Modern Consumerism*, (Oxford, U.K.: Basil Blackwell, 1989); Mary Douglass' and Baron Ishwerwood's *The World of Goods: Toward an Anthropology of Consumption* (New York: Norton, 1979); Fredric Jameson's "Postmodernism and Consumer Society," in *Postmodernism and its Discontents*, edited by Ann E. Kaplan (London: Verso, 1988); George Katona's *The Mass Consumption Society* (New York: McGraw Hill, 1964); William Leiss' *The Limits to Satisfaction: An Essay on the Problem of Needs and Commodities* (Kingston: McGill-Queens University Press, 1988); Grant McCracken's *Culture and Consumption: New Approaches to the Symbolic Character of Consumer Goods and Activities* (Bloomington: Indiana University Press, 1998); Daniel Miller's *Material Culture and Mass Consumption* (Oxford, U.K.: Basil Blackwell, 1987); Daniel Miller's *A Theory of Shopping* (Ithaca: Cornell University Press, 1998); Chandra Mukerji's *From Graven Images: Patterns of Modern Materialism* (New York: Columbia University Press, 1983); and, Don Slater's *Consumer Culture and Modernity* (Cambridge, U.K.: Polity Press, 1997).

For a comprehensive survey of the social and economic meaning of consumption, see Ben Fine's and Ellen Leopold's *The World of Consumption* (London: Routledge, 1993).

Other perspectives can be seen in: Robert Bocock's *Consumption* (London: Routledge, 1983); Rachel Bowlby's *Just Looking: Consumer Culture in Dreiser, Gissing, and Zola* (New York: Methuen, 1985) and *Shopping with Freud* (London: Routledge, 1993); Mike Featherstone's *Consumer Culture and Postmodernism* (London: Sage, 1991); Celia Lury's *Consumer Culture* (New Brunswick: Rutgers University Press, 1996); Ann Smart Martin's "Makers, Buyers and Users: Consumerism as a Material Culture Framework," *Winterthur Portfolio* (Summer/Autumn 1993) 28: 141–57; Roger Swagler's "Evolution and Application of the Term Consumerism: Themes and Variations," *Journal of Consumer Policy* 18 (1995) 2: 347–60.

Comparative Consumption

Although this volume focuses on American history, the scholar of consumption must be familiar with the excellent studies of consumption in other parts of the world. France is examined in: Leora Auslander's *Taste and Power: Furnishing Modern France* (Berkeley: University of California Press, 1996); Ellen Furlough's *Consumer Cooperation in Modern France: The Politics of Consumption* (Ithaca: Cornell University Press, 1991); Michael B. Miller's *The Bon Marche: Bourgeois Culture and the Department Store, 1869–1920* (Princeton: Princeton University Press, 1981); and Rosalind Williams' *Dreamworlds: Mass Consumption in Late Nineteenth Century France* (Berkeley: University of California Press, 1982).

Britain is studied in: John Brewer's *The Pleasures of the Imagination: English Culture in the Eighteenth Century* (New York: Farrar, Strauss, Giroux, 1997); John Benson's *The Rise of Consumer Society in Britain, 1880–1980* (London: Longman, 1994); and Lori Anne Loeb's *Consuming Angels: Advertising and Victorian Women* (New York: Oxford University Press, 1994).

Attention is drawn to other countries in: Greg Whitewell's, *Making the Market: The Rise of Consumer Society* (Melbourne, Australia: McPhee Gribble Publishers, 1989); Timothy Burke's *Lifebuoy Men, Lux Women: Commodification, Consumption, and Cleanliness in Modern Zimbabwe* (Durham: Duke University Press, 1996); and *Re-made in Japan: Everyday Life and Consumer Culture*, edited by Joseph Tobin (New Haven: Yale University Press, 1992).

Colonial and Early National America

Scholars of consumption now point to the years from the Age of Exploration through the first Industrial Revolution as perhaps the crucial period in the development of British and American consumer society. It was a time when increased demand, improved transportation, and the beginnings of mass production made consumption a mass phenonemon. Perhaps the most influential study is Neil McKendrick's John Brewer's, and J. H. Plumb's *The Birth of a Consumer Society: The Commercialization of Eighteenth-Century England* (Bloomington: Indiana University Press, 1982). The leading scholar on the American side of the transatlantic consumer revolution is T. H. Breen. Of note are his " 'Baubles of Britain': The American and Consumer Revolution of the Eighteenth Century," *Past and Present*, 119 (1988): 73–104 and "An Empire of Goods: The Anglicization of Colonial America," *Journal of British Studies* 25 (October 1986): 467–99. In addition, see Jean-Christophe Agnew's *Worlds Apart: The Market and the Theater in Anglo-American Thought, 1550–1750* (New York: Cambridge University Press, 1986); Bernard Bailyn's *The New England Merchants in the Seventeenth Century* (Cambridge: Harvard University Press, 1955); Richard Bushman's *The Refinement of America: Persons, Houses, Cities* (New York: Knopf, 1992); *Of Consuming Interests: The Style of Life in the Eighteenth Century*, edited by Cary Carson, Ronald Hoffman, and Peter J. Albert (Charlottesville: University Press of Virginia, 1994); James G. Gibb's *The Archaeology of Wealth: Consumer Behavior in Early America* (New York: Plenum Press, 1996); James Horn's *Adapting to a New World: English Society in the Seventeenth-Century Chesapeake* (Chapel Hill: University of North Carolina Press, 1994); Carole Shammas' *The Preindustrial Consumer in England and America* (New York: Oxford University Press, 1990); Joan Thirsk's *Economic Policy and Projects: The Development of a Consumer Society in Early Modern England* (Oxford: Clarendon Press, 1978); and Lorna Weatherhill's *Consumer Behavior and Material Culture in Britain, 1660–1760* (London: Routledge, 1988).

Surprisingly, we know more about consumption during the colonial and revolutionary periods than we do about consumer ideologies and practices during the "market revolution"—the commercial and social transformation of the first fifty years of the nineteenth century. Daniel Walker Howe is surely correct to suggest, in *Making the American Self: Jonathan Edwards to Abraham Lincoln* (Cambridge: Harvard University Press, 1997), that this period offered ample opportunities for "self definition to consumers." Few studies have examined the market revolution through the lens of consumption. Nonetheless, several important works on the market revolution do address the issue of consumption: Charles G. Sellers' *The Market Revolution: Jacksonian America, 1815–1846* (New York: Oxford University Press, 1991); *The Market Revolution in America: Social, Political and Religious Expressions, 1800–1880*, edited by Melvin Stokes and Stephen Conway (Charlottesville: University Press of Virginia, 1996); and Richard F. Teichgraeber III's *Sublime Thoughts/Penny Wisdom: Situating Emerson and Thoreau in the American Market* (Baltimore: Johns Hopkins University Press, 1995).

Religion

Examining the intersection of consumer society with religious practice and discourse are: Susan Curtis, *A Consuming Faith: The Social Gospel and Modern American Culture* (Baltimore: John Hopkins University Press, 1991); Frank Lambert, *Peddlar in Divinity: George Whitfield and the Transatlantic Revivals* (Princeton: Princeton University Press, 1994); R. Laurence Moore, *Selling God: American Religion in the Marketplace* (New York: Oxford University Press, 1994); Mark A. Peterson, *The Price of Redemption: The Spiritual Economy of Puritan New England* (Stanford: Stanford University Press, 1997); and Leigh Eric Schmidt, *Consumer Rites: The Buying and Selling of American Holidays* (Princeton: Princeton University Press, 1995).

Of interest are two religious based jeremiads against consumer society: John F. Kavanaugh's *Following Christ in a Consumer Society: The Spirituality of Cultural Resistance* (Maryknoll, N.Y.: Orbis Books, 1981) and John Taylor Vernon's *Enough is Enough: A Biblical Call for Moderation in a Consumer-Oriented Society* (Minneapolis: Augsburg Publishing House, 1977).

Advertising

Of all the aspects of American history, advertising has been accorded the most attention. Although the early scholarship divided along the binary of conspiratorial social control and the celebratory hagiography of the early admen, recent scholarship has presented a more nuanced perspective. The most influential studies include: William L. Bird, Jr.'s *"Better Living:" Advertising, Media, and the New Vocabulary of Business Leadership, 1935–1955* (Evanston, Ill.: Northwestern University Press, 1999); Martin P. Davidson's *Consumerist Manifesto: Advertising in Postmodern Times* (London: Routledge, 1992); Stuart Ewen's *Captains of Consciousness: Advertising and the Social Roots of the Consumer Culture* (New York: McGraw-Hill, 1976) and *PR: A Social History of Spin* (New York: Basic Books, 1996); Stephen R. Fox's *The Mirror Makers: A History of American Advertising and Its Creators* (1984; Urbana: University of Illinois Press, 1997); Marilyn Kern Foxworth's *Aunt Jemima, Uncle Ben, and Rastus: Blacks in Advertising, Yesterday, Today, and Tomorrow* (Westport, Conn.: Greenwood, 1994); Sut Jhally's *The Code of Advertising: Fetishism and the Political Economy of Meaning in the Consumer Society* (New York: St. Martins Press, 1997); Pamela Walker Laird's *Advertising Progress: American Business and the Rise of Consumer Marketing* (Baltimore: John Hopkins University Press, 1998); Jackson Lears' *Fables of Abundance: A Cultural History of Advertising in America* (New York: Basic Books, 1994); Roland Marchand's *Advertising the American Dream: Making Way for Modernity, 1920–1940* (Berkeley: University of California Press, 1985); James D. Norris' *Advertising and the Transformation of American Society,*

1865–1920 (Westport, Conn.: Greenwood Press, 1990); Daniel Pope's *The Making of Modern Advertising* (New York: Basic Books, 1983); Richard Ohmann's *Selling Culture: Magazines, Markets, and Class at the Turn of the Century* (New York: Verso, 1996); Michael Schudson's *Advertising: The Uneasy Persuasion; Its Dubious Impact on American Society* (New York: Basic Books, 1984); James B. Twitchell's *Adcult USA: The Triumph of Advertising in American Culture* (New York: Columbia University Press, 1996); and Vincent Vinikas' *Soft Soap, Hard Sell: American Hygiene in the Age of Advertisement* (Ames: Iowa State University Press, 1992).

Class and Consumption

Workers' standard of living—the empirical question: how much do workers' consume—has been a consistent theme in discussions about class, social mobility, and the American economy. See, for example, Margo Anderson, "Standards, Statuses, and Statistics: Carroll Wright and the American Standard of Living," *Advancing the Consumer Interest: A Journal of Consumer Law, Policy, and Research* 9 (Spring 1997): 4–12; John McClymer, "Late Nineteenth-Century American Working-Class Living Standards," *Journal of Interdisciplinary History* 17 (1986): 379–98; John Modell, "Patterns of Consumption, Acculturation and Family Income Strategies in Late Nineteenth Century America," in *Family and Population in Late Nineteenth-Century America*, edited by Tamara Haraven and Maris Vinovskis (Princeton: Princeton University Press, 1978): 206–40; Ted Ownby, *American Dreams in Mississippi: Consumers, Poverty, and Culture, 1830–1998* (Chapel Hill: University of North Carolina Press, 1999); Peter Shergold, *Working-Class Life: The "American Standard" in Comparative Perspective* (Pittsburgh: University of Pittsburgh Press, 1982); and Jeffrey Williamson, "Consumer Behavior in the Nineteenth Century: Carroll Wright's Massachusetts Workers in 1875," *Explorations in Entrepreneurial History* 2nd ser., 4 (1967): 98–135.

The "new labor history" placed the study of culture at the center of the analysis of working-class life. Many works about labor history have examined workers' consumption of goods, their leisure patterns, and their relationship to the middle-class culture of consumption. See, for example, Susan Porter Benson, *Counter Cultures: Saleswomen, Managers, and Customers in American Department Stores, 1890–1940* (Urbana: University of Illinois Press, 1986); Lizabeth Cohen, *Making a New Deal: Industrial Workers in Chicago, 1919–1939* (New York: Cambridge University Press, 1990); Francis Couvares, *The Remaking of Pittsburgh: Class and Culture in an Industrializing City, 1877–1919* (Pittsburgh: University of Pittsburgh Press, 1984); Paul du Gay, *Consumption and Identity at Work* (London: Sage, 1996); Ronald Edsforth, *Class Conflict and Cultural Consensus: The Making of a Mass Consumer Society in Flint, Michigan* (New Brunswick: Rutgers University Press, 1987);

Dana Frank, *Purchasing Power: Consumer Organizing, Gender, and the Seattle Labor Movement, 1919–1929* (New York: Cambridge University Press, 1994); Lawrence B. Glickman, *A Living Wage: American Workers and the Making of Consumer Society* (Ithaca: Cornell University Press, 1997) and "Workers of the World, Consume: Ira Steward and the Origins of Labor Consumerism," *International Labor and Working Class History* 52 (Fall 1997): 72–86; Susan Levine, "Workers' Wives: Gender, Class, and Consumerism in the 1920s United States," *Gender and History* 3 (Spring 1991); 45–64; Kathy Peiss, *Cheap Amusements: Working Women and Leisure in Turn-of-the-Century New York* (Philadelphia: Temple University Press, 1986); Roy Rosenzweig, *Eight Hours for What We Will: Work and Leisure in an Industrializing City, 1870–1920* (New York: Cambridge University Press, 1983); and George Sanchez, *Becoming Mexican American: Ethnicity, Culture and Identity in Chicano Los Angeles, 1900–1945* (New York: Oxford University Press, 1993).

An excellent study of the working-class demand for a shorter workday is David R. Roediger's and Phillip S. Foner's *Our Own Time: A History of American Labor and the Working Day* (New York: Verso, 1989). Other important accounts of the changing nature of leisure are: Gary Cross's *Time and Money: The Making of Consumer Culture* (New York and London: Routledge, 1993); and Benjamin Kline Hunnicut's *Kellogg's Six-Hour Day* (Philadelphia: Temple University Press, 1996) and *Work Without End: Abandoning Shorter Hours for the Right to Work* (Philadelphia: Temple University Press, 1988).

Gender, Commerce, and Culture

For a fascinating account of the pressures the new consumer ethic placed on Victorian women, see Elaine Abelson's *When Ladies Go A-Thieving: Middle-Class Shoppers in the Victorian Department Store* (New York: Oxford University Press, 1989). Other important studies which highlight gender are: Elizabeth Ewen, *Immigrant Women in the Land of Dollars: Life and Culture on the Lower East Side, 1890–1925* (New York: Monthly Review Press, 1985); Margaret Finnegan, *Selling Suffrage: Consumer Culture and Votes for Women* (New York: Columbia University Press, 1999); Miriam Formanek-Brunnell, *Made to Play House: Dolls and the Commercialization of American Girlhood, 1830–1930* (New Haven: Yale University Press, 1993); Ellen Gruber Garvey, *The Adman in the Parlor: Magazines and the Gendering of Consumer Culture, 1880s to 1910s* (New York: Oxford University Press, 1996); William Leach, "Transformations in a Culture of Consumption: Women and Department Stores, 1890–1925," *Journal of American History* 71 (September 1984): 319–42; Kathy Lee Peiss, *Hope in a Jar: The Making of America's Beauty Culture* (New York: Metropolitan Books, 1998); Jennifer Scanlon, *Inarticulate Longings: The Ladies' Home Journal, Gender, and the Promise of Consumer Culture* (New York: Routledge, 1995); and Batya Weinbaum and

Amy Bridges, "The Other Side of the Paycheck: Monopoly Capitalism and the Structure of Consumption," in *Capitalist Patriarchy and the Case for Socialist Feminism*, edited by Zillah R. Eisenstein (New York: Monthly Review Press, 1979): 190–205. For an excellent analysis of men and consumption in the postwar world, see Barbara Ehrenreich, *The Hearts of Men: American Dreams and the Flight from Commitment* (Garden City: Anchor Press, 1983).

Important treatments of the culture and the business of consumption include: Regina Lee Blaszczyk's *Imagining Consumers: Design and Innovation from Wedgwood to Corning* (Baltimore: Johns Hopkins University Press, 1999); Lendol Calder's *Financing the American Dream: A Cultural History of Consumer Credit* (Princeton: Princeton University Press, 1999); Gary Cross' *Kids' Stuff: Toys and the Changing World of American Childhood* (Cambridge: Harvard University Press, 1997); Mark Dyreson's "The Emergence of Consumer Culture and the Transformation of Physical Culture: American Sport in the 1920s," *Journal of Sport History* 16 (1989): 261–81; Ian Gordon's *Comic Strips and Consumer Culture, 1890–1945* (Washington D.C.: Smithsonian Institution Press, 1998); Neil Harris' "The Drama of Consumer Desire" in *Yankee Enterprise*, edited by Robert Post and Otto Mayr (Washington D.C.: Smithsonian Institution Press, 1981); John Kasson's *Amusing the Million: Coney Island at the Turn of the Century* (New York: Hill and Wang, 1978); William Leach's *Land of Desire: Merchants, Power, and the Rise of a New American Culture* (New York: Pantheon, 1993); Roland L. Marchand's *Creating the Corporate Soul: The Rise of Public Relations and Corporate Imagery in American Big Business* (Berkeley: University of California Press, 1998); Thomas J. Schlereth's *Victorian America: Transformations of Everyday Life, 1876–1915* (New York: HarperPerennial, 1991); and Susan Strasser's *Satisfaction Guaranteed: The Making of the American Mass Market* (New York: Pantheon, 1989).

Critiques and Celebrations

Tyler Cowen explores the contribution consumer society and commercialism make, not just to national wealth, but to aesthetic life in, *In Praise of Commercial Culture* (Cambridge: Harvard University Press, 1998). Critical perspectives can be found in: Thomas Frank's *The Conquest of Cool: Business Culture, Counterculture, and the Rise of Hip Consumerism* (Chicago: University of Chicago Press, 1997); Eugene Linden's *Affluence and Discontent: The Anatomy of Consumer Societies* (New York: Viking, 1979); Juliet Schor's "What's Wrong With Consumer Capitalism? The Joyless Economy After Twenty Years," *Critical Review* 10 (Fall 1996) 4: 495–508; Barry Schwartz's *The Costs of Living: How Market Freedom Erodes the Best Things in Life* (New York: Norton, 1994); and Alvin Wolf's *American Consumers: Is Their Anger Justified?* (Englewood Cliffs, N.J.: Prentice-Hall, 1977)

Simple Living

From the beginning, the American experiment has had its share of advocates of "simple living"—often reacting in opposition to the excesses of consumer society. Two excellent historical overviews are by David Shi: *The Simple Life: Plain Living and High Thinking in American Culture* (New York: Oxford University Press, 1985); and *In Search of the Simple Life: American Voices Past and Present* (Salt Lake City: Peregrine Smith, 1986). See also Sulevi Riukule-hto, *The Concepts of Luxury and Waste in American Radicalism, 1880–1917* (Helsinki: Finnish Academy of Science and Letters, 1999) A classic work that was very influential in the 1970s is E. F. Schumacher's *Small is Beautiful: Economics as if People Mattered* (New York: Harper And Row, 1973). Three other works in this genre are: Joe Dominguez's and Vicki Robin's *Your Money or Your Life: Transforming Your Relationship with Money and Achieving Financial Independence* (New York: Penguin, 1992); Alan Thein Durning's *How Much is Enough? The Consumer Society and the Future of the Earth* (New York: Norton, 1992); and Paul Wachtel, *The Poverty of Affluence* (Philadelphia: New Society Publishers, 1989).

African Americans: Culture, Business, and Civil Rights

African American history, like American history, has been closely intertwined with consumer society. Often, the contradictions of consumer society have weighed most heavily on blacks. The ideal of the consumer in a capitalist society was not related to race. It was the same as the ideal of the citizen in a democracy: universal. The tension between ideal and reality played an important role in African American economic and political life. For example, in the Jim Crow era blacks, often mistreated by local merchants, widely used the Sears Catalog and other mail-order shopping services because the name brands and one price system gave them better products without indignity. All the while, at the core of Jim Crow was an effort to stymie black economic achievement, meaning that African Americans were often unable to afford the products that were advertised as indispensable for modern Americans. During the Civil Rights struggle, consumption was a main arena of conflict and the ability to ride a bus, buy a meal at a lunch counter, or work where one shopped became symbols of the movement for justice. At the same time, marketing experts have repeatedly reminded merchandisers that in the aggregate, African Americans had a good deal of purchasing power. The most complete treatment of these issues is presented by Robert E. Weems, Jr. in *Desegregating the Dollar: African American Consumerism in the Twentieth Century* (New York: New York University Press, 1998). Additional works are those of: Alan R. Andreasen, *The Disadvantaged Consumer* (New York: Free Press, 1975); Edward L. Ayers, *The Promise of the New South: Life After Reconstruction* (New

York: Oxford University Press, 1992); D. Parke Gibson, *$70 Billion in the Black: America's Black Consumers* (New York: Macmillan, 1978); Grace Elizabeth Hale, *Making Whiteness: The Culture of Segregation in the South* (New York: Pantheon, 1998); Darlene Clark Hine, "The Housewives League of Detroit: Black Women and Economic Nationalism," in *Visible Women: New Essays on American Activism*, edited by Nancy A. Hewitt and Suzanne Lebsock (Urbana: University of Illinois Press, 1993): 223–41; Robin D. G. Kelley, *Race Rebels: Culture, Politics, and the Black Working Class* (New York: Free Press, 1994); August Meier and Elliot Rudwick, "The Boycott Movement against Jim Crow Streetcars in the South, 1900–1906," in *Along the Color Line: Explorations in the Black Experience* (Urbana: University of Illinois Press, 1976): 267–89 and "Negro Boycotts of Jim Crow Streetcars in Tennessee," *American Quarterly* 21 (Winter 1969): 755–63; Chip Rhodes, "Writing Up the New Negro: The Constitution of Consumer Desire in the Twenties," *Journal of American Studies* (Great Britain) 28 (1994): 191–207; and Andor Skotnes, " 'Buy Where You Can Work': Boycotting for Jobs in African American Baltimore, 1933–1934," *Journal of Social History* 27 (1994), 735–62.

Politics

Although consumer society is often accused of promoting apolitical citizens, one of the most common ways that ordinary citizens have engaged the world politically is in the realm of consumption. Indeed, the term "consumerism" is generally defined as shorthand for these various political movements.

Organized consumer movements include: from the early twentieth century, the National Consumers League; from the 1930s, Consumers Union; and from the 1960s, Ralph Nader's organizations. Two invaluable resources on the twentieth-century are: *Encyclopedia of the Consumer Movement*, edited by Stephen J. Brobeck et al. (Santa Barbara: ABC-CLIO, 1997) and *The Modern Consumer Movement: References and Resources* by Stephen J. Brobeck (New York: G. K. Hall, 1991). The most important treatment of the nineteenth-century origins of the middle-class and largely female movement is Kathryn Kish Sklar's *Florence Kelley and the Nation's Work*; Vol. 1, *The Rise of Women's Political Culture* (New Haven: Yale University Press, 1995). The "prolabor orientation" of middle-class consumer activism in the Progressive Era is discussed in David Thelen's "Patterns of Consumer Consciousness in the Progressive Movement: Robert M. LaFollette, The Antitrust Persuasion, and Labor Legislation," in *The Quest for Social Justice*, edited by Ralph M. Aderman (Madison: University of Wisconsin Press, 1983): 19–47. In addition, Leon Fink analyzes the Progressive Era "panacea of plenty" in *Progressive Intellectuals and the Dilemmas of Democratic Commitment* (Cambridge: Harvard University Press, 1997). Other important studies include: Erma Angevine's *Consumer Activists: They Made a Difference* (Mount Vernon,

N.Y.: Consumers Union Federation, 1982): Erma Angevine's *Roots of the Consumer Movement: A Chronicle of Consumer History in the Twentieth Century* (Washington D.C.: National Consumers League, 1979); Lucy Black Creighton's *Pretenders to the Throne: The Consumer Movement in the United States* (Lexington, Mass.: Lexington Books, 1976); Ralph Gaedeke's *Consumerism in the 1960s: A Study in the Development of, Underlying Reasons for, and Business Reaction to Today's Consumer Protection Movement* (Seattle: University of Washington Press, 1969); Ardith Maney and Loree Bykerk's *Consumer Politics: Protecting Public Interests on Capitol Hill* (Westport, Conn.: Greenwood Press, 1994); Robert N. Mayer's *The Consumer Movement: Guardians of the Marketplace* (Boston: Twayne, 1989); Michael Petschuk's *Revolt Against Regulation: The Rise and Pause of the Consumer Movement* (Berkeley: University of California Press, 1982); Norman Isaac Silber's *Test and Protest: The Influence of Consumers Union* (New York: Holmes and Meier, 1983); *The Consumer Movement: Lectures of Colson E. Warne* edited by Richard L. D. Morse (Manhattan, Kansas: Family Economics Trust Press, 1993); and Allis Rosenberg Wolfe's "Women, Consumerism, and the National Consumers' League," *Labor History* 16 (Summer 1975): 378–92.

Grassroots activism has been another aspect of consumer politics. Protests about the injustices of daily life have frequently involved consumer-based actions. See Dana Frank, "Housewives, Socialists, and the Politics of Food: The 1917 New York Cost-of-Living Protests," *Feminist Studies* 11 (Summer 1985): 255–85; Monroe J. Friedman, "American Consumer Boycotts in Response to Rising Food Prices: Housewives' Protests at the Grassroots Level," *Journal of Consumer Policy* 18 (1995): 55–72 and "On Promoting a Sustainable Future through Consumer Activism," *Journal of Social Issues* 51 (Winter 1995): 197; Paula Hyman, "Immigrant Women and Consumer Protest: The New York City Kosher Meat Boycott of 1902," *American Jewish History* 70 (September 1980): 91–105; Felicia Kornbluh, "To Fulfill Their 'Rightly Needs': Consumerism and the National Welfare Rights Movement," *Radical History Review* 69 (1997): 76–113; Annelise Orleck, *Common Sense and a Little Fire: Women and Working-Class Politics in the United States* (Chapel Hill: University of North Carolina Press, 1995); Esther Peterson with Winifred Conking, *Restless: The Memoirs of Labor and Consumer Activist Esther Peterson* (Washington D.C.: Caring Publishing, 1995); Annie Stein, "Postwar Consumer Boycotts," *Radical History* 9 (July 1975): 156–61; and Paula V. Ulrich, " 'Look for the Label': The International Ladies' Garment Workers' Union Label Campaign, 1959–1975," *Clothing and Textiles Research Journal* 13 (1995): 49–56.

On government policy see, Meg Jacobs, " 'How About Some Meat?': The Office of Price Administration, Consumption Politics, and State Building From the Bottom Up, 1941–1946," *Journal of American History* 84 (December 1997): 910–41.

Cultural politics was explored by Martyn J. Lee in *Consumer Culture Reborn: The Cultural Politics of Consumption* (London: Routeledge, 1993).

Consumerism Since World War II

Surveys of the period following World War II that make consumption central to their analysis include those by Otis L. Graham, Jr., *A Limited Bounty: The United States Since World War II* (New York: McGraw-Hill, 1996); James T. Patterson, *Grand Expectations: The United States, 1945–1974* (New York: Oxford University Press, 1996). For a more celebratory view, refer to Robert J. Samuelson's *The Good Life and its Discontents: The American Dream in the Age of Entitlement, 1945–1995* (New York: Times Book, 1995).

Landon Y. Jones examined the baby boom and its relation to consumer culture in *Great Expectations: America and the Baby Boom Generation* (New York: Coward, McGann and Geohegan, 1980).

Presenting excellent analyses of the "kitchen debate" and other aspects of postwar consumerism are the following authors: Eric Foner, *The Story of American Freedom* (New York: Norton, 1998); Elaine Tyler May, *Homeward Bound: American Families in the Cold War Era*, (New York: Basic Books, 1988); Karal Marling, *As Seen on TV: The Visual Culture of Everyday Life in the 1950s*, (Cambridge, Mass.: Harvard University Press 1994); and Anne Norton, "Culture of Consumption: Liberal Theory and American Popular Culture," in *Republic of Signs: Liberal Theory and American Popular Culture* (Chicago: University of Chicago Press 1993): 47–86.

The trivialization and colonization of work and leisure are addressed by Stanley Aronowitz in *False Promises: The Shaping of American Working Class Consciousness* (1973; Durham: Duke University Press, 1992).

The tension created by American businesses that attempted to co-opt and make profits out of what began as an anti-consumerist counterculture is explored by Warren Belasco in *Appetite for Change: How the Counterculture Took on the Food Industry* rev. ed. (Ithaca: Cornell University Press, 1993).

Changes in how America shops are reported by: Lizabeth Cohen in "From Town Center to Shopping Center: The Reconfiguration of Community Marketplaces in Postwar America," *American Historical Review* 101 (October 1996): 1011–43; and William Severina Kovinski in *The Malling of America: An Inside Look at the Great Consumer Paradise* (New York: William Morrow, 1985).

One of the pioneering critics of postwar affluence is examined by Daniel Horowitz in *Vance Packard and American Social Criticism* (Chapel Hill: University of North Carolina Press, 1994).

For various studies of postwar consumer culture, see Andrew Hurley, "From Hash House to Family Restaurant: The Transformation of the Diner and Post-World War II Consumer Culture," *Journal of American History* 83 (March 1997): 1282–1308; E. Ann Kaplan, *Rocking Around the Clock: Music, Television, Postmodernism, and Consumer Culture* (New York: Routledge, 1988); Karal A. Marling, *As Seen on TV: The Visual Culture of Everyday Life in the 1950s* (Cambridge: Harvard University Press, 1994); Evan Watkins, *Throwaways: Work Culture and Consumer Education* (Stanford: Stanford University Press, 1993); and Cecile Whiting, *A Taste for Pop: Pop Art, Gender, and Consumer Culture* (New York: Cambridge University Press, 1997).

For the conflicting views of two economists about the benefits of mass consumption and a consumer ethic see Stanley Lebergott's *Pursuing Happiness: American Consumers in the Twentieth Century* (Princeton: Princeton University Press, 1993); and Juliet B. Schor's *The Overworked American: The Unexpected Decline of Leisure* (New York: Basic Books, 1992) and *The Overspent American: Upscaling, Downshifting and the New Consumer* (New York: Basic Books, 1998).

Guidebooks

Consumers today can choose from a host of "guidebooks," that teach them the proper elements of shopping. Among the more popular of such texts are: *The Cheap Book: The Moneysworth Consumer Encyclopedia* (New York: Moneysworth, 1973); *Shopping for a Better World* rev. ed. by The Council on Economic Priorities (New York: Ballantine, 1991); *50 Simple Things You Can Do to Save the Earth* by The Earth Works Group (Boston: G. K. Hall, 1991); *Consumers: A Self-Defense Manual* by Stuart L. Faber (Los Angeles: Charing Cross, 1974); *The Consumer Bible: 1001 Ways to Shop Smart* by Mark Green (New York: Workman Publishers, 1995); *Marketing Madness: A Survival Guide for a Consumer Society* by Michael F. Jacobson and Laurie Ann Mazur (Boulder: Westview, 1995); *Buy American: Buy This Book* by Eric Lefcowitz (Berkeley: Ten Speed Press, 1992); *Tricks of the Trade: A Consumer Survival Guide* by Janice Lieberman (New York: Doubleday, 1998); *Inconspicuous Consumption: An Obsessive Look at the Stuff We Take for Granted, from the Everyday to the Obscure* by Paul Lukas (New York: Crown, 1997); and *The Radical Consumer's Handbook* by Goody L. Solomon (New York: Ballantine, 1972).

Contributors

Jean-Christophe Agnew, Professor of American Studies and History at Yale University, is the author of *Worlds Apart: The Market and the Theater in Anglo-American Thought, 1550–1750* (1986).

Joyce Appleby, a past president of the Organization of American Historians and the American Historical Association, is Professor of History at the University of California, Los Angeles. She has written many books about the emergence of liberal values and institutions in the United States, England, and France, including *Liberalism and Republicanism in the Historical Imagination* (1992).

James Axtell is Kenan Professor of Humanities at the College of William and Mary. He is the author of numerous books on the ethnohistory of colonial North America and on the history of education. His most recent books are *The Indians' New South: Cultural Change in the Colonial Southeast* (1997) and *The Pleasures of Academe: A Celebration and Defense of Higher Education* (1998).

Jean Baudrillard, Professor of Sociology at the University of Nanterre from 1966 to 1987, is the author of many books including, *The Consumer Society: Myths and Structures* (1997).

Wendell Berry, a writer, poet, teacher, and farmer is the author of more than thirty books.

T. H. Breen is William Smith Mason Professor of American History and chair of the History Department at Northwestern University. He has written many books on colonial America, including *Imagining the Past: East Hampton Histories* (1994). He is completing a volume on political mobilization entitled *The Baubles of Britain: Revolutionary Consumers on the Eve of Independence.*

Colin Campbell, Reader in Sociology at the University of York, is the author of *The Romantic Ethic and the Spirit of Modern Consumerism* (1987).

Lizabeth Cohen, Professor of History at Harvard University, authored *Making a New Deal: Industrial Workers in Chicago, 1919–1939* (1990) and is completing *A Consumer's Republic: The Politics of Mass Consumption in Postwar America.*

Alan Durning, director of Northwest Environment Watch in Seattle, Washington, is the author of many books including *How Much is Enough? The Consumer Society and the Future of the Earth* (1992).

John Elkington is Chairman of SustainAbility, a London-based environmental consulting firm, and co-author of *The Green Consumer Guide* (1989).

James Fallows is the author of six books, most recently *Breaking the News: How the Media Undermine American Democracy* (1996). He has written for *The Atlantic Monthly, The New Yorker* and many other magazines and was the editor of *U.S. News and World Report* for two years.

Lawrence B. Glickman, Associate Professor of History at the University of South Carolina, is the author of *A Living Wage: American Workers and the Making of Consumer Society* (1997). In addition to editing and contributing to this volume, he is completing *Use Your Buying Power for Justice*, a study of American consumer activism in the twentieth century.

Cheryl Greenberg is Associate Professor of History and Director of the American Studies Program at Trinity College in Hartford, Connecticut. She has published *"Or Does It Explode?": Black Harlem in the Great Depression* (1991) and is writing *Troubling the Waters: Black-Jewish Relations in the American Century.*

Julia Hailes is joint founder/Director of SustainAbility, a London-based environmental consulting firm, and co-author of *The Green Consumer Guide* (1989).

Andrew Heinze, Associate Professor of History and Director of the Swig Judaic Studies Program at the University of San Francisco, is the author of *Adapting to Abundance: Jewish Immigrants, Mass Consumption, and the Search for American Identity* (1990).

Joel Makower, a journalist, commentator, and editor of *The Green Business Letter* is the author of many books on environmental topics.

Elaine Tyler May, Professor of American Studies at the University of Minnesota, is the author of *Homeward Bound: American Families in the Cold War Era* (1988) among other books.

Kim Moody is Director of the Labor Education and Research Project which publishes *Labor Notes*, a monthly magazine for union activists. He is the author of *Workers in a Lean World* (1997).

H. F. Moorhouse, Professor of Sociology at the University of Glasgow, is the author of *Driving Ambition: An Analysis of the American Hot Rod Enthusiasm* (1991).

George J. Sanchez is Associate Professor of History and the Program in American Studies and Ethnicity at the University of Southern California, where he also directs the Chicano/Latino Studies Program. He is the author of *Becoming Mexican American: Ethnicity, Culture, and Identity in Chicano Los Angeles, 1890–1945* (1993) and is preparing a study of the ethnic interaction of three groups throughout the twentieth century: Mexican Americans, Japanese Americans, and Jews, in the Boyle Heights area of East Los Angeles.

Juliet B. Schor teaches economics and women's studies at Harvard University. She is the author of *The Overworked American: The Unexpected Decline of Leisure* (1992) and *The Overspent American: Upscaling, Downshifting, and the New Consumer* (1998).

Michael Schudson is Professor of Communication and Adjunct Professor of Sociology at the University of California, San Diego. He is the author of books on the news media, advertising, popular culture, and American political history. His most recent book is *The Good Citizen: A History of American Civic Life* (1998).

Mark A. Swiencicki, a doctoral candidate in sociology at the University of Connecticut, studies how the cultures of race, class, and gender are expressed through consumption.

Steven Waldman is a writer and author of *The Bill: How Legislation Really Becomes Law* (1996).

Robert E. Weems, Jr. is Associate Professor of History at the University of Missouri, Columbia. He has published extensively in the areas of African American business history and African American consumerism, including *Desegregating the Dollar: African American Consumerism in the Twentieth Century* (1998).

Raymond Williams (1921–1988) was Professor of Drama at Cambridge University and the author of many books, including *Marxism and Literature* (1977).

Index

abundance, 194
advertising, 3, 18, 42, 147, 172, 174, 182, 229–231, 316, 345–346, 351, 369, 406–407
African Americans, 3, 4, 114, 154, 158–161, 222, 329, 410–411
    black migration, 317–318
    Civil Rights Movement, 5–6, 8, 18, 316, 320
    as consumers, 316–323
    "Don't Buy Where You Can't Work" Campaigns, 241–268
alienation, 277–278
American Revolution, 2, 100–124
    and commercial public sphere, 120–121
    and consumption, 101–102, 108
    and imperial relation with Great Britain, 100, 103, 112
    republicanism, 106
    trade and liberty, 108
    and virtue, 119–120
automobile, 344, 347–348

"baby boom," 5, 9
bachelor clubs, 219–222
Bellamy, Edward, 4, 399
Boorstin, Daniel, 3, 5, 152, 390
boycotts, 13, 54, 86, 160, 241, 316, 369
    non-importation movement, 2, 101, 107, 111–115, 350–351

Carter, Jimmy, 342
chain stores, 147, 150–152
Chicago, 147–163
Cold War, 298–300
Communism, 298–300, 303, 341, 353
Communist Party, 259–262
consumer(s)
    modern, 22
    traditional, 22
consumer revolution
    English, 85–86, 378–379

consumer society, 18, 185
    American ambivalence toward, 1–2, 342
    critiques, 342–354, 409
    periodization, 2–7, 11–12, 377–382, 389–392
consumerism, 1, 306
    modern, 25–26
    problem of, 21–22
consumption
    and capitalism, 17–18
    and choice, 359–366
    and collective action, 54–55
    and community, 3–4
    critics of, 134
    and economic well-being, 52
    and ethics, 20
    and freedom, 13, 53, 368
    and gender (men and women), 12
    and globalization, 329–330, 354–356
    historiography of, 9–10, 209–212, 373–392, 399–414
    and modernity, 130
    and passivity, 367–368
    and politics, 4–5, 103, 350–351, 363–364, 368–369, 388–389, 411–412
    and privacy, 142
    relation to production, 19, 47, 49, 51, 53, 351–352, 356
    and sociability, 108, 137
    as a system, 48–53
    as waste, 17–18, 78
    and work, 12, 277, 309–310, 349–350, 407–408
counterculture, 26–27
cosmetics, 216
credit, 50, 149, 202–203, 283

daydreaming, 24–25
debt, 95
department stores, 4, 34, 227

economic policy, Asian v. Anglo American, 57–77
economics, 19, 22, 39
Eisenhower, Dwight D., 52
environmentalism, 78–81, 333–337, 358, 375
Ewen, Stuart, 349–351, 375–377

family life, 298–313
famine, 130–131
fashion, 22–23, 29
food, 367–372
Ford, Henry and "Fordism," 5, 347
fraternal orders, 222–223
free trade, 330–331
frugality, 52, 134

Galbraith, John Kenneth, 39, 41–45, 50
GI Bill, 303
Gibson, D. Parke, 319–321
goods, 33

hedonism, 22–24, 380–381
Holland, 373–382
Horowitz, Daniel, 352–353
"hot rod" subculture, 282–295
housewives, 244, 307

immigrants, 4, 147–163, 170–186, 190–203
    becoming "American," 191, 195–197
    shifting source of, 191
Indians (North American), 86–96
    acculturation, 94
    alcohol, 92–93
    cloth, 90–91
    firearms, 92
    food, 91
    mirrors, 93
    pelts, 87–88
    revitalization movements, 95–96

Japan, 58
Jews, 192–203
    anti-Semitism, 254–255
Johnson, James H., 319–320

Kennedy, John F., 6
"kitchen debate," 6, 8, 298–300
Korea, 58

Lasch, Christopher, 345–347, 351–352
leisure, 3–4, 19, 278–290, 306, 326–327
Levittown, 307
Los Angeles, 170–186
luxury, 101–102, 134–136, 141, 192, 201

malls, 35–38
Malthus, Thomas, 139–141
markets, 63–64
Marshall, T. H., 39
Marx, Karl, 39, 343–344

mass consumption, 21, 142, 328
mass culture, 147
McDonald's, 336, 341
men as consumers, 207–234
Mexicans and Mexican Americans, 154, 170–186
movies, 148, 152–154, 172–173, 178, 183
music, 170, 175
    jazz, 160–161

NAACP, 247, 258
Nader, Ralph, 5, 8
needs, 20, 23, 40, 44, 47, 346
Nixon, Richard M., 298–300, 302, 305, 317
novelty, 25–26, 402

obsolescence (planned), 22, 347–348, 375

pleasure, 23, 47–48
post-consumer society, 79
population growth, 131
Potter, David, 7–8, 11
Powell, Adam Clayton, 244, 259, 262, 263

radio, 148, 155–158, 171, 181, 316
Reich, Robert, 67–72
religion, 405–406
Riesman, David, 47, 289
Roosevelt, Franklin D., 5, 8, 342

Schama, Simon, 373–378
shopping, 172
"simple life," 6, 110, 343, 409–410
Sinclair, Upton, 4, 399
Smith, Adam, 137–138, 343–344, 353
sports, 217–219
suburbia, 298–313
Susman, Warren, 387–390

tobacco, 131
tourism, 29–30

Urban League, 246–247, 250

Veblen, Thorstein, 4, 12, 21, 379–381, 399

wants, 22, 343, 379
    artificial, 95
Weber, Max, 51, 138
whiteness, 3, 305
women as consumers, 86, 115, 117, 179, 192, 207–208, 221, 228, 231, 244, 294, 408–409
work ethic, 278–282, 290
workers, 331–332
    ethnic workers, 149–163, 382–384
    and mass consumption, 328
Wright, Richard, 66

youth culture, 172, 282, 287